The Royal Photographic Society

PORTFOLIO**THREE**

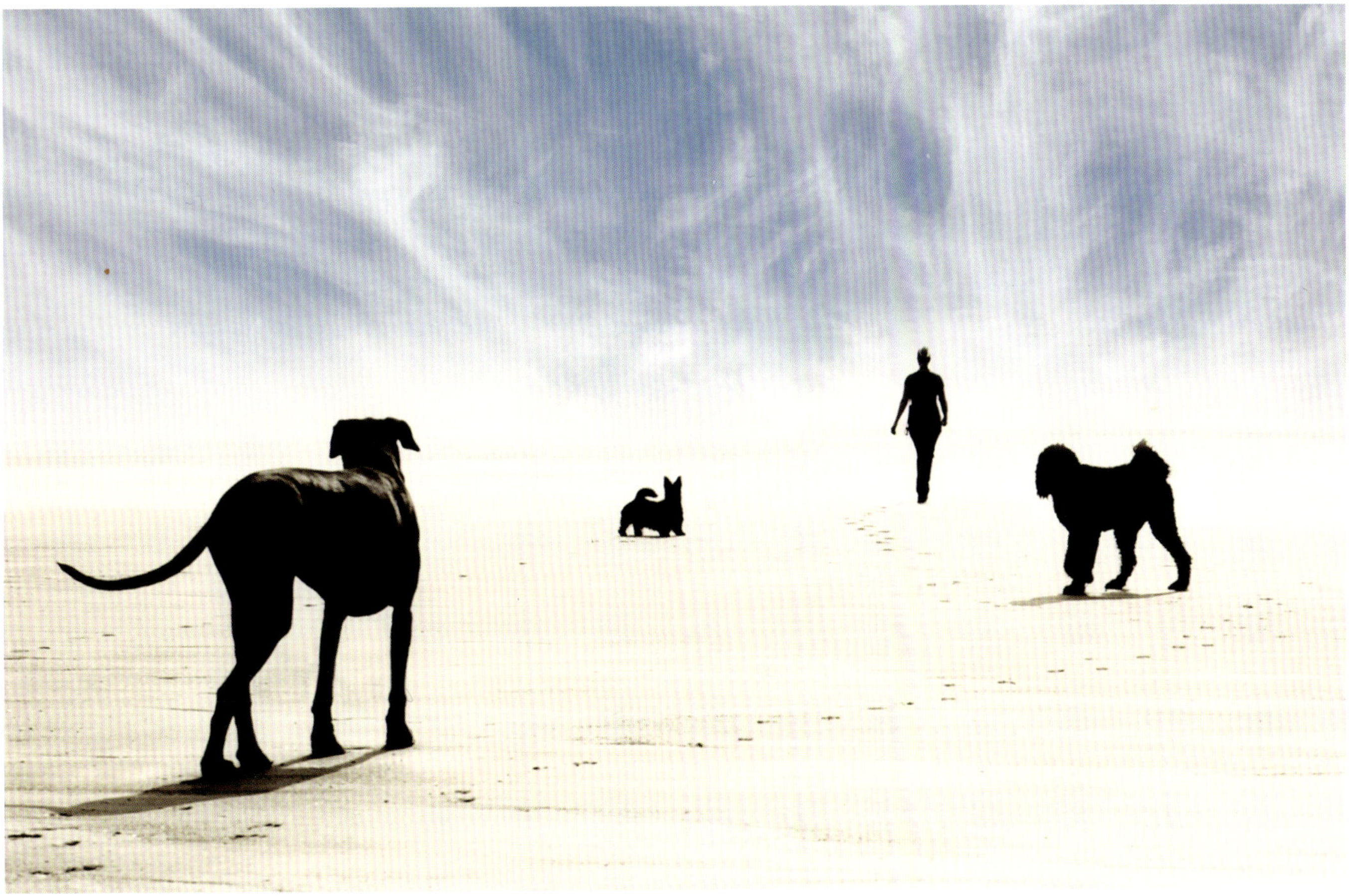

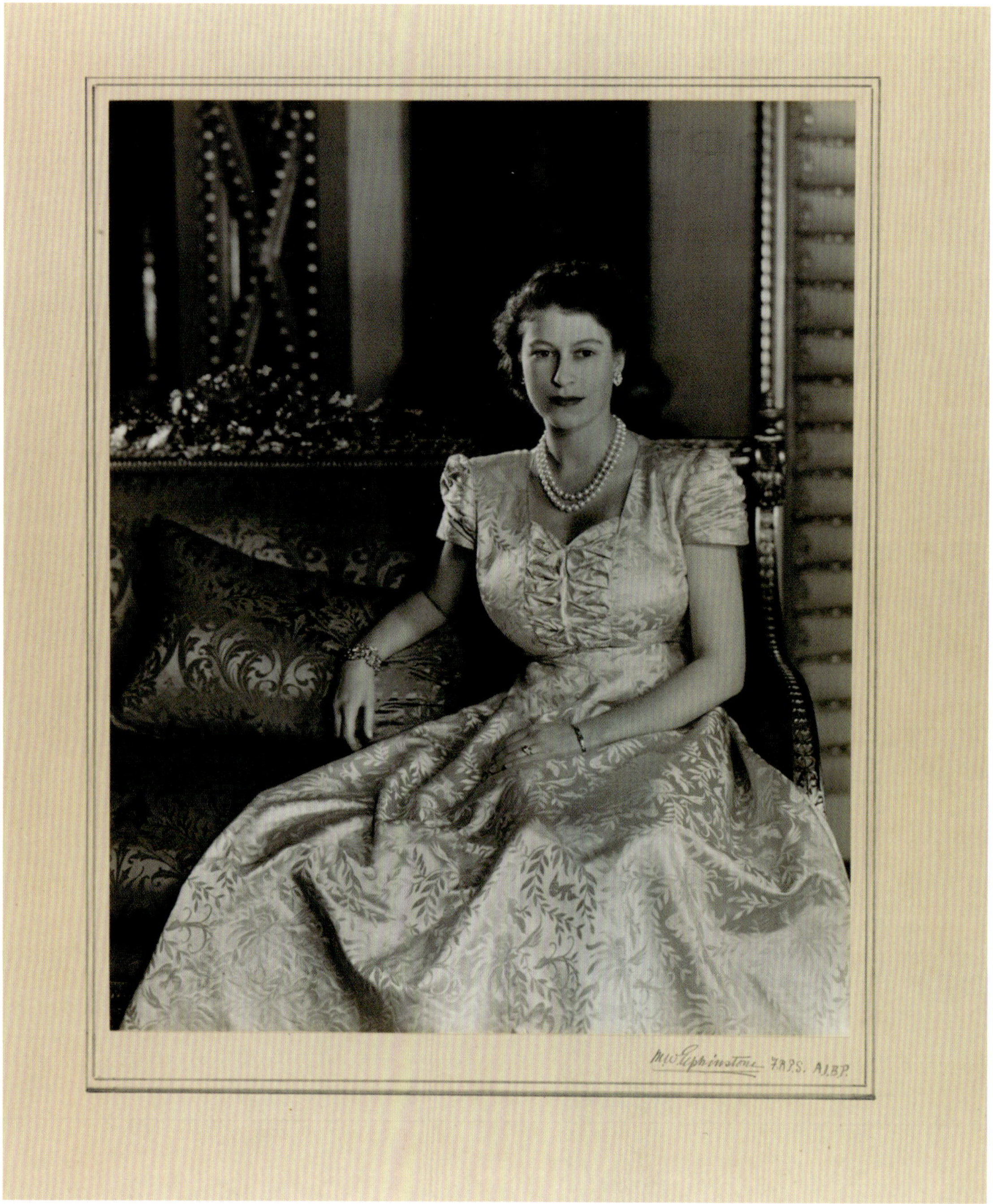

HON. MOUNTSTUART WILLIAM FULLERTON ELPHINSTONE FRPS (1871-1957)

'Her Majesty Queen Elizabeth II'

From The Royal Photographic Society Collection at the National Media Museum

The Royal Photographic Society

PORTFOLIO**THREE**

Editor

Roger Reynolds Hon.FRPS

The Royal Photographic Society

Patron: Her Majesty The Queen. Incorporated by Royal Charter

Fenton House, 122 Wells Road, Bath, BA2 3AH, United Kingdom

The Royal Photographic Society
PORTFOLIO**THREE**

Published by The Royal Photographic Society
Fenton House
122 Wells Road
Bath BA2 3AH
United Kingdom
www.rps.org

Editor:
Roger Reynolds Hon.FRPS

Project Manager:
Harry Ricketts Hon.FRPS

Editorial Team:
Derek Birch ASIS FRPS; Julia Cleaver ARPS;
Roy Robertson Hon.FRPS; Rosemary Wilman Hon.FRPS

Contributing Writers:
Michael Hallett FRPS; Monica Weller FRPS;
David Cooke ARPS; Michael Pritchard FRPS

Guest Writers:
Carol Mikellides; Spike Walker ASIS FRPS; Philippa Wright;
Afzal Ansary ASIS FRPS

Design and Artwork by:
Roy Platten, Eclipse, Hemel Hempstead, England
roy.eclipse@btopenworld.com

Colour processing, printing and binding by:
Butler Tanner and Dennis Ltd, Frome, Somerset, England

ISBN 978-0-904495-05-8

FRONTISPIECE
PAUL WALKER FRPS

From the Bill Wisden MBE Hon.FRPS Fellowship of the Year 2013. © Paul Walker FRPS

CONTENTS

THE PRESIDENT

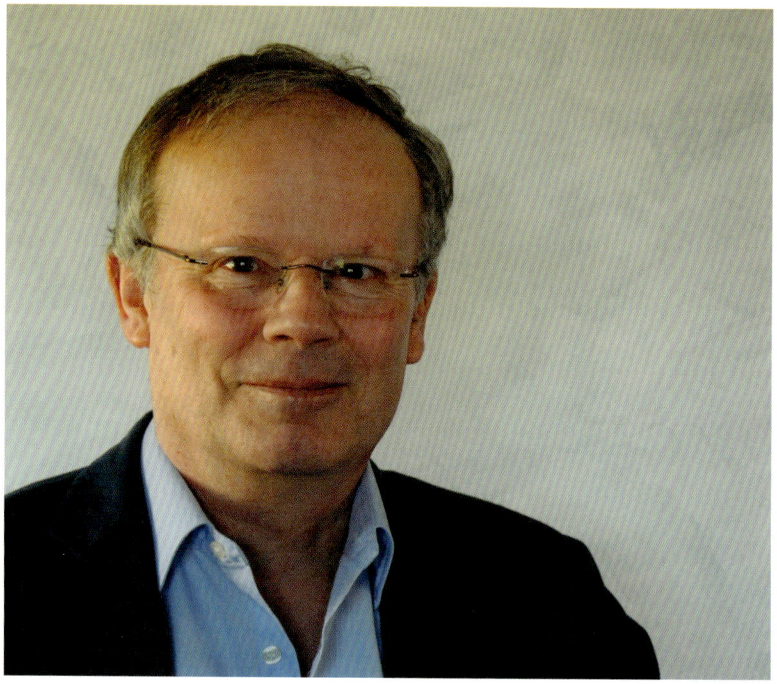

The Royal Photographic Society supports a very diverse range of activities and events – all under the banner of 'supporting the Art and Science of Photography'. There are no boundaries to being a member – it only requires an interest in photography under any one of its myriad forms. Within The Society, 14 Special Interest Groups promote and develop a number of different aspects of Photography, both by subject and by technique. There are no geographic boundaries. Through the 16 Regions and 18 Overseas Chapters, The Society arranges events, workshops and meetings throughout not only the UK and Europe, but across the world. Through the Society Awards, the highest levels of international achievement in all aspects of image making are recognised. Through the Society Bursaries younger photographers are supported in establishing themselves.

PORTFOLIO**THREE**, like its predecessors, is not intended to be a comprehensive guide to Photography. Rather, it is a snapshot of The Society in this, the 160th year since it was founded in 1853. With over 11,000 members, there was a wealth of material submitted for the Members' Gallery. The selection is designed to show the variety of the images produced by Society members, and inevitably, many outstanding images could not be included. With the Diamond Jubilee of our Patron, Her Majesty the Queen, and the London Olympics, members were also asked to submit images linked to these events.

PORTFOLIO**THREE** includes a sample of the activities of the Special Interest Groups, the Regions and the Overseas Chapters. It shows a small selection from a great many successful Distinctions Panels, some of the projects undertaken by winners of Society Bursaries, and a range of images selected from The Society's principal Exhibitions – the International Print Exhibition, the Projected Image Exhibition and the International Images of Science Exhibition.

I would like to congratulate Roger Reynolds for conceiving the idea behind the Portfolio series 9 years ago, and thank him for continuing his role as Editor – this is the third volume he has produced. Each Portfolio is a superb time capsule of the development and activities of The Society in the 21st century. I would also like to thank the Editorial team who have co-ordinated, written, and produced this publication. My thanks also to all those members who contributed the images which make this an outstanding example of the democratic and diverse Art, and the radically altered Science, that Photography has become since our Society was founded.

Enjoy the examples of the History, the Science and the Art of Photography shown here. They represent just a fraction of The Society's activities. More information about events can be found on The Society's website www.rps.org. I hope you will join us.

Roy Robertson Hon.FRPS
President

EDITOR'S INTRODUCTION

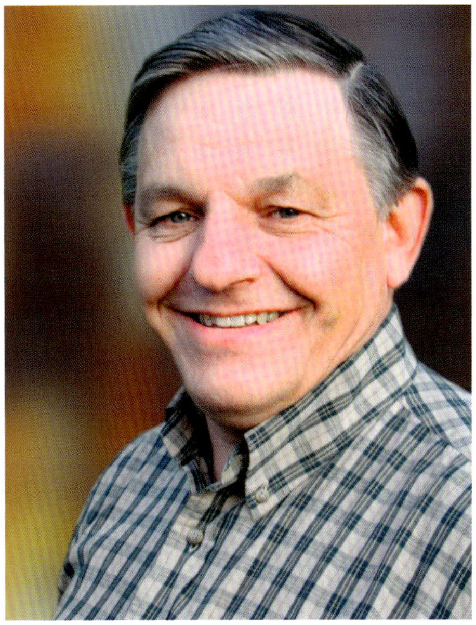

PORTFOLIO**THREE** continues the process begun in 2007 to create a living history of The Royal Photographic Society. With The Royal Photographic Society Collection now firmly established at the National Media Museum and The Society and Museum beginning a new acquisitions programme it is hoped that the Portfolio publications will in time not only be seen as an historical record of The Society's activities at the beginning of the 21st century but support the growing Royal Photographic Society Collection at Bradford.

The Portfolio series has received wide acclaim and it is now established as a significant part of recording The Society activities both currently and as an important record for the future. As editor I am indebted to the President Roy Robertson Hon.FRPS and the members of the Council for placing their trust in me once again to edit PORTFOLIO**THREE**. I hope their faith is proved to be justified and everyone enjoys the amazing content of this publication.

As in previous Portfolios the content is just a small insight into the vast programme of events and activities conducted by The Society over the last three years. The Royal Photographic Society enjoys the honoured patronage of Her Majesty Queen Elizabeth II and to mark her Diamond Jubilee we have included a superb image of Her Majesty from The Royal Photographic Society Collection. Of course 2012 was also significant for London 2012 and perhaps the finest Olympic Games ever held. In our Members' Gallery we have included images from these two events. In our Exhibitions section we have images from the Summer of Sports Exhibition which was organised to celebrate the event and this was recognised with the award of the London 2012 'Inspire Mark'.

Once again I am grateful to all of those photographers and contributors who have allowed us to feature their photography and enrich this publication. Our Portfolio section features the work of both outstanding international photographers and members. Other sections of the publication recognise the work of the Regions, Chapters and Groups, where volunteers give tirelessly to support the aims of The Society as an educational charity. Couple this with fine articles on historical aspects of the Society, the involvement in science and education and images from the extensive exhibitions programme and we have a rich variety for all to enjoy.

As editor I am delighted to feature the work of both eminent members and also world famous photographers who have been given important Society awards. I am honoured that all of those featured have freely donated their time and images to support this Portfolio. It is a measure of the importance of The Society that all of them are prepared to support such a publication. I am also most grateful to all the members of the Groups, Regions, Chapters and successful Distinction recipients who have both submitted work for consideration and allowed me to feature this in the final publication. Once again a significant section of the Portfolio is given over to the Members' Gallery which showcases the outstanding current work of the membership. I am delighted to say that there were more than 4,000 images submitted from which we made the final selection. Unfortunately we could only feature a small number of the submitted images resulting in many superb photographs not making the final selection. I personally would like to congratulate all those with images selected as well as thanking those members from all over the world who submitted such an amazing range of photographs. I am only sorry that I could not double the size of the publication to include many more.

Of course any publication such as this requires a tremendous input from a talented group of people who have been brought together to complete the project. As editor I have to pay an immense debt of gratitude to all of those who worked tirelessly to bring you this notable publication. David Cooke ARPS, Michael Hallett FRPS and Monica Weller FRPS used their immense writing talents to produce the interviews for the individual portfolios. My thanks also go to Carol Mikellides, Philippa Wright, Michael Pritchard FRPS and Spike Walker FRPS, whose contributions added so much. I am also indebted to Derek Birch ASIS FRPS, Julia Cleaver ARPS, Roy Robertson Hon.FRPS and Rosemary Wilman Hon.FRPS who as part of the editorial team have played a major part in the finished Portfolio. My thanks also go to Roy Platten, the designer, whose skill has resulted in a publication of the highest quality. Of course such a venture as this could not have happened without the support of Project Manager Harry Ricketts Hon.FRPS, who with his many years of experience in the publishing industry, was invaluable in helping me through the complicated and difficult publishing process. My task would have been far more difficult without his expert guidance and knowledge.

Finally I hope that you will enjoy PORTFOLIO**THREE** and treasure it as an important piece of photographic history.

Roger Reynolds Hon.FRPS
Editor

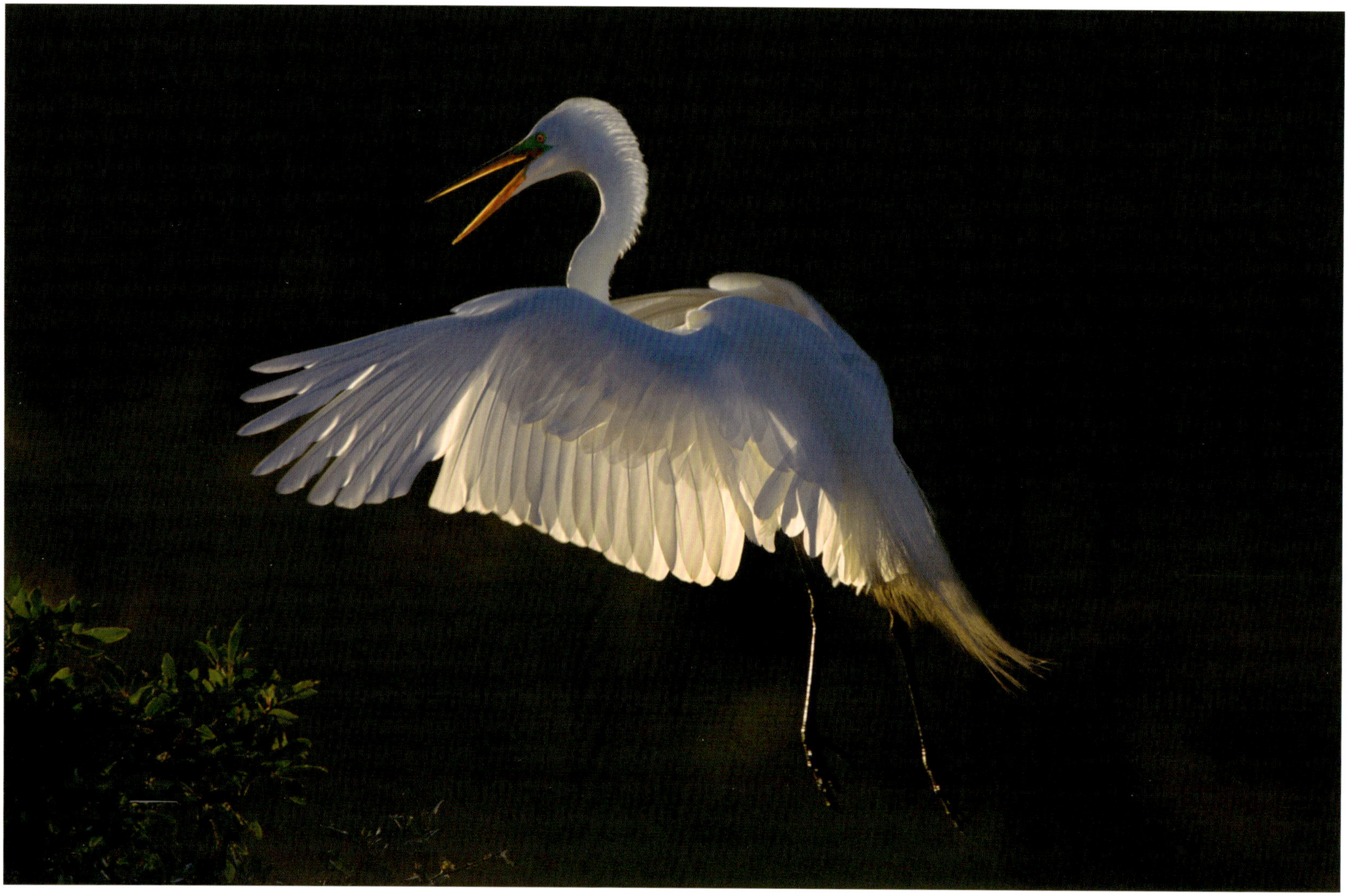

ROGER REYNOLDS Hon.FRPS
GREAT EGRET LANDING AT EVENING ROOST, FLORIDA 2012

THE PORTFOLIOS

AWARD PORTFOLIOS

The Royal Photographic Society Annual Awards recognise individual's major achievements and contributions to the art and science of photography. The Awards Ceremony is a highlight of The Society's year and is attended by many highly respected figures from the world of photography and the media.

Portfolios from recipients in 2011 and 2012

The Centenary Medal was instituted in 1993 and is awarded in recognition of a sustained, significant contribution to the art of photography. This medal also carries with it an Honorary Fellowship of The Society.

Albert Watson Hon.FRPS
Joel Meyerowitz Hon.FRPS

Honorary Fellowships are awarded to distinguished persons having, from their position or attainments, an intimate connection with the science or fine art of photography or the application thereof.

Ken Lennox Hon.FRPS
Bob Martin Hon.FRPS
Rinko Kawauchi Hon.FRPS
Jason Bell Hon.FRPS

INVITED PORTFOLIOS

A selection of portfolios and images from invited members.

Sandy Cleland FRPS
Joe Cornish Hon.FRPS
Jack Jackson FRPS
Ines Labunski Roberts FRPS
Jim Moreland FRPS
Vic Attfield FRPS and Mary Attfield FRPS

ALBERT WATSON Hon.FRPS

FIRSTS

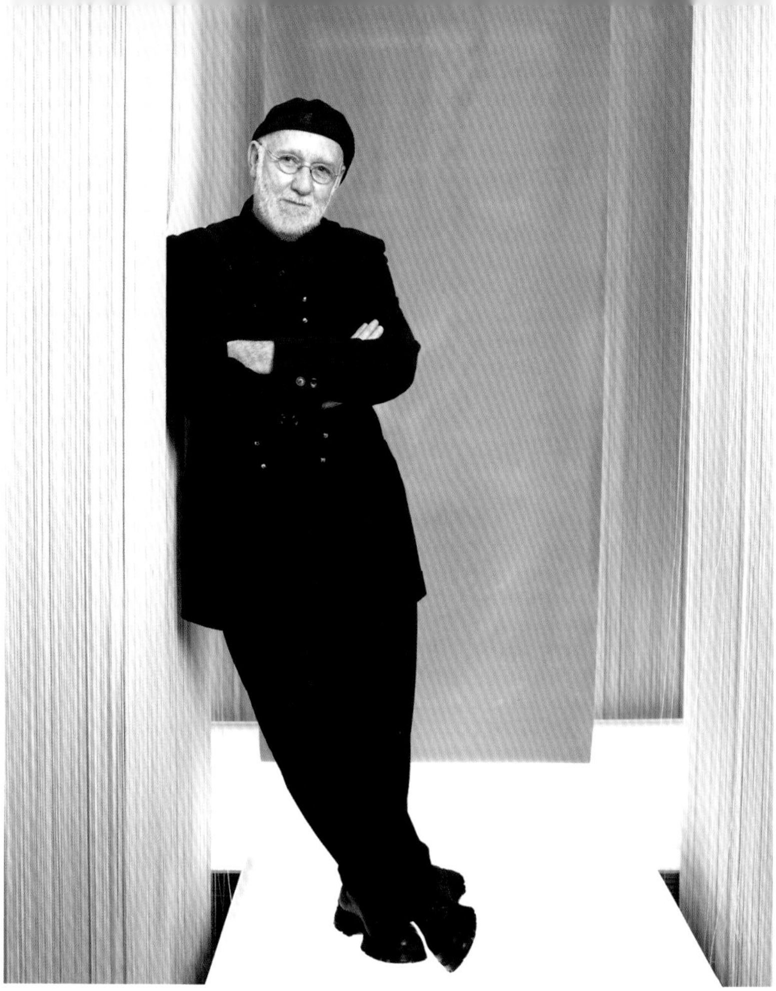

Born and raised in Scotland, Albert Watson has made his mark as one of the world's most successful fashion and commercial photographers. Over the years his images have appeared on more than one hundred covers of *Vogue* and been featured in publications from *Rolling Stone* to *Time*. He's created the photography for advertising campaigns for Levi's, Revlon and Chanel, has published five books, and since 2004 has had exhibitions around the world. In 2010 Albert was awarded the RPS Centenary Medal.

First photographs

"When I was twelve I used my father's Kodak Brownie Box camera and took four rolls of 120 film and had them processed at the chemist. I took photographs around Edinburgh and of my sister. I didn't have any further contact with a camera until I was twenty-one.

First test session

The first test was really when I studied film and television at the Royal College of Art in London in the sixties. I contacted models who wanted pictures and they came to the school. In 1970 I had a test session with Max Factor. That was very successful commercially because they bought some of the pictures. My only connection when I moved from the UK to Los Angeles, my wife Elizabeth had a teaching job and I went in as her dependent. I had one connection there: an advertising executive. He gave me the art director's name at Max Factor. I didn't have any commercial pictures of women but he did a nice thing for me. He had clothes in a closet there at Max Factor and said: "You can borrow those clothes. We'll pay for one hour for a model for you". I connected with the model. Although she was only booked for an hour I talked her into shooting all day. I took the pictures in to Max Factor. They bought some pictures and used them for ads for the 'California Blonde' makeup range.

First celebrity photograph

That picture of Alfred Hitchcock was done for the 1975 Christmas edition of *Harpers Bazaar*. He was keen on cooking and had given the magazine a recipe for Christmas goose. They wanted him holding a plate with the goose on the plate. I said it would be funnier if the goose was complete with the head. I put Christmas decorations round the goose's neck to make him festive. I'd trained as a graphic designer at Duncan of Jordanstone College of Art and Design in Dundee, then three years at film school. I'd been involved in print making and always printed my own work. As far as the photo is concerned I'd had a solid training about putting together an idea. It was one of the most important pictures. Somehow it was just the fact it was Hitchcock.

First job for Vogue

My first job for *Vogue* magazine was for their July 1976 bicentennial issue. I was given the opening to the magazine. I had been working for Condé Nast doing *GQ* and *Mademoiselle*. Eventually their editor gave me that shooting. It was a successful shoot for me with three blondes. The idea was American clothing. Pattie Hansen, Lisa Taylor and Lisa Cooper were very American-looking blondes.

First Hollywood movie poster

I did photographs for a movie called *Juice* in 1992 with Tupac Shakur. In one of the posters which was used, was a picture of Tupac Shakur with a gun. We also shot it without the gun. The gun image was better…that's what the movie was about. The gun implies violence.

First exhibition in Watson's homeland

FROZEN was at the City Arts Centre in Edinburgh in 2006 during the Edinburgh festival. There was a lot of press presence. It was a retrospective exhibition and nice to see huge posters everywhere advertising the show. Included was a series of big prints of the Standing Stones in the Orkneys, big landscape pieces. If I had all the time in the world I would do landscape work there – the trouble is it's a time consuming type of photography, dependent on things beyond your control. The weather. I chose Orkney because I liked the ageing of the stones. The fact you were looking at something that was three-and-a-half thousand years old was special. A lot of people had difficulty with my photography because they might look, for example, at a celebrity picture that I had done, then look at my landscapes, or a fashion picture, or anything from car photography to still life. They didn't know what it was about. Instead of that there was a very simple answer to it. That if you look at all my pictures they are either graphic, or cinema or a combination of the two. You can break everything down into the two categories".

Monica Weller FRPS

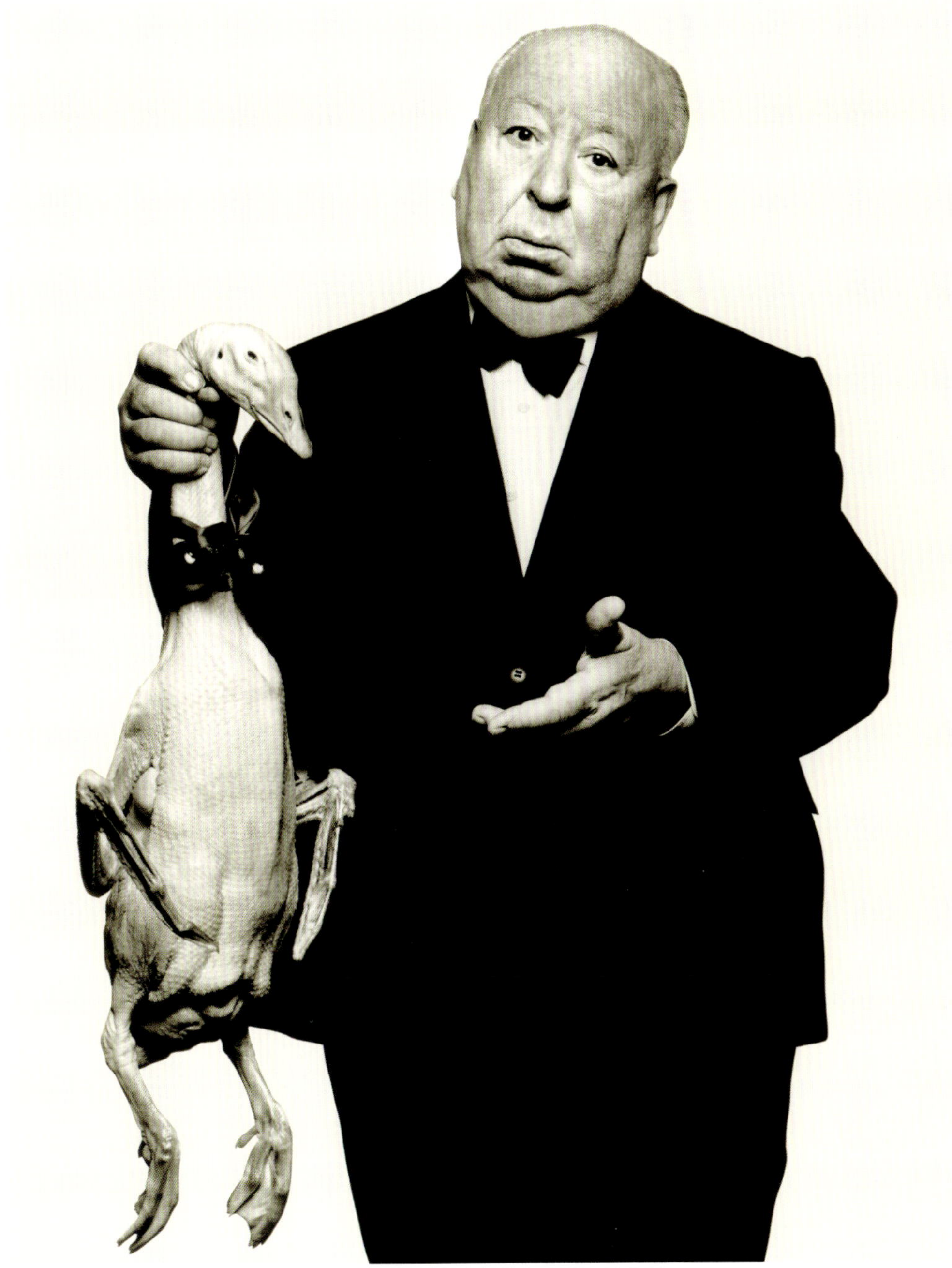

ALFRED HITCHCOCK, LOS ANGELES 1973

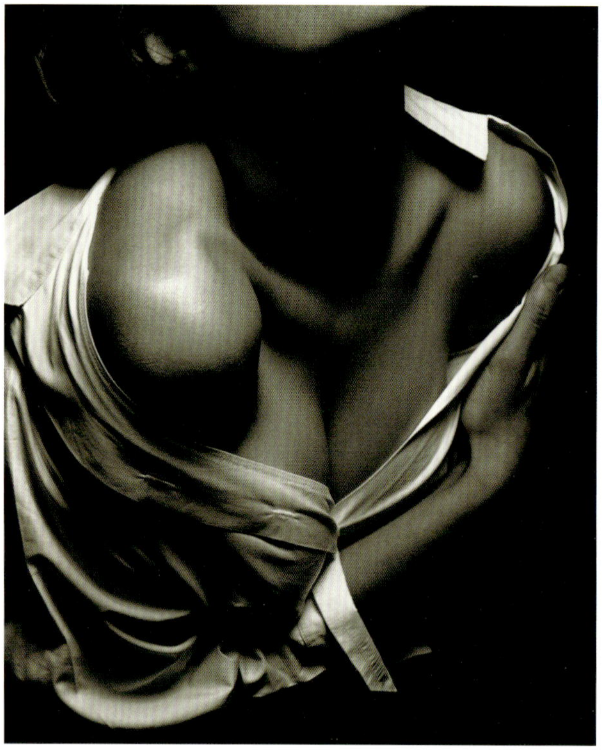

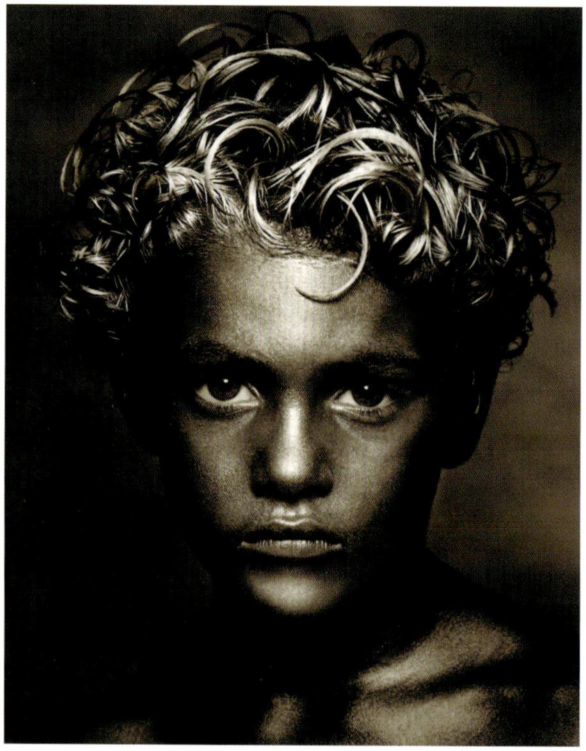

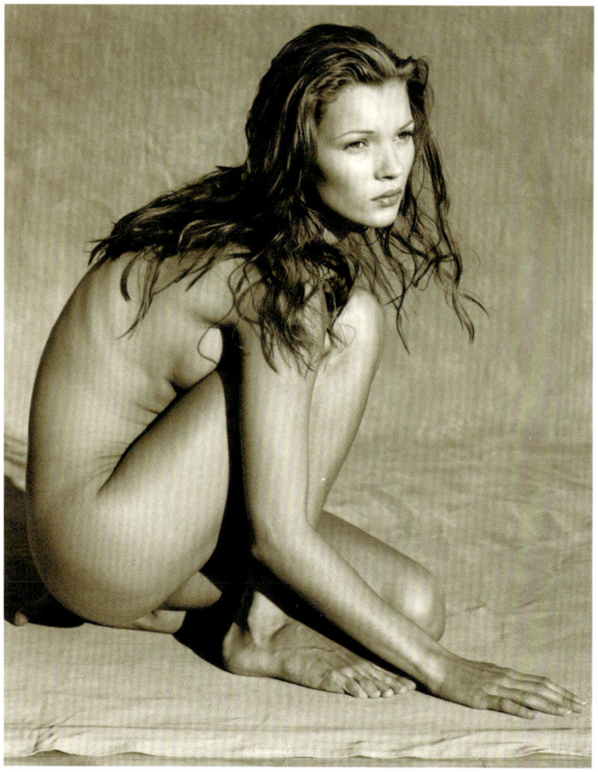

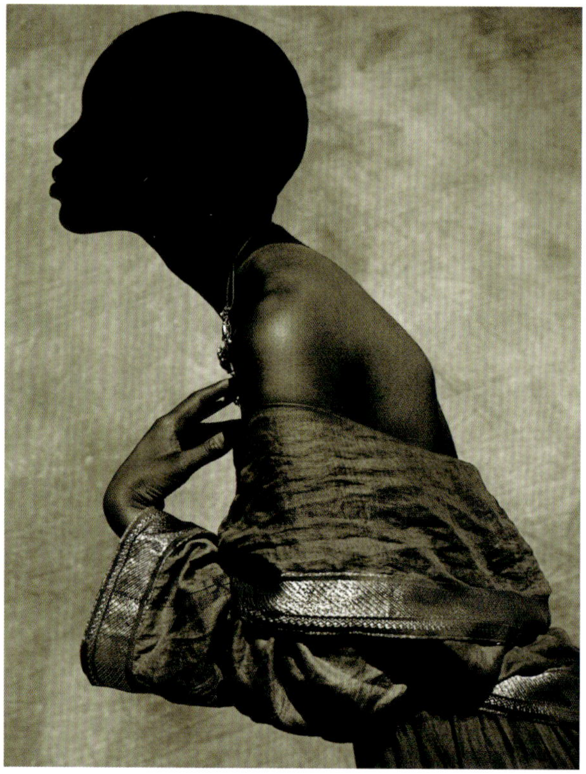

CHARLOTTE, PRADA BLOUSE, MILAN, 1986
KATE MOSS, MOROCCO, 1993

GOLDEN BOY, NEW YORK CITY, 1990
NAOMI CAMPBELL, PALM SPRINGS, 1989

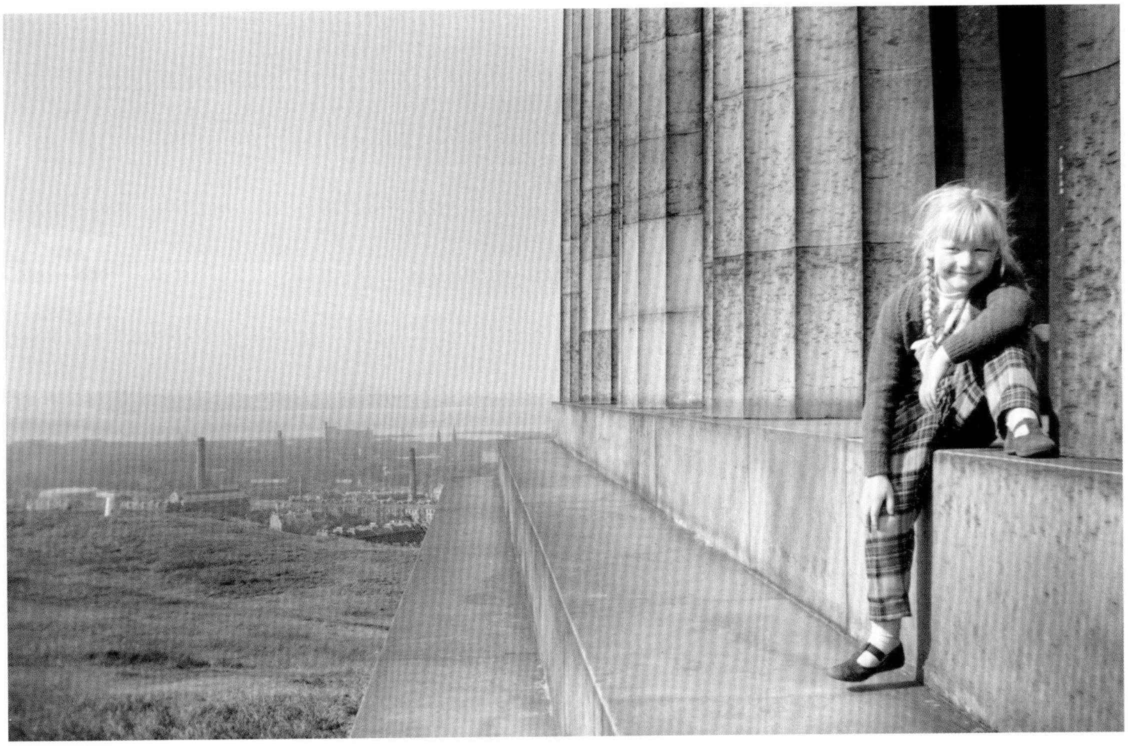

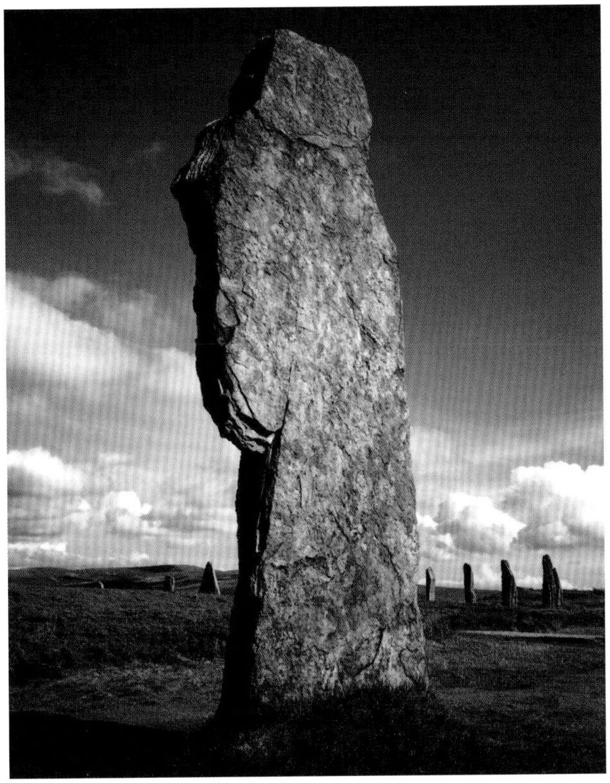

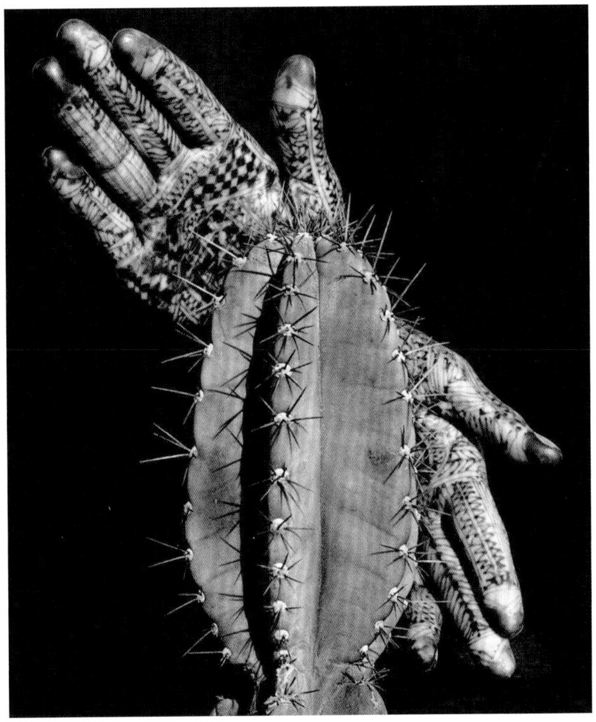

JULIE WATSON, CALTON HILL, EDINBURGH, 1954

STANDING STONE, THE ORKNEY'S, 1991

HANDS, GARDENER, DA TAMANSA, MARRAKECH, 1998

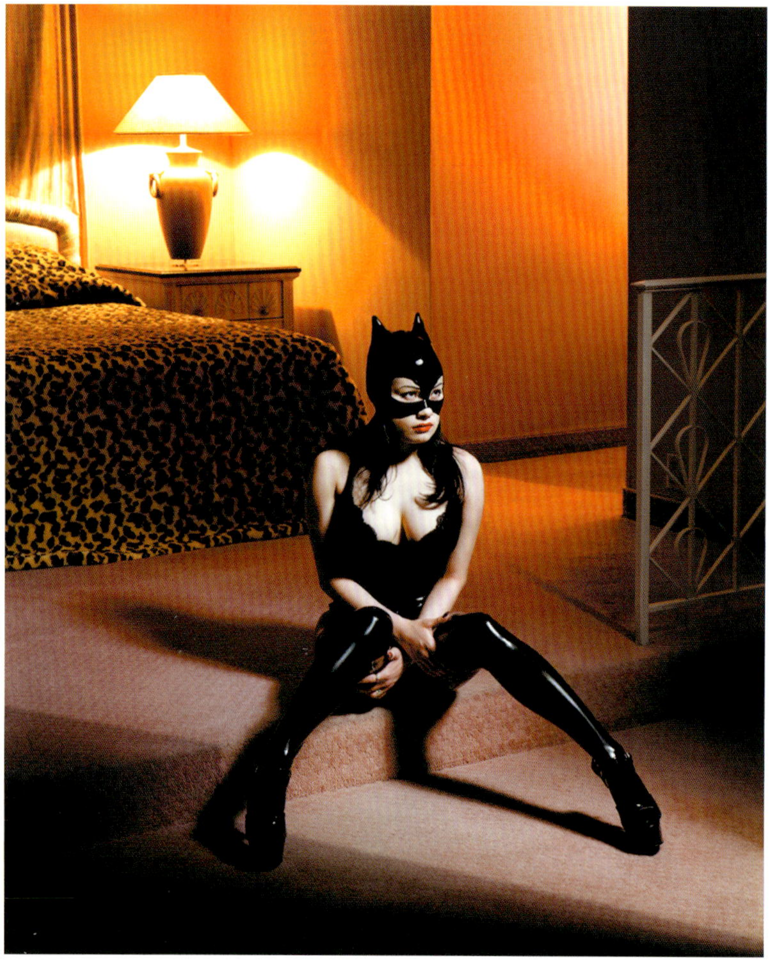

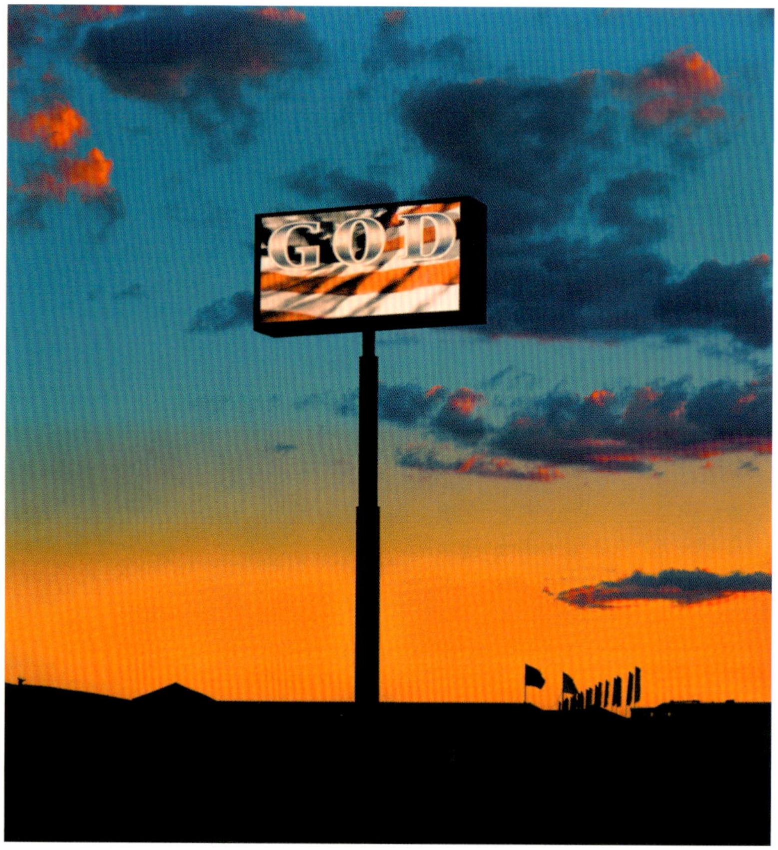

BREAUNNALN CAT MASK, LAS VEGAS HILTON, 1991

SIGN OFF INTERSTATE 15, CLARKE COUNTY, NEVADA 2001

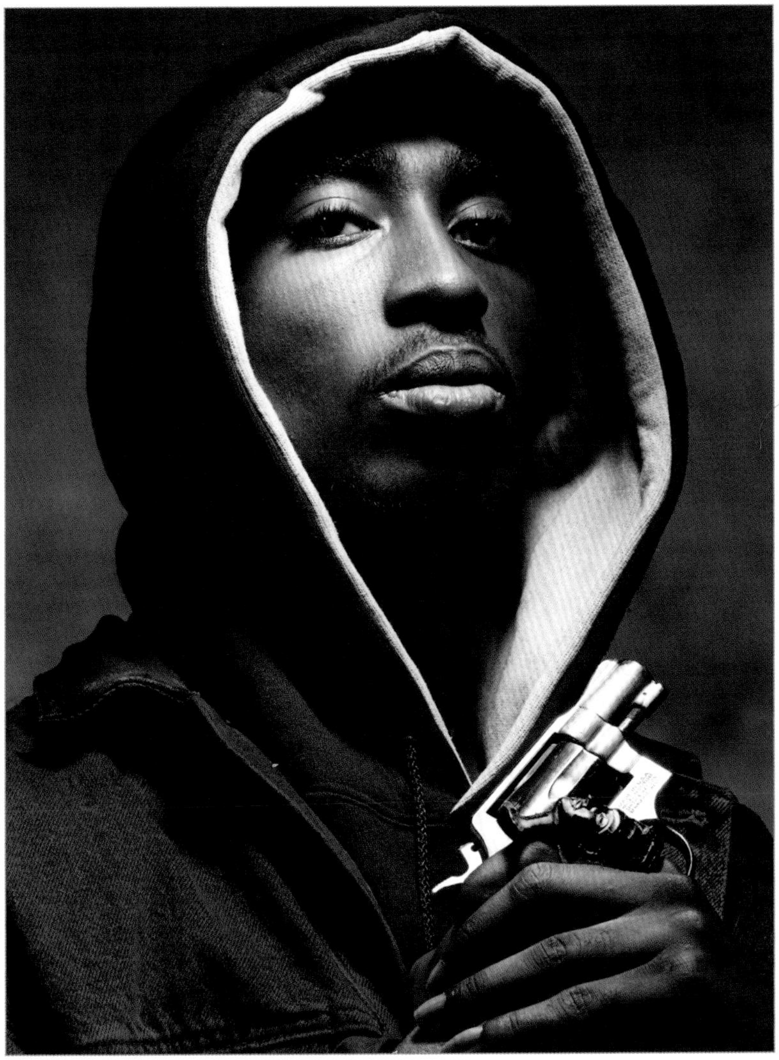

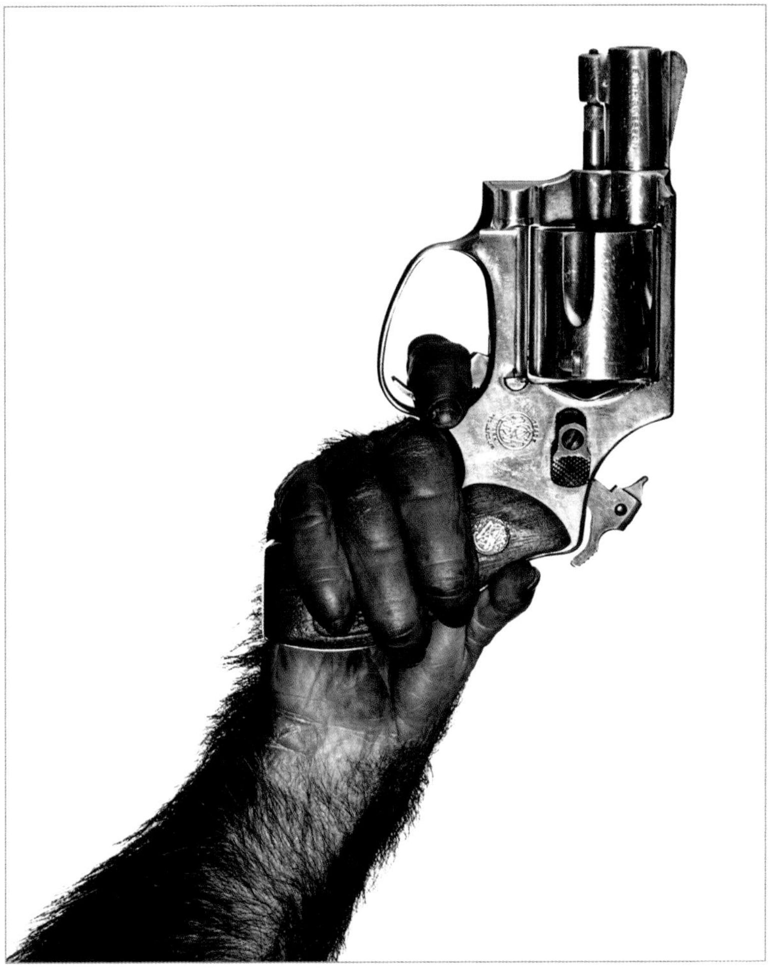

TUPAC SHAKUR, NEW YORK CITY, 1991

MONKEY WITH GUN, NEW YORK CITY, 1992

JOEL MEYEROWITZ Hon.FRPS

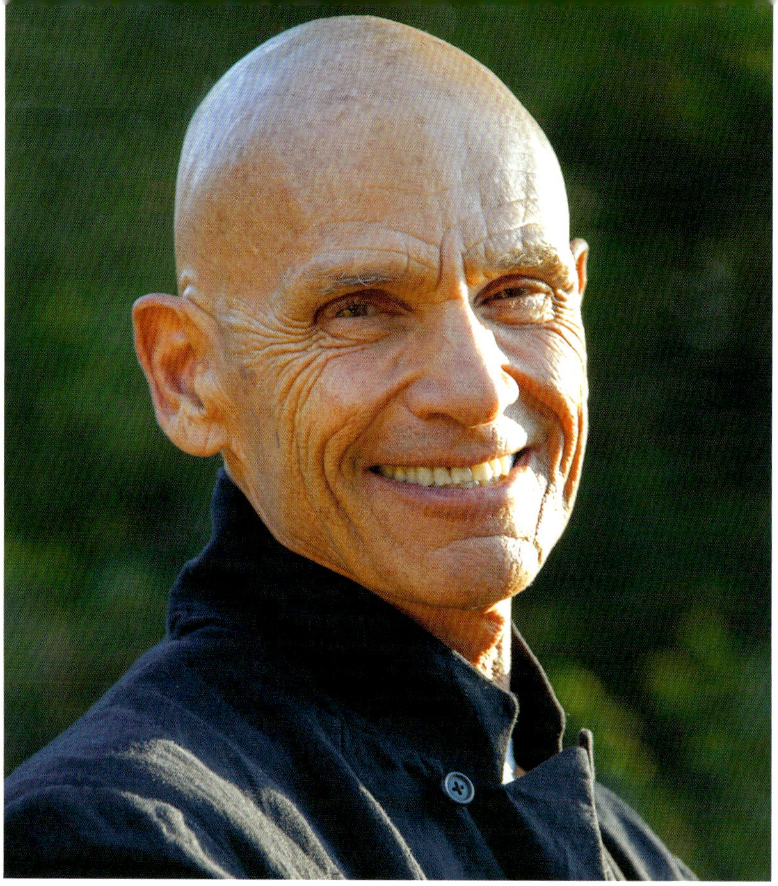

It is to do with influences and the impact of those influences. There is the element of chance and taking that chance. For Joel Meyerowitz it provided him with a perfect storm that propelled him towards photography. He was the kid who went onto the street with a borrowed Pentax, knowing nothing about photography.

It was in 1962 while art director for a small design agency in downtown Manhattan that Meyerowitz watched Robert Frank shooting a commercial assignment for a Condé Nast publication. Enthralled, he quit his job and started capturing 'inconsequential moments' in his world of colour. Nowadays, he sees himself as one of the first street photographers recording his world in movement and in colour rather than the more conventional black & white of the time. He viewed, understood and promoted the vocabulary of the street.

Born in New York in 1938, Meyerowitz believes his original ignorance of photography and its techniques and traditions worked in his favour. By 1962, he was street wise, had earned a Bachelor of Fine Arts degree from Ohio State University where he studied art history and medical drawing, was working in the media and had the enquiring and intellectual vision to make images with meaning.

Like so many other photographers of his generation and since, Robert Frank's iconic book *The Americans* provided Meyerowitz with the influence common to many photographers. For Meyerowitz, 'In the pantheon of the greats, there is Robert Frank and Eugene Atget.' He also formed an affinity with fellow photographer Tony Ray-Jones and John Szarkowski, then curator of photography at New York's Metropolitan Museum of Art.

Meyerowitz recalls that at that time when this kid from the Bronx first exposed his two rolls of colour film in 1962, there was a prejudice against that particular medium. Black & white provided a completely different mindset, and he saw himself as a sort of missionary for colour photography. He acknowledges that Ray-Jones, best known for his black & white images, was working in colour in America contemporaneous with himself. He remembers an occasion in 1962 when William Eggleston, more recently regarded as the pioneering master of colour, visited him in his apartment where they spent time looking at Meyerowitz's colour photographs and Eggleston's black & white prints. Eggleston has only recently acknowledged the impact on himself from that particular evening.

Meyerowitz's 1972 publication *Cape Light*, provides an eloquent and contemplative body of work showing the transition from seeing in terms of black & white and seeing wholly in colour. The work was made on the Cape in the Truro-Provincetown area during the summers of 1976 and 1977 with an 8 x 10 inch Deardorff view camera. The large format form allowed Meyerowitz to emphasis the light and atmosphere and play with the quality nuances provided by the subject and the process. It is this comprehensive and seminal body of work that may well survive as his most significant, and for what Meyerowitz will continue to be best known.

For Meyerowitz, it is not the high drama but the inconsequential that is important. With his photographer's interpretation, he is making the ordinary, extraordinary.

The 9/11 attacks changed so many peoples' lives, as could *Aftermath: World Trade Center Archive* published in book form in 2006, and soon to be installed as a permanent exhibition in the museum at Ground Zero. It is an amazing and mature body of work. He started on 23 September 2001 continuing to photograph for 14 hours a day. He photographed demolition crews, construction crews, first-aid crews, debris removal crews and the security crews that initially attempted to keep him off the site. The archive will be seen as part of not just the history of photography, but the history of ourselves.

Now having reached his mid-seventies, he has provided himself with what he sees as the photographers' end game, with new work exploring the ever changing building blocks of life; earth, water and sky. This bigger picture has the potential of going on forever.

Meyerowitz has received two Gugenheim Fellowships (1970, 1978) and a National Endowment for the Arts grant (1978). His work has been exhibited in one-man shows at Boston's Museum of Fine Art, the George Eastman House, and the Museum of Modern Art in NYC, all of which have acquired photographs for their permanent collections.

In September 2012, Joel Meyerowitz was awarded The Society's Centenary Medal along with The Society's Honorary Fellowship in recognition of his sustained, significant contribution to the art of photography.

Michael Hallett FRPS

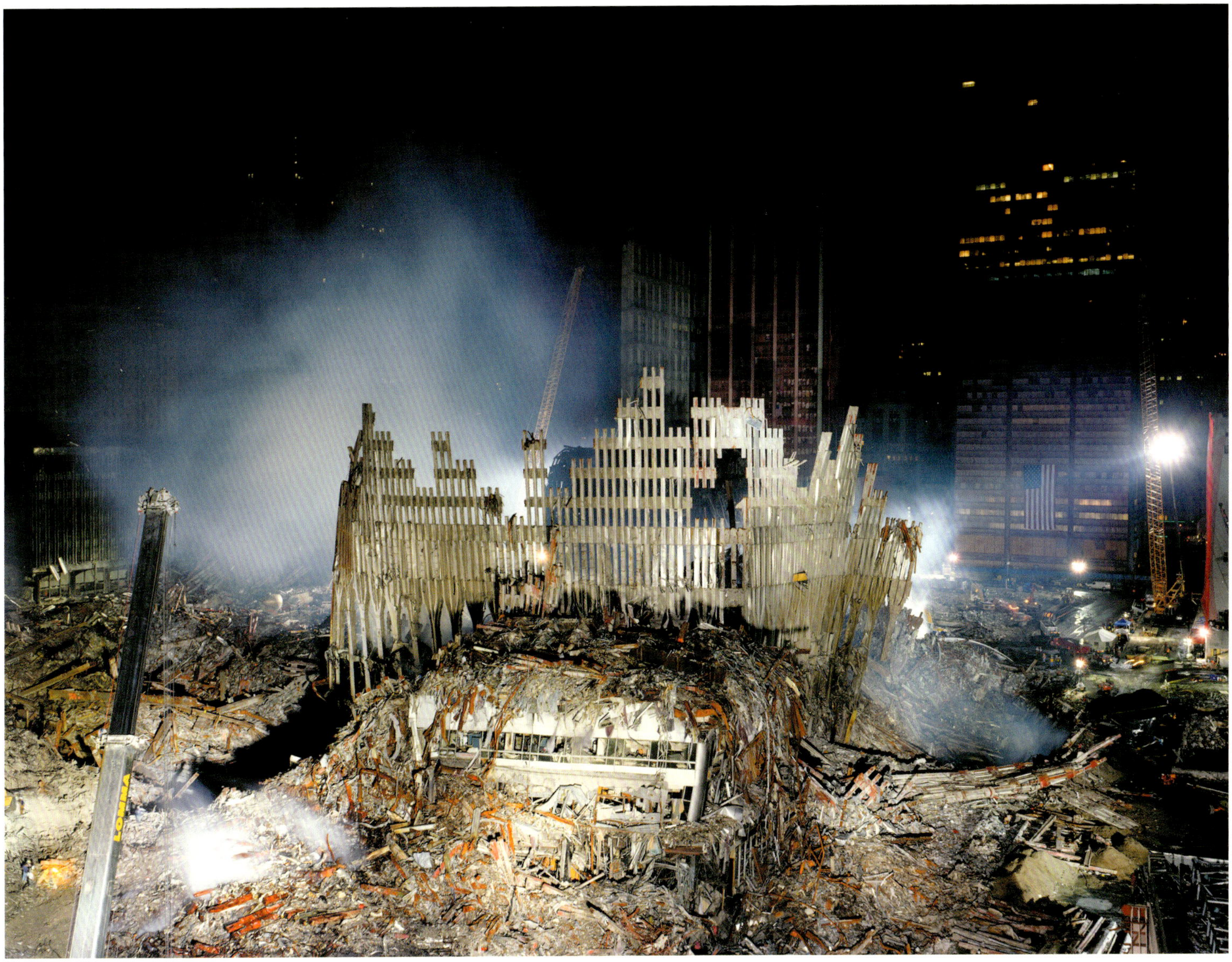

WORLD TRADE CENTRE, TWIN TOWERS

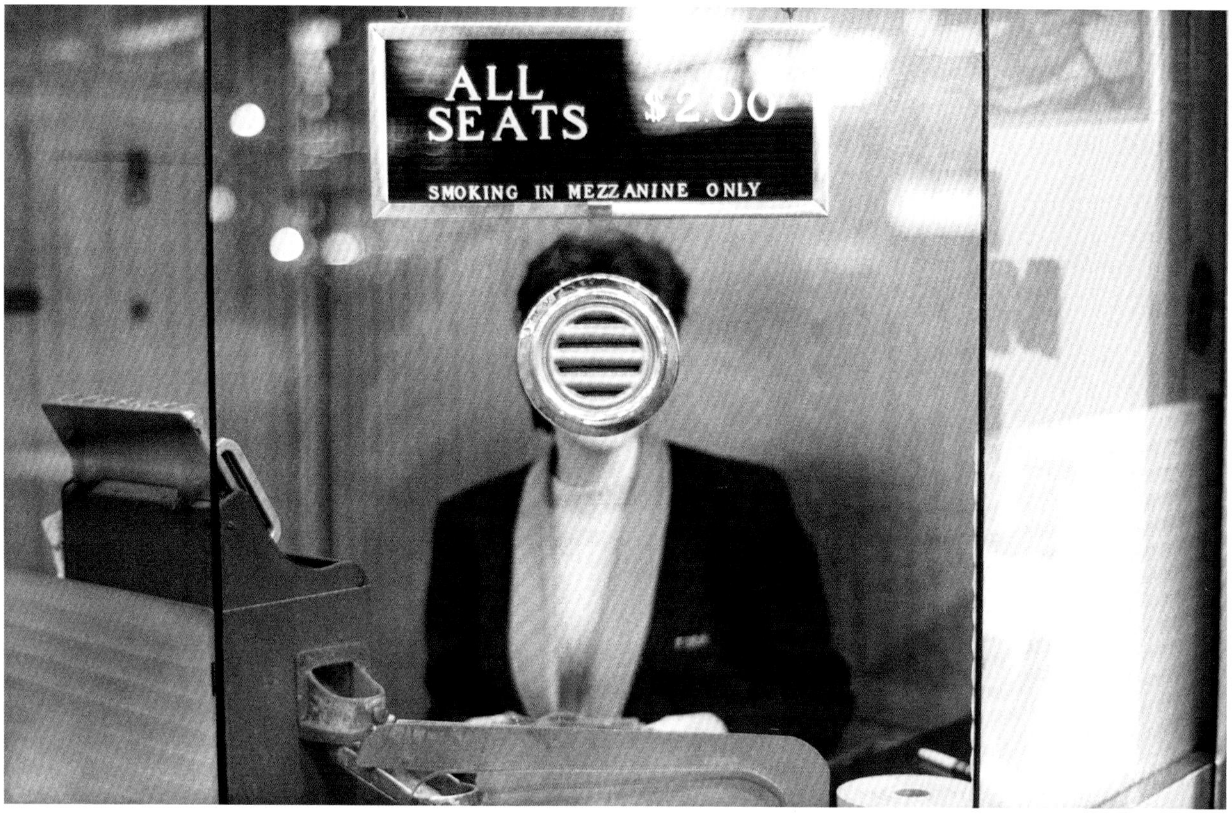

UNTITLED

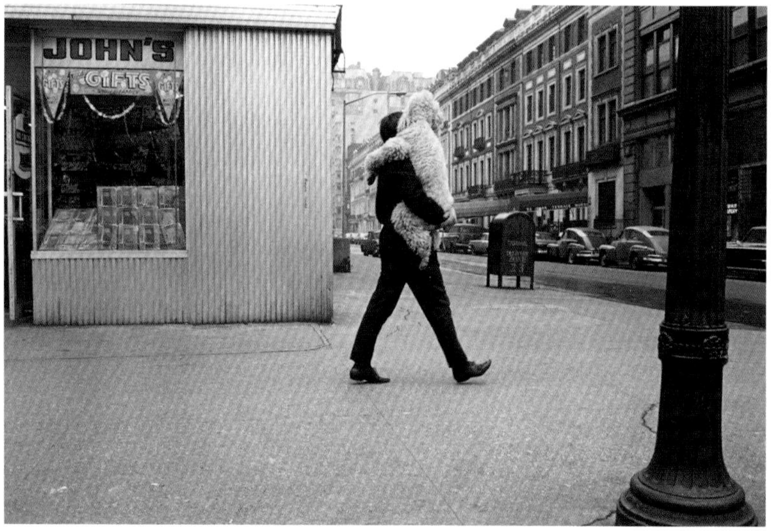

UNTITLED

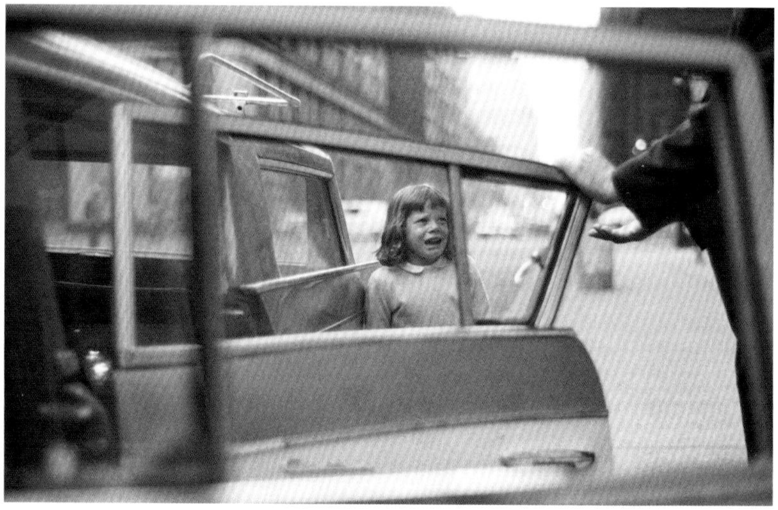

UNTITLED

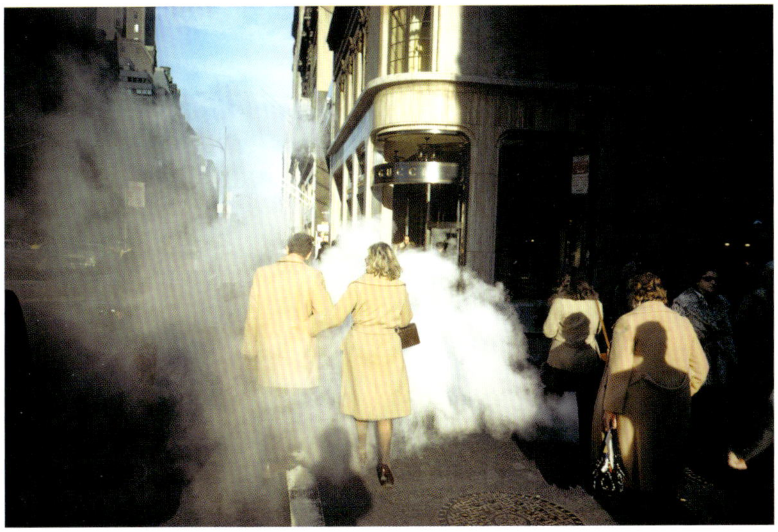

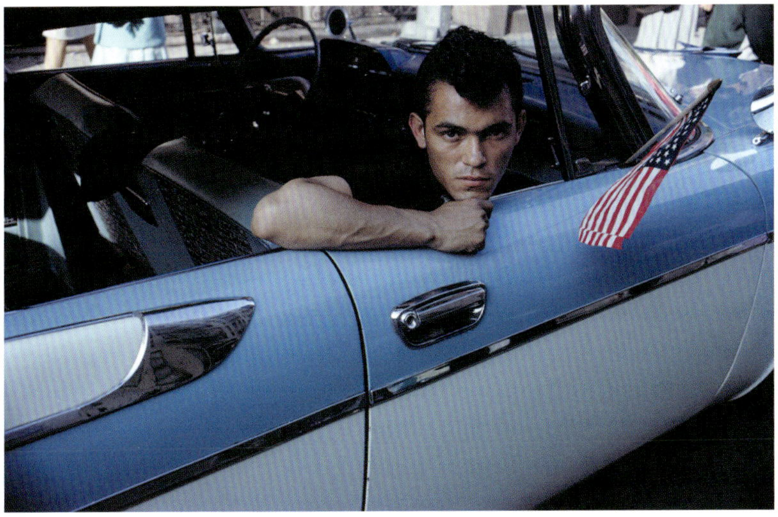

UNTITLED
UNTITLED

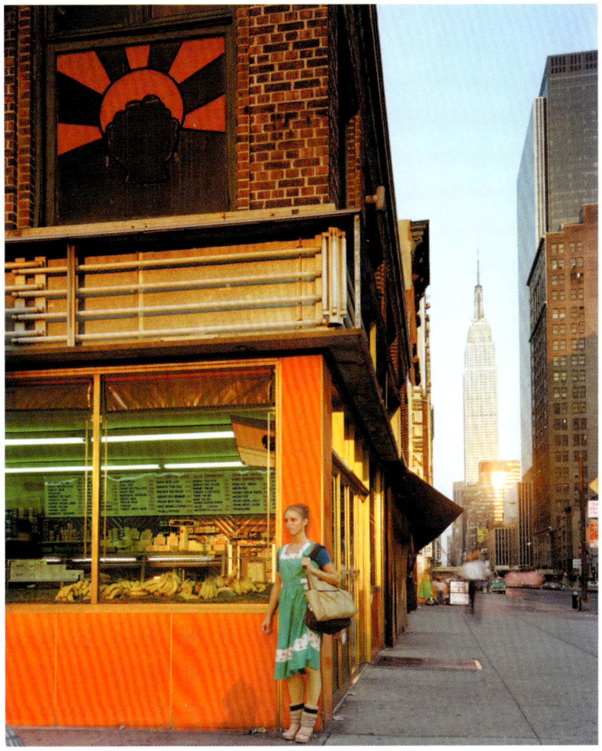

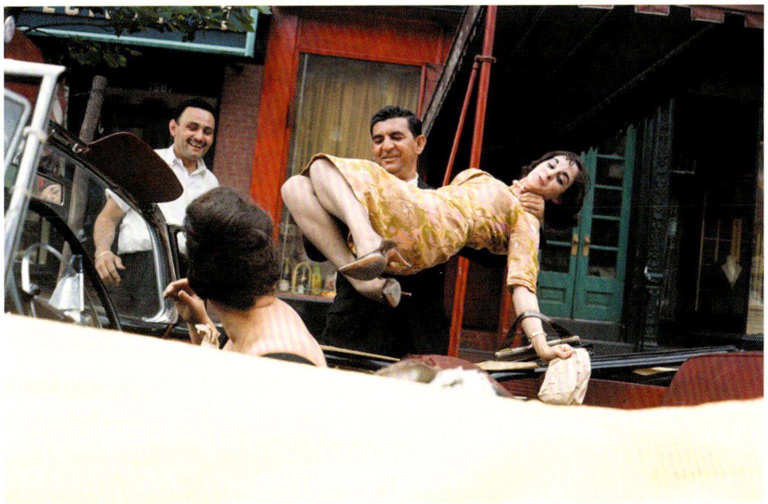

UNTITLED
UNTITLED

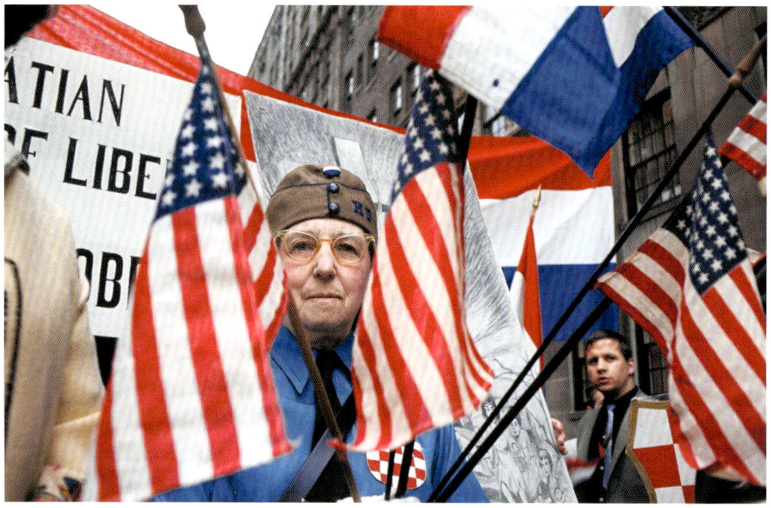

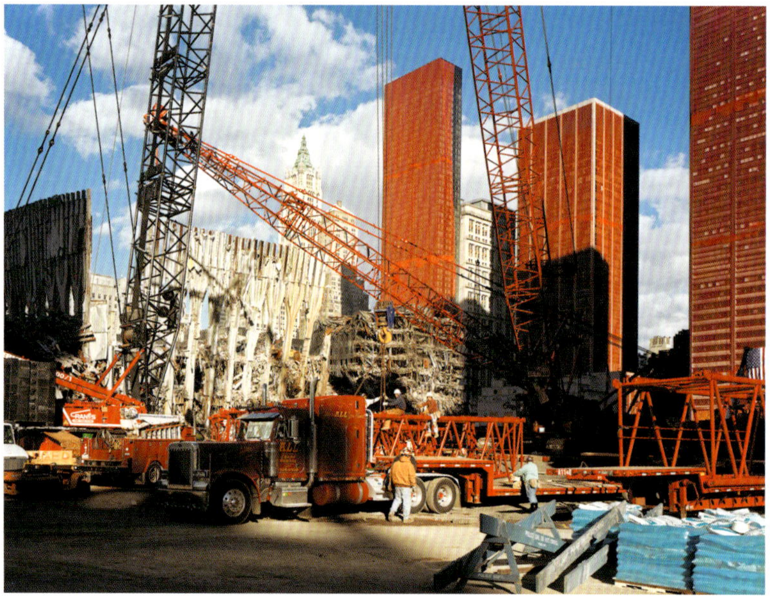

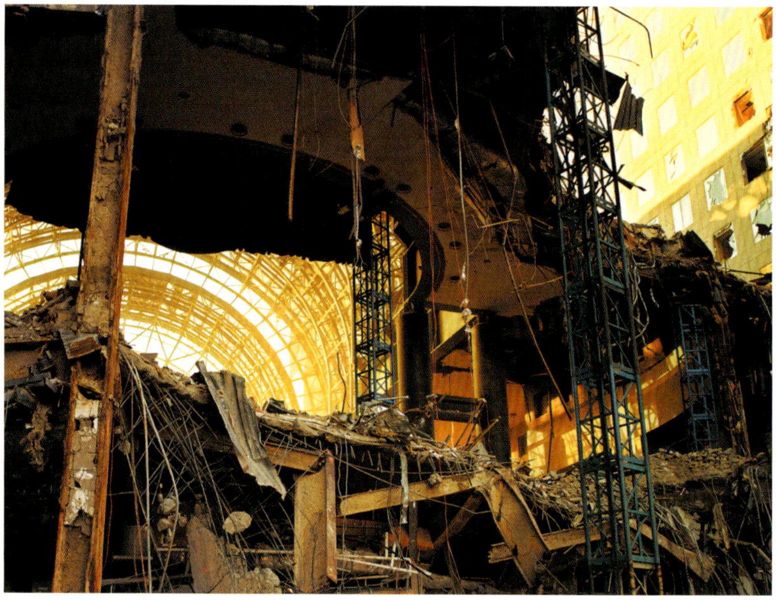

UNTITLED

AN AUTUMN AFTERNOON

UNTITLED

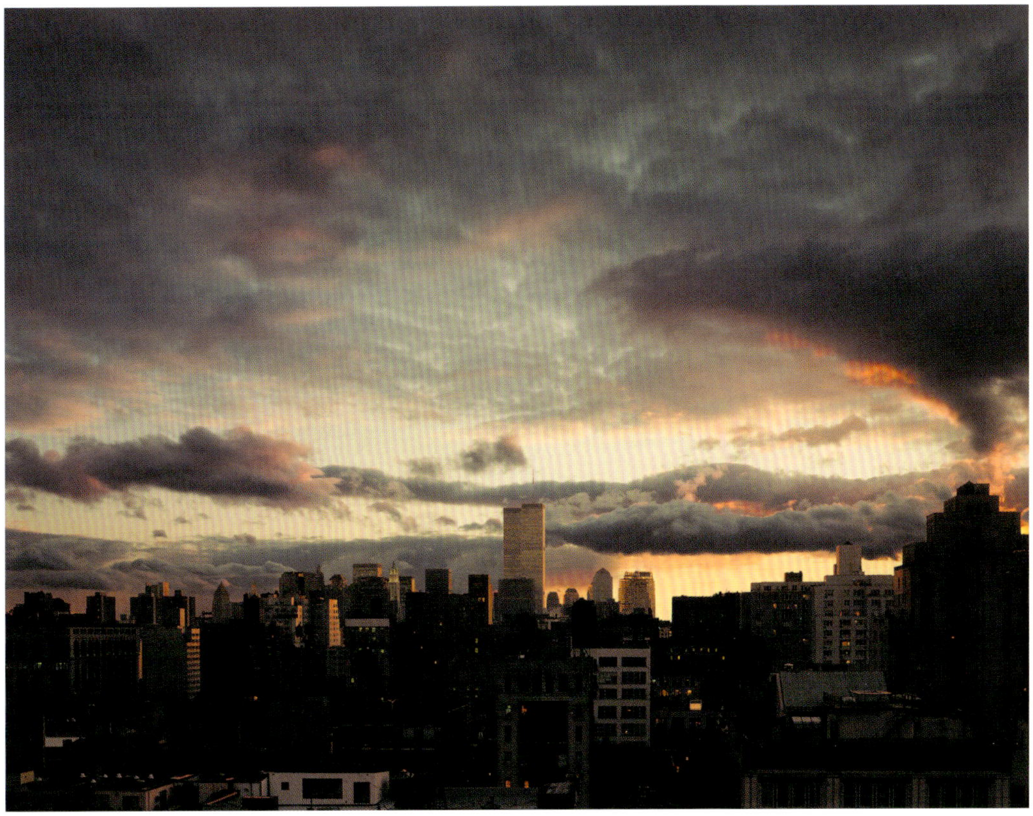

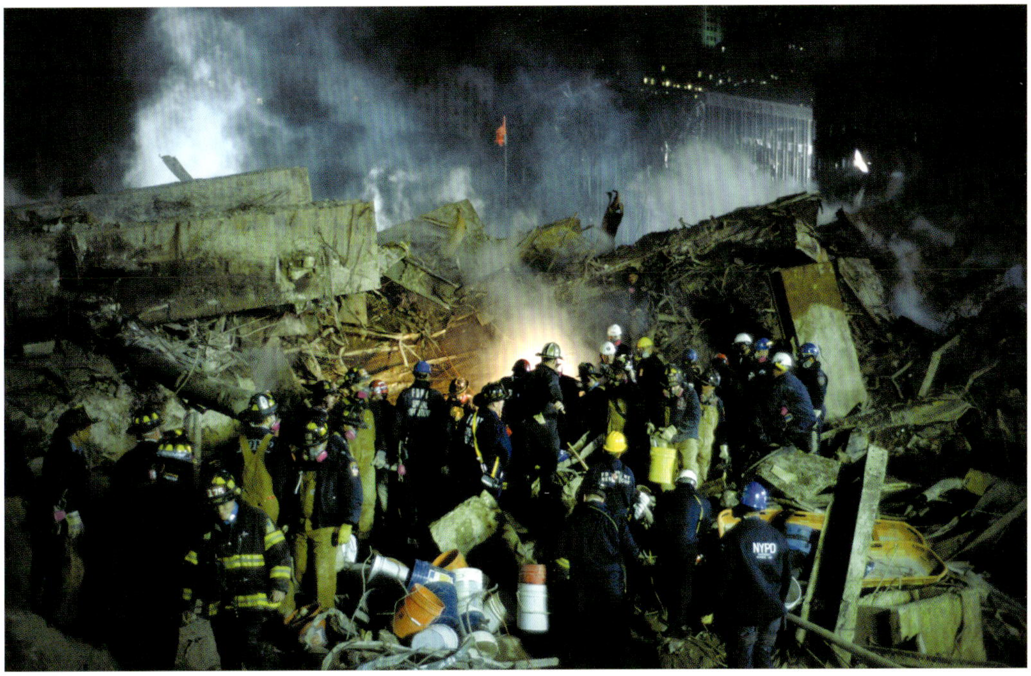

FIERY SKY, NEW YORK CITY
GROUND ZERO, NEW YORK CITY

KEN LENNOX Hon.FRPS
BEHIND THE HEADLINES

Ken Lennox was picture editor of the *News of the World* and *The Sun*. He's worked in Fleet Street for 30 years across such titles as *The Mirror*, *The Express* and *Today*. He is a professional news photographer, was awarded Royal, Sports and British Press Photographer of the Year, and captured thousands of definitive moments.

I like to do war

"It's one of these things you get hooked on. During the First Gulf War we'd been in the desert six months before the ground war started. We were in rags – uniforms in holes – underwear worn out. Kate [Adie] mentioned our underwear on the television news. All over Britain women sent packets of cotton drawers. She said "Do you want some?" "No Kate, if they found out I was wearing ladies knickers it wouldn't go down well". A few days later I was desperate and said "Yes". I wore them in the shower where you washed yourself with buckets of water. I was finishing when a tanky [tank soldier] came in. He asked what I was wearing. "Kate Adie's knickers". He looked at me strangely… then asked me to get some for him. My favourite picture of Kate is where she's posing with a group of soldiers – they loved her".

Mrs Thatcher

"It was 27 November 1990. I'd been brought back from the Gulf War. The writing was on the wall for MrsThatcher. I took my ladder to Downing Street. A spokesman came out of Number 10 with a sheet of paper. It said, "I will fight till I win". I was there until midnight then back the following day at 6.30 am. Around 1 pm she came out, made a speech then ducked to get in the car. She saw the girls at the press office window weeping buckets. Her shoulders flinched, a tear on her face. I got to the car as it moved away. She leaned forward for a last look. I took one frame. Roy Greenslade, the *Mirror's* editor, called me back to the office to talk about it. He asked: "Did you get that on your own?" I said "I haven't a clue". At midnight we'd seen the papers. If anyone else had the same image they'd have used it. *The Mirror* ran it as an exclusive for the second edition. People remember this image of Thatcher – the Iron Lady finally cracked".

Mother Teresa and Geldof make headlines

"Band Aid had topped the UK singles chart in 1984 with 'Do They Know It's Christmas' raising funds for African famine relief. Bob Geldof, Band Aid's brainchild, lived round the corner to me. I asked if he would come and see the camps in Ethiopia. He said "If you promise not to do any pictures of me with dying babies". I agreed. It was an expensive trip so we brought in ITN. We flew Geldof out in January '85. Mother Teresa was at Addis Ababa airport. She'd been asking the Ethiopian government for help. I called, "Mother Teresa. I've got Bob Geldof with me. Would you like to meet him?" She hadn't a clue who he was. I got the picture of two living saints together".

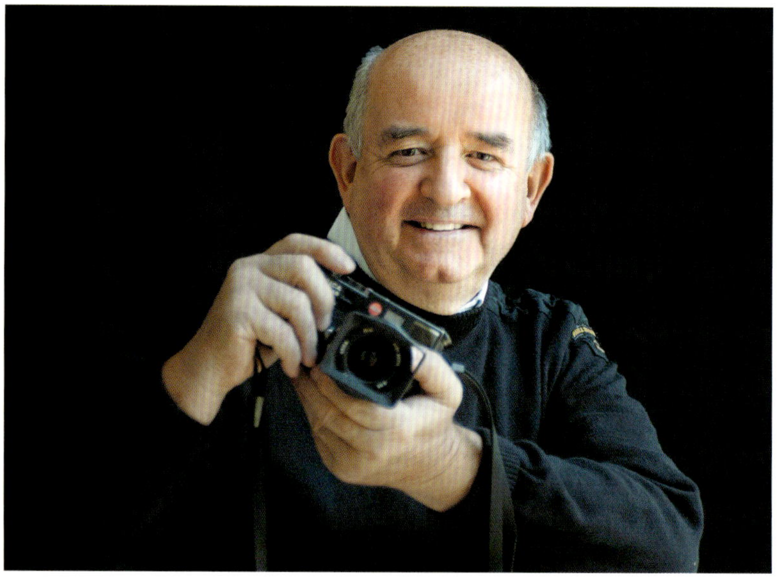

Savile Row diners

"I took a photo recently from a window in Savile Row. I'd spotted a British Telecom Outreach van and three BT workers having their lunch each day with a glass of wine, at tables set with tablecloths. It's won the Funniest Picture of the Year".

Gentleman photographer

"In 2013 I'll be 70. I'm going to become a gentleman photographer – no more commissions. I want to do something on street life and poverty in Britain, starting with poverty – lots of people are suffering. Poverty has affected me. I went up to Leeds when the social security people told me about a single lady in a council estate who'd been a bus conductress all her life, looked after her mother who'd died 2 years before and got home one day, to find the neighbours had gutted the place. She sat there wearing her clippy's outfit. I'm looking through the lens of my Hassleblad. I didn't do squalor. I did poverty. I gave her linoleum for the room, a table, chair, bedstead, a two-ringed cooker, frying pan, a cooking pot". Ken paused, overcome by emotion.

"I've been photographing war and famine for 53 years – nothing's changed. Nowadays there are fewer opportunities to see anything – we live in a cult of celebrity. Kids grow up wanting to be famous. The Press goes with what sells".

Monica Weller FRPS

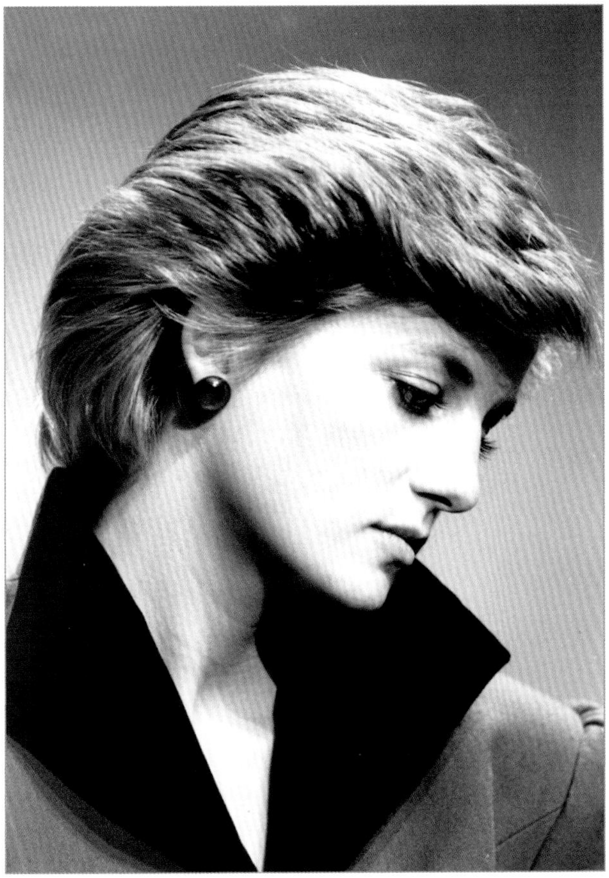

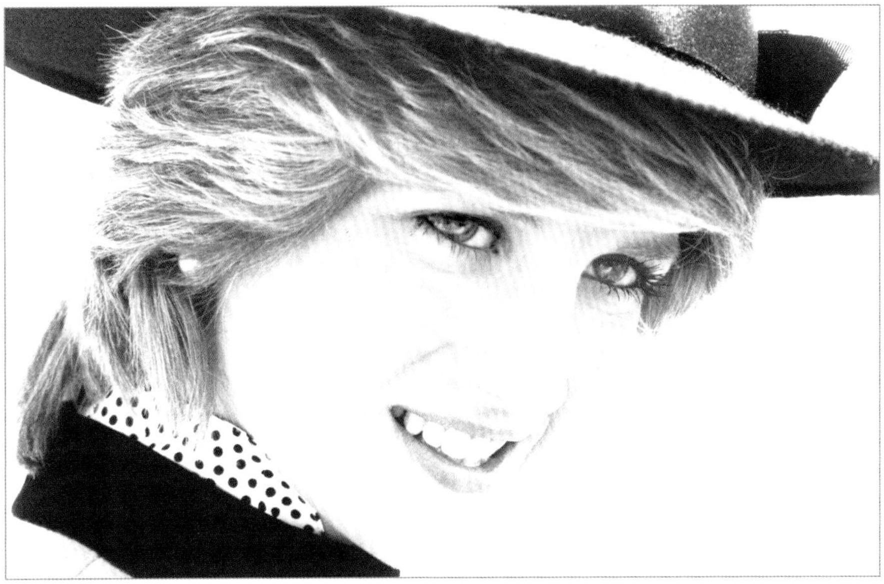

DIANA, NEW HAIR STYLE

PRINCESS DIANA IN CANADA

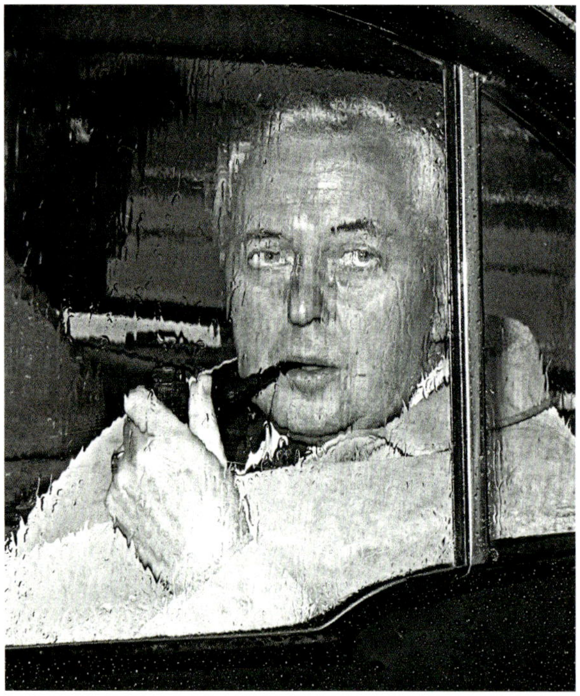

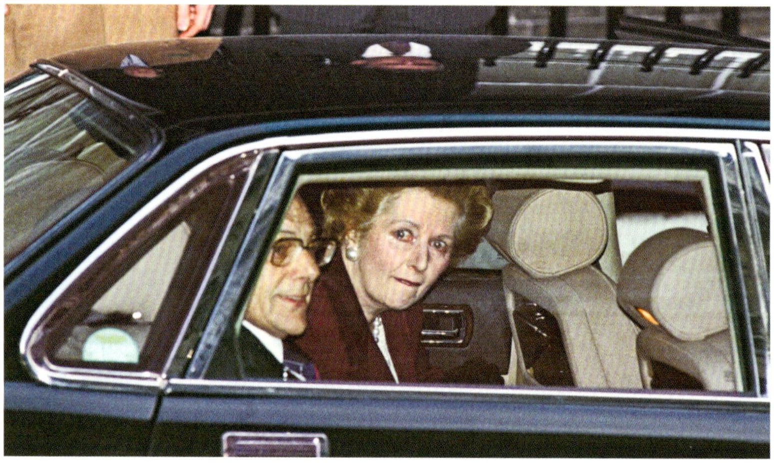

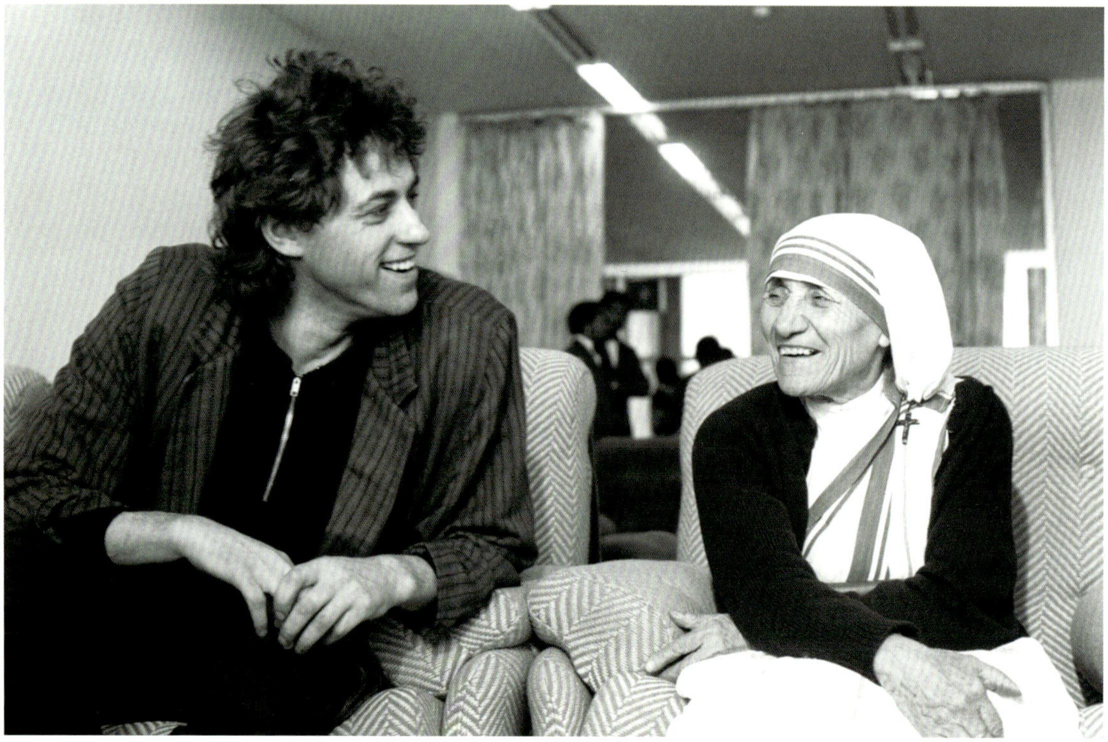

HAROLD WILSON, ELECTION CRISIS

TEARS FROM THE IRON LADY AS SHE LEAVES DOWNING STREET FOR THE LAST TIME

BOB GELDOF AND MOTHER TERESA

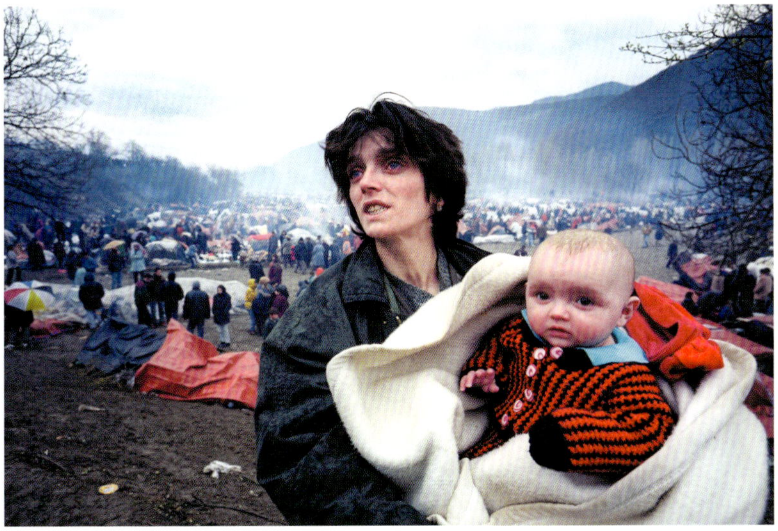

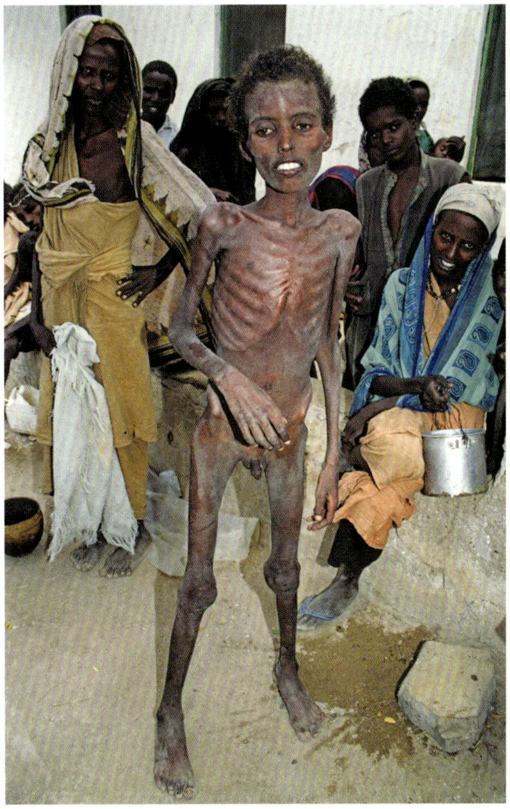

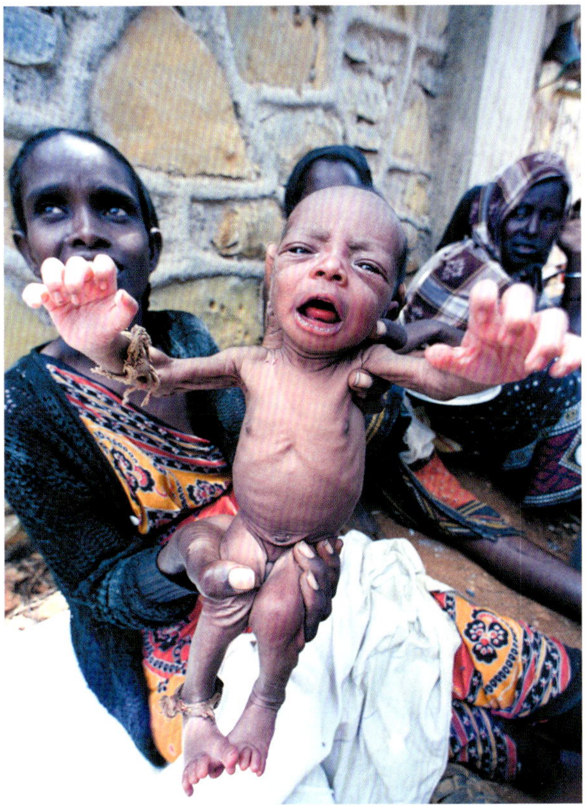

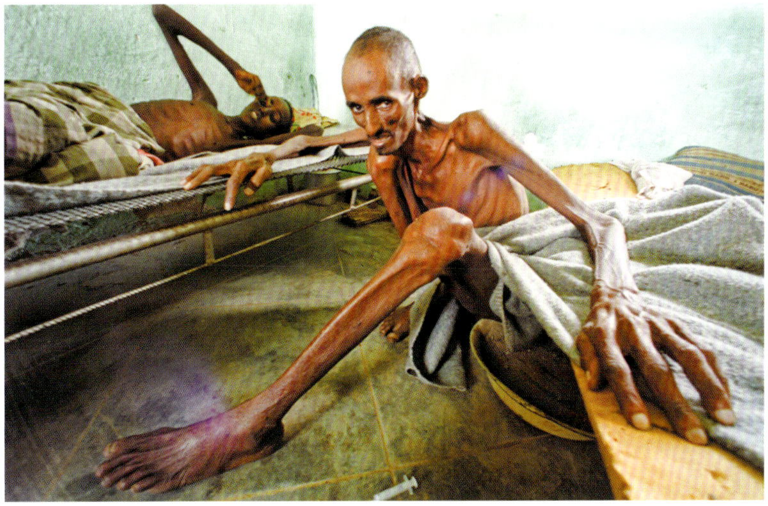

ETHNIC CLEANSING, KOSOVA
DYING BABY, SOMALIA

STARVATION, SOMALIA
STARVATION, SOMALIA

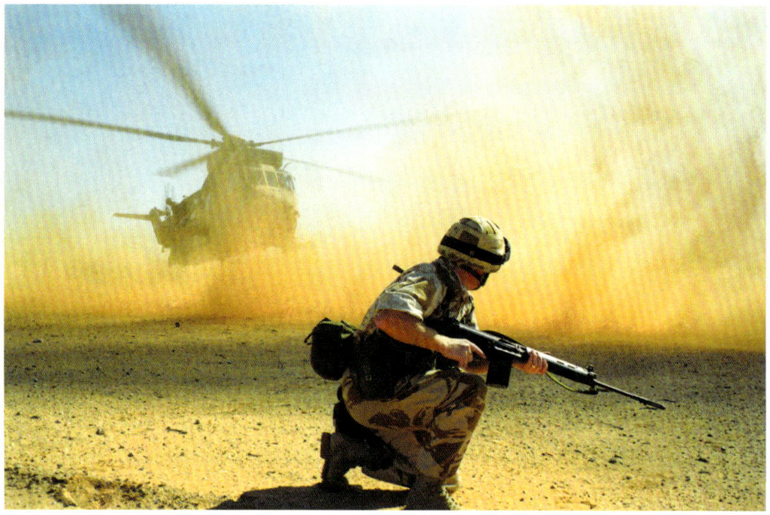

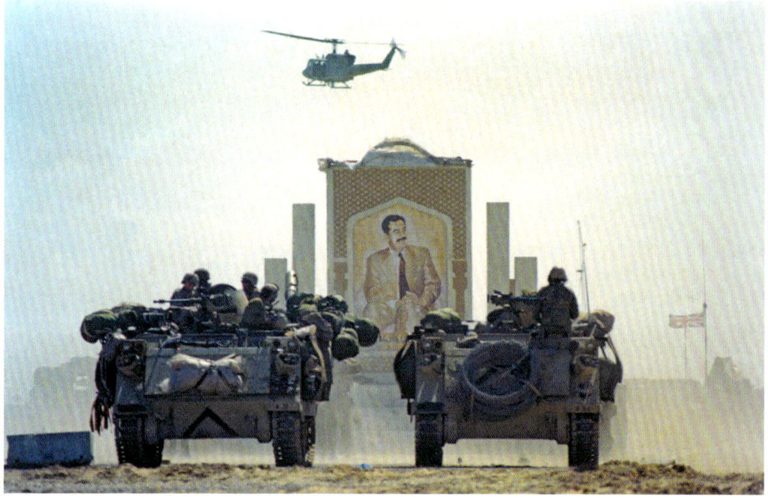

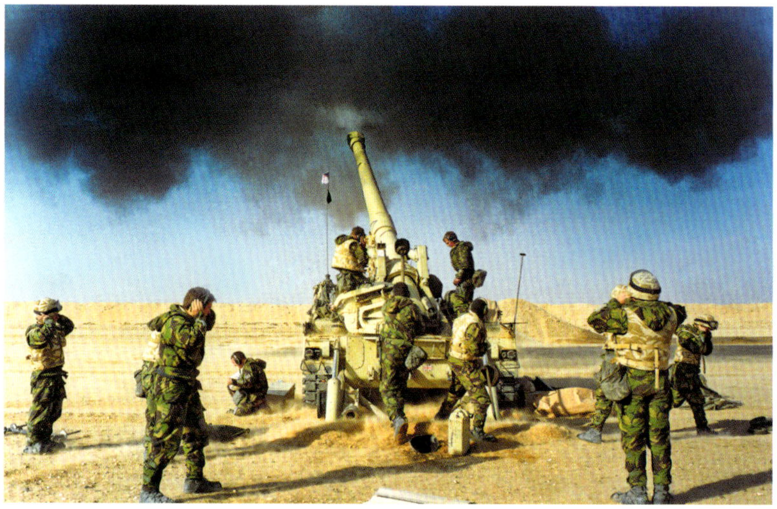

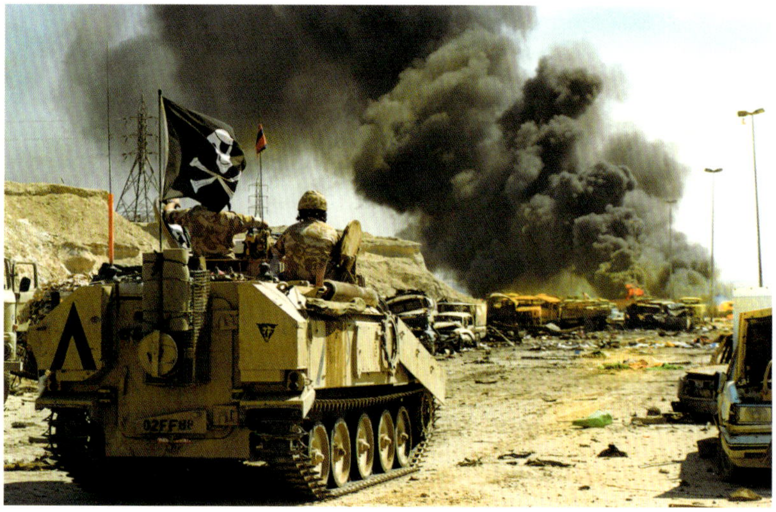

MEDIVAC, THE GULF WAR

GULF WAR ONE, THE BORDER OF KUWAIT AND IRAQ

OPENING SALVO, THE GULF WAR

BRITISH ARMOUR IN BATTLE, GULF WAR

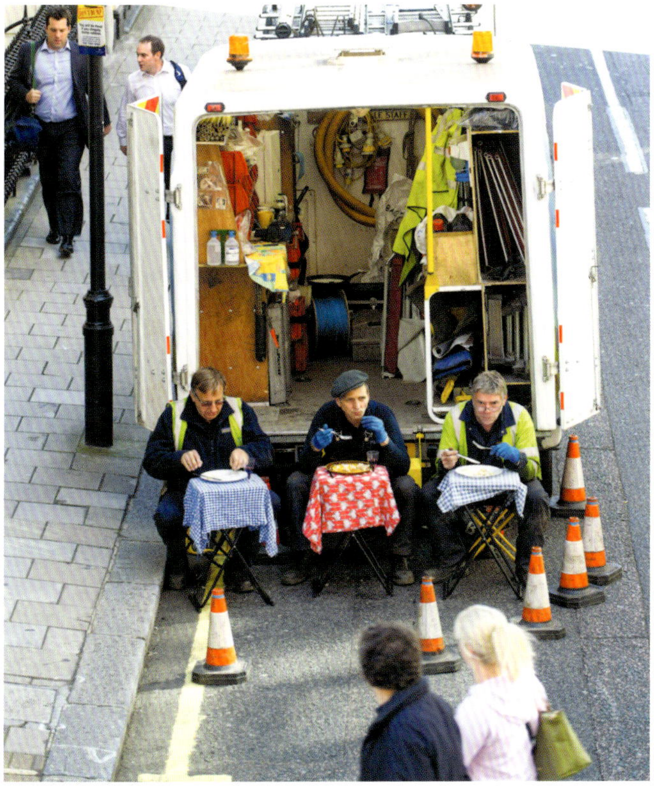

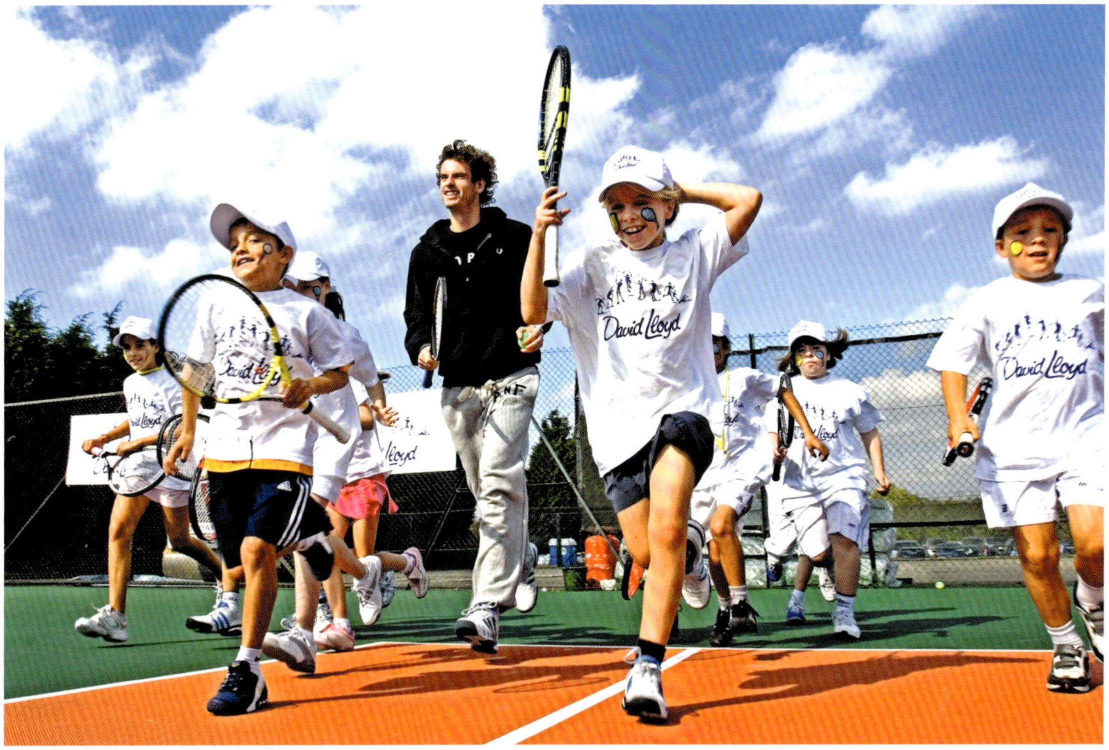

BRITISH TELECOM'S WORKMEN IN SAVILE ROW

ANDY MURRAY TRAINING TENNIS KIDS

BOB MARTIN Hon.FRPS

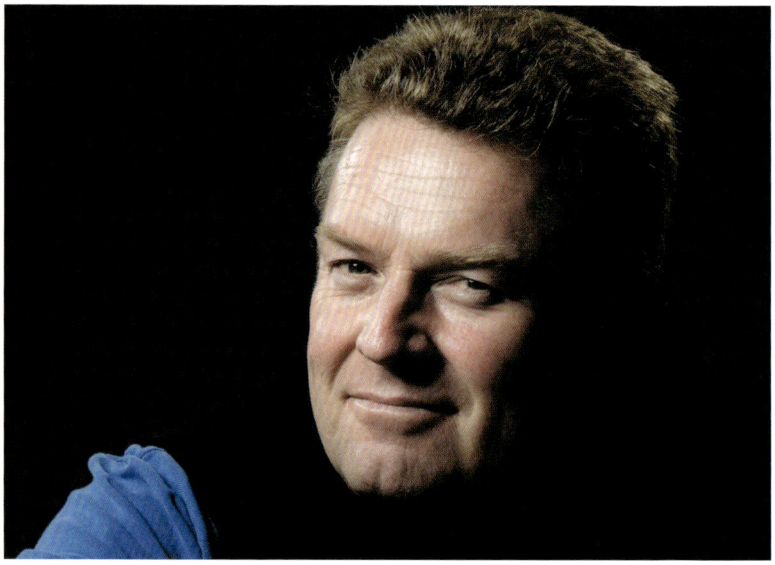

Bob Martin had an interest in photography from the age of 11. His parents encouraged him and he used to develop and print his own work in a small darkroom in a spare room. In his head, he wanted to be a vet, but he says "that involved far too much study for such as me" so, when he left school, he decided to take a year out and, as his father put it, 'get the photography out of me'. He says he never really finished that gap year.

In the following years, he had several jobs, including working at the Allsport Photographic Agency and for the American magazine *Sports Illustrated*. In 2011, he became the Photo Chief for the London Olympic Games.

Bob was always interested in taking pictures but he was not a sports 'nut' or sports fan; he was more attracted by the picture taking. "That's the way I drifted", he told me.

One thing that strikes me about Bob Martin's photography is that it is not just the action that he is capturing; it has an almost innate sense of fine art. All the images are beautiful and well composed.

"I really like composition", he told me, "and I like to think that my pictures have good composition. A lot of sports photography is about capturing the moment and a lot of that is being in the right place at the right time but good sports photography is about taking into account composition and content and taking action happening within that space. The most fantastic picture of someone flying through the air will be awful if the background is disturbing or the composition is bad".

Bob works with his business partner, Tom. "It makes life easier to work with other people" he says, "photography can be a very lonely existence. When I worked in a big agency, we would sit talking about our pictures every Monday and part of what drove you is that, if you had a bad shoot one weekend, you'd have the mickey taken out of you on a Monday. That meeting was part of what shaped me as a photographer: the fact that you were in competition with your pals to produce".

Bob covers the photography for Wimbledon and he wants his photographs to show Wimbledon off. When he takes an action shot of a player that shot says 'Wimbledon'.

Bob was invited to take over there when John Lyth, who was in charge of photography at the time, retired. Slowly, he started to change things. "As a club", he says, "Wimbledon has a very good relationship with photography and it's considered to be one of the best events in the World to go to for facilities. The photography is now very creative. So much so that the last two coffee table books for which we did all the photography won Best Illustrated Sports Book of the Year in 2010 and 2012".

I asked him if his role in the Olympics was similar to Wimbledon. "Exactly the same", he replied, "doing Wimbledon made me very popular in the British market because the photographers thought that if it was like Wimbledon it would be a good Olympics. Because it was in London and I'm English, I felt I should do it and it was a roaring success with the photographers. It's been very highly heralded as being the best Olympics ever for photography".

At the Olympics, he picked many spots he would go to, but he was disappointed how few people went to the more unusual ones. "You had a hundred people at the finish of the hundred metres, or at the final bend in races. We had some good positions but just one or two people went to these spots, not the number I would like to think would if the opportunity was there".

He has been Sports Photographer of the Year three times in the British awards and twice in the USA including 2012. When he started out, he had no idea that he would end up winning awards.

I wondered if there was one award he particularly cherished having won. "Yes", he replied, "The World Press Award for Sports. I've only won it once and it was for the photograph of the swimmer diving in where he'd left his legs behind at Athens Olympics in 2004. It's my most famous picture".

Bob is writing a book on his photography. He has worked on many books before but there is always a compromise and he wants to do one without compromise.

I asked him about the future. "In ten years time I'll be 64 and I want to be retired. In reality, though, I don't think I'll retire ever, I'll just slow down. I'm not going to be climbing the mountain to do a ski race but I'm still going to be in the valley. I'll still take pictures whilst I feel I bring something to the table when I get my cameras out", he concluded.

David Cooke ARPS

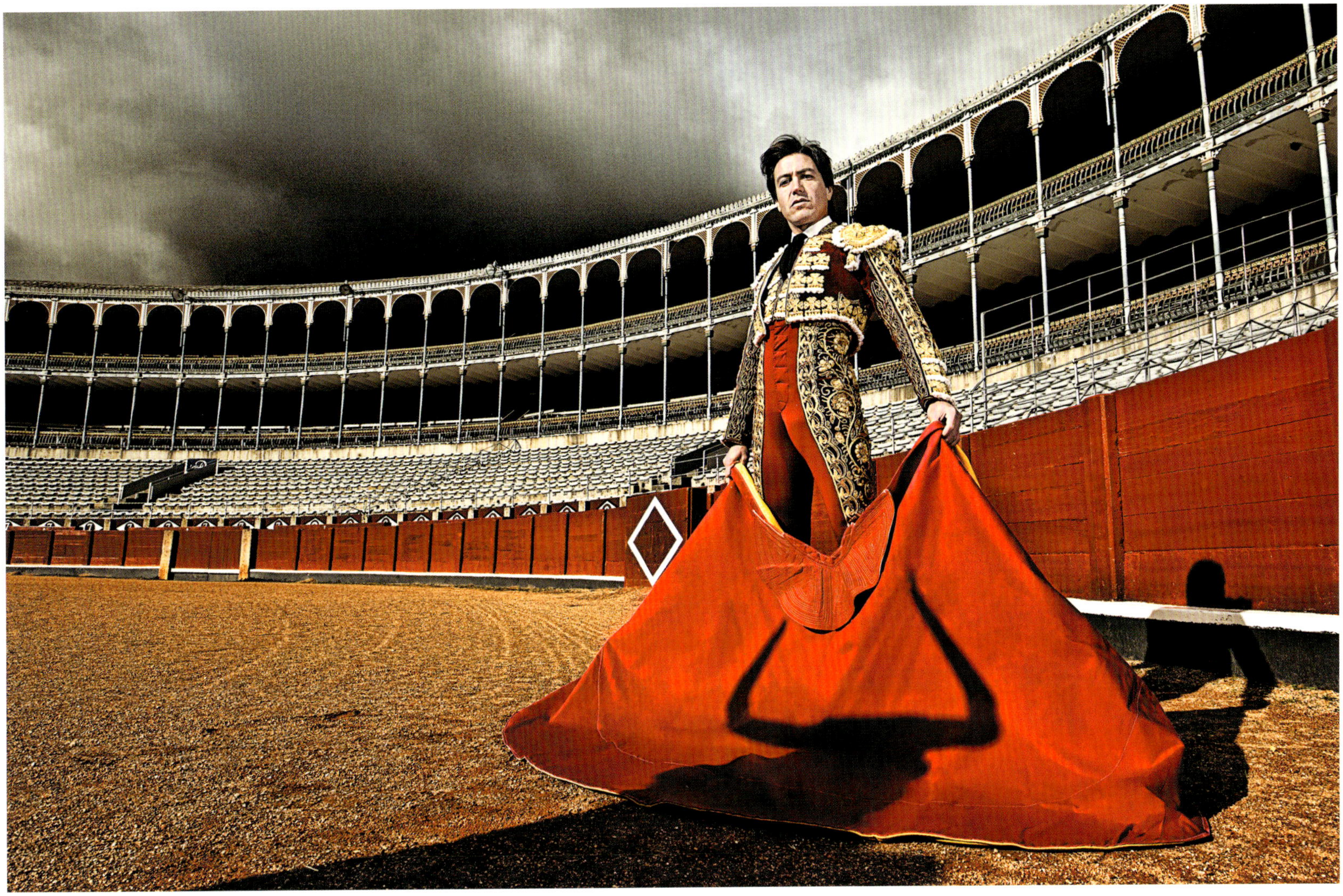

MATADOR

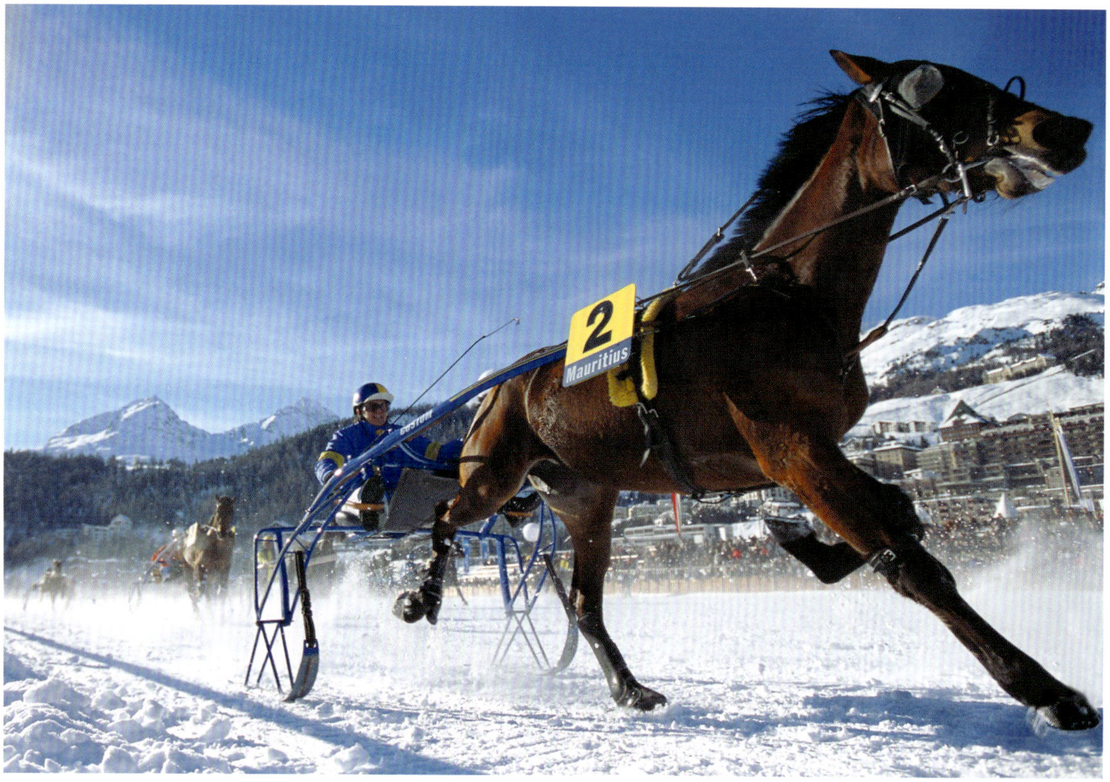

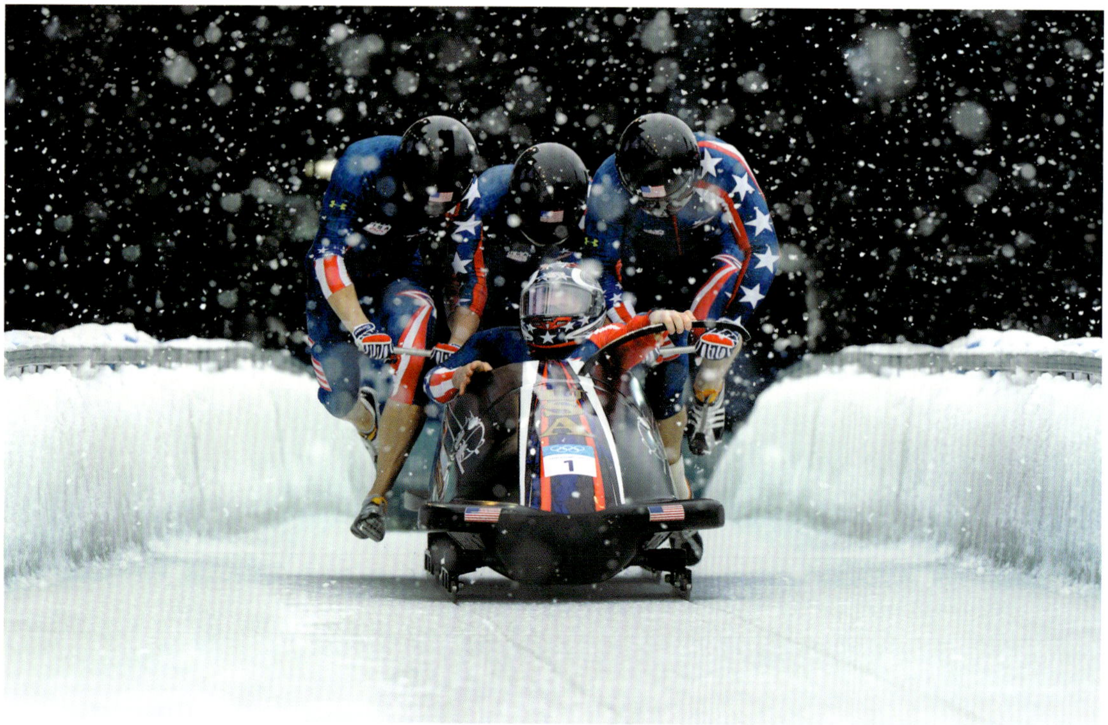

TRAPS AT ST MORITZ
USA BOB SLEIGH

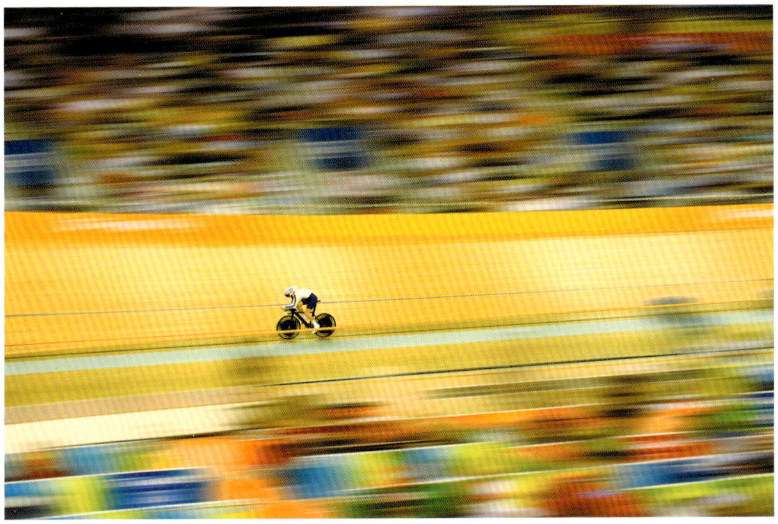

UNTITLED

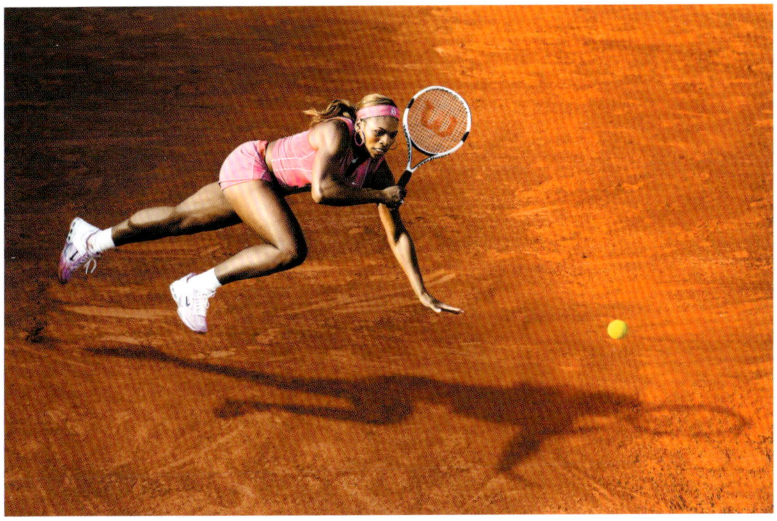

SERENA WILLIAMS

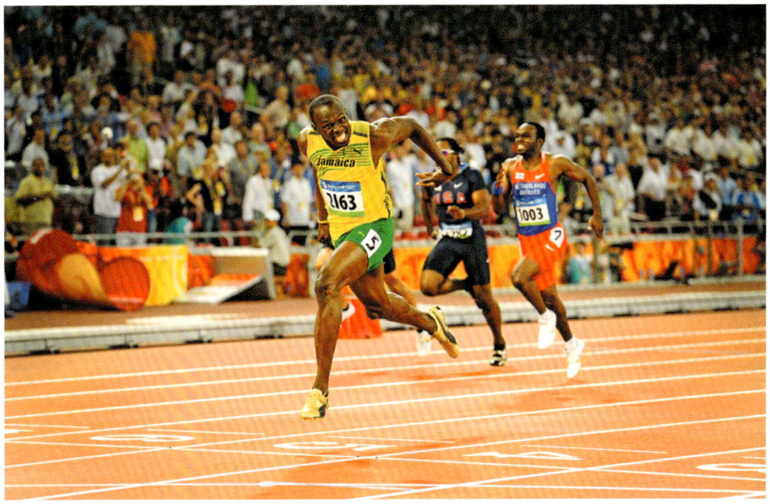

USAIN BOLT

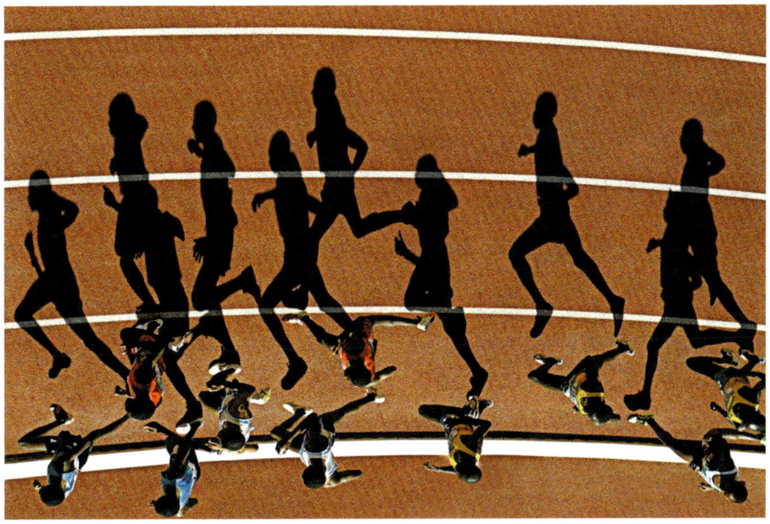

UNTITLED

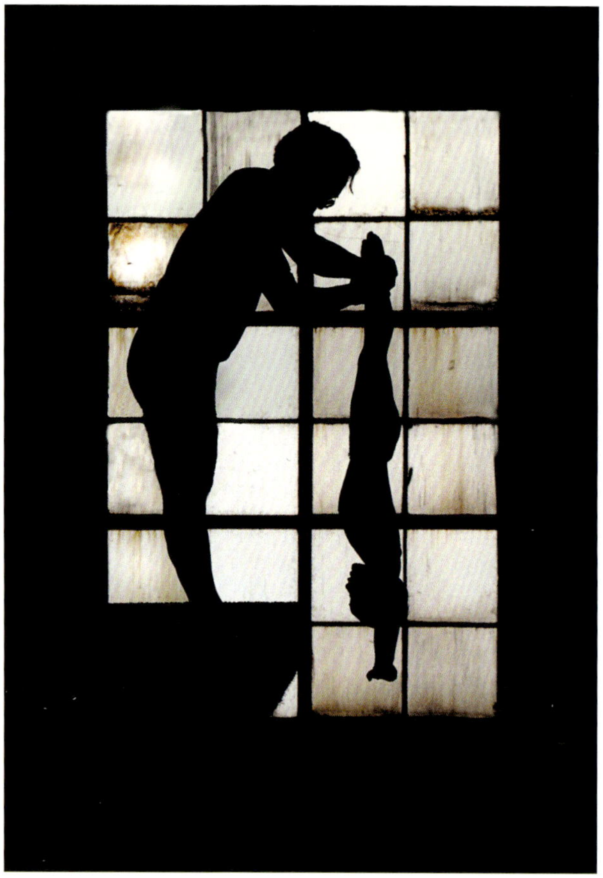

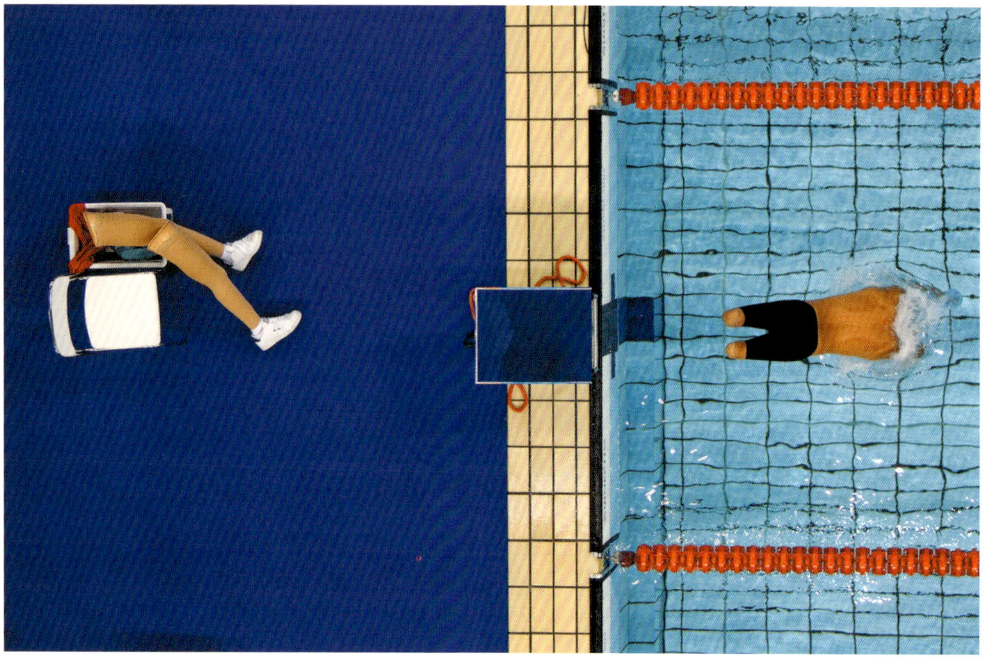

CHINESE DIVER
DISABLED SWIMMER

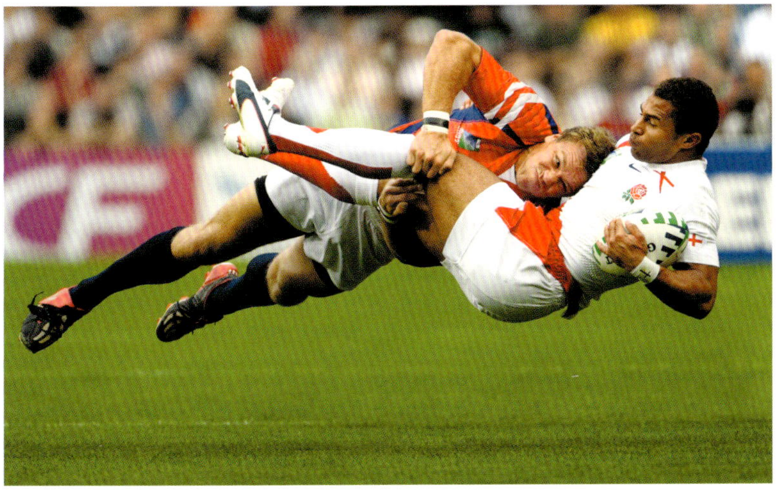

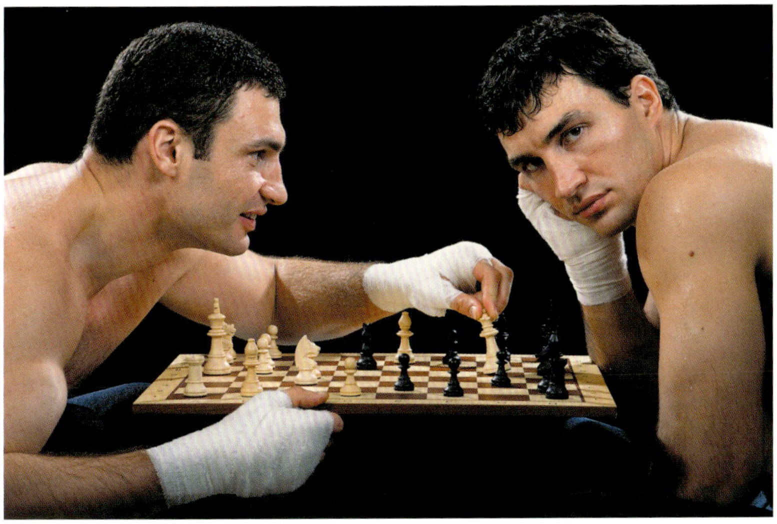

UNTITLED

THE KLITSCHKO BROTHERS

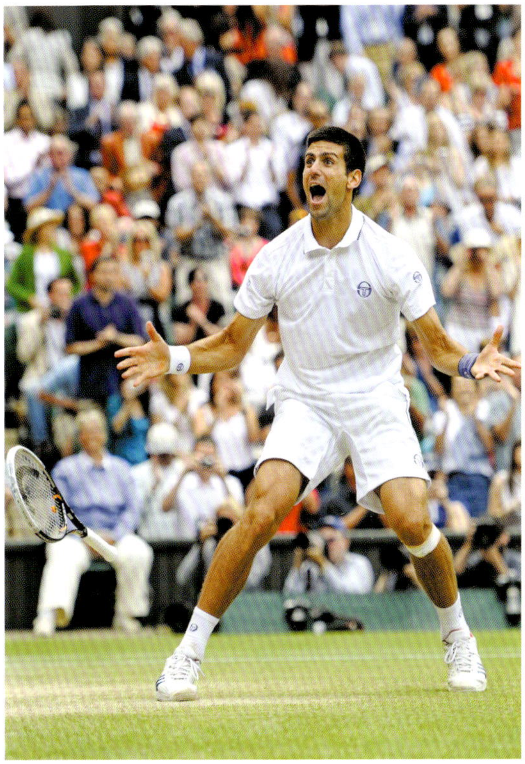

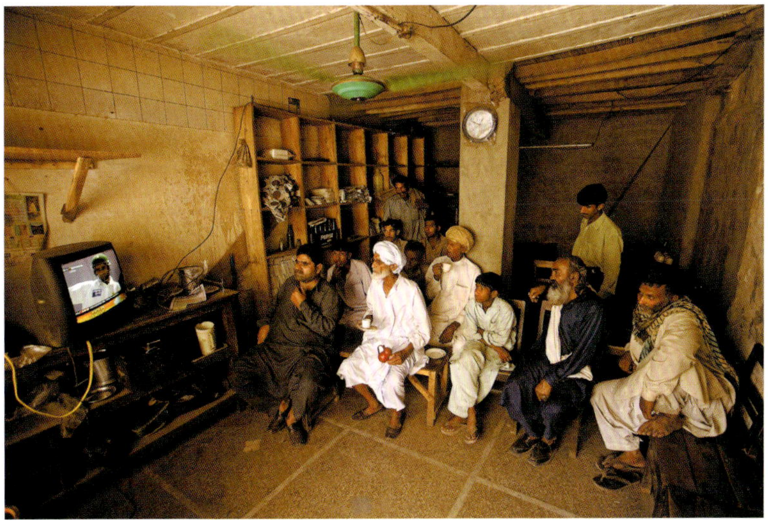

NOVAK DJOKOVIC

UNTITLED

RINKO KAWAUCHI Hon.FRPS
ILLUMINANCE

In 2012, Rinko Kawauchi was awarded The Society's Honorary Fellowship. When we met at the Awards Ceremony held in London at the Royal Society in September 2012, we talked about her work.

Kawauchi's photographs earned her a place on the four-strong shortlist for the 2012 Deutsche Börse Photography Prize. Her photographs deserve our attention because they map our appetites and fears, they transmit our times.

Rinko Kawauchi is a poet of the intimate and the everyday. The work on show at the Photographers' Gallery as part of the Deutsche Börse award comes from two recent series, *Illuminance* (2007-9) and *Iridescence* (2010). Light, often opaque and glowing, and movement are two constants, but so too is a quiet stillness that, in Kawauchi's best photographs, you can almost hear. 'I prefer to listen to the small voices in the world, those which whisper,' she writes in her artist's statement; '...my eyes naturally focus on small things.' In so doing she brings these to an unanticipated visual dominance.

Rinko Kawauchi (born 1972, Japan), began making photographs at the age of 19. Enrolled on a graphic design course at Seian University of Art & Design, she initially used her camera in her spare time. Photography eventually took over, and after graduating she began working in the photography department of an advertising agency, before moving to a Tokyo studio to shoot 'packaging and artworks'. She used every spare moment to study others' work. 'I respected photographers who had originality and a great and strong eye,' she says. Her first solo exhibition was in Japan in 1998.

In 2001 she published three books simultaneously: *Utatane* (which translates as Catnap), *Hanabi* (Fireworks) and *Hanako*, a study of a young girl. In Japan, photo-books are the primary form of publication and take precedence over exhibitions. It was therefore a natural first step for Kawauchi, who still lives and works in Tokyo, and who had been hand-making her own books for years. Such accomplished bodies of work coming seemingly from nowhere, startled her audience and she won international acclaim.

Further publications include *Aila* (2004), followed in 2005 by The Eyes The Ears, *Cui Cui*, an intimate recording of her family life, and *Rinko Diary I* and *II* (2005/2006), a collection of her mobile phone images she had posted daily on her blog. In 2010 *Murmuration* was published, the result of a commission by the Brighton Photo Biennial. Her most recent publication, *Light and Shadow* (2012) is a self-published project in aid of survivors of the Tohoku earthquake.

Although she has used 35mm, large-format and panoramic cameras, she has settled on the twin-lens medium-format Rolleiflex. She says it is 'a good match for me. It hardly makes a sound when I push the shutter, and it is cute and classic.'

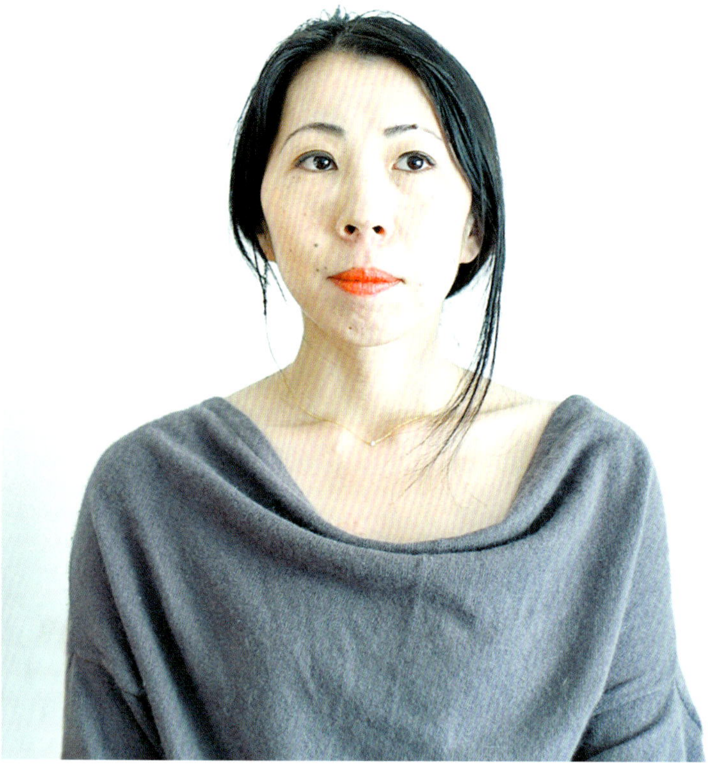

Her photographs revel in highly charged sensations, which she reveals from the most mundane circumstances and objects. The results can be eerie, even queasy. Her photographs have been compared to haiku poems, which use the precise description of ordinary things to reveal a weightier meaning.

Many of her images show things that are fragile, transient, such as fountain jets, the smoke from a firework, ripples, rain, a bubble. She examines the way light performs in patterns, reflections, dazzles, streaks, through gauze, through clouds, through water, through glass, and providing the reason why the book is titled *Illuminance*.

The key to Kawauchi's work is the order in which the images appear. She prints a small version of every photograph and lays them on the floor. 'First I choose the key image for the book and then I choose the next one and the next, over and over to create a composition.' The images work best in pairs and are designed to sit so in the book: 'Seeing images next to each other opens up the imagination and gives birth to something else.' Sometimes she will set up a shot from scratch – the lit cigarette is one – to be a match for one she has taken serendipitously. Often the link is simply their colour, which has a candy-like intensity throughout, although she says this is the way she sees colour naturally.

It is helpful to view her images and their sequence as a piece of carefully scored music. Note follows note, phrase follows phrase. The structure controls the mood of the work and the way we respond to it. 'I feel things in harmonies,' she says.

Michael Hallett FRPS

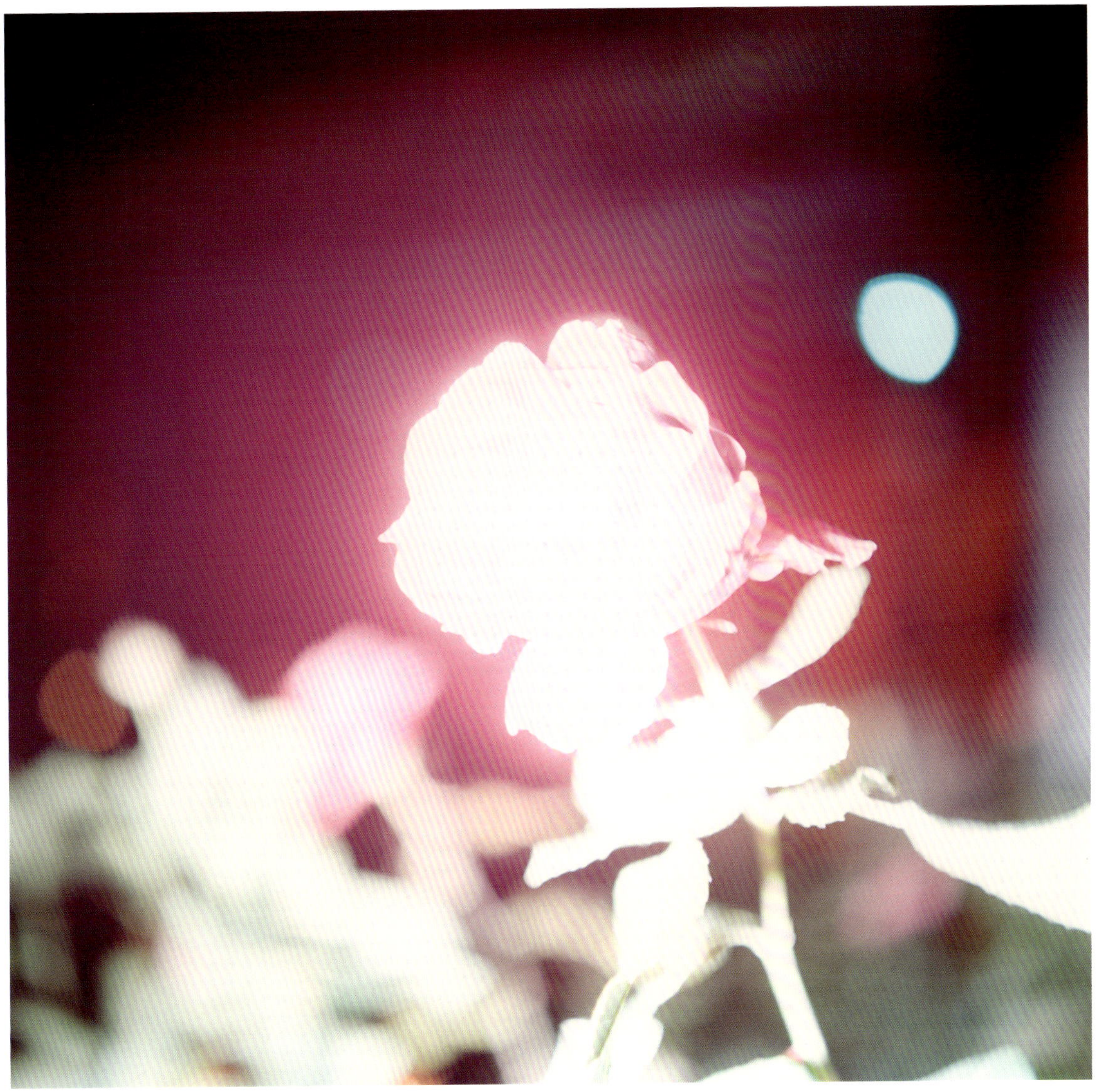

UNTITLED, FROM THE SERIES OF **"ILLUMINANCE"** 2009

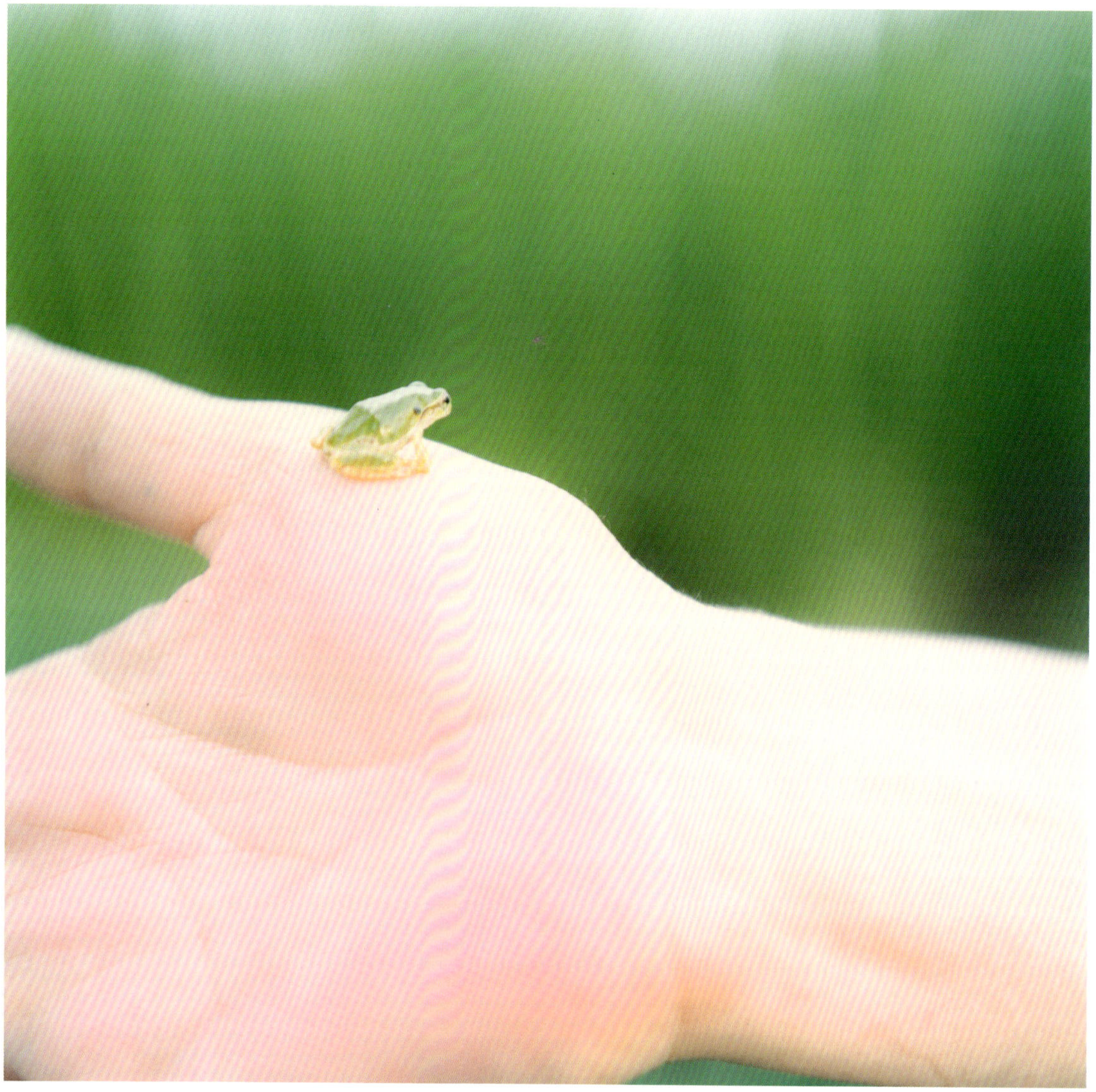

UNTITLED, FROM THE SERIES OF **"ILLUMINANCE"** 2009

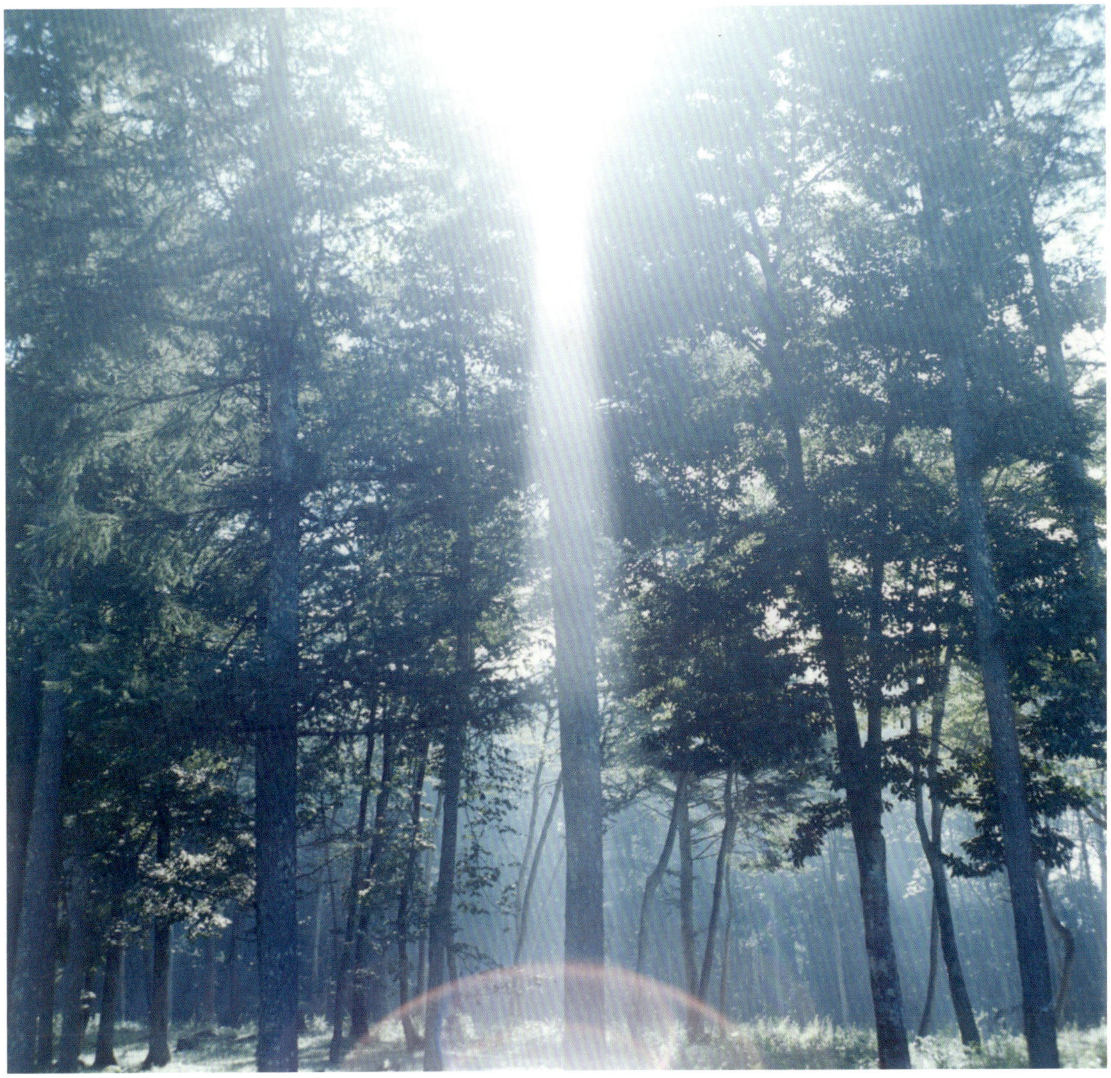

UNTITLED, FROM THE SERIES OF **"ILLUMINANCE"** 2009

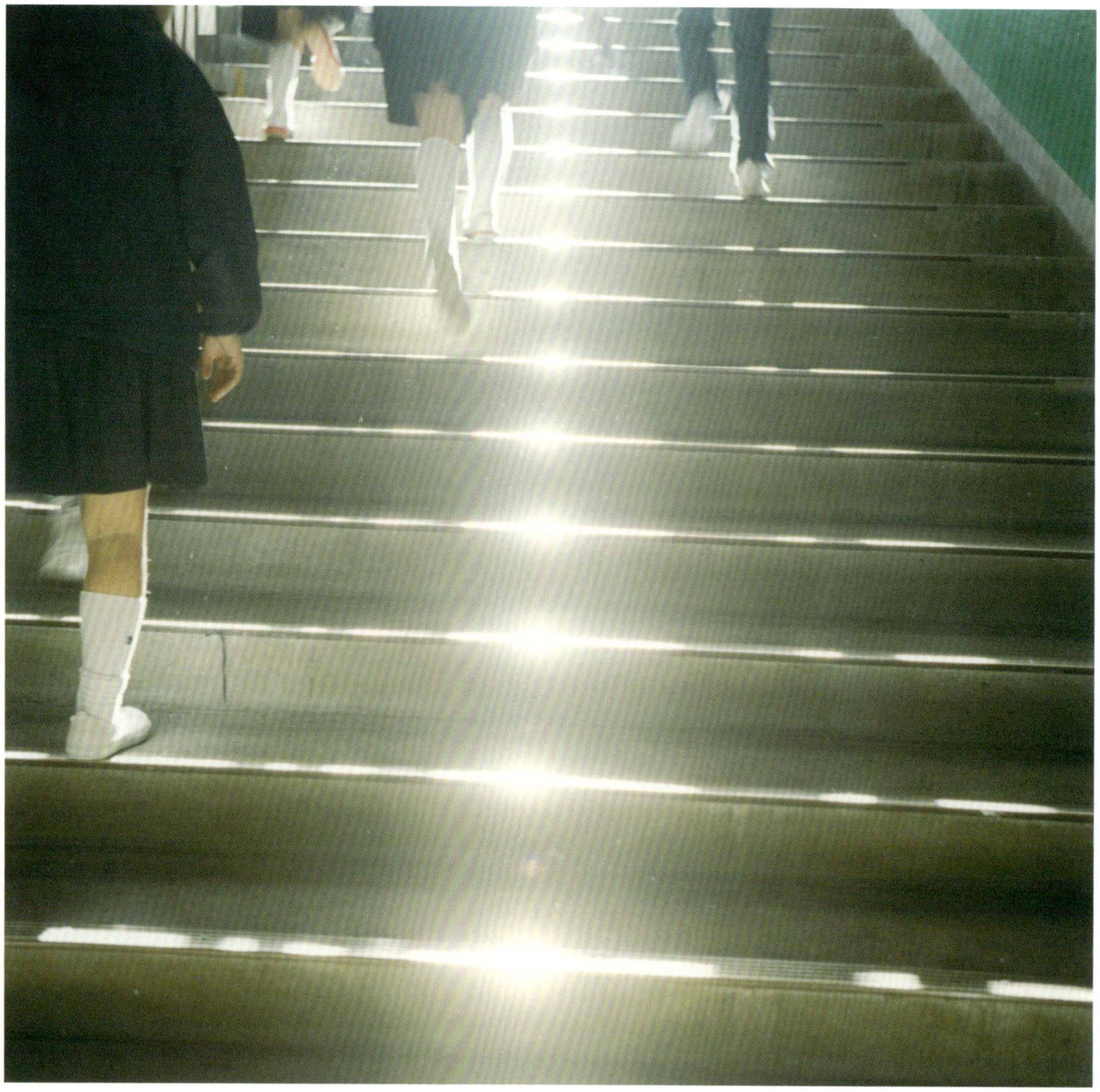

UNTITLED, FROM THE SERIES OF **"ILLUMINANCE"** 2009

UNTITLED, FROM THE SERIES OF **“ILLUMINANCE”** 2009

JASON BELL Hon.FRPS

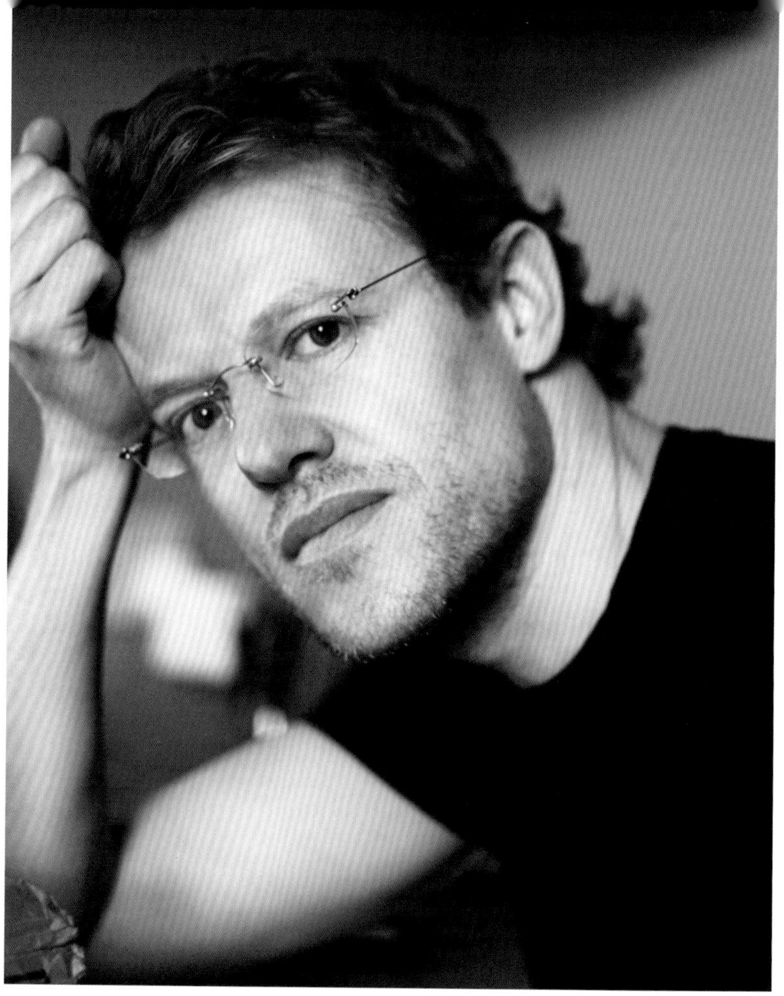

As we sat in his London Studio, I asked Jason Bell how he got into photography. "In one sense", he replied, "I didn't get into photography – it was always part of who I was." When he looks back, he realises that a significant moment was when he was given the key to the school darkroom at the age of 13. "That was Pandora's Box and this magic world opened up to me," he recalls.

"I remember devising a still life with bottles and things in my bedroom, taking a picture and processing it to make a print. For me the magic of that journey from beginning to end, totally threw me."

Jason studied politics, philosophy and economics at Oxford. As soon as he arrived, he got involved in the University Newspaper and Magazine and quickly became the photo editor of both. After university, he worked for some small magazines in London but was also temping to pay the rent. Eventually, he started to work for the *Sunday Times* so was able to stop doing other work.

There was then a steady progression and the first commission he got for the *Sunday Times Magazine* was Kate Winslet for the cover. "She'd just done 'Titanic' and this was a big deal for me", he said. As things progressed, he started to work for more and more magazines, including *Esquire* and *Harpers*.

He was still very young, only 21 but he wanted to work for *Vogue* and *Vanity Fair* and felt a bit stuck in London. His agent said he should to go to the States. He got a place in New York and started to work for *American Vogue* and *Vanity Fair*. When he came back, he worked for *British Vogue*. He feels that it all started to feed itself.

Jason sees himself as a portrait photographer rather than a fashion photographer. "For me, the most important thing is the person", he says, "I always research the people I'm photographing quite carefully so I know what they do".

He tries to do as much as possible in camera. "There's no substitute for sorting it out at the time so you can see that it's working or not working. You set up the situation to make it all work, you just push in a little bit of magic on the day, and you get something even better than you planned", he said.

I wondered how much getting the little bit of magic was to do with the relationship between him and the person he was taking the photographs of. "It's crucial", he said, "I find myself saying to people 'I can't do this without you – we have to do this together'. I encourage them to get involved".

Jason has many photographs in the National Portrait Gallery Permanent Collection. When he conceived the *Englishman in New York* book, he contacted the Gallery to see if they were interested in the concept for an exhibition. Their positive response helped him to get the book going.

The idea resulted from a shoot he did on the Met Ball for *American Vogue* on 'Anglomania'. He was shooting several English models in an English Tearoom in the West Village. The couple running it told him that there were over 100,000 English people living in New York and he wondered why so many English people had come here and what did they do here. He thought it would make an interesting project and started researching it. It grew from there.

His exhibition at the National Portrait Gallery lasted eight months.

I asked Jason how his videos fit in with his stills work. "A lot of my stills work is very narrative so it wasn't a very big stretch. For instance, there is a shoot I did with Courtney Love for *Vanity Fair* and I had a whole narrative idea in my head. She was living in England at the time and I decided that we would reference Alice in Wonderland. I conceived the whole thing so to shoot a video wasn't a big deal and it was a very good fit. The Courtney Love video was on the VanityFair.com website for quite a while.

What is clear though, is that he doesn't wish to move out of stills and do something else. "When I think about the thing I fell in love with, it's a picture on the wall. I've always loved movies but there's something about the way you can't put them on the wall that has always held me back. The photograph as the object, the print, still feels key to me".

Jason has some landscapes on this website, which are very different from his normal work. "It's ironic, in a way, that the main reason I became a photographer was Ansell Adams. I would pour over his photographs as a child and I absolutely loved his stuff. I remember being incredibly excited about that and thinking I want to be a photographer".

There is a marriage of the videos / stills work in a Royal Opera House campaign that he has done over the last 7 years. "They are opera and ballet stars in incredible settings and I think that you need to be a bit of a landscape photographer for that particular campaign. I think it shows in the work".

"We've had some moments on that campaign. I remember we were at a shoot in China with an opera star. The weather came in, it's snowing, and we're wearing Converse sneakers. Snow is coming down and you shouldn't really have opera stars standing in the cold. I worry she's going to walk off the set thinking 'I can't do this, my voice is so precious'. I'm freaking out a little bit, feeling we're not going to get this. But we do and there's the thrill of feeling we did it".

He is very conscious though not to work too much because he believes that if you are shooting 300 days a year, you are not producing great work on day 300. "I need the time to be able to think how do I want to do a shoot, where do I want to do it, how's it going to feel? If you are going from job to job that gets squeezed out".

Jason has now been a photographer for over 20 years and feels that a sort of calmness has crept in. "I don't feel so neurotic about it anymore. I remember finding it all much more frightening when I was starting out and now I have a deeper sense that it's all going to be OK", he said.

David Cooke ARPS

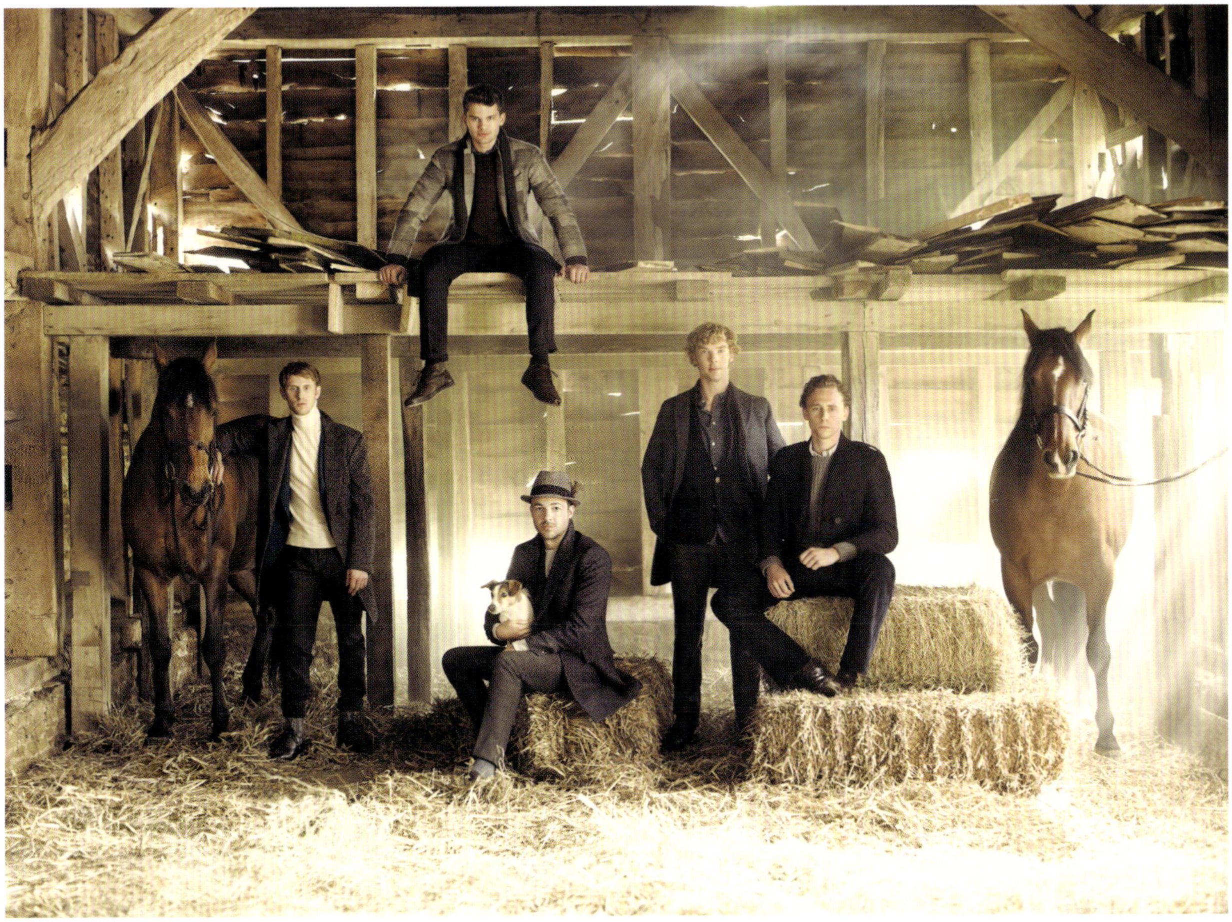

WAR HORSE FOR VANITY FAIR

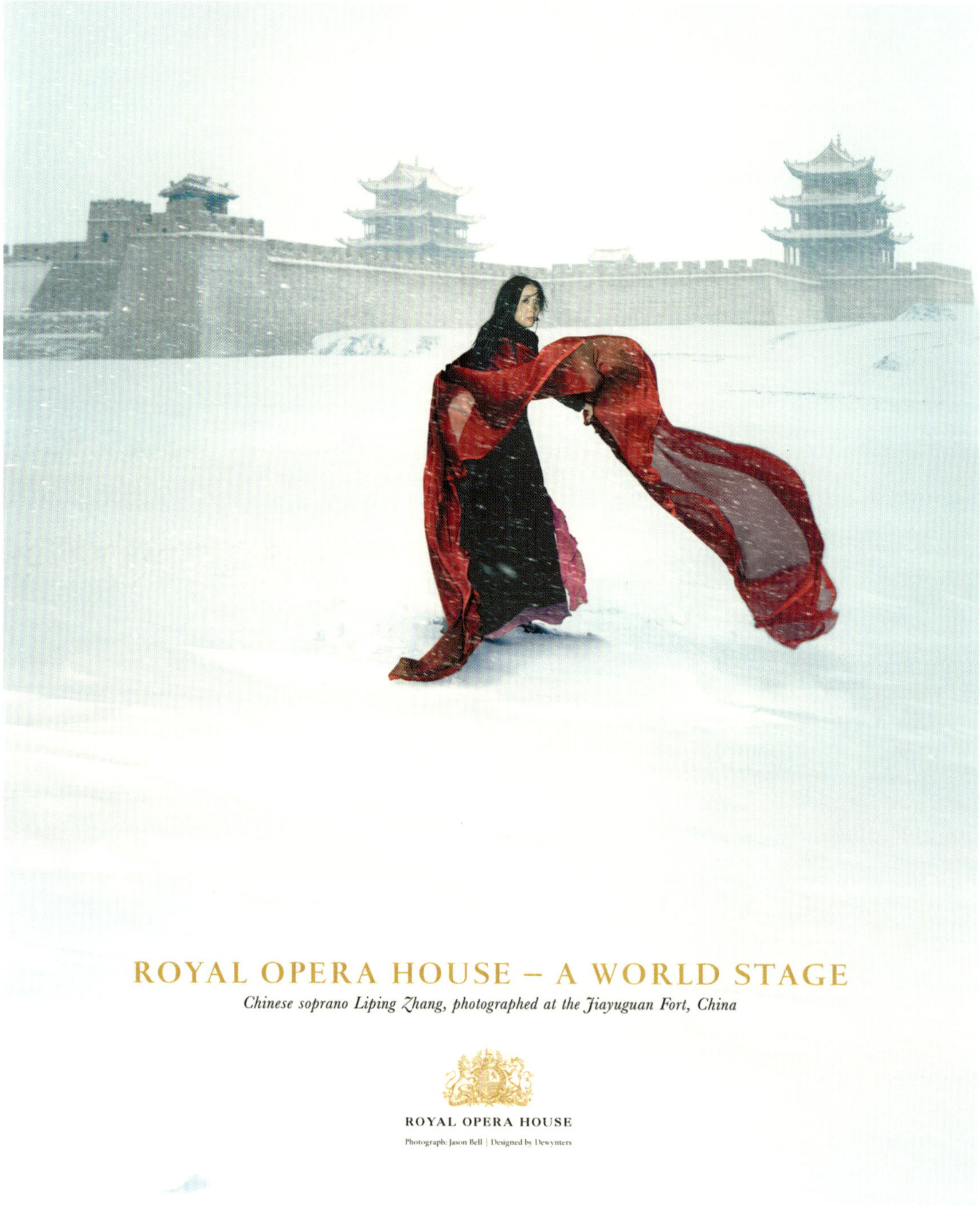

ROYAL OPERA HOUSE, LIPING ZHANG, CHINA

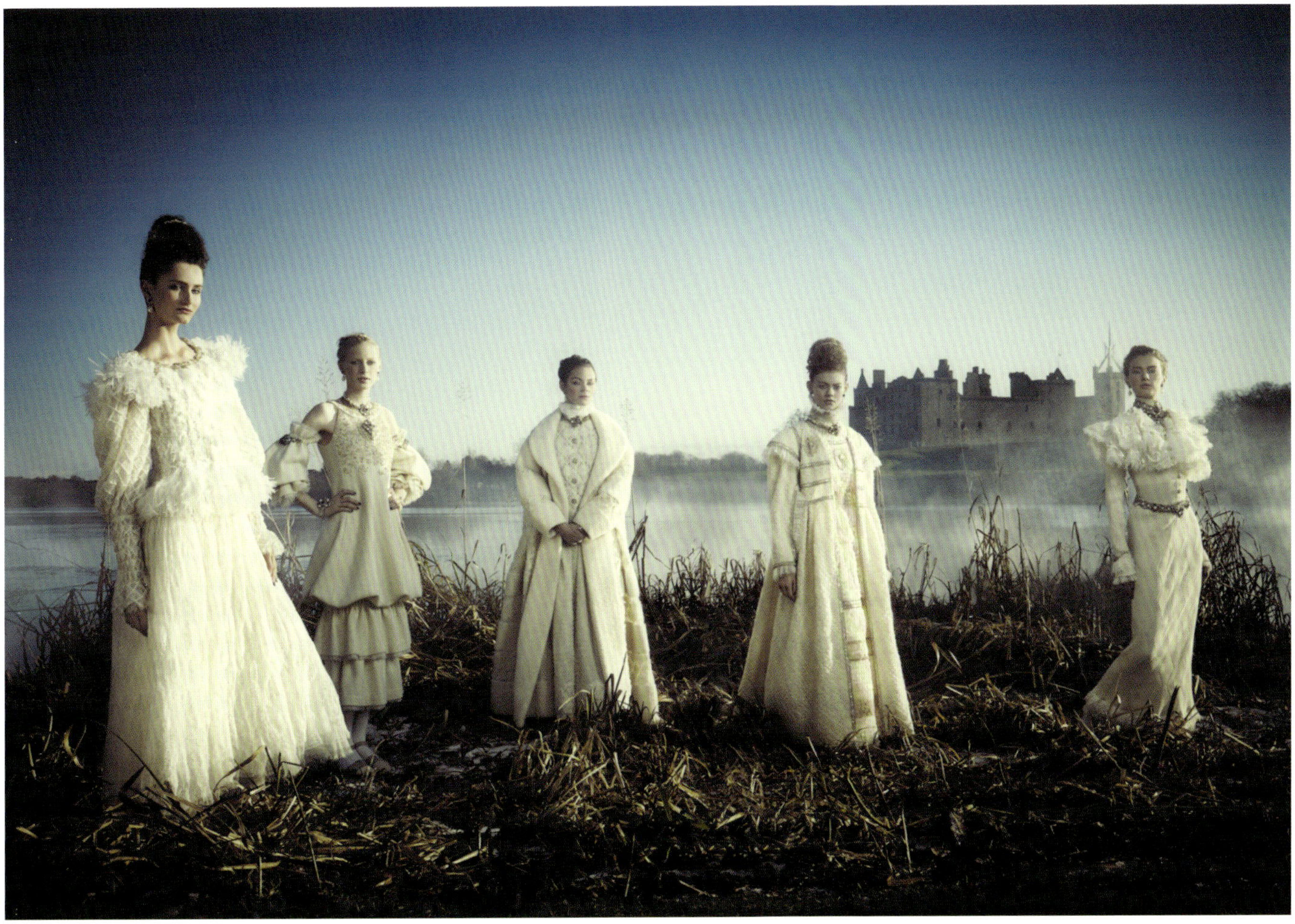

CHANEL METIERS D'ART COLLECTION FOR VANITY FAIR

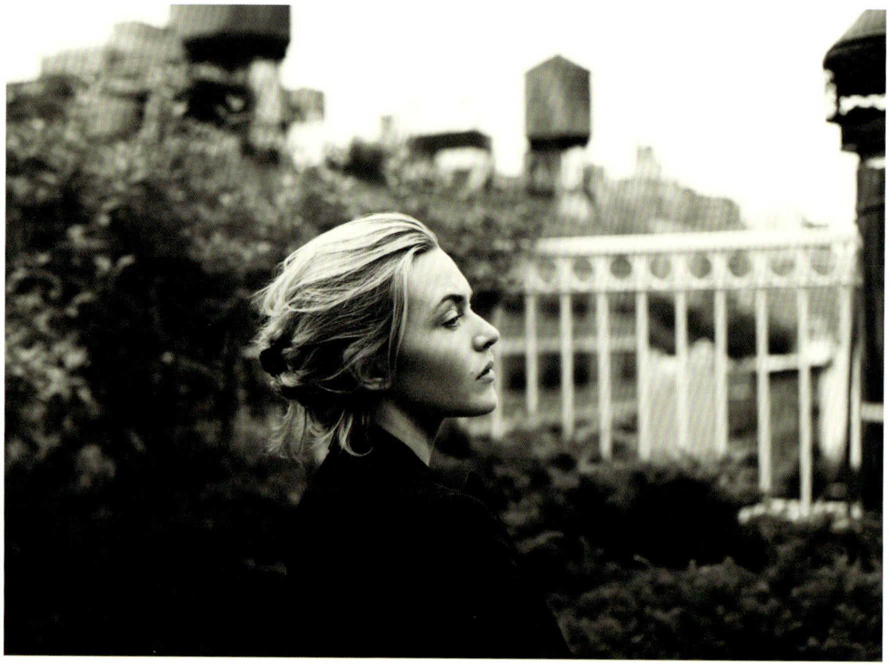

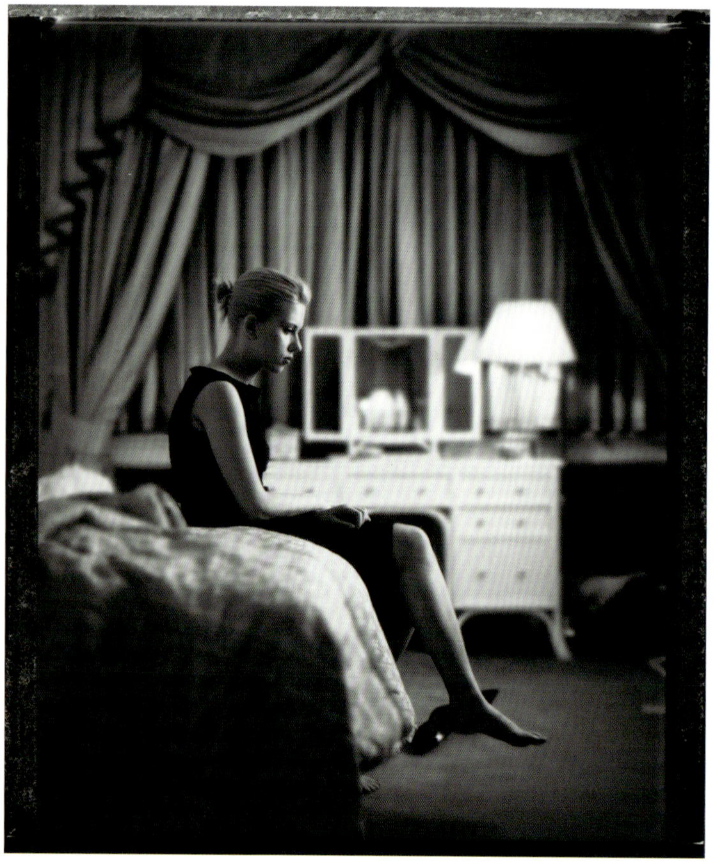

KATE WINSLET
SCARLETT JOHANSSON

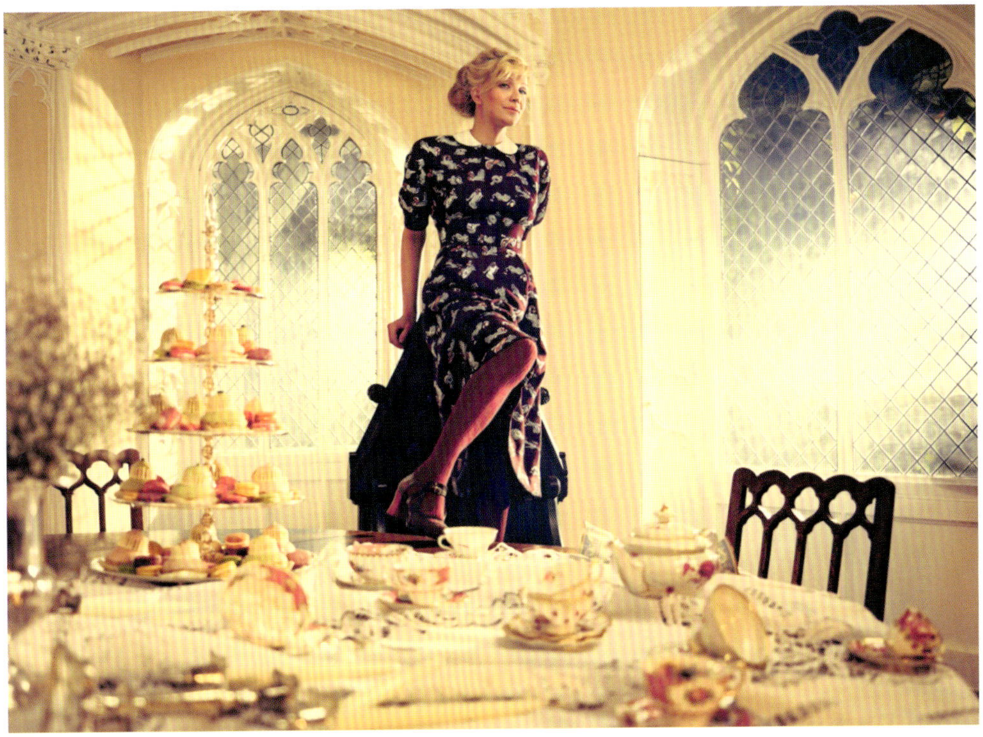

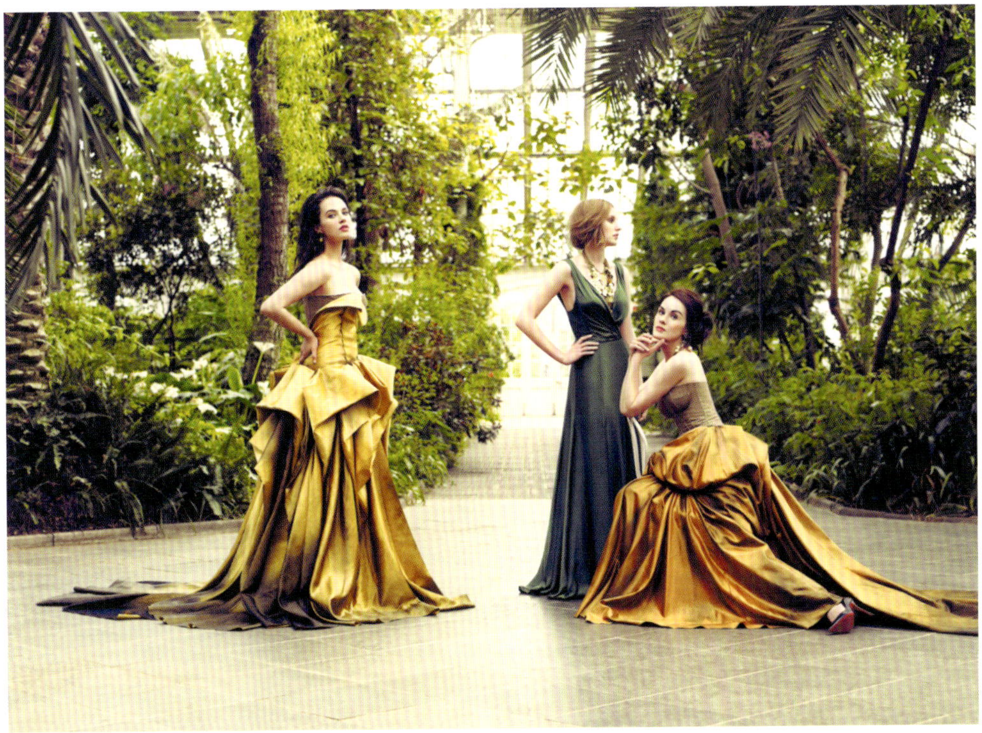

COURTNEY LOVE

DOWNTON ABBEY FOR VOGUE

SANDY CLELAND FRPS

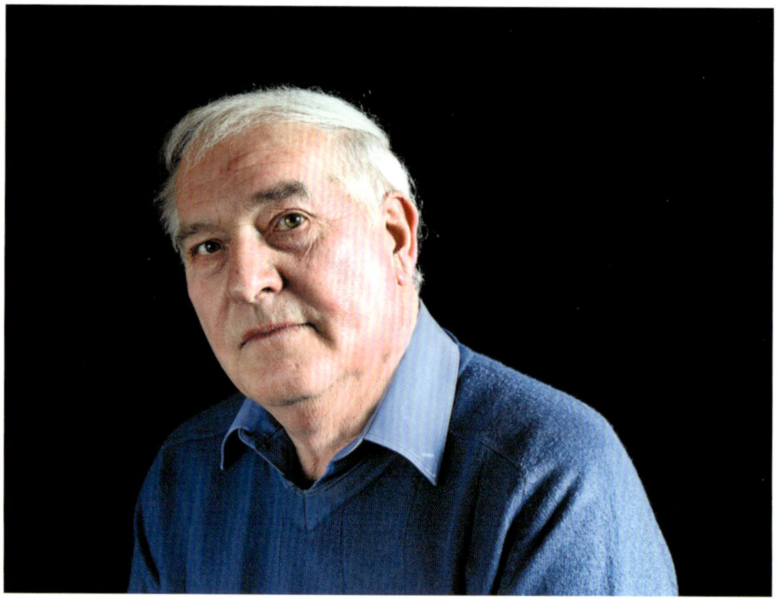

Sandy Cleland was 13 when he first started taking photographs. He was inspired by television programmes like "Look" with Peter Scott and the "On Safari" series with Armand and Michaela Dennis.

His father bought him an 8mm cine camera and he went up to Linlithgow Loch with it. He saw some Grebe and started photographing them. "I couldn't understand when the film came back why they were just dots in the water when everyone else on the television had them. At that time, I didn't realise there were telephoto lenses and I got quite a shock".

He went onto stills after that. "My first camera was a Praktica 4F and I got a Schacht macro Travenar lens. In those days, you mentioned a macro lens and nobody knew what they were. It was a manual preset as everything was. That's when you learned your trade. I had to make my own flash rigs using old Sunpak GX17 flash guns. You build up the knowledge that way. These days you can buy things off the shelf but you couldn't then".

Natural history has always been and still is his main interest. His RPS Associateship in 1980 and his Fellowship in 1986 were both awarded as nature slides.

He finds nature photography fascinating and it is very much a learning experience for him. Often he will take a photograph first and then he reads up about the subject. "As you are reading, you find out something else that is interesting, so you try to photograph that".

He tends to use a tripod, maybe using a bit of fill flash. "It slows you down but slowing you down is a good thing because everything is fast nowadays and I think as photographers we should slow down a bit and think about our pictures. Good photography comes from the heart. I always find that my best photography comes from what I really want to do".

He likes working close to home and many of his images are taken within a five-mile radius of home, where there is quite a variation in habitat, woodland, hills and moorland.

He knows his own patch well. "I've been to the Serengeti and places like that but I never feel they're my patches because the guide's taken you there whereas when I'm on my own patch I know what's there".

He was outside a lot too, when he worked for the Scottish Agricultural College on grassland. "Just going about different farms and the hills where we did the reclamation work, I found places and things to photograph". People often ask how he finds things to photograph. "People look but they don't see", he told me, "I think you have to train yourself to look".

Sandy has been shooting digital since 2006. Moving to digital proved to be a renaissance in his photography. "After a number of years, you tend to get staid and this just opened many other doors for me. In 2006 we went to Kenya and I took a digital camera and the 35mm, and the film is still in the camera".

"It's allowed me to do things I wouldn't have tried before. The light gathering capacity for a start, you can take pictures in conditions you would never have considered – and you can take chances. Swallows in flight, dragonflies in flight. You'd rattle through film and get nothing whereas with digital, you can try these things. If it doesn't work it doesn't matter".

He still shoots as though he is shooting slides. "I do very little in Photoshop unless I do some of the more creative stuff. I think if you shoot as though you do very little in the computer then that's the best way to do it. I still don't use the motor drive – I think it's the Scot in me still thinking I'm burning film".

Sandy likes to work in panels and themes now. "The subject chooses me" he says, "I wander around looking for things to happen and ideas just keep popping up". His panels cover many subjects including character studies at the Edinburgh Festival, a car boot sale, shutters and crazed walls in Montmartre. He uses them in lectures and explains that working in panels makes you think a bit more. "Obviously", he says, "there's the sudden image that you get, something that just happens and you can't make a panel of that because it's instant and it's that one moment. But the things like the shutters and the car boot sale, they develop themselves into a panel. I try everything. I think that's the great thing about being an amateur, I can do what I want. It's my time".

He spends a lot of that time volunteering for The Royal Photographic Society which is very important to him. He has been involved with the Licentiateship Panel as a panel member and a Chairman as well as being a member of the Associateship and Fellowship Panel for Natural History. At present he is a member of the Distinctions Advisory Board and the Fellowship Board.

In 2005 he was awarded the Fenton Medal for his outstanding contribution to The Society.

David Cooke ARPS

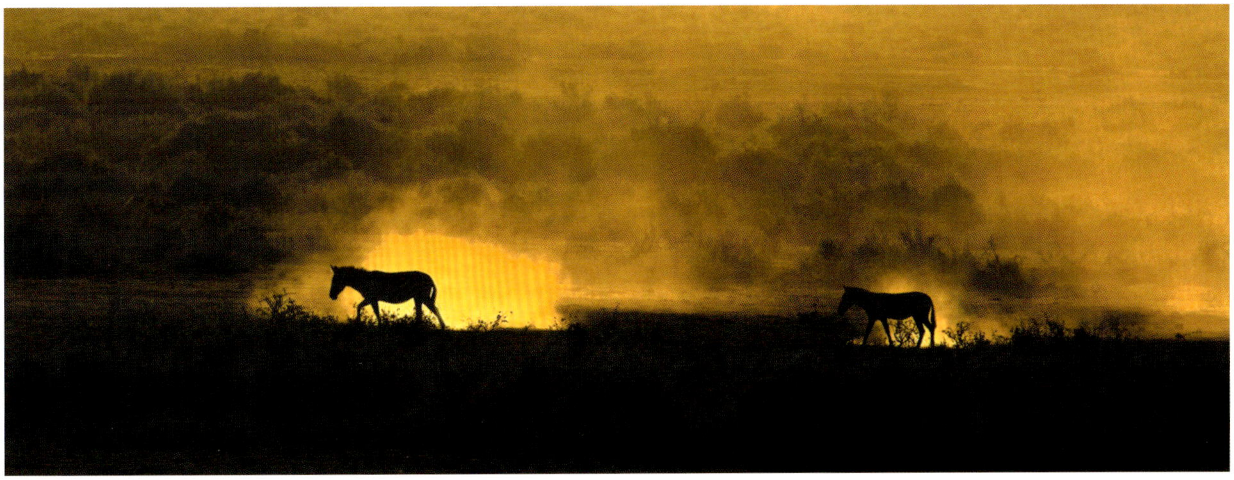

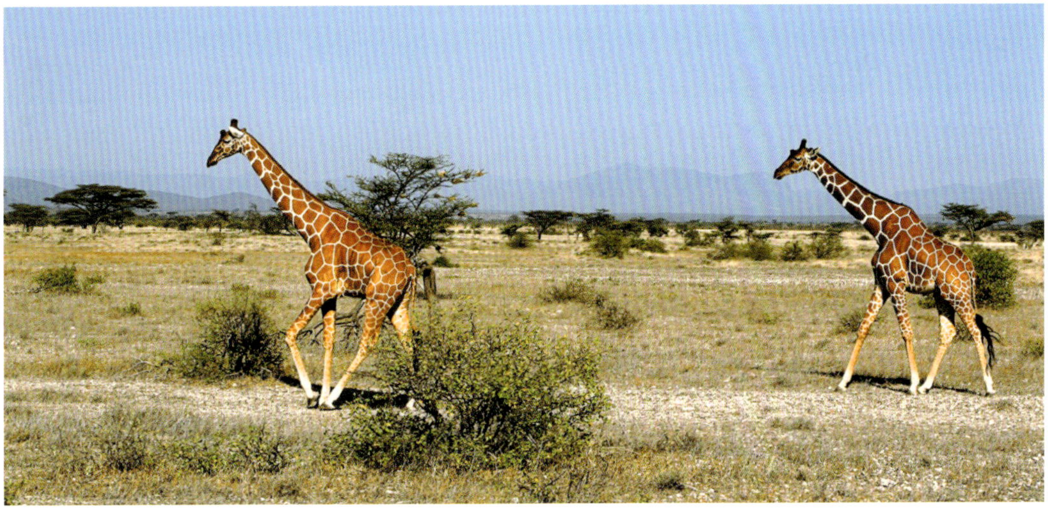

BURCHELL'S ZEBRAS IN DROUGHT
BLACK HORSE
RETICULATED GIRAFFES, SAMBURU

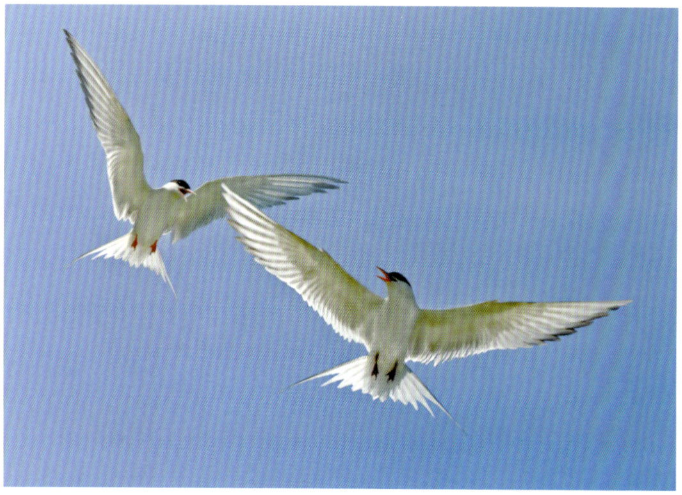

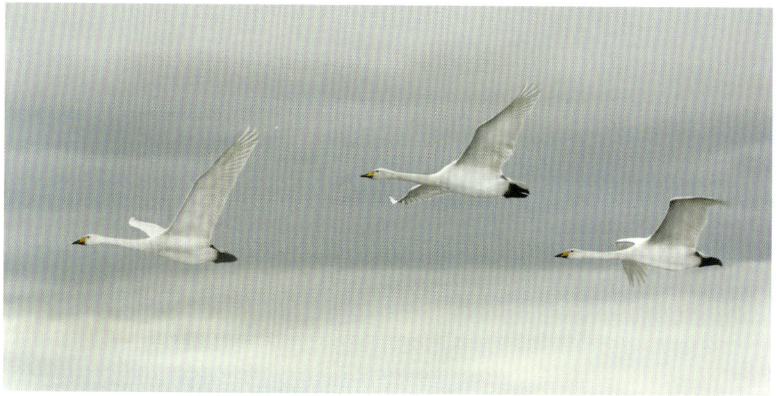

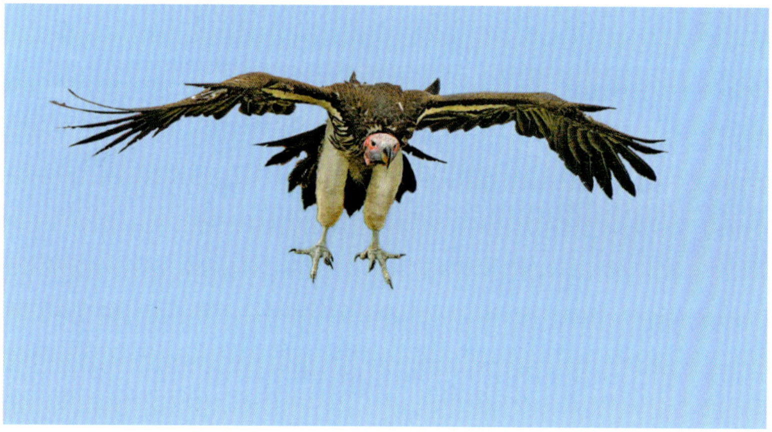

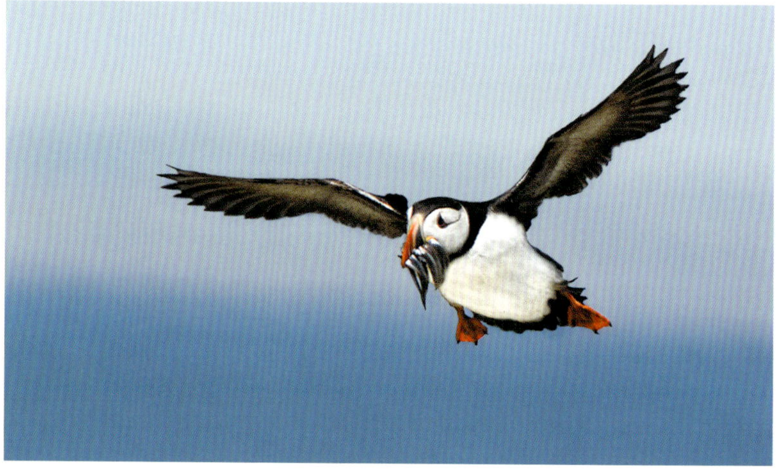

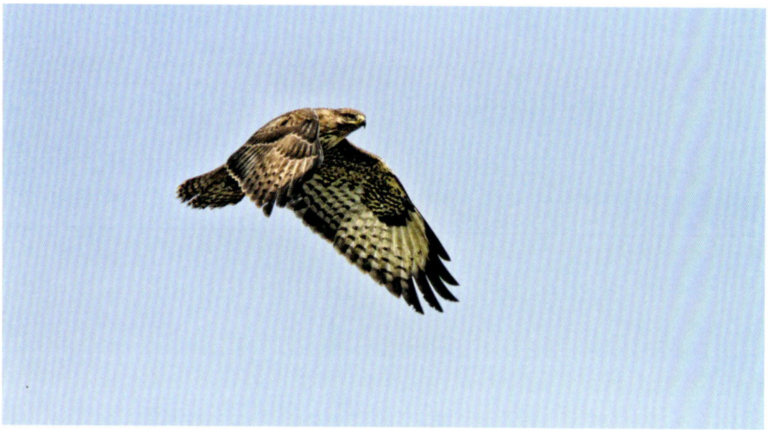

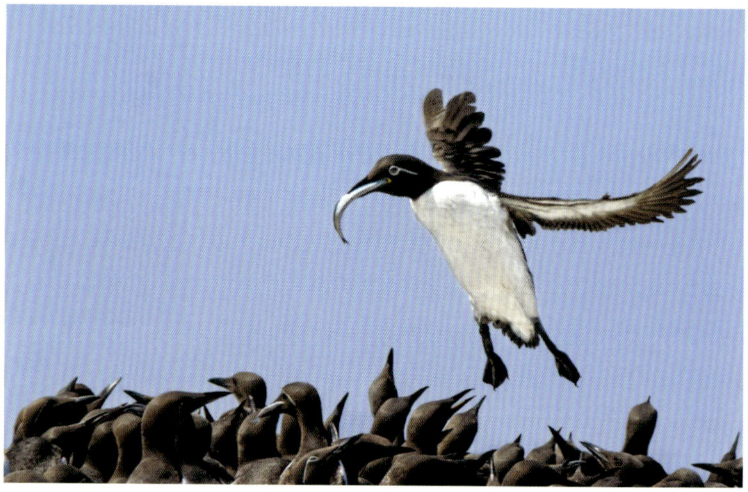

ARCTIC TERNS JOUSTING
WHITE HEADED VULTURE
BUZZARD

WHOOPER SWANS
PUFFIN IN FLIGHT
BRIDLED GUILLEMOT ARRIVING WITH FISH

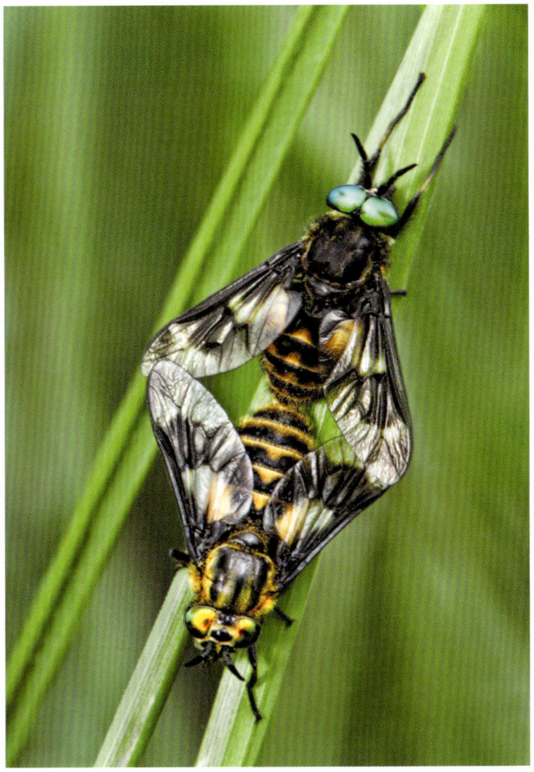

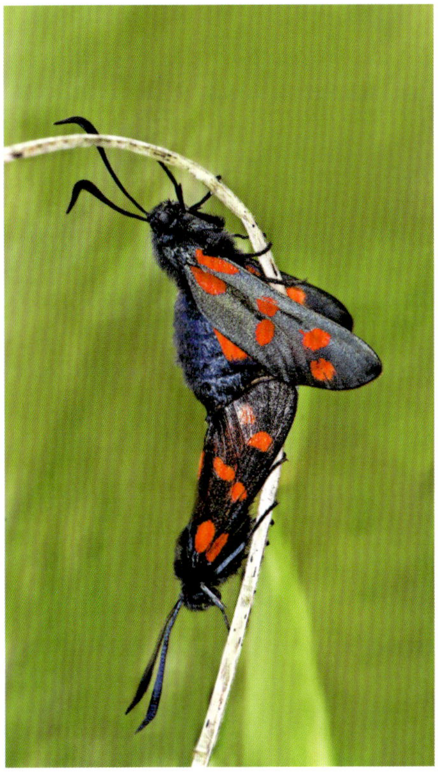

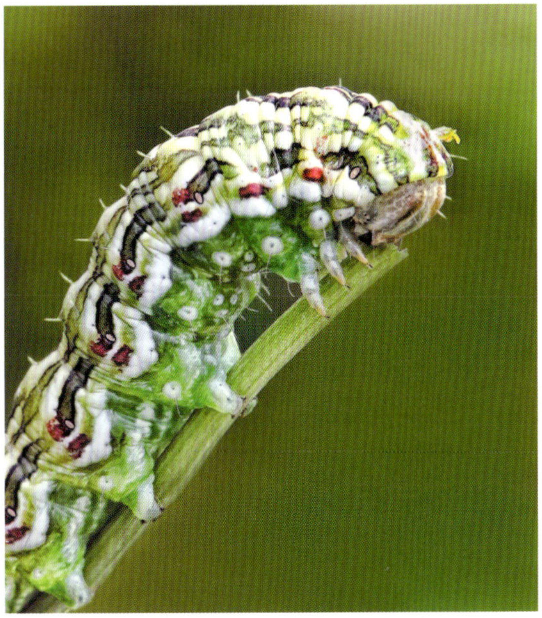

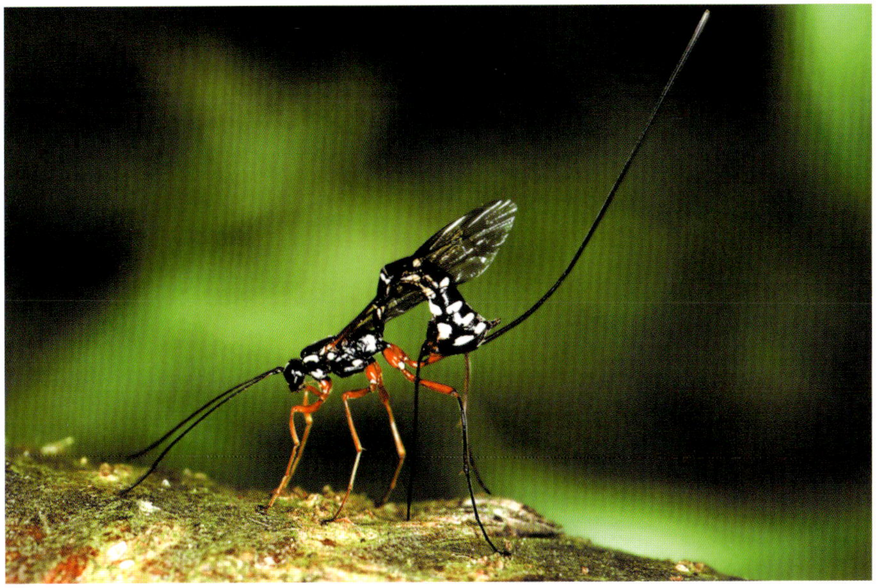

TABANID FLIES MATING

CHAMOMILE SHARK MOTH CATERPILLAR

SIX SPOT BURNET MOTHS MATING

ICHNEUMON FLY OVIPOSITING

JOE CORNISH Hon.FRPS

A JOURNEY

From Joe Cornish's hand-written journals.

On the Life of a Landscape Photographer

...Means getting up in the dark, seeing the day break, feeling the cold, the wind, the early sun, the colour of the morning. My memories of working outside are – perhaps a contradiction in terms of memory – intensely physical. Usually it's damp, cold, especially by the sea. Most places to which I am drawn are at least a bit wild. The air: clean, fresh. The weather dominates my photographic experience as it must.

On Being Creative, Or is It?

...Is what I do actually creative at all? Possibly not. My principal goal is to be the faithful eye witness. But to what? Eye witness to our own, my very own, point of view. I find views; that is simply my job. What do they stand for? Does it matter? Who cares? Why do others sometimes seek out my tripod footprints? Am I striking some kind of chord? And can a faithful eye witness, someone who essentially prints a close version of what lay before the camera (at least in terms of a graphic 2-D representation) actually be creative? If so, what is my creativity, what is my point of view? Am I really just an illustrator? A view finder?

What I Use

...I've photographed landscapes ever since I've had a camera and I still find it endlessly beguiling, at times frustrating, but mostly – inspiring. I've used dozens of cameras, mainly film, 35 mm, medium and large format; now I use a Linhof Techno view camera, and I am using the Phase One IQ 180 mounted on it, my digital equivalent of large format film. It's an odd sort of hybrid, with some drawbacks from the smaller viewing area (compared to 5x4inch), but also massive advantages from the security and flexibility of digital capture and post production.

On Awakening the Senses

...For the last few years I've become more and more interested in, and concerned about, our relationship with nature, both as individuals and as a society. Surely, human beings are too remote from the natural world? The subject of my latest project has the working title, Awakening the Senses. The idea is to convey the physicality of nature – its textures and colours, cold and warmth, wet and dry, its space, its atmosphere.

On a Trek in India – 1st July 2012

LEH to KARGIL (via Mulbek, our campsite tonight)

...What happens if you drive a road through the highest mountains on earth? A journey – almost literally – beyond description. We travelled through a dozen different geological theatres of the Indus Valley including a monastery stop. And the spectacular junction of the Zanskar and Indus rivers. But then we branch off the Indus gorge and up a side one and we are in the Himalayan badlands – the road is astonishing – a miracle of engineering, probably built at least partly by slave labour – here are road builders' encampments every four miles, but no sign of amenities, food, facilities.

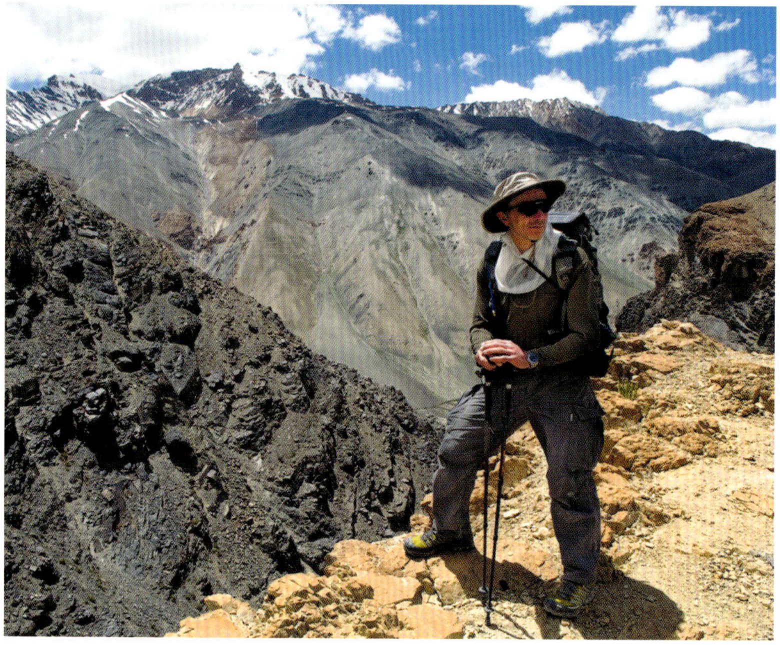

Room with a view, Testa

...We rested here for two nights and a full day before resuming our trek, the campsite in a charming spot sheltered by willow trees. The village sits on a broad, shallow slope of alluvial rock, high above the river that cuts through the valley. Fed by simple cut channels of glacial meltwater, walled fields are green with sunlit crops.

Abandoned kitchen, Testa

...The afternoon of our rest day at Testa included the joy of a hot shower. Madan provided us each with a large bucket of hot water, and we took turns (with comparative privacy in a narrow latrine-type tent) using a large mug as a convenient ladle. It's amazing how essentials we take for granted at home acquire the status of rarefied luxury on trek.

Zanskari, Weaver and Grandson

...This was (our friend and Zanskari native) Tanzin's moment, for Testa is his home. We spent a relaxing afternoon, beginning at the family residence visiting his Mum; and later in the village, strolling, meeting local people who graciously allowed us to photograph them, children too...but the highlight beyond doubt was being shown inside one of the villager's houses, and then being served tea (and a taste of chang, the local brew). The details of their winter lives is almost indescribable, whole families packed inside a dark back room, the outside temperature -20ºC on average, with their yaks in a room beside or below to give heat and dried yak dung the only source of fuel for the fire.

Joe Cornish went to Reading University where he studied Fine Art. Here he discovered photography having never touched a camera before. He is now one of the UK's foremost photographers known for his large format landscapes.

Monica Weller FRPS

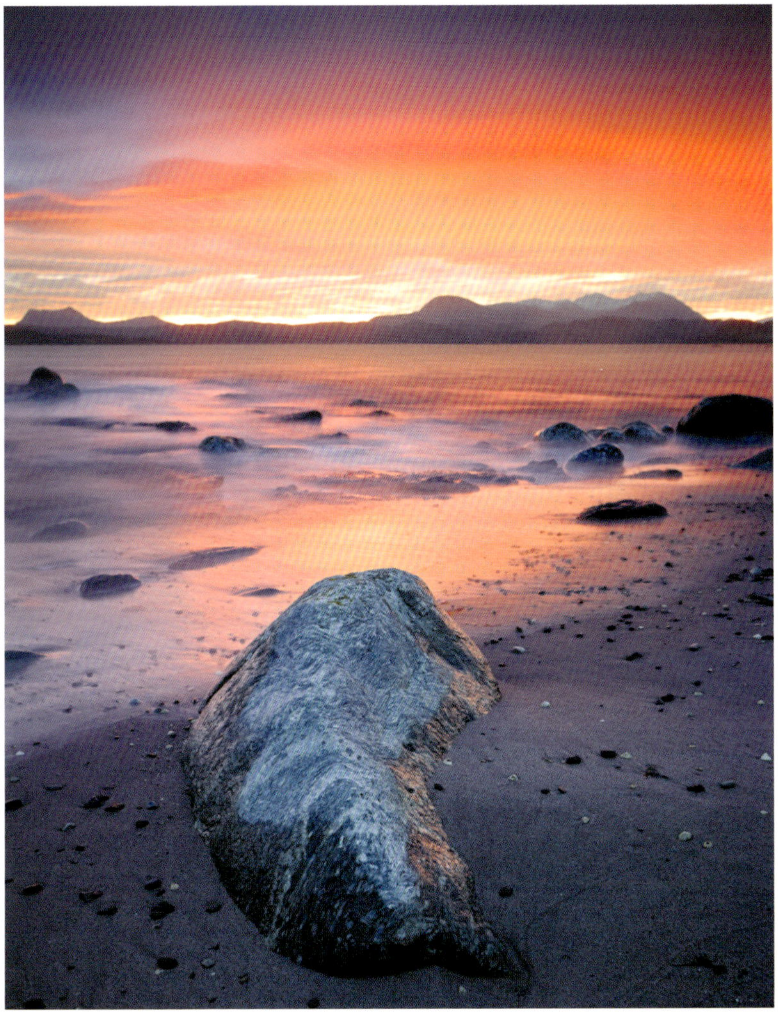

RECLINING ROCK AT SUNRISE

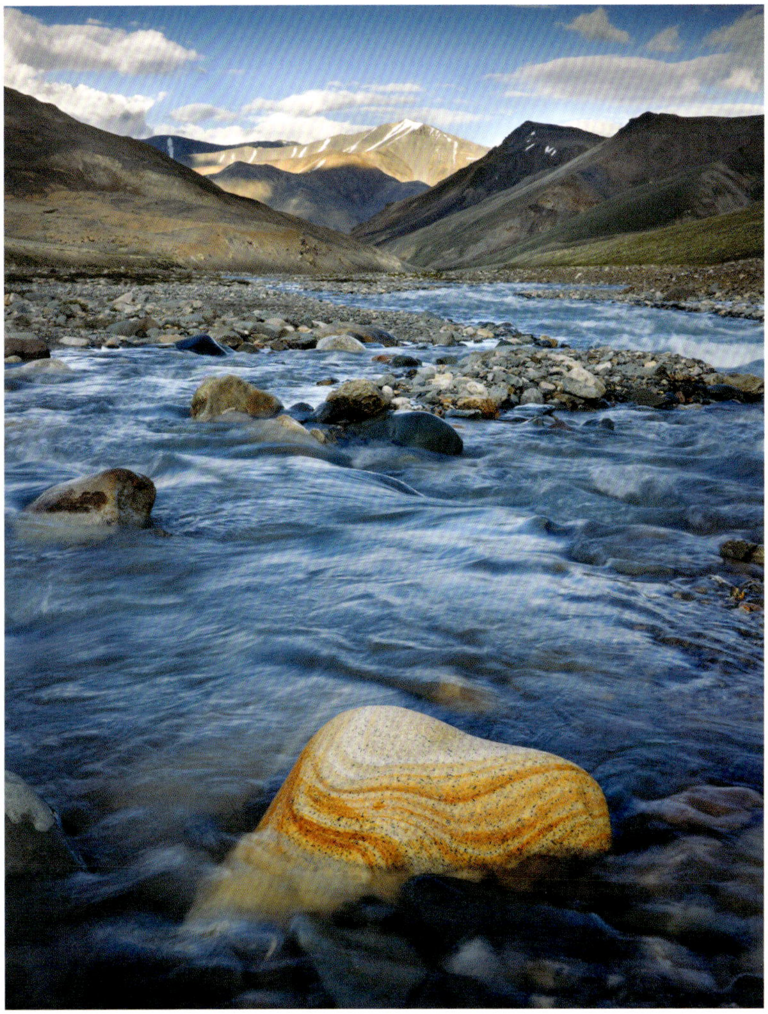

CHHUMIK NAKPO RIVERSCAPE

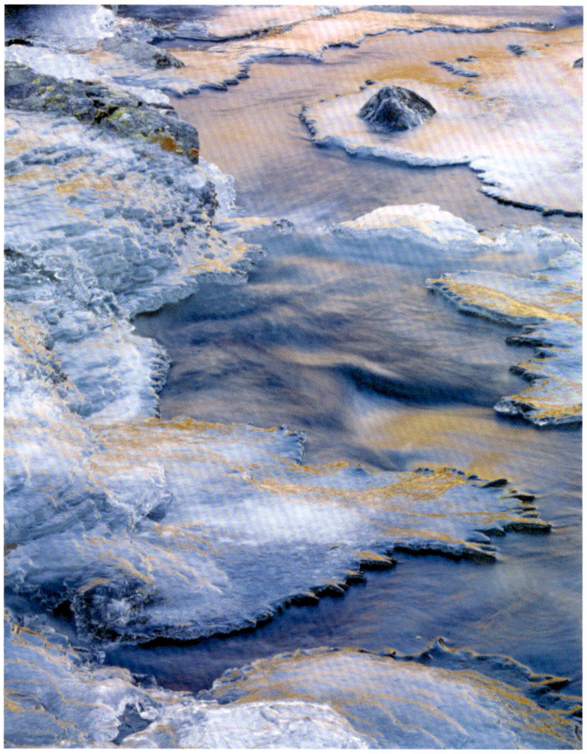

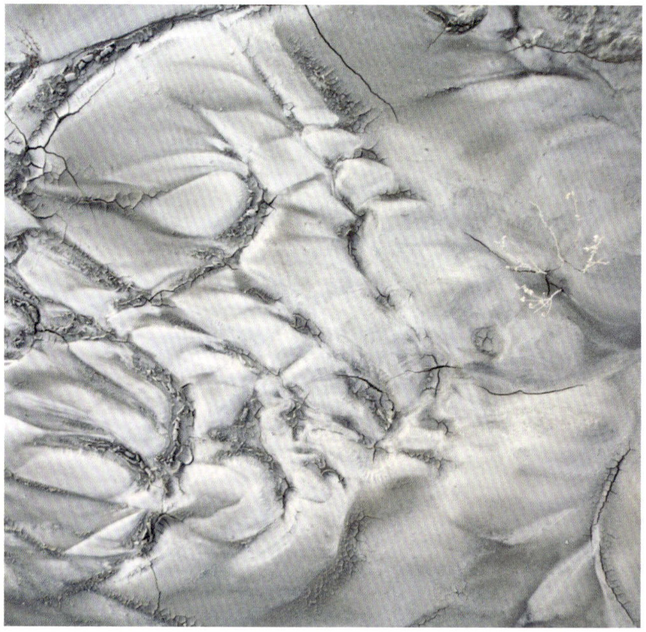

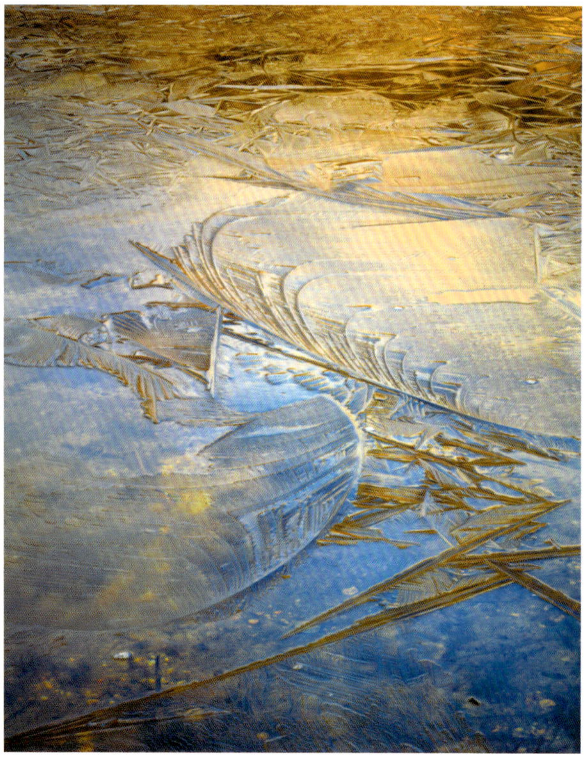

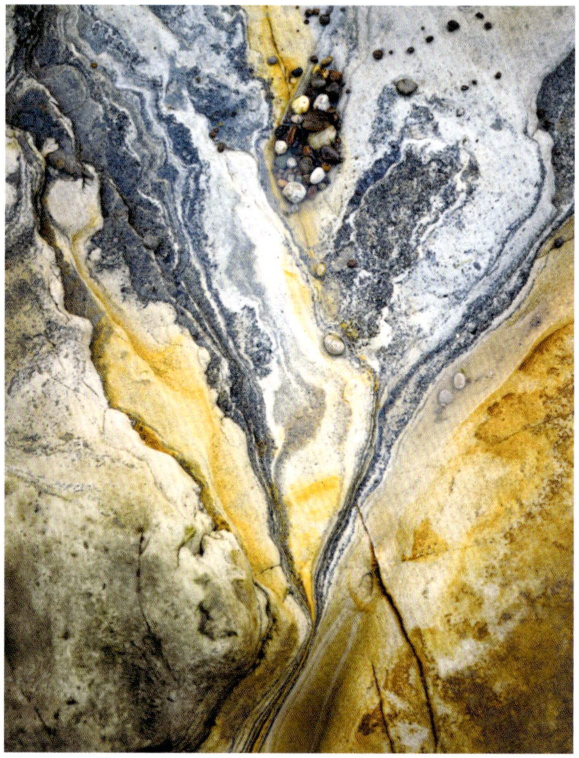

COLOURS OF WINTER, NANT BOCHLWYD

ICE DETAIL, LOCH CLAIR

BISTI MUD FLOW

CORNELIAN ROCK ABSTRACTION

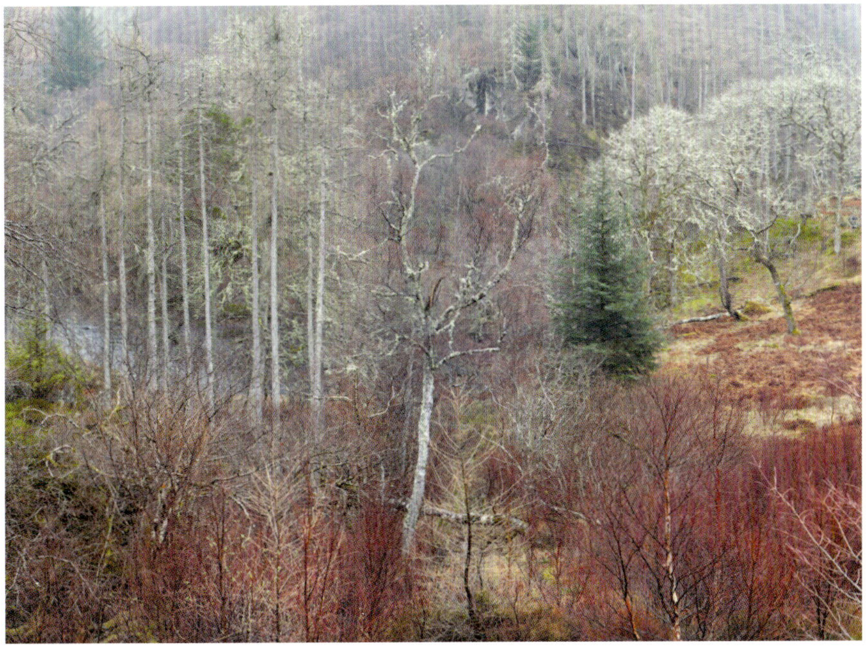

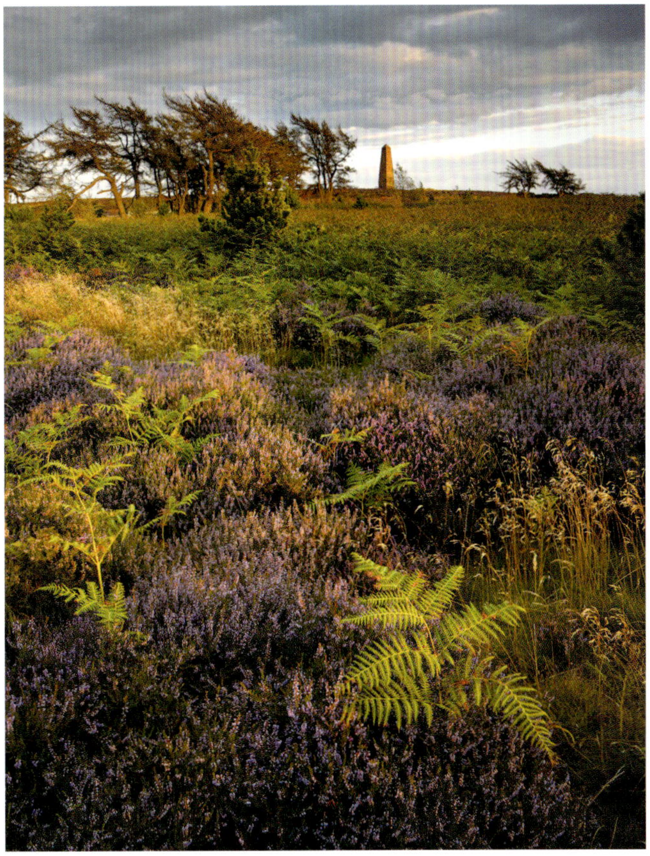

GAIRLOCH WOODS IN THE RAIN
CAPTAIN COOK'S MONUMENT

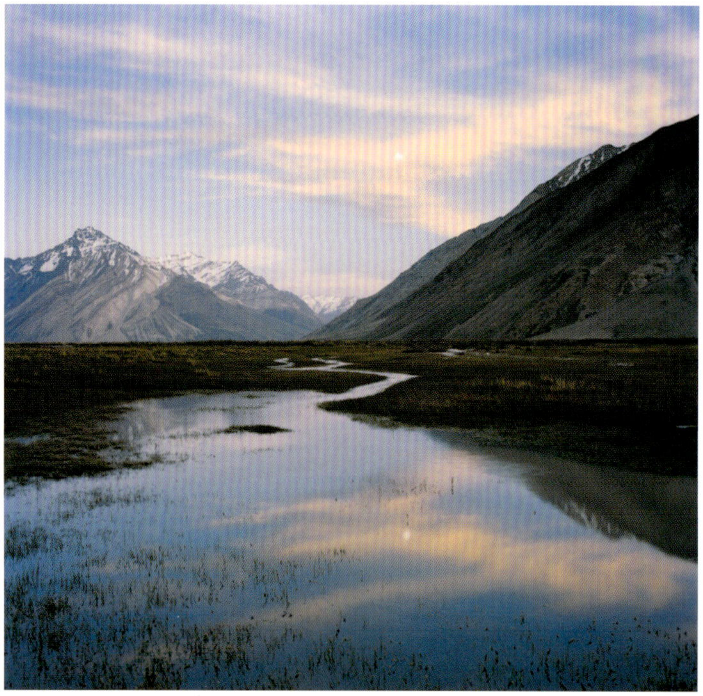

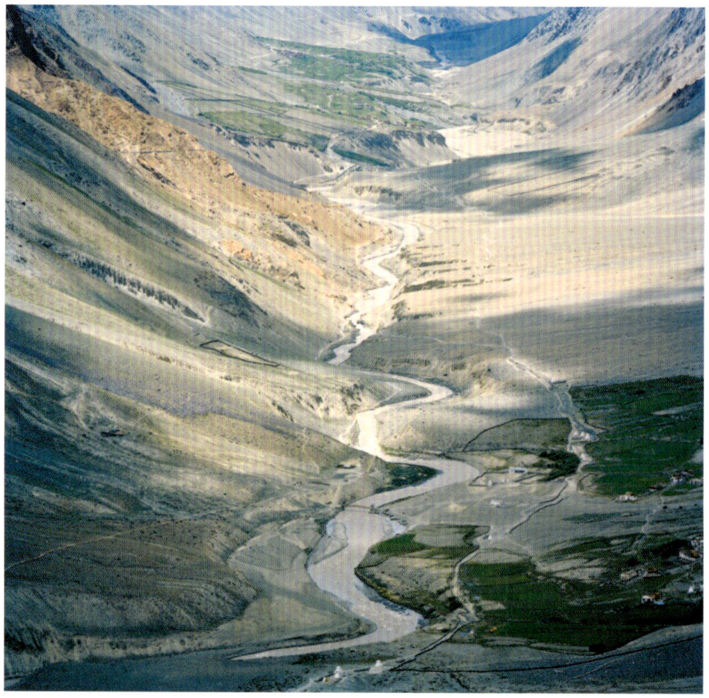

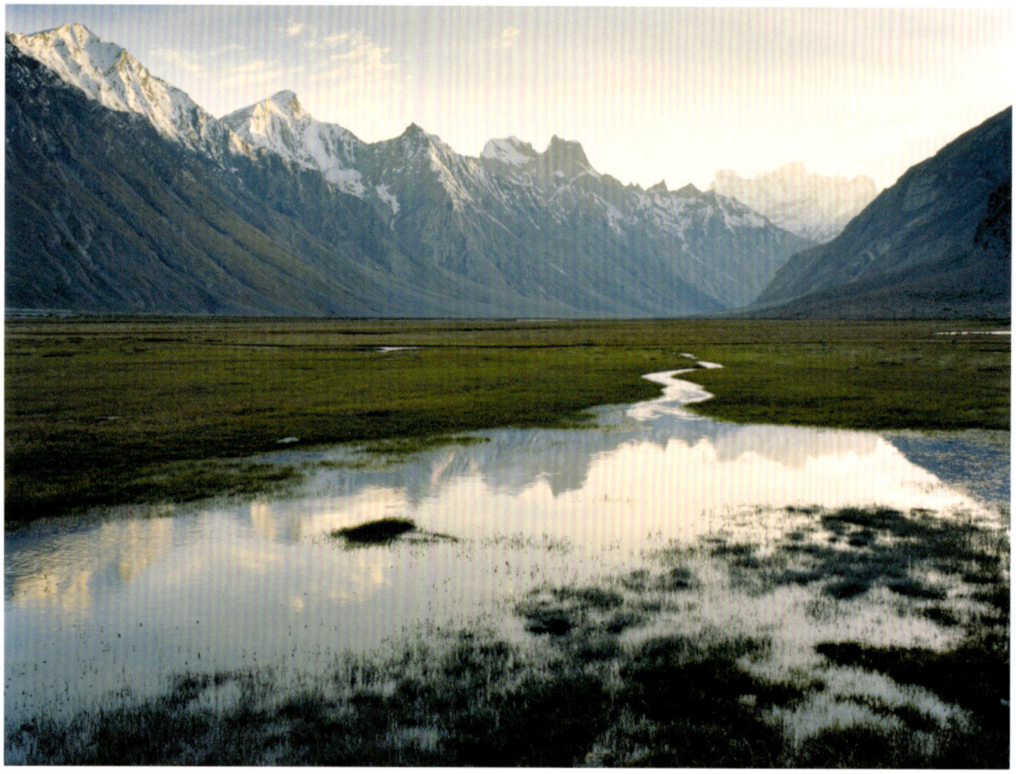

RANGDUM MOONRISE

ZANSKAR VALLEY FROM HEARTBREAK HILL

RANGDUM EVENING

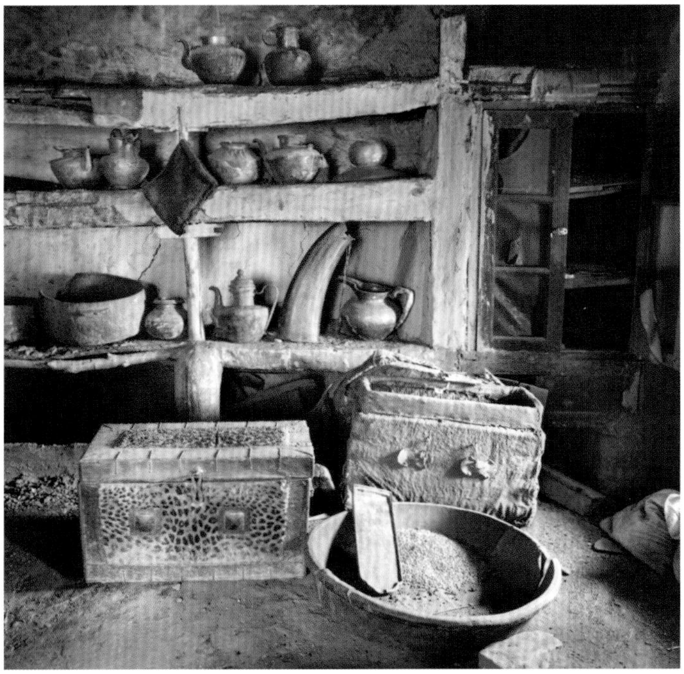

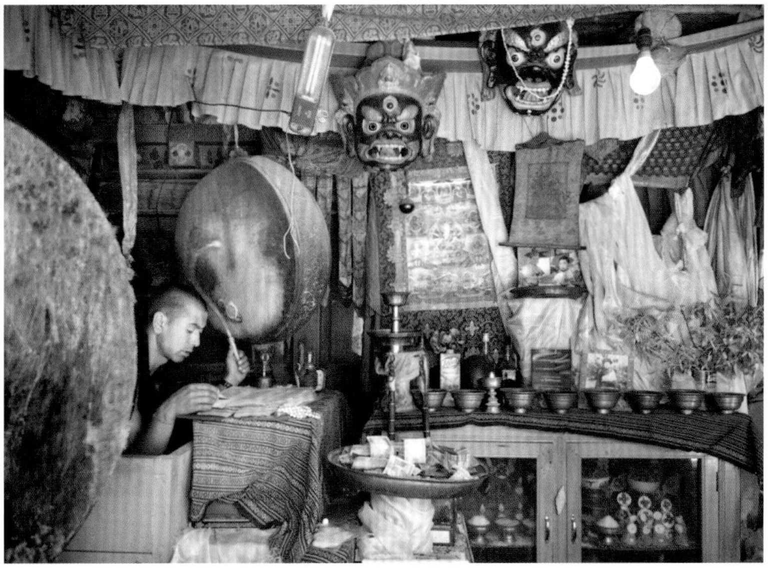

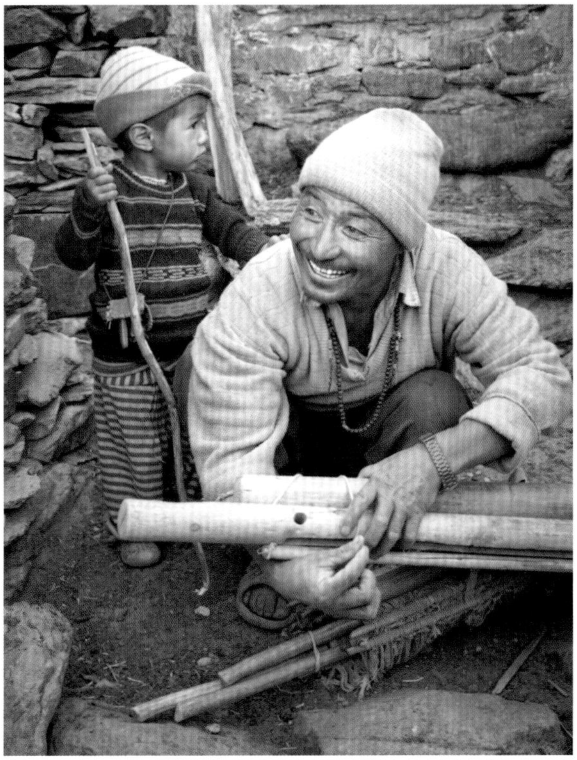

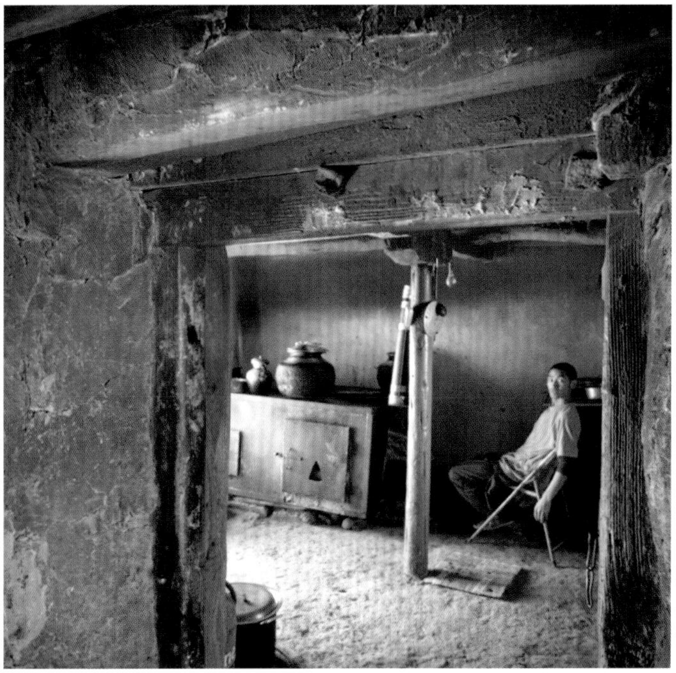

ABANDONED KITCHEN, TESTA

ZANSKARI WEAVER WITH GRANDSON

BHUDDISTS DRUM, HEMIS MONASTERY

RANGDUM KITCHEN

JACK JACKSON FRPS

JACK JACKSON'S STORE CUPBOARD

Mountaineer, diver, photographer, worldwide lecturer, award-winning author, consultant to the Royal Geographical Society's Expedition Advisory Centre, Jack Jackson FRPS has travelled the remoter areas of the world since 1967, both on his own account and as leader of scientific, cultural and tourist expeditions.

I embarked on a 15-mile car journey in the familiar, green landscape of the south of England to meet Jack Jackson, the adventurer. As I stepped through the front door of their home one thing was obvious: I'd entered a store cupboard of Jack's adventures. Shelves from floor to ceiling bulge with reference books, all with scientific names, which Jack says are vital for picture sales of fish and invertebrates to identify photographs he's taken. Copious numbers of the stacked books have been written or edited by Jack and contain his photographs, including *The 4-Wheel Drive Book, Complete Diving Manual, Diving the World's Coral Reefs, The Underwater Photography Manual*. I glanced at piles of magazines and newspapers under tables that together represent Jack's achievements. Titles from *Amateur Photographer and British Journal of Photography to Wanderlust, Scuba Globe Pacific* and *Land Rover International, The Times* and *Telegraph*, all contain his articles and photographs.

Jack says he dislikes small talk, talks technical (including photography), talks straight and is very pc. He shows me a copy of *Off Road 4-Wheel Drive Book*, described as the authoritative book on 4-wheel drive vehicles, their off road and expedition use. "Because of our trips made overland to India and Annapurna it was suggested I should write a 4-wheel drive manual. Gentry Books who first commissioned it thought it would work. I said it wouldn't. When I sat down to write, it just came flowing out of my head. It took six months to write and was published in 1982. The publisher offered me a price, it sounded good. We've made more money from that book than any others. The title was bought by Haynes the car manual publishers and reprinted under their label in 1985 and updated three times".

Jack's first real experience of adventuring was climbing in Norway in 1963. Then in 1967 he found the call of adventure and his love for mountains too strong and gave up his profession as an industrial chemist for expeditions: "I'd done a lot of climbing when I was still at school. I had it in me as a school boy to be an adventurer. It was all the books I got out of the library, like Scott of the Antarctic, probably an escape from home life". I asked if his parents encouraged him. "No, they took no interest. Even National Service was an escape. I was not really a soldier but a chemist running laboratories in mainland Europe. I played sport and ran a photographic club but I had to do the soldiering drills to get the rank of sergeant".

I asked Jack which one artefact from his adventures meant the most to him. He pointed to a brass, captain's porthole on the wall. "We were running a Scuba diving operation in the Sudan, taking tourists diving to the wreck of the Umbria, the Italian ship that went down in the 2nd World War.

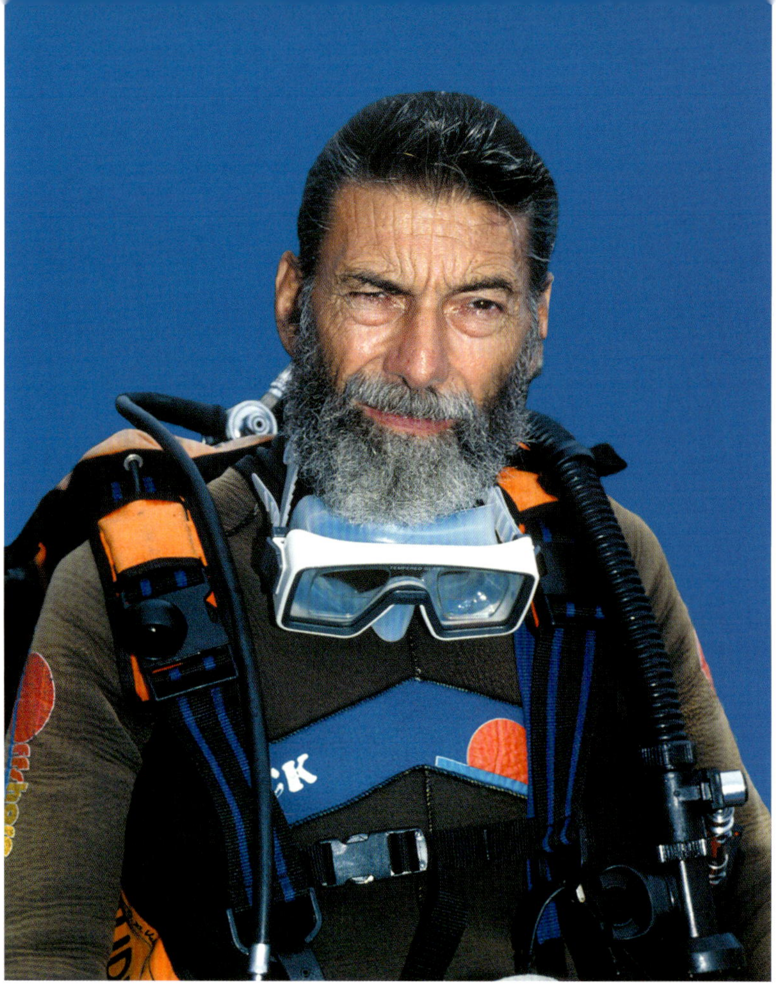

We took three portholes all covered in barnacles and registered them with the Maritime and Coastguard Agency". Mounted behind the glass of the porthole is his photograph of a grey reef shark. "I used to specialise in shark photography. I met him [the shark] several times in the Sudan. I did get nipped, one bit my ankle but I carried on".

I asked which of his photographs was his favourite. "The iceberg in the middle of the frozen sea in East Greenland – you can't tell it's frozen by looking at it. It was April and cold. Prior to this we'd been organising trips to the Sahara Desert and climbing in Afghanistan and Pakistan, combining Land Rover and water trips. A friend, who'd been in the Royal Marines and had done climbing expeditions in the Arctic, came out of the navy. We decided to get together. He'd got all the equipment. Away we went. The photo shows us taking our gear on dog sleighs to the mountain where we climbed. It is all ice except for the dark bits which are volcanic ash".

Jack spent years as a member of the various Society Distinctions panels, Documentary, Travel and Professional and Applied. In 2012 he received the RPS Fenton Medal. "My initial reaction was: they've made a mistake. I haven't done enough to deserve it". He added "It's photography that makes me tick. I know I'm good. I'm a bit obsessed… I just love adventure. My advice to anyone who's interested: Just do it. You might die in the process…you'd die happy!

Monica Weller FRPS

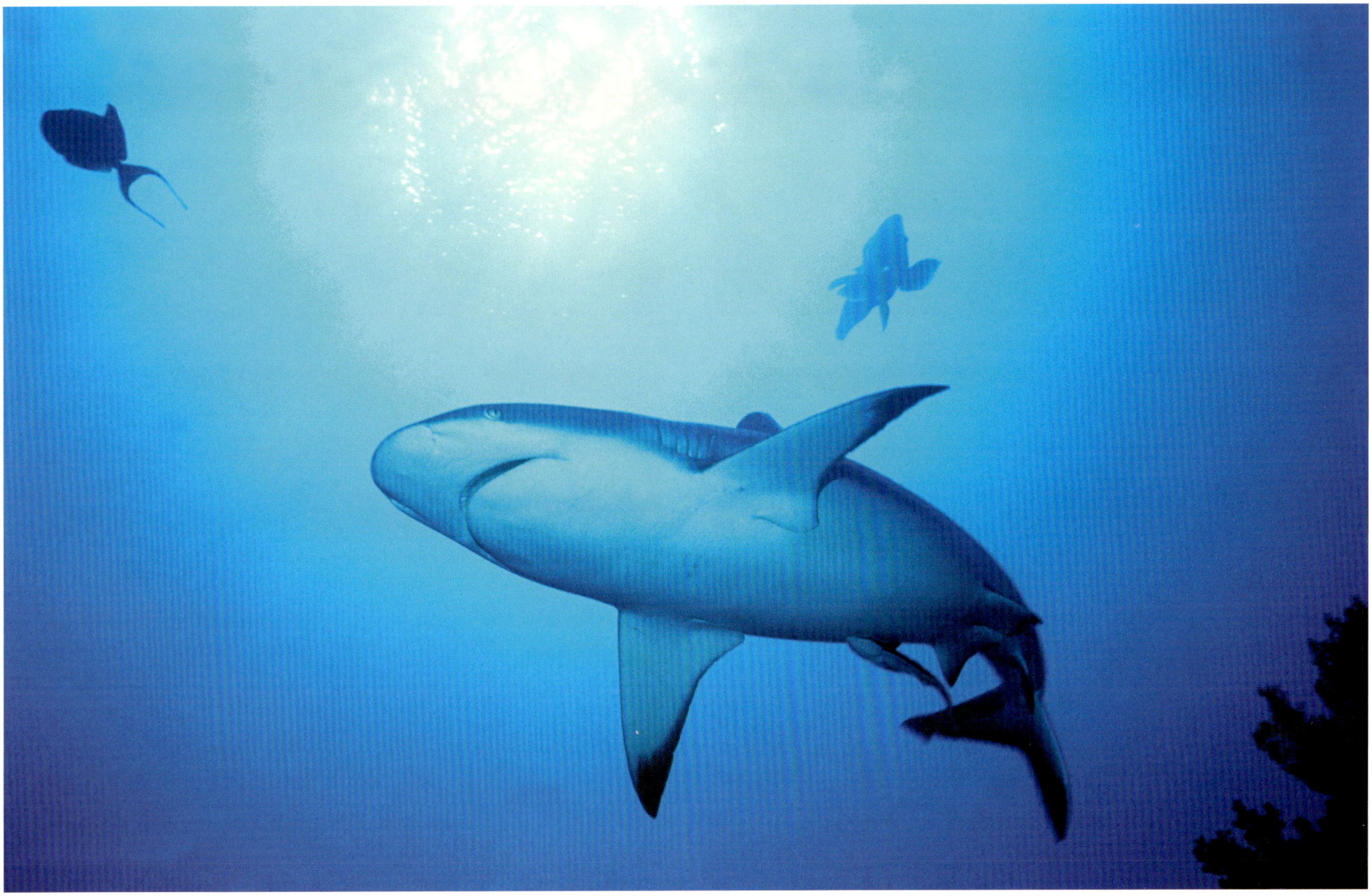

GREY REEF SHARK AGAINST SUN, SUDAN, RED SEA

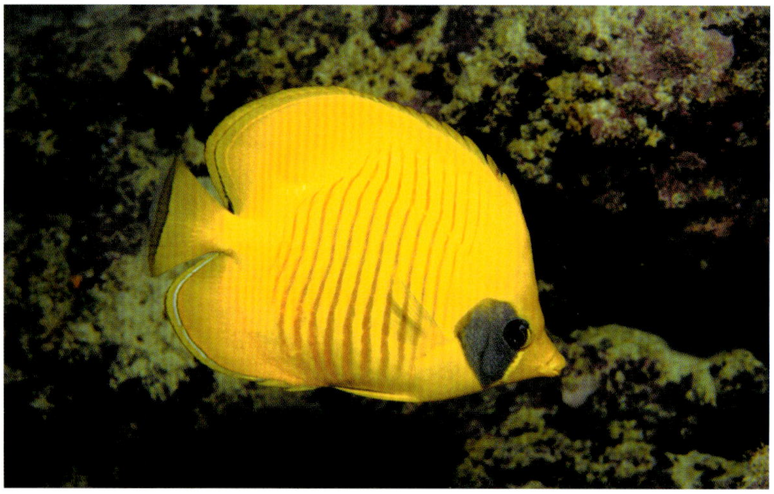

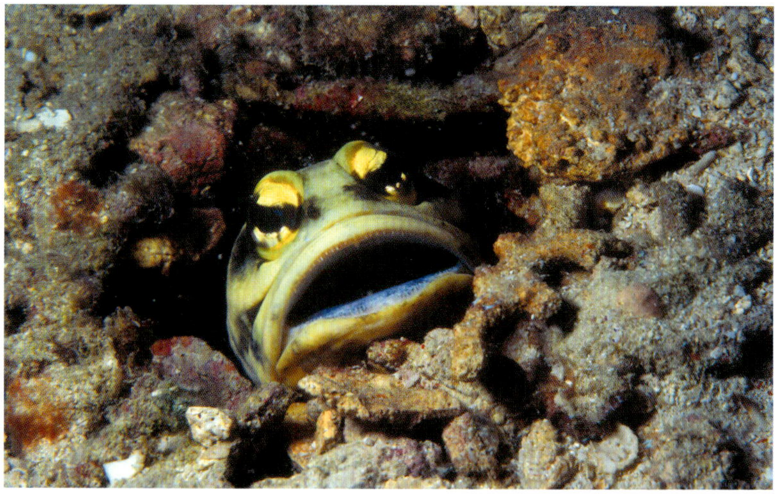

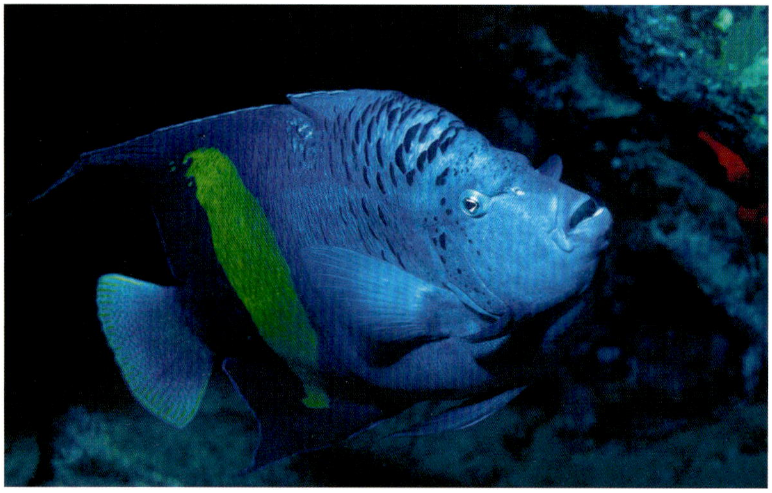

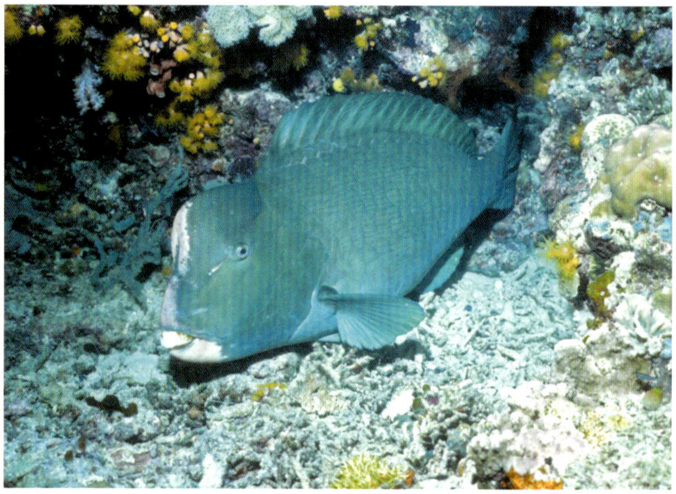

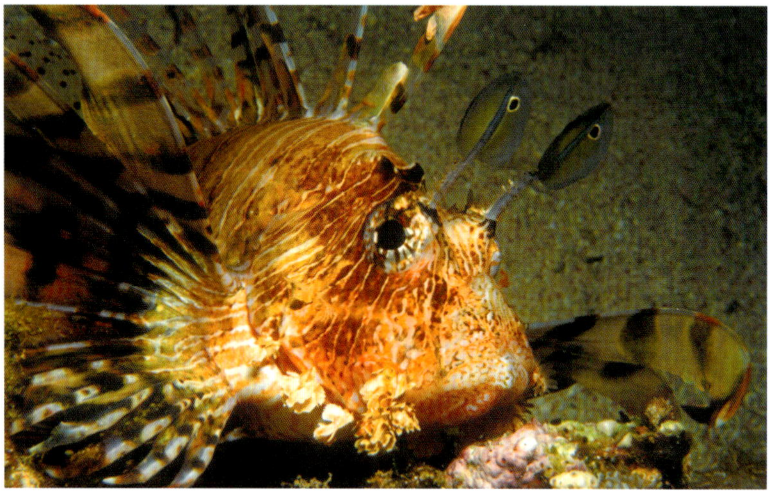

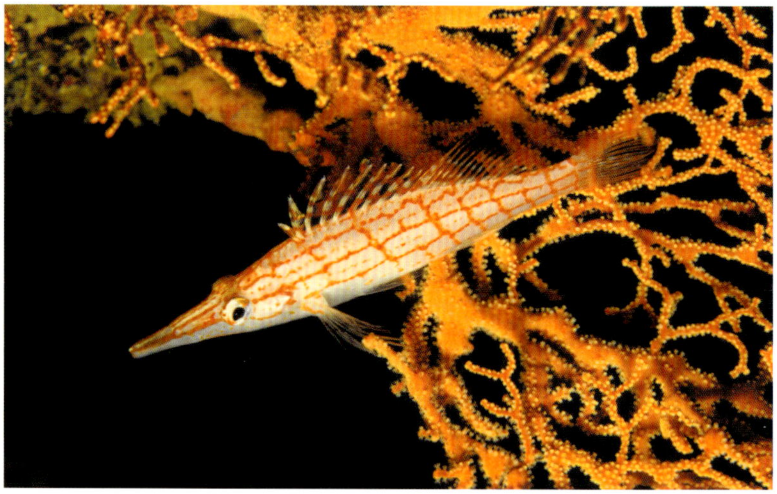

MASKED BUTTERFLY, RED SEA, EGYPT
YELLOWBAR (HALF MOON) ANGEL FISH, RED SEA, SUDAN
LIONFISH, DAEDALUS REEF, RED SEA, EGYPT

JAWFISH, LANKAYAN, SULU SEA, SABAH, BORNEO
SLEEPING BUMPHEAD PARROTFISH, AT NIGHT SPADAN, SABAH, BORNEO
LONGNOSE HAWKFISH, SPADAN, SABAH, BORNEO

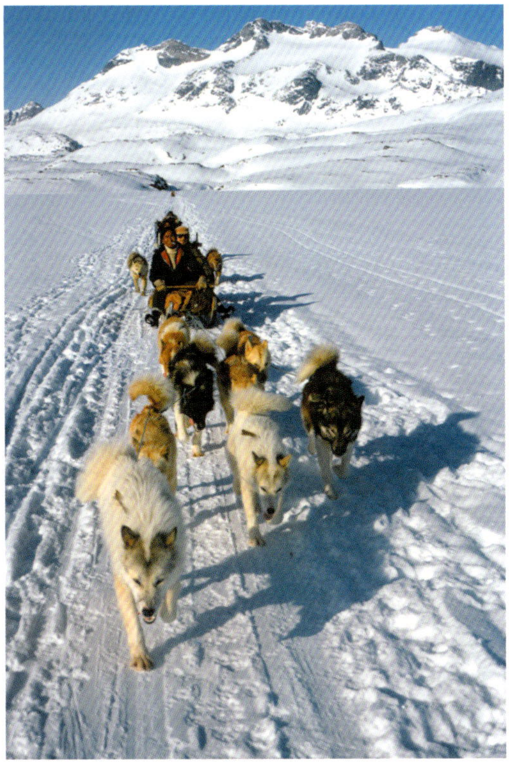

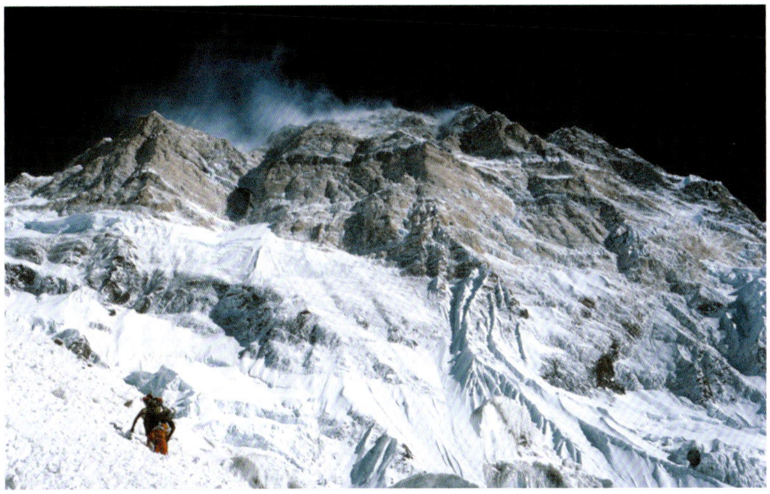

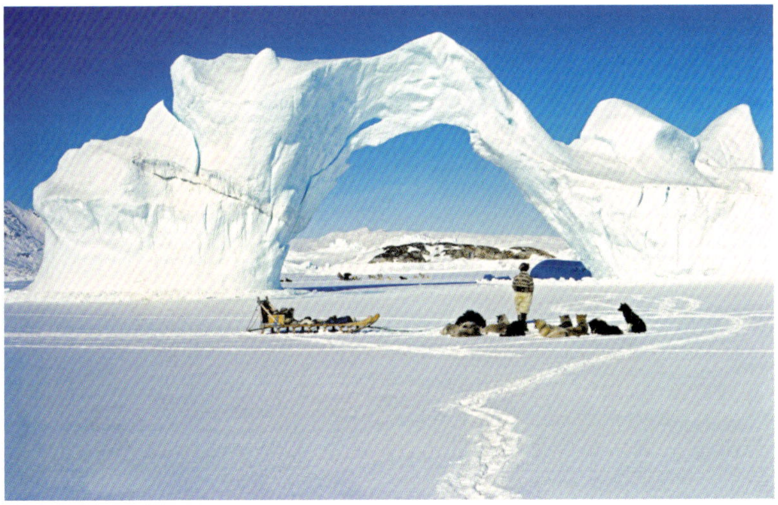

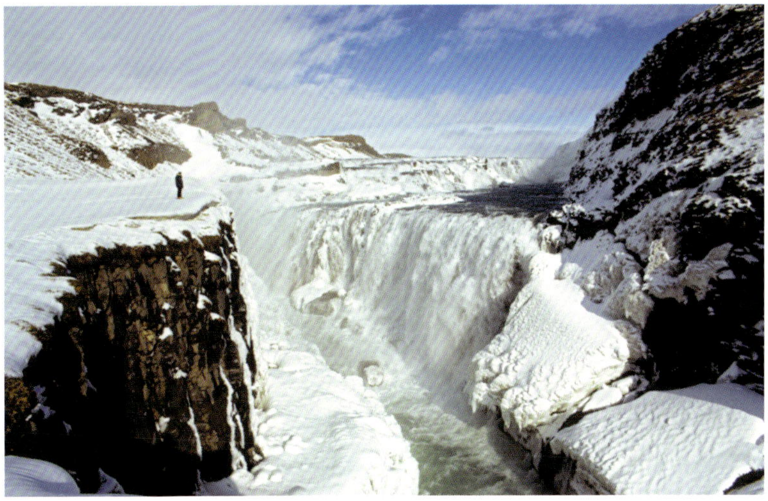

DOG SLEDGE, EAST GREENLAND

DOG SLEDGE AND ICEBERG, EAST GREENLAND

CLIMBING TO CAMP 3, ANNAPURNA SOUTH FACE, NEPAL

GULLFOSS IN WINTER, ICELAND

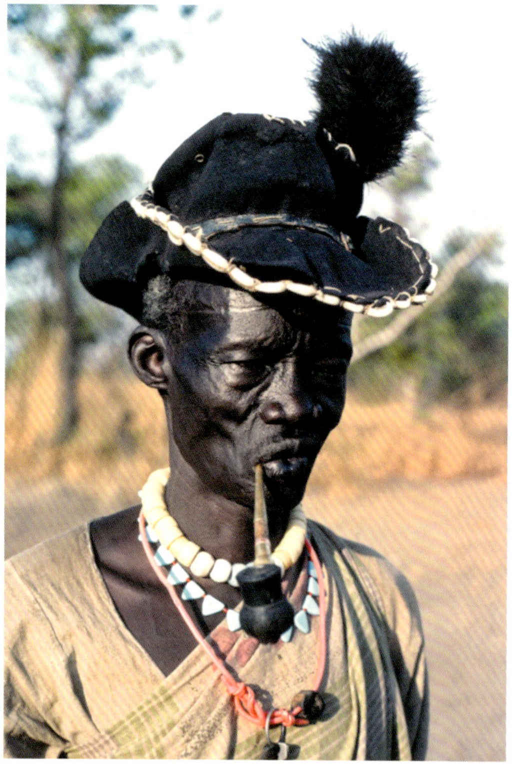

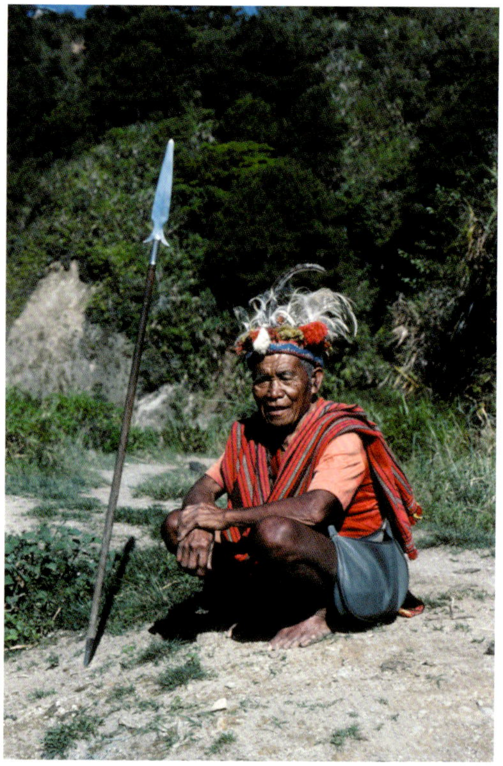

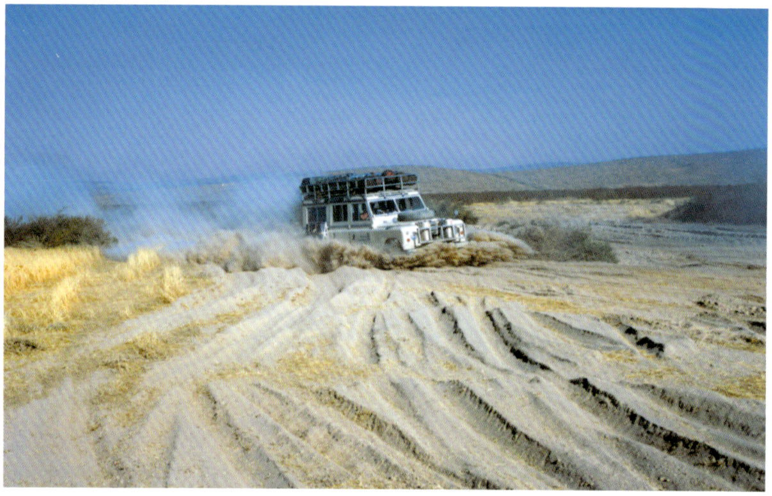

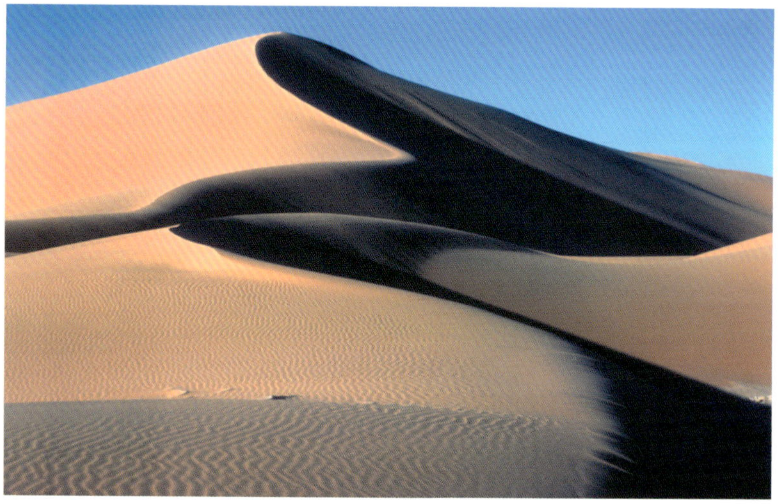

DINKA MAN, SUDAN

LANDROVER THROUGH BULL DUST,
DASHT E LAILI DESERT, NORTHERN AFGANISTAN

IFUGAO MAN, PHILIPPINES

BEAUTIFUL SHAPES, SAND DUNES,
THE SAHARA, ERG BOUHARET, ALGERIA,

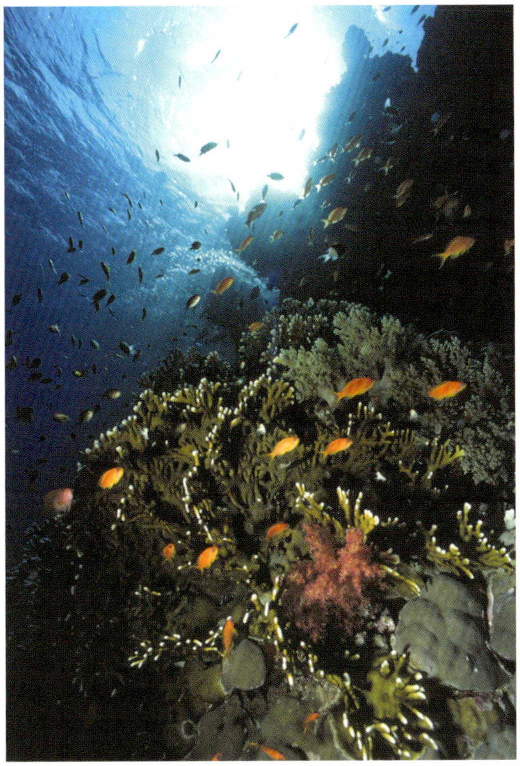

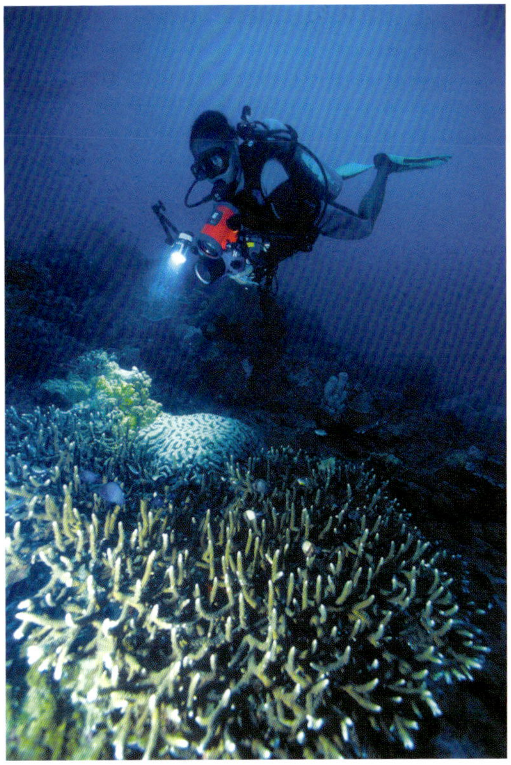

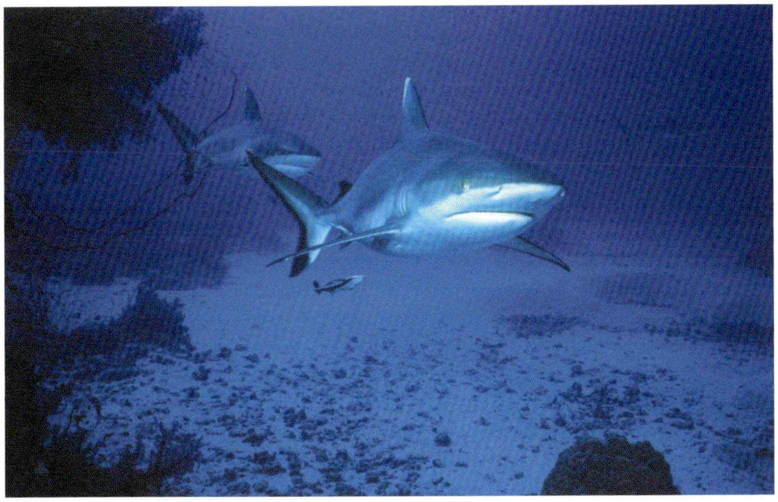

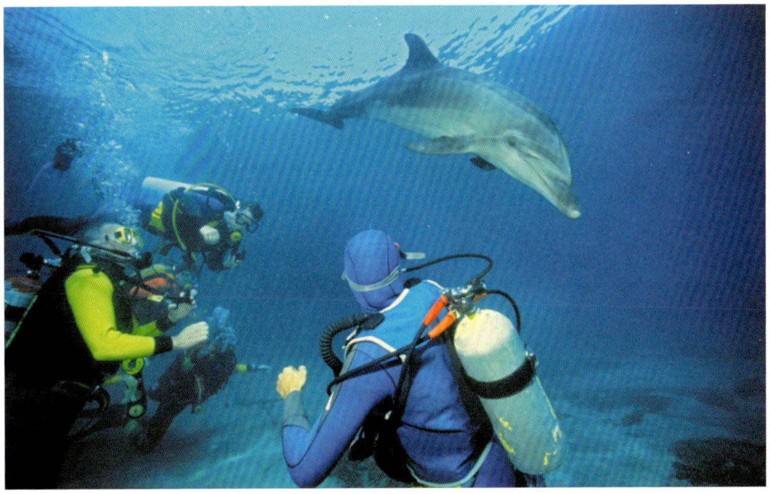

REEFSCAPE, RED SEA, EGYPT

GREY REEF SHARK, RED SEA, SUDAN

AMILLSON BARAGUS OVER STONY CORALS, LANKAYAN, SULU SEA, SABAH, BORNEO

BOTTLENOSE DOLPHIN & DIVERS, GULF OF AQABA, RED SEA, ISRAEL

INES LABUNSKI ROBERTS FRPS

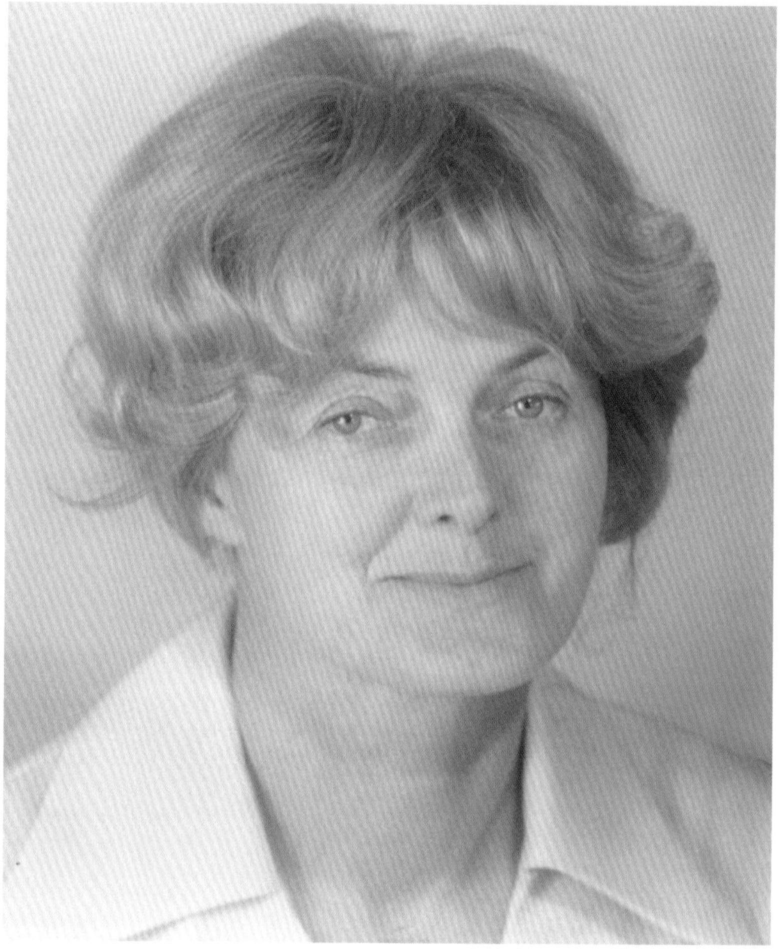

For Ines Roberts, photography is part of her life, just like breathing and eating. She explains: 'It is not just defined by carrying a camera and collecting photographs in thousands, that is just a small part of it. It is a constant involvement of seeing and discovering the world around me.'

Ines Labunski Roberts has lived in Santa Barbara since 1966. She was born in Danzig, now Poland. A year before the war ended, her mother abandoned their home in Zoppot and fled with her two children through Poland, Austria, and finally to the Danish border to avoid the Russian Army. Roberts was educated in Germany and England. She studied medicine in England, ambitions that were abandoned on meeting her husband, Gilbert.

Living in Scotland she joined the local camera club in Stirling, and with the exception of support offered there, is a self-taught photographer. Her husband designed a 'fuse and dissolve' unit for her slide-music presentations, and since 1972, she has produced 35 such slide shows, the majority having been premiered at the Santa Barbara Museum of Art. Her first show, 'The Four Seasons of Sequoia' receive a standing ovation at the PSA International Convention of Photography in San Francisco.

In 1988 she was elected a Nominee for the Californian Art Advocate. She received her Fellowship of the Royal Photographic Society in 1992, with invited membership of the London Salon of Photography in 1996. In 2002 and 2003 she was overall winner in the Royal Aero Club Trust Photographic Competition. She was a winner in the BBC Wildlife Photographer of the Year Competition in 2003 and again in 2007. Away from photography, both she and her husband were enthusiastic hang-glider pilots with Ines enjoying nearly 700 flights between 1979 and some ten years ago when she stopped flying.

Over the years, her photographs have been published as feature articles in Canada, England, Germany, Holland, Japan, Mexico and the USA. In particular, her articles and photographs are published regularly in *Natur Foto* (Germany) and *Nature Photo* (USA).

'I really have no preferred subject matter. In that way I am not selective and I do not ignore certain categories in photography. Something has to call me, may catch my attention, speak to me, and then I am responding to what I see. This could be anything – a flower, or a wide landscape, a face in its pensive mood or a little busy insect. It may be an unusual cloud formation or a pattern of lines and texture in the sand or rock. It could be a dilapidated old hamlet – so sad in its desertion – or the embalming light on a crisp modern building. It may also be a very mundane item in my kitchen momentarily changed by the light.'

'Santa Barbara is a very peaceful and unusual town and we are surrounded by nature, with the Pacific in front of us and the mountain ranges behind. I sometimes miss the Seasons, but one can always step into the car, leave the balmy coast and reach wild, cold winter terrain in a few hours.'

'I deeply love nature subjects, I feel so at home and become absorbed in a natural terrain and wilderness. I am overwhelmed by the harmonious beauty of form and lines created by the wind in the dunes, and the quiet simplicity of a snow-landscape. Also the truly miraculous sight of the so hostile desert temporarily transformed into glorious bloom after adequate rainfall.'

"It could be anything, but I strongly believe that any photograph, of whatever subject matter, has to contain more than just an obvious reality or be a factual documentary. Something in the image has to allude to another meaning and involve my imagination. It should always hint at yet another reality than the obvious. Just an old flower or a tree could become a metaphor or symbol of life. It should be thought provoking and widening.

'In the beginning I never know what the final image or outcome will be, as one step in the creative involvement suggests and leads to the next, and I respond to what feels right, looks good and is meaningful to me.'

'Afterwards when I am looking at the images that I photographed, they should again speak to me and move me, or sometimes invite me to see and discover yet other possibilities of expression and meaning.'

Michael Hallett FRPS

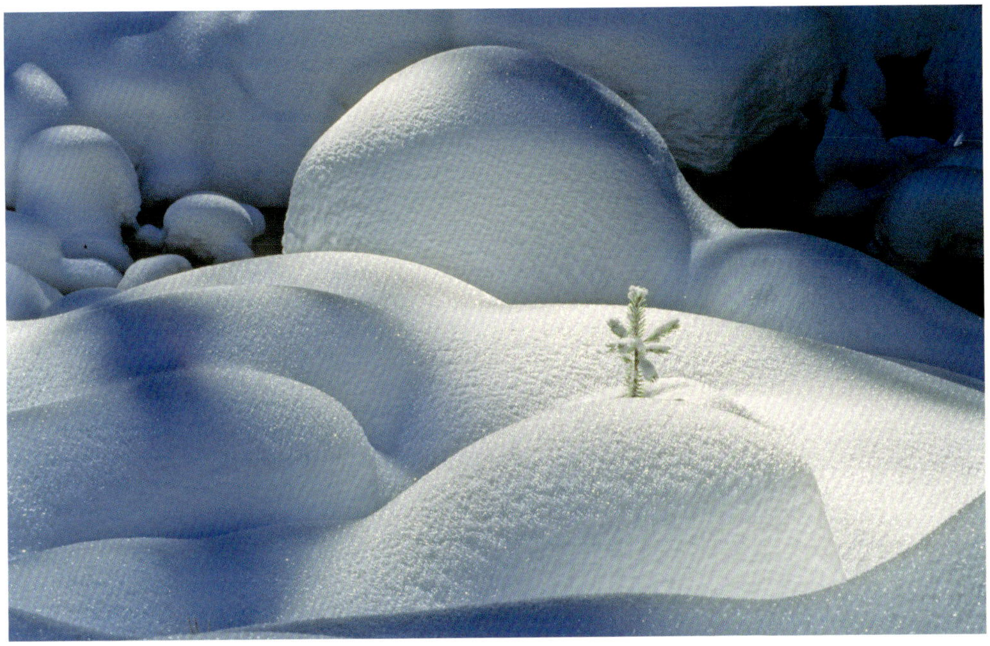

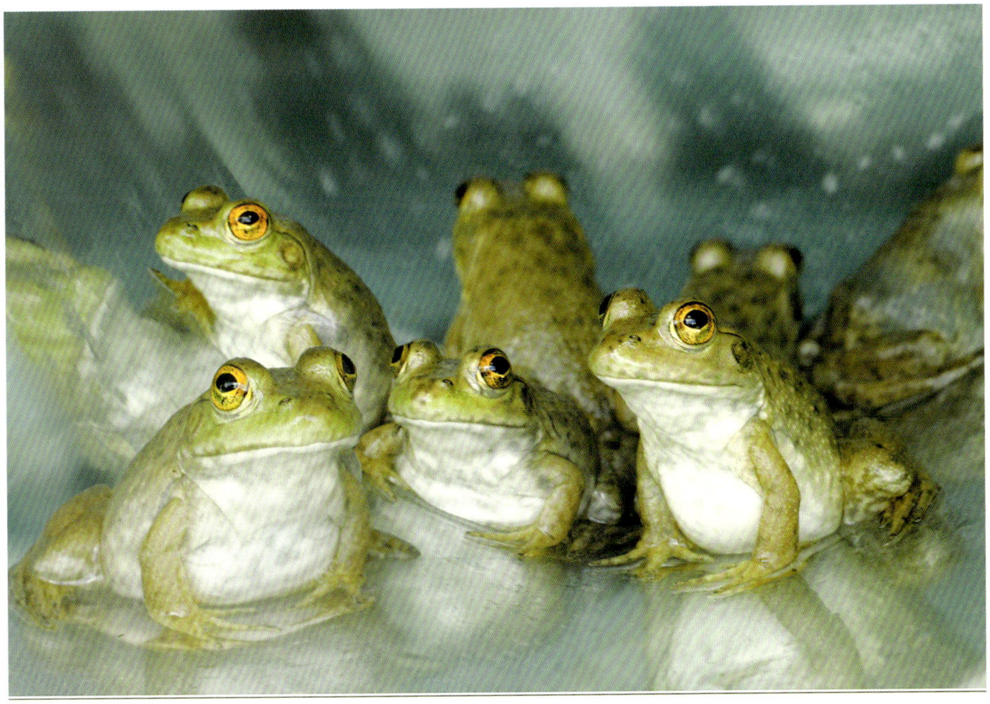

FIR ON SNOW MOULUORS
FROG REFUGE

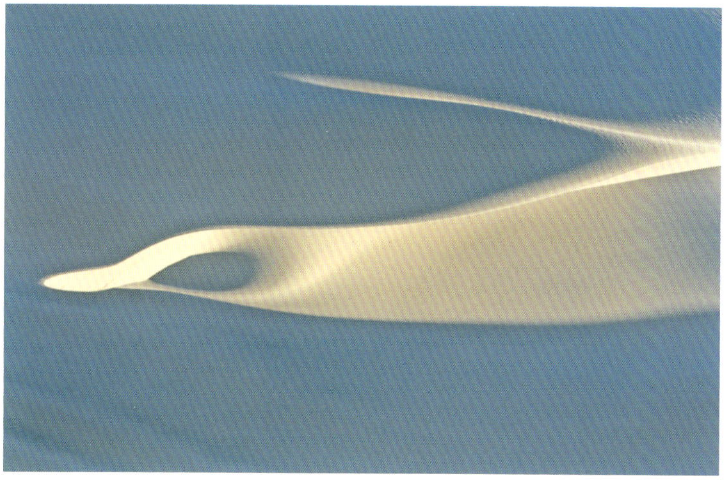

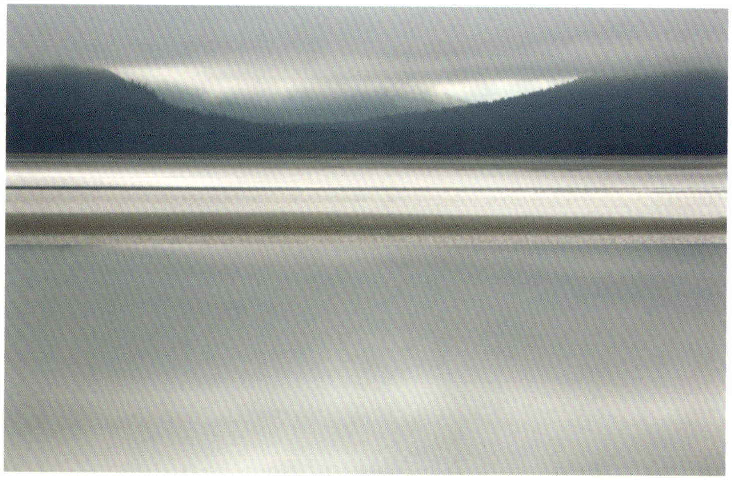

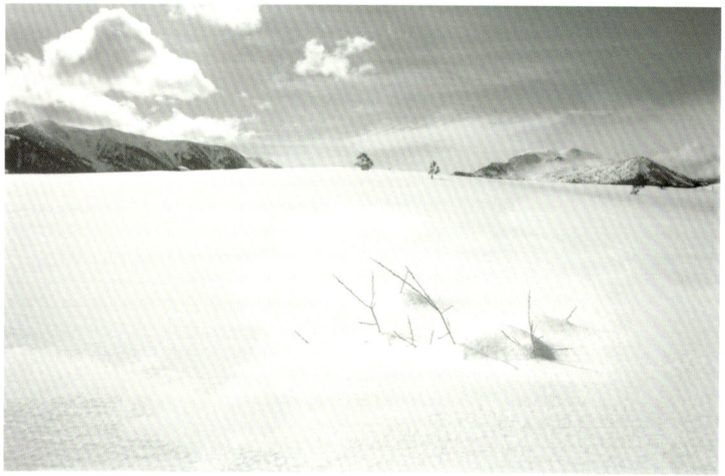

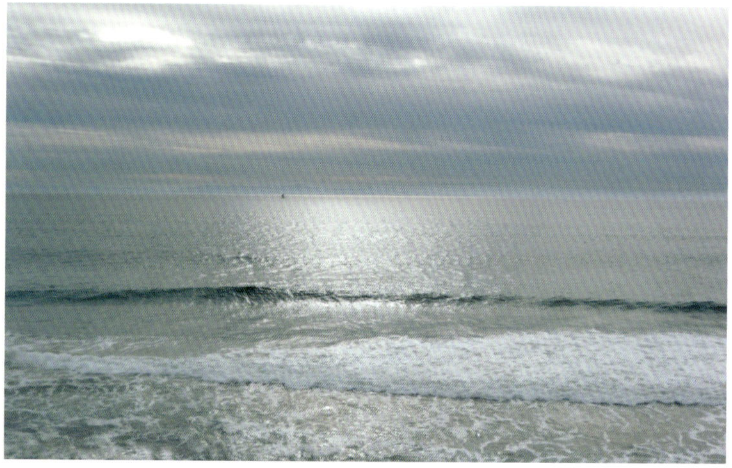

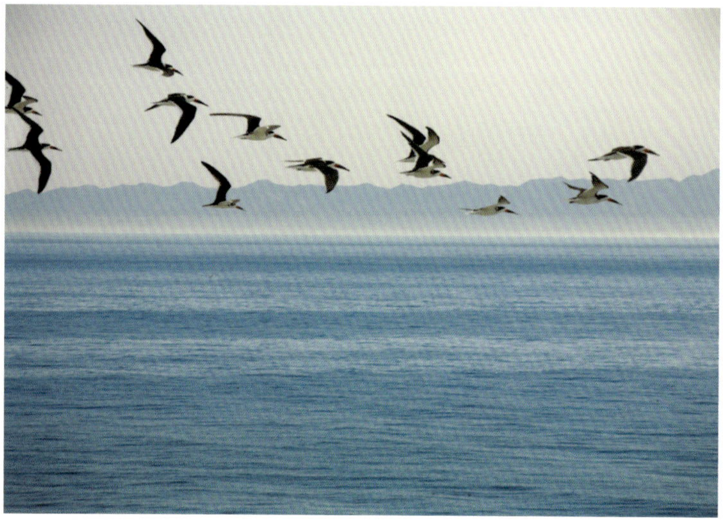

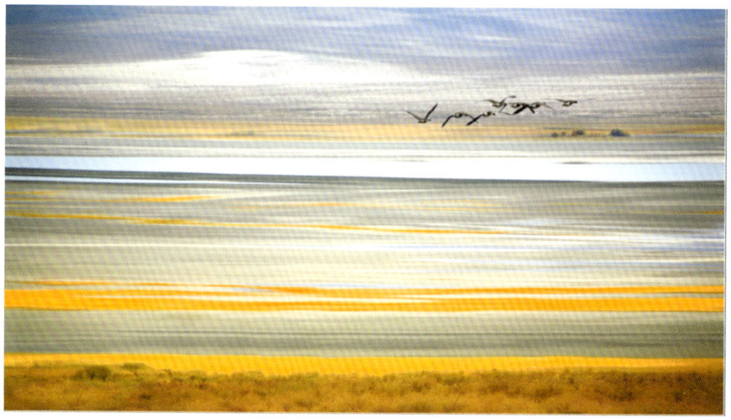

DUNE DETAIL
STILLNESS
OCEAN AND SKIMMERS

LAKE IN ALASKA
OCEAN VIEW
DRYLAKE OWENS VALLEY

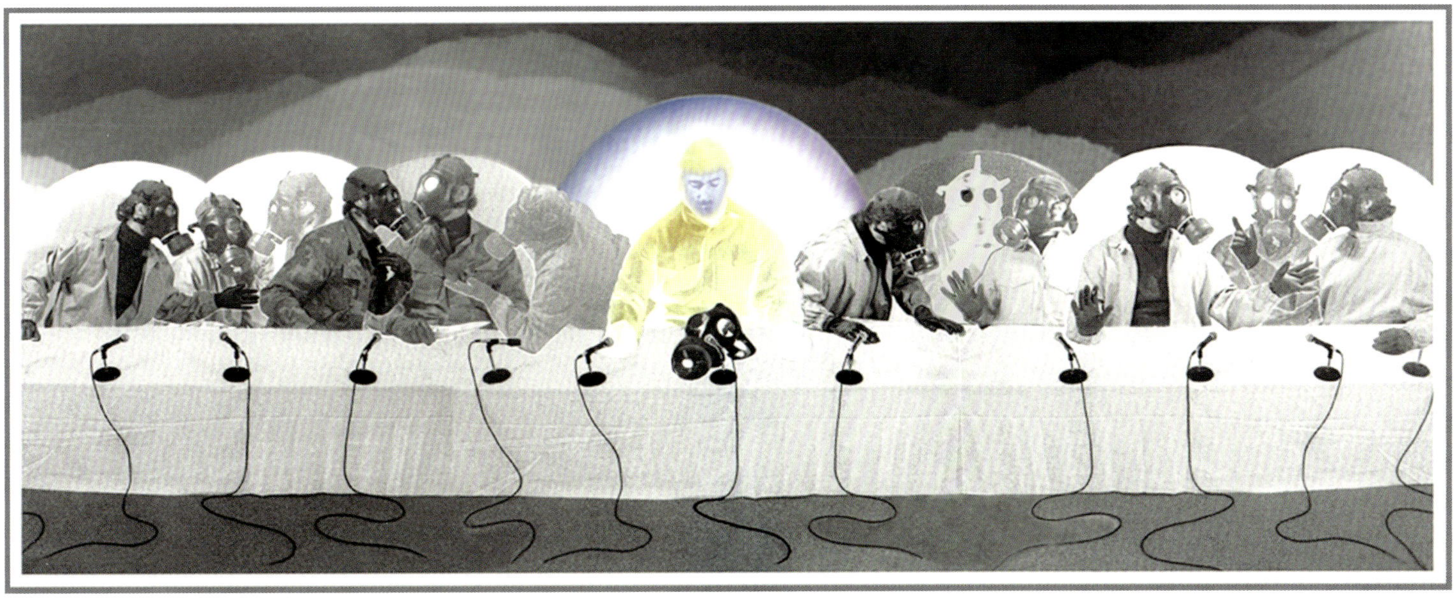

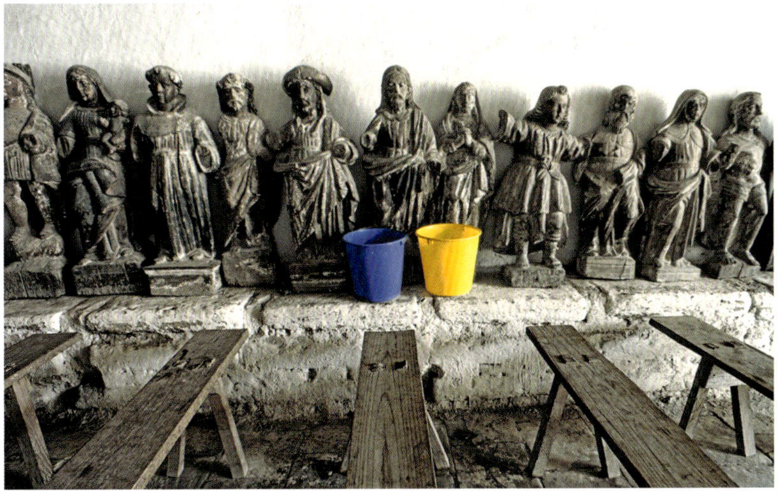

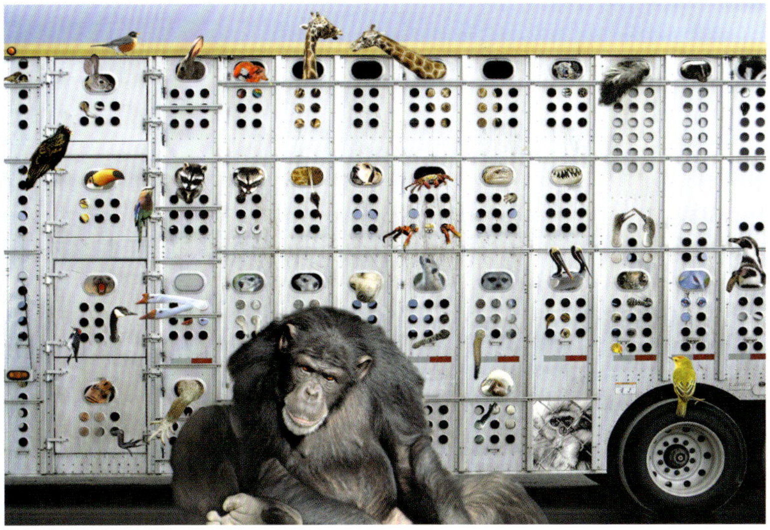

MASQUERADE OF INDECISION

SAINTS WITH BUCKETS, GUATEMALA

MODERN NOAH'S ARK

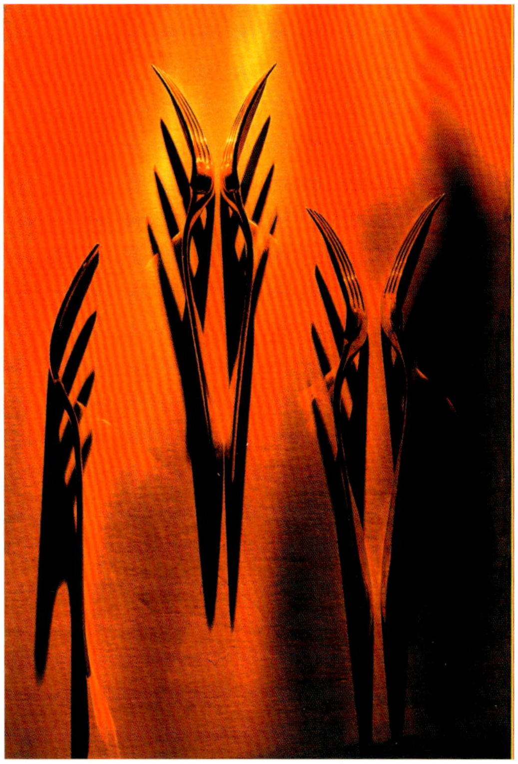

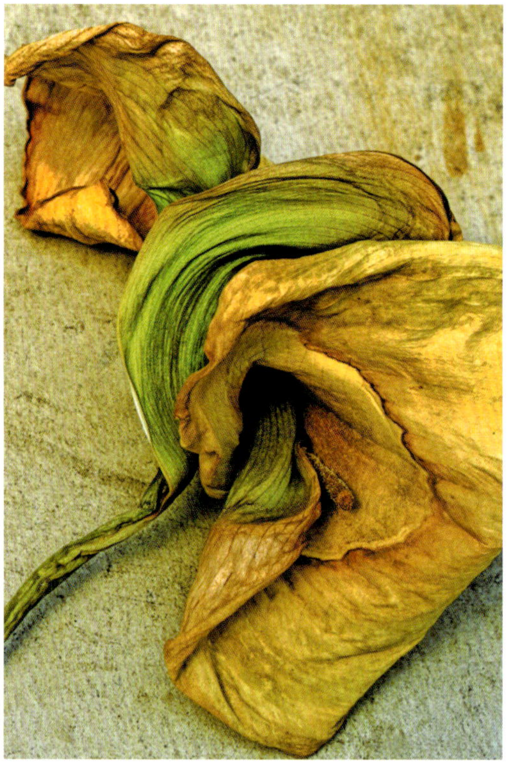

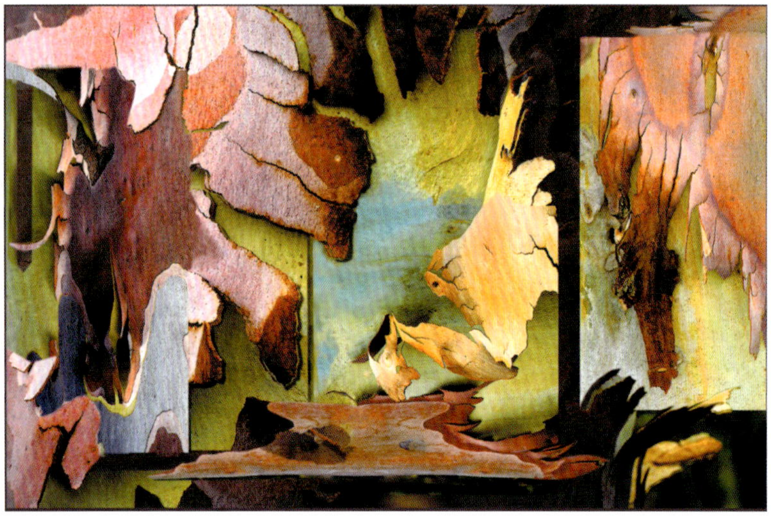

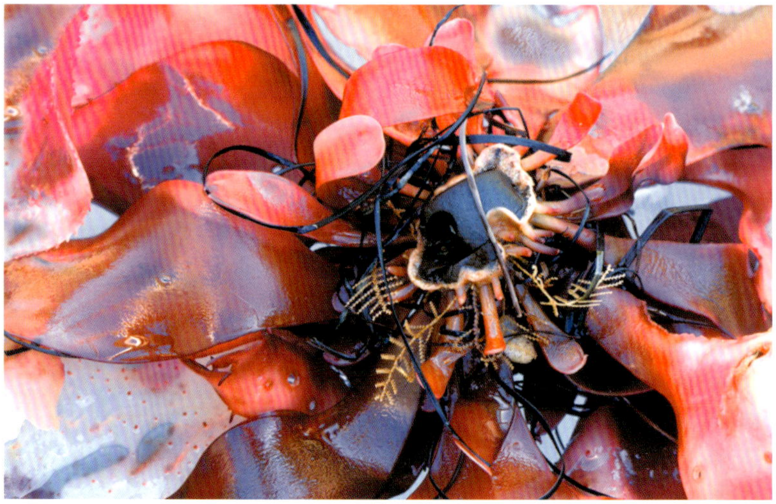

ABSTRACT – FORKS IN GOLDEN LIGHT
PEELING BARK OF THE EUCALYPTUS TREE

DEAD CALLA
KELP AT LOW TIDE

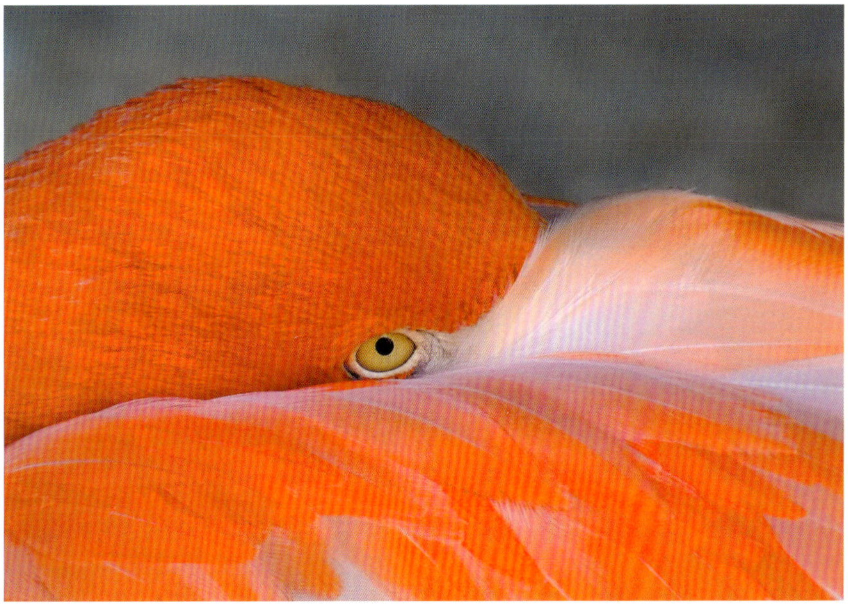

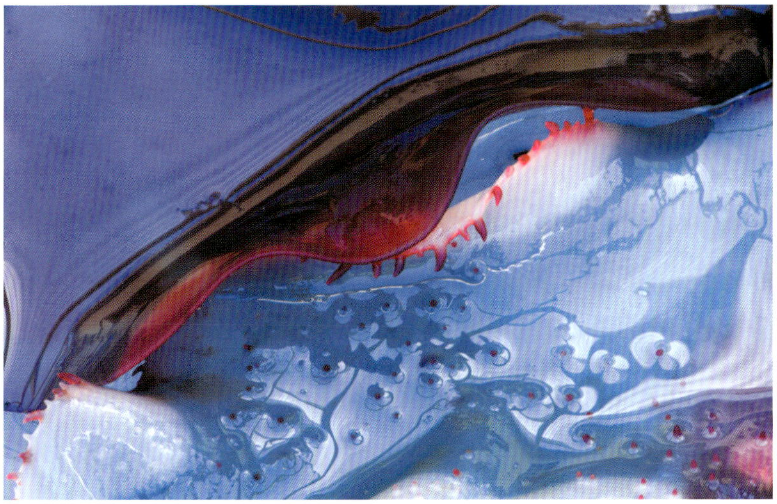

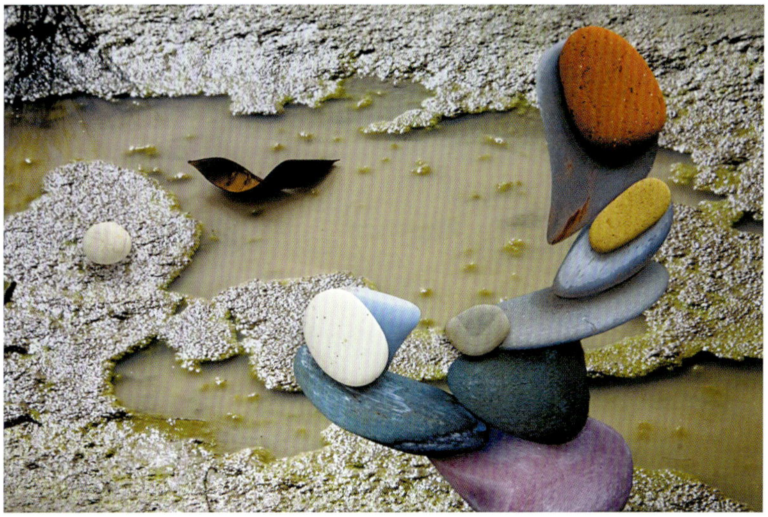

I AM WATCHING YOU

ABSTRACT – FLOATING KELP

NEW IDEA

JIM MORELAND FRPS

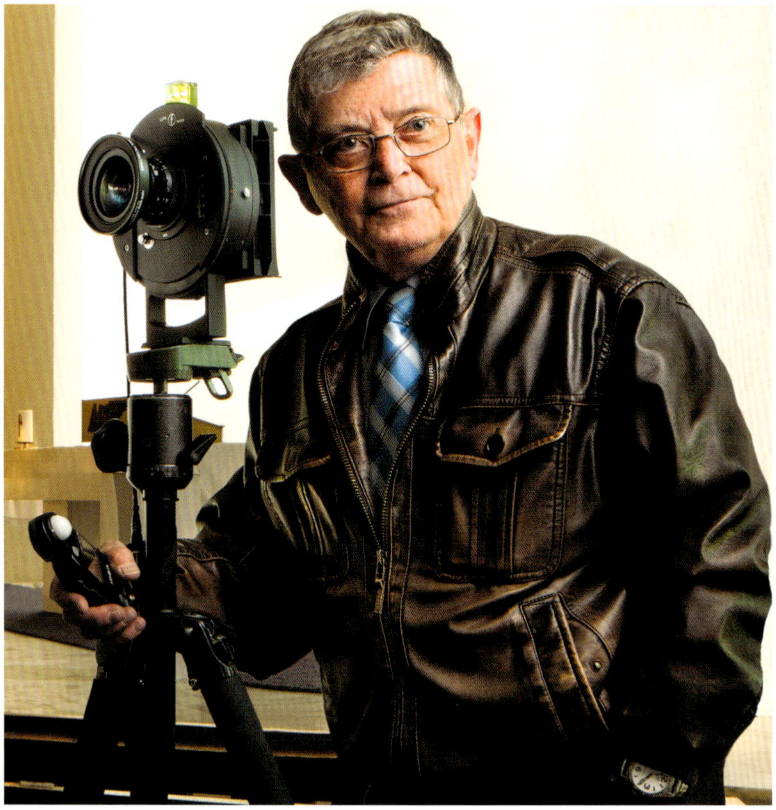

Jim Moreland first got involved in photography in the mid-60s when he went on a tour of Ireland in a car he borrowed from his father. He was with a friend, and his girlfriend, who is now his wife. His friend was very keen on photography and was taking photographs and talking about f8 and f5.6 and f11. "I had no idea what he was talking about", Jim told me, "I'd never seen a camera like that in my life and I was amazed when he took the lenses off. We started talking and I became intrigued with the technical side of it. When we came back from holidays, we went to his darkroom. He put a piece of paper in the enlarger, exposed it and put it in what I thought was water. I saw the image coming up and I've never forgotten that. It had an amazing impact me. It all developed from there. Photography became an obsession.

By the 1970s, he decided to take up photography full time. "In a way it was quite stupid", he said, "and a professional friend told me it was difficult to make a living out of photography". He went ahead anyway. He left his job as an office machine technician and took a significant drop in salary to get a job in a local photographic studio and then with a local professional photographer. His belief was justified. Soon afterwards, he won the first place in the Architecture section of the Ilford Print Awards and received a cheque for £1000. At the time, he was earning about £800 a year. It was the first time that a photographer from Northern Ireland had won this award. In 1974, he saw in the local paper that the Northern Ireland Electricity Service (NIES) were expanding and they wanted a professional photographer to run their new photographic department. Jim applied for the job and got it.

He spent the next 20 years at the NIES. He had a lot of freedom and loved the variety of what he did. "You never knew what you were going to be asked to do from one day to the next. Sometimes there was nothing down to do for a couple of days so I would go out to take landscapes to put in the offices. Some of those photographs are still around", he told me. During his time at the NIES, he won two further Ilford Awards in the Commercial and Portraiture sections.

He met the late Larry Bartlett who was the main speaker in the Ilford Roadshows and became one of junior speakers. "Larry was amazing" he said, "He helped me to get the quality of printing that is required for British Institute of Professional Photography (BIPP) Fellowship level". Jim's BIPP Fellowship panel was successful on its first attempt and he won the award for the most outstanding panel of the year.

The morning after the award ceremony in Bath, he came across the RPS Headquarters and spent some time talking to the staff. Within weeks, he had become a member and considers it one of the best decisions he has made. Soon afterwards, he was awarded his RPS Fellowship, which was in the Pictorial category.

He loves strong backlighting or directional lighting. "I like prints to bounce off the wall and hit you without being over contrasty", he says, and he takes a lot of time and effort to get that. "I like good blacks, juicy blacks. I'm not looking for a long range of intermediate tones, highlights to shadows. I compress it. I could easily print something which to me would be much flatter but would give a much better range of tones but that's not my style".

He was invited to sit as a panel member for RPS distinctions in the Applied and Professional category and he did this for 12 years. He is now on the Fellowship Board and the Distinctions Advisory Board and was awarded the RPS Fenton Medal in 2011.

Jim likes helping others. "For years", he says, "I was fanatical at competing to win awards and prestige, but this past 6 or 7 years, I haven't entered competitions and I've concentrated on helping people to get their RPS distinctions. I give many talks to help people improve their photography, particularly if its monochrome. I get a good buzz about helping people. I love the adrenaline it gives me when people achieve their distinctions".

I asked him, what he wanted people to get out of his work. "Enthusiasm", he replied without hesitation. "The one thing you can't buy is enthusiasm. You can buy the most fantastic equipment but you have to have the buzz, the passion and the enthusiasm to set about trying to do something properly. You need to go out and get stuck in and make lots of mistakes because that's the way you learn".

Jim's enthusiasm and passion for photography is the same now as it was when he decided to give up his full-time job for a career in photography many years ago. He hopes he'll still be doing what he's doing now in five years' time: taking photographs in monochrome, shooting film, and lecturing. "I love lecturing, especially if you get a big crowd" he added.

David Cooke ARPS

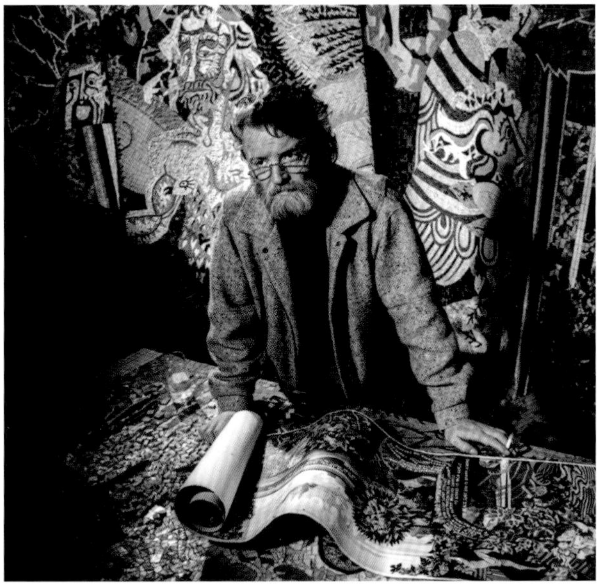

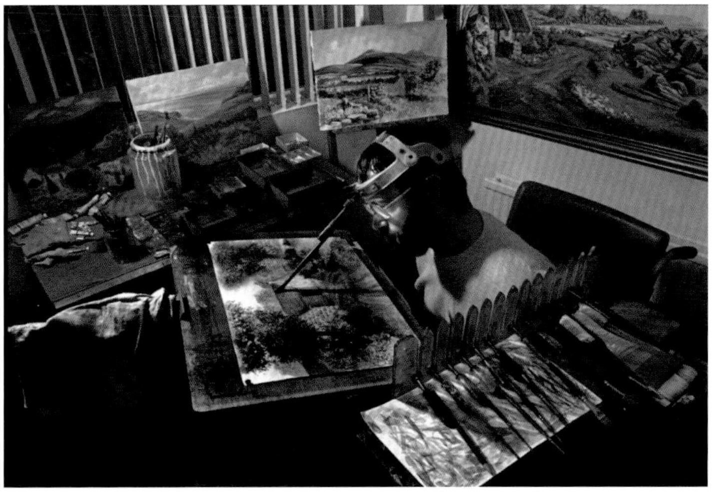

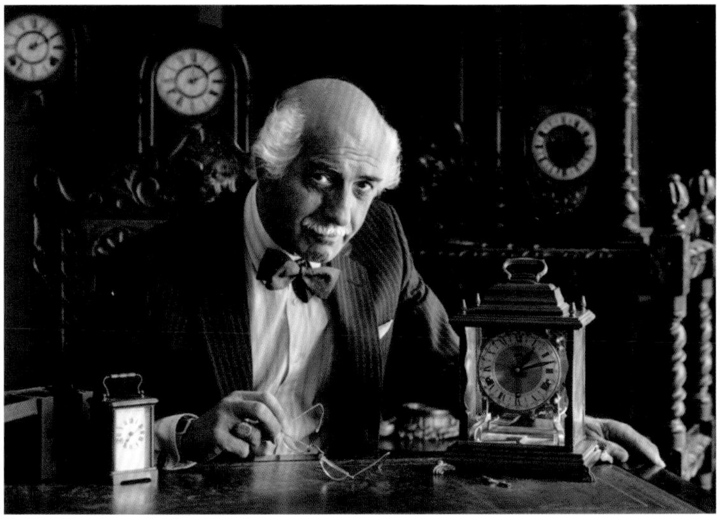

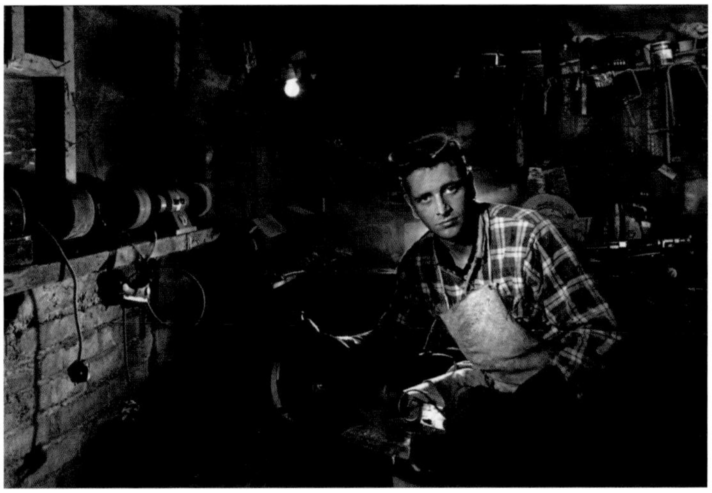

MOSAIC DESIGNER

THE VALUER

TRUE GRIT

THE WORKER

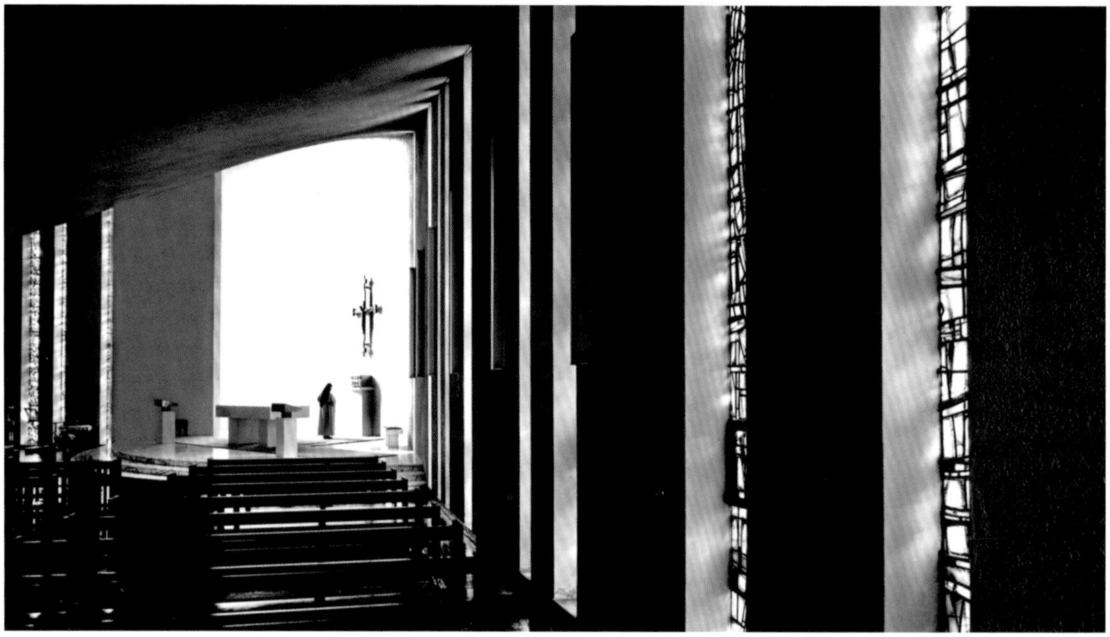

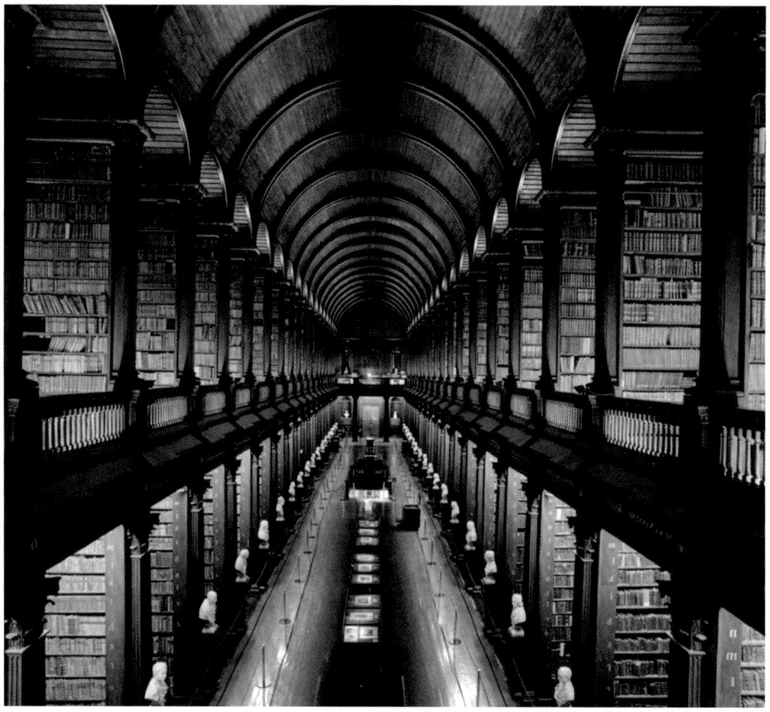

SILENT PAYERS

TRINITY LIBRARY

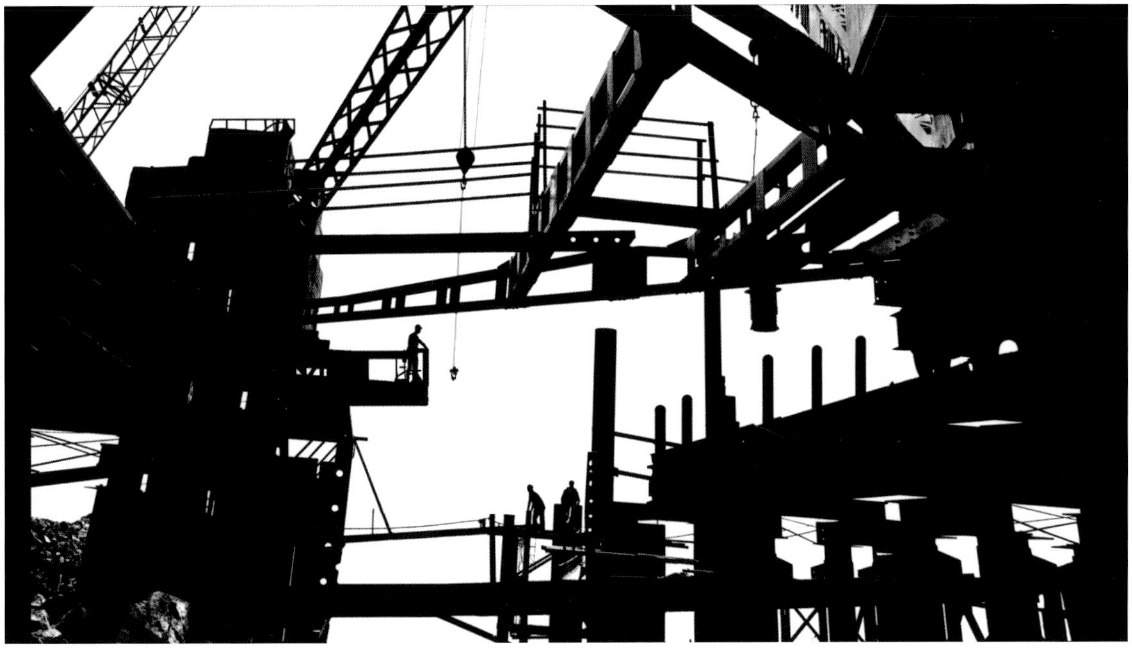

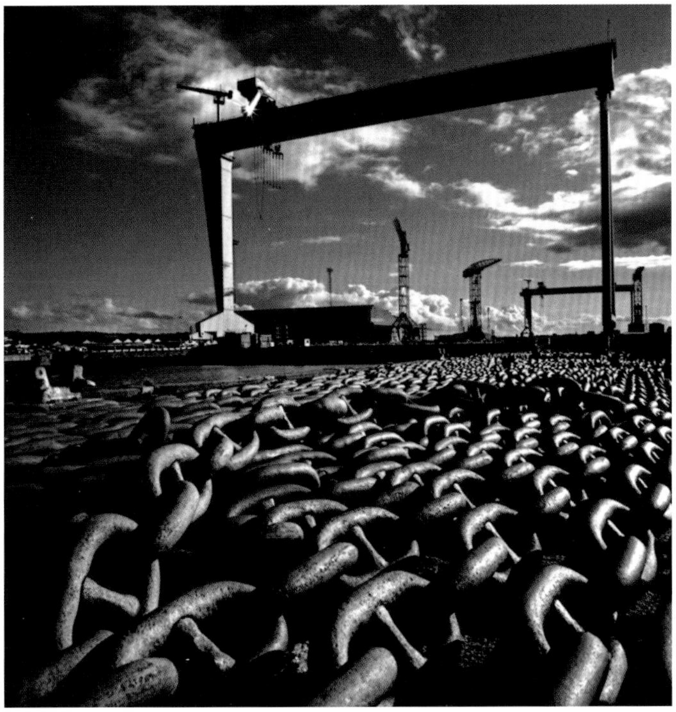

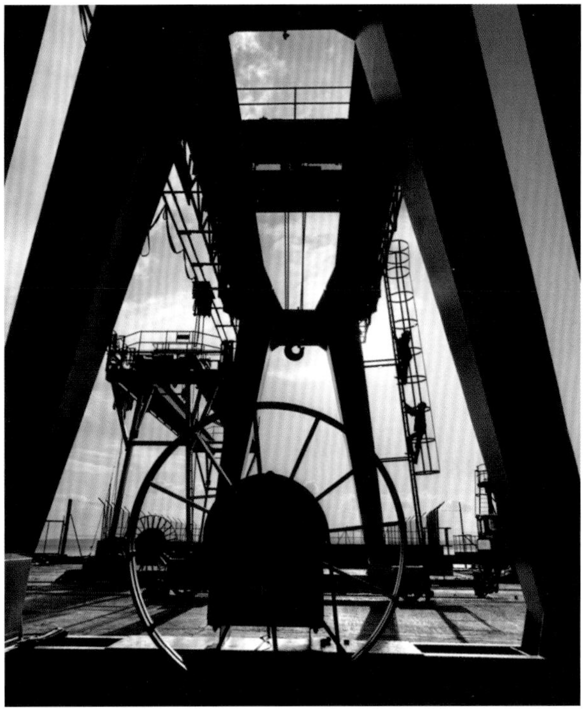

INDUSTRIAL GRAPHIC

THE SLEEPING GIANT, HARLAND AND WOLF

GOLIATH

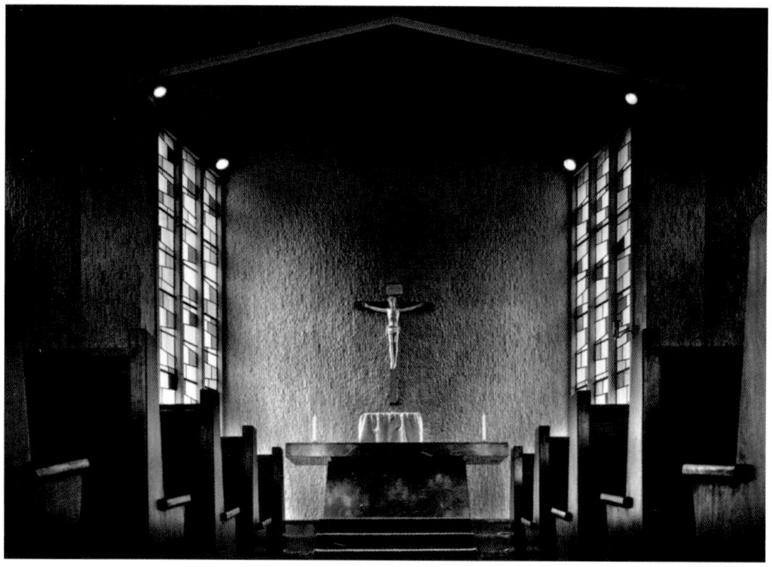

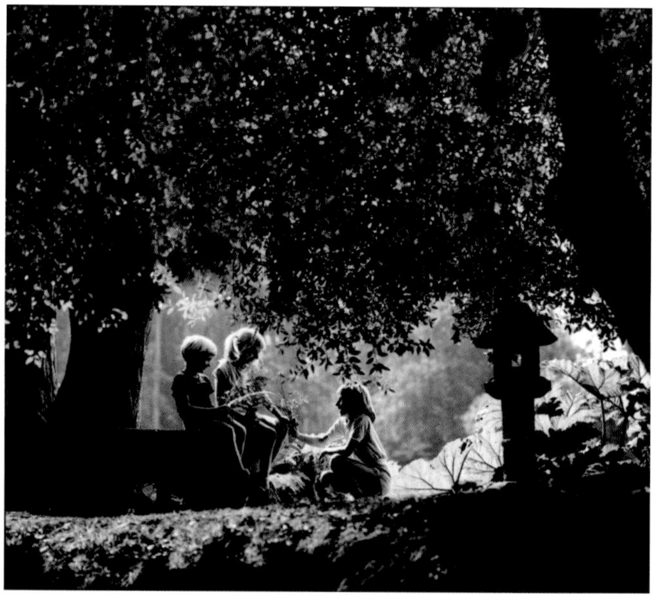

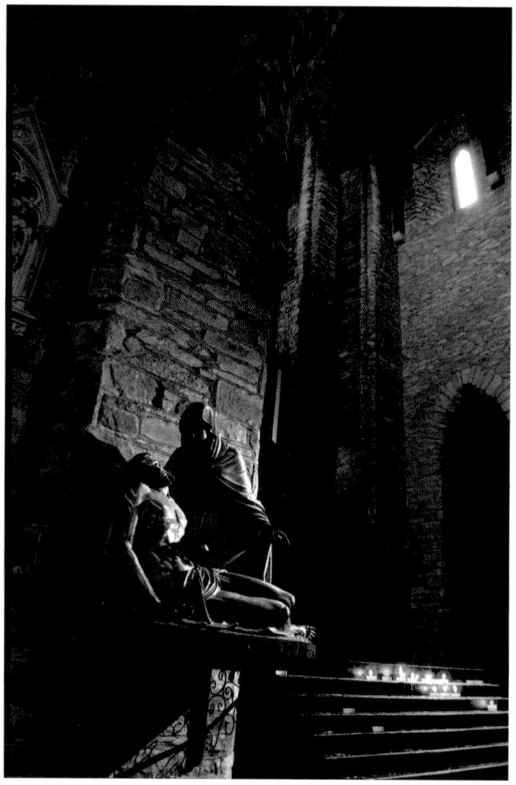

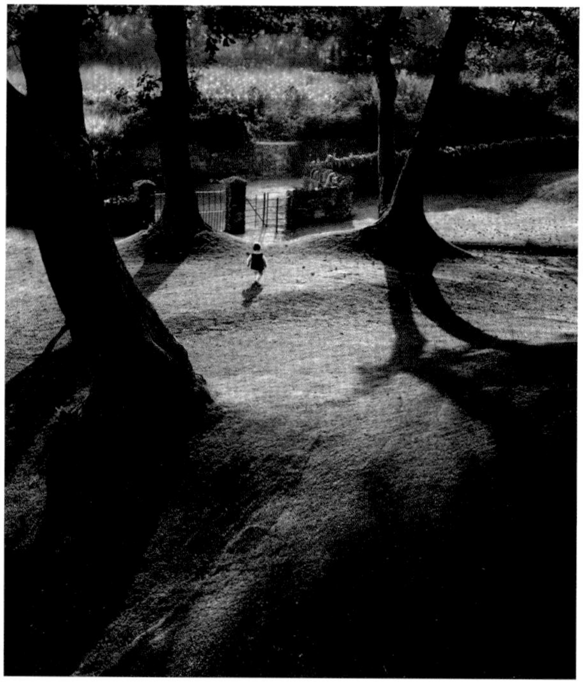

BEHOLD THE MAN
THE PIETA

PLAY TIME
CHILDHOOD FANTASY

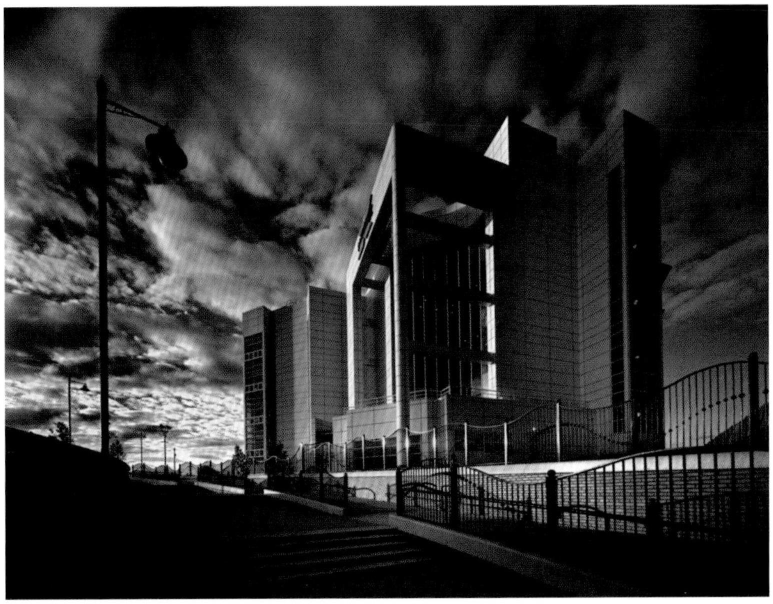

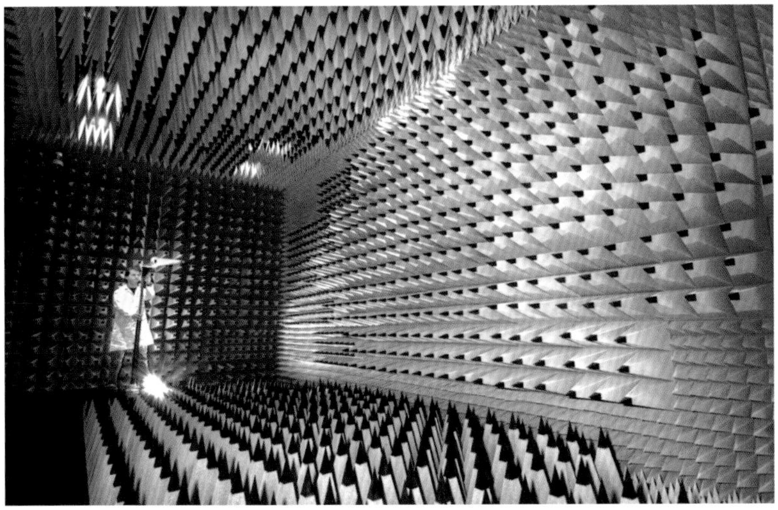

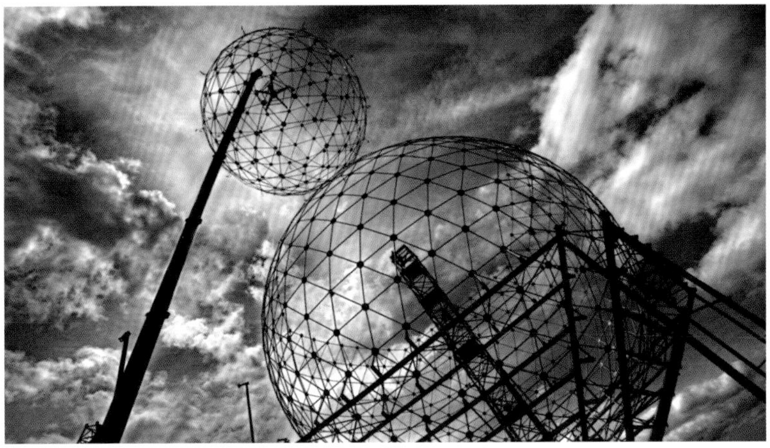

HALIFAX HEADQUARTERS

SOUND ROOM

THE RISING

VIC ATTFIELD FRPS AND MARY ATTFIELD FRPS

When Mary Attfield first spoke to me of her photography, she was very clear that while she and Vic were a married couple, as photographers they were certainly not joined at the hip.

What was particularly evident was a parallel agonising between the various mediums of monochrome versus colour, and the place of the more recent digital processes. What was abundantly obvious was their emphasis and joy of craftsmanship of the mounted print on the wall, which was exposed in their joint 100 print retrospective exhibition recently.

Vic Attfield FRPS

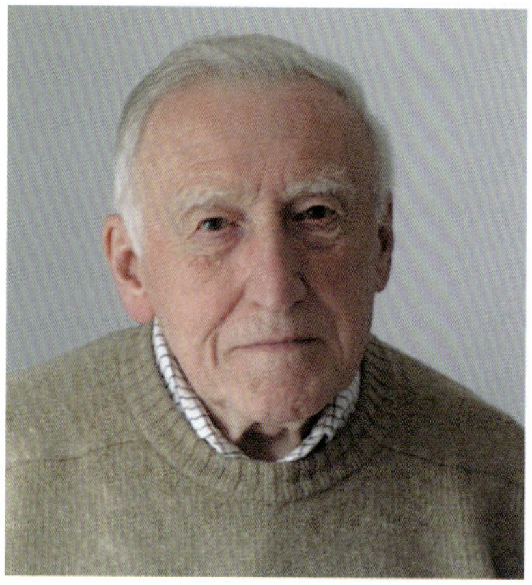

Vic Attfield's first passion was designing, building and flying free flight model aircraft, and occupied most of his spare time. As this did not suit his changing life style, he was subsequently 'encouraged' to take up photography instead. As it turned out, this became even more of a passion and has remained so ever since. His working career has been in engineering, on piping design and plant layout for the petroleum and petrochemical industries, such as oil refineries and offshore platforms.

Originally working in monochrome and occasionally in colour he has confined his photography solely to monochrome over the past decade or more. He feels that the introduction of colour gets in the way of what he is trying to communicate and that the graphic quality of black & white suits his type of subject matter.

Often his images are of landscapes, an interest that combines well with a love of walking. But mainly these days he concentrates on what can be loosely described as 'street photography'. He feels that with the increasing pace of life and quickly changing environment and lifestyles, the recording of these moments in time are becoming much more important than in the past.

In using 35mm film format he realizes the importance of filling the frame at the taking stage, so is very careful to include only those elements that give a balance within the frame and in conveying the feelings or mood of the subject. Vic has also developed the instinct of visualising the finished print at the taking stage. A great believer in thoroughly knowing the functions of your equipment, Vic has been using the same manual SLR cameras and lenses for over 30 years. Because of this, picture taking has become so automatic that full concentration can be made on taking the subject.

Mary Attfield FRPS

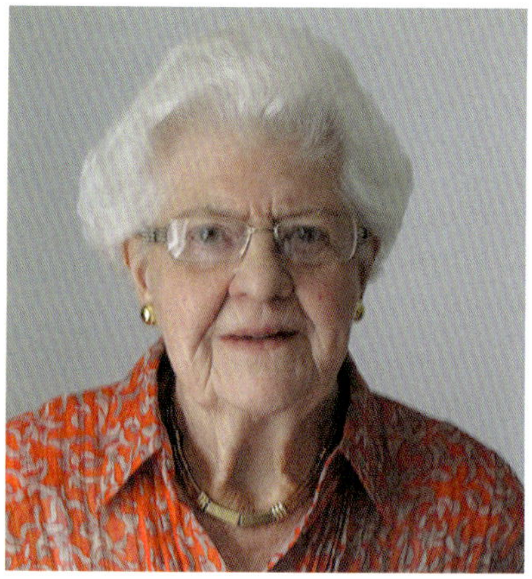

After an education in science and law, Mary had a career in industrial training and education development. She took up photography as an antidote to the pressures of work.

Mary's explains. 'Having always had an interest in paintings, sculpture, colour and design but lacking the ability to be truly creative in any of these fields, photography has proved to be the ideal outlet for the more creative side of my makeup. A fascination with human nature has been the other driving force behind my work.'

'Colour was my first concern. While working solely in the medium of colour slides, in which my only input was at the taking stage, I moved towards a limited colour range and awareness of design and space in the picture frame. When I took up monochrome photography in the early-90s, this led naturally to an initial concentration on design, perspective and lighting, themes that I pursued without the inclusion of a human element.'

'Portraying people in colour had never really appealed to me because I found them too distracting. Gradually and without realising it, I became more confident about incorporating people in my monochrome pictures.'

'What fascinates me now is the transience of moments in time and the intriguing way in which people react to one another and their surroundings. I hope such photographs will also say something to future generations about the way we live now. I want my pictures to transmit what I think and feel when taking them and to portray something about the human condition. Whether they do or not is another matter!'

'A manual camera, two lenses and two filters are my standard equipment. More would reduce the mobility and speed of reaction I need. Some people carry a camera everywhere. I do not. I need to concentrate fully in order to see things properly, so prefer to devote times specifically to photography and to work entirely on my own, without time constraints.'

Mary Attfield died on 28 October 2012, a short while after our conversation. Vic and Mary's retrospective exhibition was on show at the Smethwick Photographic Society for the month of November 2012.

Michael Hallett FRPS

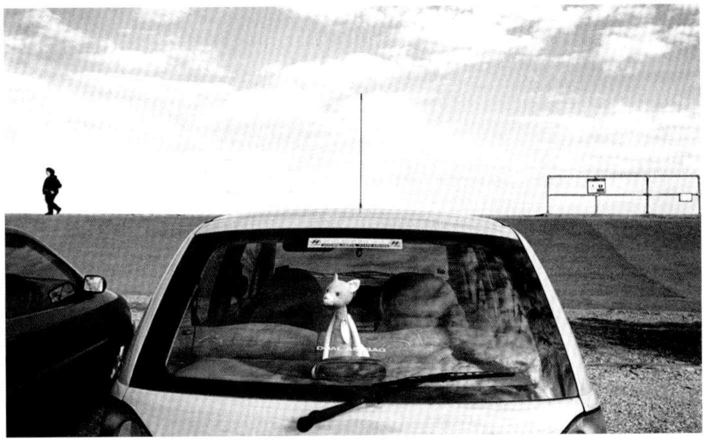

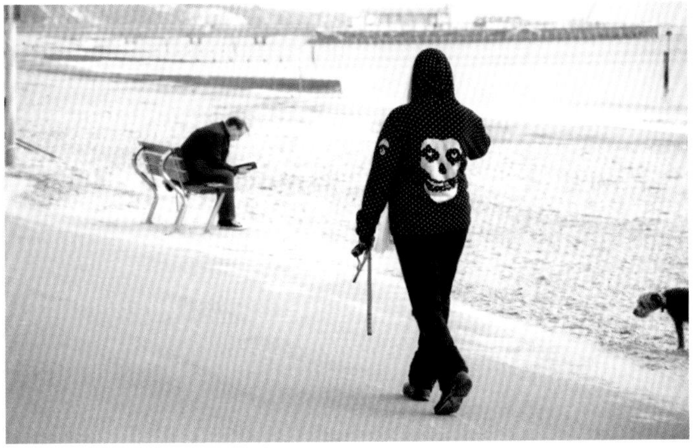

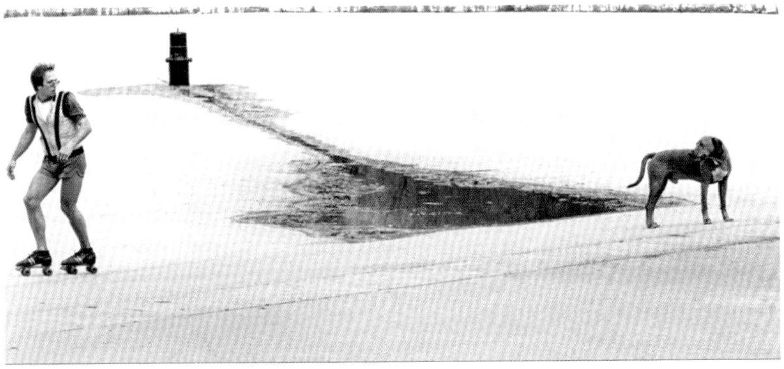

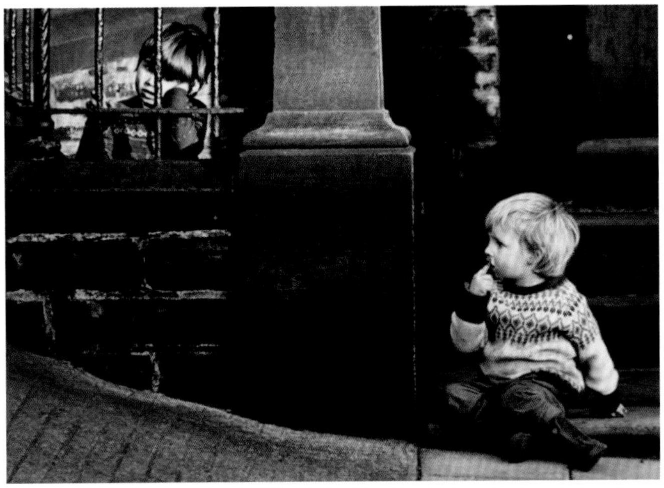

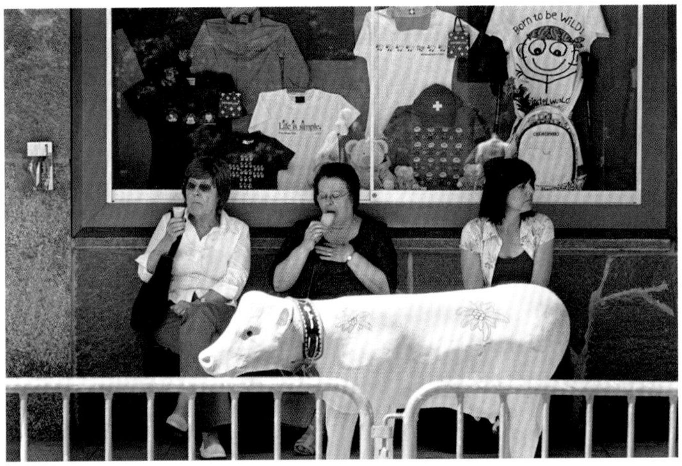

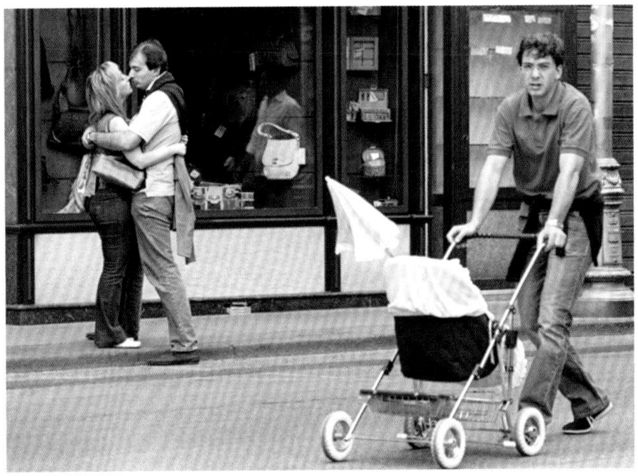

VIC ATTFIELD FRPS

MASCOT
DOG WALKER
IT WASN'T ME

CHILD OF HEBDEN BRIDGE
GRINDELWALD
CONSEQUENCES

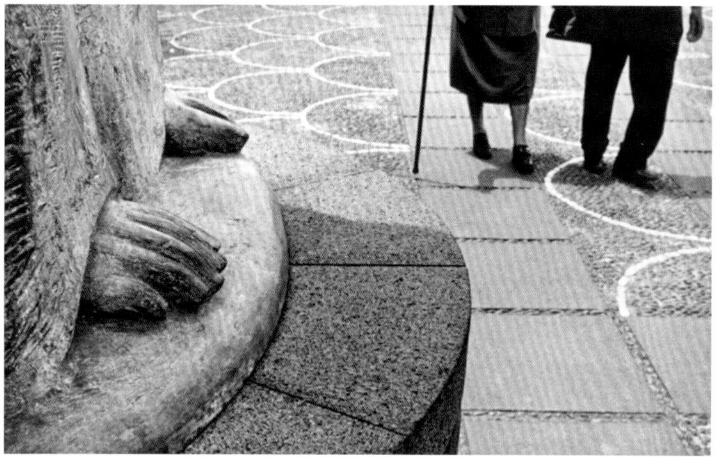

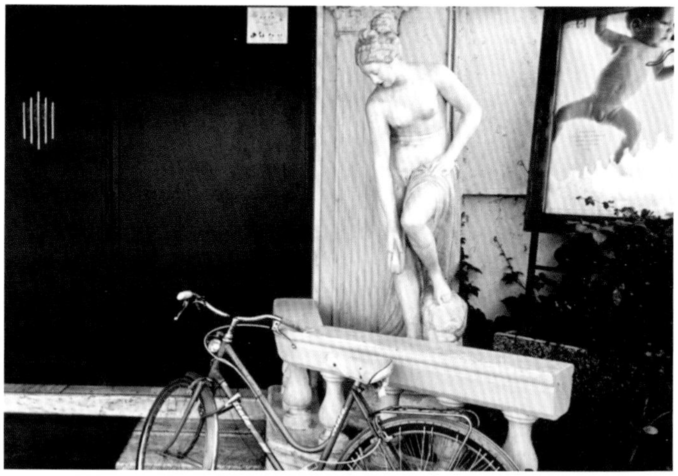

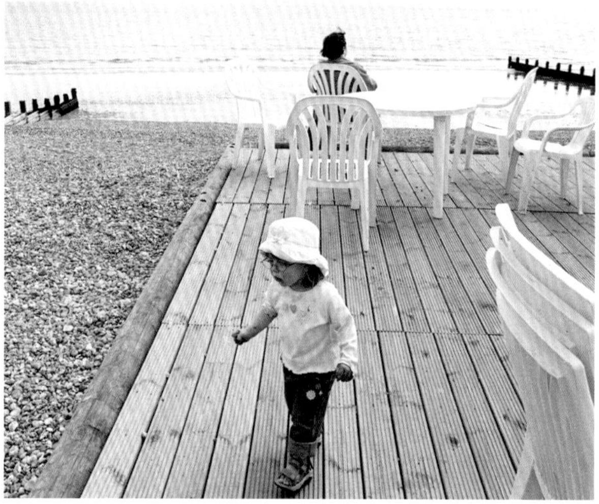

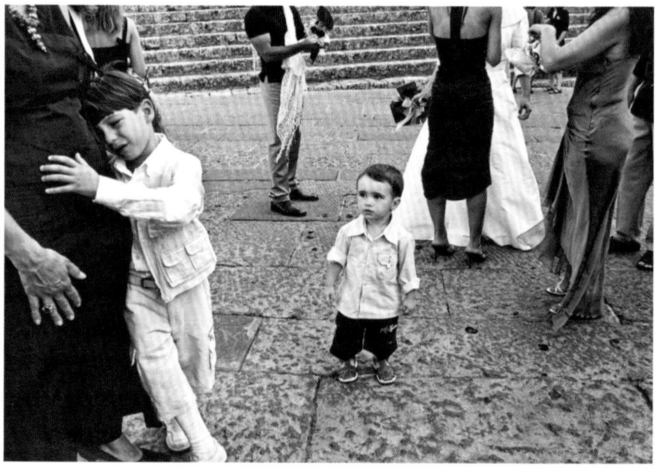

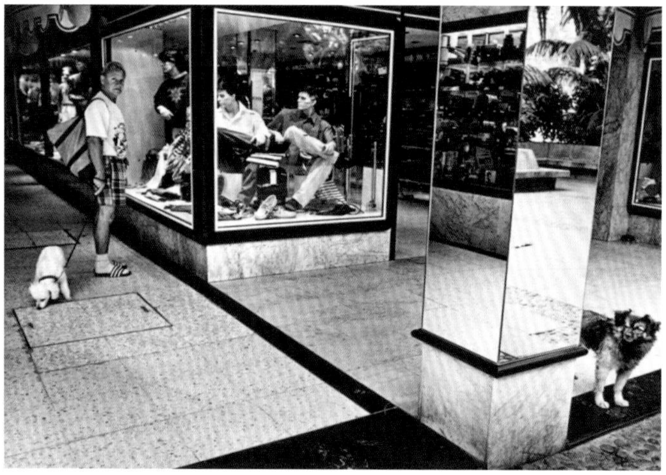

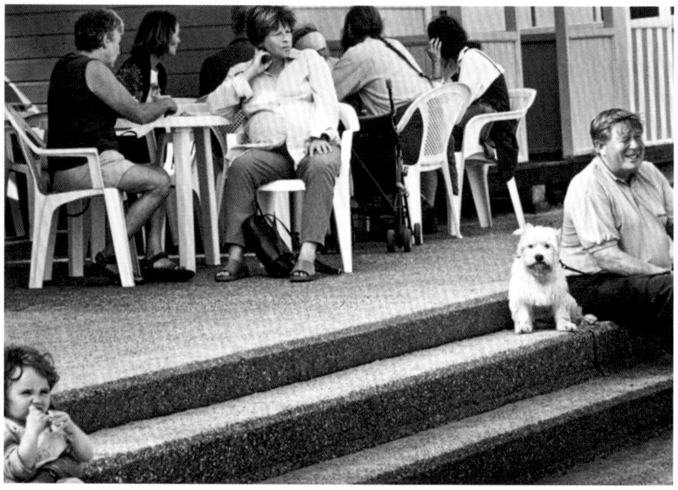

MARY ATTFIELD FRPS

FEET

A MIND OF HER OWN

CONTRASTS

LIFE CYCLE

MUMMY'S BOY

ON THE SEA FRONT

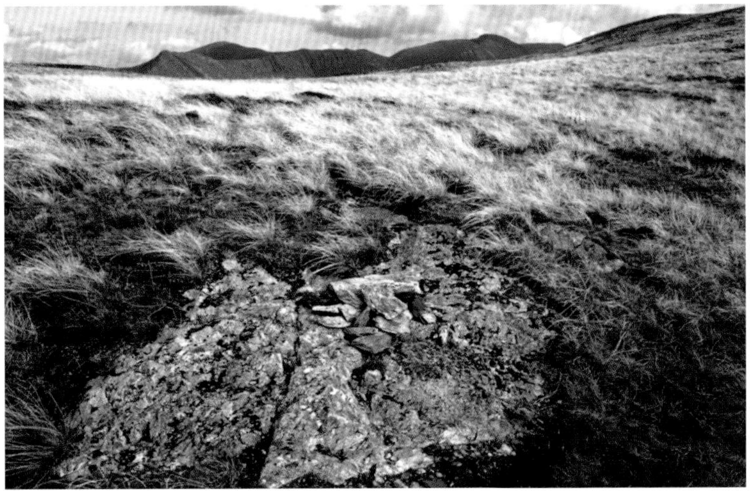

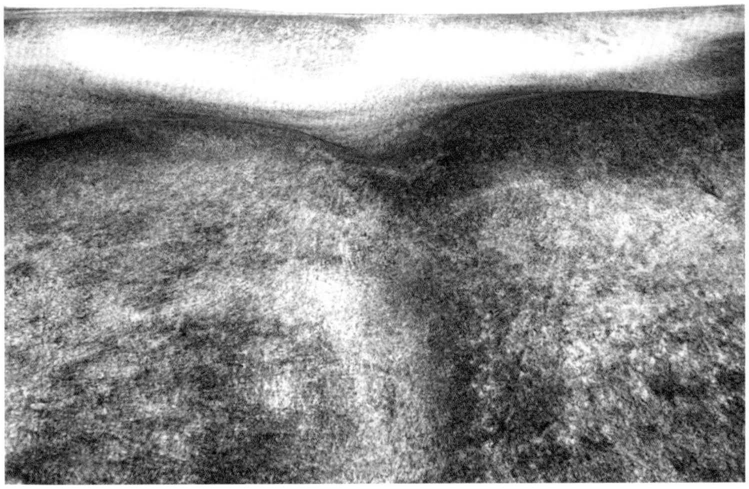

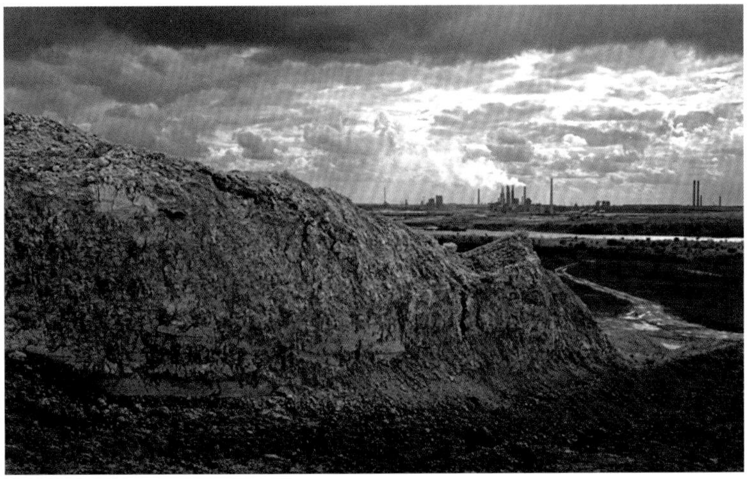

VIC ATTFIELD FRPS

DALES OUTCROP

SANDBAGS, DUNWICH

VANISHING COUNTRYSIDE

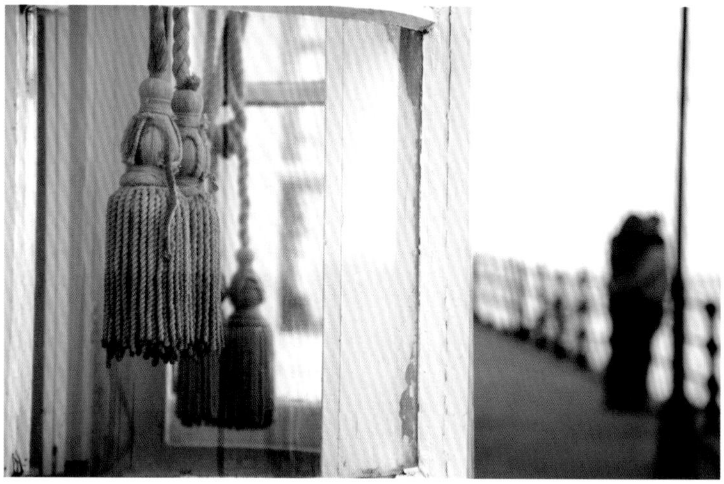

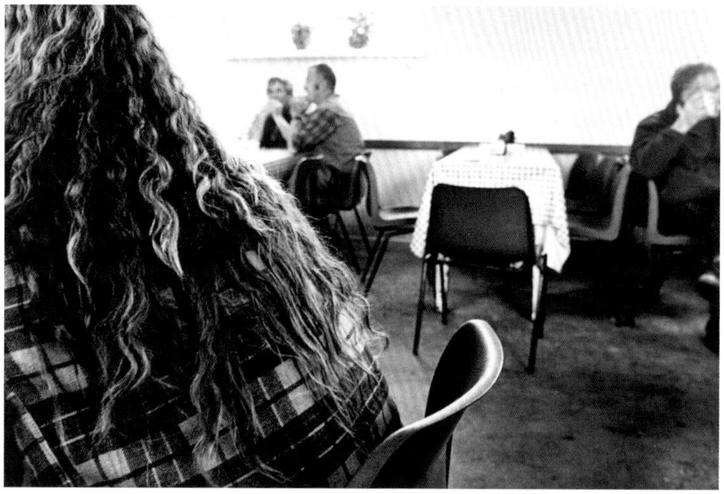

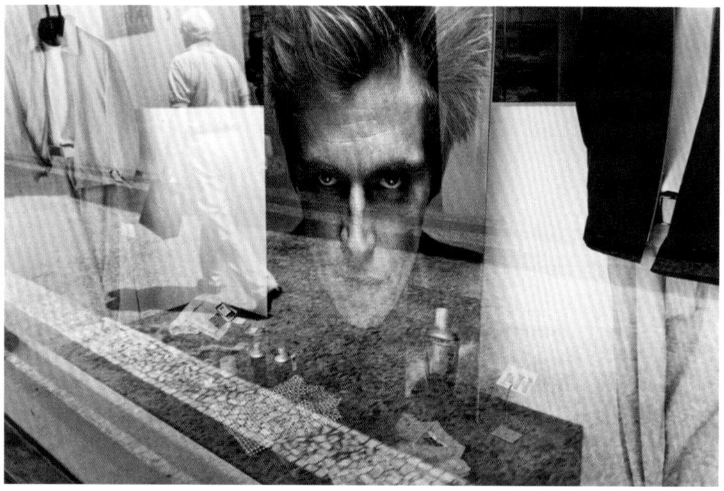

MARY ATTFIELD FRPS

SEASIDE ROMANACE

SEPARATE TABLES

MENSWEAR

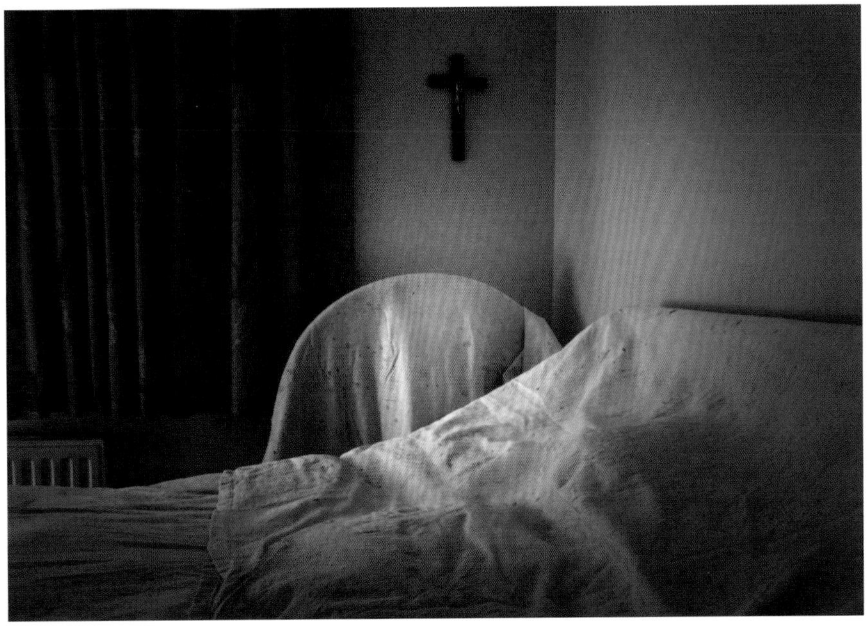

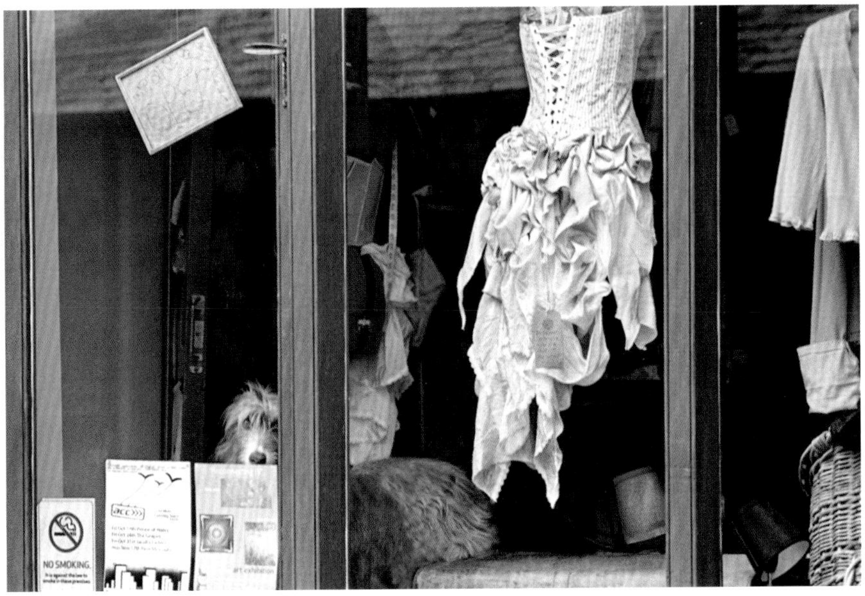

VIC ATTFIELD FRPS

THE SILENT ROOM

CORSET WITH DOG

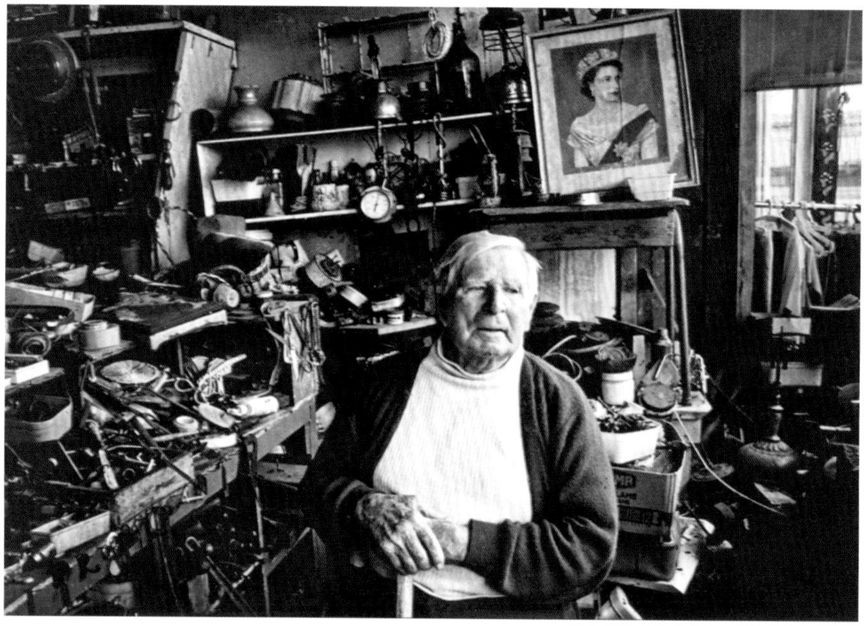

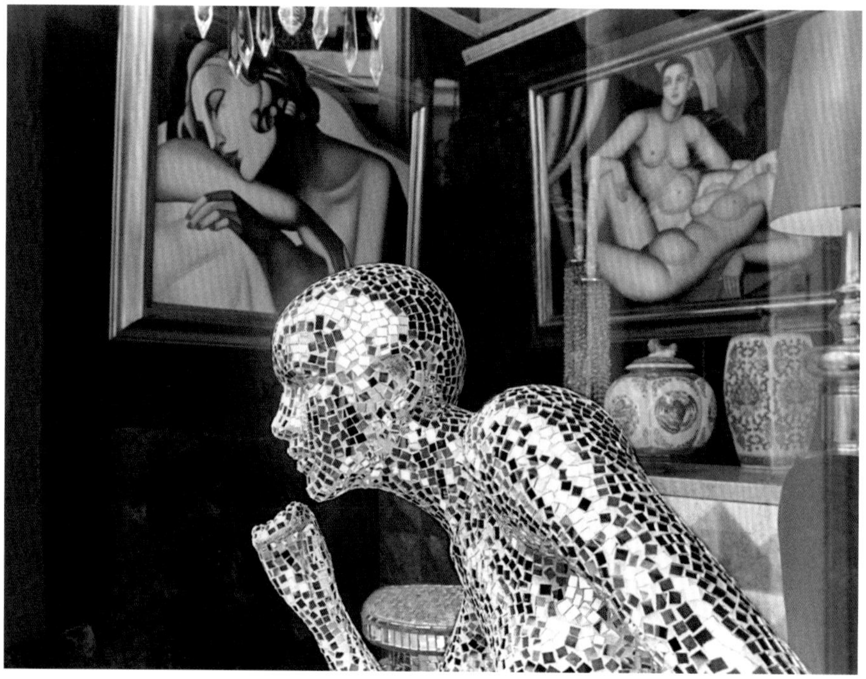

MARY ATTFIELD FRPS

CHARLES HUTLEY

INTERIOR DECORATION

SOCIETY DISTINCTIONS AND QUALIFICATIONS

The Royal Photographic Society's Distinctions are recognised as measures of achievement throughout the world.

When you work towards a Distinction you will improve your photographic skills and also know that once you have been successful the quality of your work will be recognised worldwide.

Distinctions are awarded either on the basis of a portfolio of work which may be photographic images or it may be research, or by successful completion of a recognised course.

There are three levels of Distinction and, in addition, the Imaging Scientist Qualifications which are specifically aimed at engineers, scientists and technologists and provide vocational qualifications relevant to a professional career in imaging science.

The three levels of Distinction are:

Licentiate: The Licentiateship (LRPS) is normally the entry level Distinction and is awarded for a good level of basic skill and competence.

Associate: The Associateship (ARPS) is awarded for a high standard of technical competence and individual creative ability.

Fellow: The Fellowship (FRPS) is awarded for exceptional standards of excellence and distinguished ability.

The award of a Distinction entitles members to use the letters LRPS, ARPS or FRPS after their name. An application for a Distinction of the Society is made in one of the following disciplines:

Still Photography
Research, Education and Application of Photography

Science (awarded as appropriate with the Imaging Scientist Qualifications)

In the case of Still Photography the Associate Fellowship applications are assessed in the following sub categories:

Professional and Applied (includes architecture, illustrative, portraiture, theatrical, wedding photography, Documentary and Visual Journalism and Moving Image)

Contemporary
Natural History
Creative Production (Formerly Printing)
Travel
Visual Art
Each application is assessed by an expert Panel appointed for the discipline or category concerned.

The Bill Wisden MBE Hon.FRPS Fellowship of the Year

In 2012 the Society introduced an award for the most outstanding fellowship of the year. The award is named in honour of Bill Wisden MBE Hon.FRPS in recognition of more that forty five years voluntary service in support of the Society distinction. The recipient is selected by the Society's Fellowship Board from among all of the successful Fellowship. The first two recipients are featured in this section.

2012 Dawn McKeown FRPS
2013 Paul Walker FRPS

LICENTIATE AWARD
IVAN BARRETT LRPS PORTFOLIO

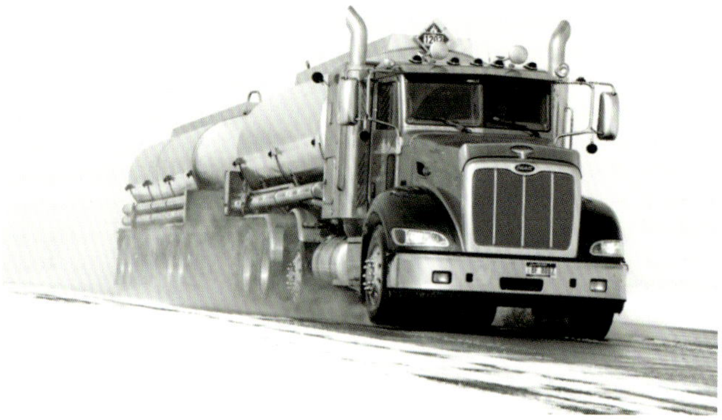

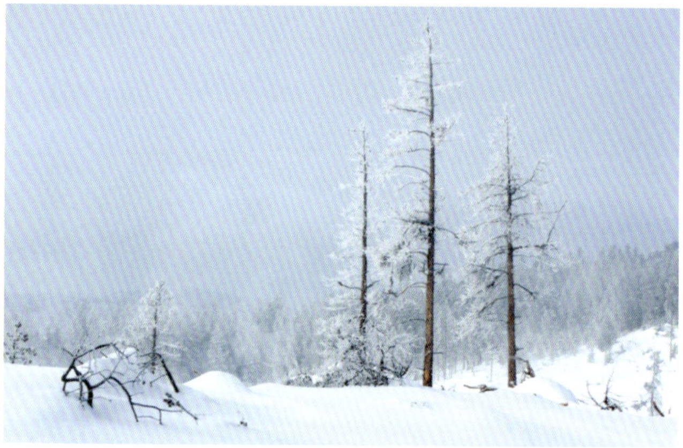

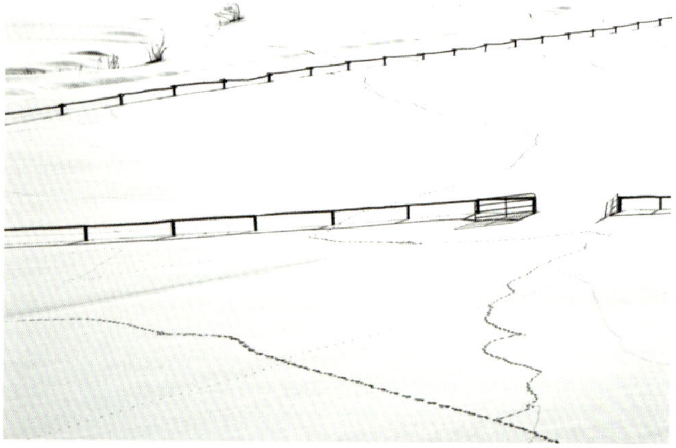

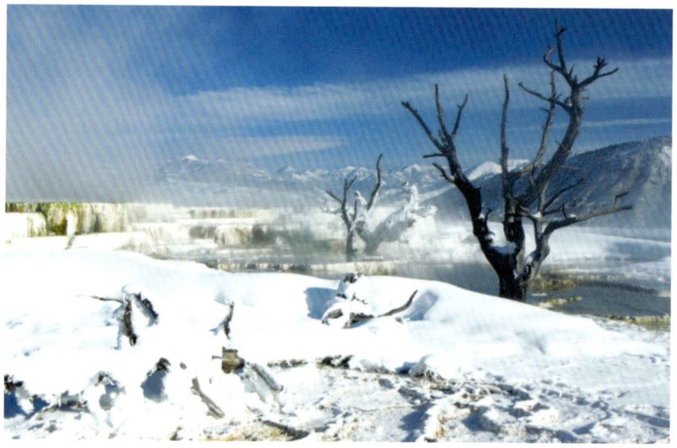

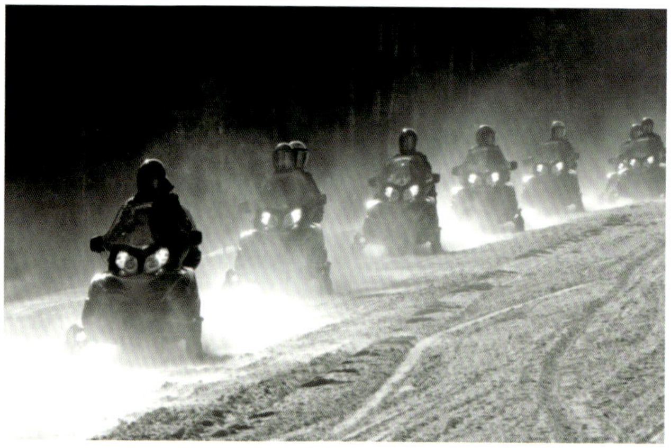

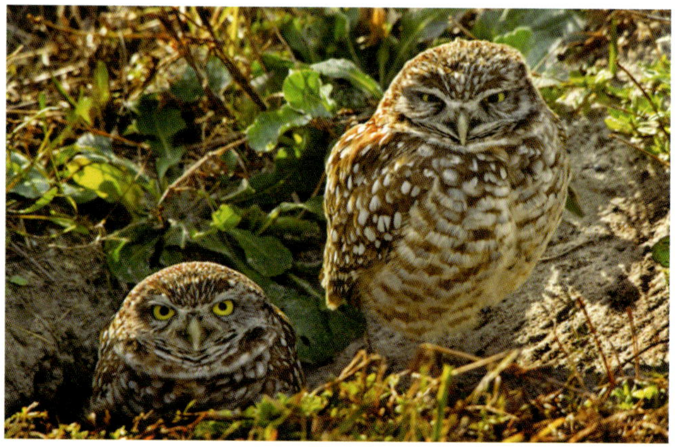

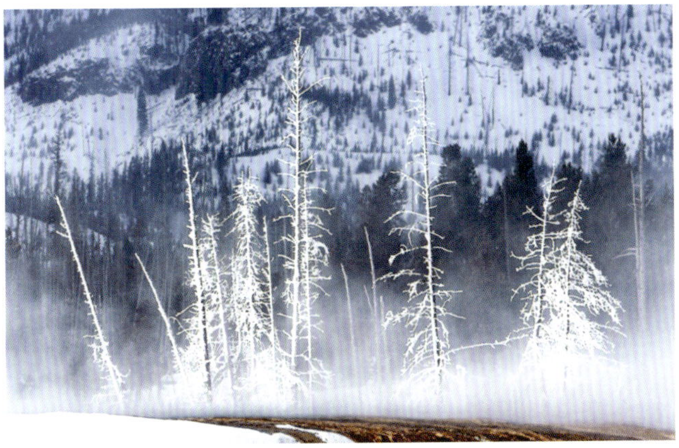

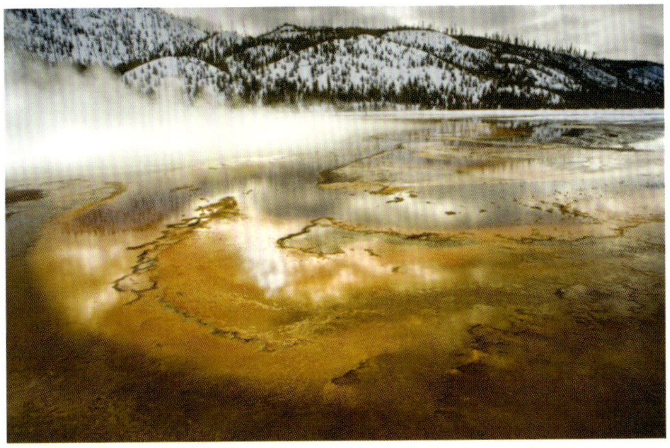

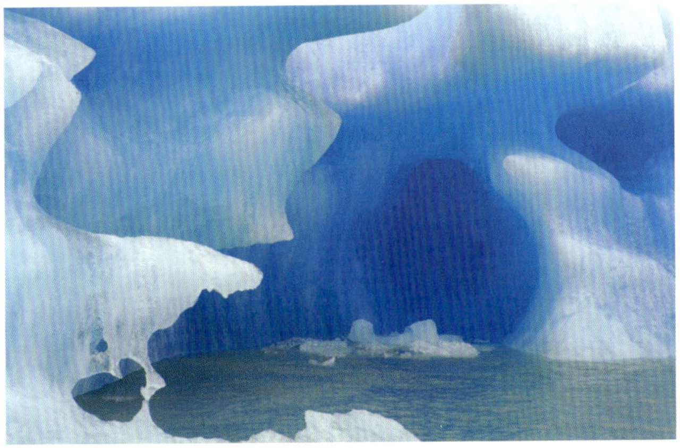

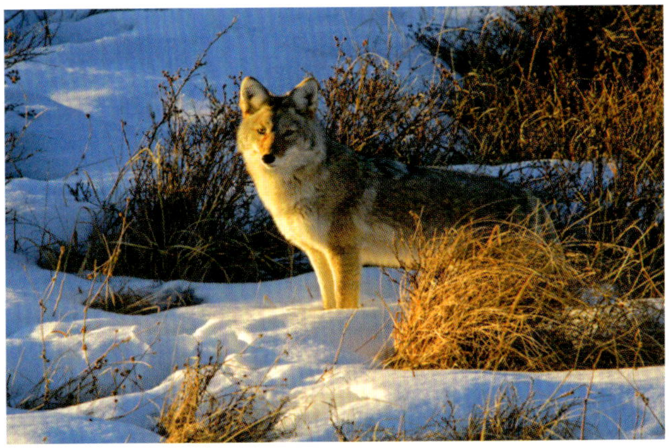

Hanging Plan

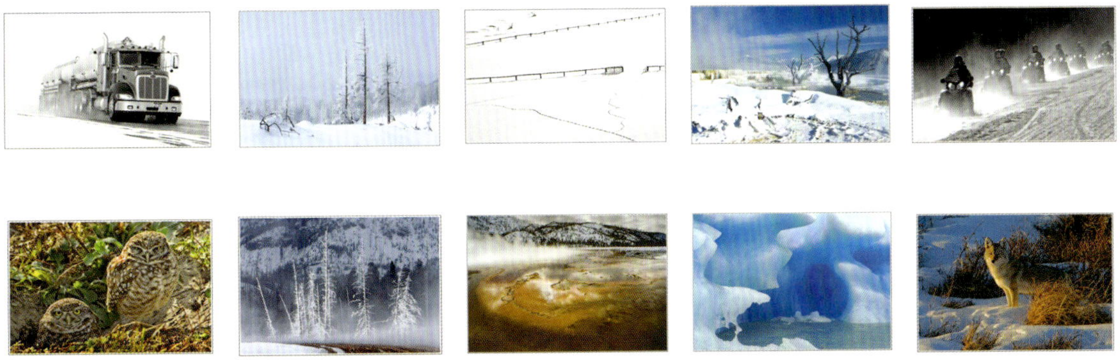

LICENTIATE AWARD
SASKIA SLAVIN LRPS PORTFOLIO

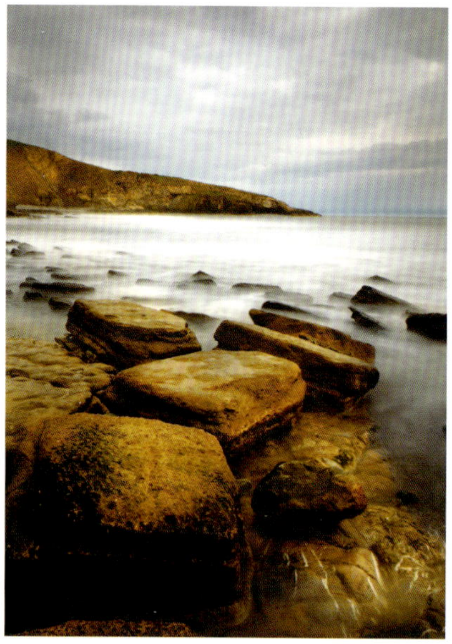

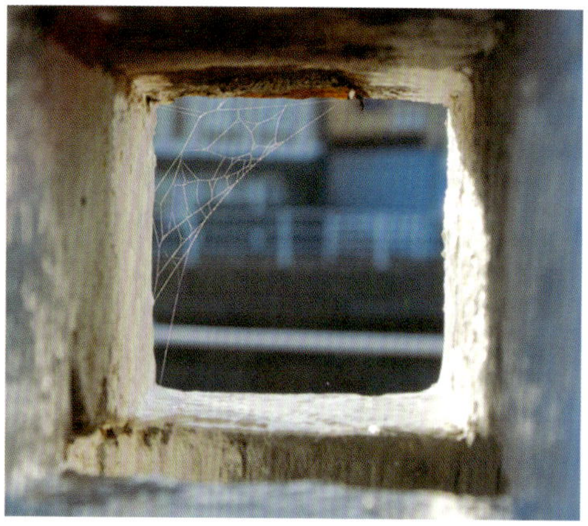

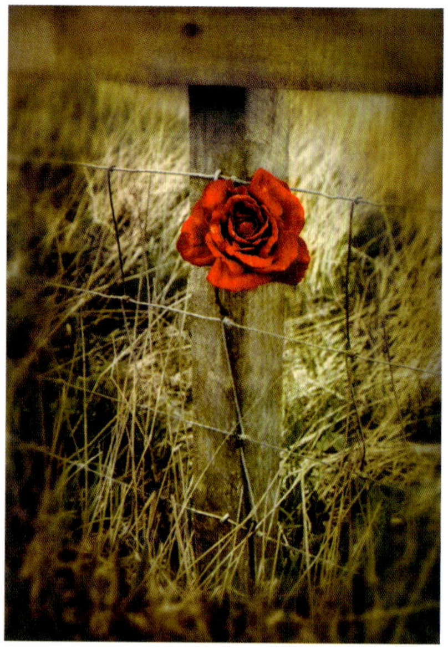

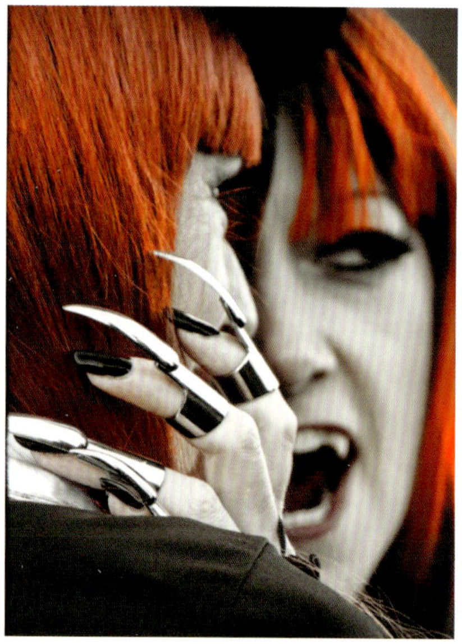

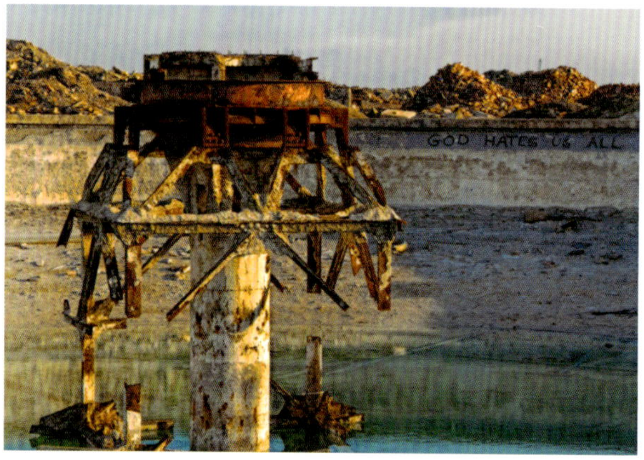

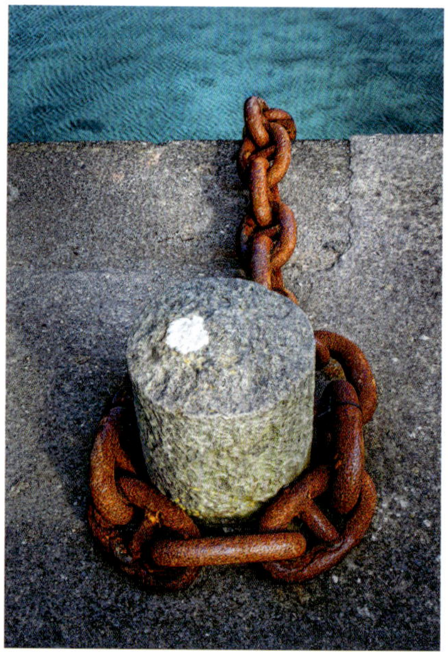

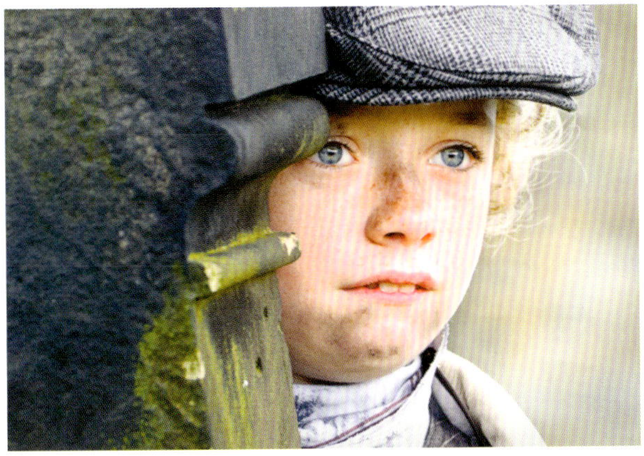

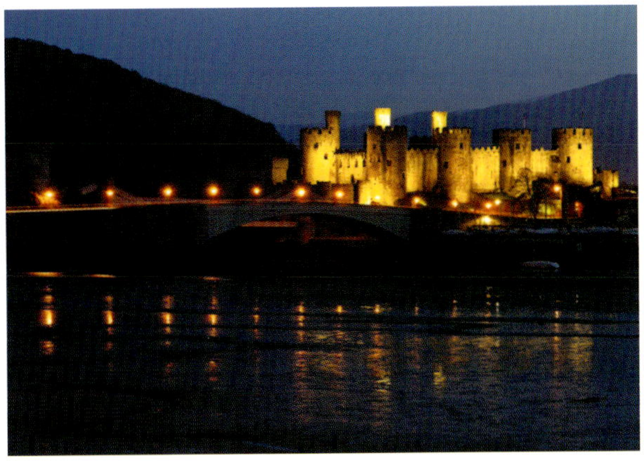

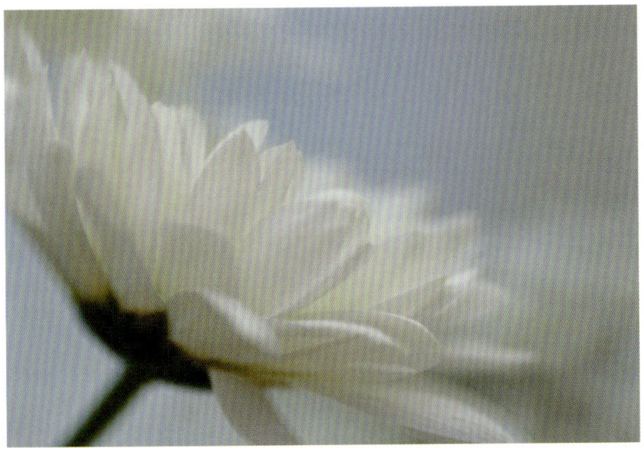

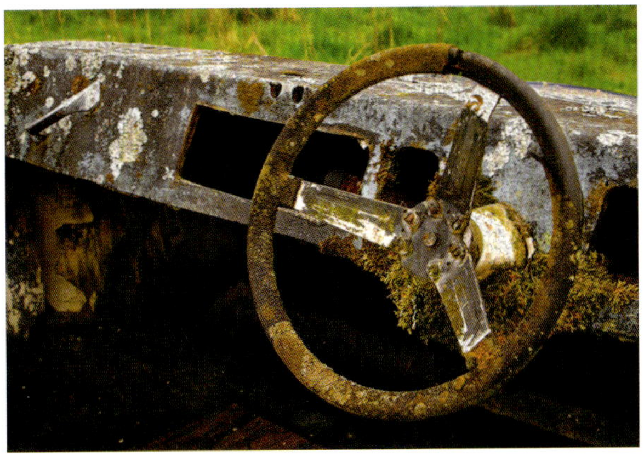

Hanging Plan

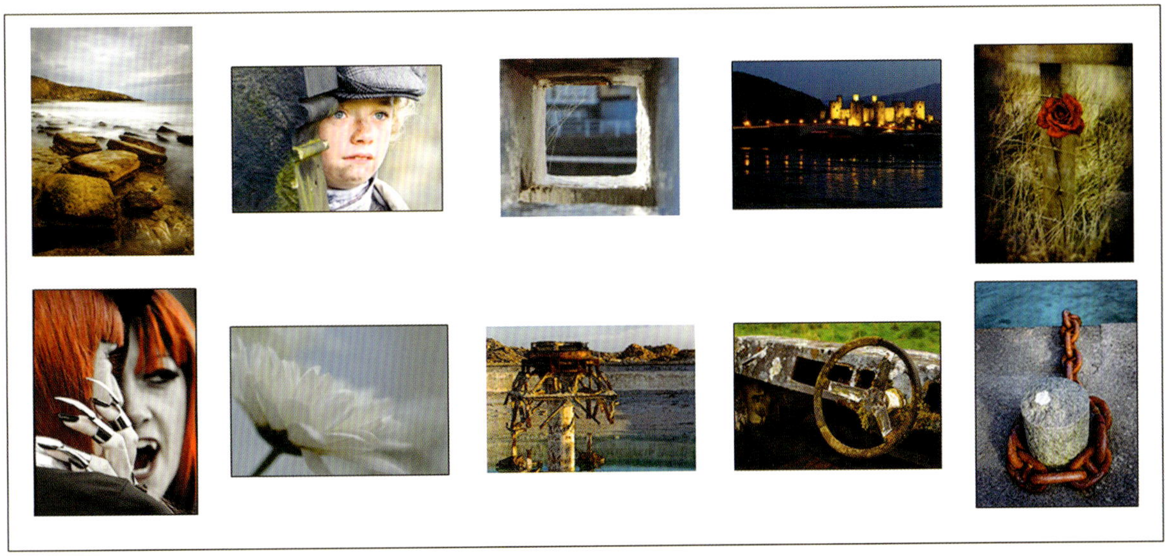

EDMUND FELLOWS ARPS
NATURAL HISTORY PORTFOLIO

I am a life long birdwatcher. I strive to share my enthusiasm with other people, and to show them the beauty and the wonder of the life of birds. My panel of pictures shows Scottish birds, varying from the very common to the more hard to find. Many of them were photographed in places where birds are used to people and can be readily approached. Some of these locations were in Norway, where species scarce in Scotland are sometimes more numerous. About half of these pictures were obtained within a couple of miles of my home in Dumfriesshire. Much of the enjoyment of my photography comes from the preparatory bird watching.

I frequently use hides in order to photograph birds in action. I take great care that my bird watching and photography does not disrupt the activities of the birds, as they go about their natural lives. When photographing birds, protected under Schedule 1 of the Protection of Birds Act, near their nests, I always obtain a permit from Scottish Natural Heritage. Such a permit was obtained for the merlin photograph.

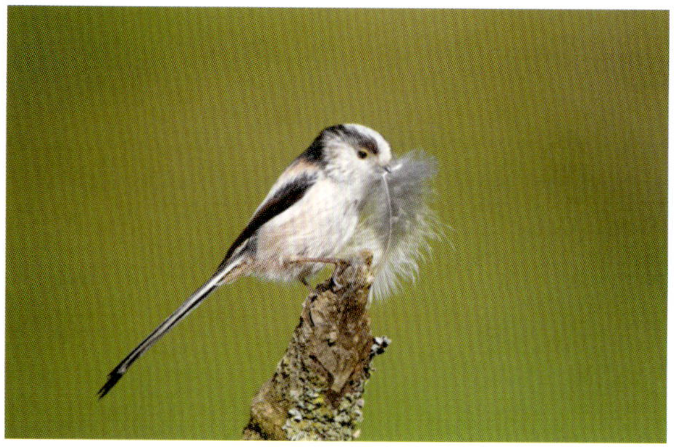

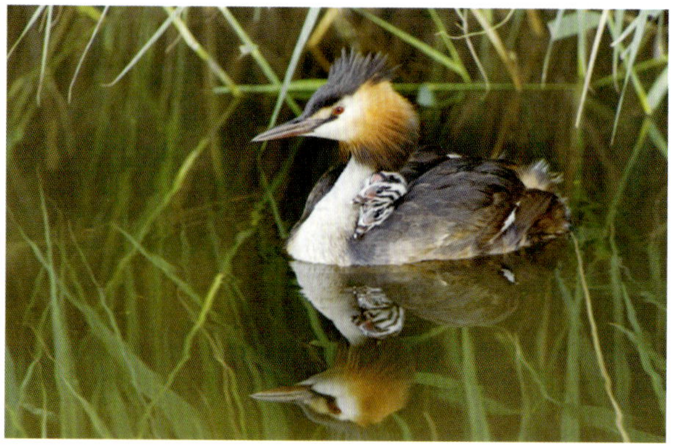

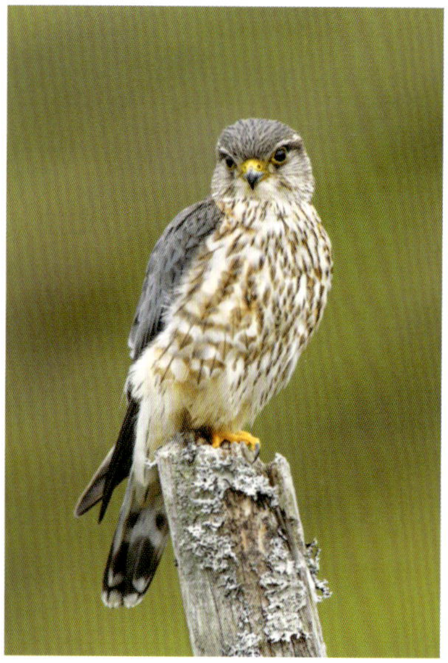

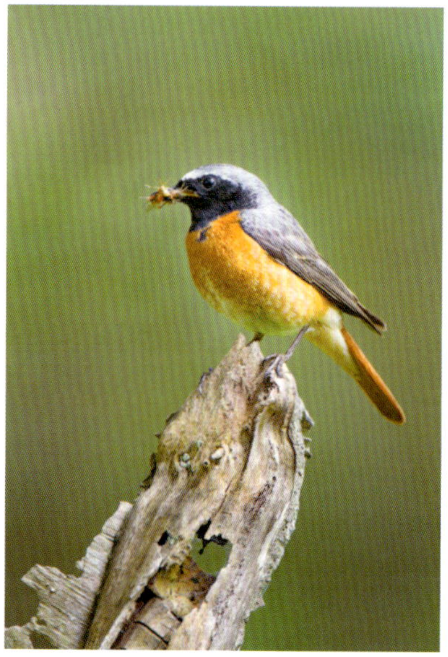

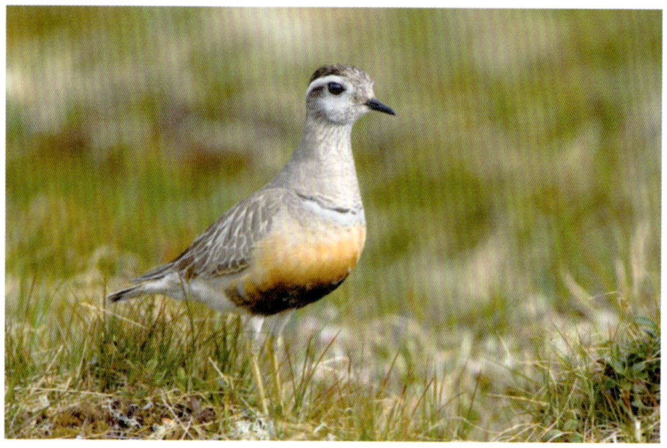

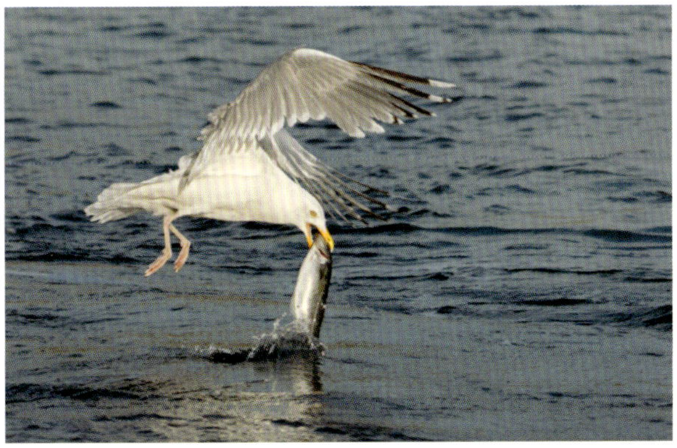

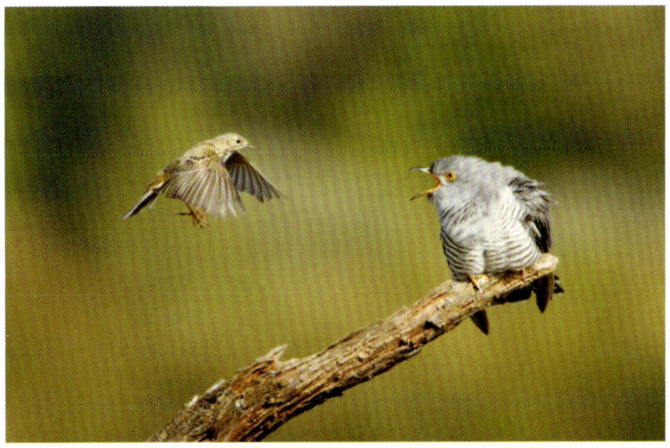

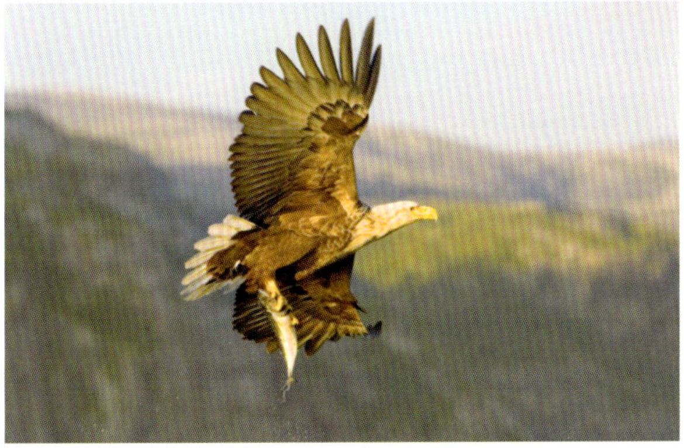

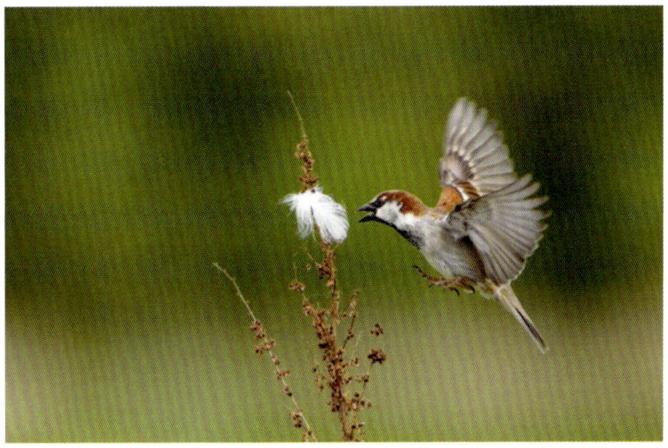

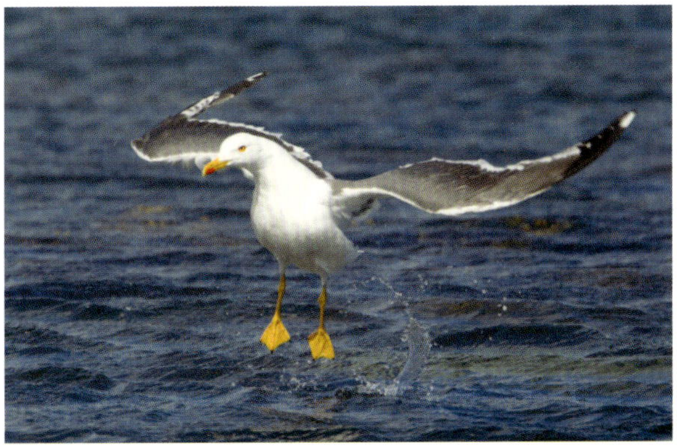

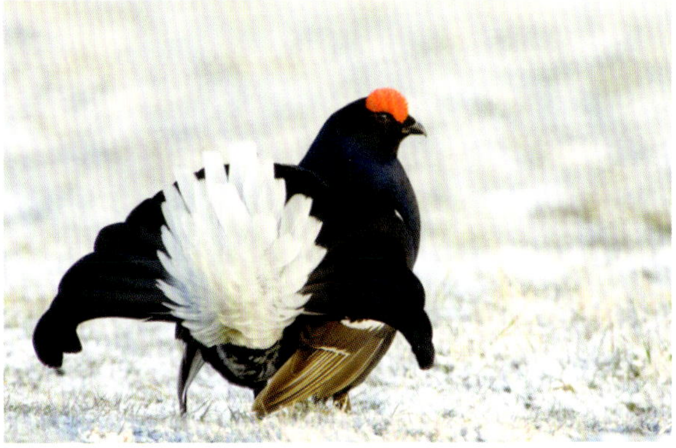

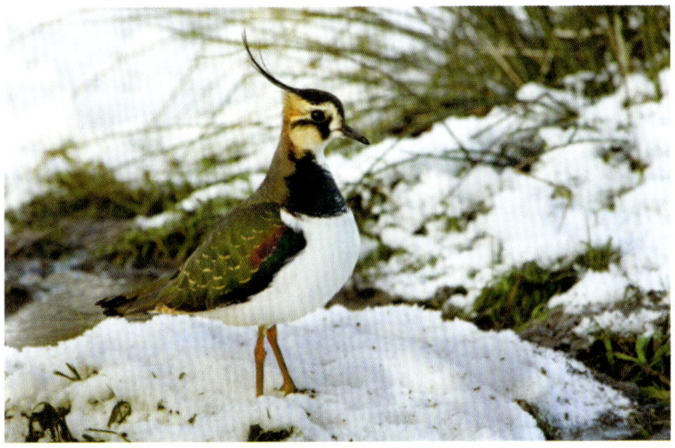

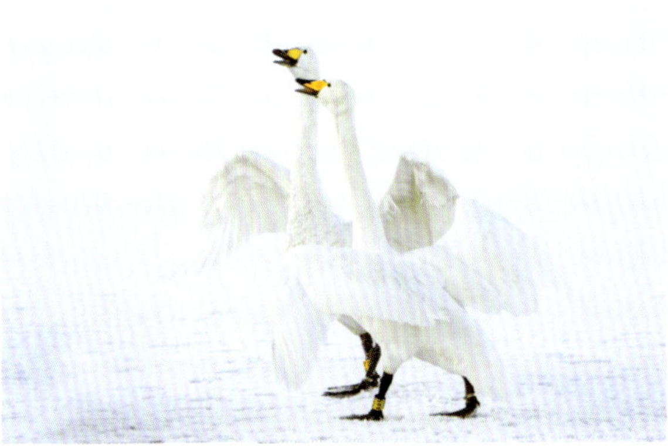

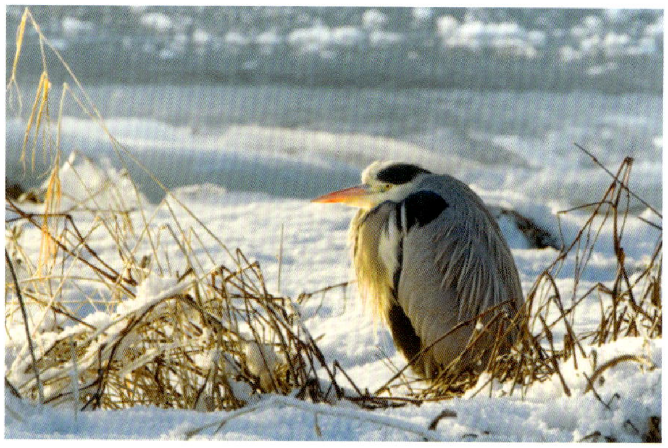

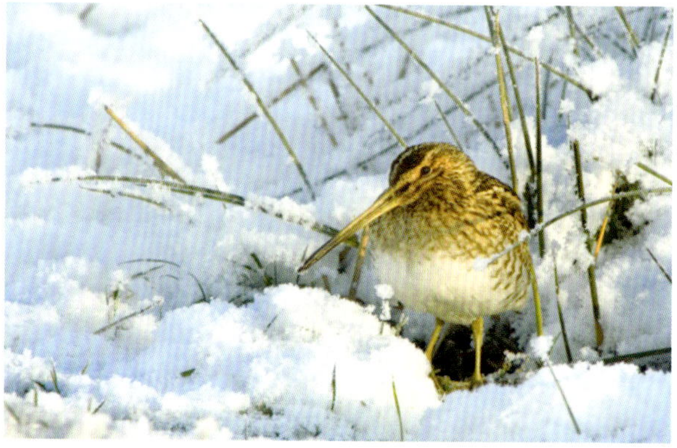

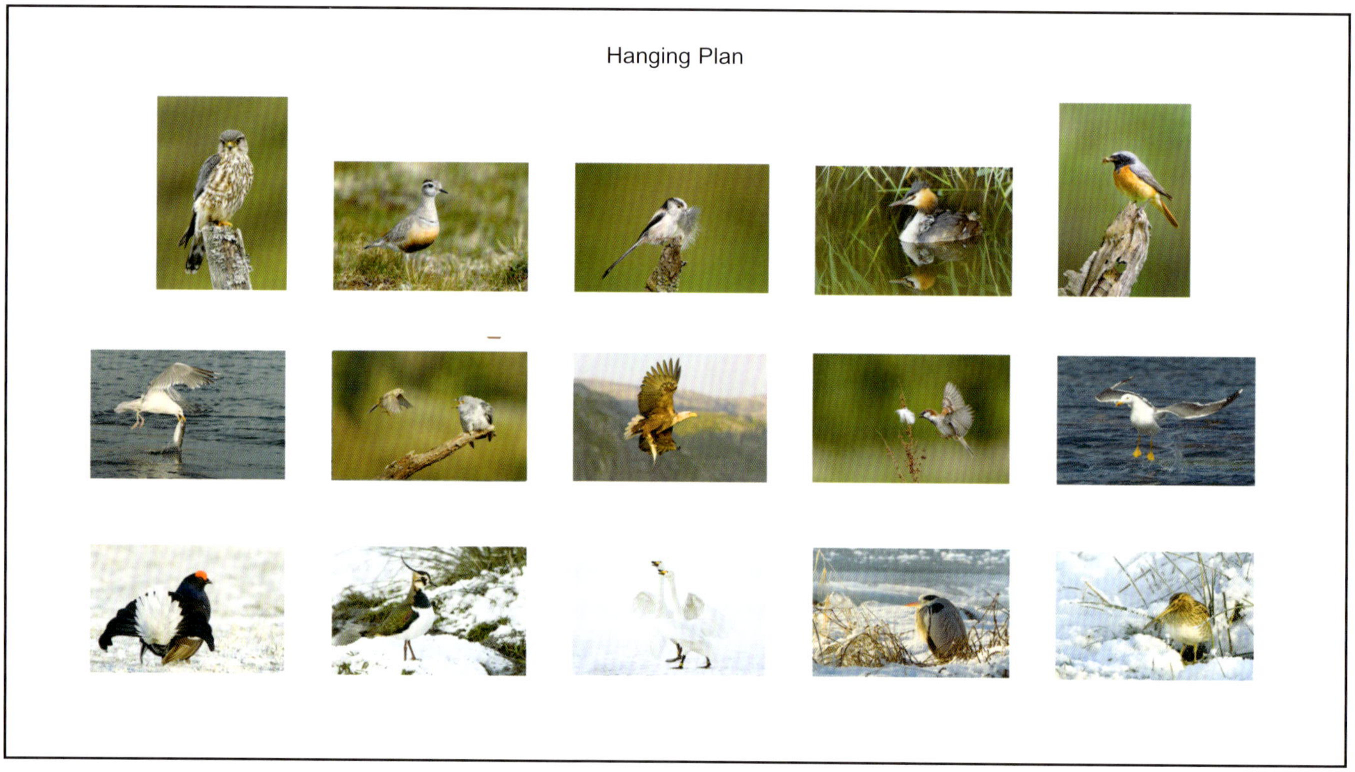
Hanging Plan

NICHOLAS HILL ARPS

PROFESSIONAL AND APPLIED PORTFOLIO

In Cuba professional boxing is prohibited but during the last 30 years of amateur competition the country has won 27 Olympic gold medals, more than any other nation. As a third world country success is rewarded with prestige. After a fighting career is over many become involved in training, thus ensuring their knowledge is passed down to the next generation. I spent three days at the Rafael Trejo gym located on the outskirts of Havana. The facilities have scant resource yet are shared by young hopefuls, Olympic contenders, and past winners who regard boxing as a team sport. I set out to document these athletes as they trained and fought together, trying to capture the humility, skill, technique and respect they possess.

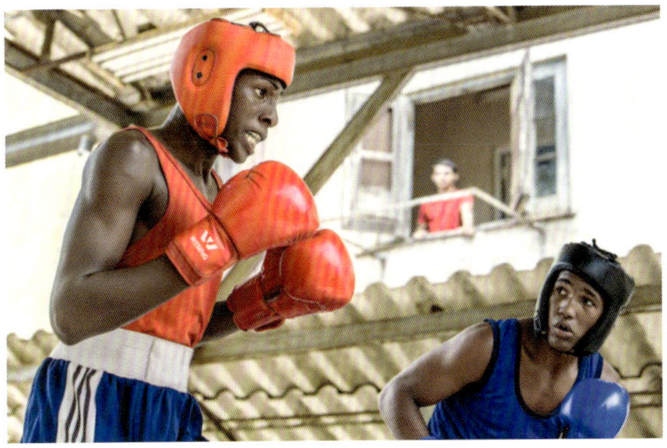

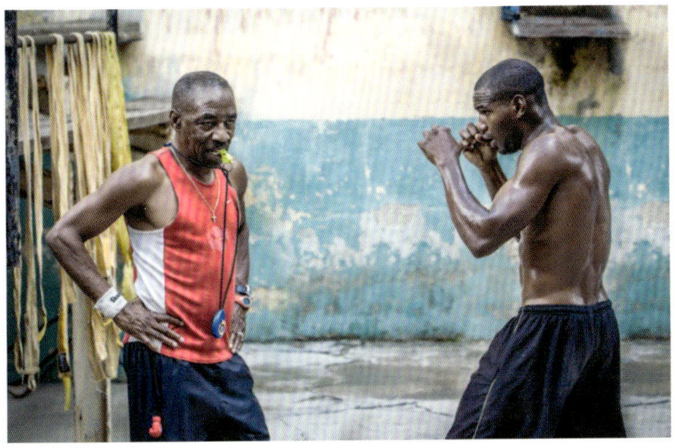

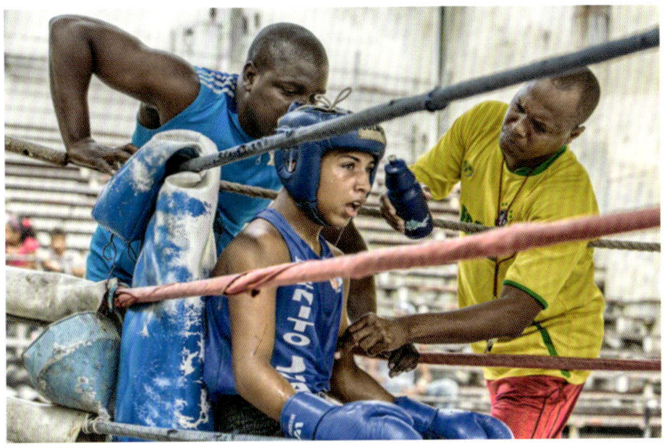

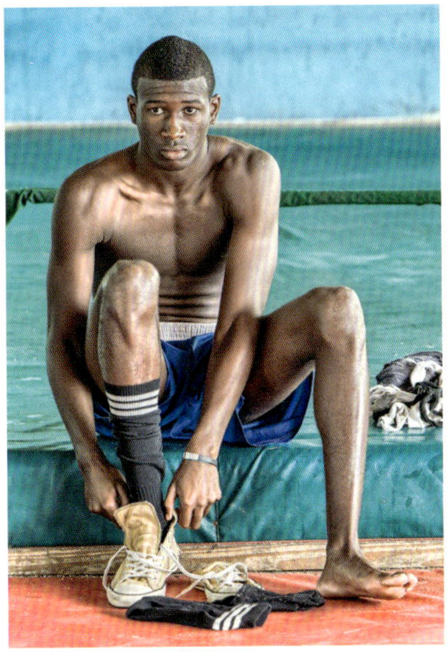

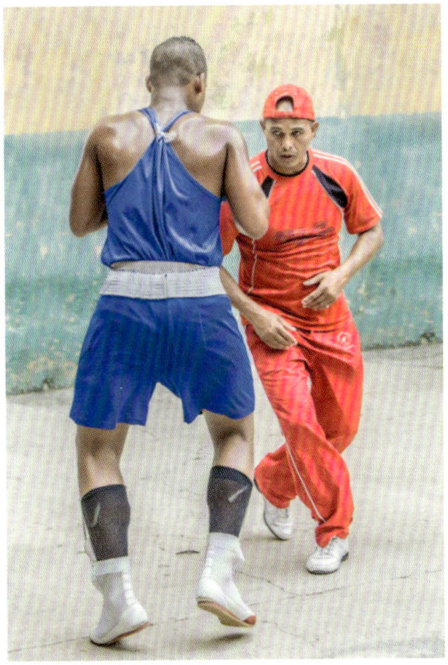

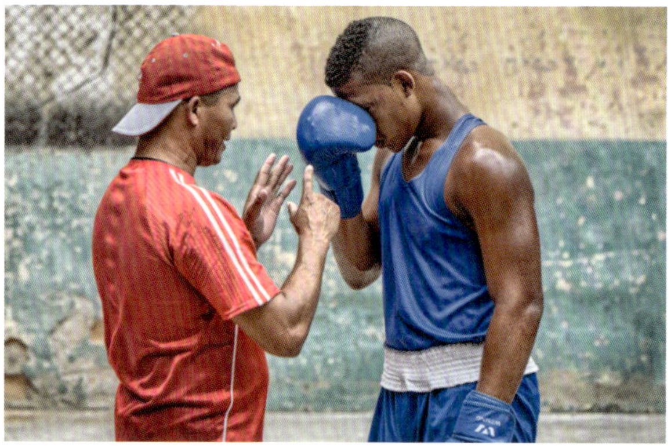

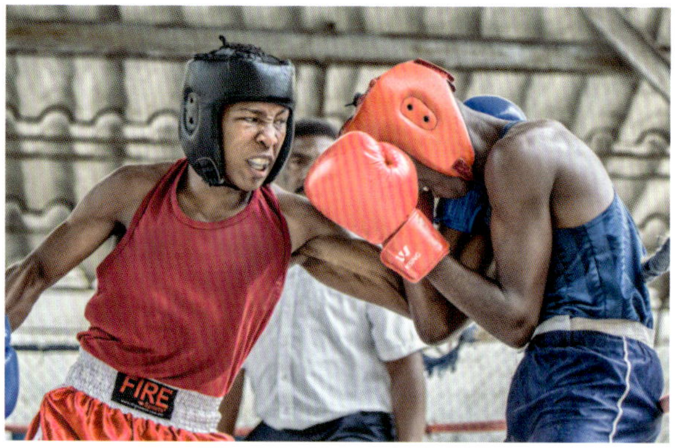
FIRE

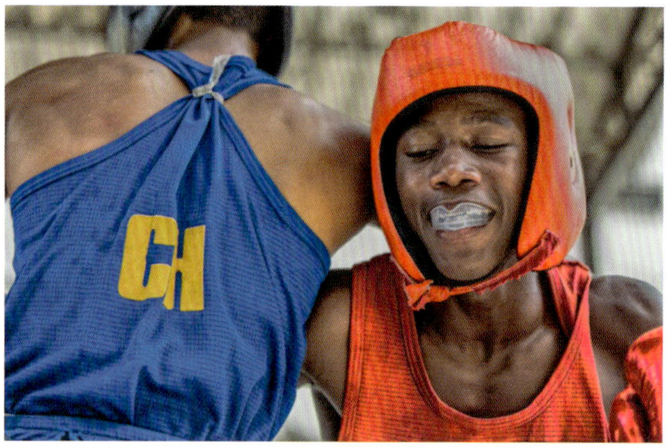
CH

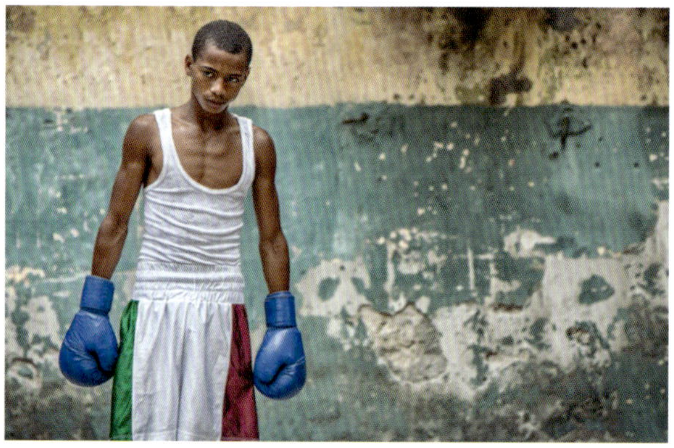

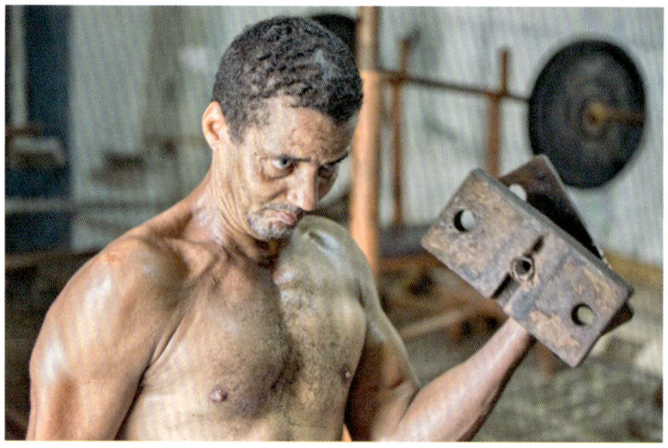

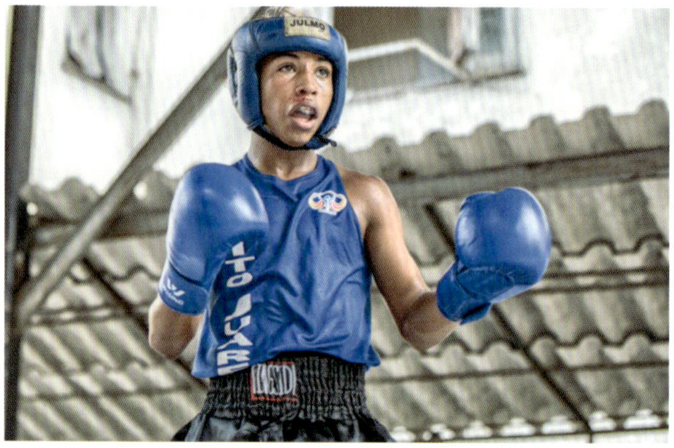

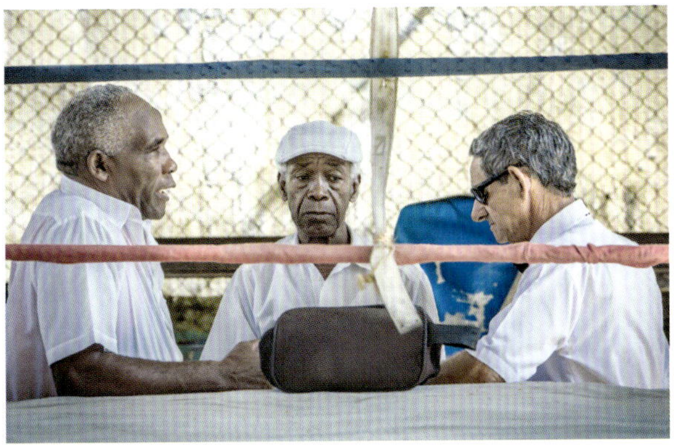

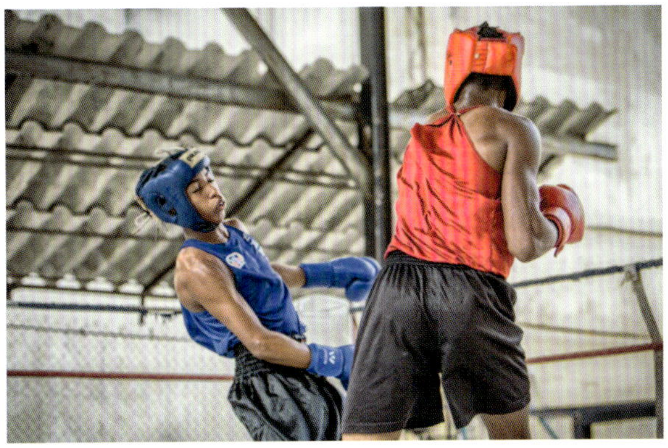

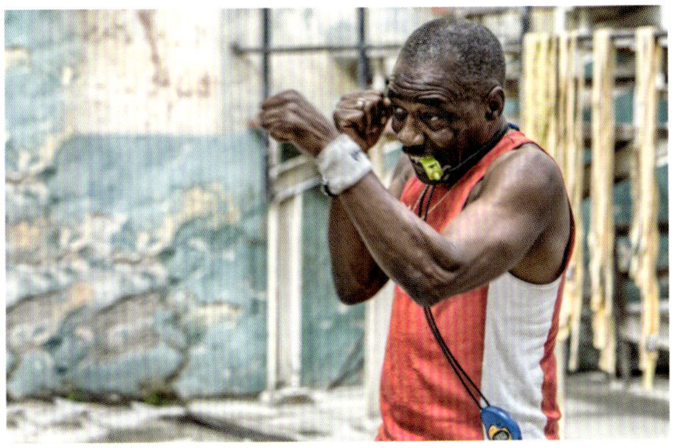

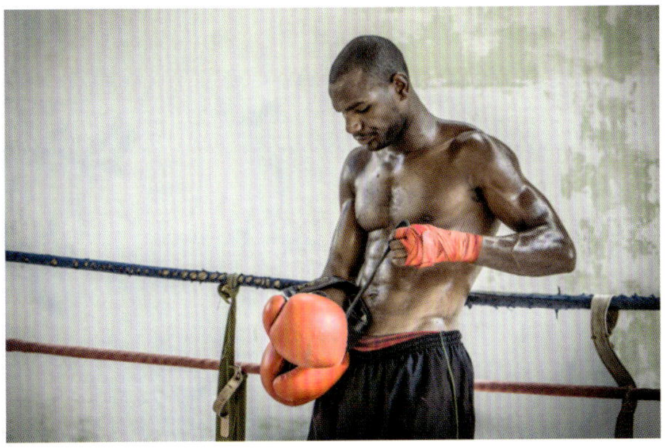

Hanging Plan

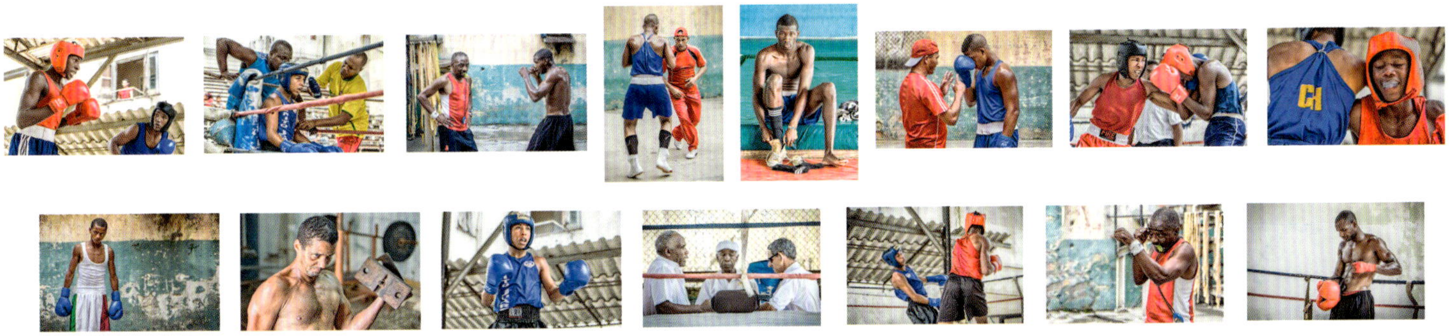

DAWN McKEOWN FRPS PROFESSIONAL AND APPLIED
BILL WISDEN MBE Hon.FRPS FELLOWSHIP OF THE YEAR 2012

As a Professional portrait photographer, my everyday job is capturing people.

They range from tiny, premature, new born babies to dads and mums.

My work is split between images for the people themselves and stock images with a theme, for instance "temptation" or "speak no evil".

The panel is printed on a warm, museum quality archival paper.

I would like to think that every image in the panel would be a talking point if displayed as wall décor in any room.

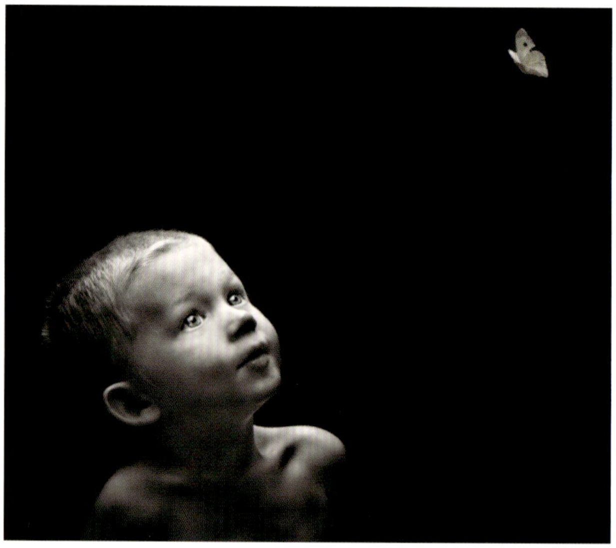

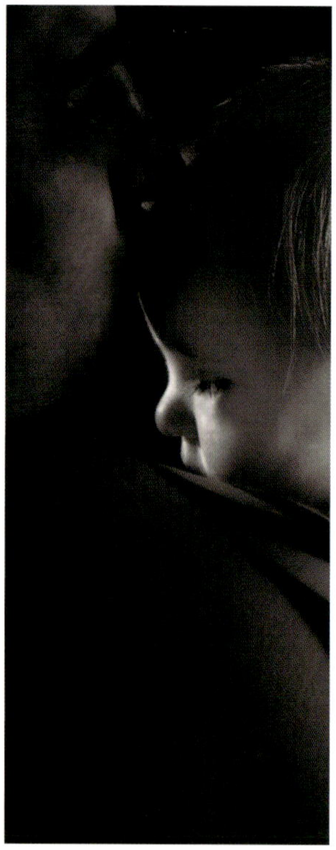

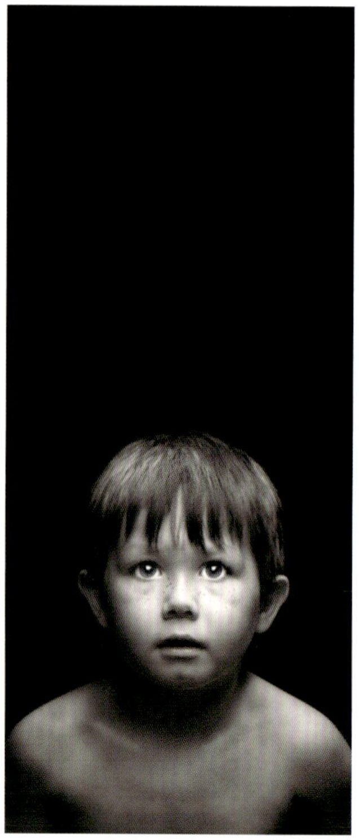

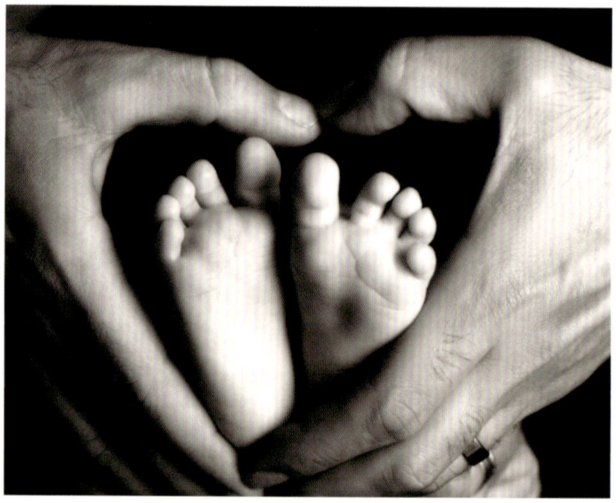

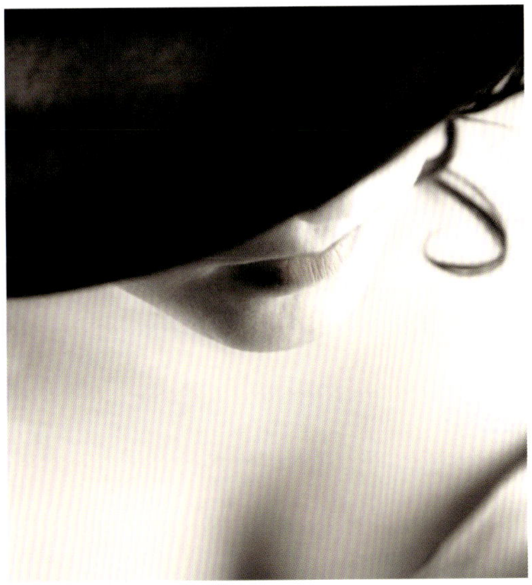

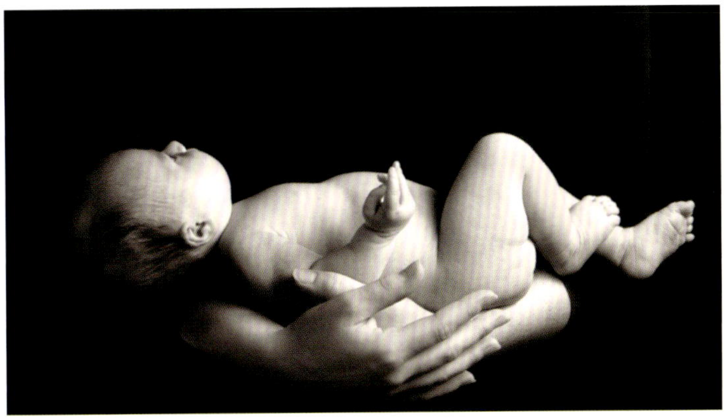

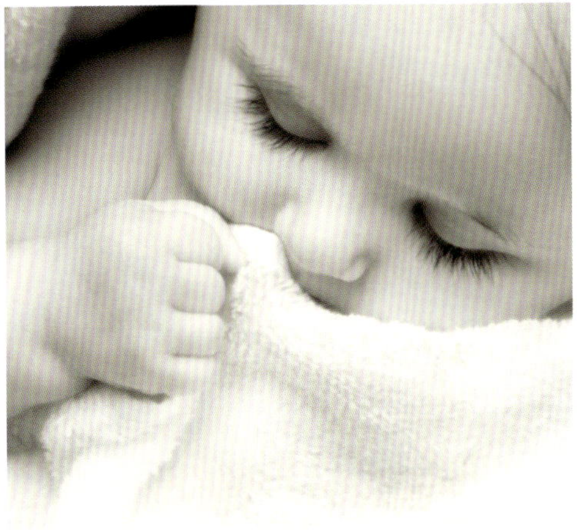

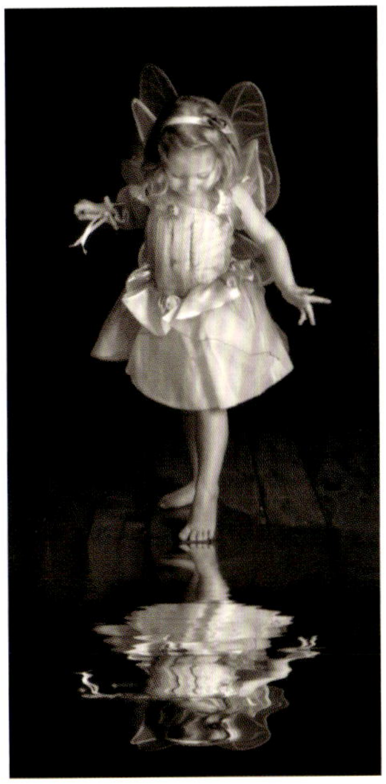

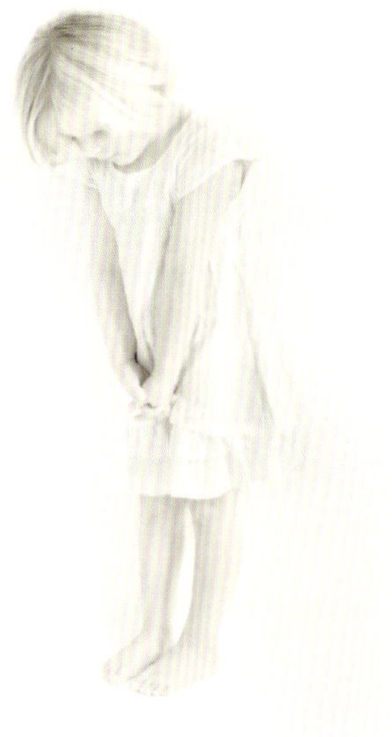

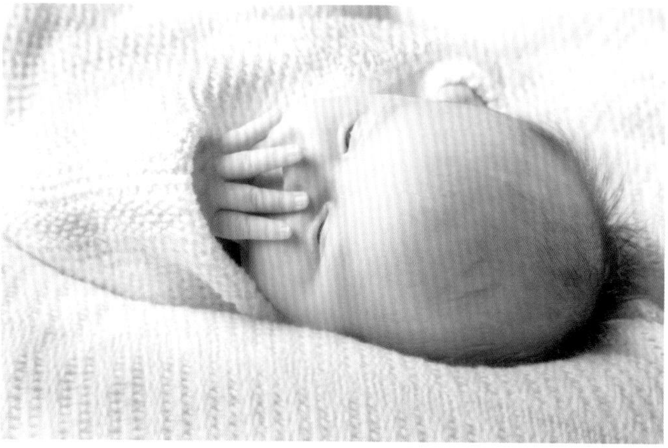

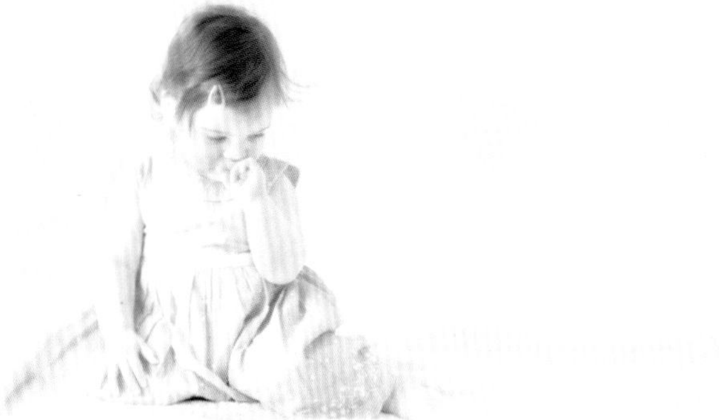

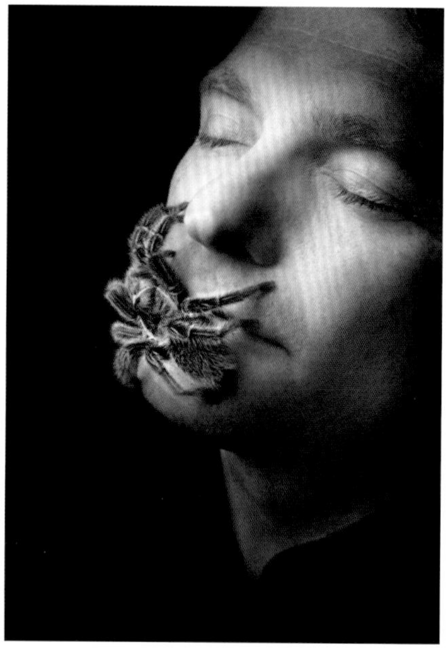

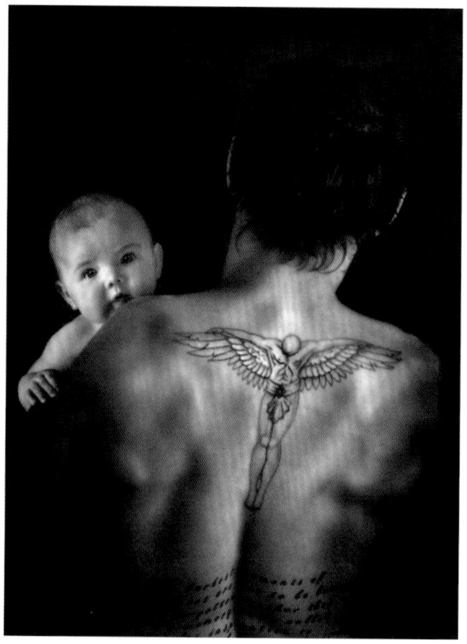

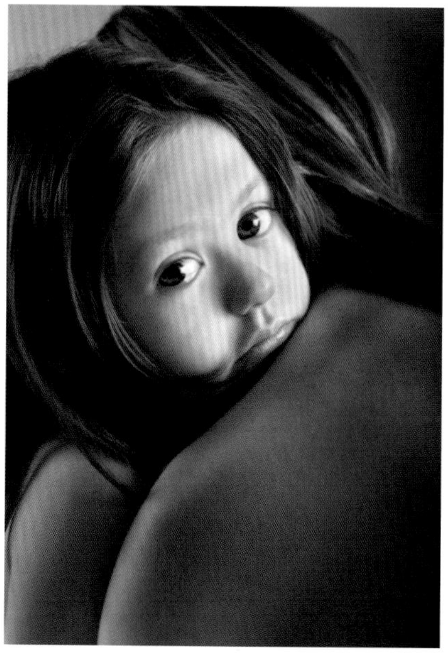

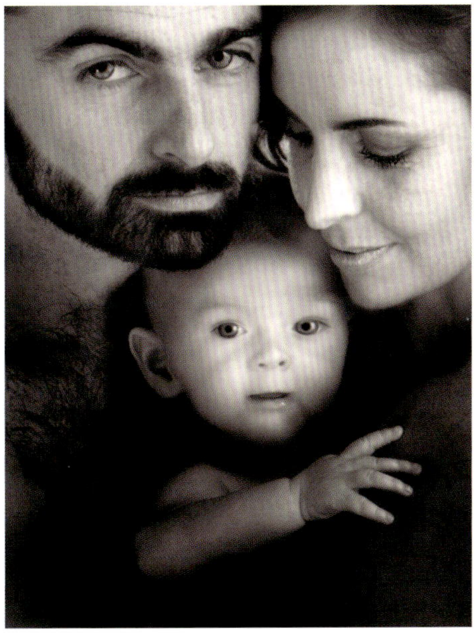

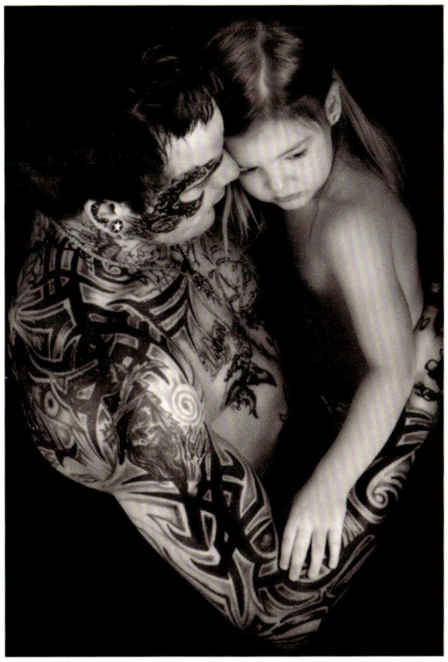

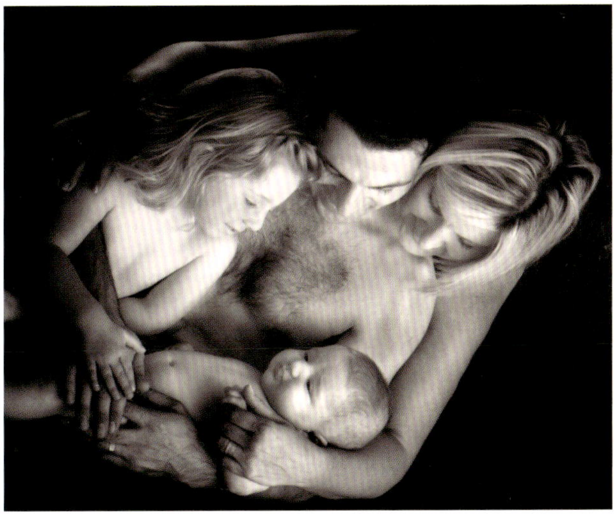

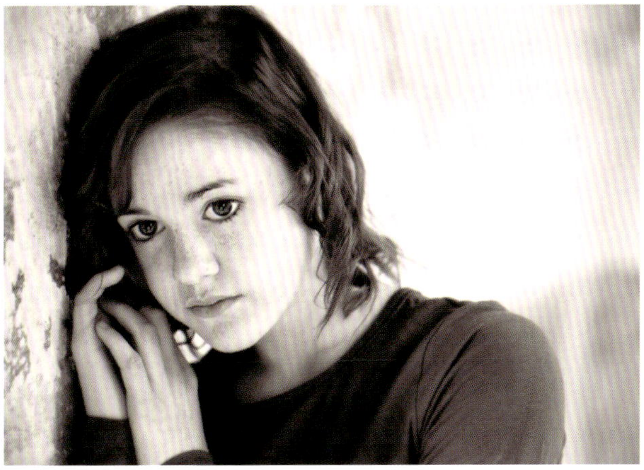

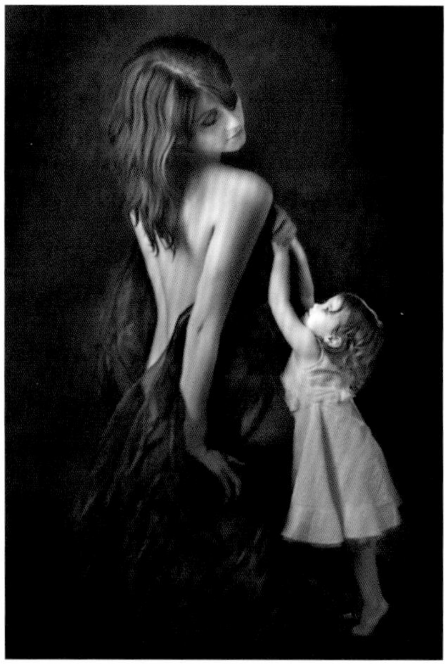

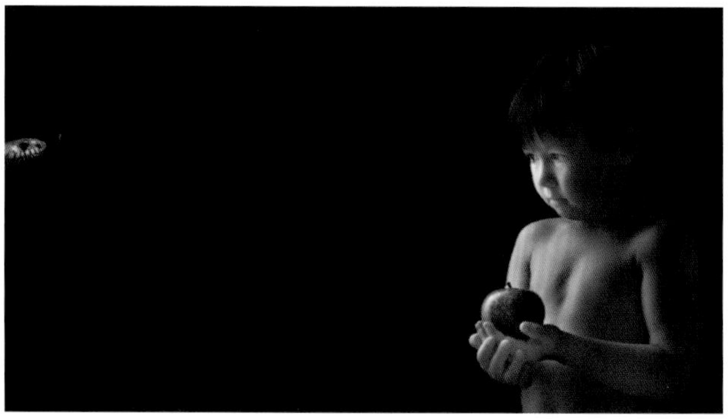

Hanging Plan

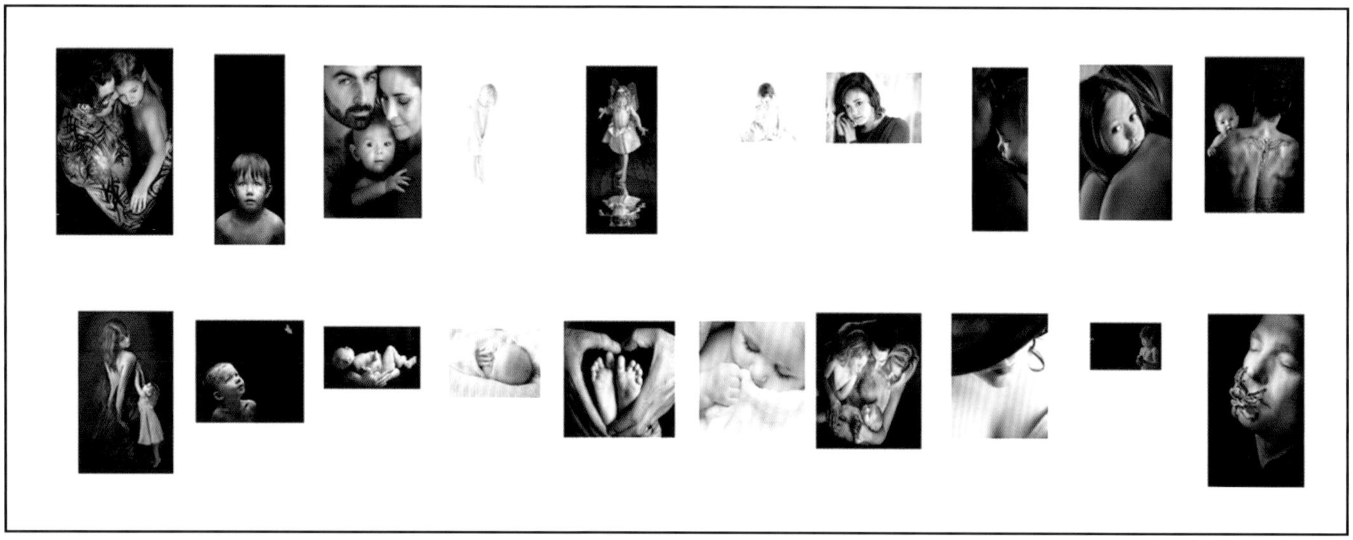

PAUL WALKER FRPS PROFESSIONAL AND APPLIED
BILL WISDEN MBE Hon.FRPS FELLOWSHIP OF THE YEAR 2013

My passion has always been the photography of dogs in a non-studio environment, whether it be the home, hills, beach or local park.

Although this has its challenges both in respect of the dogs' own obedience and the owners "handling ability" in varied environments, it has led to numerous commissions that have only further increased my enthusiasm for dog photography.

This panel is in three parts and it represents the variability in commissioned work and diversity of dog photography I am often engaged with. The top tier represents the companionship aspect of people and their dogs. The middle tier represents the dynamic action that is so often fleetingly seen when conducting assignments and lastly the bottom tier representing the anthropomorphic side of dogs which are often sought after by greeting card companies.

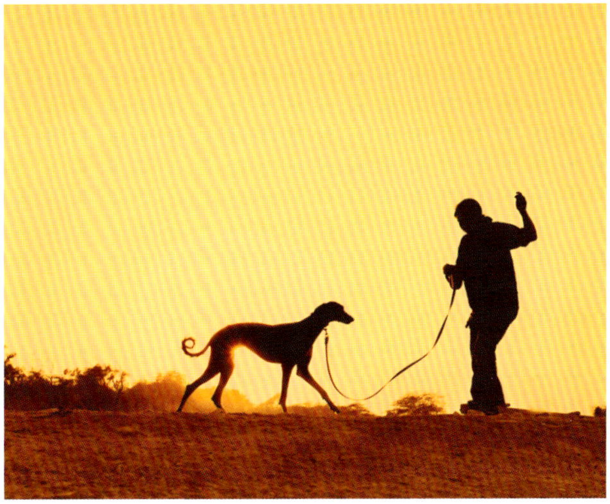

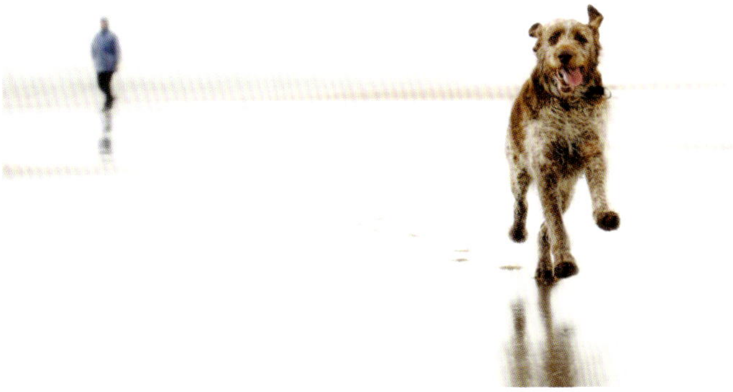

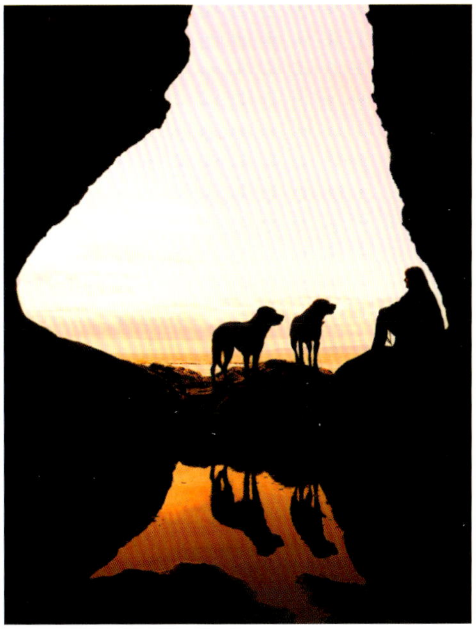

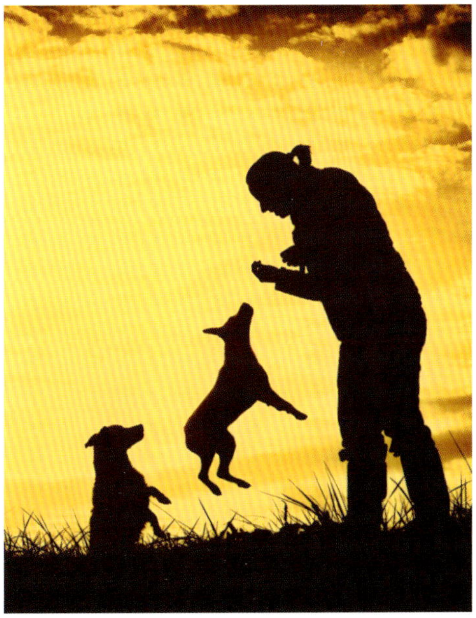

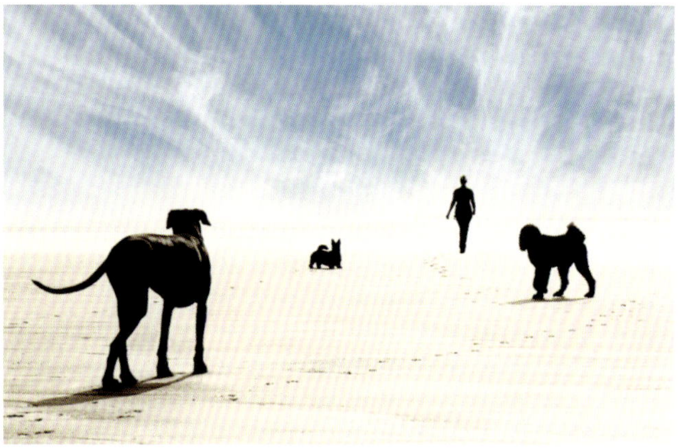

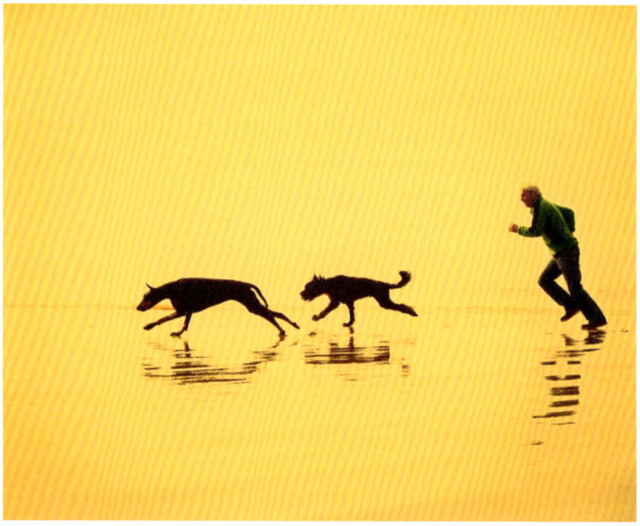

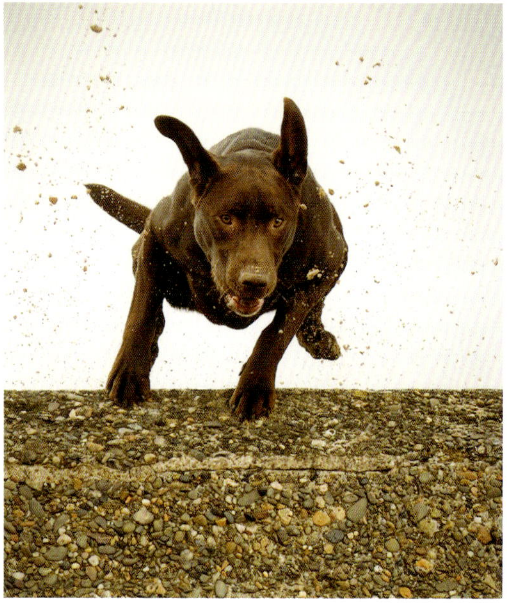

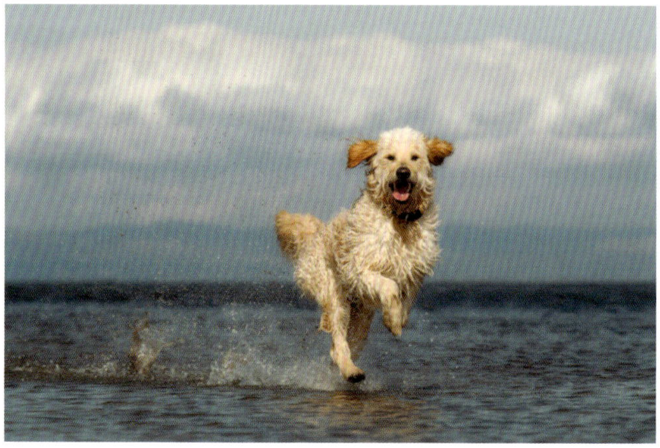

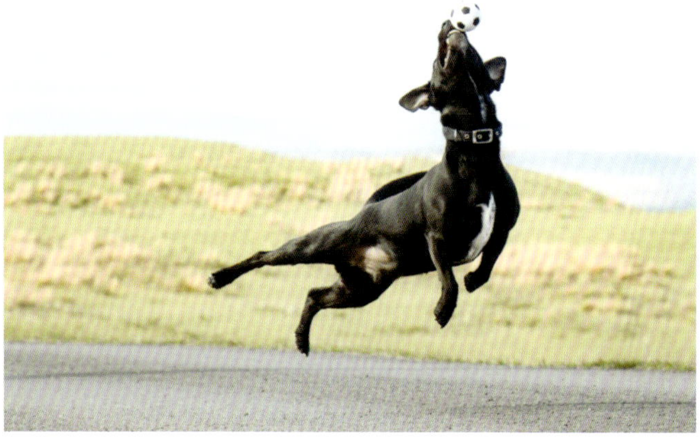

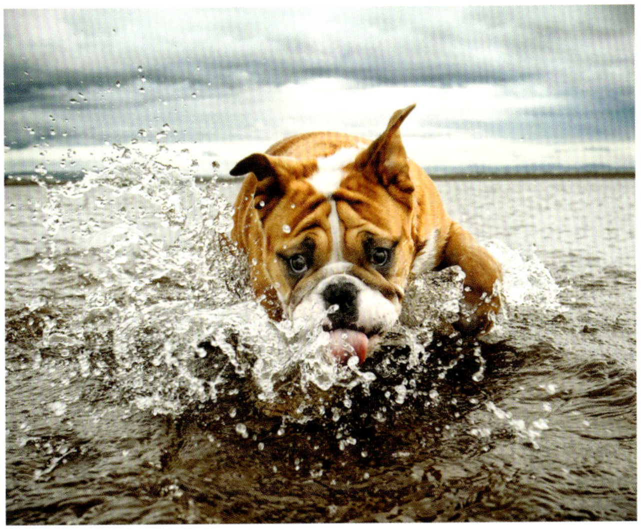

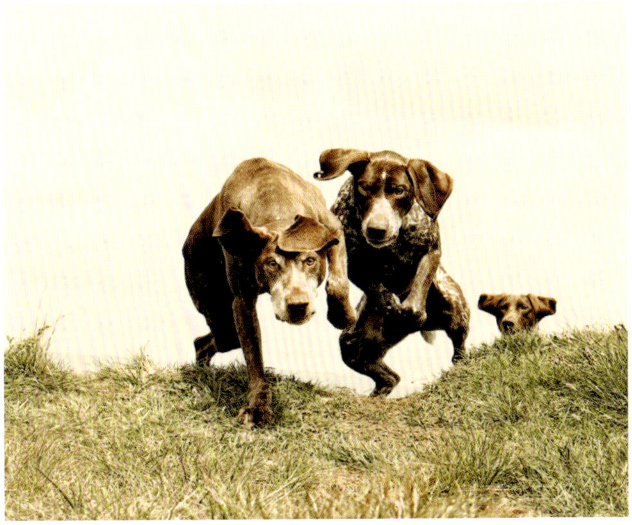

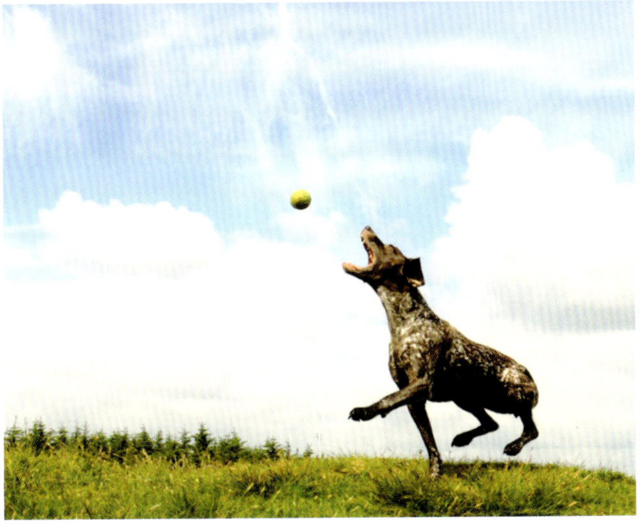

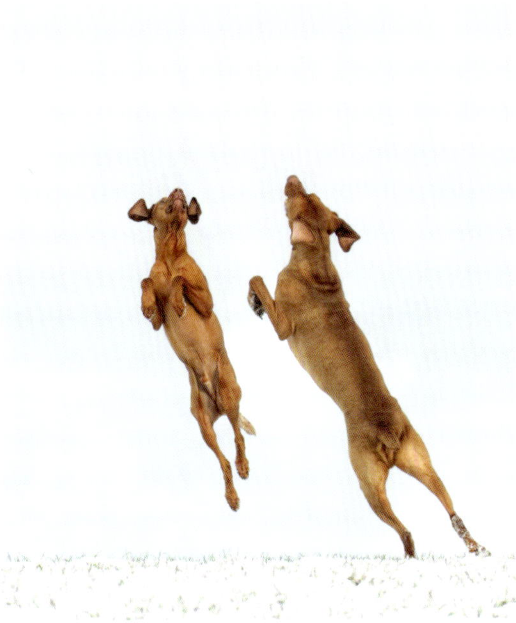

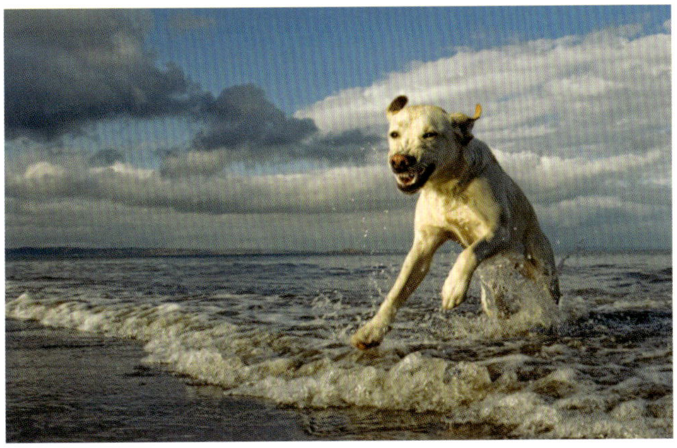

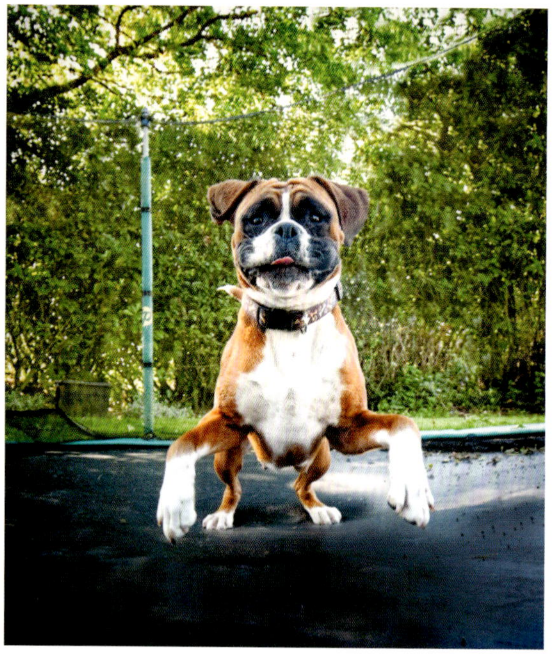

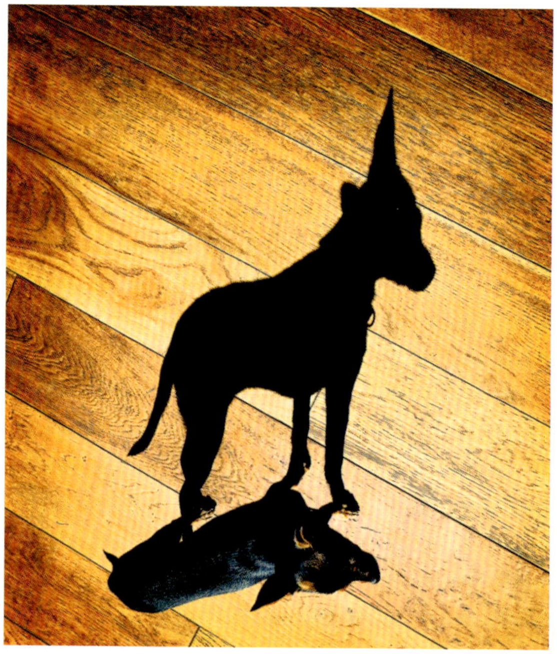

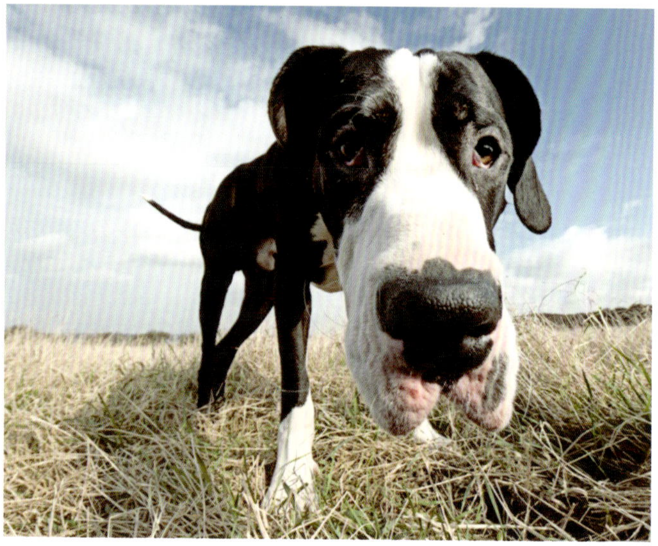

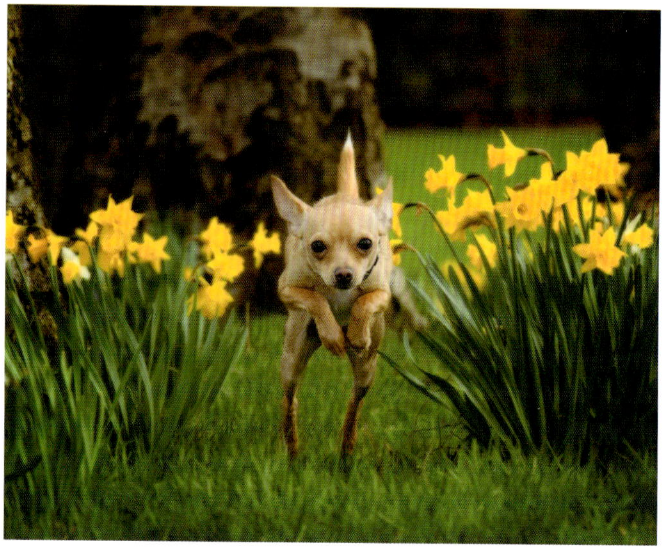

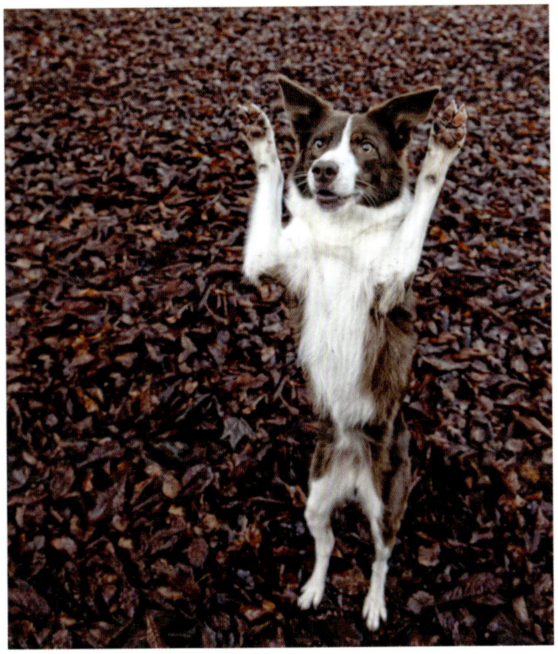

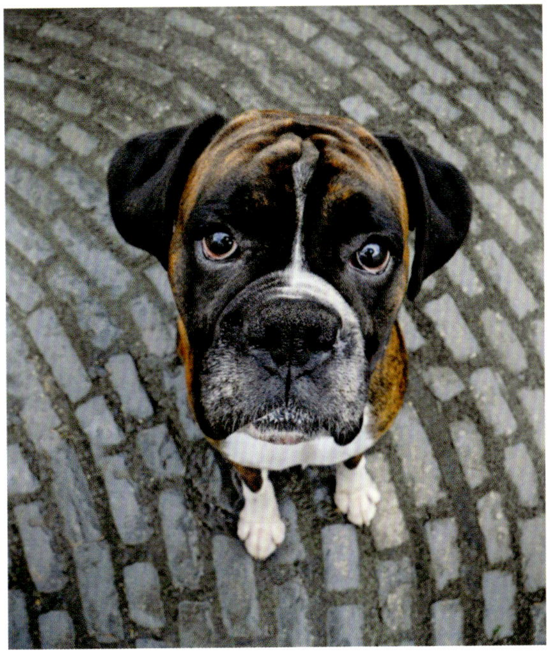

Hanging Plan

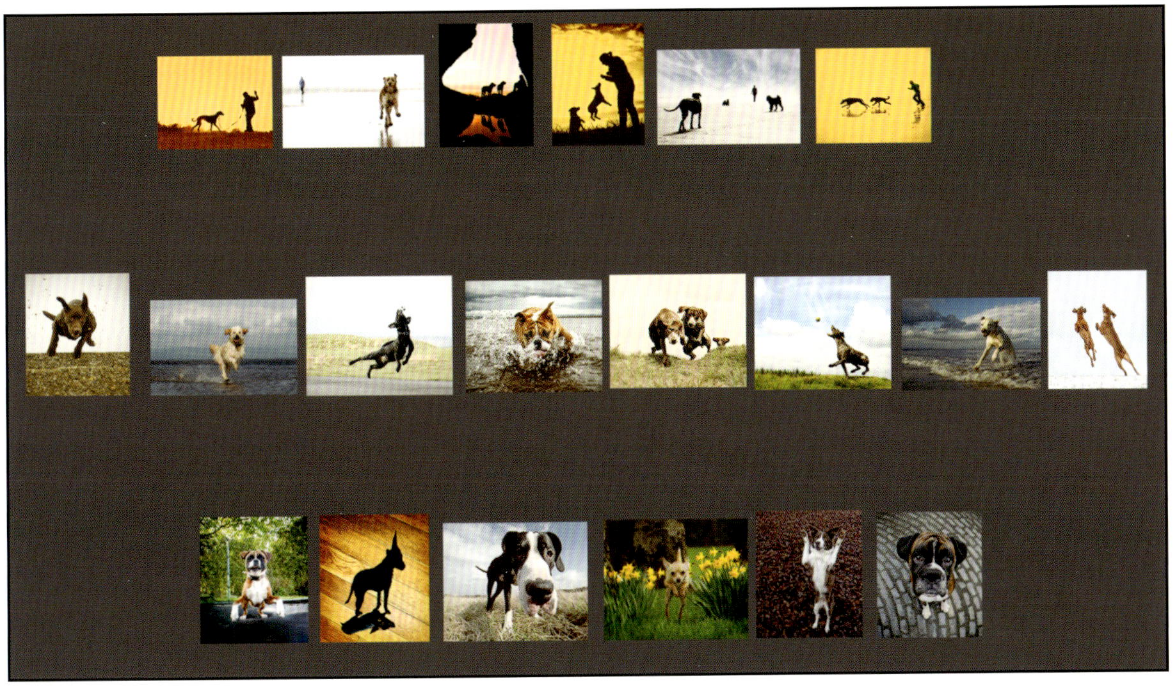

MARK MUMFORD FRPS

VISUAL ART PORTFOLIO

Looking for enlightenment, a personal exploration.

My panel is an exploration of surreal imagery using religious symbolism from beginning to end, literally. The first image represents new life, death, good and evil. Other images depict enlightenment, nirvana, discovery, Heaven and Hell, Catholicism, Jewish, Muslim, Buddhism and Hindu religions. The final image in the panel depicts the end of everything, Armageddon. Or is it the end, or just a combination of many photographs? An exercise in stretching my imagination and creative ability by using ordinary photographic images to form bizarre creations which question religions, faiths and reality. You will see images within images, strange perspectives, a multitude of layers, a multitude of meaning and interpretations. Is good bad? Is black white? Does white still represent good? Are birds birds or are they angels?

I personally find religious iconography and those who dress in robes and cloths of their religious beliefs to be fascinating and yet somewhat bizarre.

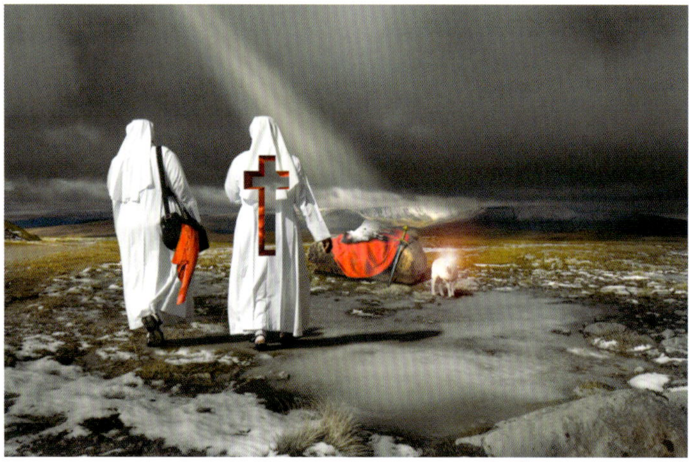

I was brought up a Christian but now question religion and find it illogical, but have used my knowledge of religion and its strange practices to create this panel.

Religion.... what a shame that what is supposed to be good, can turn out to be so bad and a major cause of conflict thought this wonderful world we live in. Spiritual enlightenment along with love, joy and peace can still be found through religious belief but unfortunately so is darkness, hate, despair, bigotry, sadness and war. These are some of the things I have tried to depict and explored in this surreal panel of work.

"May your God go with you", Dave Allan.

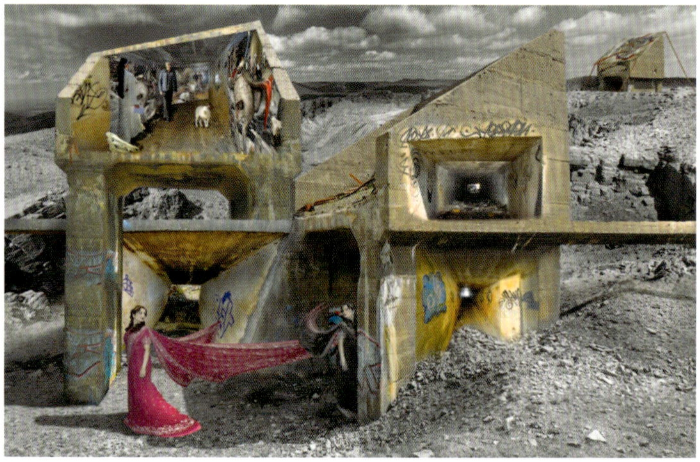

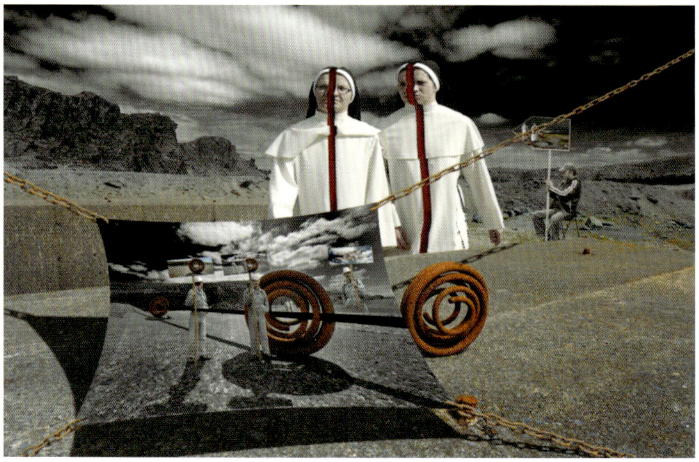

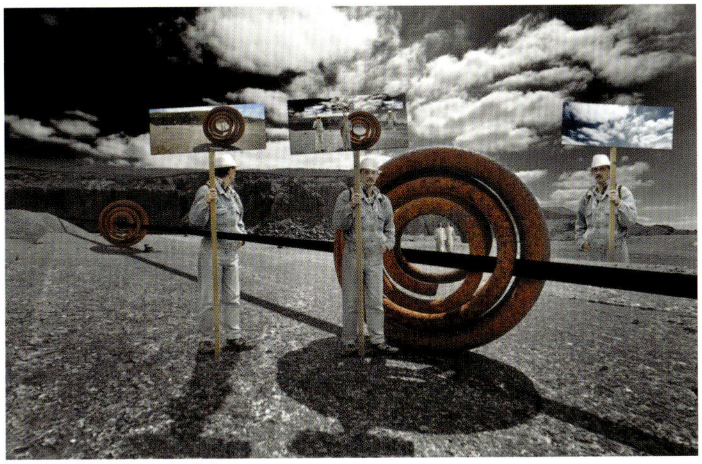

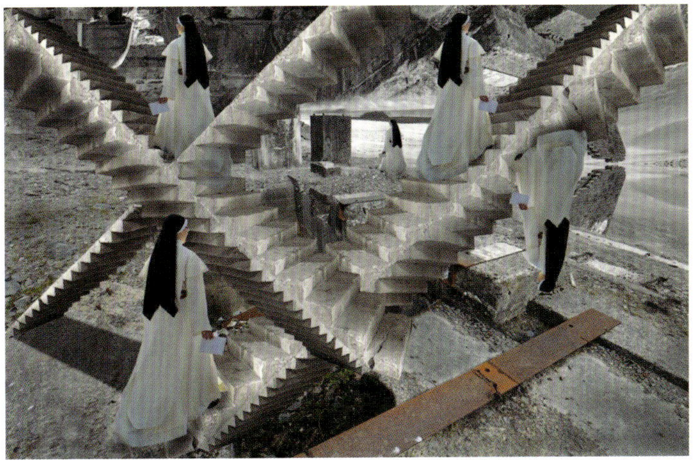

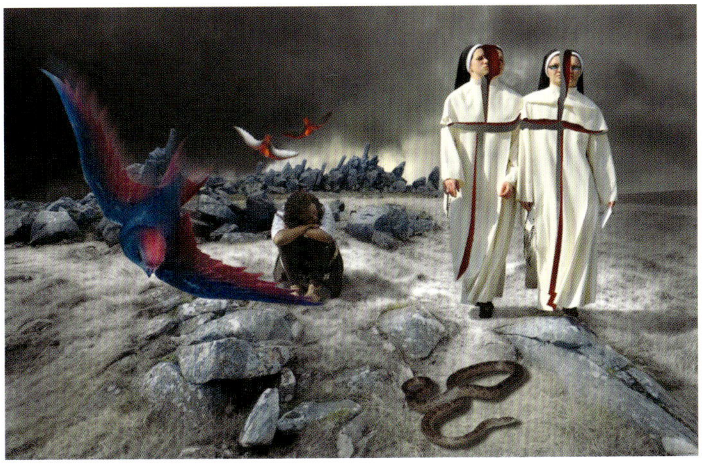

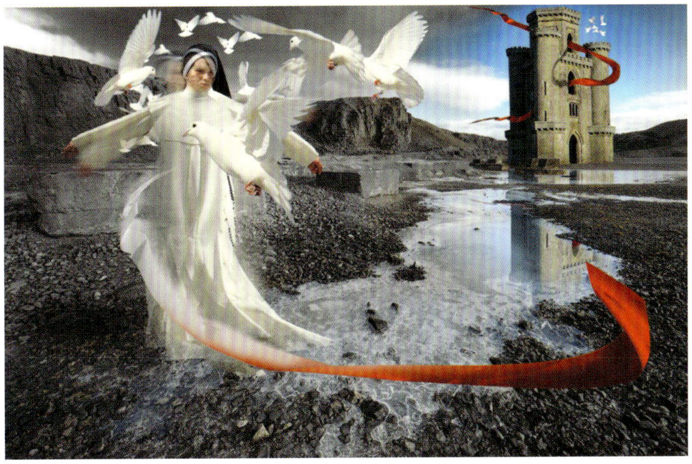

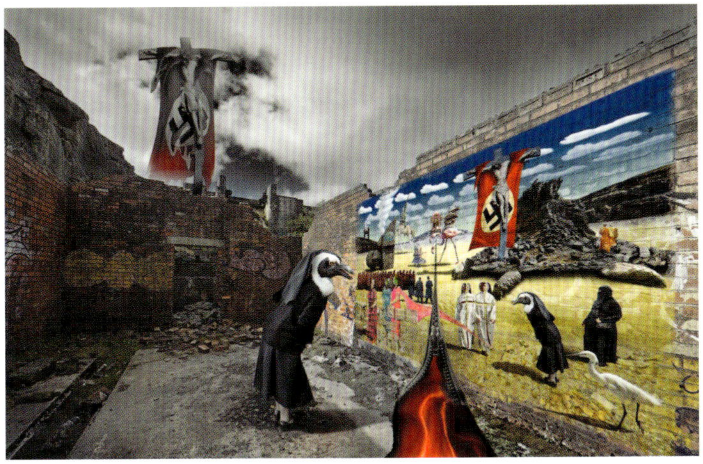

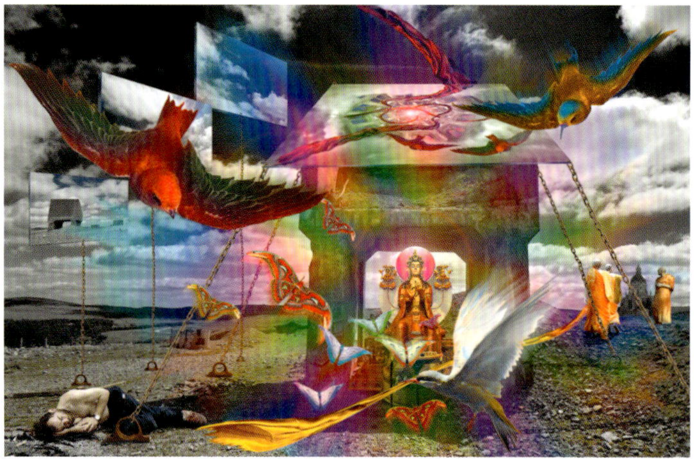

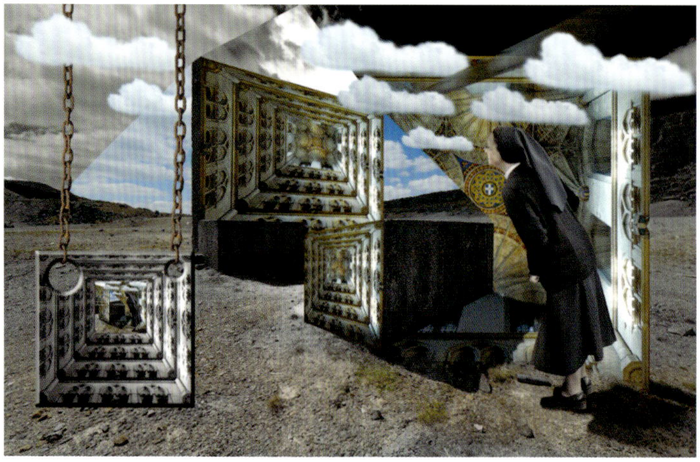

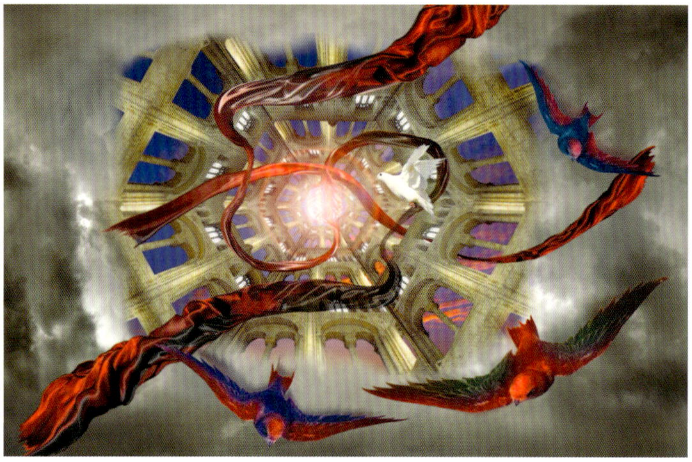

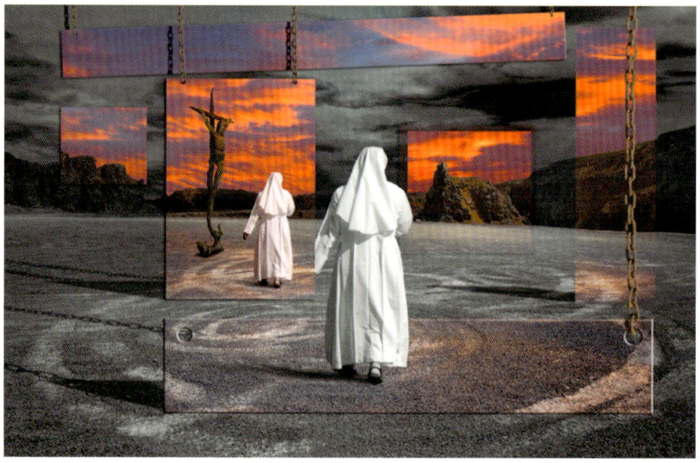

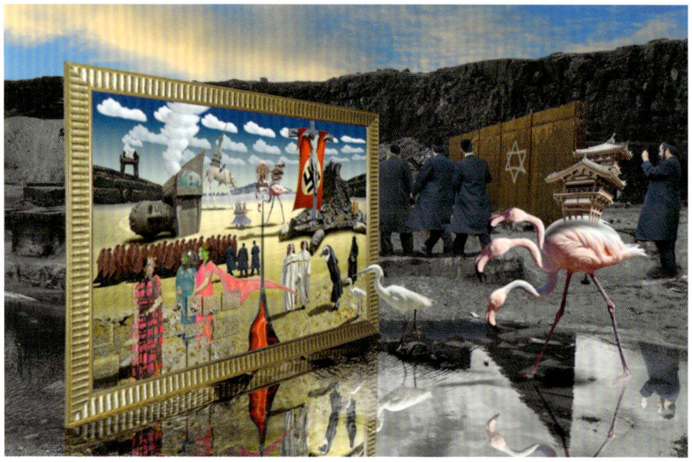

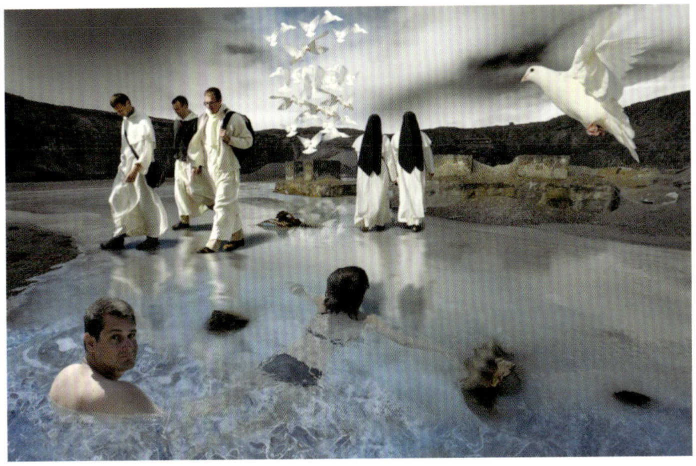

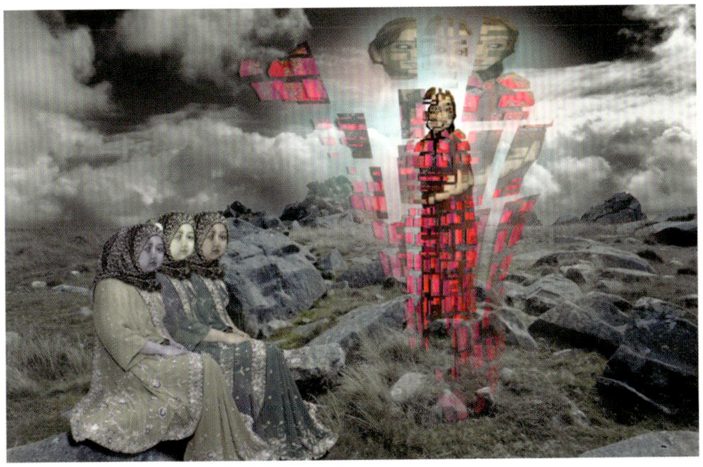

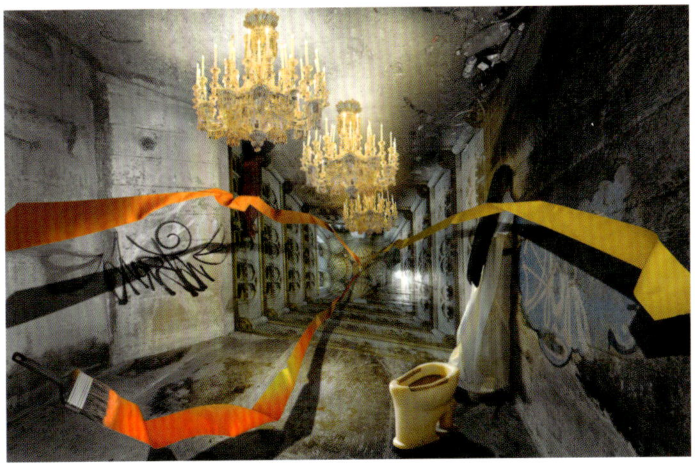

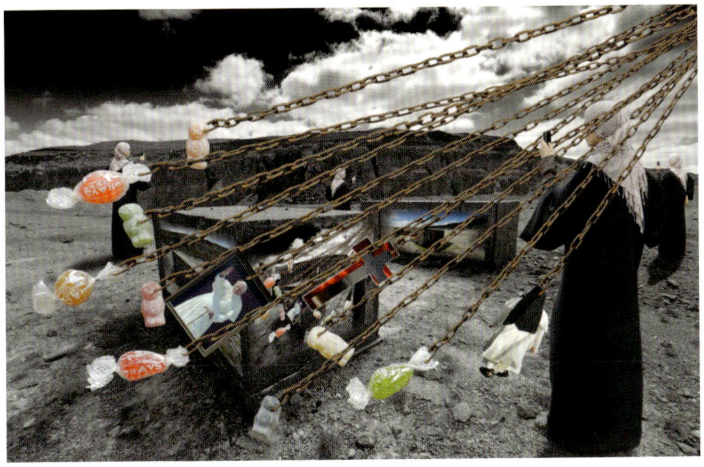

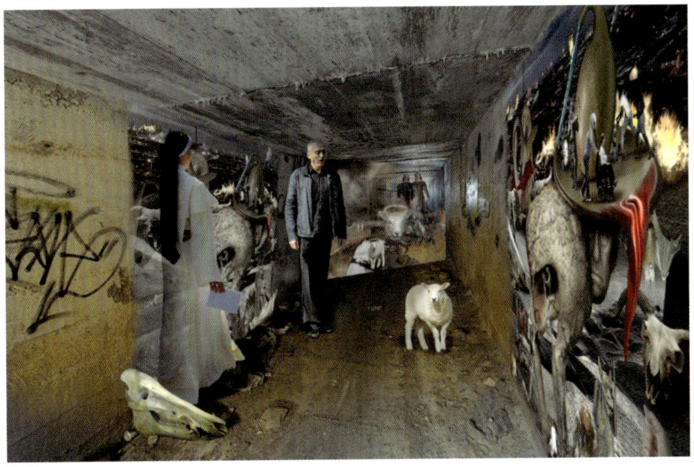

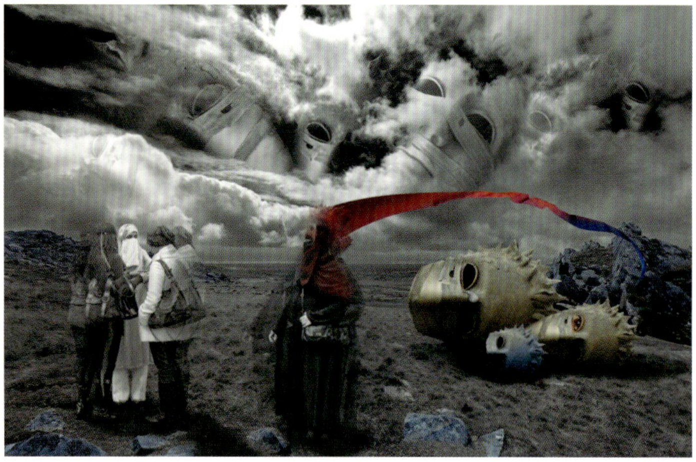

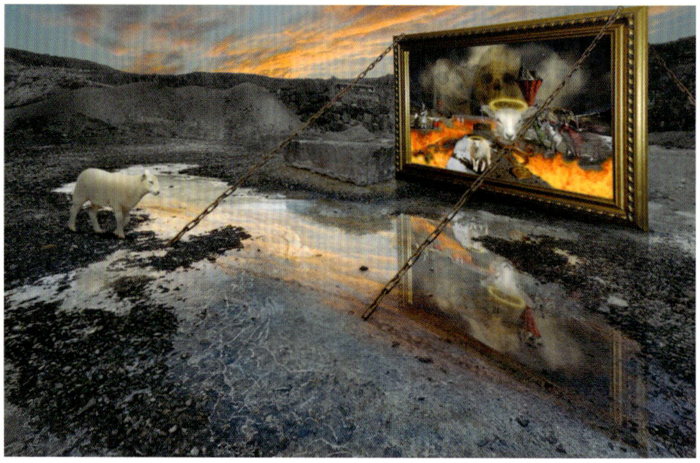

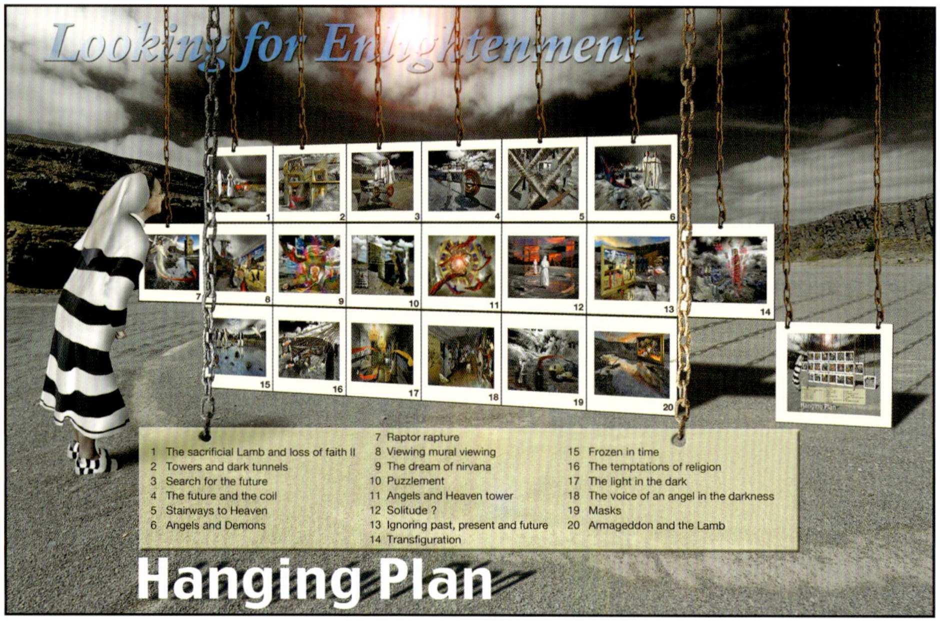
Looking for Enlightenment
1 The sacrificial Lamb and loss of faith II
2 Towers and dark tunnels
3 Search for the future
4 The future and the coil
5 Stairways to Heaven
6 Angels and Demons
7 Raptor rapture
8 Viewing mural viewing
9 The dream of nirvana
10 Puzzlement
11 Angels and Heaven tower
12 Solitude ?
13 Ignoring past, present and future
14 Transfiguration
15 Frozen in time
16 The temptations of religion
17 The light in the dark
18 The voice of an angel in the darkness
19 Masks
20 Armageddon and the Lamb
Hanging Plan

HISTORY AND EDUCATION

The past shapes the future

The Photographic Society was founded in 1853, and became The Royal Photographic Society in 1894. In 2004, The Society was granted a Royal Charter.

Since 1853 its aim has been promote both the Art and Science of photography through the exchange of ideas and experience.

History of The Society and photography is found within The Society's Collection at the National Media Museum, comprising over 270,000 images, 6000 items of photographic equipment and myriad photographic books, periodicals, correspondence and catalogues. The Collection is recognised internationally for its historical importance.

160th Anniversary

Since The Society was founded in 1853 and 2013 sees the celebration of its 160th anniversary, Michael Pritchard FRPS looks back at those 160 years.

Distinctions History

The Royal Photographic Society has offered photographic Distinctions for many years. Today The Society's Distinctions are recognised throughout the world as the 'Gold Standard'. In 2012 more than 1,200 people from all around the globe sought to achieve their Licentiateship, Associateship or Fellowship. Carol Mikellides, better known to members as Carol Agar, the retired long-time manager of The Society Distinctions Department, looks back over the history of these Society Distinctions.

The Bursaries

One aspect of The Society's current educational remit is to support and encourage younger photographers and students to achieve Distinctions and excel in their field. The bursaries supported by both The Society and sponsors are offered annually. Two initiatives in place for postgraduate study and a social documentary travel project are highlighted here.

Huw Wahl ARPS – The Postgraduate Bursary

Neil Hall – The Joan Wakelin Bursary

The Conservation and Preservation of Joseph Nicéphore Niépce's Photographs

Three of the earliest known photographs from Joseph Nicéphore Niépce are held in The Royal Photographic Society Collection at the National Medium Museum in Bradford. Former Curator Philippa Wright explains how the research, preservation and conservation of these priceless images have been handled in recent years.

Acquisitions to The Society Collection

An active acquisitions policy was put in place in 2010 to ensure the Collection remains live and continues to grow. Rosemary Wilman Hon.FRPS explains the process.

THE PHOTOGRAPHIC SOCIETY

ITS ORIGINS AND JOURNAL

In 2013 The Royal Photographic Society celebrated its 160th anniversary evolving as the interests and needs of its members have changed and, particularly, as photography itself has changed. It continues to fulfil its original aims of 'promoting the art and science of photography' through a programme of meetings, exhibitions, and through its wider educational programme.

Origins

The Photographic Society was not the first photographic society but it was the first to be formally organised and to have been in continuous existence to the present day. The Edinburgh Calotype Club was formed in 1843 and consisted of 'keen experimentalists'. Its dozen members met to look at calotypes, to discuss photographic art and to socialise. In London the publisher Joseph Cundall, with Robert Hunt, started the Calotype Society – later known as the Photographic Club – in 1847. This, again, was a gathering of around a dozen photographers or 'gentlemen amateurs' who met regularly to discuss their experiments in photography and to exchange photographs. In mid-1852 the Leeds Photographic Society was formed, operating under properly constituted rules.

The Great Exhibition of 1851 exhibited photography as both a fine art and as a branch of science and over 700 photographs were shown as well as cameras, lenses and associated photographic apparatus. The Exhibition raised awareness of photography as an art form and by late 1851 there was a campaign underway to establish a photographic society in London.

The main difficulty the committee faced was to convince Henry Fox Talbot to release members from any restriction imposed by his calotype patent. Robert Hunt met with him but no agreement was reached. Reconciling Talbot's interpretation of the patent laws with those of the committee proved impossible and their efforts were adjourned indefinitely.

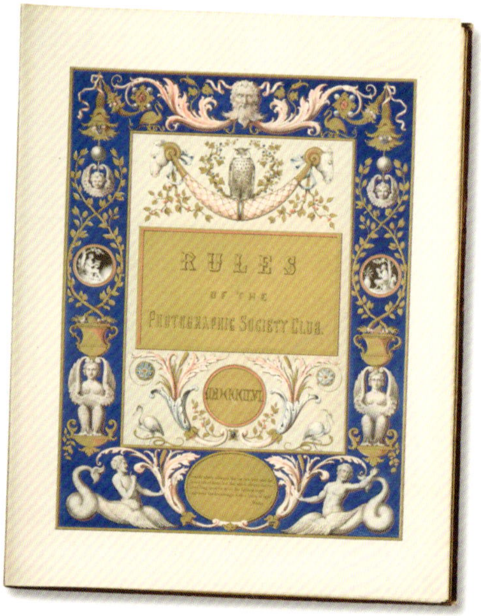

Rules of The Photographic Society Club, 1856, from The Lord Chief Baron's [Sir Frederick Pollock FRS] copy of The Photographic Society Club album. Made up of Society members the Club was designed 'to promote union and friendly feeling amongst members of the Photographic Society'. Its members met and dined together five times a year, including one which took place in the country at a venue 'favourable to photographic pursuits'.

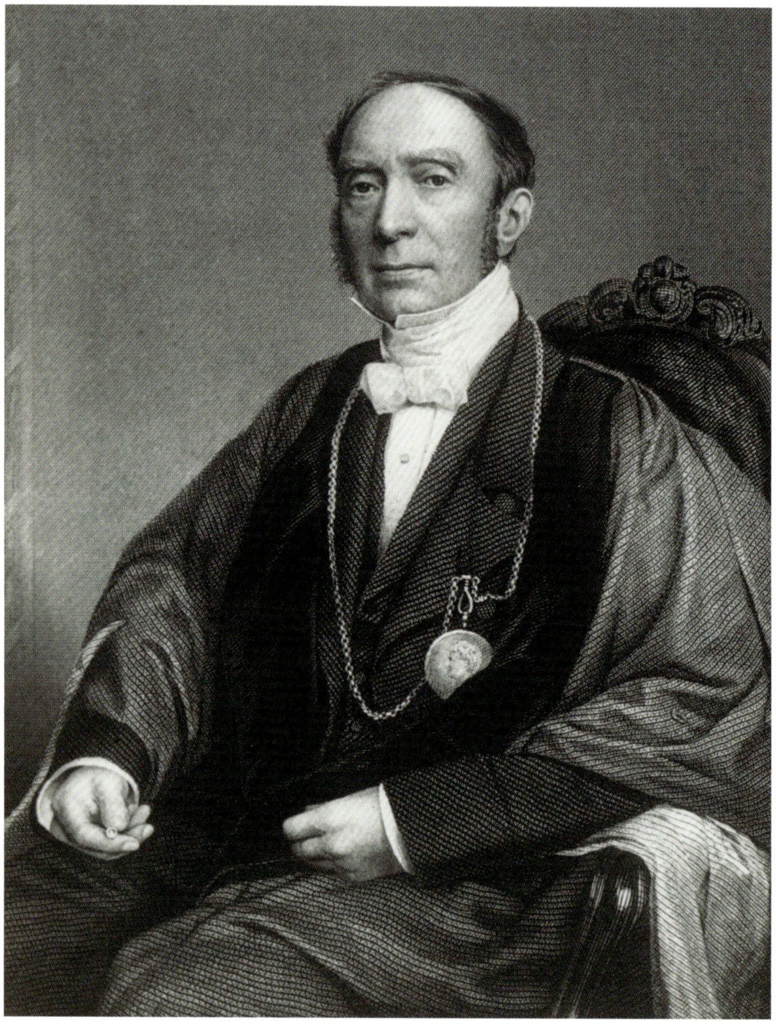

Sir Charles Eastlake, The Society's first president.

Despite this setback discussions continued under the auspices of the Society of Arts with Sir Charles Eastlake, director of the National Gallery, and Lord Rosse, president of the Royal Society, taking the lead as official representatives of art and science in the UK. After two months an agreement was reached. In a formal letter dated 30 July 1852 Talbot acknowledged the impact of the Great Exhibition as heralding a new era for photography and he presented his invention to the country.

Later that year the Society of Arts held the first exhibition devoted to the art and science of photography. Opening on 22 December 1852 nearly four hundred photographs were shown and such was its success it was extended to meet the public demand.

The inaugural meeting

The committee that had attempted to form a photographic society earlier in 1852 was resurrected following the agreement with Talbot. It recommended the establishment of a photographic society and placed advertisements in newspapers announcing an inaugural meeting on Thursday, 20 January 1853 in the Great Rooms of the Society of Arts in London. The meeting was open to 'ladies and gentlemen interested in Photography'.

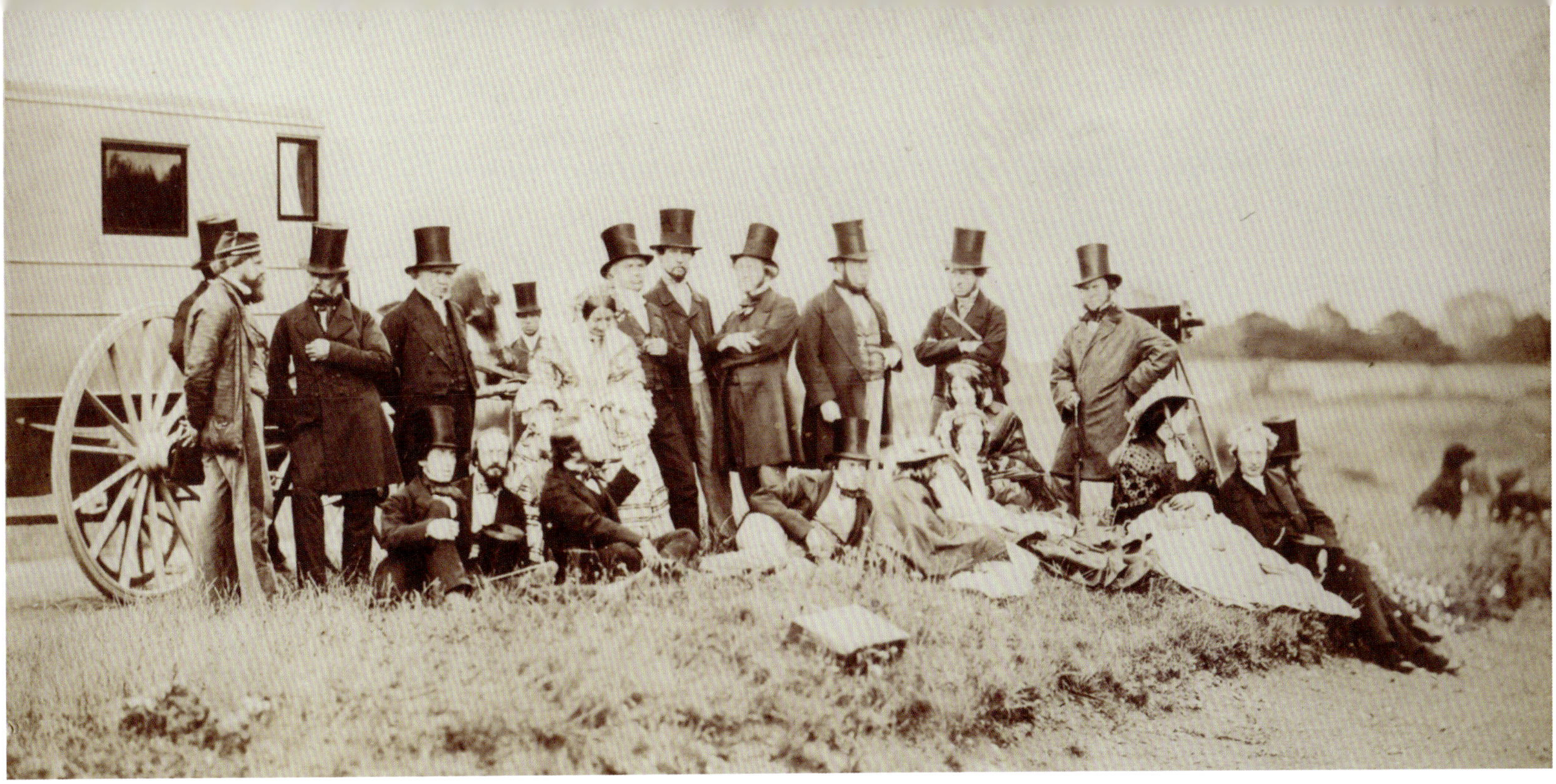

Roger Fenton, Members of the Photographic Society at Hampton Court, 1856.

The chair was taken by Sir Charles Eastlake with Roger Fenton acting as Honorary Secretary to the provisional committee. Eastlake addressed the meeting and thanked Talbot for having 'thrown open his invention to the enterprise of men or science, of amateurs and artists'. Fenton then read a report describing previous attempts to form a society and the meeting then confirmed the establishment of The Photographic Society.

The first proper meeting of the new Photographic Society was held on 3 February 1853 at which new members were elected, papers read and photographs 'chiefly of wood scenery, taken by Sir William J Newton were exhibited'. The first annual general meeting was held on 2 February 1854.

Exhibitions

Producing a photography exhibition was a key objective for the new Society. The Society of Arts had proposed that The Society cooperate with it in a plan for forming a collection of photography to be sent around the country for exhibition. The Society's Council agreed to support this but it was also keen to mount its own exhibition of photography in London. The difficulty of securing suitable premises delayed it and Council resolved that 'in consequence of it not being possible to obtain suitable Rooms' it would postpone its exhibition of photographs to the latter part of the year.

On 1 December Fenton was able to report that he had engaged the rooms of the Society of British Artists in Suffolk Street, Pall Mall, for an exhibition during January and February 1854 at a rent of £25 per month. The Queen Victoria and Prince Albert were given a private tour by the President, Sir Charles Eastlake, and Fenton and they bought several prints. It opened to the public on 4 January 1854. In February Council agreed that the 'working classes' could be admitted in the evenings at a cost of 3d per person and that this was to be advertised in The Times until the exhibition's close at the end of February.

Royal Patronage

At The Society's fifth Ordinary meeting on 2 June 1853 Fenton read an extract from the 12 May Council minutes which noted the Council considered 'it is of the highest importance to the interests of the Photographic Society that H.M. the Queen and H.R.H. The Prince Albert should become patrons of The Society'. Buckingham Palace confirmed their accepted in a letter dated 30 May which informed the Society 'that the Queen and Prince will willingly give their Patronage to the Photographic Society'.

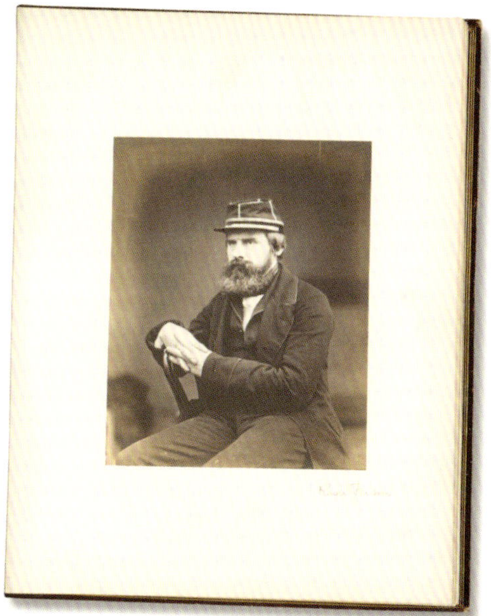

Roger Fenton, 1856, from The Lord Chief Baron's [Sir Frederick Pollock FRS] copy of The Photographic Society Club album.

This raised the question of whether The Society's name should be changed to reflect the Royal patronage. The Council minutes of 16 June recorded that 'the subject of the assumption of the title of "Royal Photographic Society" having been considered. Resolved 'that it is not expedient to take any further steps in that matter for the present'. The Society eventually became 'Royal' in 1894.

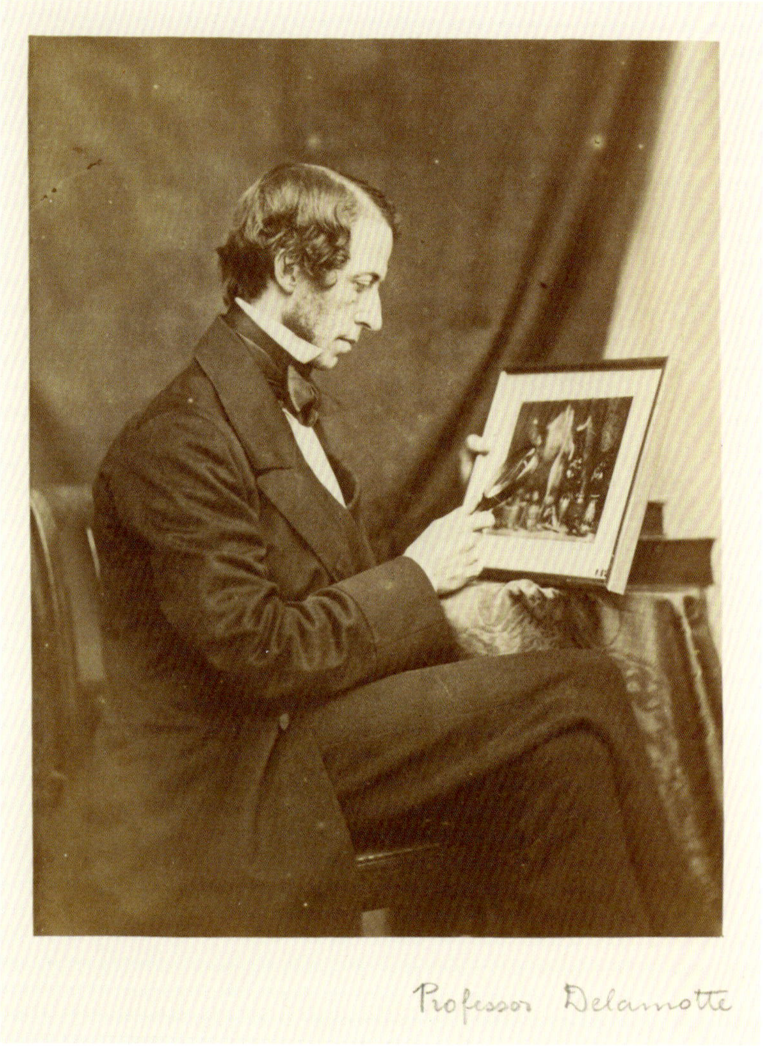

Portrait of Philip Henry Delamotte, 1856. Delamotte was an early member of the Society and exhibited regularly from its first exhibition in 1854.

Journal

The need to publish a journal was also a key aim and has been seen as essential even before The Society was set up. Council appointed a publication committee at its 10 February 1853 meeting. It resolved that 'a Journal be established for the dissemination among the members of this Society of the communications made at the Ordinary meetings and of information bearing upon the interests of the Photographic Art and that the Journal be published monthly'. The committee was authorised 'to make the best and most economical arrangements with a respectable firm for the printing and publication of the Journal of the Society'.

The committee resolved on 16 February to propose to Council that 'the proceedings of the Society ought to be published under the name of "The Journal of the Photographic Society" '. It also proposed that the Journal should appear promptly after each meeting and 1000 copies be printed of the first number so that free copies could be sent to all the Clubs of London and to scientific and literary institutions, thereafter 500 copies would be printed. The first number of the Journal was ready by the 3 March.

Such was the demand for the Journal that a second edition of 800 copies of the first number was ordered and throughout the first year reprints and larger print runs of the Journal were approved. By the end of 1853 it was 'ordered that the standing number of the Journal now printed be 4000 and that the back numbers as they may require printing be made up to 4000'. By May 1854 the print run was reduced to 2750 with the Journal stereotyped for future re-printing if required. Consideration was also given to publishing the Journal twice a month and this was agreed on 21 April.

To the future

The Photographic Society had a busy first year. Council was preoccupied with ensuring that papers were ready for meetings and with setting up the administrative procedures of the new Society. The finances of The Society do not feature significantly in the Council minutes but the Journal report of the first annual meeting held on 2 February 1854 reported cash and assets at a healthy £406 17s.

Much like today The Society was approached by other organisations as a point of contact for photographic advice. The need to publish a Journal and to produce an exhibition were The Society's two main concerns and both were successfully realised continuing to the present day.

The work undertaken by Fenton and the other members of The Photographic Society's Council in the first year did much to establish The Society on a sound long-term footing. Over the following years The Society had occasional financial or internal crises which it successfully weathered. The aims of The Society and how it achieves these have evolved and continue to do so as photographic imaging changes. Despite this Fenton and the members of the first Council would still recognise The Society today as the direct descendent of their Society.

As part of its 160th anniversary The Society has digitised its Journal from 1853-2013, in excess of 30,000 pages. The journals are fully searchable and are an important contribution to photographic scholarship as well as a resource for local and family historians. The Society is pleased to acknowledge the support of a long-standing member in realising this project.

Dr Michael Pritchard FRPS

Acknowledgment

Toni Booth, Colin Harding and Brian Liddy at the National Media Museum, Bradford.

HISTORY OF THE SOCIETY DISTINCTIONS

On 20th January 1853, soon after the dawn of photography, The Photographic Society of London held its inaugural meeting. Originally founded as a scientific society, its aims were summarised as 'the advancement of photography'. In 1894 by Her Majesty's command, the Society became 'The Royal Photographic Society of Great Britain' and in 2004 was granted a Royal Charter.

The Fellowship: the beginning

Membership of The Society has always been open to anyone interested in photography. By the 1890s it was felt that competence in the practice and development of photography should be recognised; consequently, in 1895, the Fellowship (FRPS) was introduced. During the first year, members of The Society were able to claim admission as Fellows without the submission of evidence; of 549 members, 156 applied and were made Fellows. Subsequently members had to submit their qualifications to Council.

By the turn of the century an Admissions Committee had been appointed comprising eighteen Fellows of The Society, half to consider qualifications relating to science, and half to consider pictorial qualifications.

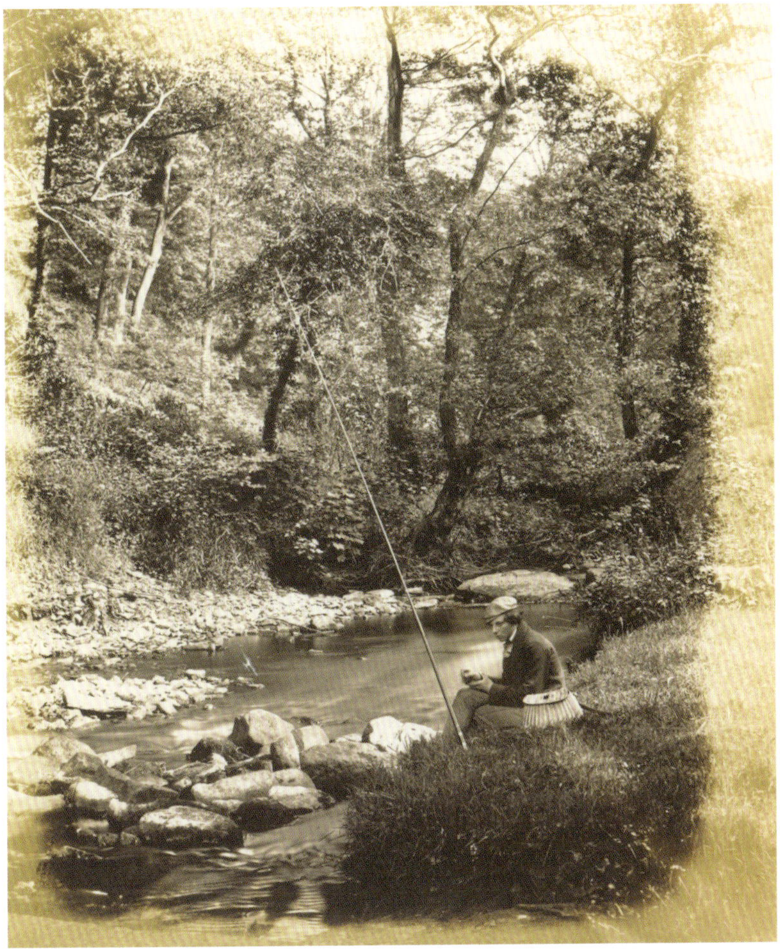

John Dilwyn Llewelyn FRPS Piscator (Albumen Print) c1855

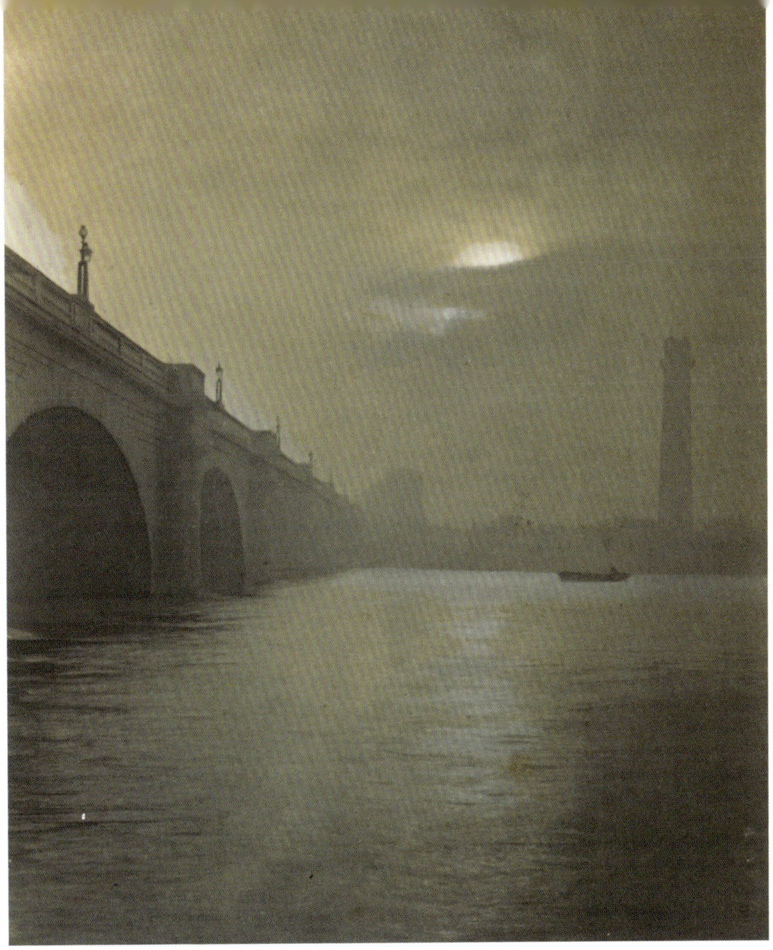

Frederick Hollyer FRPS Waterloo Bridge (Platinum Print) 1877

Candidates had to be recommended by two Fellows of The Society, who would confirm their 'personal or social eligibility'; consideration of technical or pictorial qualifications being left to the committee who reported to Council. Council discussed these reports at one meeting, but only voted at the following meeting; (not until 1940 did discussion and voting take place at the same meeting); two-thirds of the vote was required in order to be successful.

By 1909 membership of The Society was just over 1,000 of which 188 were Fellows. Applications for the Fellowship had become more formalised requiring a statement of qualifications under one or more of the following:

a) *Original investigations, improvements or inventions adding to photographic knowledge in either theory or practice*

b) *Educational work*

c) *Technical work, e.g. the application of photography in the various arts and sciences, and in record work of all kinds*

d) *Pictorial work*

e) *Professional portraiture*

f) *Other qualifications*

Applicants were asked to submit as much evidence as possible including details of any examinations or awards achieved relating to photography, published papers, examples of work, etc.

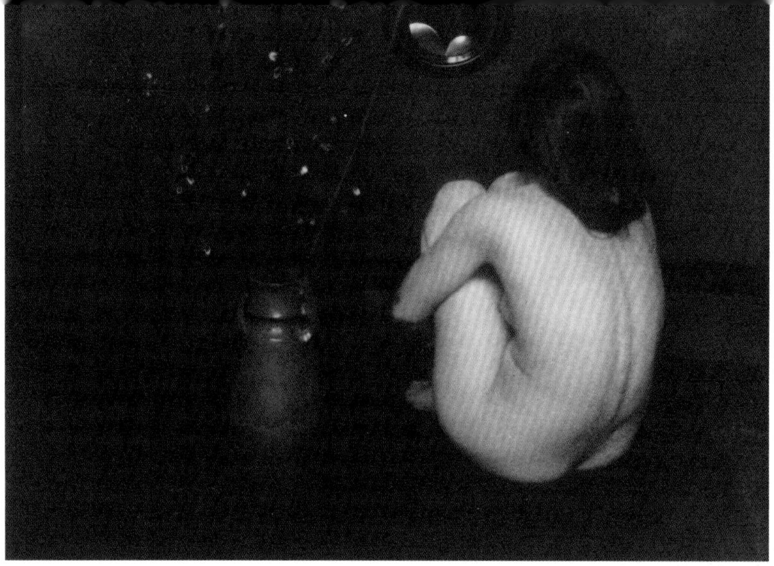

Edward Steichan FRPS Torso, Paris (Photogravure) 1902

The Associateship: the early years

The Associateship (ARPS) was introduced in 1924. The President, J. Dudley Johnston, wrote:

> *"There are a great many able photographers who, by the very nature of their work, would never be likely to receive the Fellowship, but for whom the Associateship will be very appropriate, and something in the nature of a certificate of proficiency."*

Only members could apply for the Associateship, and only Associates for the Fellowship.

By 1940 the number of Associateship applications had risen from 55 to around 140 a year and were submitted under the following headings:

A. Pictorial Photography, including Portraiture

B. Commercial, Advertising, Press and Record Photography and Photo-Engraving

C. Colour Photography

D. Natural History Photography (Animal, Botanical, Entomological, etc.)

E. Kinematography

F. Scientific Photography, including Photomicrography, Aerial survey, Astronomical, Meteorological, Medicine, X-Ray work, etc.

G. Scientific Research on Photographic subjects

H. Work on Photography of a definitely educational character

Assessors with appropriate expertise were appointed and each Section voted separately; their recommendations were reported to Council and three quarters of Council's vote was required to be successful.

Requirements

Until the end of the 1930s there were no regulations regarding the quantity of work to be submitted for the Distinctions and there was no application fee until the 1950s: initiallly10s 6d, which covered entries in any number of categories made at the same time.

In 1939, in Sections (later known as 'Categories') where evidence was principally in the form of images (i.e. Pictorial, Commercial, Colour, Nature) applicants had to submit "not less than six and not more than twelve" images; this was changed the following year to: "not less than twelve". The requirement for a *fixed* number of images – twelve for both Associateship and Fellowship – was introduced in 1950 and successful prints were franked: 'Accepted for the Associateship (or Fellowship) of The Royal Photographic Society' (this practice was discontinued in 1960). Twelve years later, in 1962, the number of images required to apply for the Fellowship was increased to eighteen. Submissions of colour transparencies had additionally, until 1985, to include six prints as supporting evidence. The final change in the quantity of work required came 30 years later, in 1992, when it was increased to fifteen and twenty respectively for Associateship and Fellowship.

Applicants for the Associateship had to demonstrate that they were 'thoroughly competent' and 'well above average in their photography'; for the Fellowship, exceptional work was expected as well as evidence of a sound judgement in self-appraisal.

In his Presidential Address, 1967, G W G Maclennan FRPS stated:

> *"For the Fellowship, exceptionally, when the photographic reputation and work of a photographer are known to be above reproach, Council has the right to waive submission of evidence."*

This was later formalised into the Direct Application for Fellowship which, instead of the submission of work, is based on the applicant's established reputation, requiring support from a sponsor and referees.

While the majority of Distinction applications were individual, until 1989 joint applications for Fellowship were permissible where "the circumstances of work performance are such that none of the applicants could have completed it alone."

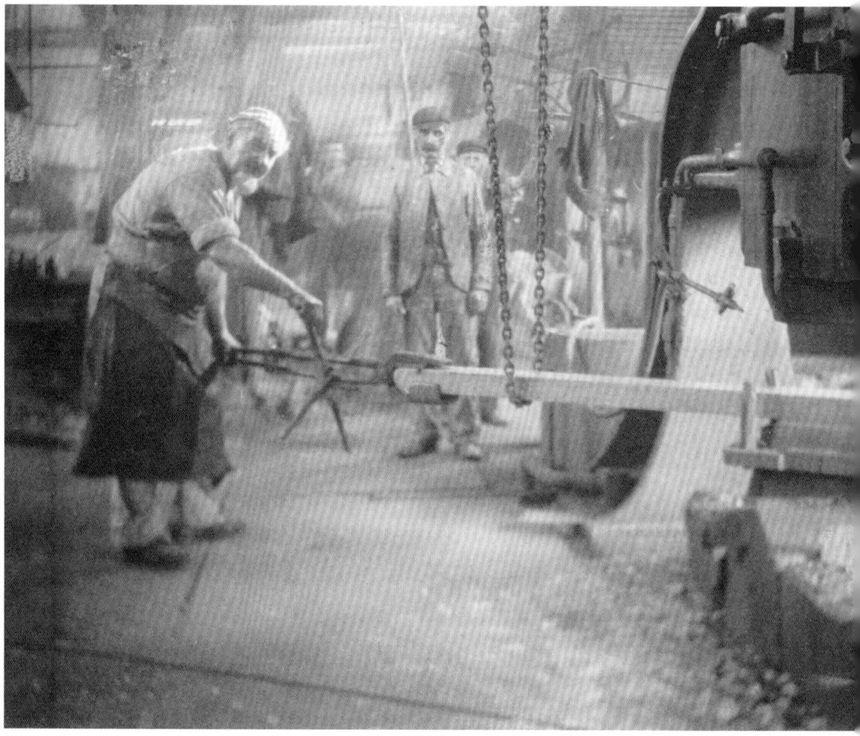

Alvin Langdon Coburn FRPS Forging Steel (Platinum Print) 1905

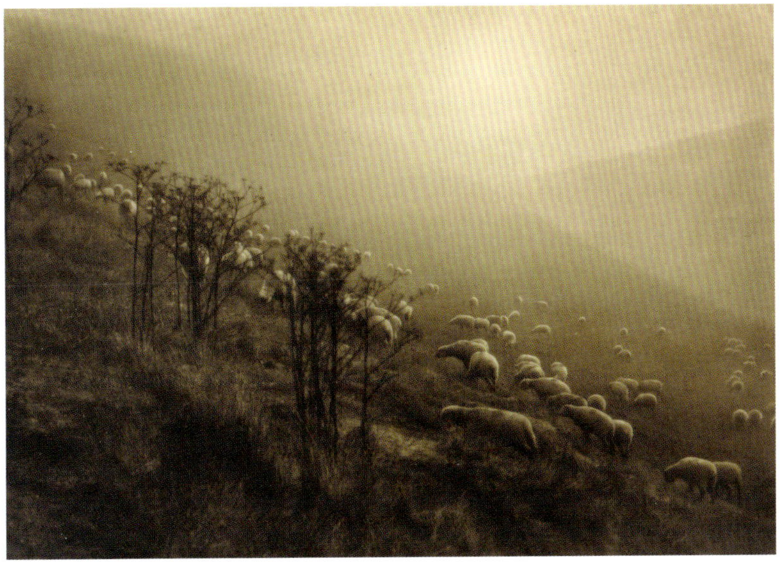

Charles Job FRPS Morning mist on Sussex Downs (Carbon Print) 1905

Initial Advice and Guidance

Only in the 1940s was consideration given to providing guidance for applicants. Panel Chairmen were asked to prepare general reports on their own meetings for publication in the Journal. It was soon evident that these reports were of limited value since the same faults kept occurring. As an interim measure it was decided to give advice only to a) overseas applicants; b) those who had failed on more than one previous occasion and c) applicants who were very close to the required standard. In an attempt to assist applicants, exhibitions of successful work were held at The Society's Headquarters and later in the regions.

Concern that written comments could be misleading led to Council's decision after four years, to stop commentaries altogether. However, demand for feedback prevailed and one of the first proposals of the Distinctions Co-ordinating Committee (appointed in 1958) was that unsuccessful Associateship applicants should receive a form listing the most common faults with ticks indicating where the submission failed as well as indicating which images were not up to the required standard.

Introduction of the Licentiateship

The ten years to 1947 saw a huge increase in the membership of The Society, from 2,500 to over 6,000 then remaining fairly static until the mid 1970s. During the same period the number of Distinction applications averaged around 480 a year; the Pictorial category attracting the largest number of applications.

The 1970s proved to be momentous years for The Society. In 1970, in response to growing criticisms, a Commission (comprising senior members of The Society) was set up to consider all aspects of membership; to discover what members wanted from The Society and how they thought it should develop. A major outcome was the establishment of the Licentiateship (LRPS) in 1972:

> *"The Associateship is awarded for a high degree of competence in one of twelve different fields of photography and is primarily a Distinction for the specialist; the Licentiateship will be awarded on the basis of practical photographic ability in either still or motion picture work and will therefore provide recognition for the good all-rounder."*

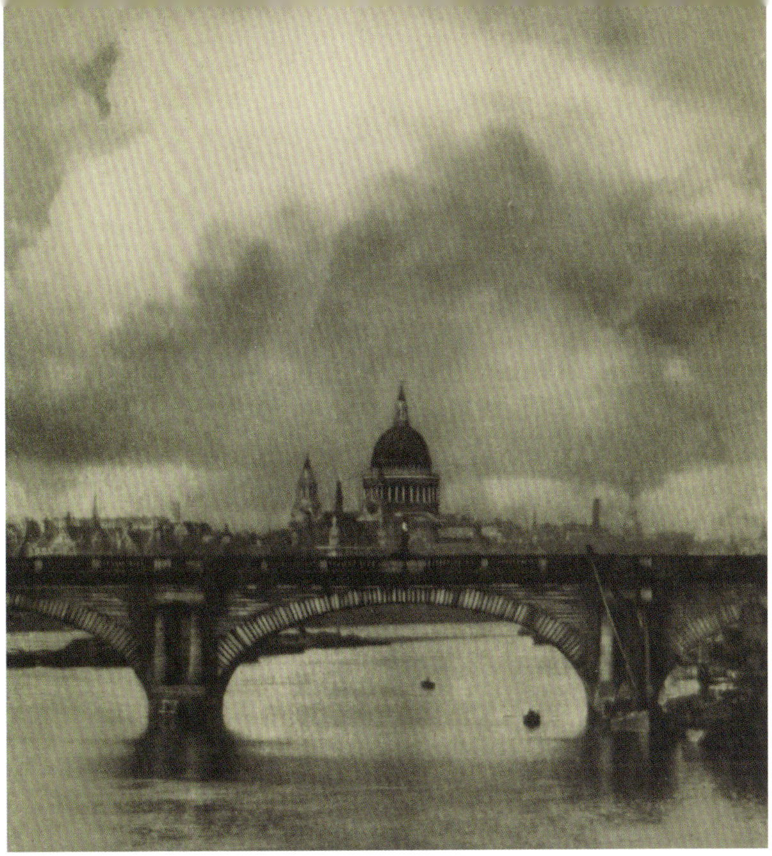

Alvin Langdon Coburn FRPS St Paul's from river 1905

From the start ten images were required for the Licentiateship in stills photography, 'entirely the work of the applicant'. A major innovation, was the opening of these assessments to an audience and from 1974 'Towards the Distinctions' Photographic Advisory Evenings were also organised – the forerunners of today's Distinctions Advisory Days.

For the first time a Society Distinction was open to those who did not take photographs but could display alternative specialised skills, e.g. colour printers, film editors, etc. An exemption scheme was also introduced: applicants were exempt from submitting practical work if they could provide evidence of passing an appropriate photographic examination.

In 1978 trade-processed colour prints were accepted, but applicants were advised that other aspects of their photography, e.g. lighting, composition, would be more critically assessed.

Despite the success of the public Licentiateship assessments, it was not until 1978 in Coventry that an audience watched an Associateship and Fellowship Slide-Sound Sequences Panel – the first public meeting outside London. Again it was enthusiastically received, but a further five years elapsed before the next occasion – an Associateship Nature Panel chaired by Heather Angel FRPS (subsequently awarded the Honorary Fellowship following her two years as President of The Society (1984-1986); only the second woman to hold this office, the first being Professor Margaret Harker Hon.FRPS in 1958.) Audiences were gradually accepted at all assessments.

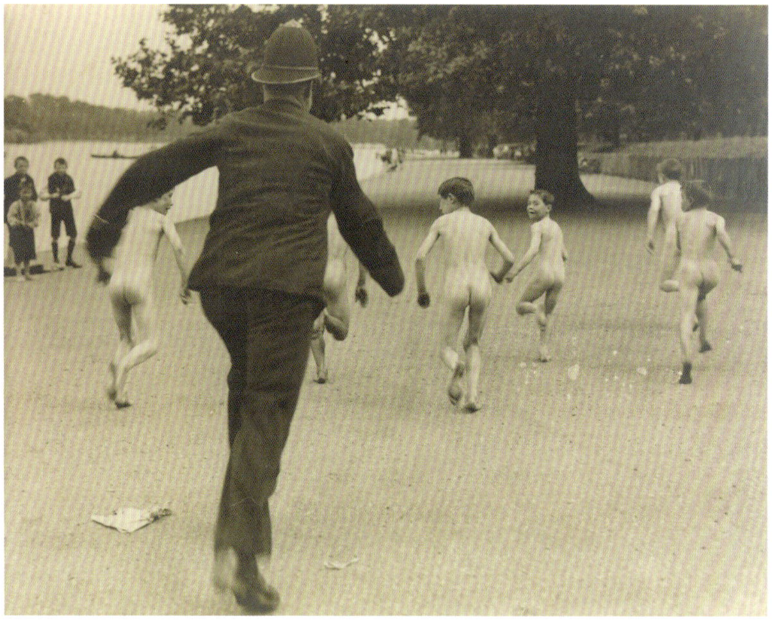

Charles Job FRPS Morning mist on Sussex Downs (Carbon Print) 1905

National Centre

The mid 1970s were difficult years for the UK – 25% inflation, regular strikes and power cuts – and for The Society, a deficit in 1974 more than doubled the following year to over £13,000 facing it with an acute cash-flow crisis and the possibility of closure. Radical steps were taken – principally reducing publication of the Journal from twelve to six issues a year and increasing subscriptions.

Since its formation The Society's headquarters had always been in London. While in Princes Gate, a prestigious property overlooking Hyde Park, the local authority ruled that the building should be converted to residential use so The Society was forced to move. Temporary offices were found in Maddox Street until it could move to its new home at 14 South Audley Street in Mayfair, officially opened in November 1970 by HRH Princess Margaret, accompanied by her husband, the professional photographer, Lord Snowdon.

After ten years it became obvious that The Society could no longer afford to remain in London. An appeal to the photographic community throughout the world was launched, raising over £400,000 towards the establishment of The RPS National Centre of Photography which was eventually located in The Octagon, an 18th century Grade 1 listed building in the centre of the World Heritage City of Bath. At her own request, the official opening ceremony in April 1981 was performed by HRH Princess Margaret.

The Growth of the Distinctions

The number of Distinctions applications gradually increased through the 1980s to a peak in 1991, of 1,547 (730 of which were for the Licentiateship) – a 15% increase. A major contribution to these record figures was the acceptance of the City & Guilds 9231 scheme for Licentiateship exemption; a modular scheme, it was aimed at the recreational as well as the serious amateur photographer and as many as 38% of Licentiateship applications came via this scheme. Following this success, an equivalent exemption scheme for the Associateship was introduced in 1994, a degree in photography being the benchmark.

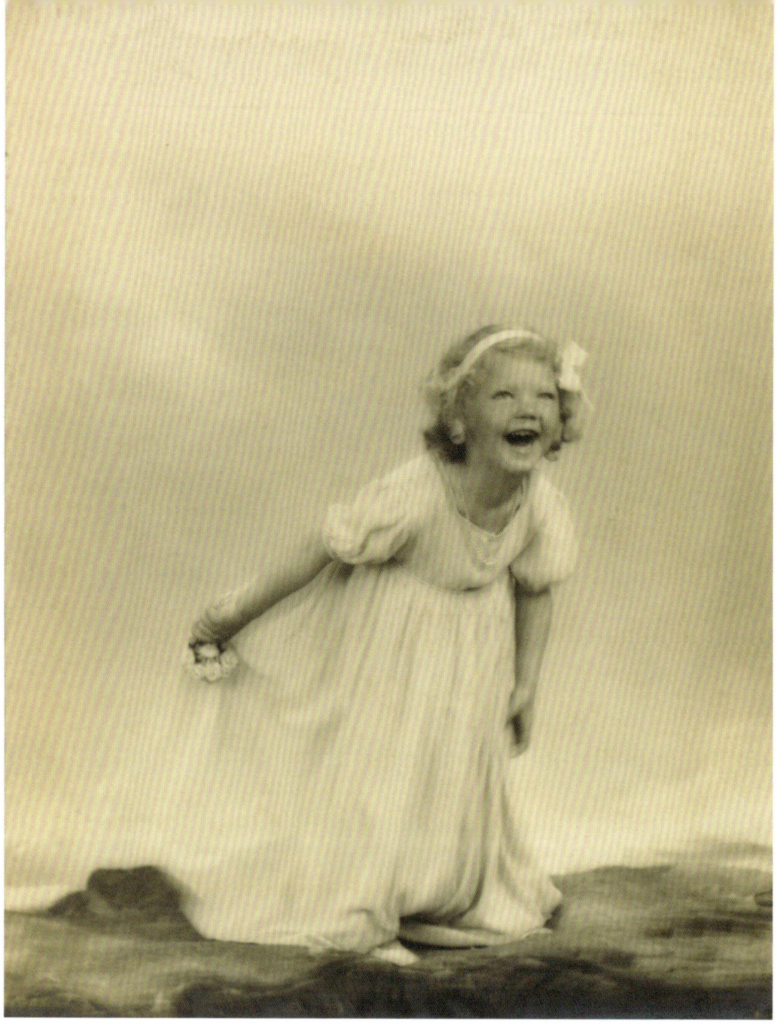

Marcus Adams FRPS Charm of childhood (Cloro-Bromide Print) 1930

In order further to encourage membership of The Society, in 1986 non-members were allowed to apply for the Licentiateship on the understanding that if they were successful, the Distinction would be awarded only when they joined The Society. This was later applied to the Associateship.

The popularity of the Licentiateship led to an increase in the number of assessments held each year both in Bath and throughout the UK. A particularly exciting venture in 1993 was a Panel and workshop held in Hong Kong at the instigation of the Hong Kong Tourist Board which was enthusiastically received.

Recognising the importance of the Distinctions to The Society, successive Councils have endeavoured to improve the assessment process, aiming for fairness and consistency for all applicants while maintaining standards across a wide range of subject matter and format. There have been many changes in the scope and nature of the Associateship and Fellowship categories; some have been disbanded through lack of interest, e.g. Graphic Art Processes, while others have been renamed in order to clarify their scope, e.g. the History of Photography. Originally part of the Education category, its title changed to: 'History of Photography & Critical Writing'; later merging into an 'Academic' Panel which has now developed into the 'Research, Education & Application of Photography' Panel.

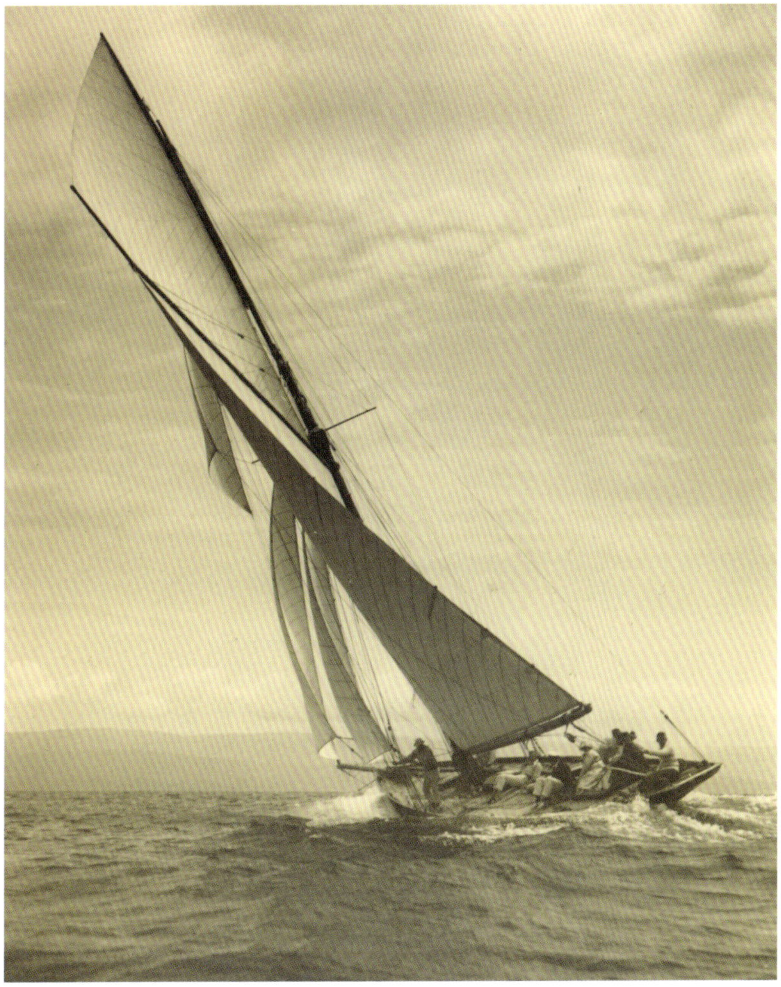

G L A Blair FRPS The 'Verve' (Bromide Print) 1930

From the start, the Pictorial category attracted the largest number of submissions and briefly in 1990 it was renamed 'Pictorial and General' in order to accommodate photographers who enjoyed a wide variety of work. The Panel's range was so diverse, it divided into 'Visual Art: Pictorial' and 'Visual Art: Contemporary' with the intention of reverting eventually to form one Visual Art Panel. It was soon recognised that the differences in philosophy were too great and they remained as separate categories: 'Contemporary' and 'Visual Art'.

Imaging Scientist Qualifications were introduced in 1993. They provide a structure leading to professional qualifications for engineers, scientists and technologists whose professional activities are concerned with quantitative or mechanic aspects of imaging systems or their applications. Successful applicants also receive an equivalent Society Distinction.

It has always been important for The Society to keep abreast of current developments. For the Distinctions, the Contemporary Panel encourages diverse forms of submission and was the first to accept installations as applications. In 2002, the first digital submissions on CD were accepted for the Licentiateship; and two years later for the Associateship. Increasingly the internet is used to disseminate information and provide advice and guidance; a comprehensive document covering all aspects of the Distinctions process is available to download from the RPS website as well as several interactive CDs.

Committees

The Distinctions Co-ordinating Committee (DCC) comprising the Chairmen of all the Panels, was appointed in 1958 to meet once a year to discuss any matters of concern. However, a need was identified for a body responsible for the overall monitoring of standards of the Distinctions, independent of the Chairmen. In 1993 the Distinctions Moderating Board (DMB) was formed.

The Distinctions Moderating Board comprised five suitably experienced Fellows, plus two non-members of The Society (appointed principally to ensure that The Society kept abreast with developments in the educational/photographic world). Its primary role was to maintain equalisation of standards across the Distinctions and it incorporated the Validations Committee which had advised on educational matters, particularly with regard to the exemption schemes.

The Distinctions Advisory Board (DAB) later replaced the DMB and extended its role to advise and monitor all aspects of the Distinctions and make recommendations to Council. It first met in 1996 to discuss Quality Management and all documentation relating to the Distinctions was revised. In line with this process, a proposal was mooted to adopt a criteria-based marking system for the Distinctions in order to ensure a more consistent method of assessment and provide a more accurate system of feedback to applicants. Using the existing criteria, a marking sheet was produced which each assessor would complete for every applicant. Following a pilot in April 1997, this form of assessment has continued ever since.

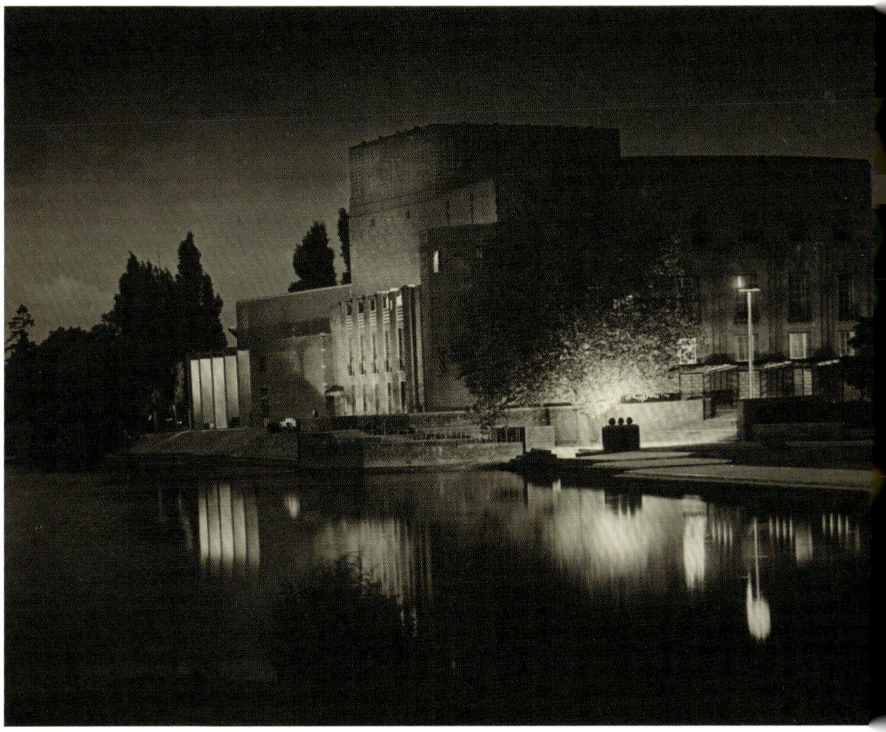

John Ahern FRPS The Shakespeare Theatre, Stratford upon Avon 1930

BURSARIES

HUW WAHL ARPS

The RPS Postgraduate Bursary supports postgraduate students undertaking photographic research or studying Masters Courses in photography at UK colleges and universities. The bursary winner in 2011 was Huw Wahl ARPS.

"Instead of doing a BA I became a bicycle courier" said Wahl "and to express myself creatively I took photographs". Later he gained a place at the University of Central Lancashire for an MA in photography. He said "The RPS Postgraduate Bursary gave me a supportive backing. Without it I would never have achieved my final project".

For his MA Wahl investigated the use of photography within the Israel/Palestine conflict. He interviewed photographers there from photojournalists to activists and artists who had "experimental and philosophical considerations for the potential of the image in their work". Wahl said that through listening to them the project opened up questions regarding representation, victimhood and photography in the media. He made images with his black and white film camera, questioning his role within the spectacle of oppression, and edited his audio recording alongside his images. His aim was to produce a piece that would encourage the viewer to question the photographer's role.

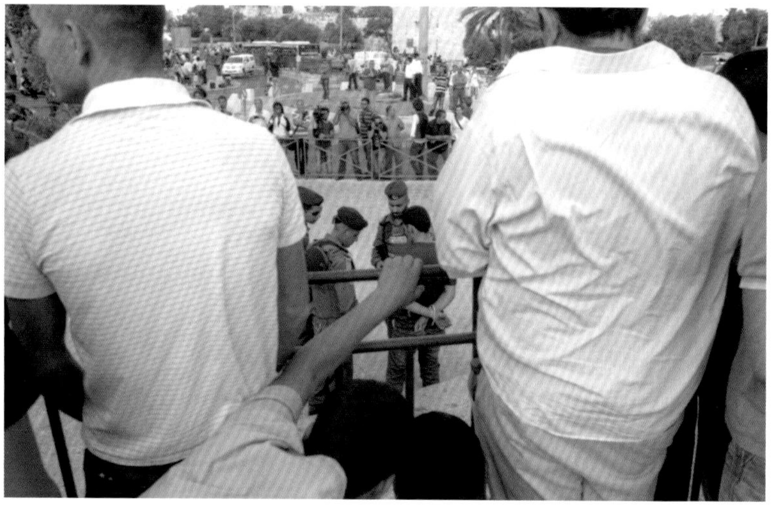

Wahl's work has been shown internationally in several film festivals. Since gaining his MA he has worked on projects involving film and photography inspired by disciplines such as anthropology and documentary. He is part of a collective called 'Castles Build in Sand' who produced a documentary about the DIY music culture in Manchester, and is interested in collaborations where he can "further explore photography in a questioning manner, through the mixture of text, film, sound and image".

Monica Weller FRPS

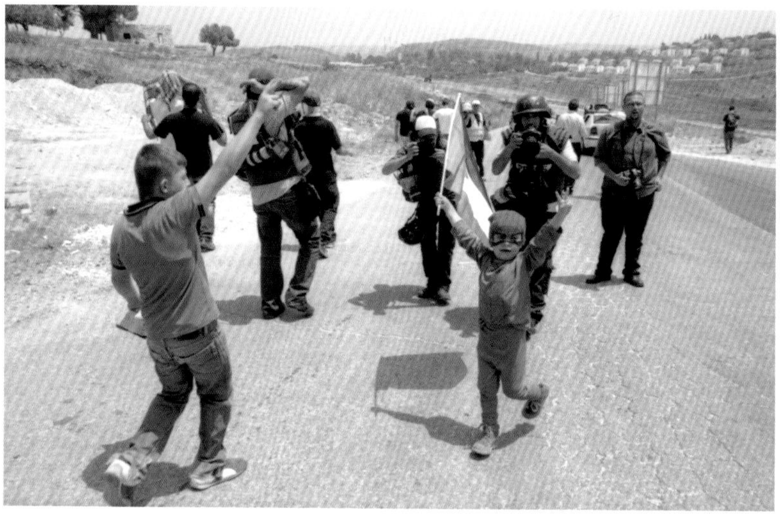

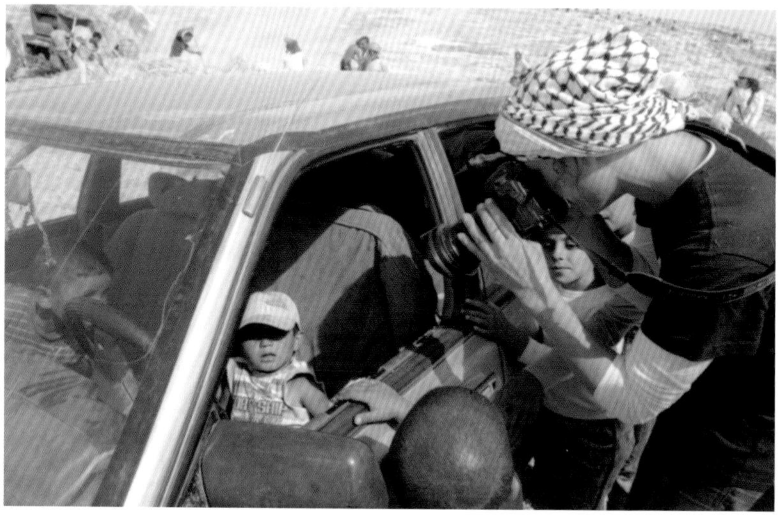

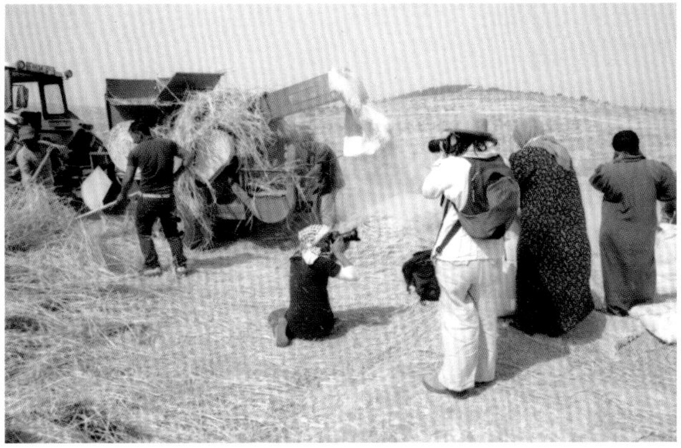

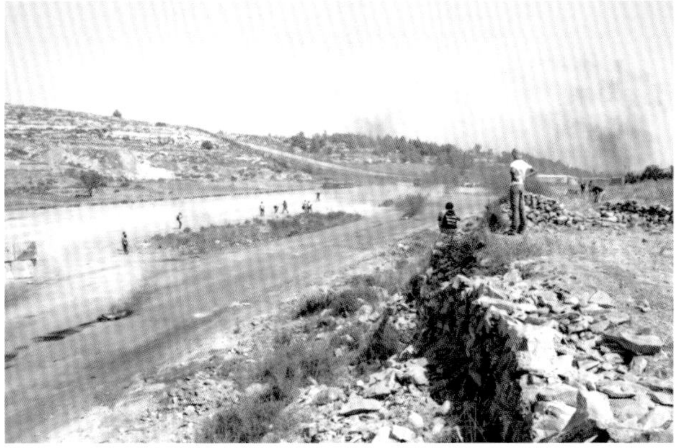

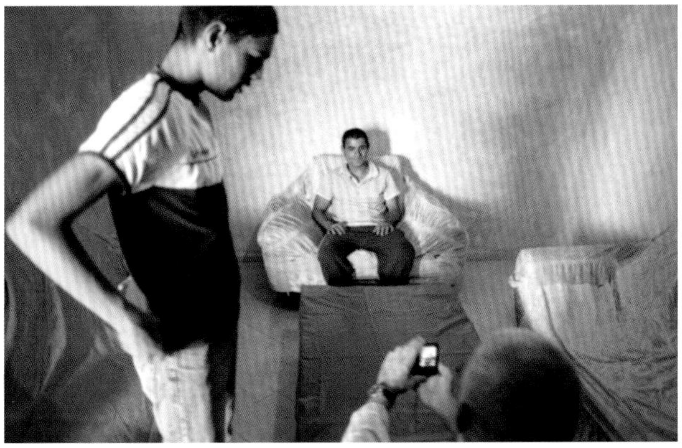

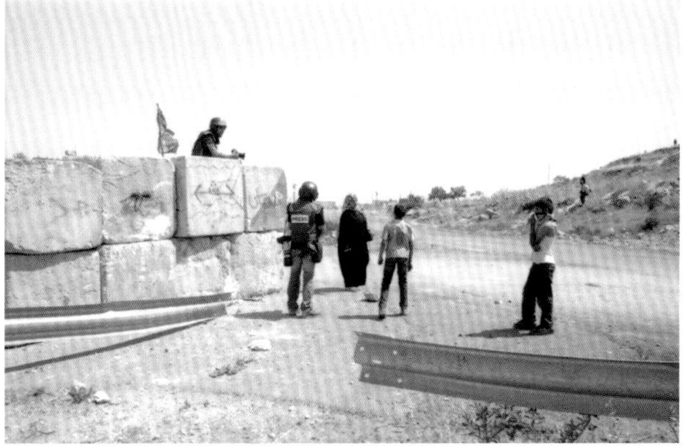

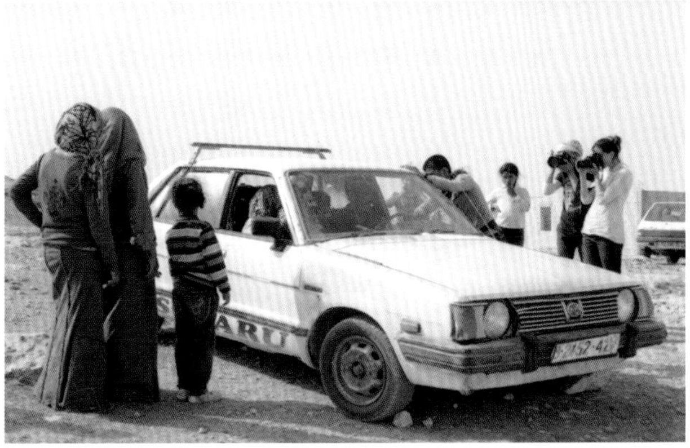

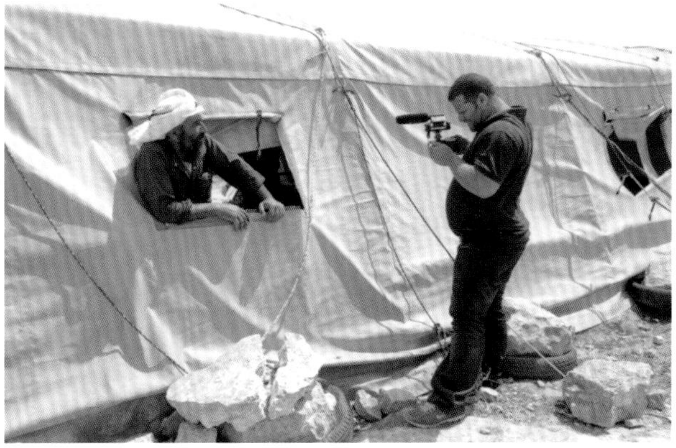

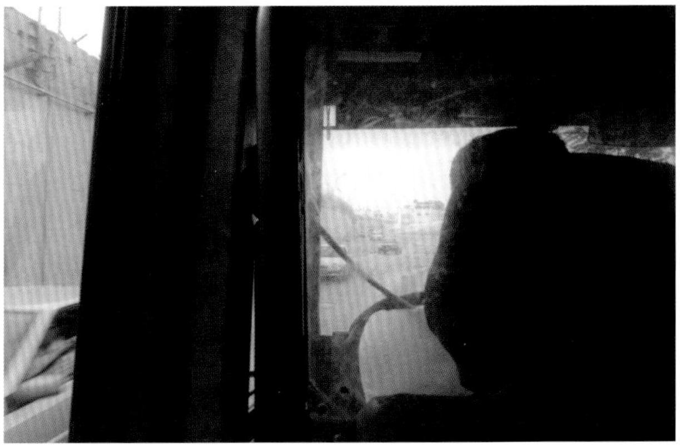

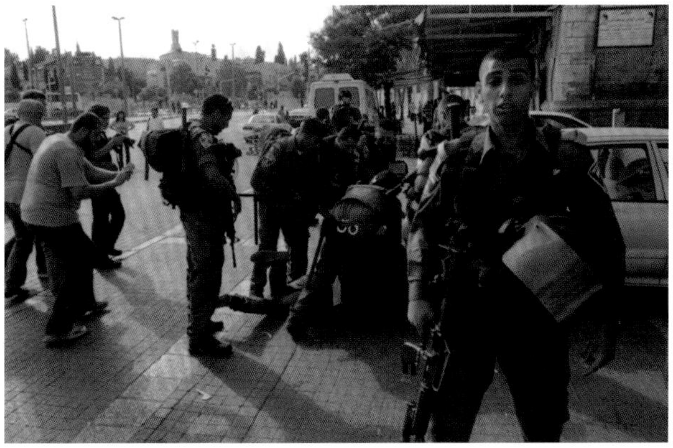

BURSARIES

NEIL HALL

The Joan Wakelin Bursary offers photographers £2,000 for the best proposal for a photographic essay on an overseas social documentary issue. It is supported by *The Guardian*. The photographic essay is published by *Guardian News* and *Media* and The RPS *Journal*. Neil Hall was the recipient of the award in 2011.

The Atacama desert in Northen Chile is the driest place in the world. Local people there are reversing the trend of desertification by harvesting coastal fog in large nets. "Fog water is pure for drinking, useful for agriculture and has been used to transform arid patches of desert to fertile land" said Hall. Water which is in high demand from mining industries is currently piped hundreds of miles from the Andes mountains. "Harvesting fog water has the potential to change parts of the desert into gardens, offering a clean, cheap and sustainable resource for the future".

Hall, a freelance photographer who has worked in local and international news and editorial photography since 2006 said, "I found the Wakelin Bursary to be an excellent showcase for my work and offers a chance for photographers to display their abilities and fulfill their potential". He now covers all aspects of London news as a stringer for the Reuters news agency alongside regular commissions from UK newspapers and magazines.

Since being awarded the bursary Hall's work won First Prize in the Live News category at the 2011 Press Photographer's Year awards. He was shortlisted as the 2012 news photographer of the year by the UK Picture Editors Guild.

Monica Weller FRPS

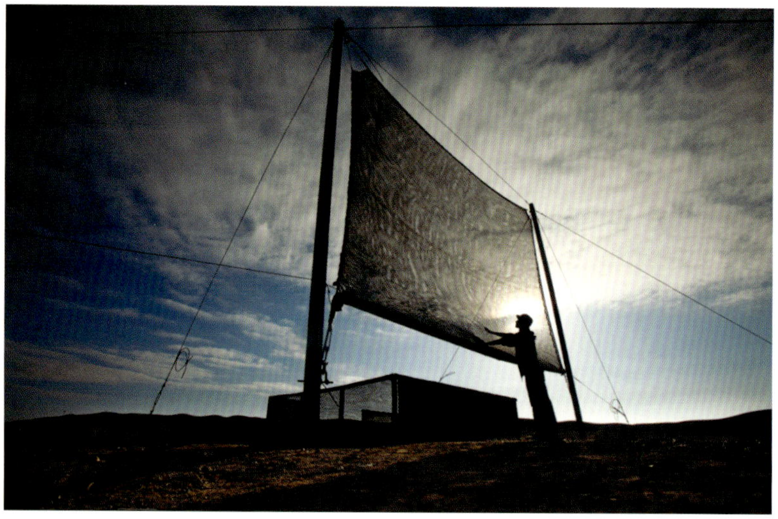

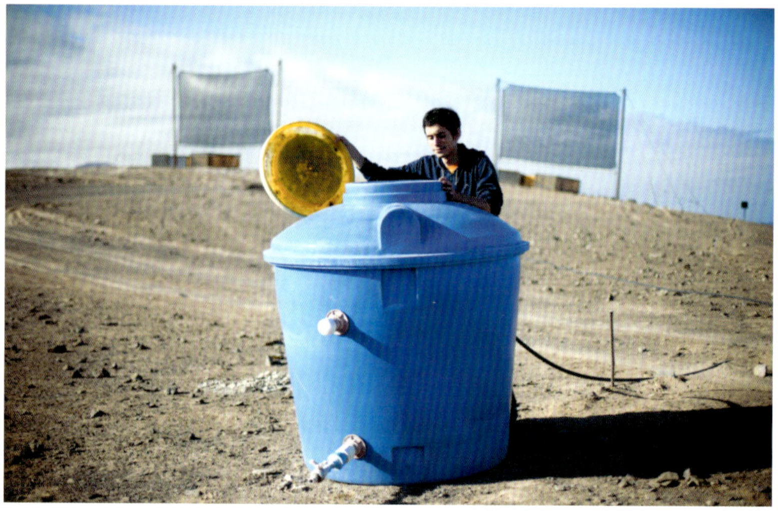

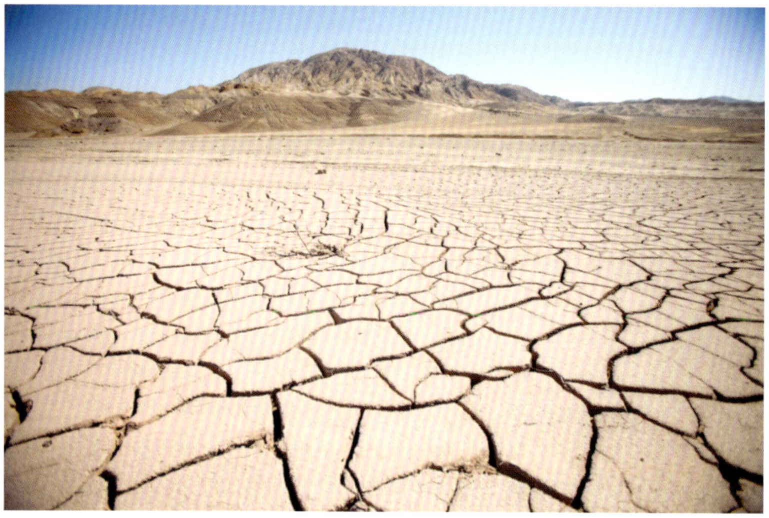

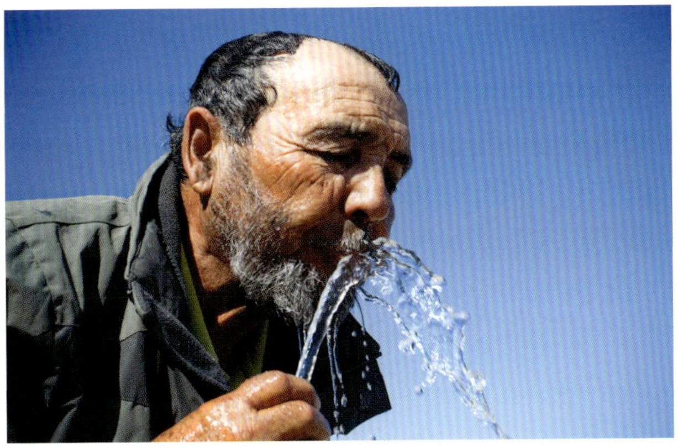

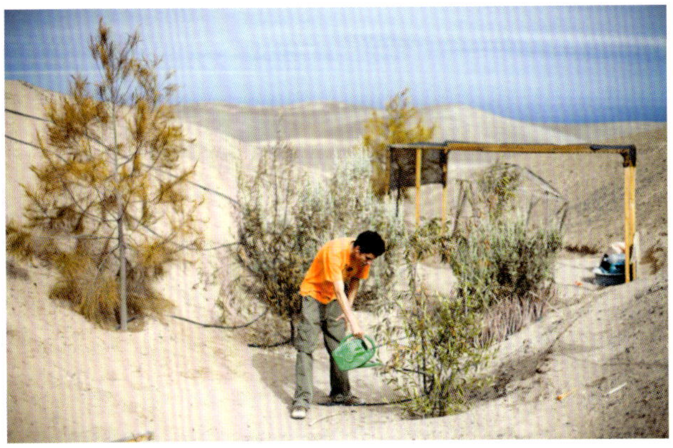

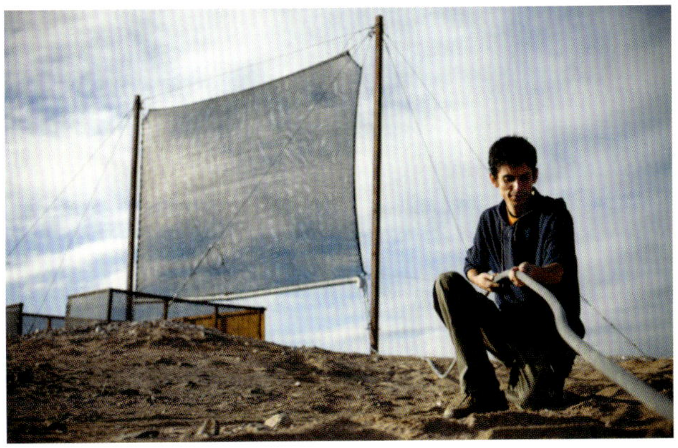

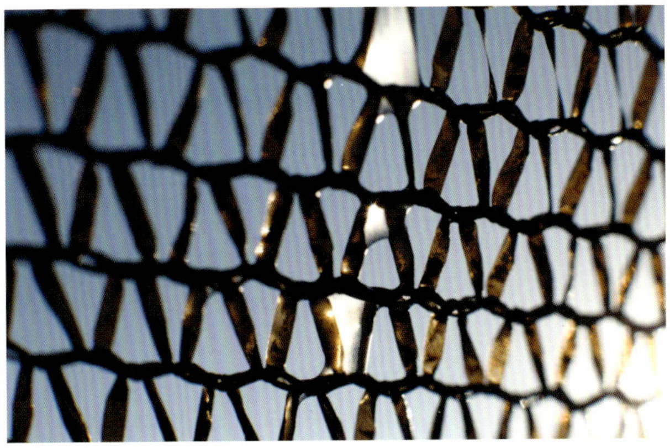

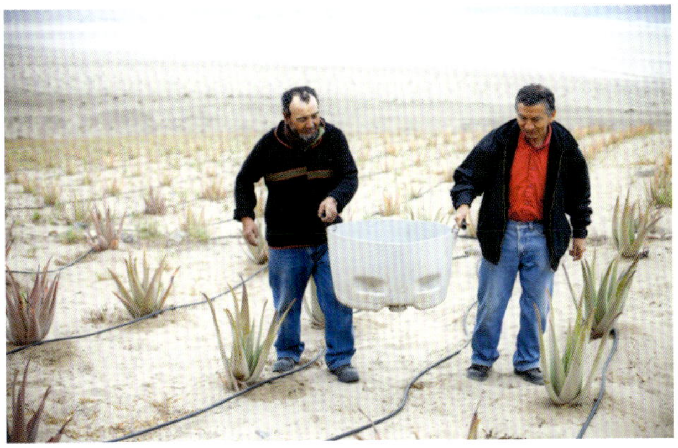

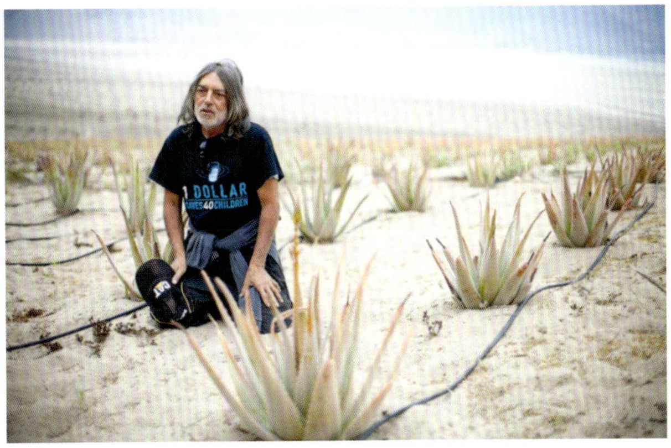
1 DOLLAR

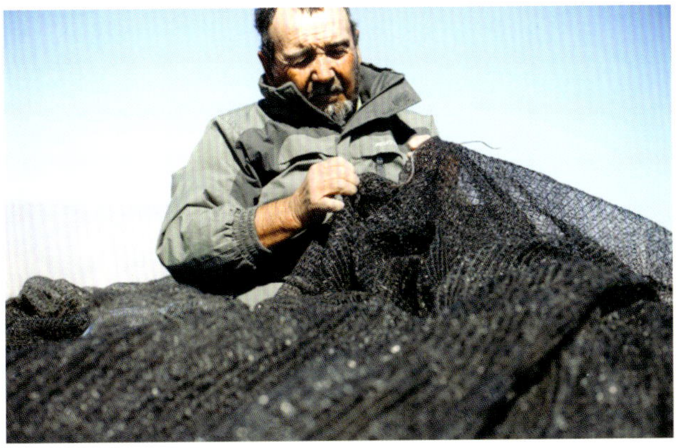

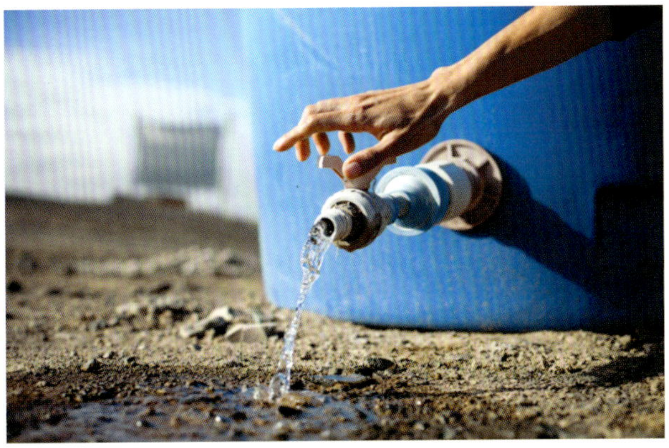

THE CONSERVATION AND PRESERVATION OF JOSEPH NICÉPHORE NIÉPCE'S PHOTOGRAPHS

PHILIPPA WRIGHT, FORMER CURATOR OF PHOTOGRAPHS, NATIONAL MEDIA MUSEUM

The three Niépce photographic plates from The Royal Photographic Society (RPS) Collection held at the National Media Museum (NMeM) are vitally important in the early history and development of photography. Titled *Le Cardinal d'Amboise* (1826), *Un Clair de Lune* (Moonlight) (c.1827), and *Christ Carrying his Cross* (c.1827) they belong to a small number of pre-1839 photographic artefacts that are of the highest importance for the world's cultural and photographic heritage.

These Niépce plates were the focus of an extensive scientific and historical research project conducted between 2006-2010 by the Getty Conservation Institute (GCI), Los Angeles, USA, and the National Media Museum (NMeM), Bradford. This culminated in ground-breaking results being presented at the *Niépce in England* conference held at the NMeM in October 2010.

The provenance of the three plates is well documented. In 1827 Niépce came to England to visit his ailing brother. He hoped to present his experiments in photography to the Royal Society of London however these presentations, as far as is known, never took place. Niépce returned to France in 1828 leaving the plates with his friend and supporter Franz Bauer. He died in 1833 unrecognized for his invention. The plates were given to the RPS and added to its Collection in 1924, moving to the National Museum of Photography, Film and Television, now the NMeM in 2002.

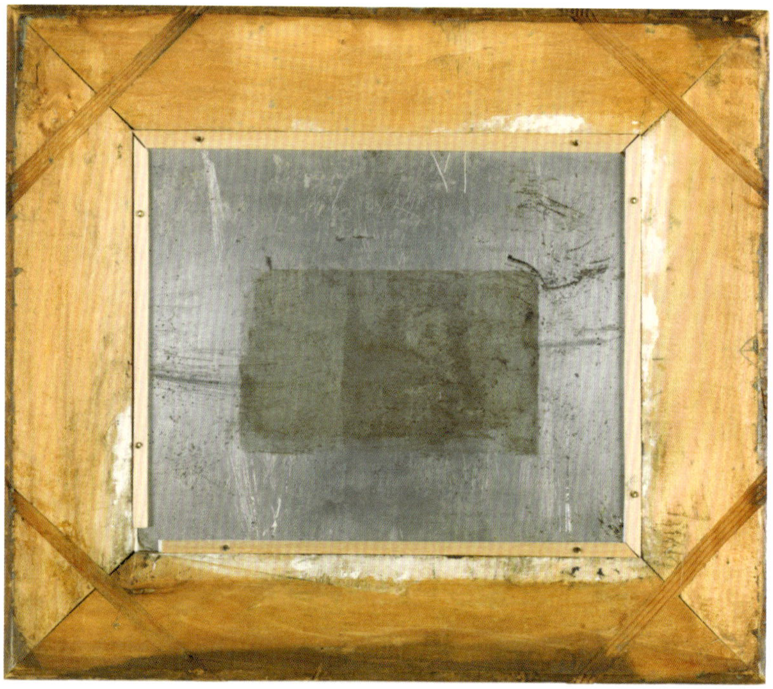

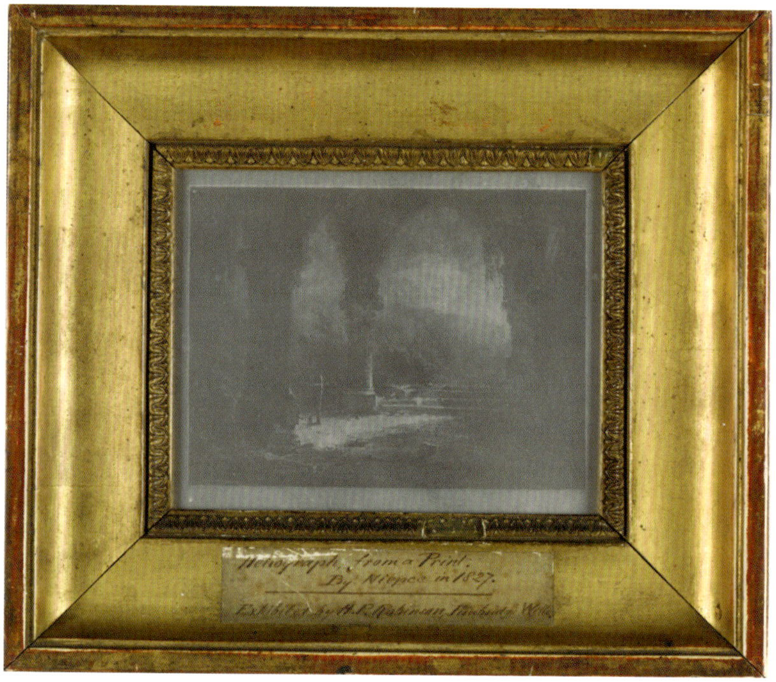

Between 2007-2010 the GCI team with key members Dr Dusan Stulik, senior scientist, and Art Kaplan, research laboratory associate, carried out scientific analysis of the plates. The *Cardinal* and *Christ* plates had been taken out of their frames prior to the RPS Collection being moved to the NMeM in 2002. In 2008, the project team made the decision to open the frame containing *Un Clair de Lune* in order to carry out analysis of all the plates.

An array of experts from different disciplines was invited to assess the plates, their frames and associated elements. This also included Isabella Kocum, frame conservator at the National Gallery, London, Peter Bower, a forensic paper historian, London, and Philip Gilhooley, an independent fingerprint consultant and lecturer in forensic science at Liverpool John Moores University. Their knowledge confirmed that the frames, papers and fingerprints were contemporary to the plates.

Scientific analysis revealed the unexpected discovery that the plates were each produced by different photographic processes, two of which were previously unrecorded. The *Le Cardinal d'Amboise* was, as expected, a heliogravure on pewter. However *Christ Carrying his Cross* was also made using bitumen which was lightly etched and was itself a unique image and had never been inked or used as a printing plate. The analysis of *Un Clair de Lune* was a revelation, for it was made not with bitumen but with resin obtained by heating oil of lavender, and had not been etched. It was a unique image, ironically, taken from an engraving of an original painting by Daguerre. This meant that a third photographic process had been

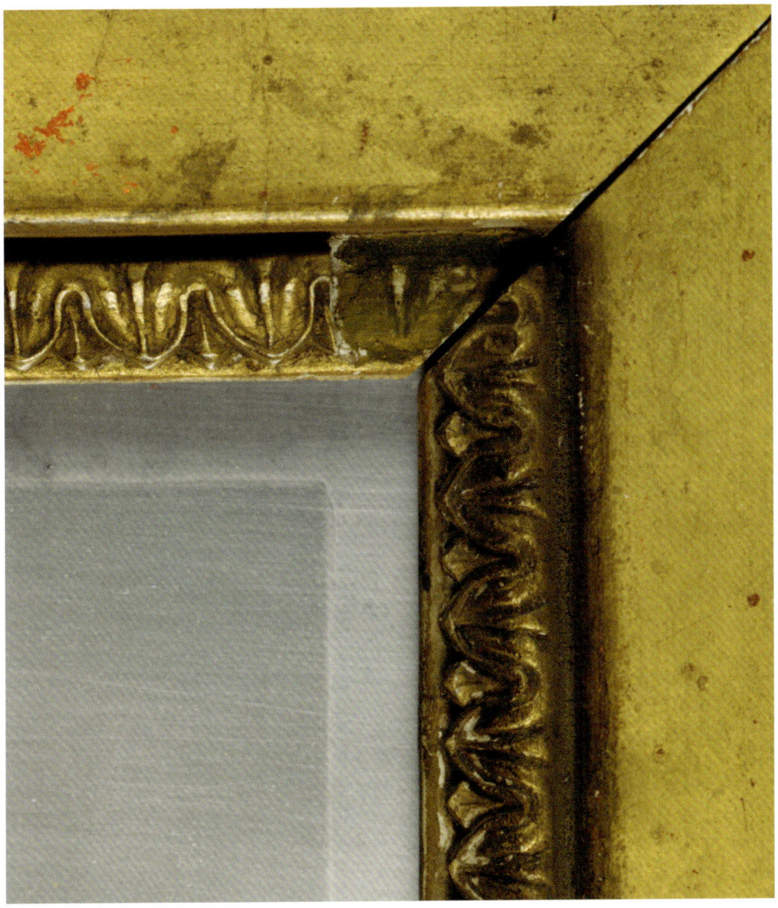

developed by Niépce that was similar to his physautotype process, although an example of it was not previously thought to be extant. The first mention of the physautotype process only occurs in 1830, much later than the date of this plate (c.1827).

The future preservation of these plates was central to the investigation. During the conservation process the maximum amount of information about the photographs was gathered. Great effort was taken to ensure that the integrities of the original materials were not compromised, but enhanced by sympathetic conservation methods and materials. All constituent parts were conserved where necessary and appropriate materials and methods for reassembly were used.

The ground breaking discoveries were announced to the photographic, scientific, curatorial and conservation communities at the *Niépce in England* conference in 2010. The plates, conserved papers and frames, and illustrations of the research and scientific analysis undertaken were displayed at the NMeM throughout the conference. This gave the delegates a once in a life time opportunity to view the plates out of their frames.

After the conference, in 2011, Susie Clark, the lead conservator for the project, and Isabella Kocum reassembled the plates into their frames having left the conserved frames to 'off gas' for several months. Prior to reframing they constructed a prototype frame using a steel plate as a substitute for the photographic plates. This worked well and this prototype was used as the model for reframing the plates.

Separately between 2003 and 2006 the GCI team had researched, designed and constructed a highly sophisticated low oxygen and stable environment display case for the long time preservation of the 'world's first photograph' by Niépce, which is in the Gernsheim Collection at the Harry Ransom Center, Texas. The NMeM curators and collaborating conservators approached the same GCI team with the idea of developing a similar preservation strategy for the three RPS plates.

The resulting display case, funded by The Royal Photographic Society's Colour, Historical and Imaging Science Groups, and developed jointly by the NMeM-GCI team and a number of other UK specialists and consultants will:

- provide a stable low-oxygen environment for both the display and long term preservation of all three plates
- will allow for the monitoring and recording of temperature, pressure and light levels and will provide a means, in the future, for monitoring oxygen levels inside of the display case
- be equipped with an external, low-UV, low-heat lighting system with case design also allowing for the installation of an internal LED lighting system if needed
- require minimal maintenance and monitoring. The case will perform for several years before needing maintenance
- will be easy to move within the NMeM with the plates secured within the case, and facilitate transport outside of the museum
- provide a high level of security against theft, burglary or unauthorized handling.

During 2012 a prototype case was constructed to determine the best viewing angle for the plates and the completed case will be installed during 2013.

ACQUISITIONS TO THE SOCIETY COLLECTION

Queen Victoria's husband, Prince Albert, a staunch supporter of The Society, suggested that The Society collect photographs to record the rapid technical progress. This was later supplemented by books and apparatus. John Dudley Johnson, twice President and Curator of the Collection for 31 years from 1924, collected currently and retrospectively, steering the Collection in the direction of pictorialism, establishing one of the world's most important photographic collections. The inclusion of contextual information and artefacts makes the Collection of extraordinary value to researchers.

In June 2002 a Heritage Lottery Fund grant was announced transferring the Collection to the National Museum of Photography, Film and Television, now the National Media Museum, part of the National Museum of Science and Industry. Combined with the Museum's Collection it is recognised as one of the most important worldwide.

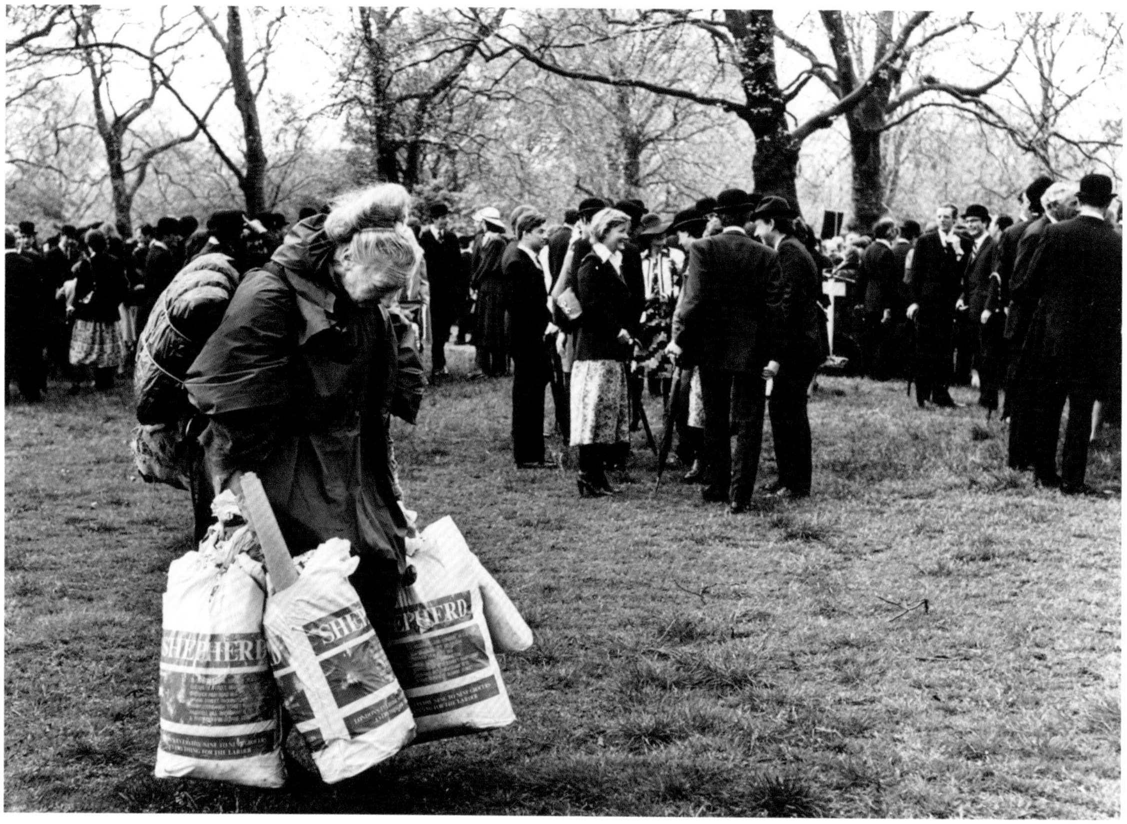

'Hats off to a Lady' (acquired 2011: The Royal Photographic Society Collection at the National Media Museum)

For some time before the transfer proactive acquisitions were rare, however, the Agreement referred to a 'live' and growing collection. In 2010 the Acquisitions Group, with representatives of The Society and Museum, established an Acquisitions Policy, with initial acquisitions in 2011. Work is acquired through an invitation to donate images or other items (eg. books or scientific equipment). Following established practice contextual information about the member, their photography and Society role is included.

The Museum will accept: one Fellowship each year; an image from new Honorary Fellows; the Gold Medal image from the International Print Exhibition; a summary of each President's term, an image and portrait. The Acquisitions Group has invited a few members whose photography is at the highest level who are significant to The Society's history; or their activity and work has either materially enhanced or interpreted modern photographic techniques or research; or they have considerably contributed to the public understanding of photography. The Group also considers the work of recently deceased Fellows who fit these criteria.

Bill Carden FRPS

Bill played a significant role in The Distinction process. A member of the inaugural Licentiate Panel in 1972, he took over as Chair in 1982, successfully managing the Panel until 1991. He was invited to join the newly formed Distinctions Advisory Board in 1993, and chairing a working party that, with professional guidance, developed the criteria based marking system for Licentiate Panel assessment. He served on Council from 1990-92. Six images were acquired after his death in 2009.

A master of observation, capturing the moment and monochrome printing Bill wrote about his photography: 'My pictures do not extensively make a comment which is the real world of the Documentary Photographer, nevertheless there is more than a brave attempt to communicate something of importance about my subjective observations and a message to leave the viewer with some understanding of the time when the pictures were taken. Many of my pictures may appear organised, even theatrical – the essential ingredient is the ability to "will" something to happen when the stage is set. There is no resort to change anything, certainly not for Pictorial reasons, only to tell the truth with sincerity.'

SOCIETY EXHIBITIONS

The traditions of the International Print and Projected Image Exhibitions have continued as The Society's Exhibition programme has expanded in the last three years, adding an International Images for Science Exhibition and a London 2012 Cultural Olympiad competition.

The International Print Exhibition, reaching its 155th year in 2012, continues to raise debate through its intent to show new and innovative work alongside more traditional approaches. The Projected Image Exhibition received its last Slide entries in 2010 and now receiving more entries it continues to flourish, and like the Print Exhibition new work is encouraged. Images from the 2010, 2011 and 2012 Exhibitions together with the 2011 and 2013 Members' Print Exhibitions are shown on the following pages and demonstrate how image making is continuing to develop. The 2013 Members' Print Exhibition, held biennially since 2003, used the new on-line facility for initial selection leading to a touring Print Exhibition.

Awarded the London 2012 'Inspire Mark' Celebrate a Summer of Sport was The Society's contribution to the Cultural Olympiad. This provided an opportunity for The Society to establish an on-line entry facility for ongoing projects. Selected images from the final London Exhibition are shown at the end of this section.

inspired by London 2012

In 2011, The International Images for Science Exhibition was held for the first time. Although within the Exhibition Department's remit it is showcased in the Science section of this Portfolio.

In addition to Society Exhibitions, Groups, Regions and Overseas Chapters organise a wide range of other Exhibitions over the course of the year; and in Fenton House, individual members have the opportunity to present exhibitions of their own photography.

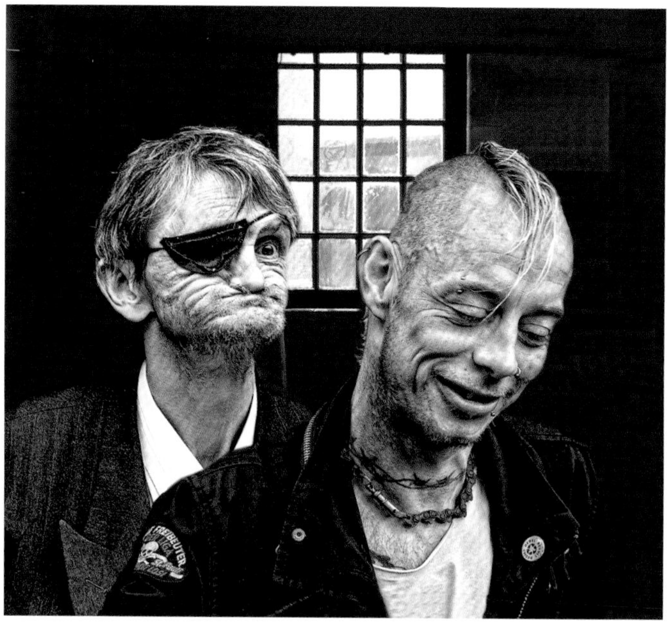

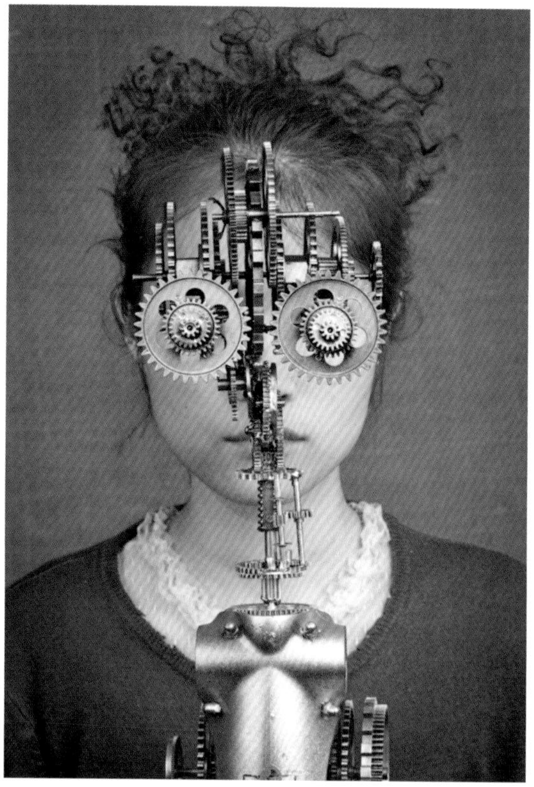

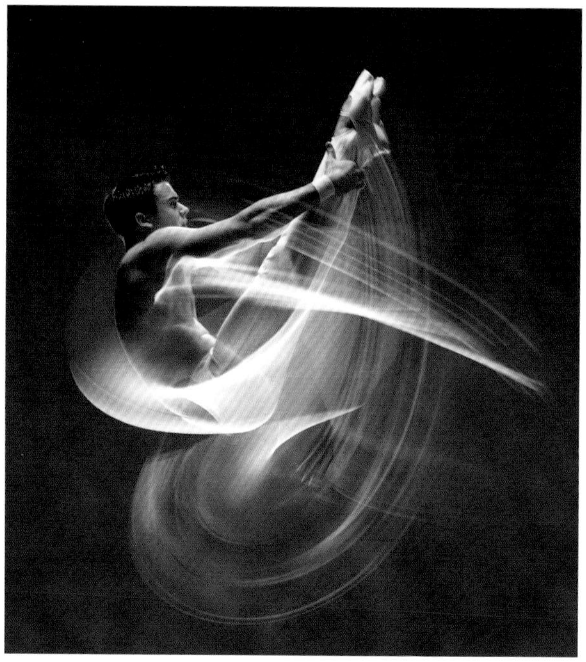

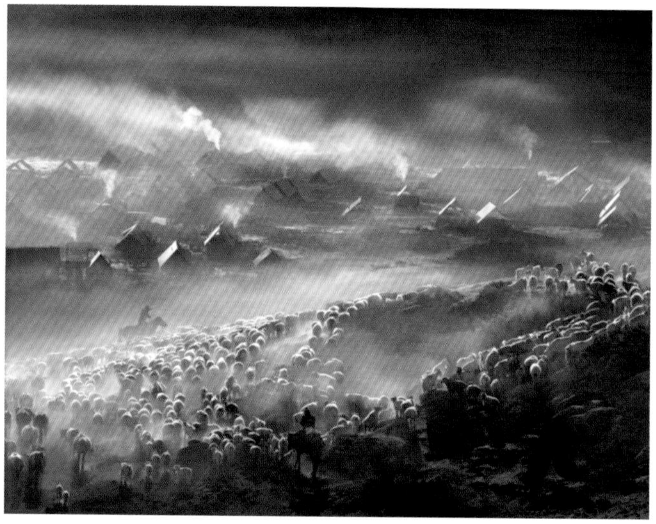

SANDY CLELAND FRPS UK
RAY MASSEY FRPS UK

MICHAEL RYAN CHINA
ZHANG HONGLIN CHINA

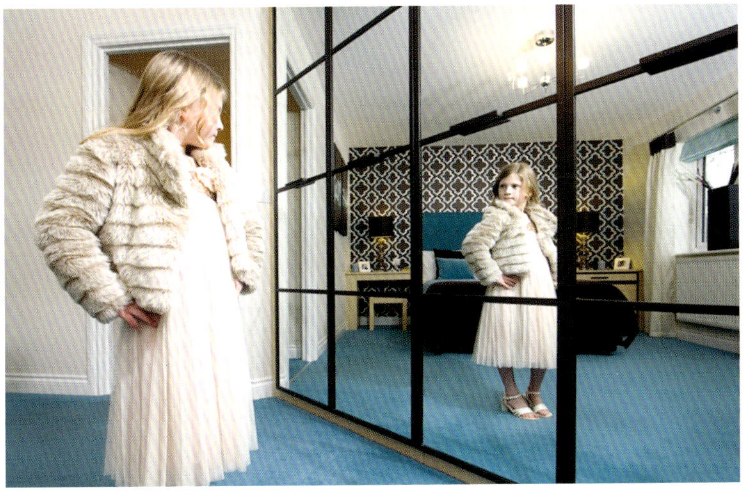

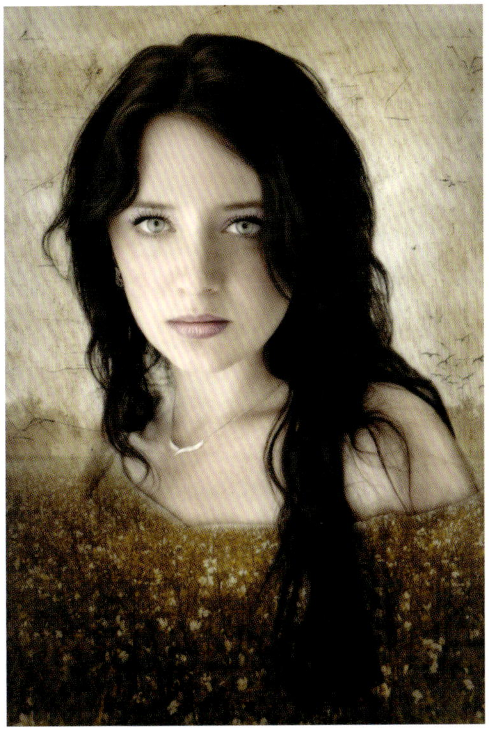

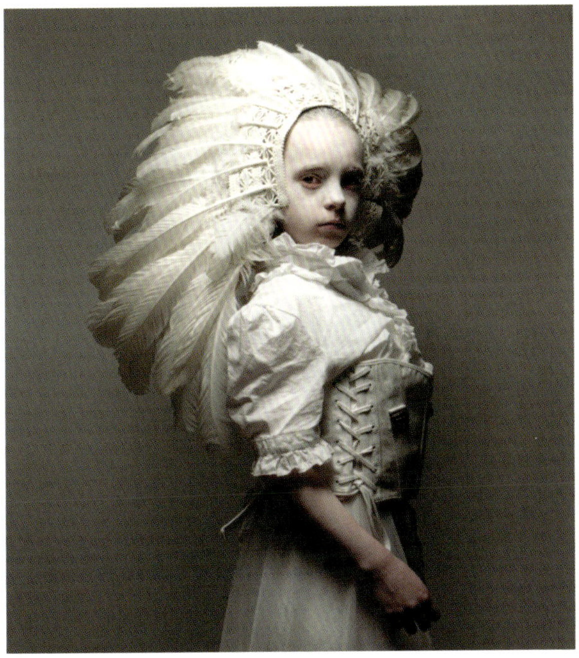

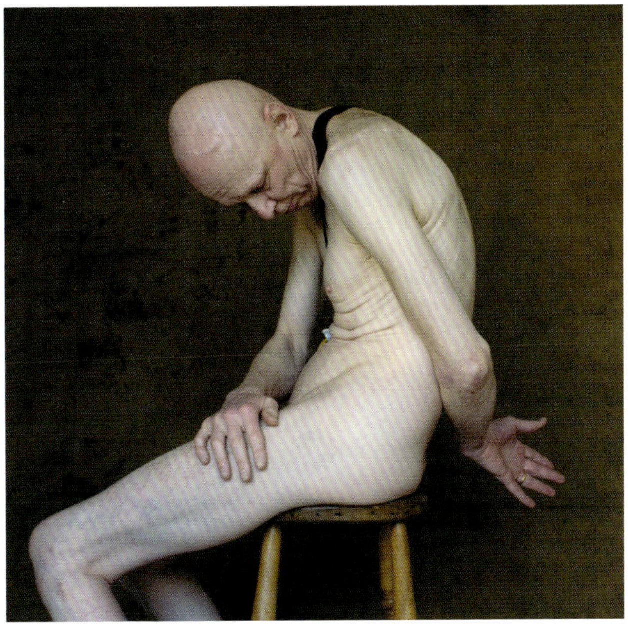

CHARLEY MURRELL UK
JUSTYNA NERYNG UK

ROB EVANS UK
CLARE PARK UK

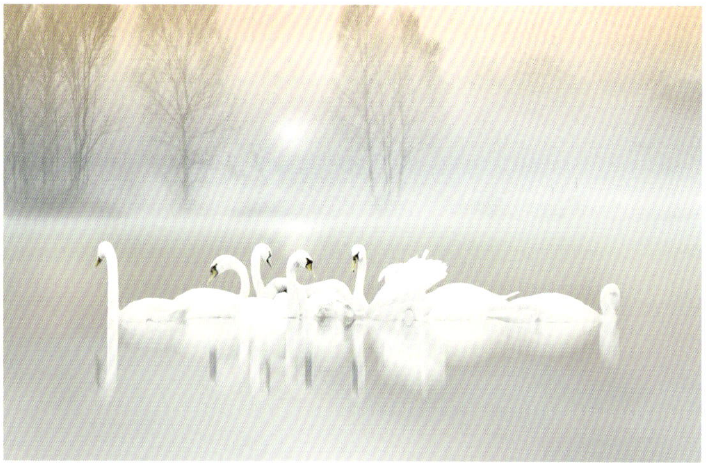

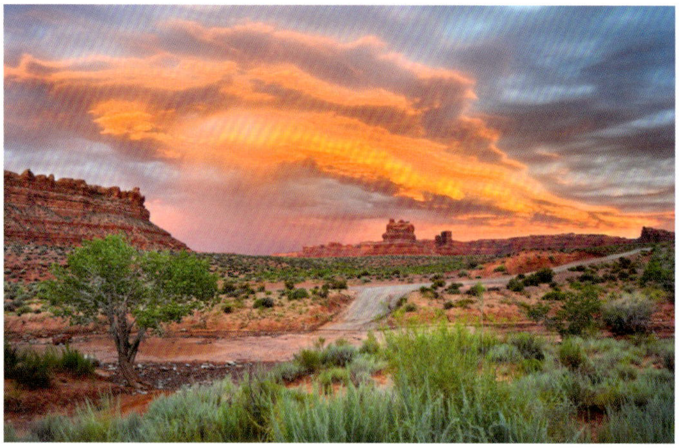

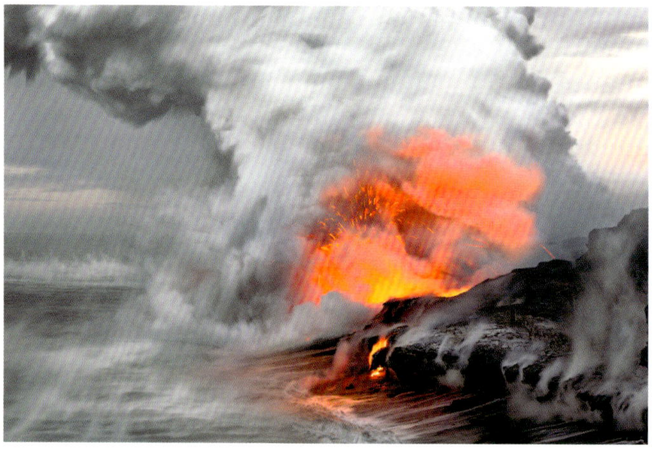

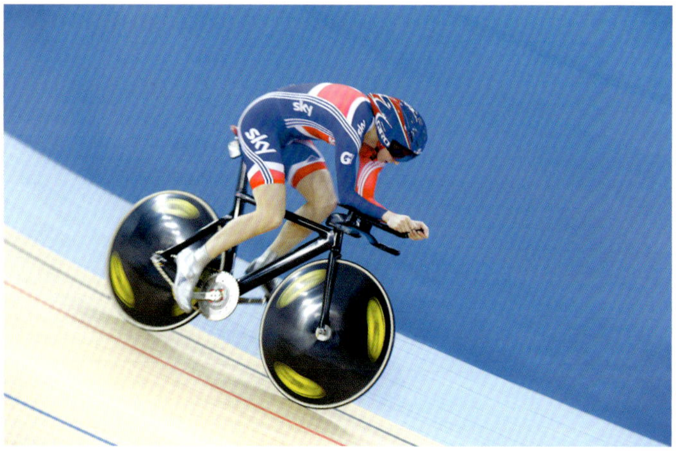

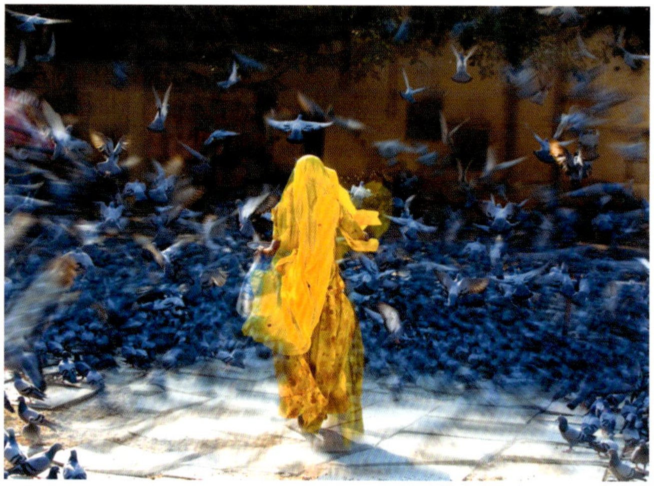

MICHAEL MAGUIRE FRPS UK

SAM CORNISH UK

DAVID WILKINSON ARPS UK

PETER LIK FRPS USA

FAT CHEN HONG KONG

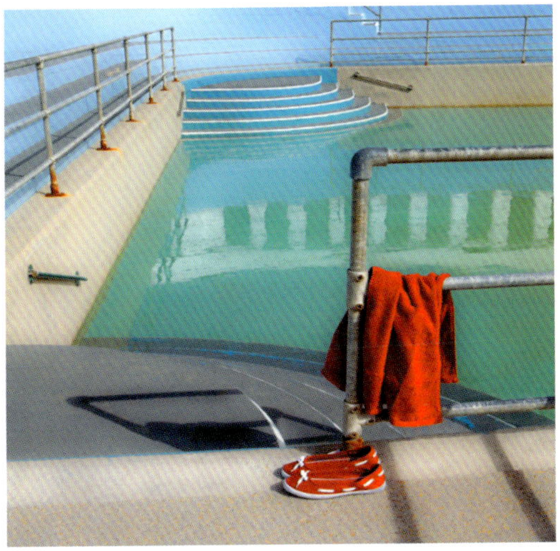

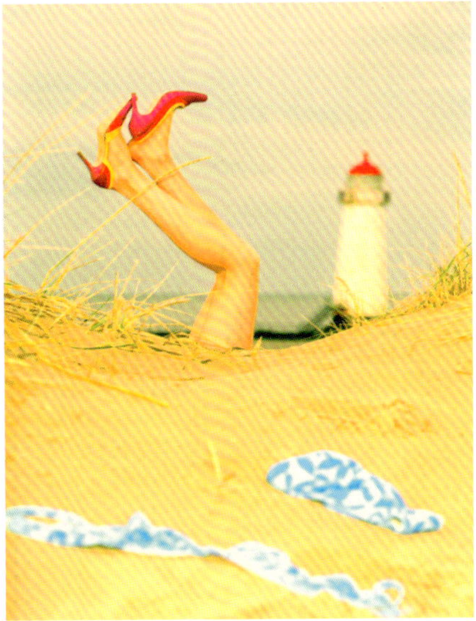

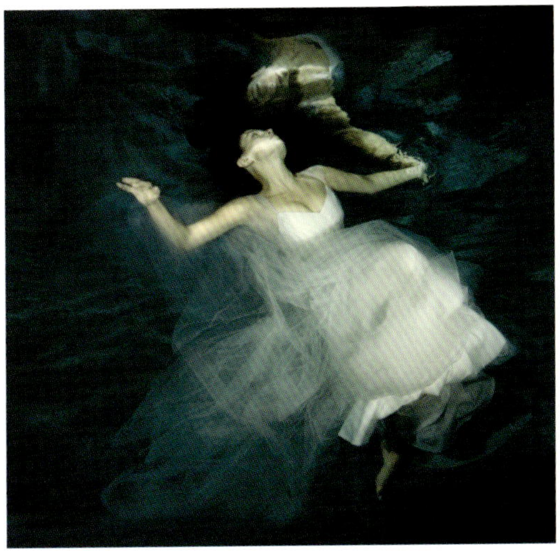

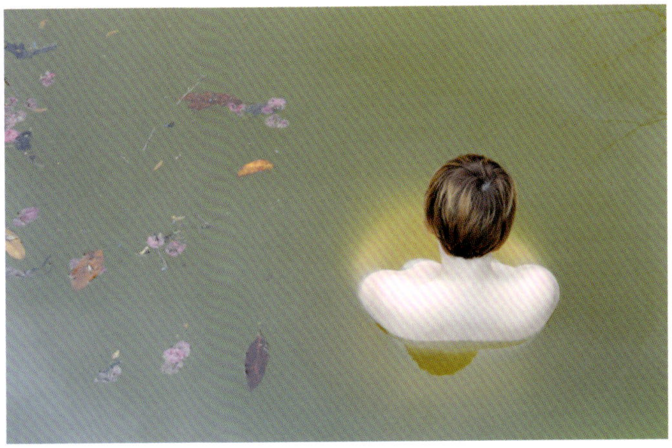

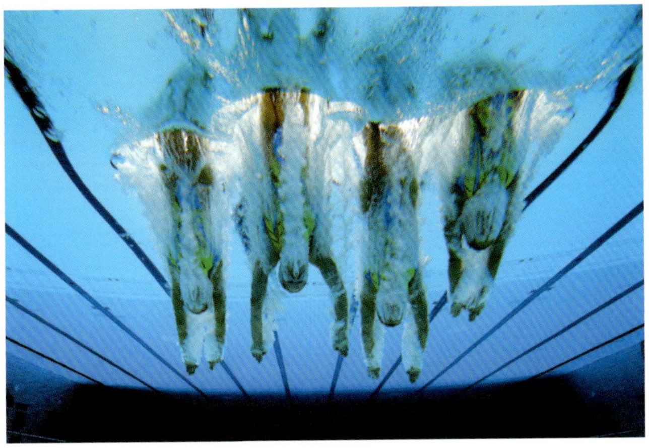

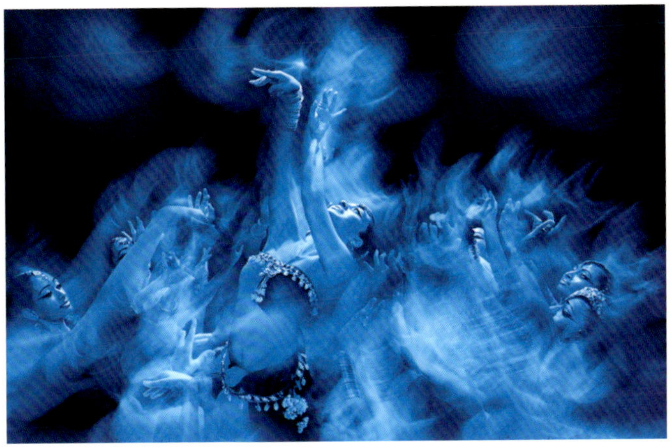

SUSAN BROWN FRPS UK
SERGEY BUSLENKO FRPS UKRAINE
MARC ASPLAND FRPS UK

GARY SHERIDAN ARPS UK
MICHELLE CHAPLOW LRPS SPAIN
HENRY RAJAKARUNA SRI LANKA

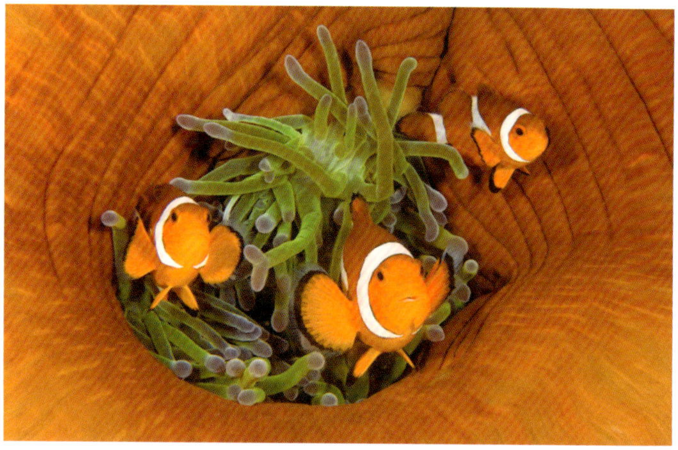

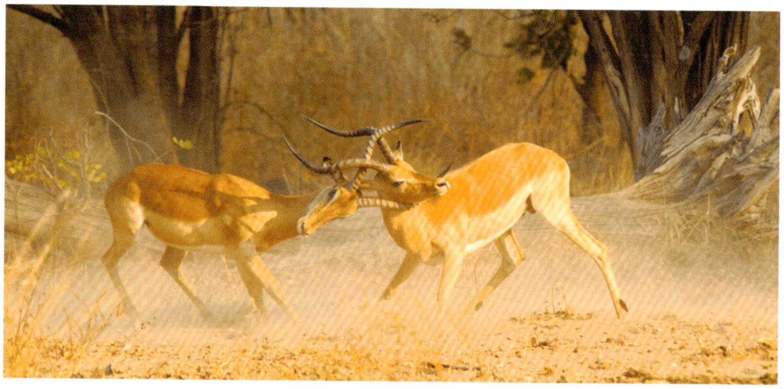

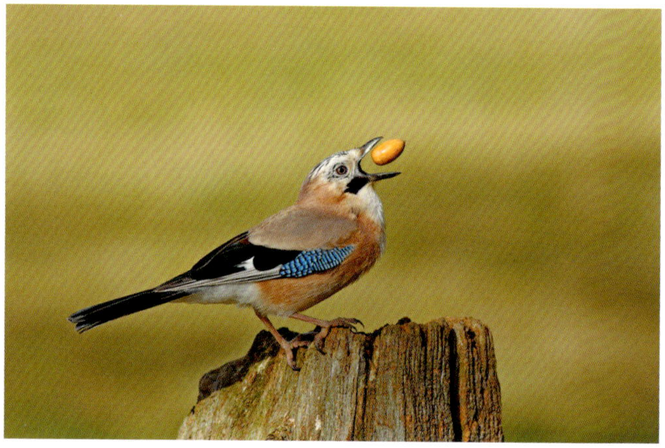

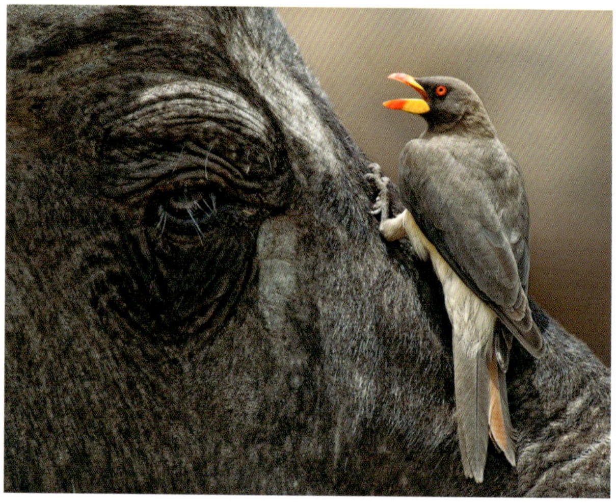

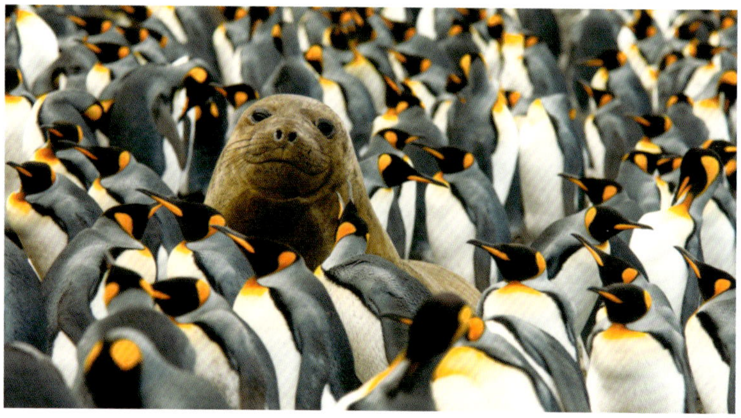

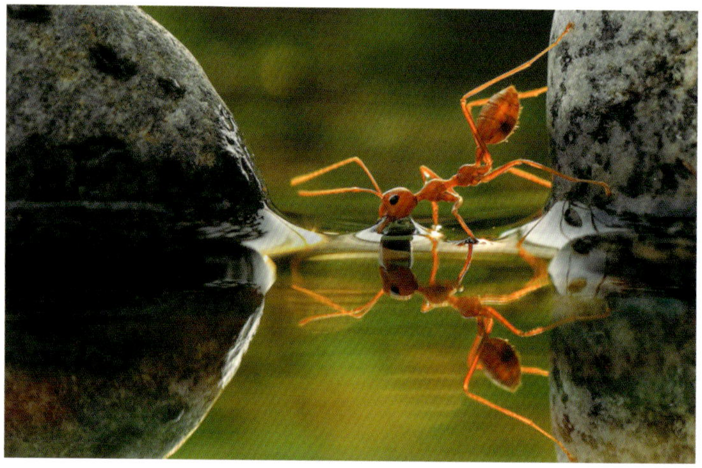

LEN DEELEY FRPS UK
MIKE WILKES FRPS UK
GUNTHER RIEHLE GERMANY

GORDON UPRICHARD UK
IAN WHISTON UK
VINCENTIUS FERDINAND INDONESIA

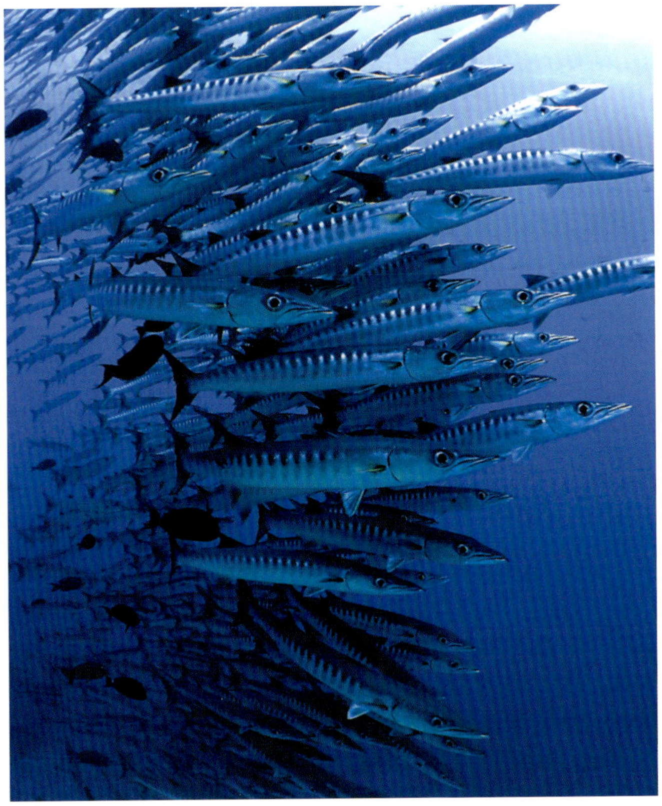

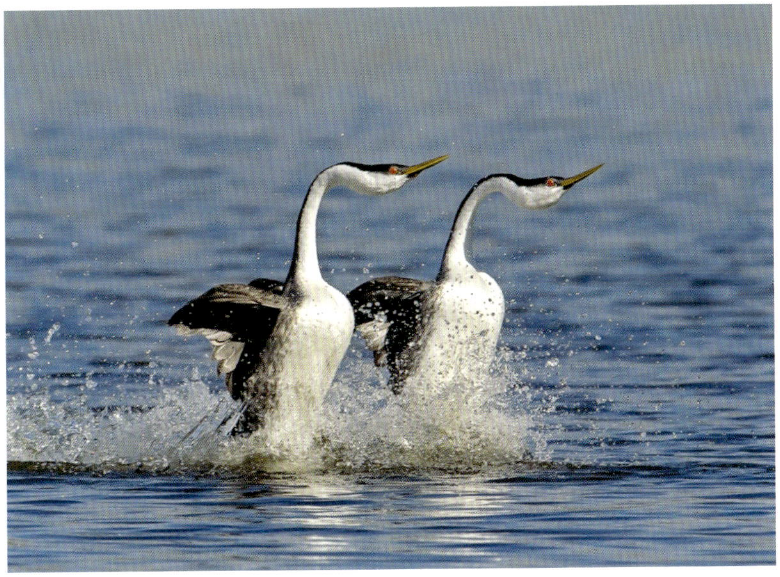

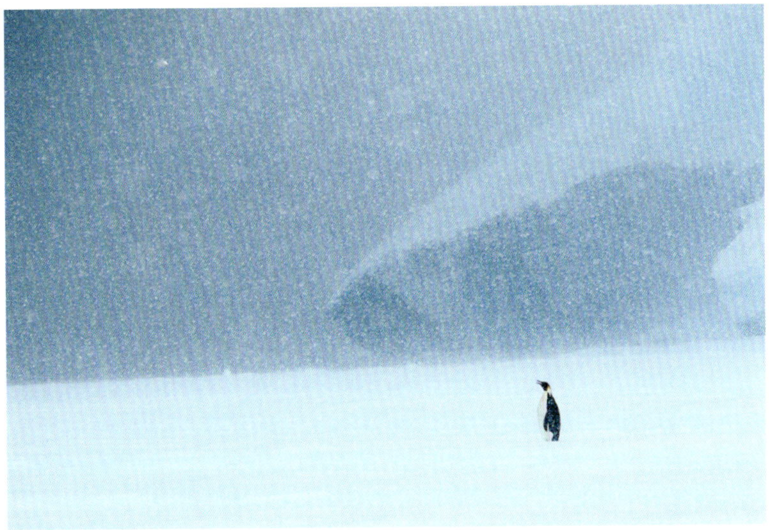

YU MA USA

JACKIE CAMPBELL EIRE

ANDREW GASSON ARPS UK

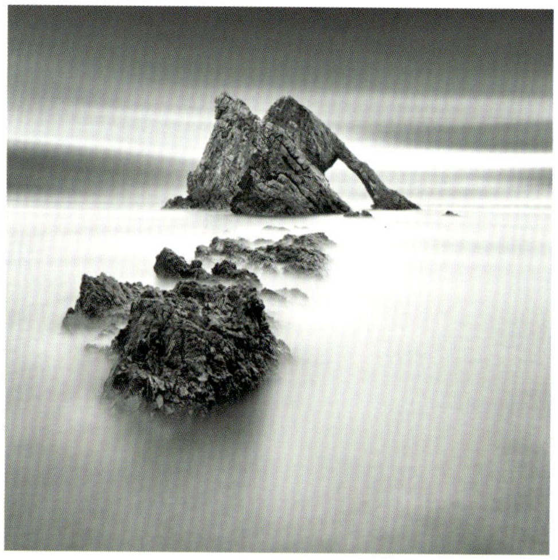

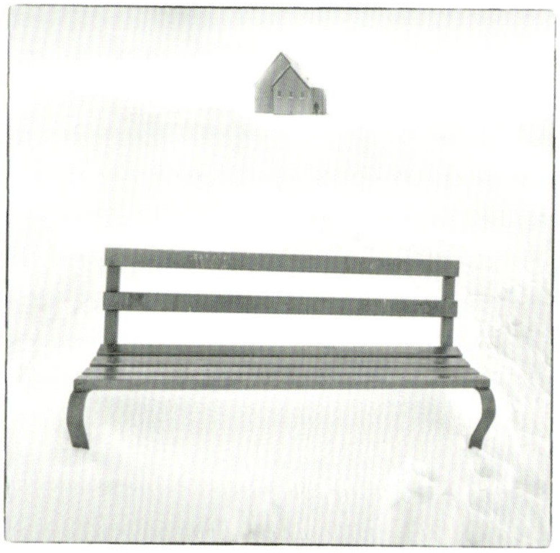

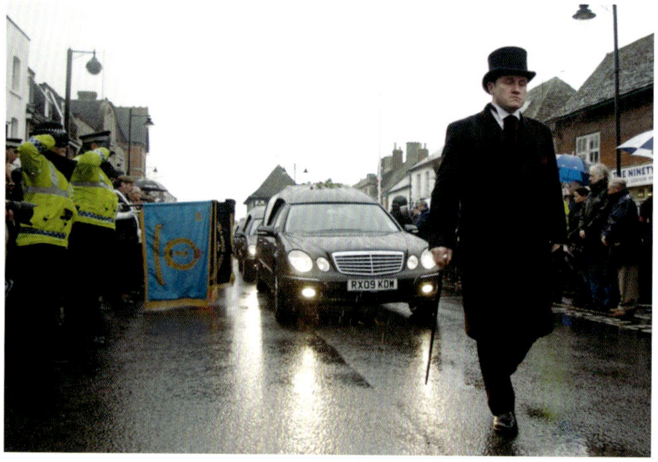

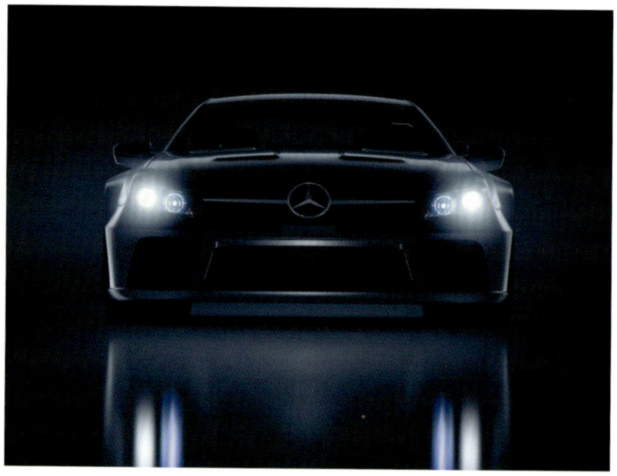

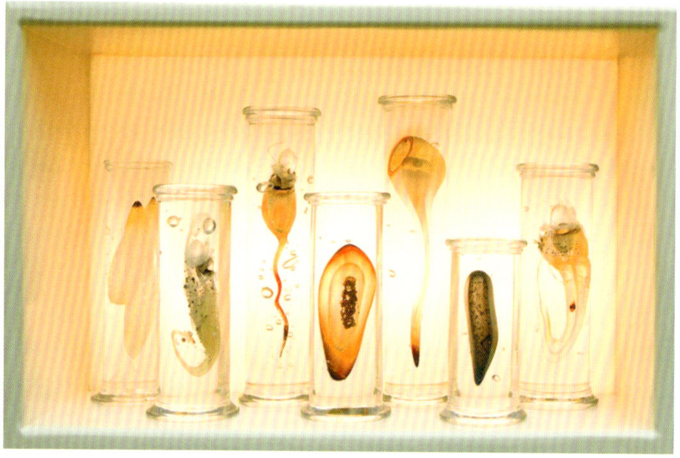

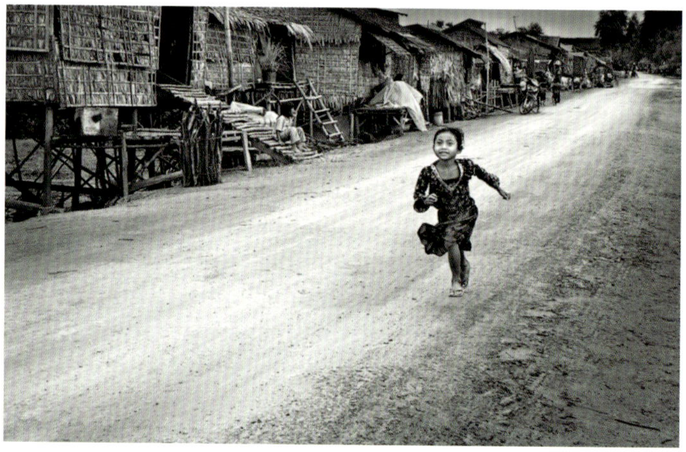

MICHEL RAJKOVIC FRANCE
DAVID PEARCE UK
YIN WONG ARPS UK

JOHN ROBERTSON UK
CHRIS BAILEY FRPS UK
CHRISSIE WESTGATE FRPS UK

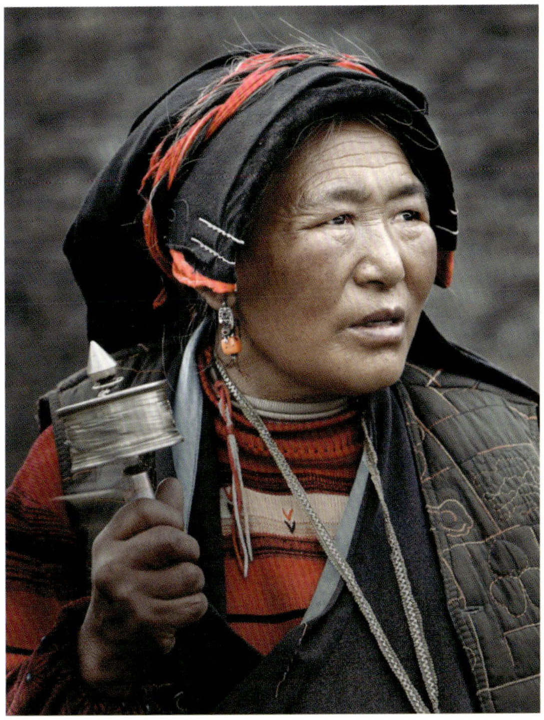

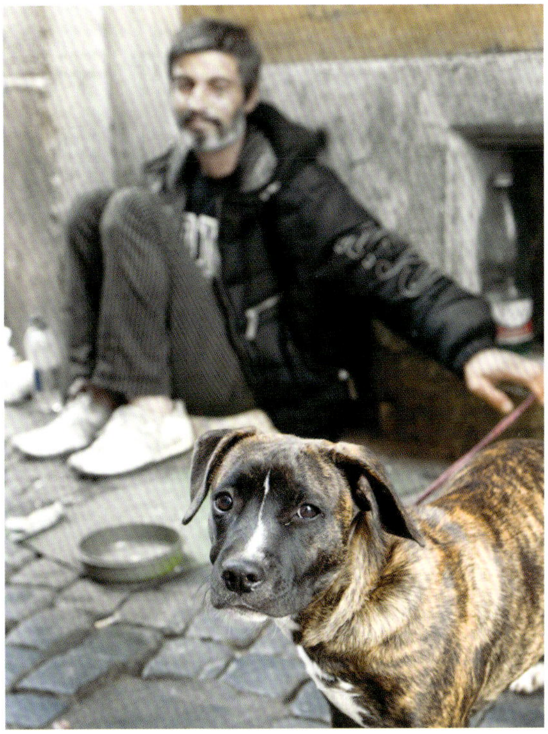

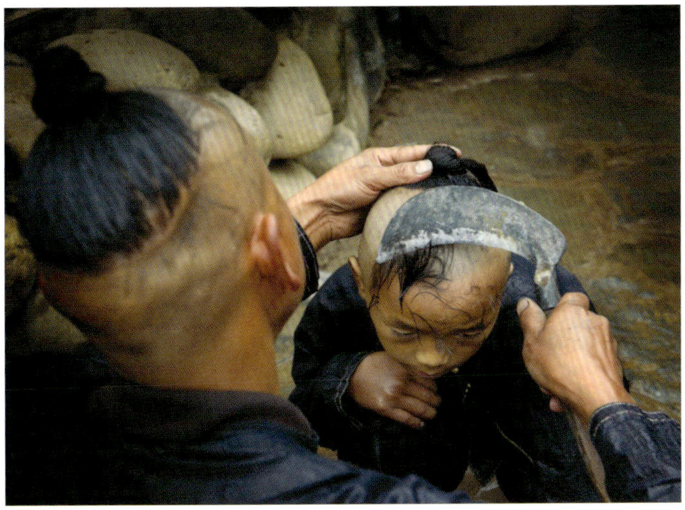

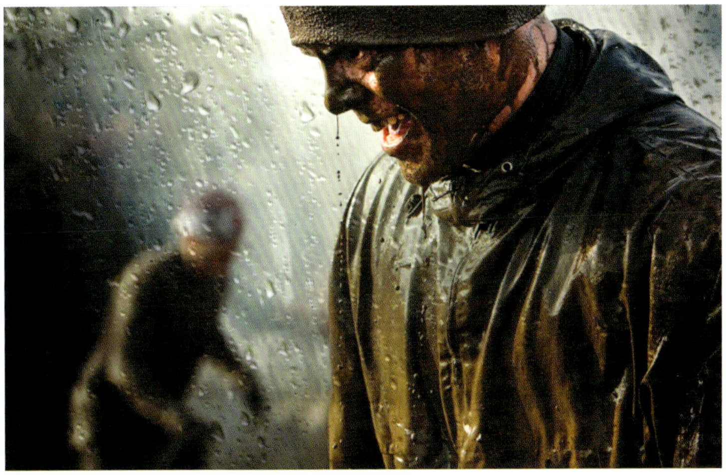

GENQUAN XU CHINA
YEOW-KWANG YEO FRPS SINGAPORE

NICK SCOTT FRPS UK
JOE BRENNAN UK

CELEBRATE A SUMMER OF SPORT

The Society celebrated the London 2012 Olympic and Paralympic Games with an online photographic competition, awarded the London 2012 'Inspire Mark'.

inspired by London 2012

Celebrate a Summer of Sport was open to entry worldwide and aimed to encourage people in the UK and across the world to record all aspects of sport and play in their own countries and communities – from informal, fun activities to local, national and international organised sporting events and competitions.

The competition was in 2 Stages: Sport for All (this page) and Spirit of the Games (opposite page), the medal winners shown here. Further selected images from the exhibition shown in London during November 2012, as part of the London 2012 Cultural Olympiad programme, are overleaf.

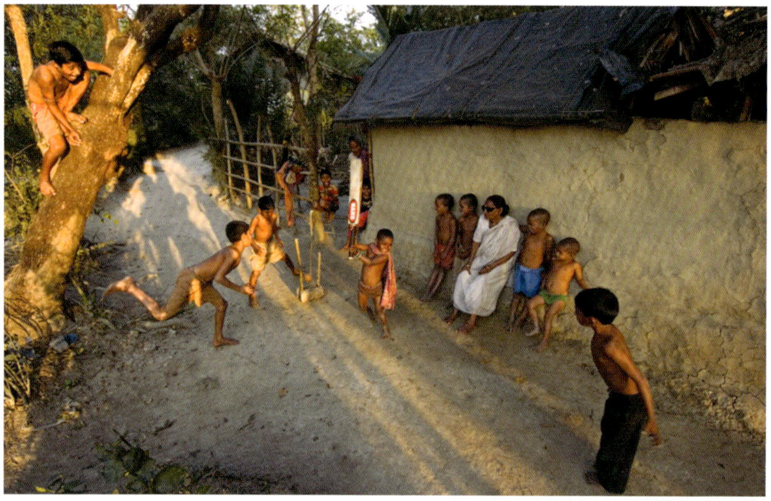

Rural Cricket **SUDIPTO DAS** INDIA

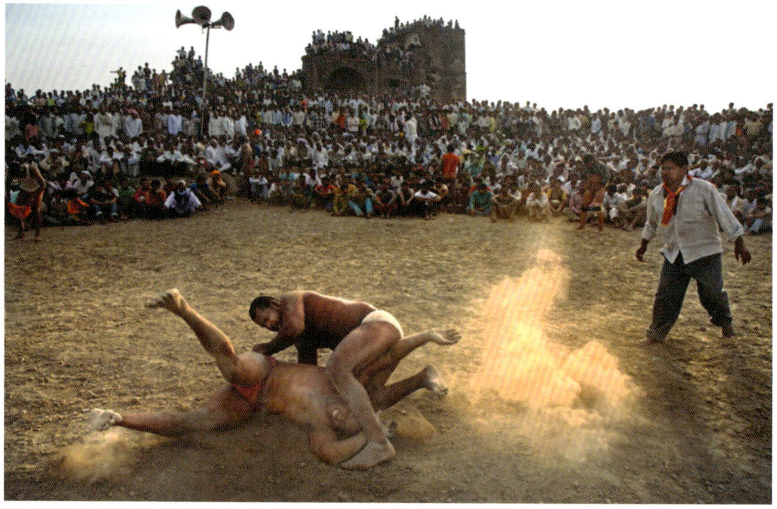

Free Style **SOMENATH MUKHOPADHYAY** INDIA

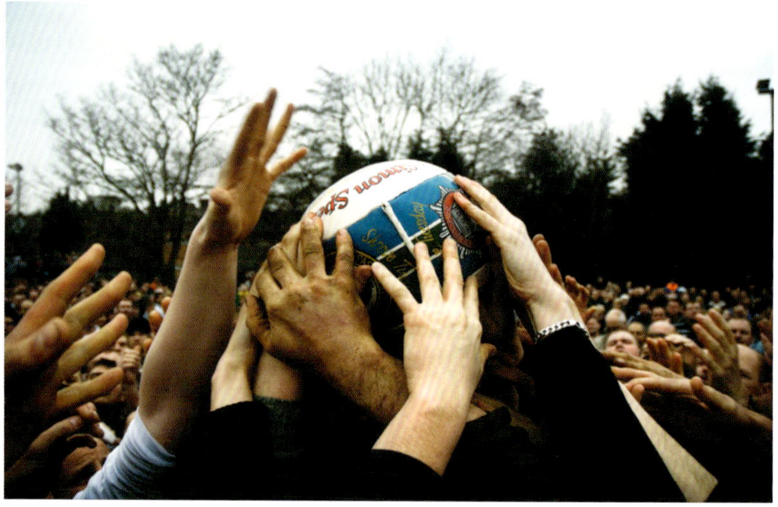

The Hug **SCOTT WEBSTER** UK

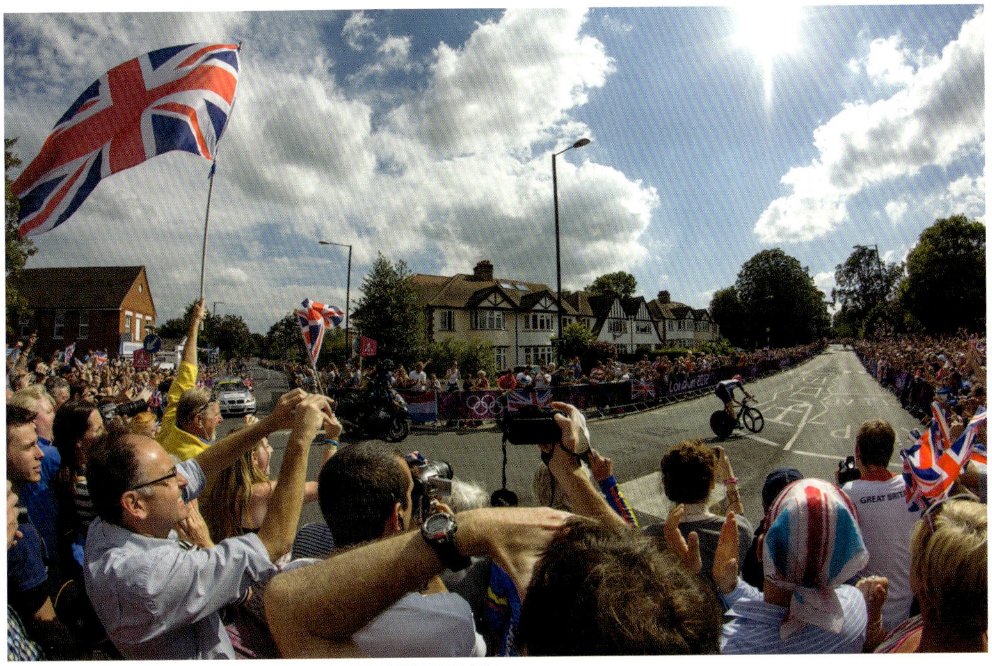

Wiggomania on Strawberry Hill **PHILIP PARRISH** UK

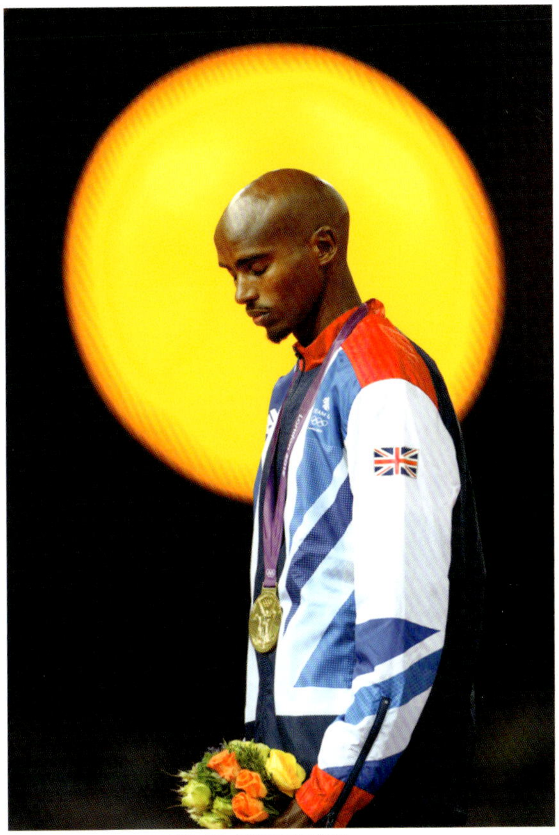

Golden Moment **TIM CLAYTON** USA

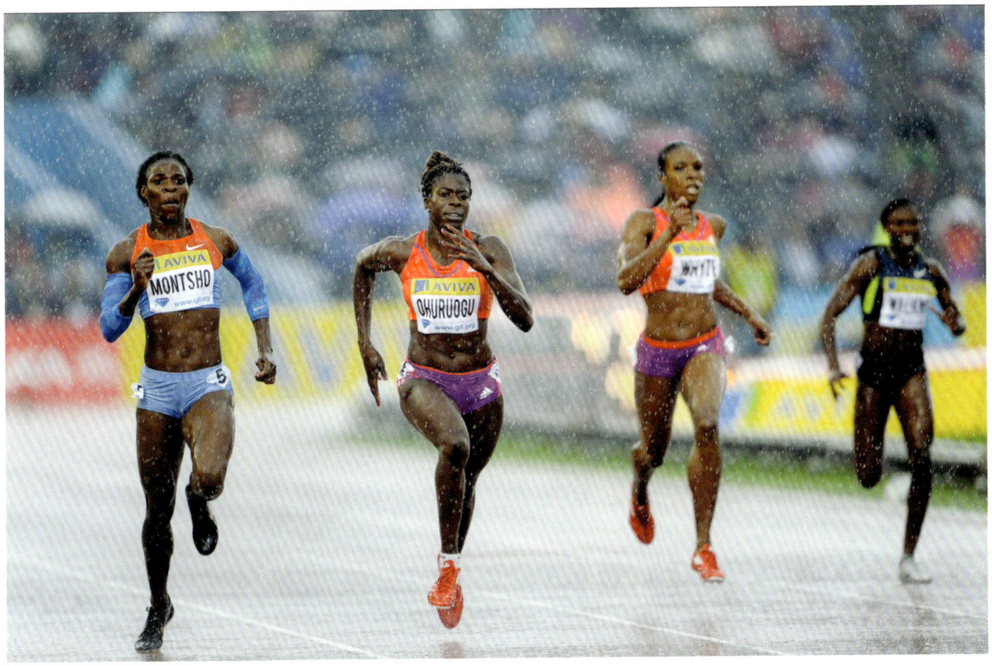

Victory Over Arch Rival **HARISH CHAVDA** UK

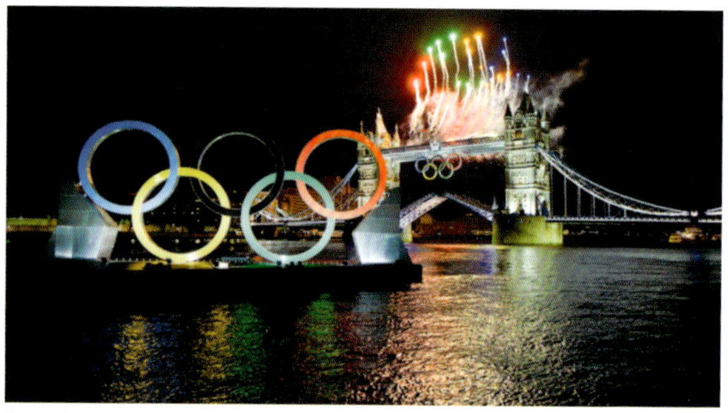

The Beginning **CHAIYASITH JUNJUERDEE** THAILAND

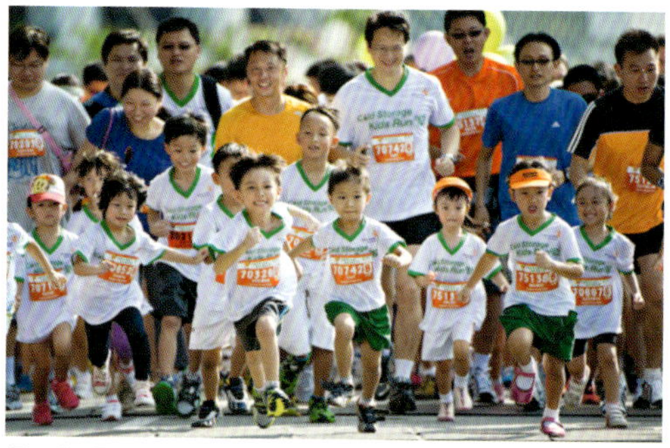

Family Run **LIEW TONG LENG ARPS** SINGAPORE

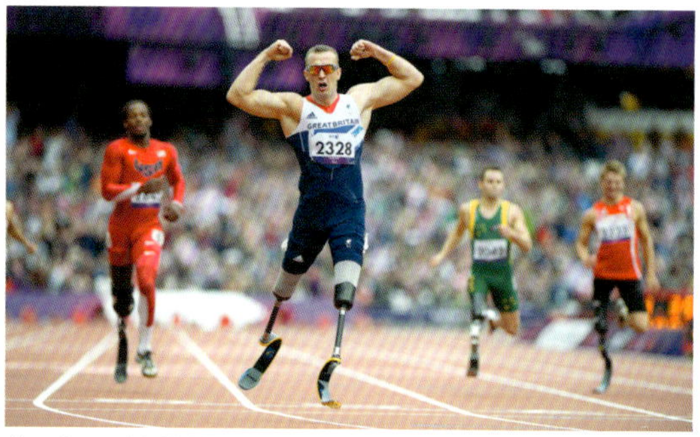

I've Done It! **MARK PAIN** UK

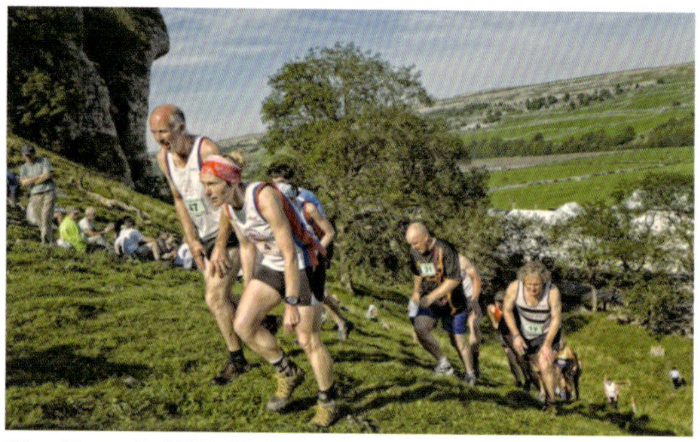

The Struggle **TIM MUNSEY** UK

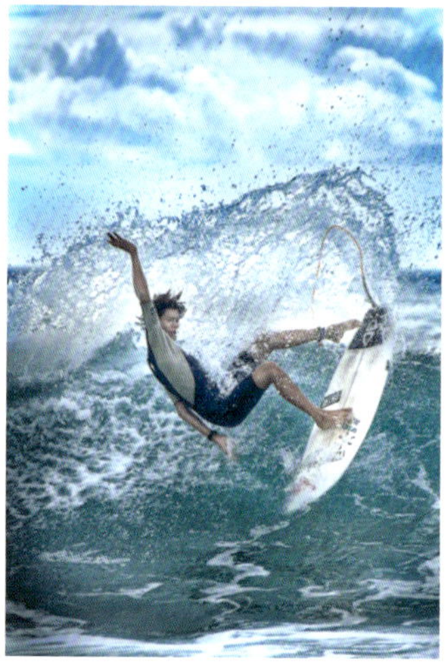

Water Ballet **DIANNE ENGLISH** AUSTRALIA

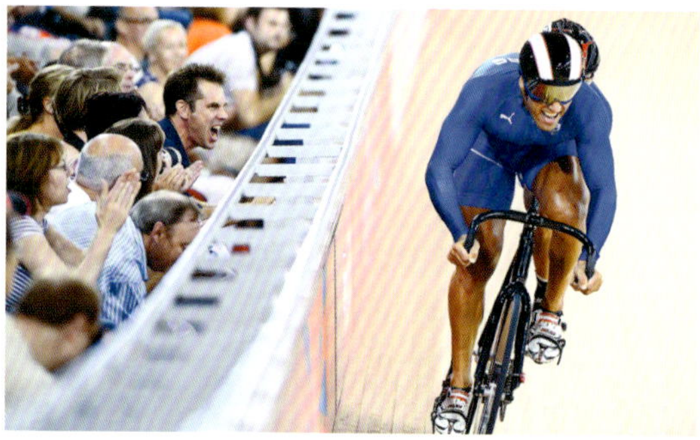

Determination of the Athlete – Passion of the Crowd
JUSTIN SETTERFIELD UK

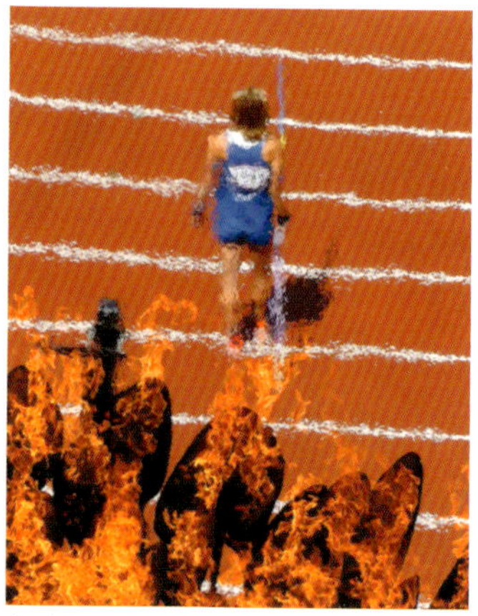

In the Heat of Competition
GRAHAM WOOLLVEN UK

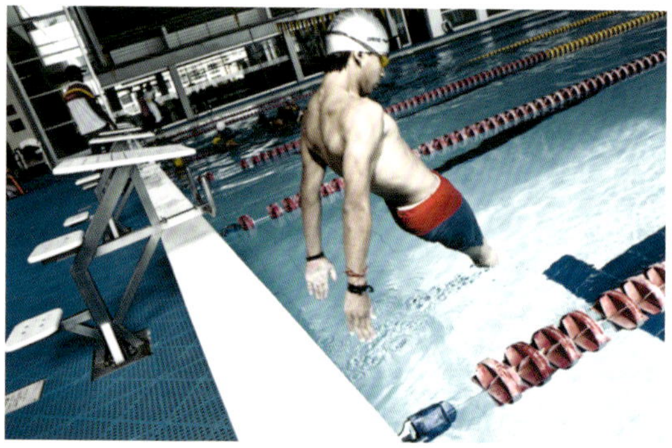

Swimmer **OLIVIO ARGENTI FRPS** ITALY

SCIENCE

Science has always been an important aspect of The Royal Photographic Society since its foundation when it was stated that The Society's object "is the promotion of the Art and Science of Photography". The Society has an internationally recognised Qualifications and Distinctions programme for those in imaging science and scientific imaging. In this section we look at two aspects of The Society's work in the field of science.

International Images for Science Exhibition 2011

Activities of The Royal Photographic Society have always reflected the developments in the science of imaging and many scientific studies have been presented, discussed and recorded in regular issues of its Journals. Recently it was also recognised that sharing scientific images with the wider community would enhance the understanding of the important developments in many technical areas. As explained by Afzal Ansary ASIS FRPS, who instigated this major event, The Society was able to present fifty stunning images in this exhibition. From its inception it was highly regarded and developed a range of venues in the UK and overseas. Its success also gained support for The Society from organisations including the UK Scientific and Technical Facilities Council to make the public more aware of scientific work, leading to a second Society exhibition opening in the 2013 British Science Week. In this feature we are able to share a selection of ten of the original impressive images.

'Spikeberg' Illumination

Spike Walker ASIS FRPS was the recipient of The Society's 2010 Combined Royal Colleges Medal recognising his outstanding contribution to photography – photomicrography – and its application in the service of medicine.

He had his first basic microscope as a young boy, then a couple of years later he was given an older but optically superior instrument which he used to make his first photomicrographs, by direct projection onto bromide paper, in his early teens. His scientific interest continued and, after obtaining his BSc degree in Zoology, he became a teacher who taught biology until his early retirement in 1989. Throughout this time his skill in microscopy developed and for many later years Spike worked with traditional photomicrography. However his conversion to digital began, and as quoted in The Society's Awards statement, "he is now realising his lifelong goal – to present images from the microscope as being worth looking at in their own right".

This article explains his development of illumination techniques to enhance microscopy images.

INTERNATIONAL IMAGES FOR SCIENCE EXHIBITION 2011

This broad set of fifty stunning Images for Science, from which we are able to show ten high quality selections, was the first Society exhibition in this field for many years. After its initial launch at Fenton House in Bath in September 2011, it attracted extensive media coverage and travelled to a series of venues within the United Kingdom and overseas. Early in 2012 in London it was shown to a selected audience in the Palace of Westminster and received public viewing when exhibited at the Royal Albert Hall. Selected images were also shown outdoors as very large prints in St Andrews Square in Edinburgh as part of the "Invisible Worlds" exhibition, being seen by more than 140,000 people. Some of the images from the exhibition have since been selected for a front cover of The Society's Journal and many of its Imaging Science Journals. The success of this newly organised International Images for Science Exhibition exceeded all expectations.

These images are not only outstanding records of seldom seen objects or events but they also provide a bank of scientific information. Words are usually not able to express or indicate all the information that a photograph can show. Therefore, scientists have always needed to communicate their discoveries by pictorial documentation in the form of photographs. In fact, the application of photography to science is almost as old as photography itself.

In recent years, the original analogue photography has evolved into highly sophisticated digital imaging systems, with the capability of yielding excellent results for diagnosis, evaluation, measurement, assessment and investigation. Because of these prolific developments in digital technology there are now more and better means of showing work in this field than ever before. Many used to say, 'if you can see it, it can be photographed'. Now we can say, 'even if you cannot see it, we most likely can photograph it'.

Myriad advances that we take for granted have been made possible through scientific applications of imaging. They range from extreme microphotography, such as atomic force microscopy used for imaging in nanometres (billionths of a metre), to macrophotography such as satellite imagery, recording photographs of the Earth and images of the universe. The list of scientific applications of photography is endless, spanning spectra from radiation, X-ray, ultraviolet (UV), visible light and infrared (IR), and recording in times from long and slow imaging through time-lapse to high speed – the names of specialist techniques could fill pages. The old adage that necessity is the mother of invention has resulted in the discovery of new and better methods of recording images through advances in sophisticated optical instrumentation together with novel techniques for recording invisible radiation. Since photography's inception, its users have constantly extended its limits, applying it to recording and visualising that which human eyes cannot perceive, from minute objects too small to be seen with a microscope, to objects too far away to be seen with a telescope, and events that occur too rapidly or too slowly for us to visualise.

Scientists and technologists need such imagery not just for their research and development work, but also for pictorial documentation, communication, presentations and publications to share their results and discoveries. Here are just a couple of examples giving an idea of the range of practical imaging – remote controlled cameras can go where humans cannot and can transmit images to provide vital information – cameras in space can transmit information on ecology and climate issues – in medical imaging, tiny pill-sized CMOS cameras can be swallowed by patients and travel harmlessly through their gastrointestinal tracts, transmitting valuable diagnostic images.

Building on the success of this Exhibition, The Society partnered with the United Kingdom's Science and Technology Facilities Council in 2013 for a second Exhibition "International Images for Science : An exhibition of the world's best scientific photographs", launched in September 2013 at the Great North Museum, Hancock, as part of the annual British Science Festival hosted by the city of Newcastle.

Dr Afzal Ansary ASIS FRPS
Exhibition Co-ordinator

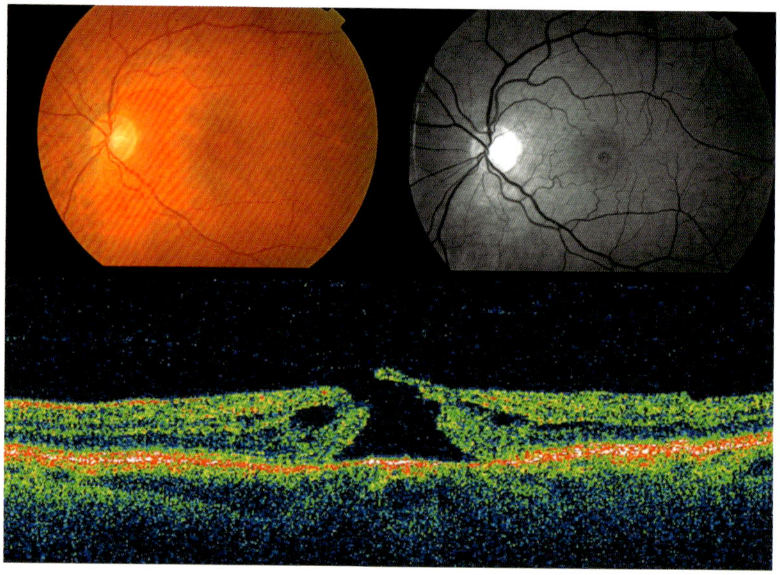

Macular Hole : 2009

KIM BAXTER, *Media Studio, Cambridge University Hospitals NHS Foundation Trust, England*

A macular hole seen in the retina of a patient's eye. The macula is the faint ring-shaped area seen in the colour retinal photograph (top left) and more clearly defined in the red-free photograph (top right). At the bottom is a colour-coded optical coherence tomogram (OCT), a virtual 'slice' through the tissue of the macula made with infrared radiation, that clearly shows the hole (black) in the tissue of the retina (green). These images are used to plan corrective surgery on the macula to restore the patient's high-resolution vision.

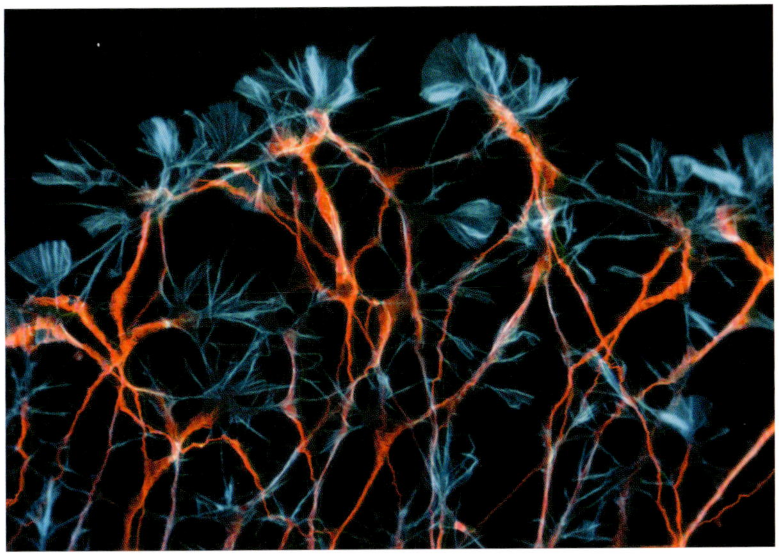

Neurons : 2000 *(left)*

HEITI PAVES, ***Department of Gene Technology, Tallinn University of Technology, Estonia***

Sensory nerve cells from a rat embryo grown in culture. These cells, also called neurons, were stained with chemicals that bind with specific proteins then fluoresce in characteristic colours under ultraviolet radiation. Here the blue colours show microfilaments, the smallest component of the cell's cytoskeleton structure, while the red colours show the larger neurofilaments. This image was captured using an Olympus fluorescence microscope.

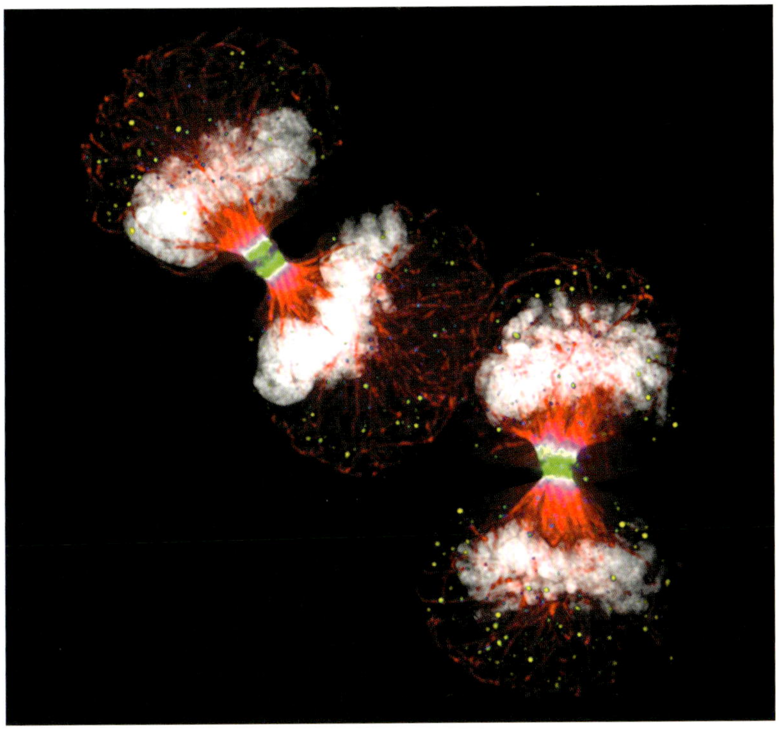

Two in Telophase : 2003

PAUL ANDREWS, ***University of Dundee, Scotland***

Two HeLa human cervical cancer cells are captured here in telophase, a stage in cell division, fluorescing under ultraviolet radiation. In each cell there are two bundles of DNA wrapped up as chromosomes (white) that will form the nuclei of the daughter cells. These are connected with microtubules (red). At the very center of each cell, where they are about to divide, is a protein called Aurora B (green) that may be a target for new chemotherapy drugs. This image was created by restoration deconvolution microscopy. By knowing the characteristics of the lens system it is possible to reconstruct even out-of-focus spots of light to how they should look in focus, then assemble them in a stack to reconstruct the 3D structure.

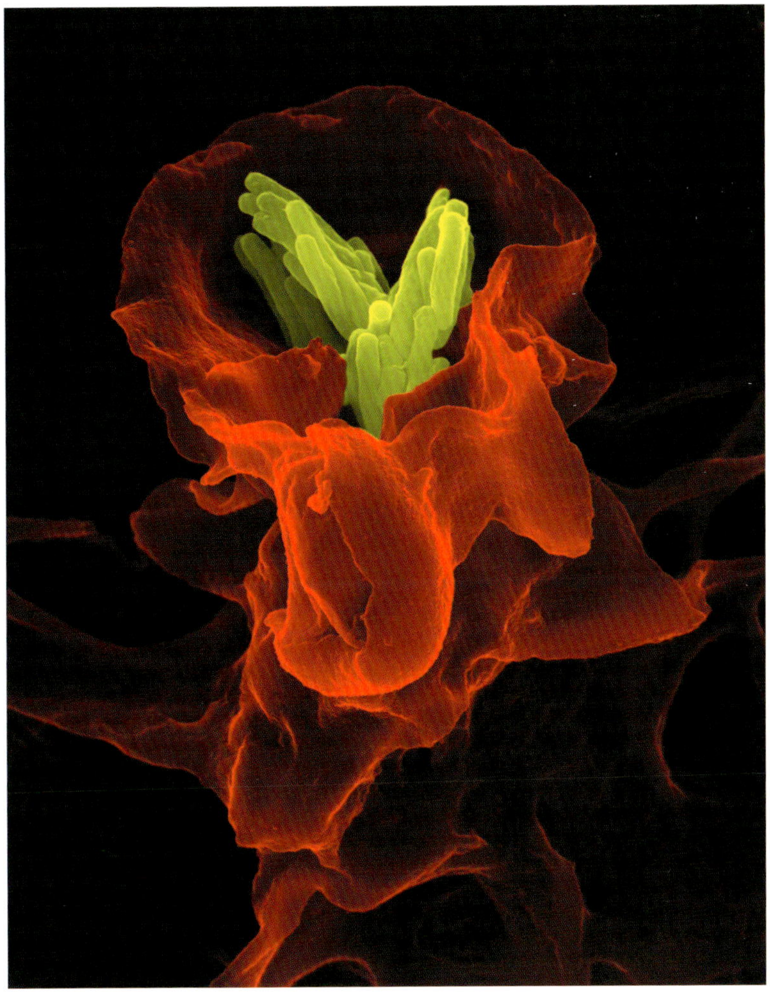

TB Macrophage : 2009

VOLKER BRINKMANN, ***Max Planck Institute for Infection Biology, Germany***

A macrophage is a white blood cell used by the body to engulf invading cells and destroy them. Here a macrophage (red) is enveloping some Mycobacterium tuberculosis bacteria (yellow). M. tuberculosis, the causative agent of TB, has found a way to survive inside macrophages and thus defeat the body's defences. This image was captured using a scanning electron microscope and was then digitally colourised to differentiate the cell types.

Fibonacci's Series on Butterfly Egg (Lysandra Bellargus) : 2010

MARTIN OEGGERLI, *Micronaut, Switzerland*

Scanning electron micrograph of an egg of an Adonis Blue butterfly (Lysandra bellargus) on a leaf. The spiraling pattern of aeropyles in the casing of the egg is governed by the Fibonacci series. This is in a sequence of numbers described by Leonardo Fibonacci in 1202. The series starts with a zero and a one, thereafter the next number is the sum of the previous two (0, 1, 1, 2, 3, 5, 8, 13, etc.). This sequence appears in a variety of biological settings such as branching in trees, the fruitlets of a pineapple and the pattern of florets in a sunflower. The original monochrome image was digitally colourised to reflect the colours seen in nature.

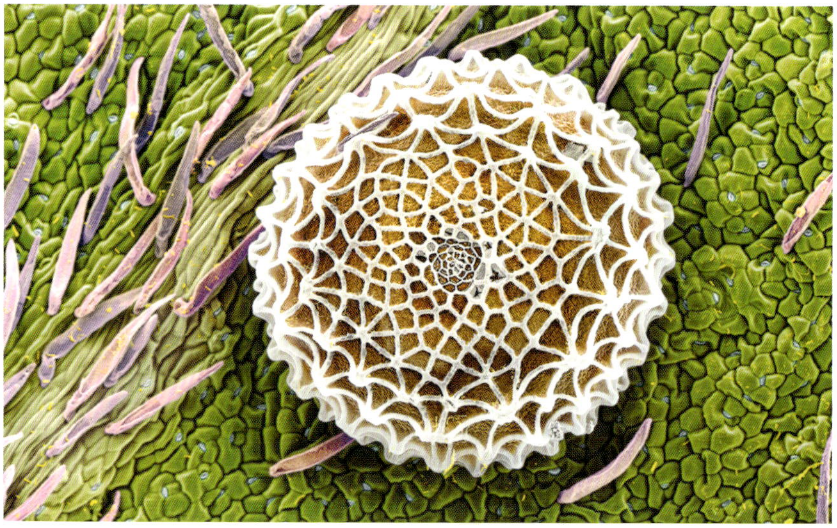

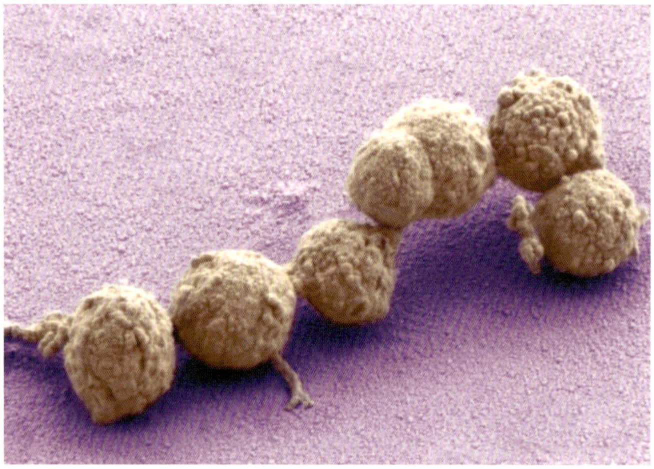

The First Synthetic Form of Life : 2010

THOMAS DEERINCK, *National Center for Microscopy and Imaging Research, UC San Diego, CA, USA*

Captured at the very limit of magnification in a scanning electron microscope, this is one of the first ever images of a man-made life form – Mycoplasma mycoides JCVI-syn1.0. These few cells are the result of 15 years of research and an investment of over £20 million, yet their significance cannot be overstated. The process involved synthesizing the 1.2 billion base-pair genome of M. mycoides and implanting it into a single M. capricolum cell. The new genome took over the cell which behaved like natural M. mycoides. The technology is intended to enable the creation of bacterial and algal strains with commercial usefulness, such as biofuel production or removal of pollution. The original monochrome scanning electron micrograph was digitally colourised for aesthetic effect.

Shock Diamonds : 2011

HARALD KLEINE, *School of Engineering and Information Technology, University of New South Wales, Australia*

Four high-speed jets of air exiting an industrial blowpipe used in steel making. The pressure inside the pipe means that the exiting air is traveling supersonically. Inside the air jets the static pressure is lower than in the surrounding air, so the boundary between them initially billows outwards before collapsing inward. This sets up a complex reflecting system of shock waves inside the jet, where they converge we see 'shock diamonds'. Here the patterns of changing air density are revealed using a colour schlieren system in which the colours relate to the direction of the density gradient present. The system was illuminated using an electronic flash with a duration of around 200 microseconds (two ten-thousandths of a second).

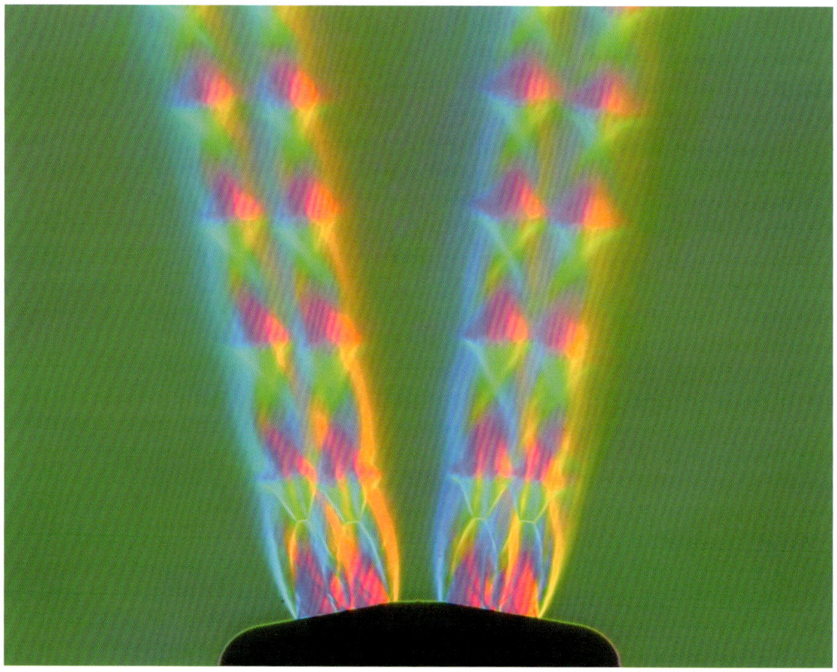

Aesthetic Imperfections : 2008 *(right)*

HANS U. DANZEBRINK, *Physikalisch-technische Bundesanstalt, Braunschweig, Germany*

Imperfections in the arrangement of polystyrene nanospheres in a photonic crystal are captured in this image. The magnification is truly impressive – these nanospheres are about 200 nanometres (billionths of a metre) in diameter, or 300 times smaller than a human hair. Photonic crystals are found in nature, for example in the iridescence of opal, but are also manufactured for things such as lens coatings and inks and sophisticated light guides. This image was created from data gathered by an atomic force microscope, in which surface height data are converted into a 3D model and digitally colour coded.

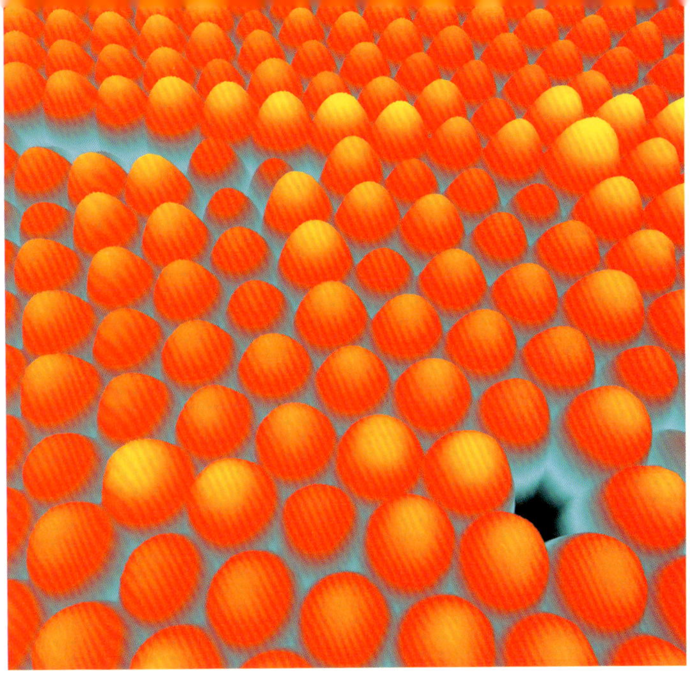

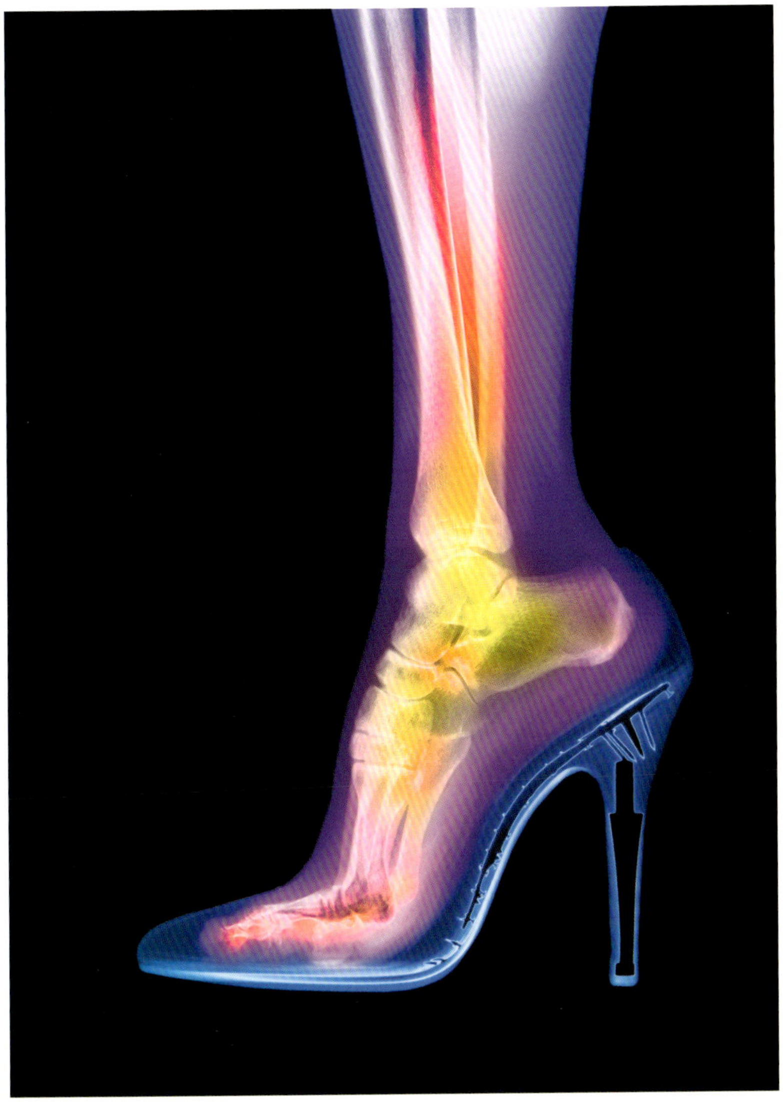

Stiletto (femme-fatale) : 1998

HUGH TURVEY, *Artist in Residence, British Institute of Radiology, London, England*

The distortion the human foot is subjected to when wearing a stiletto shoe is very clear in this X-ray image. The Xogram technique used here involves making multiple X-ray exposures at different densities which are then digitally combined and colourised by the artist.

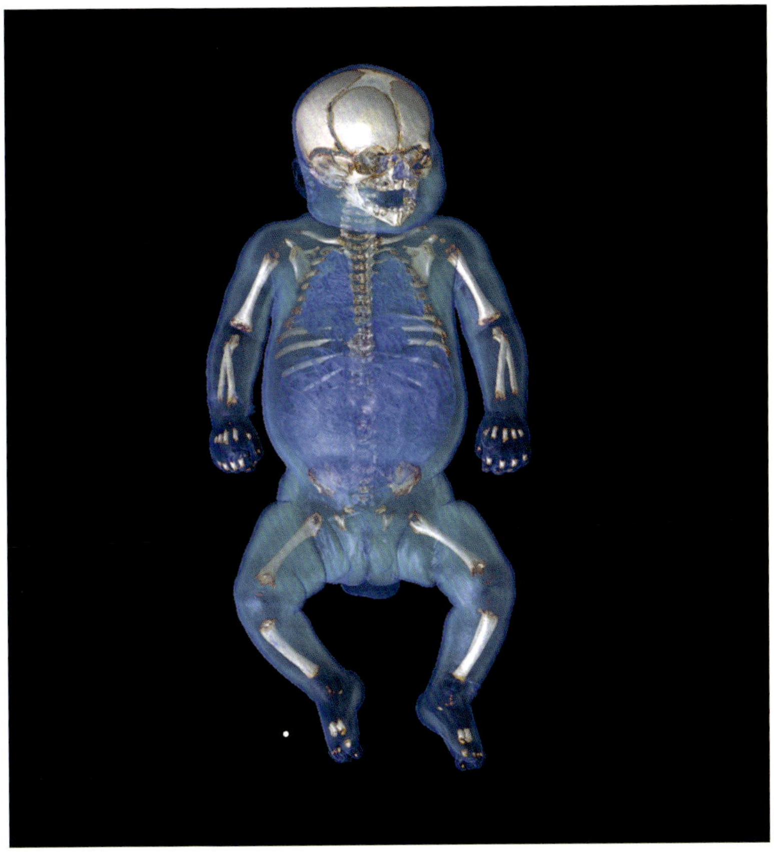

Child Postmortem Examination : 2011

ANDERS PERSSON: *Center for Medical Image Science and Visualisation (CMIV), Hälsouniversitetet / Radiologi Linköpings Universitet, Sweden*

Here virtual autopsy has been carried out with the aid of three-dimensional X-ray techniques. The skull and other bones are clearly seen. Whole body virtual autopsy was performed and the examination ruled out child abuse as the cause of death. The findings were verified with a conventional autopsy. With this technique virtual and bloodless autopsies are now being performed on suspected victims of crime.

'SPIKEBERG' ILLUMINATION

SPIKE WALKER ASIS FRPS, RECIPIENT OF THE SOCIETY'S 2010 COMBINED ROYAL COLLEGES MEDAL

Many photographers to whom I have lectured on the subject of photomicrography have been surprised to hear that the great majority of optical microscopes are designed exclusively for the examination of transparent material by transmitted light – surprised because most common materials, be they pieces of wood or people or rocks, are more-or-less opaque. Fortunately however, most can be rendered transparent if they can be sliced, ground, squashed or smeared thinly enough but, as is often the case, solving one problem immediately generates another. Light may now pass through the specimen but its constituent parts are often so similar optically that any details of structure which we might hope to make out are virtually invisible. Blood in a test tube, when held up to the light, is seen plainly as a murky, deep-red fluid, but when reduced to a dried smear on a glass slide not much more than a micrometre thick, it becomes practically invisible even with the most 'powerful' microscope. The red cells which en masse gave its intense hue are individually transparent and almost colourless. Consequently, what we now need is a so-called 'contrast enhancement technique' – a way of making the most of any differences, chemical or physical, that do exist between the object's components, so that we can see them.

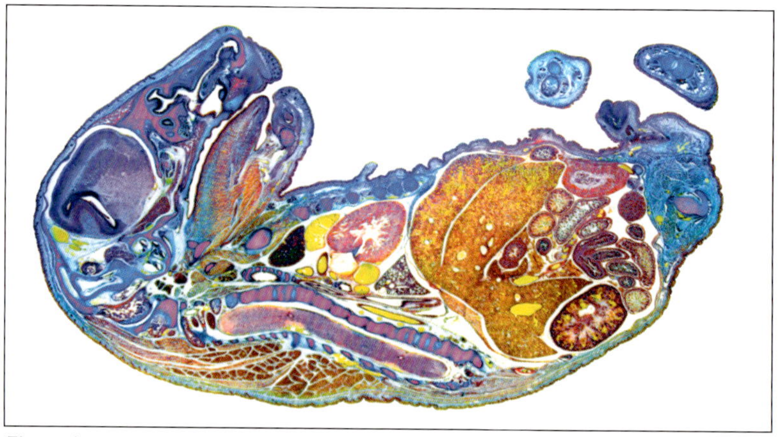
Figure 1

For organic objects, ranging from bacterial smears to sections of leaves and brains, a time-honoured method is to use carefully-chosen dyes or mixtures of dyes to stain them differentially (Figure 1). This remains the method of choice across a wide range of biomedical disciplines but it has the disadvantage of often involving complex preparatory procedures which usually 'kill' them.

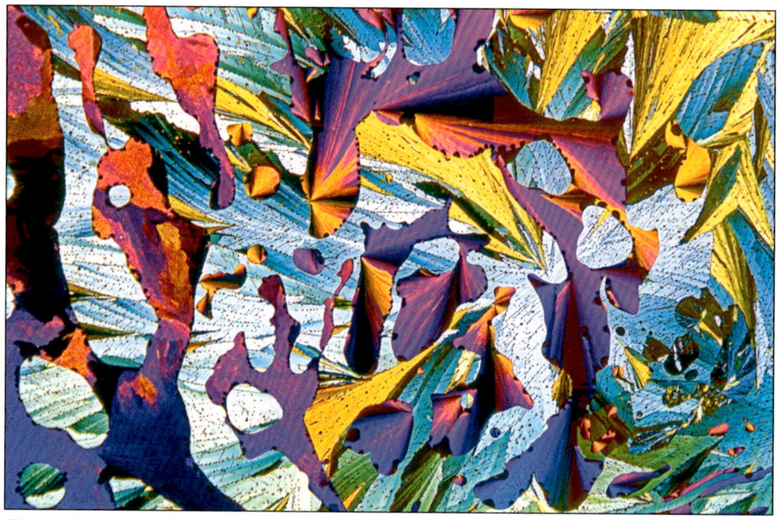
Figure 2

Other techniques, often with the advantage of being less invasive, exploit optical rather than chemical variations within the material and range from cheap and do-it-yourself to those that are complex and out-of-reach except for well-heeled research institutions. 'Spikeberg' belongs to the former category.

An easy but potentially very informative technique simply involves placing a piece of linear polarizing sheet below the specimen and another above the objective lens, and then rotating one of them until the light passing through the lower filter is extinguished. Many materials with an orderly molecular structure, including bone, plant-cell walls, and crystals (including rock-forming minerals) then show against a black background, often in brilliant colours (Figures 2 & 3).

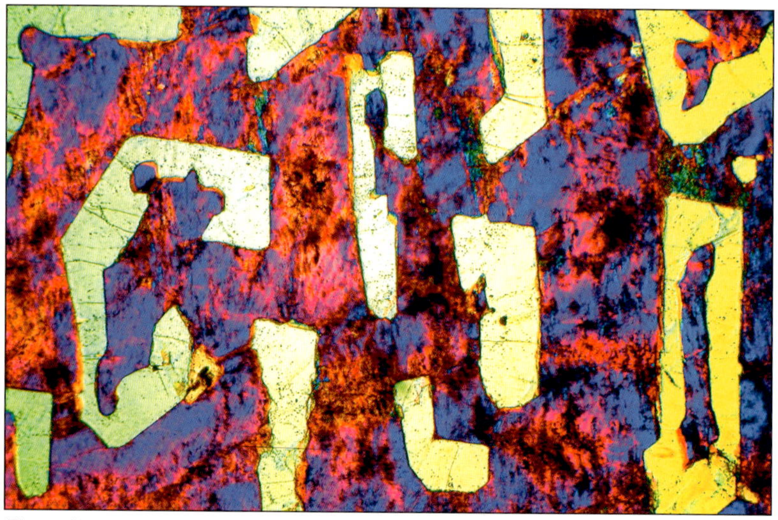
Figure 3

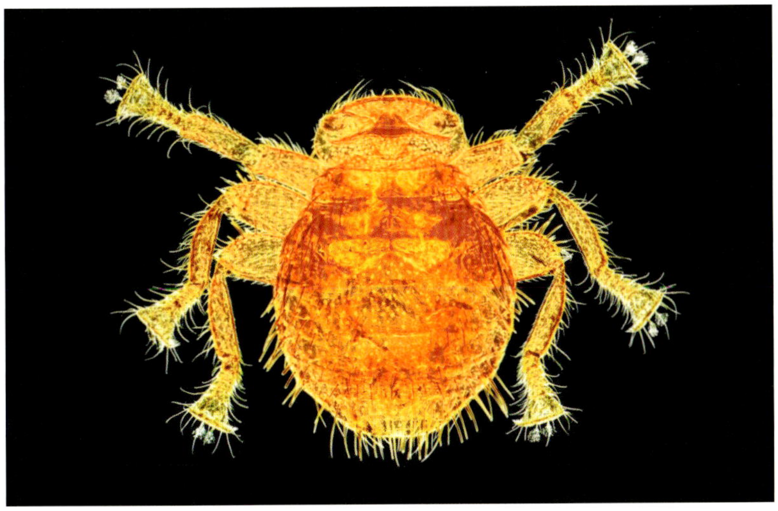

Figure 4

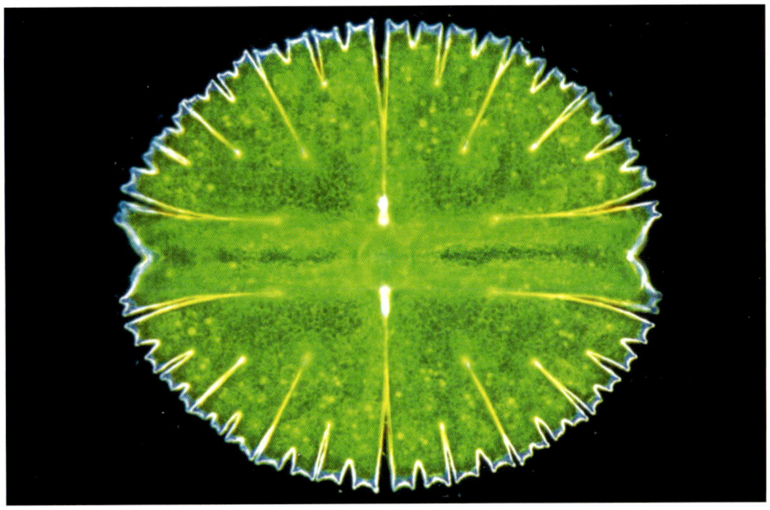

Figure 5

All other contrast enhancement techniques that come to mind require the presence of a condenser below the stage on which the object sits. This consists of a more-or-less complex optical system which illuminates the specimen and, by means of an iris diaphragm beneath it, controls the working aperture of the objective (which usually lacks an iris of its own). Excessively closing this diaphragm greatly increases the visibility of colourless and transparent objects but at the expense of diffraction effects which destroy the resolution of fine detail. On the other hand, excessive opening of the aperture diaphragm, which would normally flood the image with light, can yield excellent contrast with objectives of low to medium magnification if enough of the central rays are occluded by means of an opaque 'patch stop'. This is called 'darkground' or 'darkfield' illumination because, when the condenser is properly adjusted, the object appears to shine brilliantly against a black background (Figures 4 & 5). At its most basic, the method requires nothing more sophisticated than a disc of clear, colourless glass or plastic in the filter tray beneath the condenser, supporting a smaller, central disc of say, black paper, though a large number of alternatives have been suggested, from small coins to insulation tape and even, in extremis, a finger end. However, the focusing of the condenser, the diameter and centration of the patch stop – and absolute optical cleanliness – are critical for good results. (It is usually necessary to adapt the condenser for 'low power' operation by removing its top lens or swinging in an auxiliary lens.) The mechanism involved is simple enough – the light passing through the clear outer annulus is diffracted by the specimen to enter the aperture of the objective. With no specimen in position, the field of view will appear uniformly black. If the patch stop diameter is too large for the objective/condenser combination the image will not be bright enough or even non-existent – if too small, only the centre of the field will be dark.

In 1898, Julius Rheinberg published an account[1] of three novel methods of contrast enhancement which he called collectively 'Multiple Colour Illumination', one of which (his 'low power' method) lives on and bears his name. This is derived from the darkground technique outlined above but employs a filter with a deeply-coloured patch stop instead of a black one and usually an annulus in a lighter contrasting colour instead of a colourless one. Thus a filter made up of a dark blue patch stop surrounded by a pale yellow annulus should render a colourless object yellow against a blue background (Figures 6, 7, & 8). The annulus may be divided into two or four sectors of alternating colours to produce striking images of objects such as feathers or finely woven textiles if properly orientated with respect to the filter.

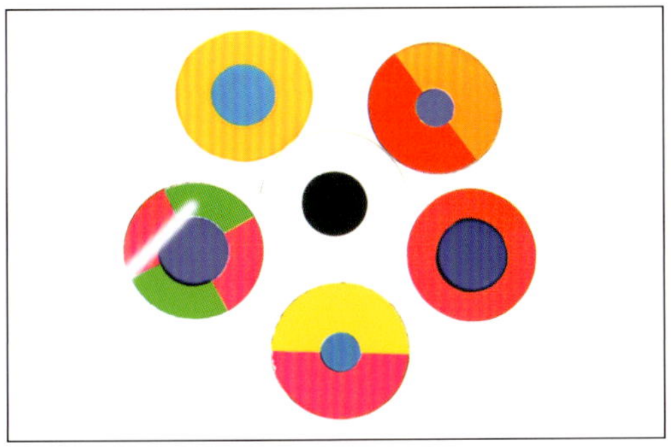

Figure 6

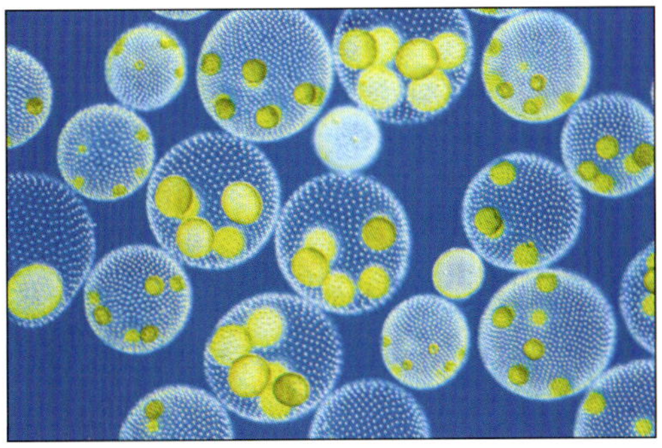

Figure 7

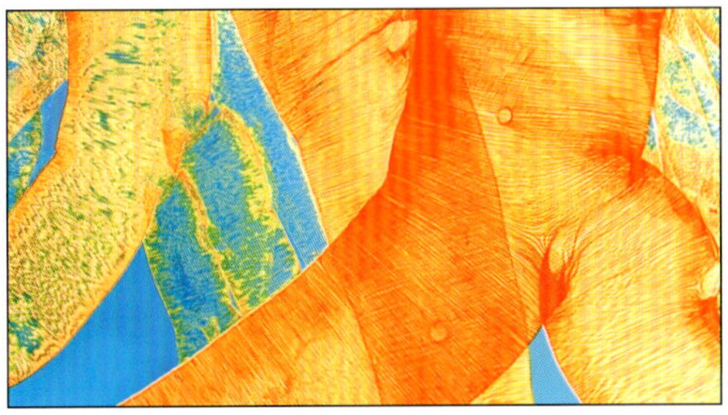

Figure 8

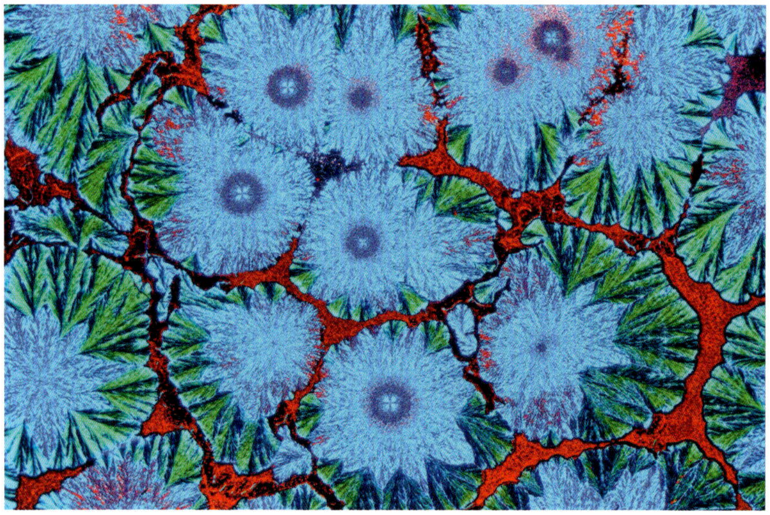

Figure 9

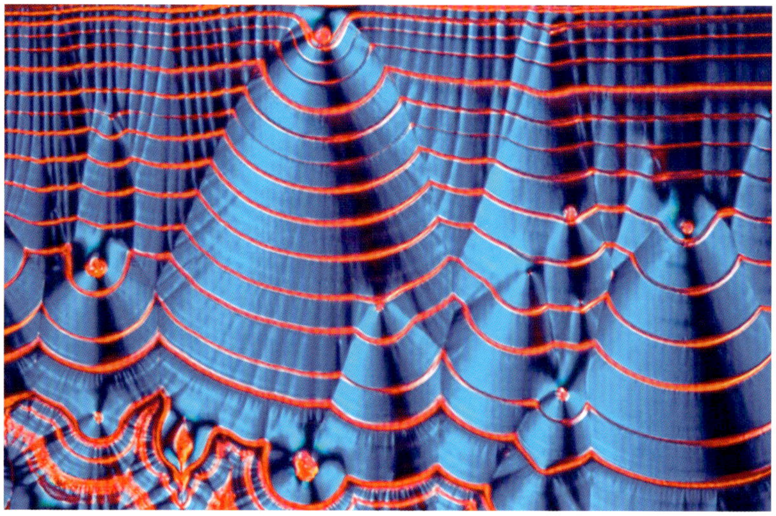

Figure 10

Rheinberg Illumination has spawned a large number of variants, of which 'Spikeberg' is one which I devised about 25 years ago as part of an attempt to catch the eye of judges in international photomicrography competitions that I entered. Long before the days of Photoshop it yielded unusual colour combinations which, in combination with the results of one-or-two other optical tricks[2], suitably disgruntled some of the opposition. It manages to combine the effects of crossed polars and Rheinberg Illumination in such a fashion that crystalline components of the object, for example, appear in either blue, green and cyan, or red, magenta and blue, while those which merely diffract the light, such as cracks and striae, are given complementary colours (Figures 9, 10, 11 & 12). The construction of the filter is remarkably simple, consisting of a patch stop which is approximately magenta in colour, surrounded by a green or yellow (or green and yellow) annulus, or a cyan one surrounded by red or yellow and/or orange. So far this would give nothing more than a typical Rheinberg image and the novel effects result from the presence of a second patch stop, of linear polarizing material, on top of the coloured one, orientated so that it is crossed with another polarizing filter (the analyser) above the objective. When the two are fully crossed the background should appear black, otherwise it will be some shade of magenta or cyan, the depth of which varies with the orientation of the patch stop (or analyser if rotatable).

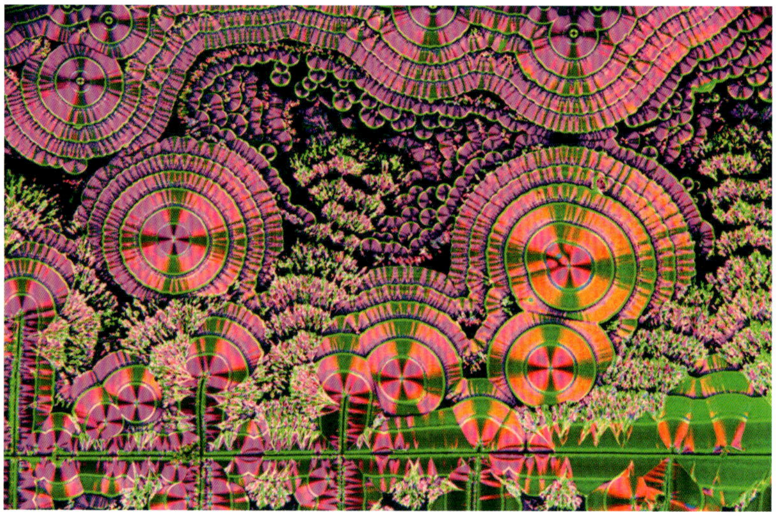

Figure 11

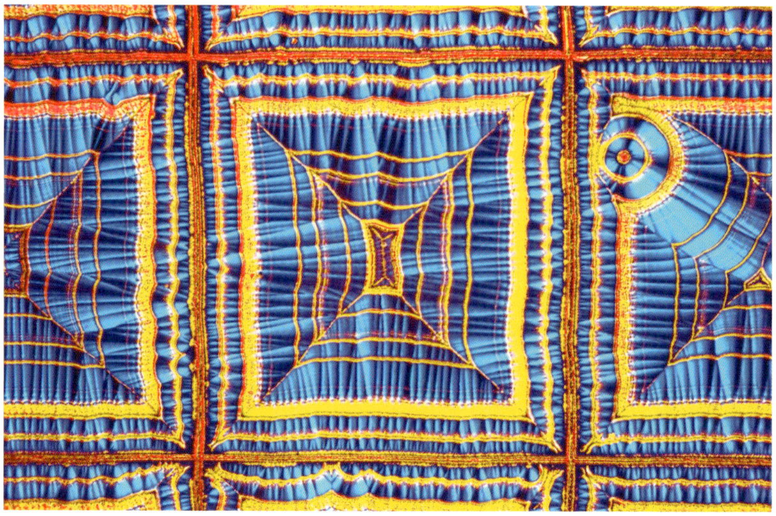

Figure 12

1 *The Illustrated Annual of Microscopy*, (Lund, Humphries & Co.) pp 44 – 50.

2 Figure 10 shows crystals of vitamin C grown from dilute aqueous solution, photographed using a filter with a bluish-cyan patch stop and red annulus. Their point of origin can be seen as a crystal dust particle, top centre. Breathing on the crystals as they developed (at one minute intervals) provided extra water of crystallization which temporarily boosted their growth rate but made them fine enough to diffract the red light from the annulus.

Figure 11 used a magenta patch stop and green annulus.

Figure 12 used a similar filter but with a yellow and red annulus. In this case, the film of supersaturated solution was quickly scratched with a needle to form a pattern of approximately 1.5 mm squares, before breathing on the preparation. The crystals grew at the same rates from each side – hence the mitred corners!

REGIONS AND CHAPTERS

The Society's Regions and Chapters organise local events, meetings, exhibitions and competitions. Members are assigned to a Region on a postcode basis or, where possible, a Chapter based on country and are encouraged to attend local meetings and events. Each Region and Chapter has a local Organiser.

Regions meet regularly, often with guest speakers, arrange Distinctions Advisory Days, field trips, hold exhibitions of their work and publish regular newsletters for their members. In the British Isles there are eighteen Regions including Eire.

Chapters can be formed in any country where a sufficient number of members wish to join together to arrange events on behalf of The Society. In the last three years new Chapters have been formed in Indonesia, Italy, Shangtuf (China) and Switzerland. Currently The Society has Chapters in many countries including a significant number in the Asian, European and American continents.

This section features work from:

THE NORTH WEST REGION

Covering the North West of England and the Isle of Man, this Region has over 700 members. This features a selection of images from some of the Region's members.

THE GERMAN CHAPTER

Members of the Chapter showcase images from their current project 'White'.

THE JAPAN CHAPTER

The Japan Chapter is one of the longest established of The Society's overseas chapters, having being formed in 1966. Here the Chapter showcases images that reflect Japanese culture and members' individual styles.

NORTH WEST REGION

REGIONAL ORGANISER: AFZAL ANSARY ASIS FRPS

Known as a friendly Region, the North West, including the Isle of Man, has over 700 members. We previously had as many as 12 to 14 events per annum but have now narrowed down our activities to focus on quality rather than quantity.

Annual events include Portrait Days and spring and autumn landscape events in the Lake District, which provide an excellent opportunity to photograph its glorious colours and light in the two seasons. One Portrait Day provided an opportunity to photograph body builders. A Monochrome Group has been running for about four years with speakers and visits, including the Pete Kelly Studio in Stockport to see a demonstration on photographic encaustic, which is a process of encasing photos in beeswax. We are currently arranging events to develop and improve members' photographic skills and encourage them to work for Society Distinctions. Distinctions Advisory Days are also very much in demand and we hold at least one every year.

Our members regularly enter The Society's Annual International Print and International Projected Image Exhibitions and The Society's Biennial Members' Print Exhibition, with a high level of success. Each year The Society's International Projected Image Exhibition is shown in Chester Zoo. The North West was the first Region to host the official opening away from Bath. Attended by many of the award winners it was a very successful day.

We make great use of the social aspects of being part of The Society. Each December we have a Christmas lunch and a quiz with a speaker to entertain us. Most of all, we endeavour to ensure that photography is great fun.

Fortunately, I have very supportive committee members who give unstinting service. We were delighted that Sylvia Jones, our treasurer for many years who has given support beyond the call of duty, was awarded The Society's 2011 Members Award.

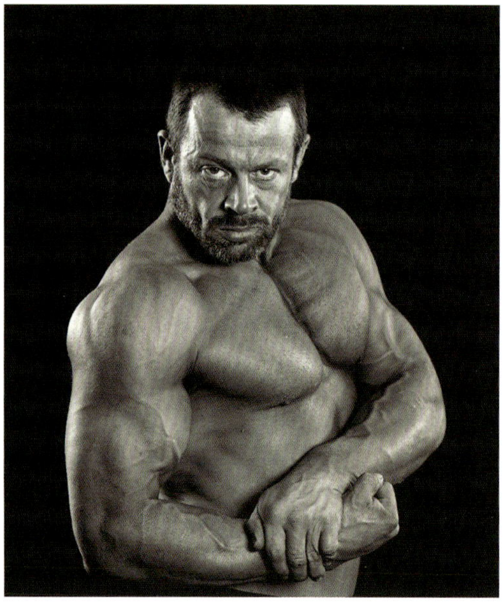

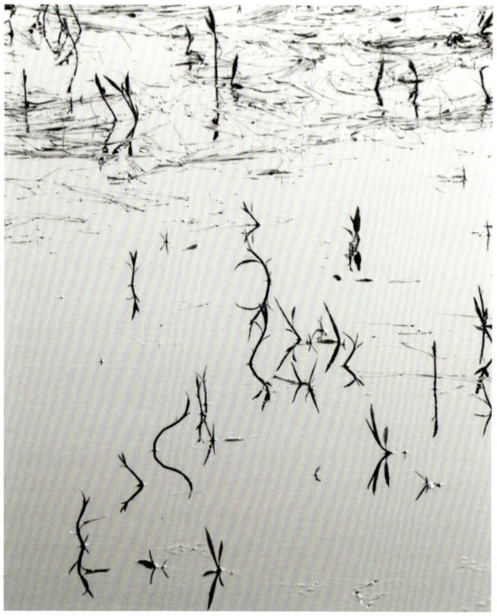

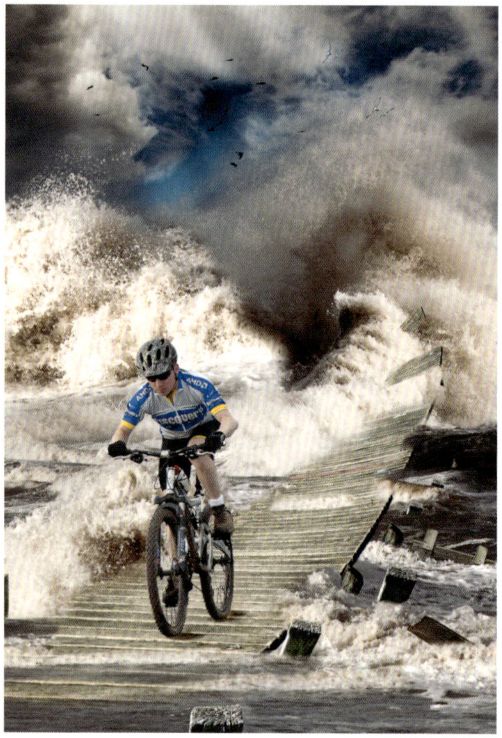

ALAN ANGEL FRPS

BEN GORMAN ARPS

MIKE MCNAMEE FRPS

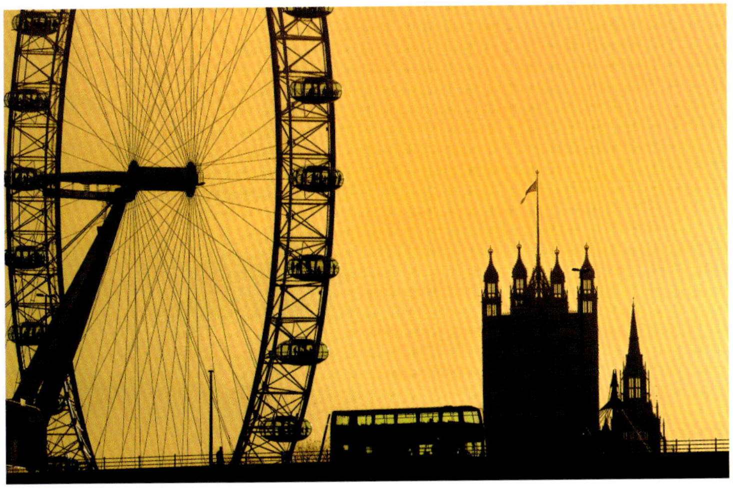

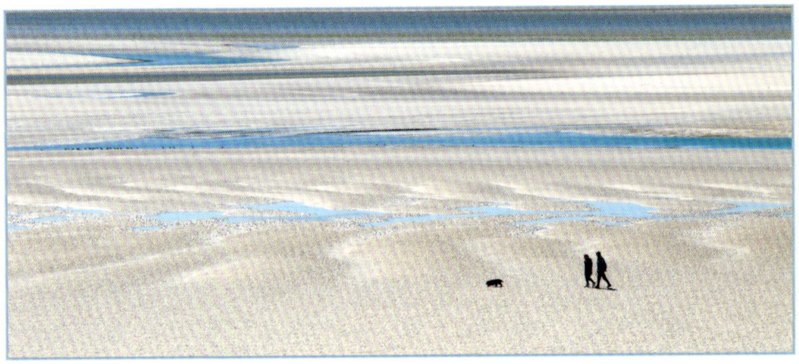

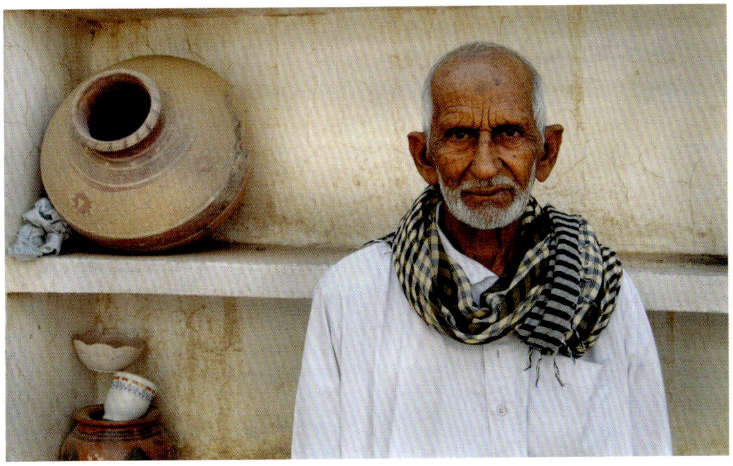

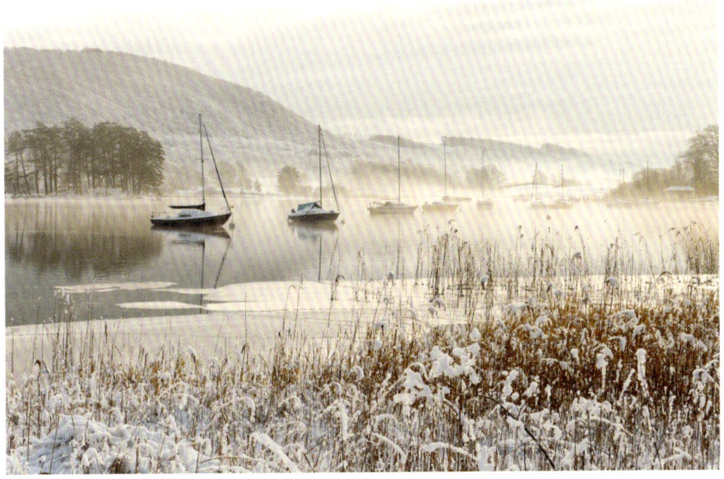

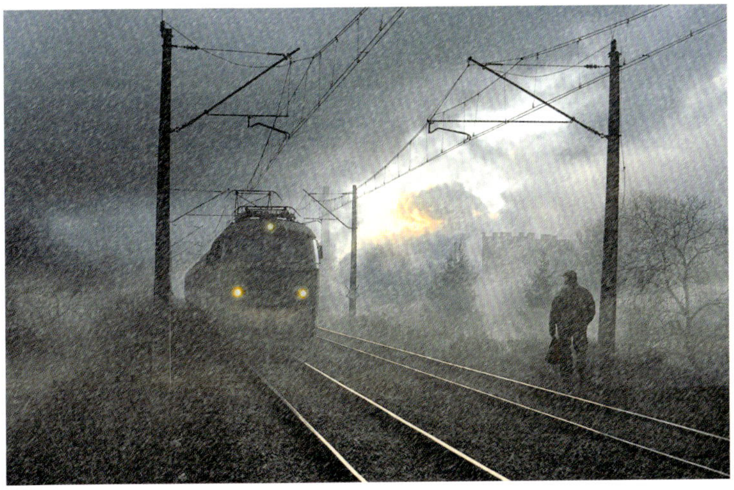

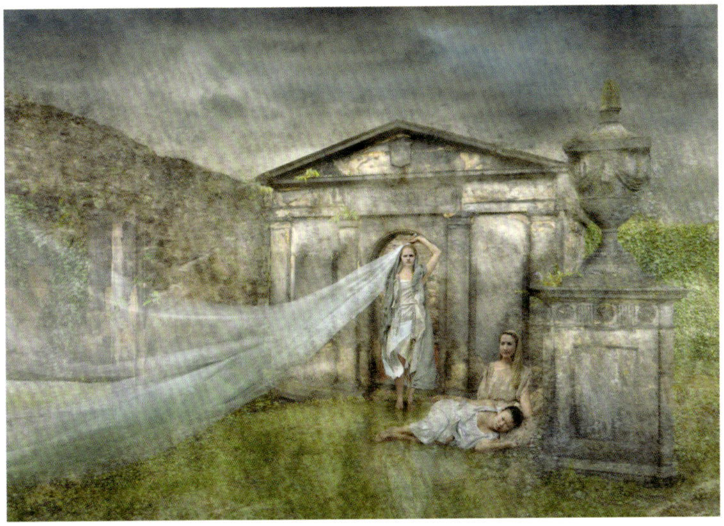

CHRIS CHARNOCK ARPS
AFZAL ANSARY ASIS FRPS
PHIL CHARNOCK FRPS

SYLVIA JONES
DAVID BRIGGS ARPS
GWEN CHARNOCK FRPS

GERMAN CHAPTER

CHAPTER ORGANISER: TONY CUTLER LRPS

The German Chapter was formed in 2009 following discussions with members of The Society resident in Germany. From the very beginning it was decided that the Chapter should organise photographic projects on a regular basis with the idea of holding exhibitions in various locations throughout Germany, thereby making The Society more known to the general public. It was also intended that members should be given the opportunity to explore specific photographic areas, thus broadening their skills and knowledge.

The first exhibition with the theme 'Spectators' opened at the Theatre Museum in Düsseldorf in February 2009 with more than 100 images from 14 photographers. This was also shown at the Park Theatre in Iserlohn. Encouraged by these successes a second theme 'Letters' was chosen and a new exhibition opened in the Märkischen Bank, Menden, in June 2012. Parallel to these activities members organised several workshops including a Portrait Workshop, a Distinctions Advisory weekend with Panel members travelling from the UK and a visit for Travel Group members.

To encourage young photographers, show parents what can be achieved and publicise The Society we organised a school competition entitled 'To be young'. Images by students aged 11-16 taken on iPhones, iPads and cameras were exhibited at the Hohenlimburg School and a 2012 calendar was published. For a second exhibition in Hagen Chapter members added their images on the theme 'Getting Old'. Copies of PORTFOLIO**TWO** were presented to the first placed in each age group and all winners were invited to spend a day at a studio where they had a great time learning about potrait photography. Finally everyone visited an exhibition of monochrome photographs in Düsseldorf.

The photographs that are displayed here are taken from the current project 'White' which has been running since the beginning of 2012. Once again over 100 photographs have been placed on file with subjects ranging from a typical snow scene to a high key portrait and a selection will form the Chapter's next exhibition.

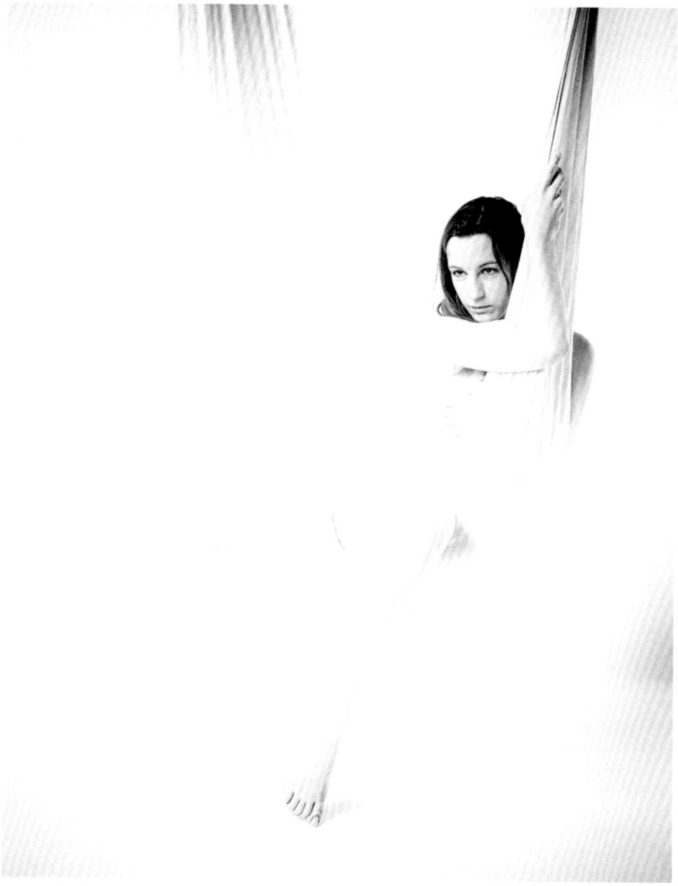

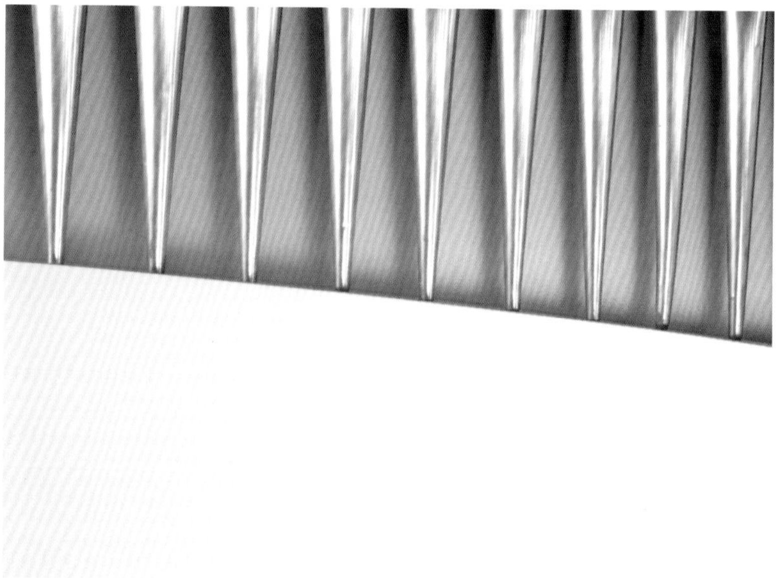

NICKOLAUS GREUNHERZ
ANDREAS PFEIFFER

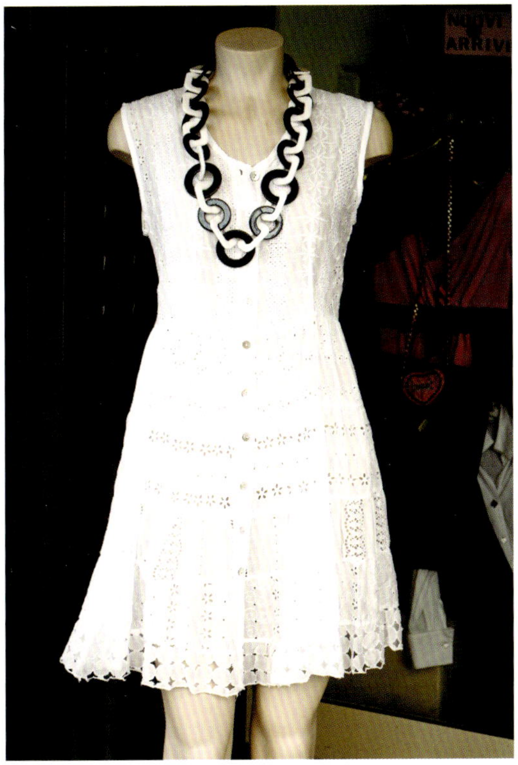

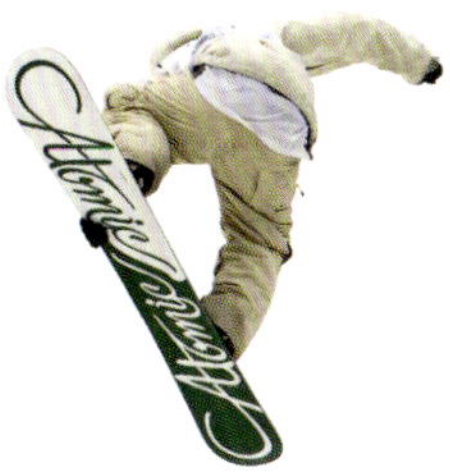

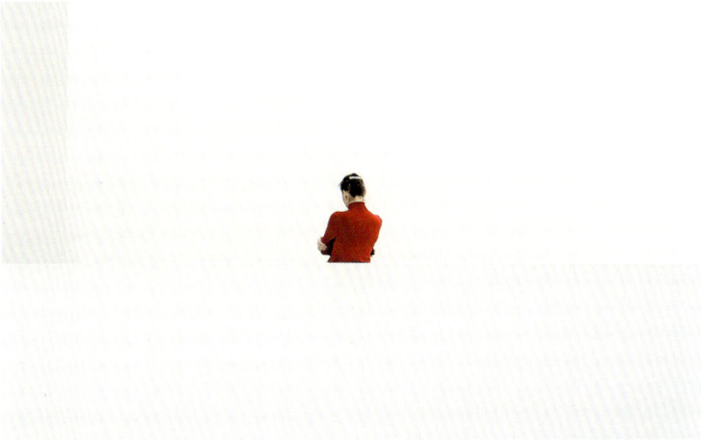

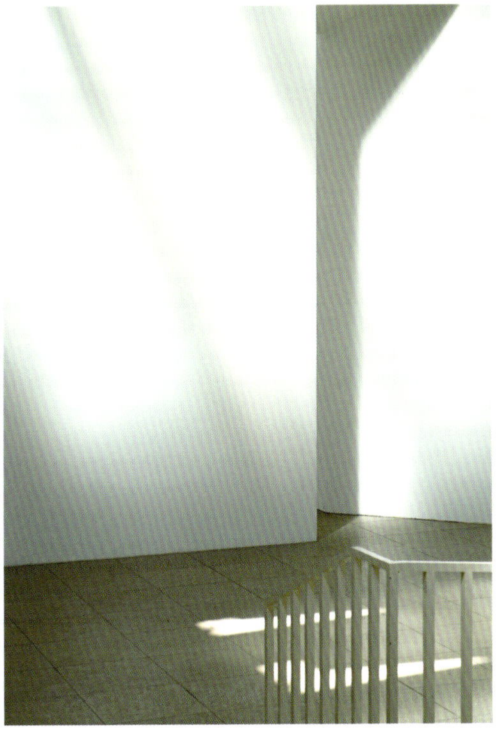

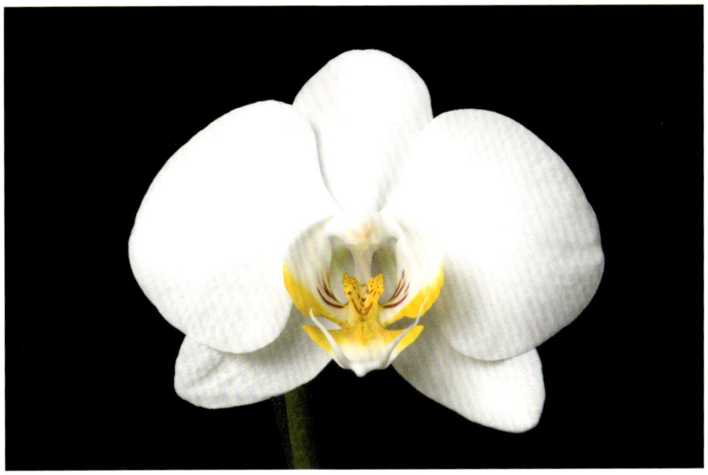

TONY CUTLER LRPS
SIEGFRIED RUBBERT LRPS

PAUL JOYCE LRPS
PAUL JOYCE LRPS
TONY CUTLER LRPS

JAPAN CHAPTER

CHAIRMAN: YOSHIKAZU HAYASHI

The Japan Chapter of The Royal Photographic Society (RPSJ) was founded in September 1996 and has had a number of eminent members. Talking about our activities, the Chapter holds lectures and photography tours, an annual exhibition event, and publishes its RPSJ journal three times a year in addition to issuing news on the website www.rps-japan.org. Talks are usually by members about their experiences, with individual photo exhibitions. The annual assembly is abundant and informative, providing an opportunity to meet socially and share expertise. Members are encouraged to apply for Society Distinctions and the Chapter is working to increase membership, particularly encouraging junior members.

The Chapter's 11th exhibition in March 2013 was held in the gallery at the Frameman Exhibition Salon in Ginza, Tokyo with the theme "What is British like" following the 2012 10th exhibition "Feel British", displaying images which feature feelings as much as possible – a challenge to reflect a British-style spirit that the photographer has located in Japan or elsewhere. It was an opportunity for our members to rediscover Great Britain. Visitors to the gallery include the Japanese who have experienced the British lifestyle, British businessmen, students from home and overseas working and studying in Japan.

Members have been successful in major exhibitions, both in Japan and elsewhere. We wish to mention the recent remarkable news that some members were awarded the Gran Prix (grand prize) at the most traditional photography exhibition in Japan. The Society was also delighted that I was able to attend the opening of the 152nd and 153rd RPS International Print Exhibitions in London in 2011 and 2012, meeting with Society trustees and staff and receiving both Allen & Overy Awards.

The images we have shown for PORTFOLIO**THREE** reflect Japanese culture and our members' individual styles.

Translated by Yoshio Miyake, Secretary to Mr Hayashi

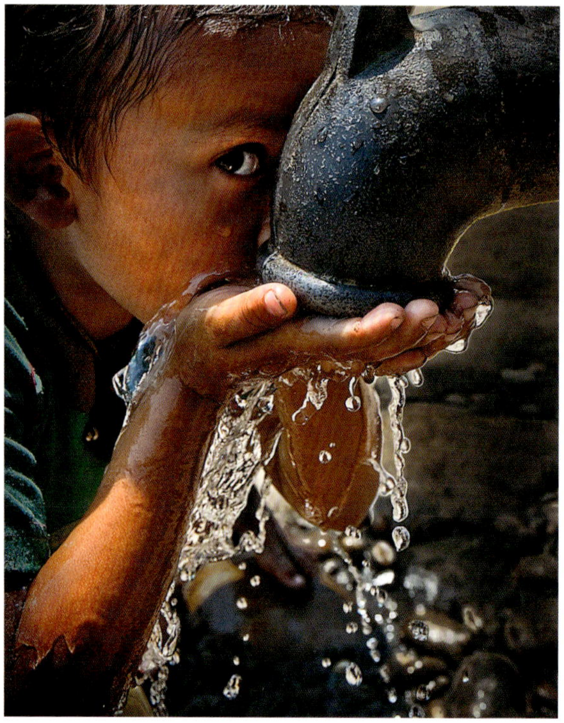

ISAMU MINODA

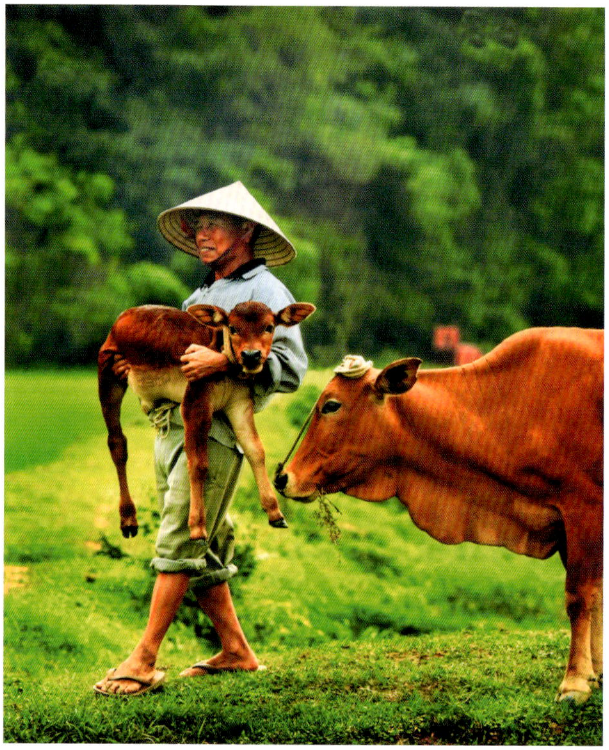

KAZUO SAITA

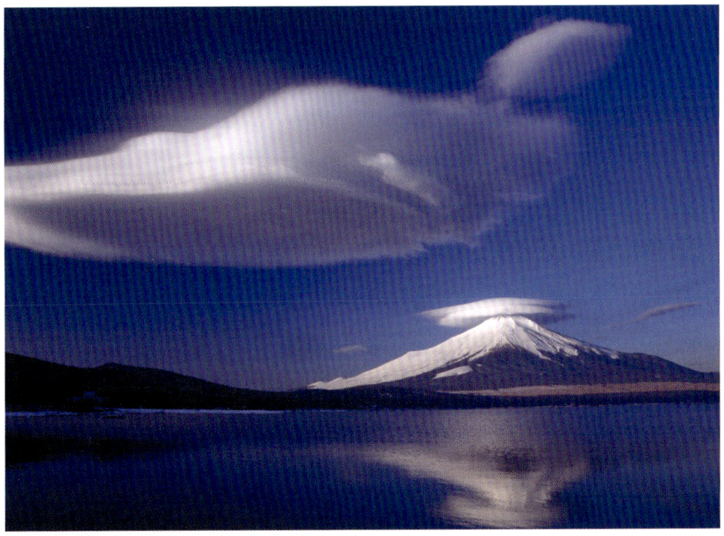

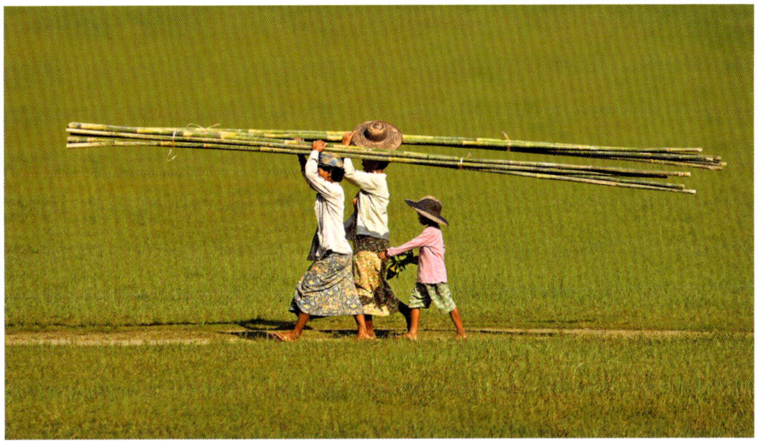

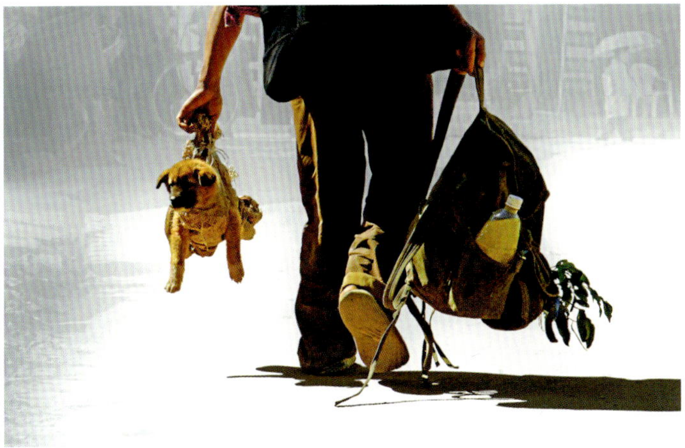

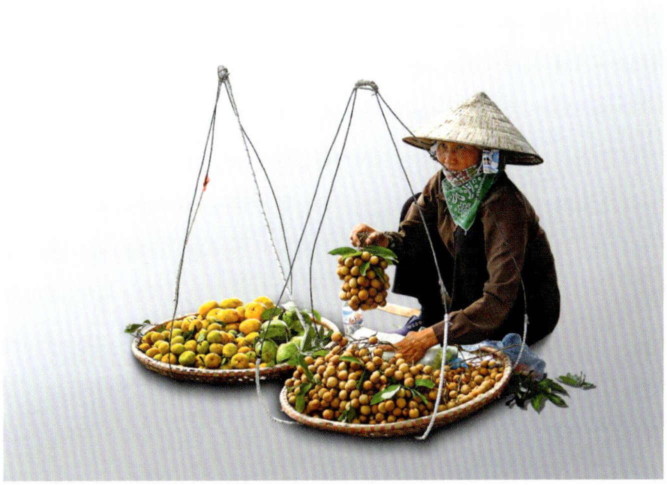

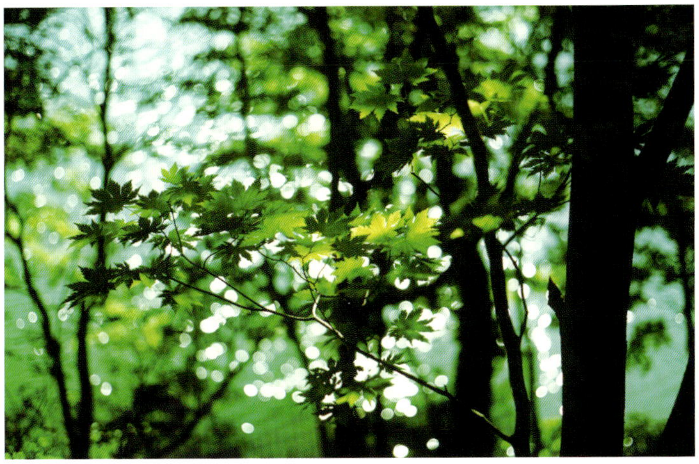

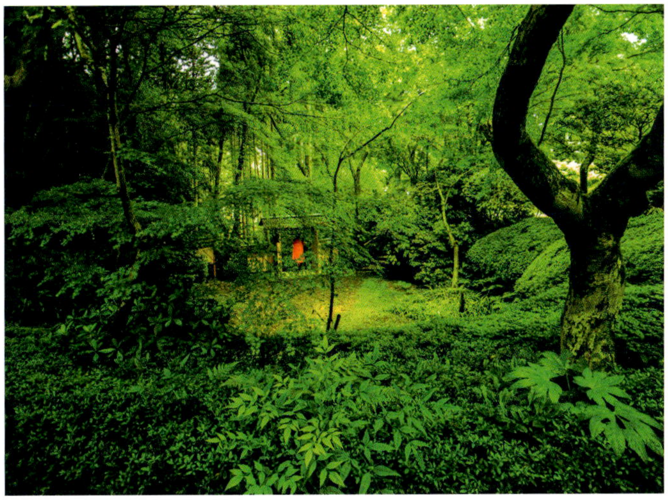

SEIKO MORI
YOSHIKASU HAYASHI
KENICHI KAWAMURA

YOSHIKASU HAYASHI
ISAMU MINODA
HIROSHI ISHIGURO

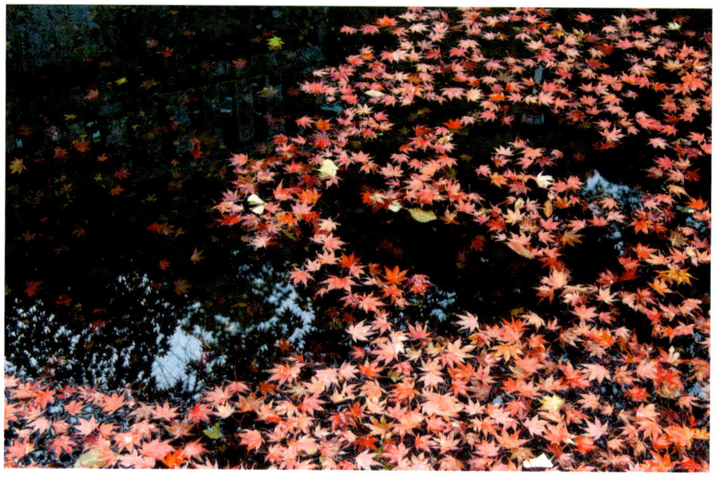

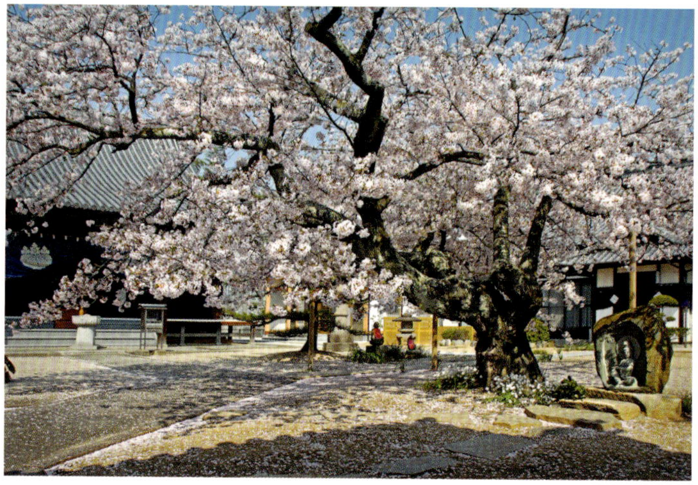

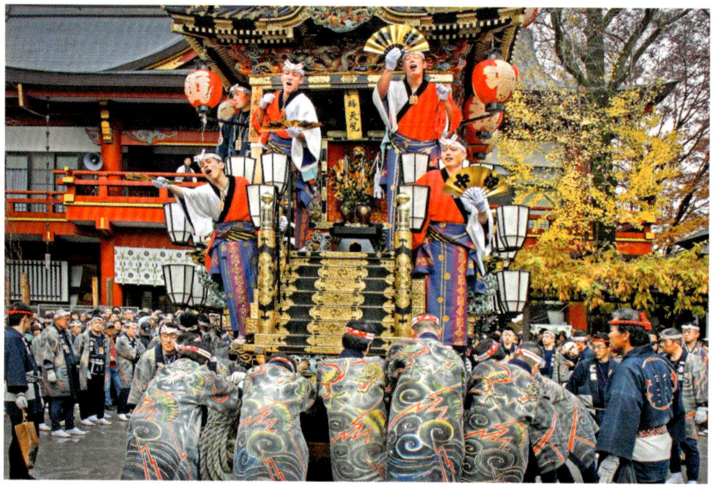

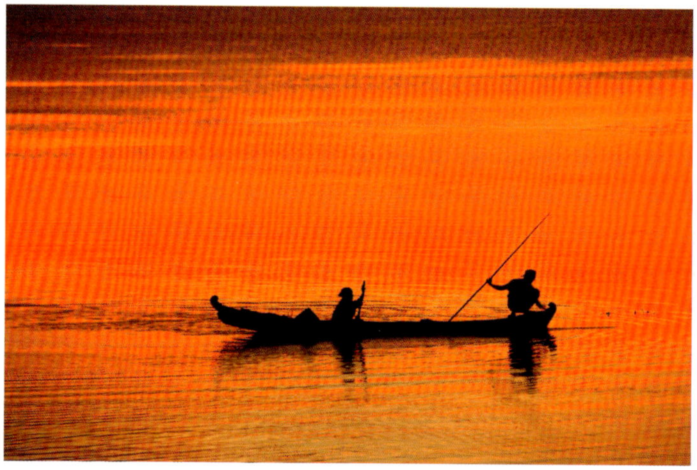

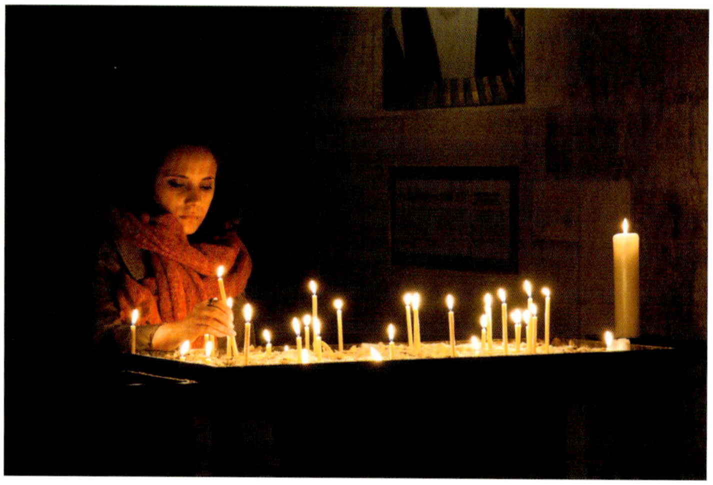

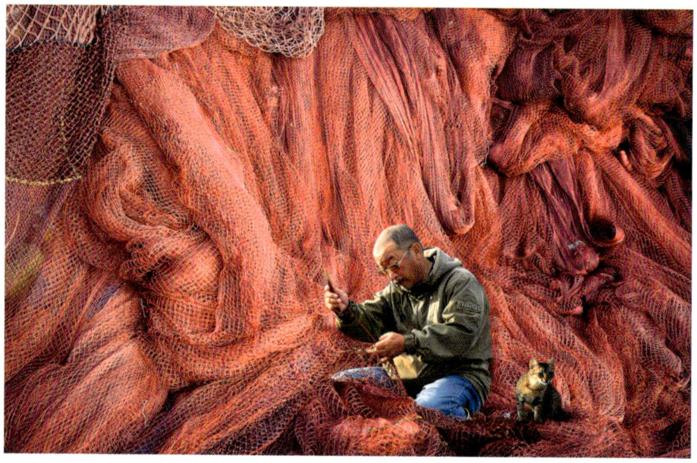

HIBIYA YOSHIO LRPS
EKIKO MASUDA
HIBIYA YOSHIO LRPS

EKIKO MASUDA
KASUMI DOBASHI
TETSUKO ISHIBASHI

SPECIAL INTEREST GROUPS

The Special Interest Groups offer additional services and resources covering many different aspects of the art and science of photography. Each Group offers its members a variety of activities relevant to that special interest, usually including events, exhibitions, and newsletters. Several Groups have postal or web portfolios and members are encouraged to enter work.

Many Groups will give advice and guidance on how to improve your photographic skills and you will certainly have the opportunity to meet with like-minded photographers.

For a small additional fee members are encouraged to join one or more Special Interest Groups. For new members The Society offers the opportunity to join one Group at no cost in their first year of membership.

Featured in this section is work from two of the fourteen Special Interest Groups:

Archaeology and Heritage Group
Featuring a small selection of images from Group members.

Nature Group
Richard Revels FRPS explains the challenges and approaches of photographing insects in flight.

ARCHAEOLOGY AND HERITAGE GROUP

CHAIRMAN: R KEITH EVANS FRPS

Founded in 1974 as the Archaeology Group, the Archaeology and Heritage Group has since expanded to include a wide variety of heritage interests and activities.

These range from the photography and recording of archaeological discoveries to that of buildings, artefacts, transport, and military and industrial heritage.

The Group offers a varied programme of visits to places of historical interest – six or seven each year – and lectures on relevant topics and photographic techniques. A twice-yearly journal, Heritage Photography, is mailed to all members, and a periodical print exhibition takes place: in 2012, as part of British Archaeology Fortnight, this focused on Church Architecture and Heritage.

Many of our members make practical use of their skills in this genre of applied photography. Several provide pictures to the photo libraries of The National Trust, English Heritage and the RIBA; others regularly lecture or write for the technical or academic press.

In the past few years, members have enjoyed the opportunity to photograph in such diverse locations as Ely, Guildford and Hereford cathedrals, military museums at Duxford, Chatham and Woolwich Arsenal, preserved steam railways and numerous great houses of The National Trust; the pictures shown here typify the Group's wide range of interests.

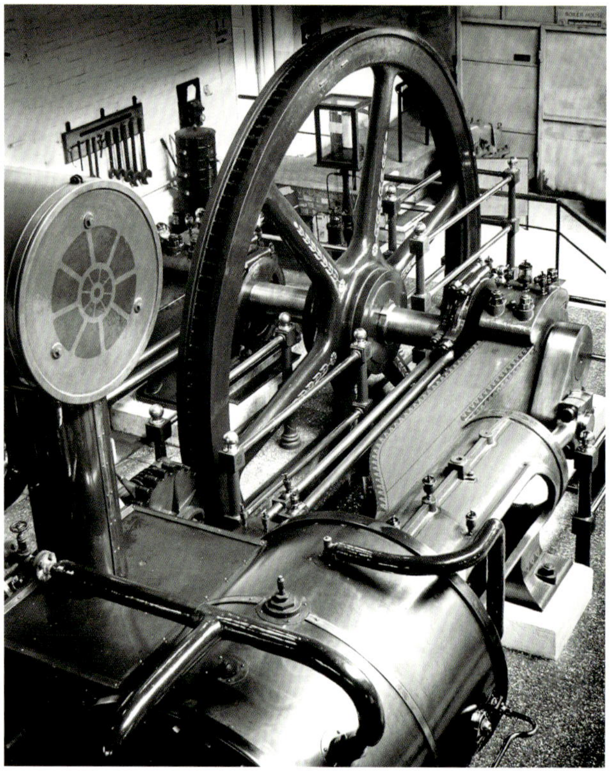

KEITH EVANS FRPS
CROSS-COMPOUND STATIONARY ENGINE, 1910

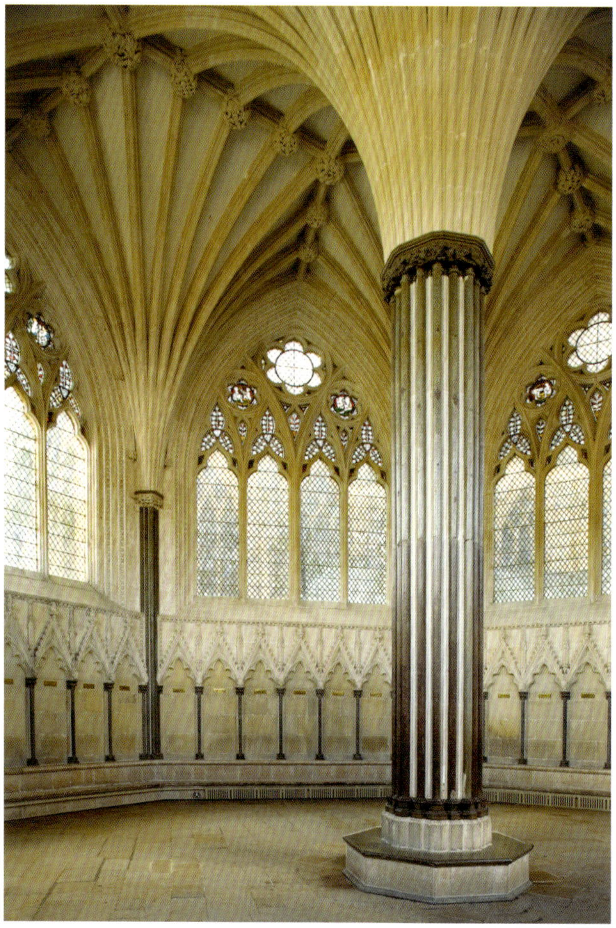

CLIVE TANNER FRPS
THE CHAPTER HOUSE, WELLS CATHEDRAL

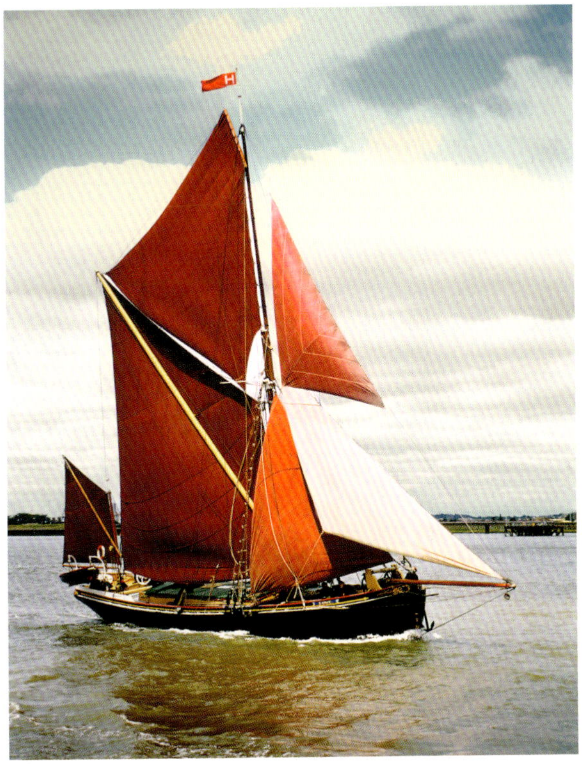

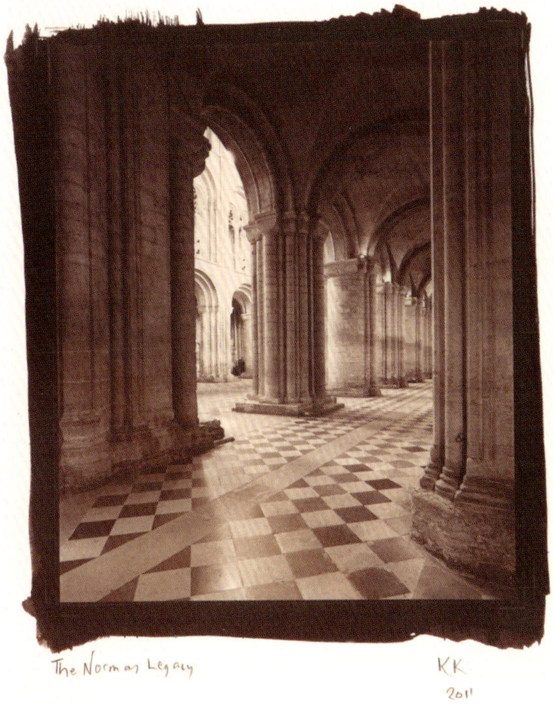

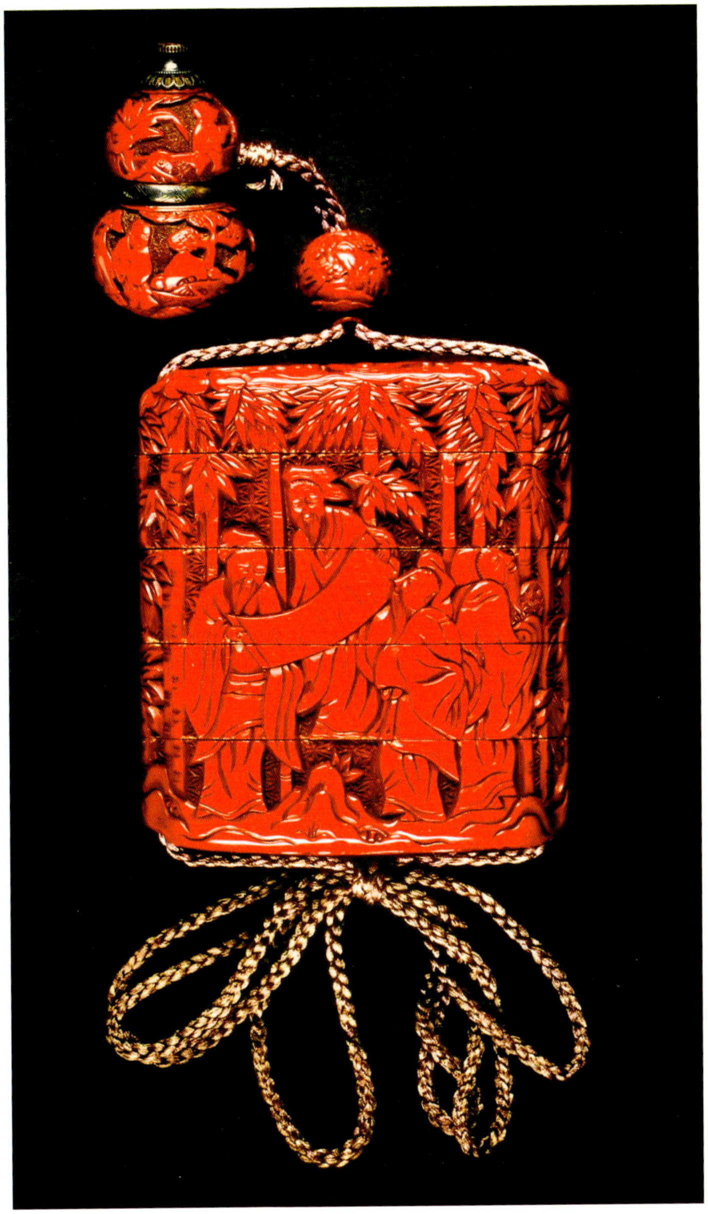

KEITH EVANS FRPS
SPRITSAIL BARGE 'EDME', HARWICH – BUILT IN 1898

KEN KEEN FRPS
ELY CATHEDRAL – 'THE NORMAN LEGACY'

CLIVE TANNER FRPS
19TH CENTURY JAPANESE INRO, NETSUKE AND OJIME

NATURE GROUP
CHAIRMAN: TONY BOND FRPS

Founded in January 1976 under the Chairmanship of Heather Angel Hon. FRPS the Nature Group's aim has remained 'to bring together photographers, naturalists and biologists who will encourage each other, by a cross fertilisation of ideas and techniques, to broaden their approaches to this branch of photography'. The Group has a membership of around six hundred, largely in this country but with members from the four quarters of the globe. Today the Group comprises the whole spectrum of abilities ranging from some of the most eminent and well-known professionals; respected tour leaders, natural history authors with several books to their name; contributors to magazines; lecturers etc., to those who are just starting out.

The Group publishes its Journal 'The Iris' three times a year, and holds an annual exhibition and lecture meetings, including a biennial Chairman's day, with high quality invited speakers. A weekend residential field meeting and a wide range of day field meetings are organised by individual Nature Group members. A biennial Nature Photography Convention which attracts a broad spectrum of delegates is held jointly with organisations including the Nature Photographers' Portfolio, the Zoological Photography Club and the Nature Photographers' Society.

The advent of digital photography and the rapid increase in the capability of cameras and lenses has led to a dramatic increase in the number of photographers recording the natural world. As a result superb images of birds in flight and of large mammals behaving in often spectacular ways are now commonplace. While many Nature Group members are interested in birds and mammals, a few concentrate on smaller subjects nearer to home, and Richard Revels FRPS is one such member. We have chosen a selection of his images of insects in flight as an example of images which are away from the mainstream.

Richard Revels FRPS has been interested in insects and their behaviour from boyhood and these photographs are taken, using three different techniques, to show insects in flight. Manual focus was used except where autofocus is stated.

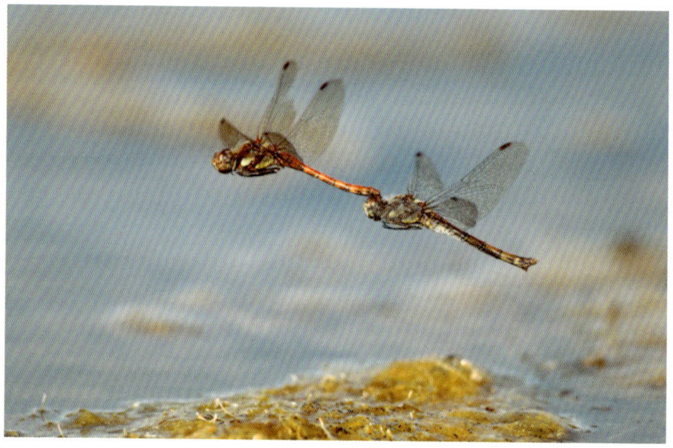

Common Darter Dragonflies in tandem

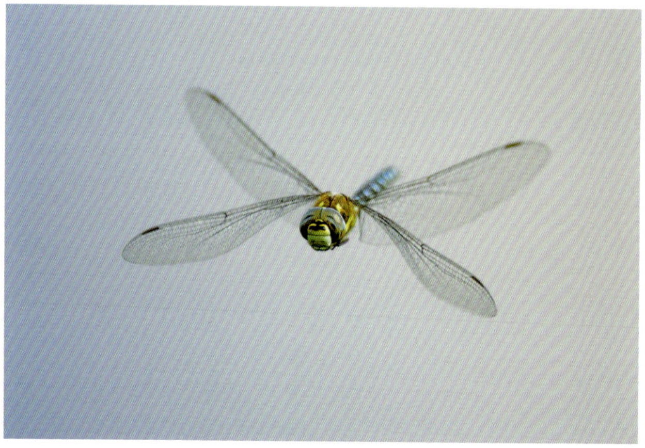

Migrant Hawker Dragonfly hovering

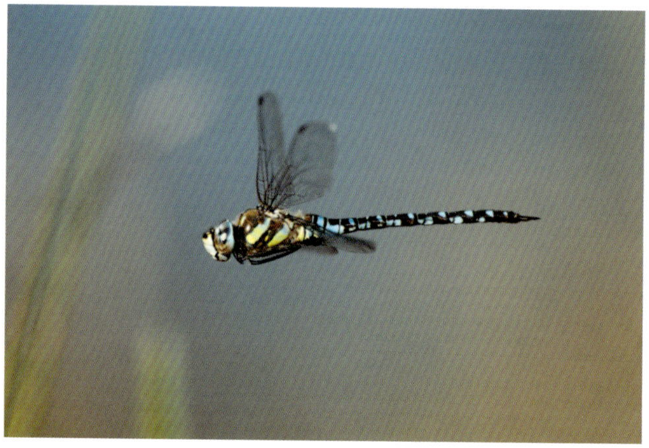

Migrant Hawker Dragonfly hovering

These images were taken using a 500mm telephoto lens with an extension tube to enable closer focusing. Using a fairly high ISO rating (usually 800 ISO) allows the use of a shutter speed of at least 1/1000th of a second. Autofocus was used for these Dragonflies as they flew or hovered around a lake.

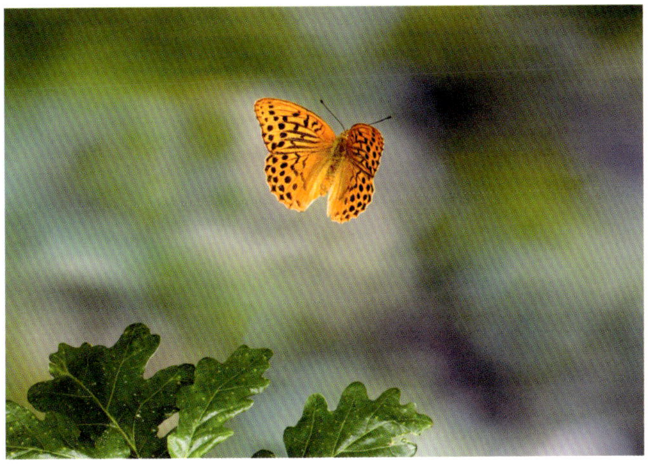

Silver-washed Fritillary butterfly flying from oak leaves.

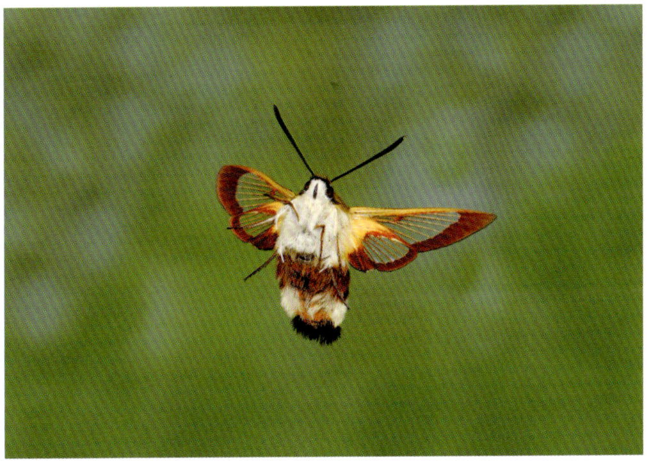

Broad-bordered Bee Hawk-moth in flight

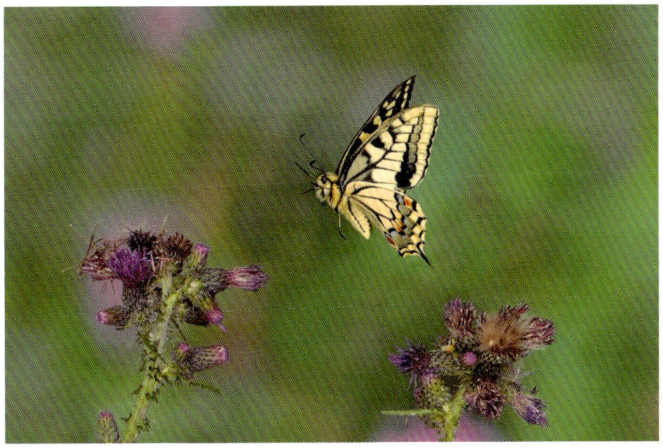

Swallowtail butterfly flying to thistle

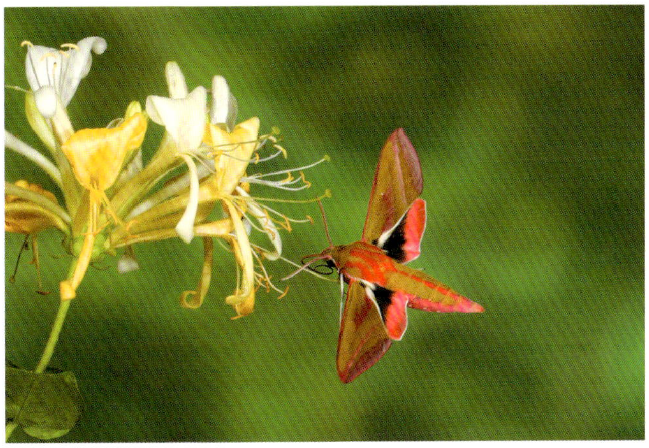

Elephant Hawk-moth feeding at honeysuckle

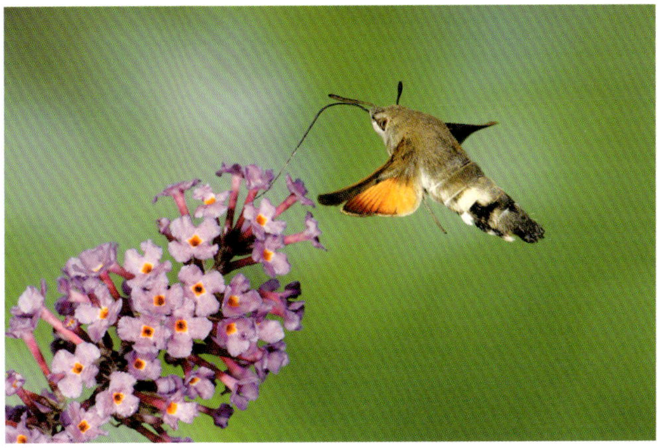

Hummingbird Hawk-moth feeding at buddleia

This series was taken using a flight cage in the studio, using a 180mm macro lens with flash as the light source – one master flash unit and five or six slave units. Autofocus was only used to take the Hummingbird Hawk-moth as it flew around and fed on the buddleia flowers. The other images were taken after manually pre-focusing in an area where I expected the insect to fly.

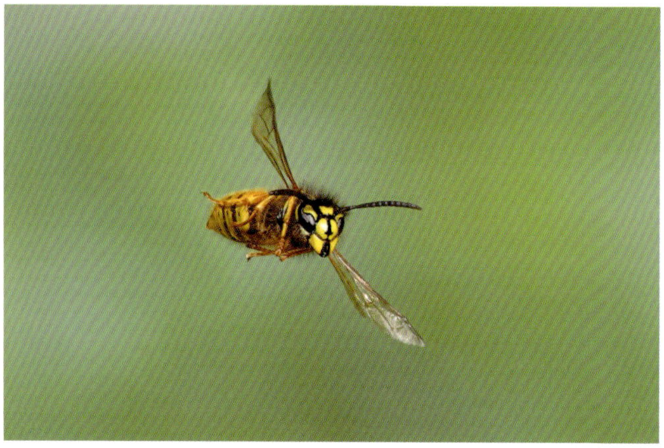

Common Wasp in flight

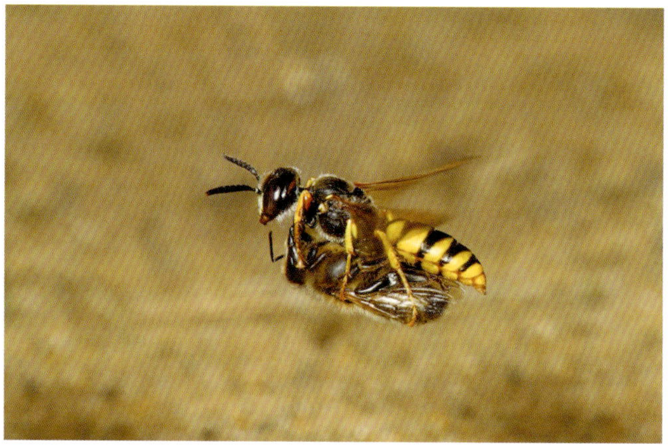

Bee Wolf Wasp with Honeybee prey

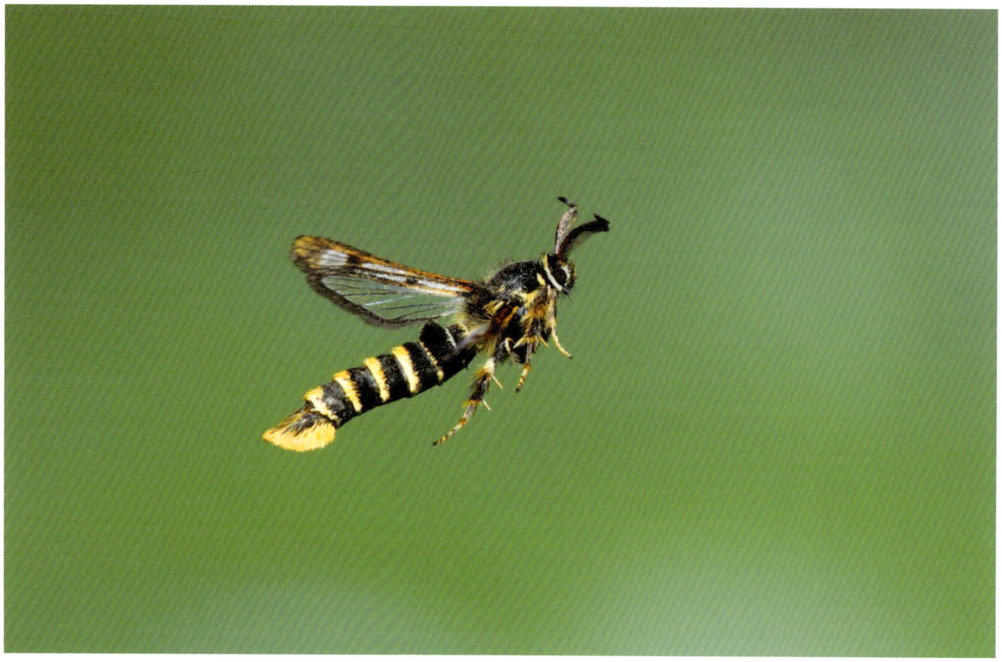

Raspberry Clearwing moth

These images were taken outdoors in the wild, again using the 180mm macro lens with flash as the light source. For the Bee Wolf Wasp flying with its Honeybee prey, just 2 flash units were used, one on a bracket the other on the camera hotshoe. The Common Wasp was photographed as it flew around an over-ripe apple, 7 flash units were used to freeze this insect in flight. The same technique was used to take the Raspberry Clearwing moth flying to a pheromone lure in a garden near to raspberry canes.

MEMBERS' GALLERY

A selection of images submitted by members

An invitation to submit images for the Members' Gallery was provided to all The Society's members. The impressive presentation of the previous Portfolios stimulated many members to submit their work for PORTFOLIO**THREE** and over 4,000 images were received, covering many genres and approaches to photography. Every picture was considered by the selection panel who struggled to reduce the numbers to a short list of outstanding images, not all of which could be included in this Gallery.

The final selection was designed to show the excellent talents of the membership and the diversity of subject matter and approach.

Those who have work included can rightly be proud of this achievement.

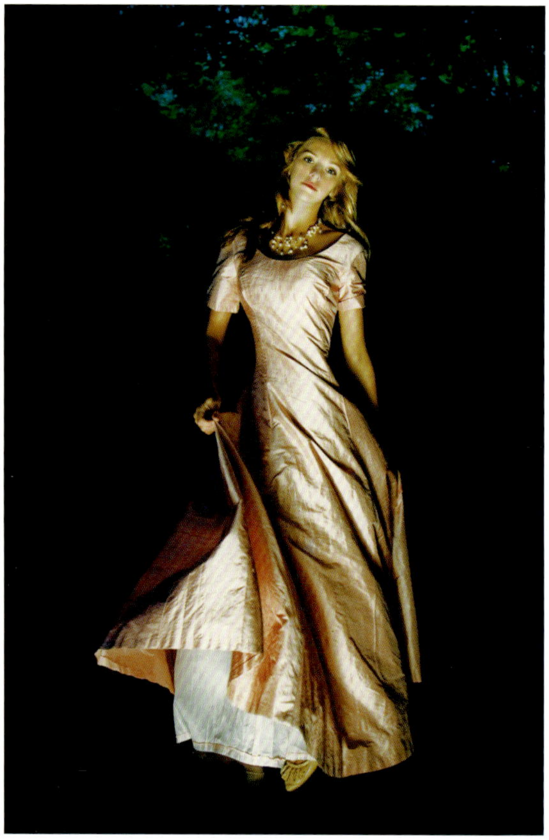

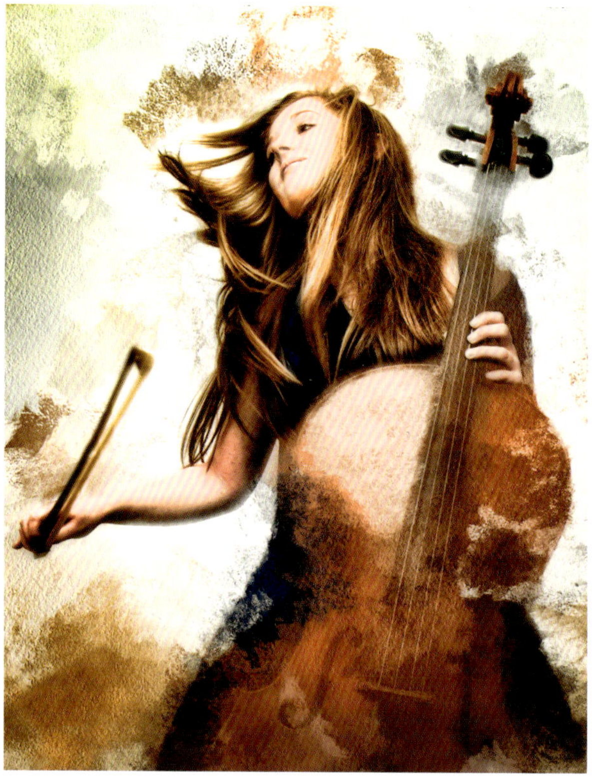

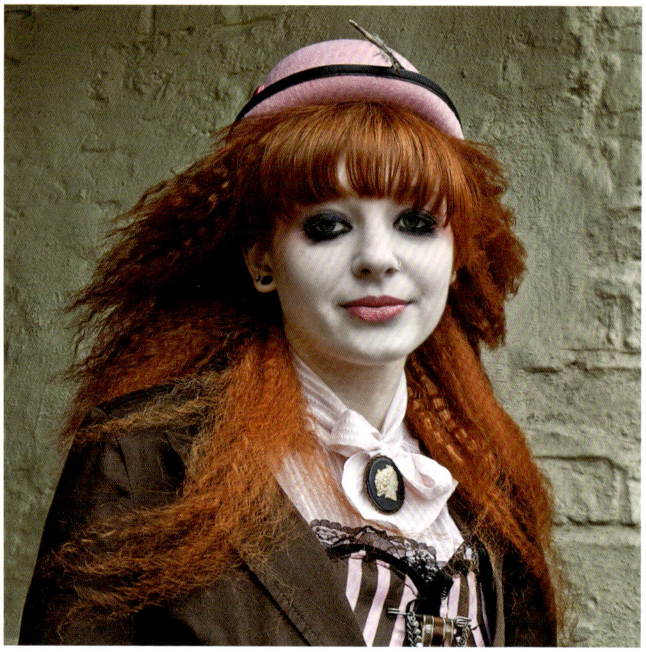

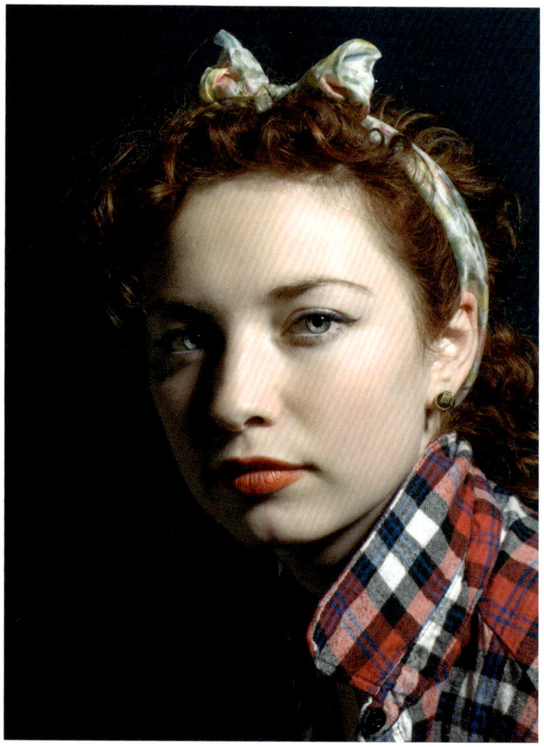

JULIA CLEAVER ARPS UK
BARBARA HILL ARPS UK

STEPHEN LLOYD LRPS UK
TREVOR HIDDEN UK

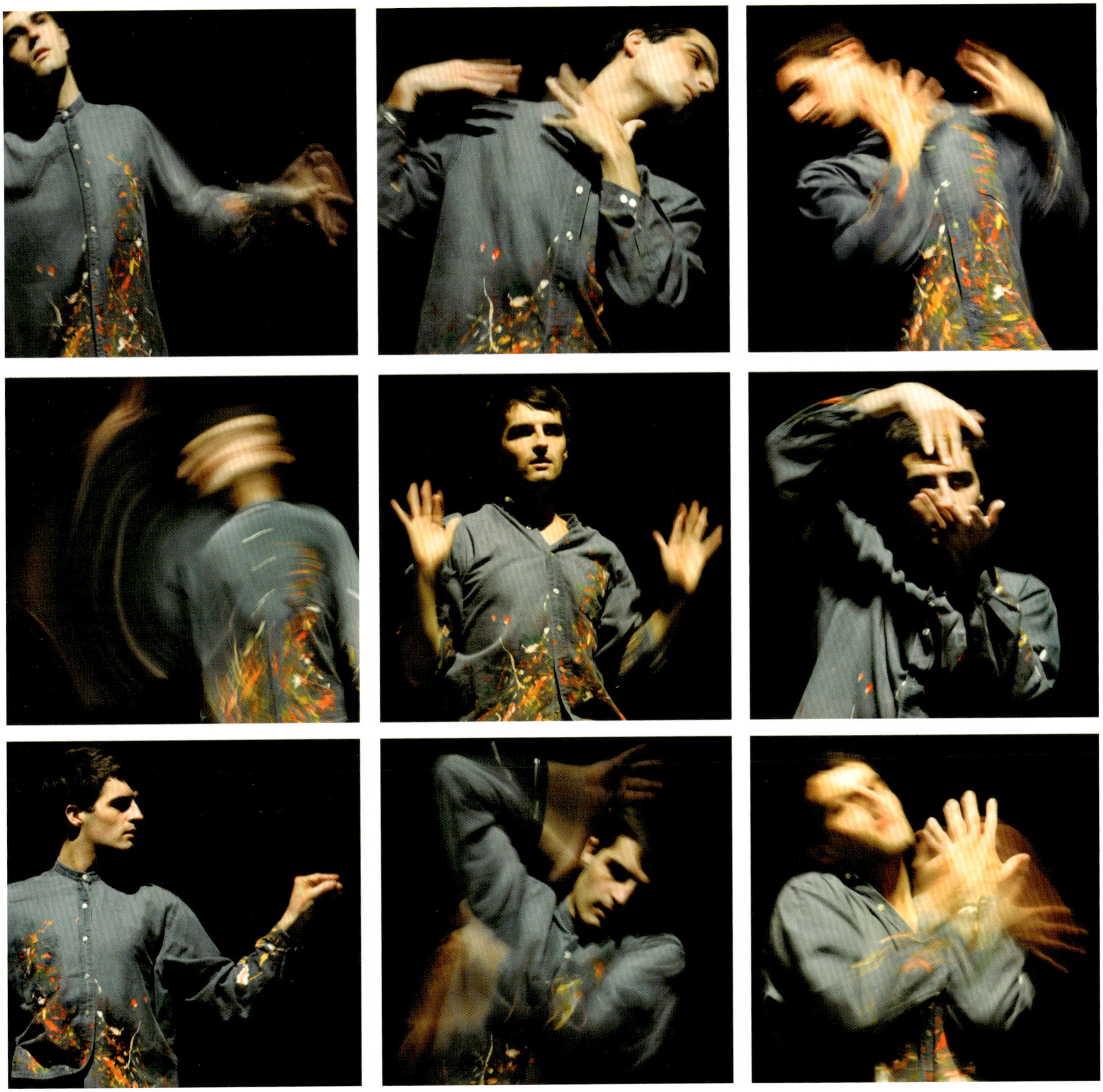

ROY ROBERTSON Hon.FRPS UK

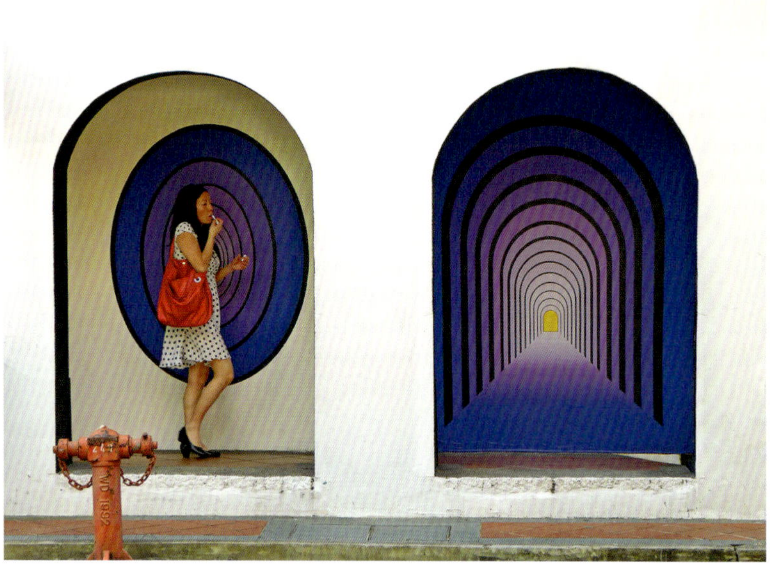

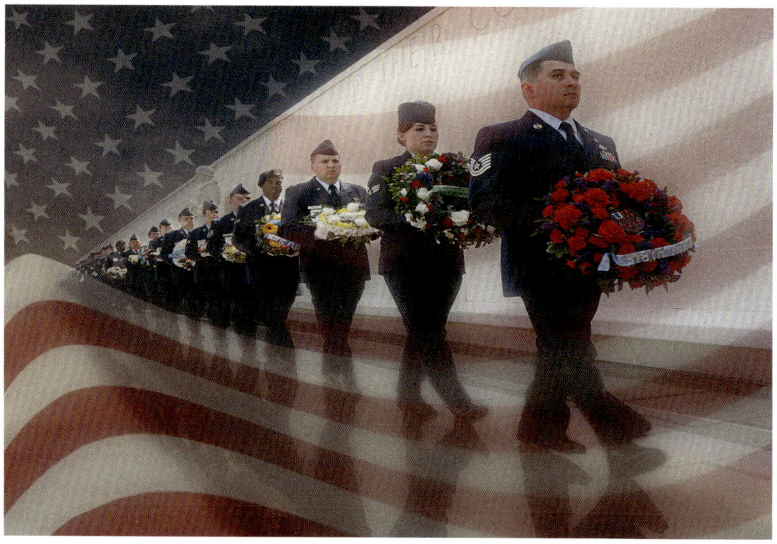

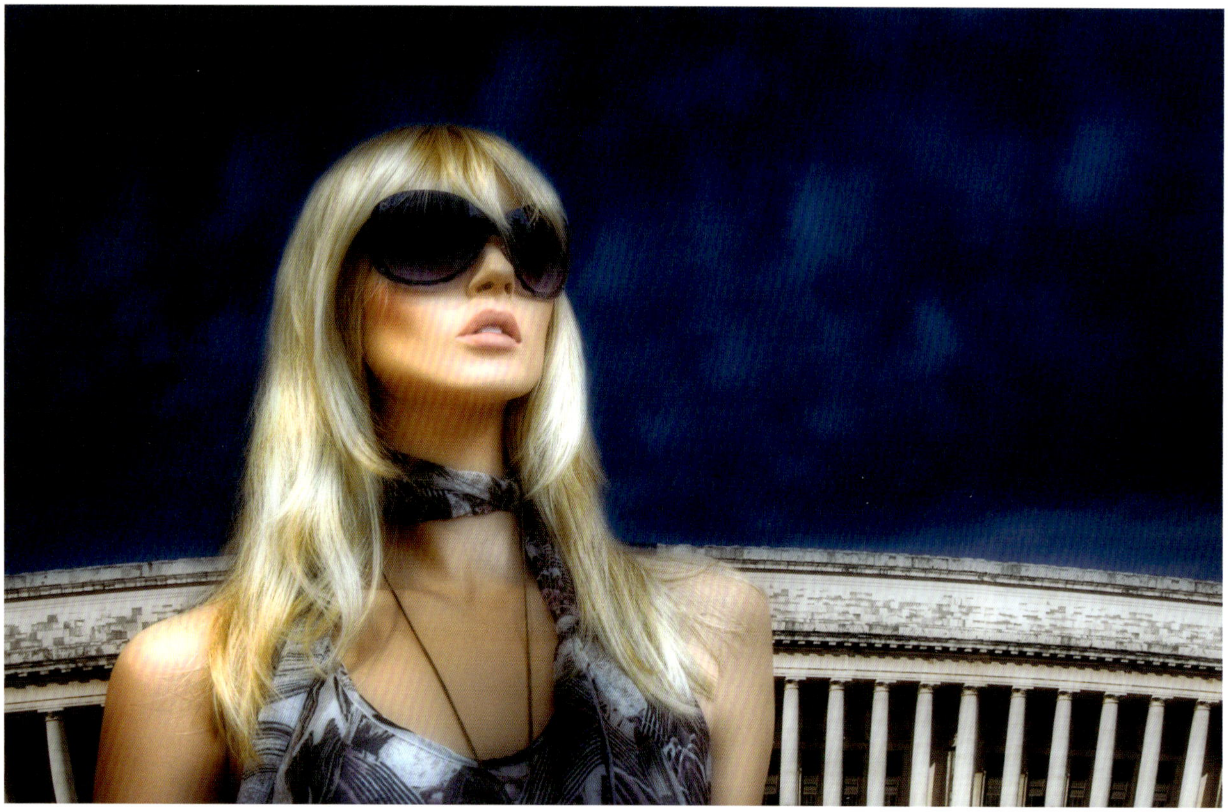

AH SOOI WONG FRPS SINGAPORE
LEO PALMER FRPS UK

COLIN HARRISON FRPS UK

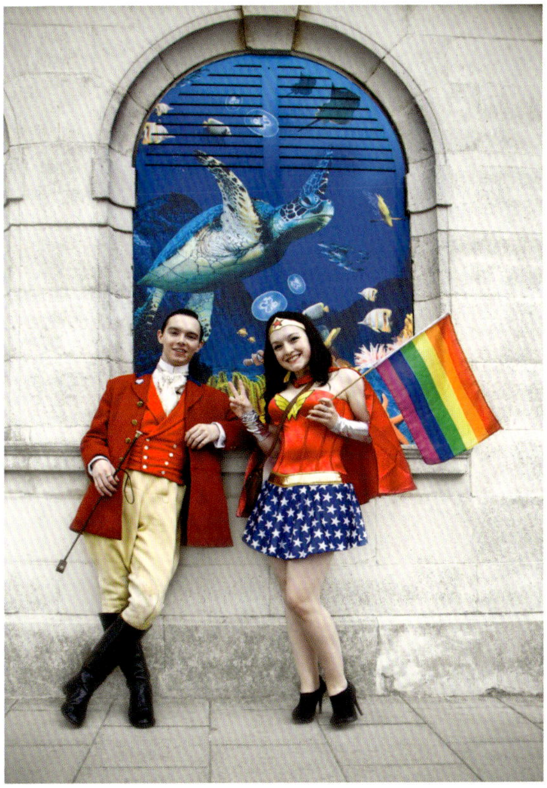

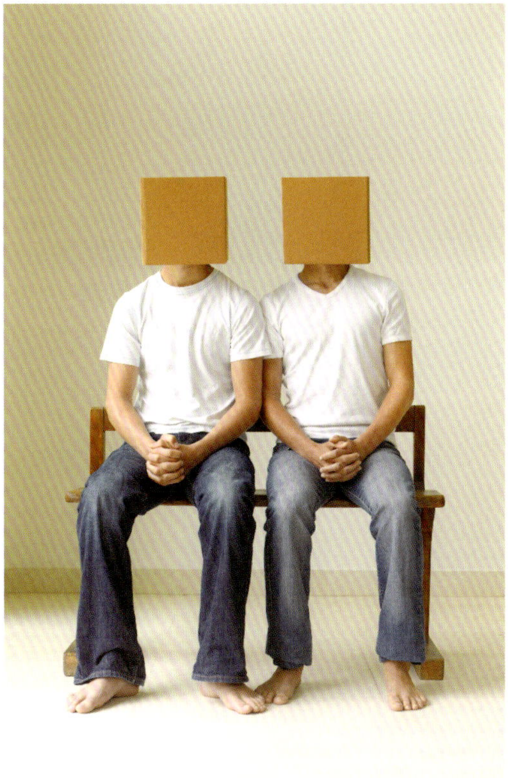

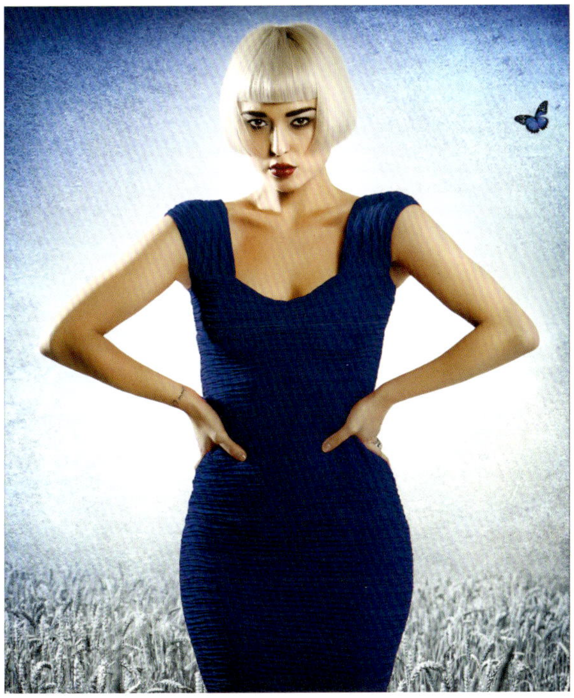

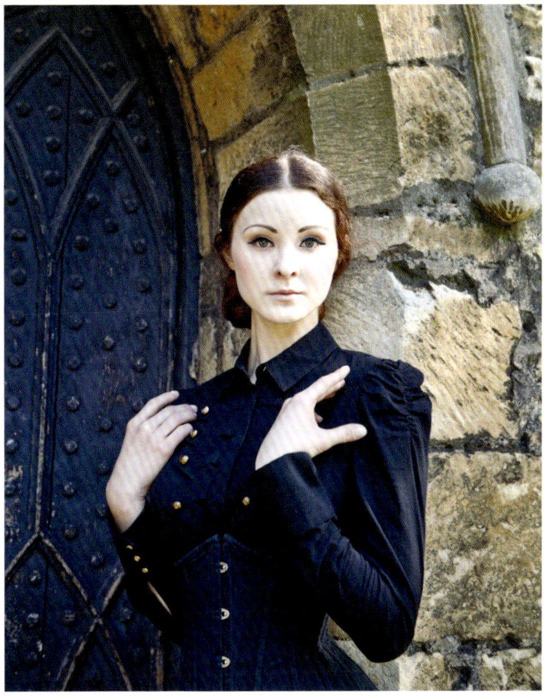

BOB WEBZELL ARPS UK
ROSS McKELVEY ARPS UK

PETER DAZELEY FRPS UK
BARBARA HILL ARPS UK

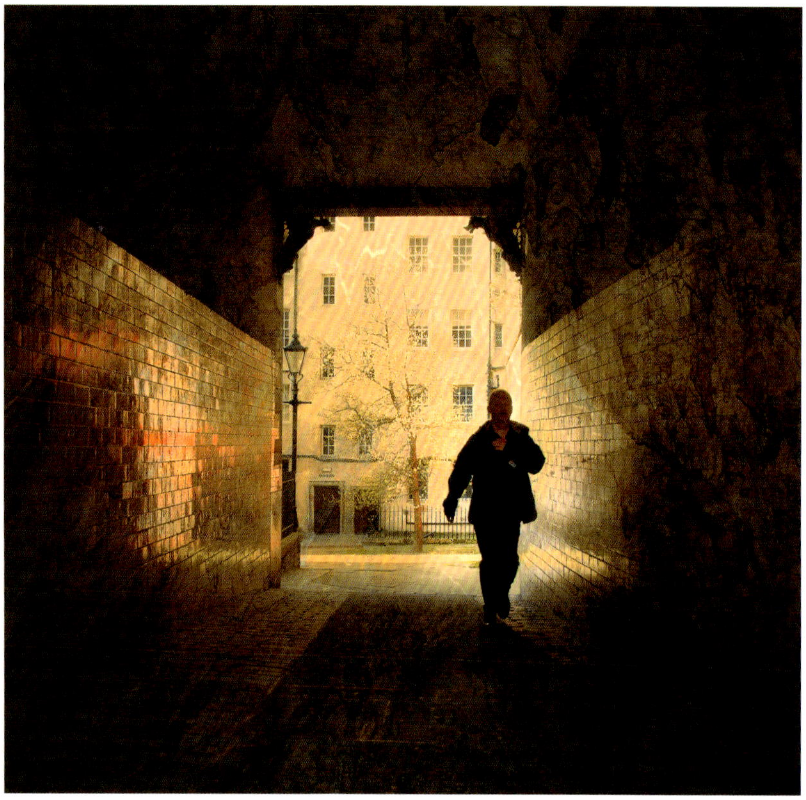

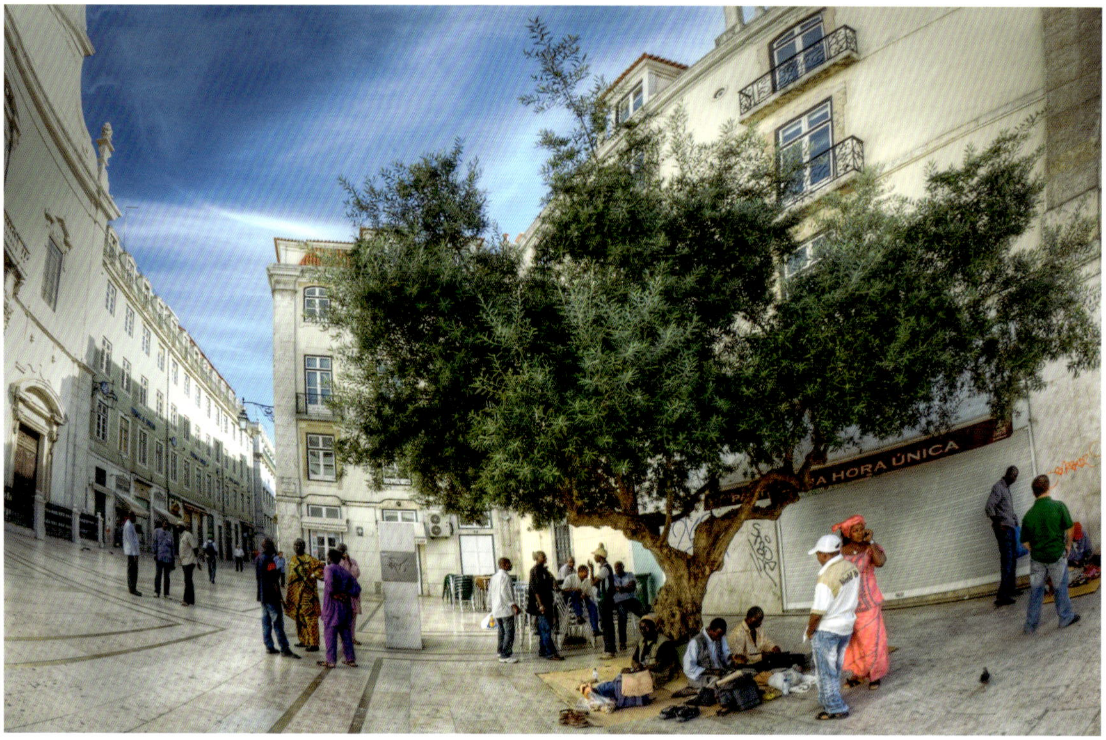

DAVID COOKE ARPS UK
CAROL PALMER ARPS UK

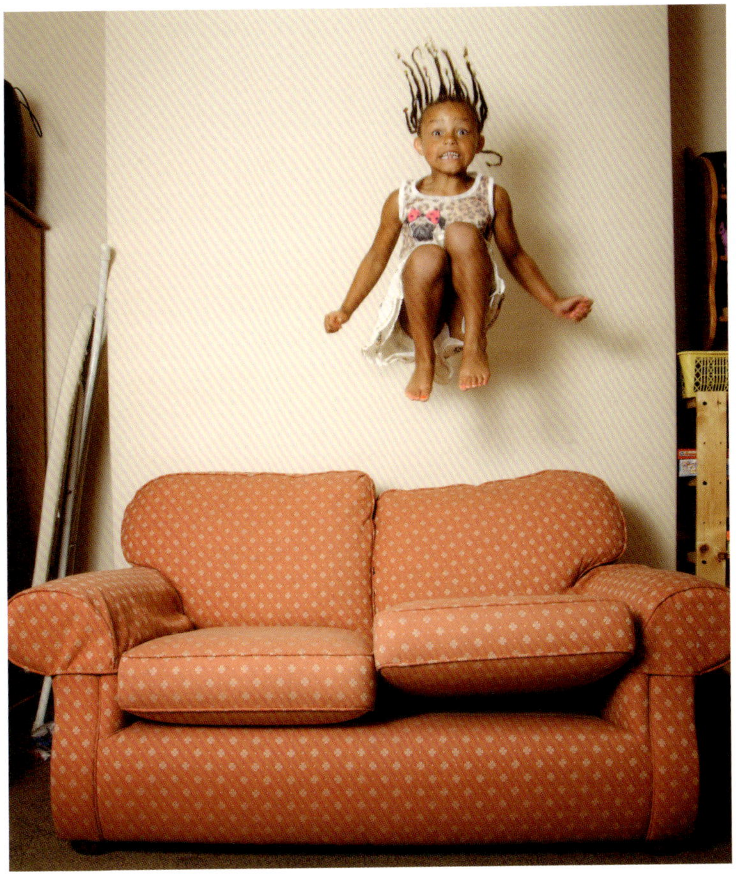

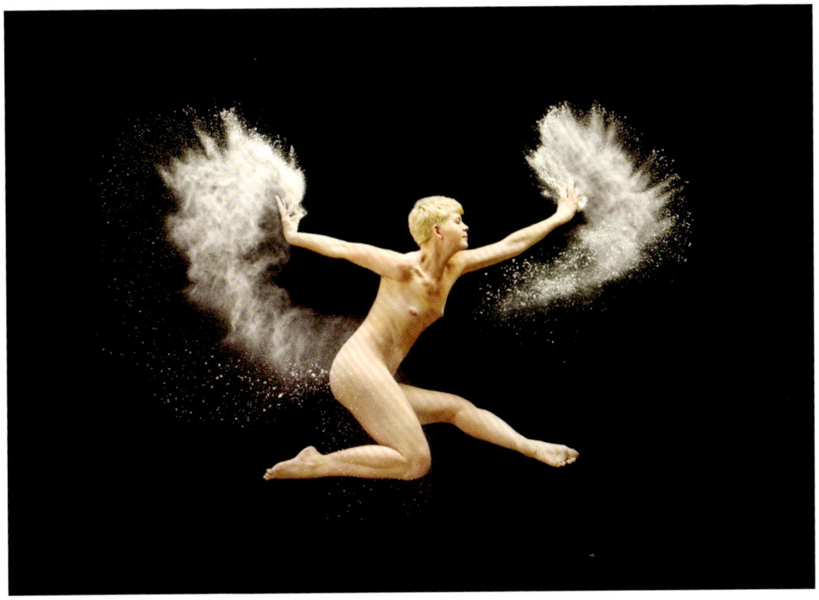

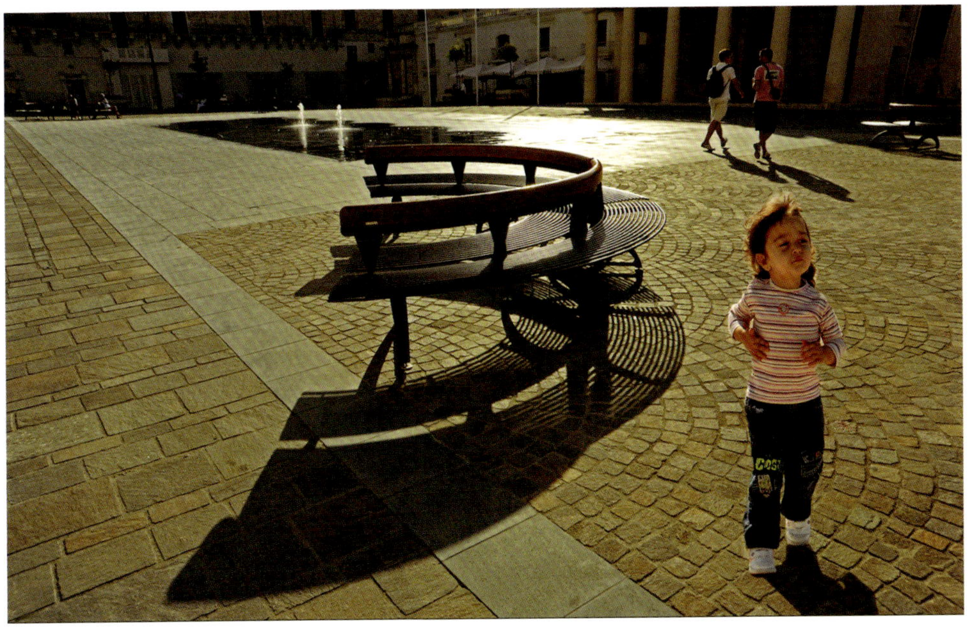

RAY GROVER ARPS UK

PETER DAZELEY FRPS UK

GEOFF SMITH ARPS UK

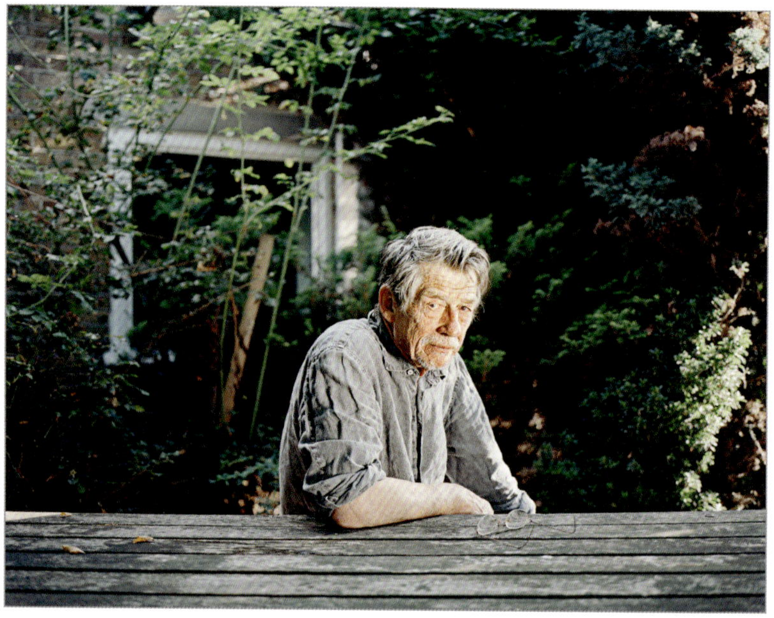

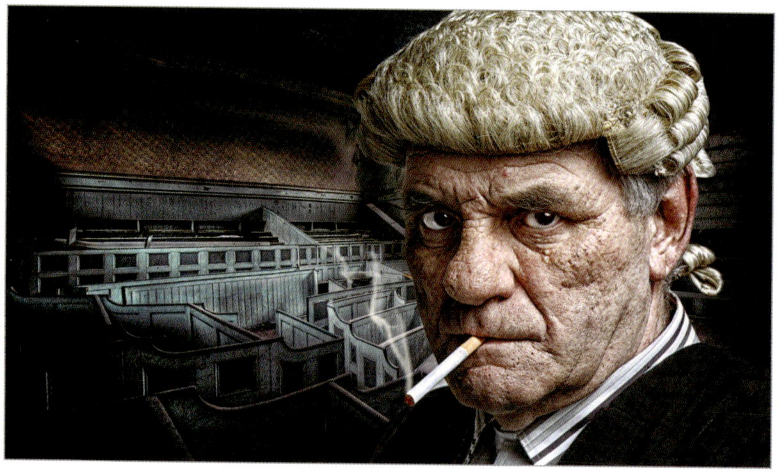

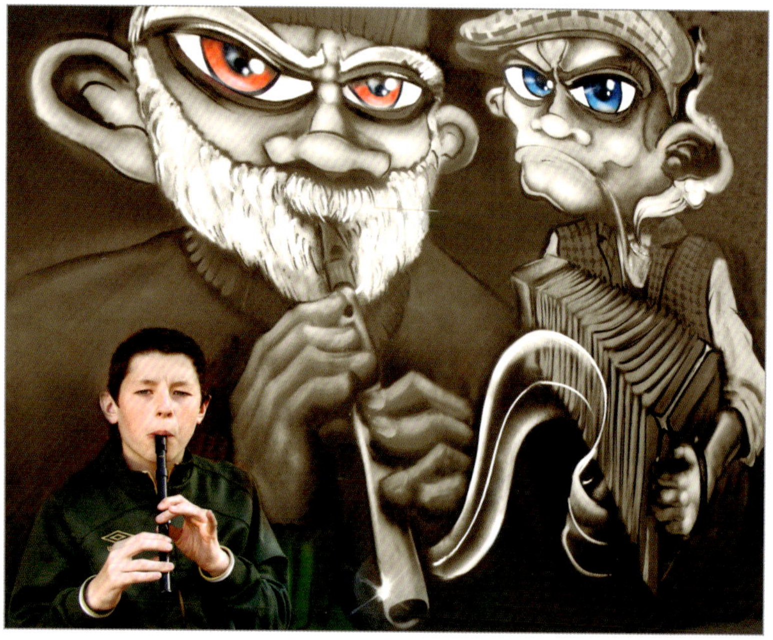

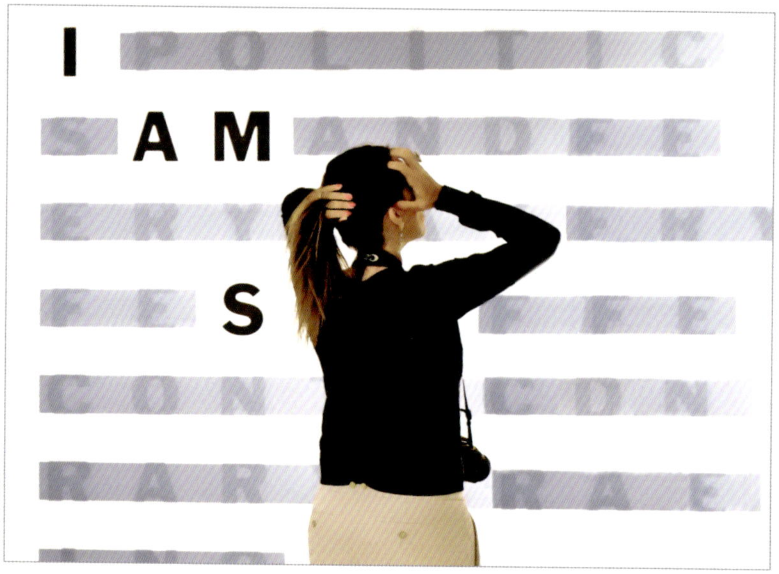

THOMAS BALL ARPS UK
MARGARET SALISBURY FRPS UK

ROSS McKELVEY ARPS UK
KAREN BERRY FRPS UK

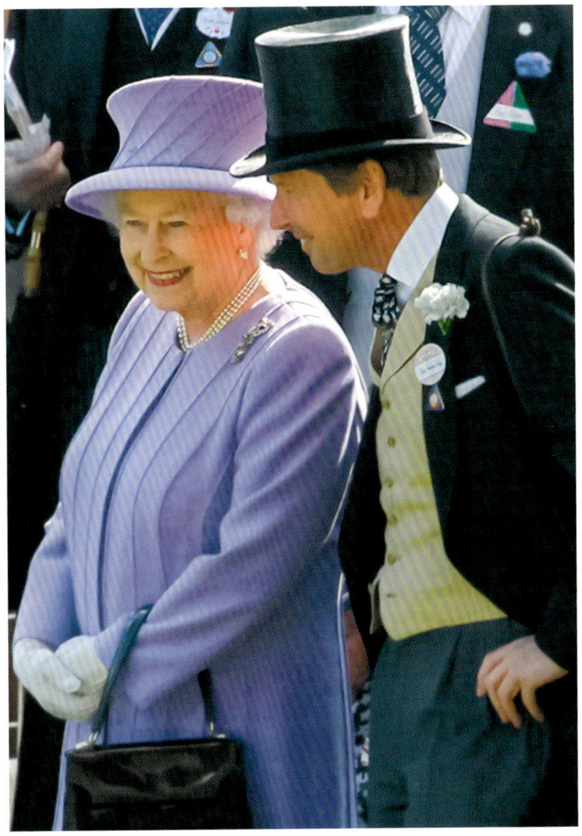

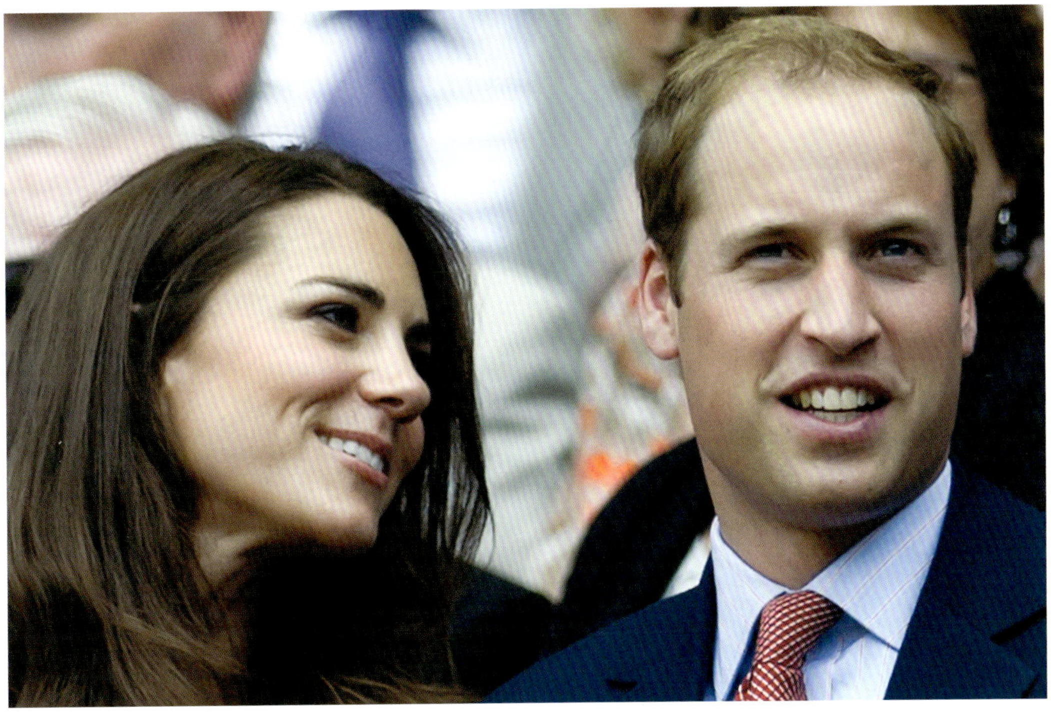

EDDY LANE ARPS UK
DUNCAN GROVE FRPS UK

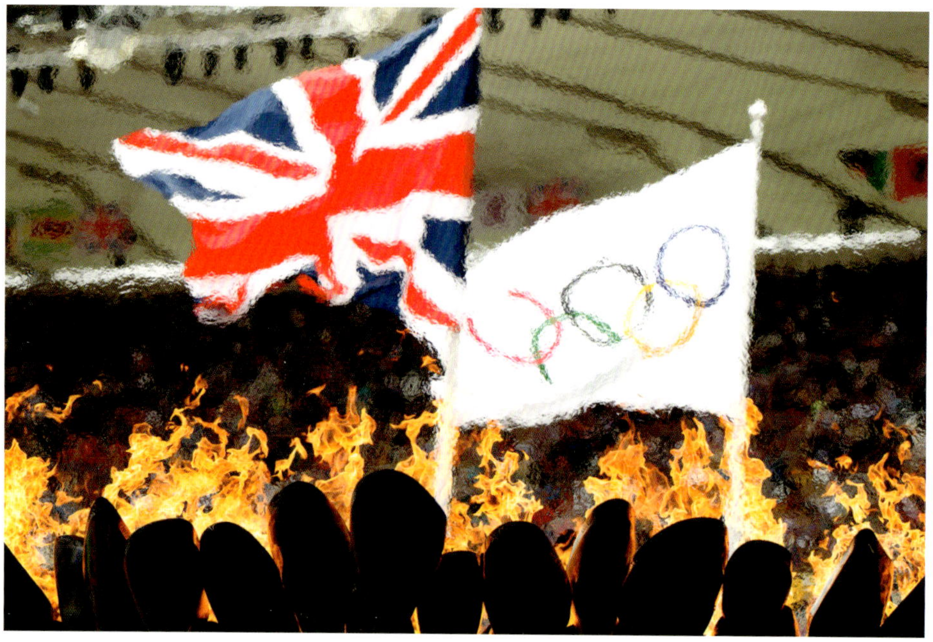

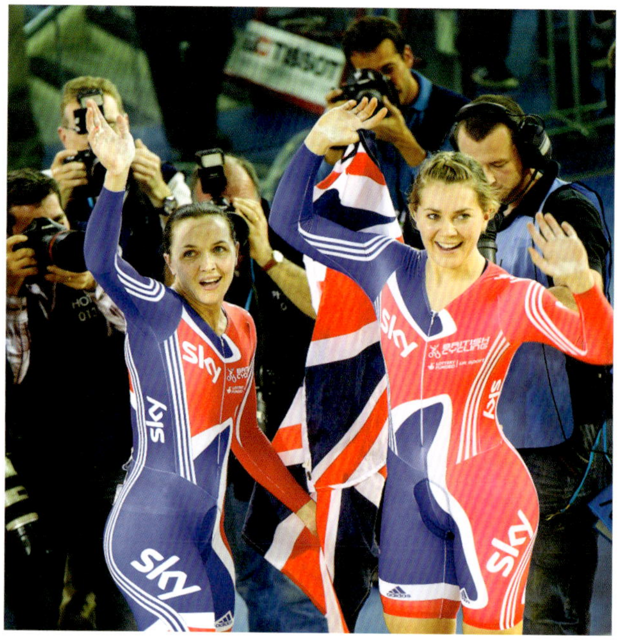

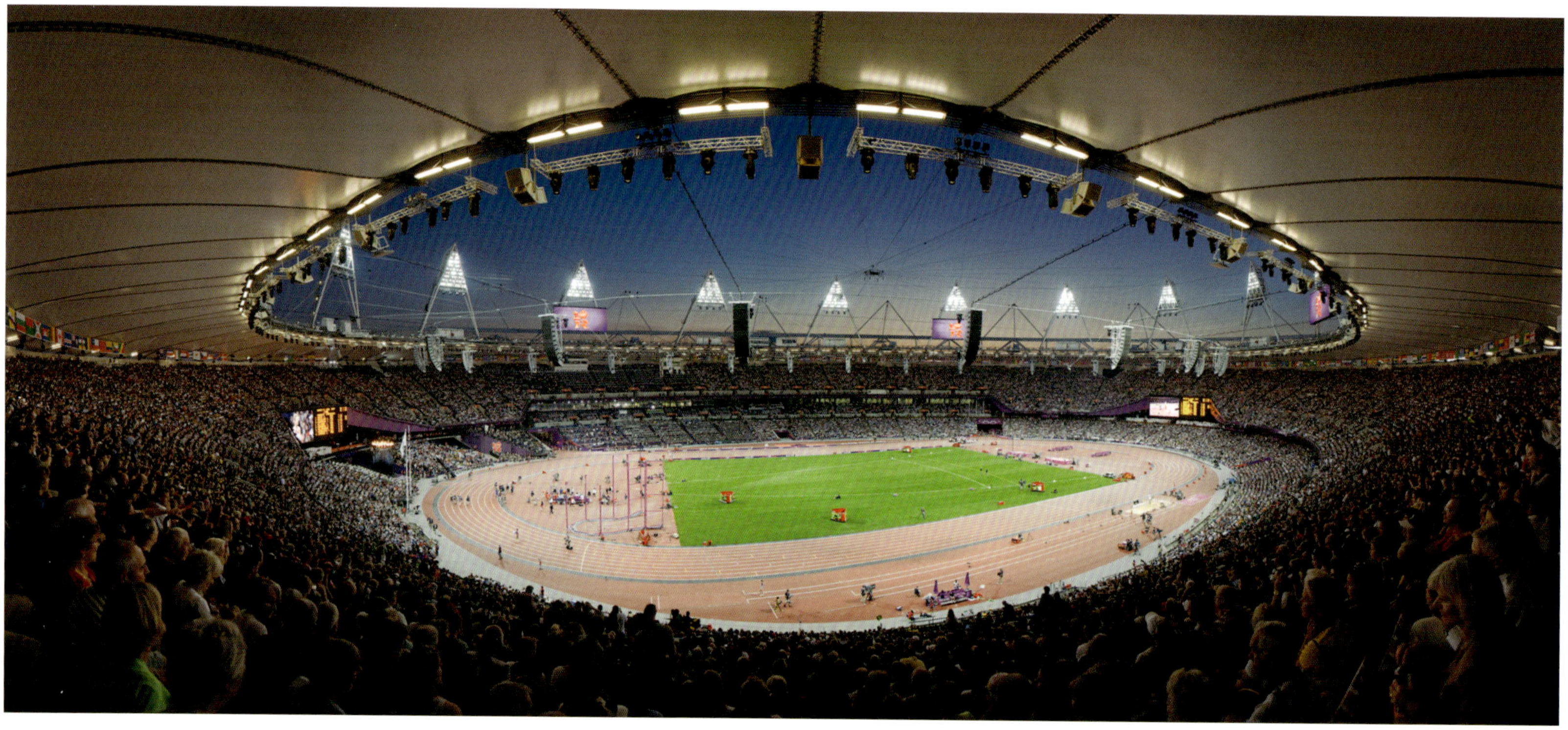

NEIL HALL UK
RICHARD HALL LRPS UK

BOB PEARSON FRPS UK

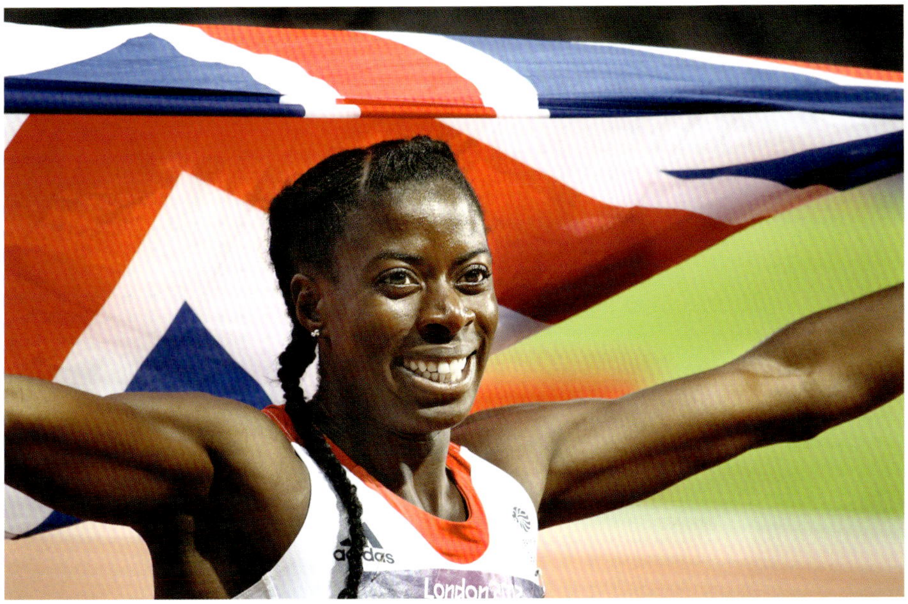

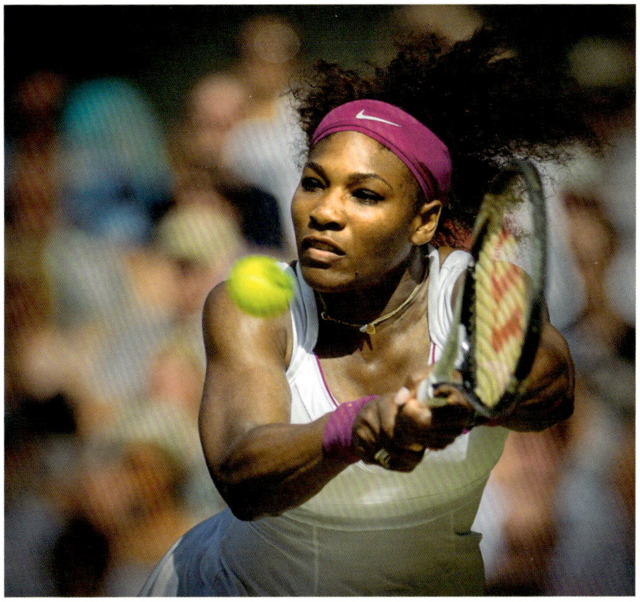

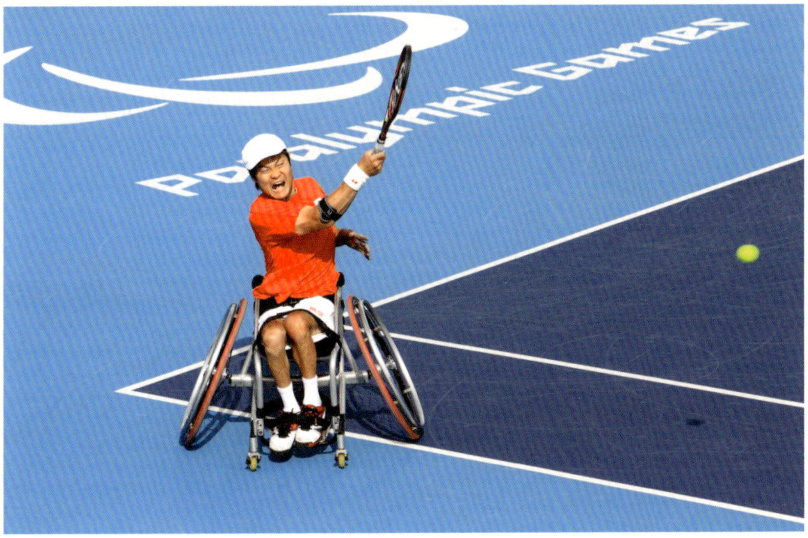

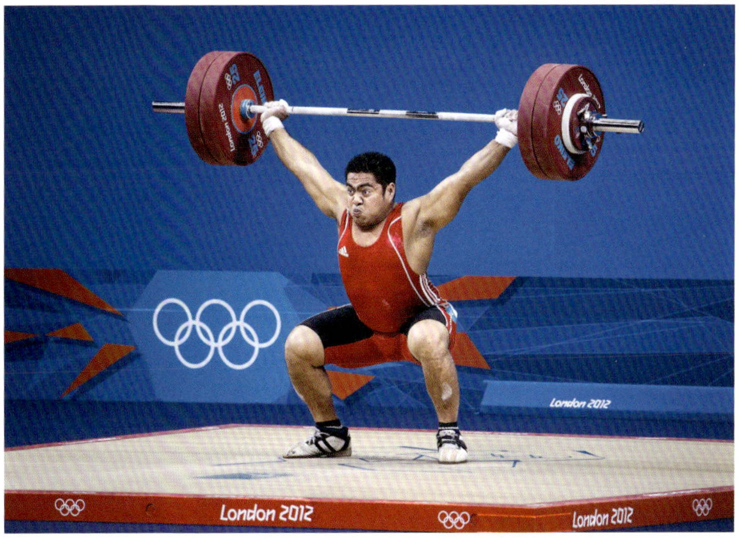

JON MARTIN UK
PAUL KEENE FRPS UK

DUNCAN GROVE FRPS UK
JON MARTIN UK

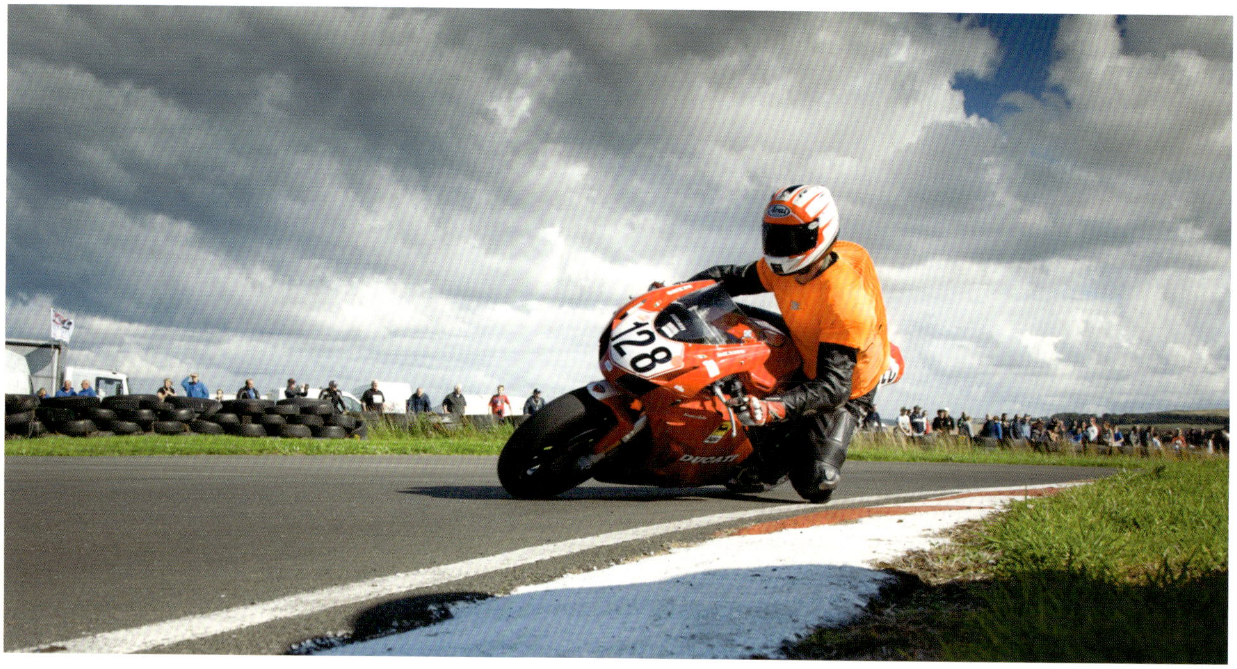

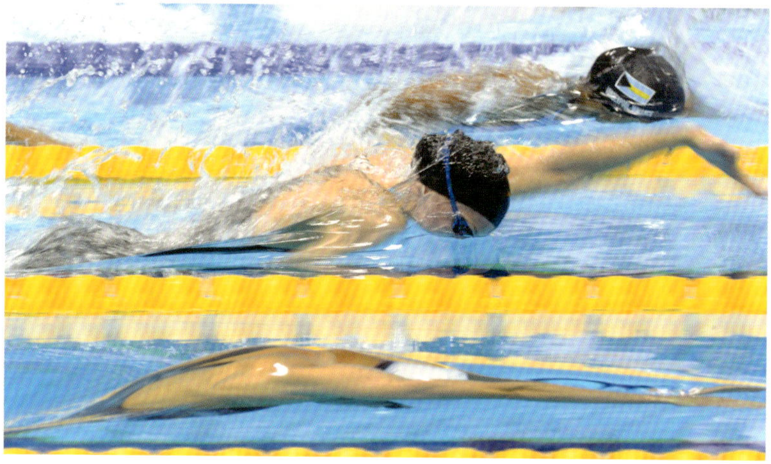

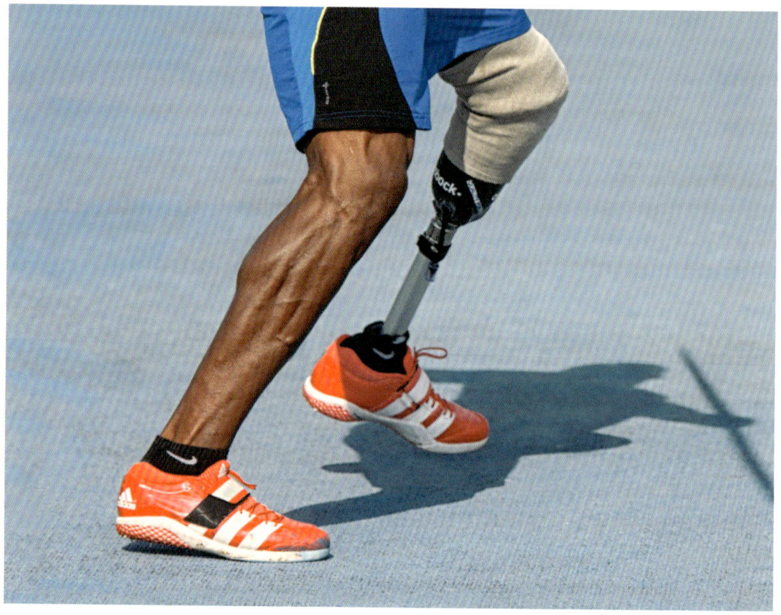

NICOLA HARKNESS ARPS UK
STUART ROBINSON FRPS UK

JOHN BULPITT FRPS UK

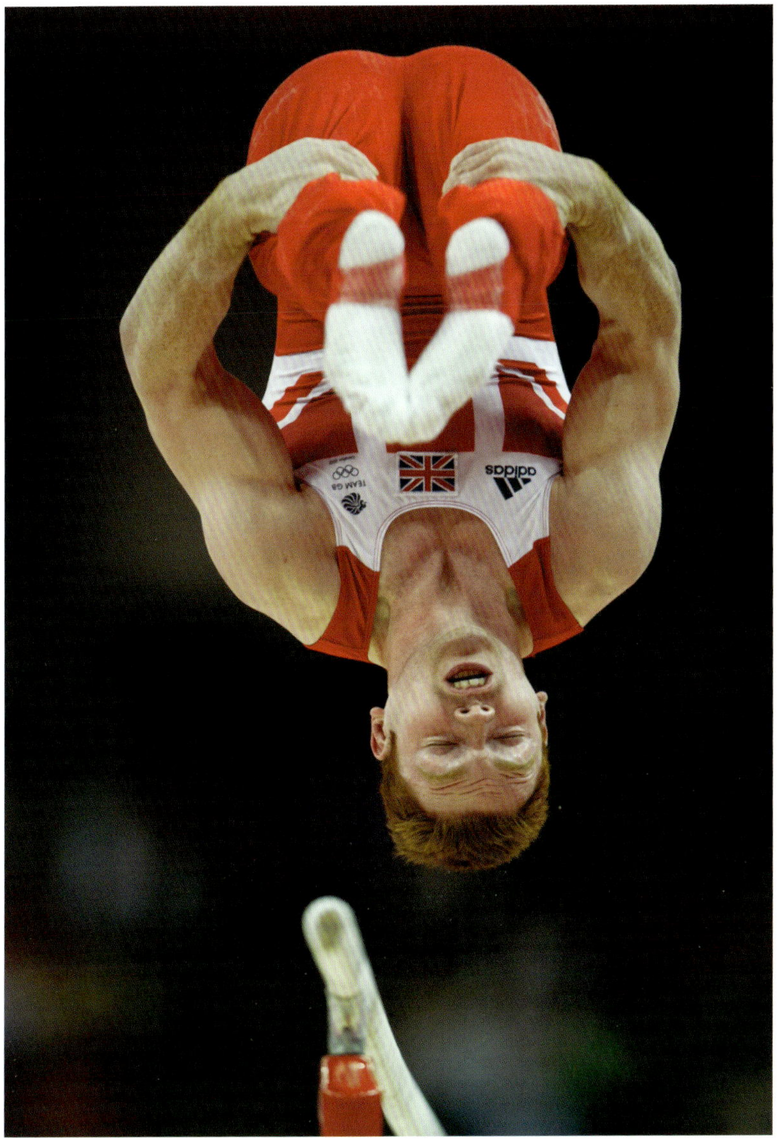

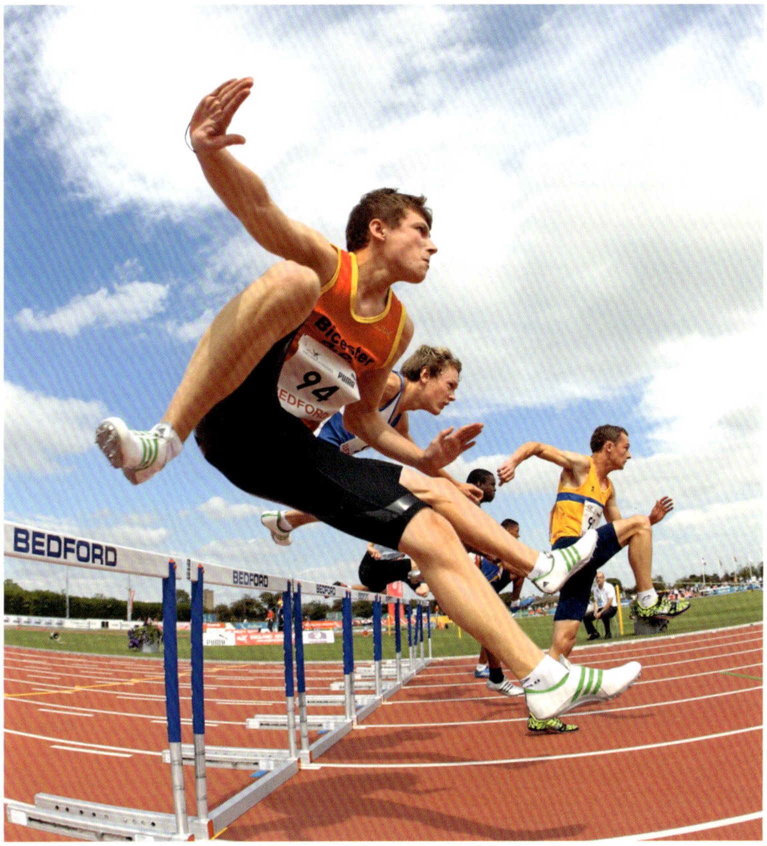

STUART ROBINSON FRPS UK

JOHN BULPITT FRPS UK

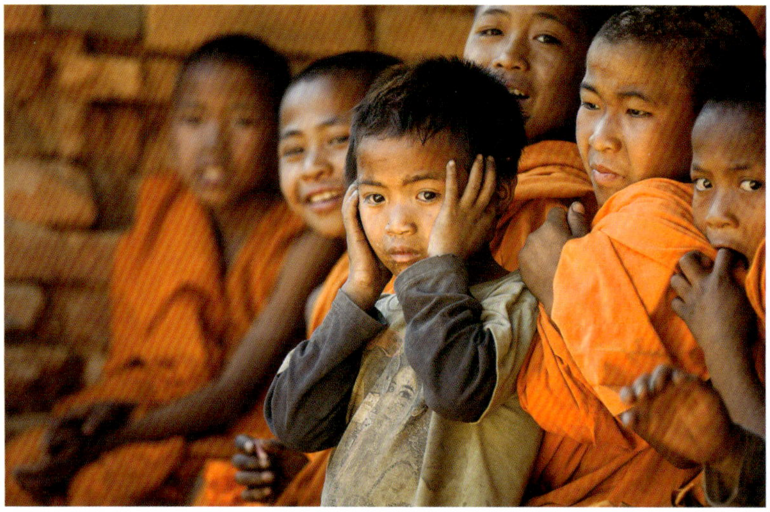

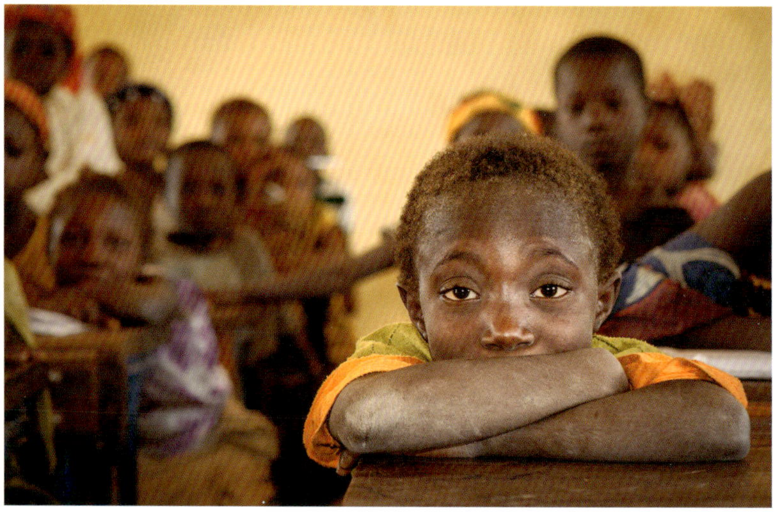

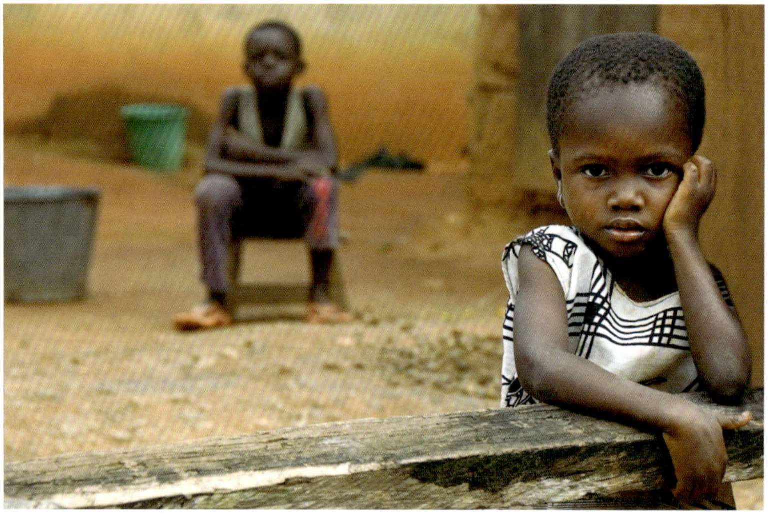

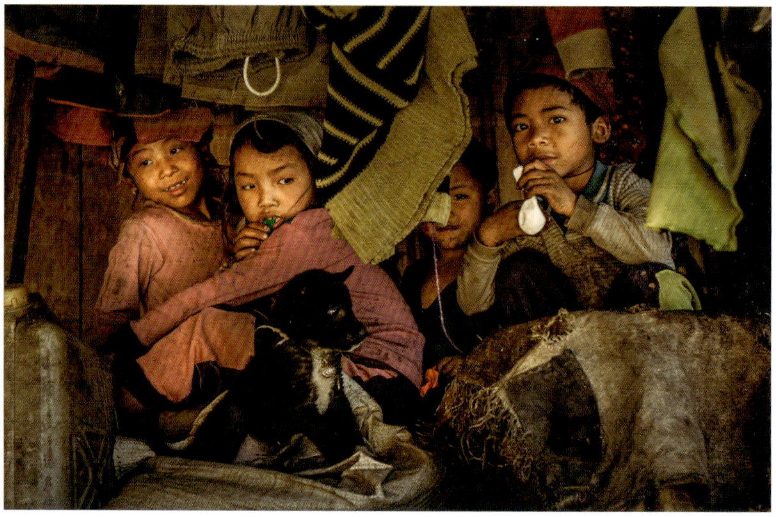

HAZEL FROST ARPS UK
MARGARET SALISBURY FRPS UK

HAZEL FROST ARPS UK
JAMES FROST FRPS UK

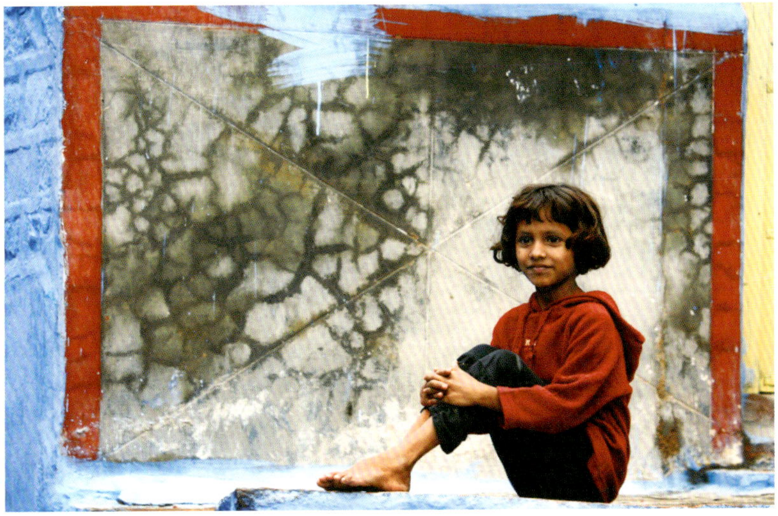

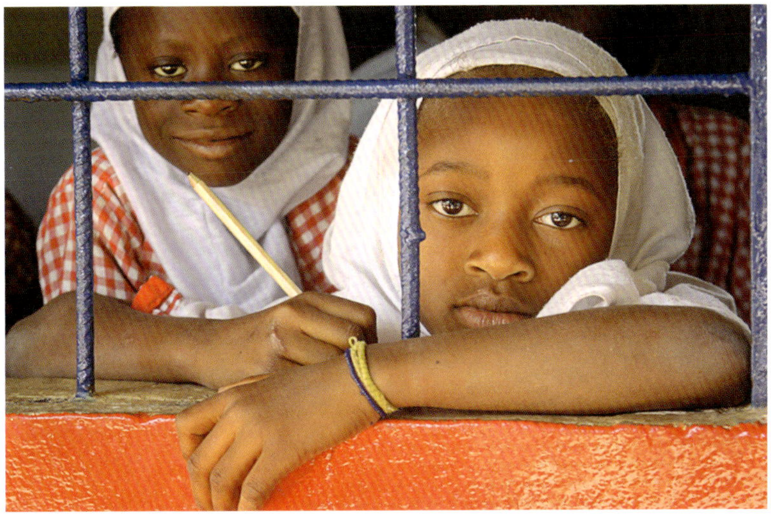

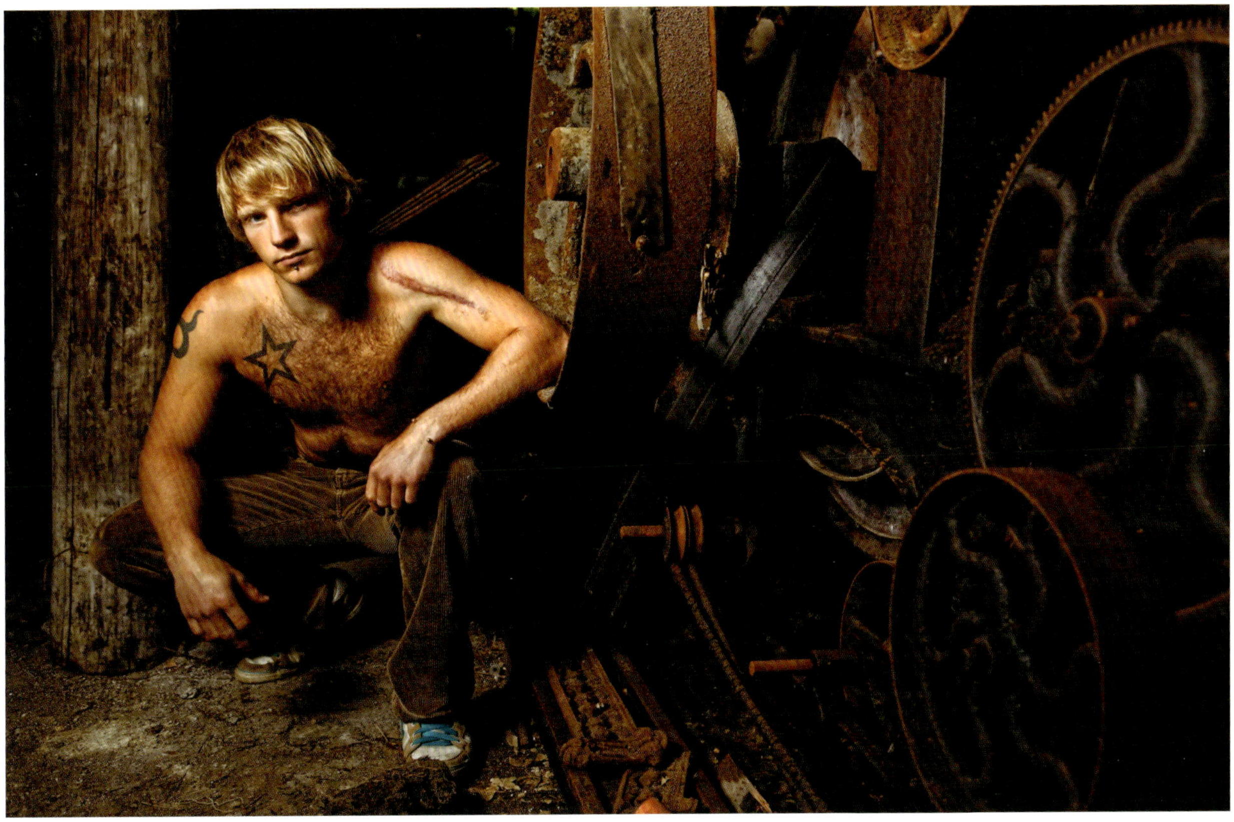

MING LAI CHUNG ARPS HONG KONG

CHRIS ELLISON LRPS UK

IAN O'NEILL LRPS UK

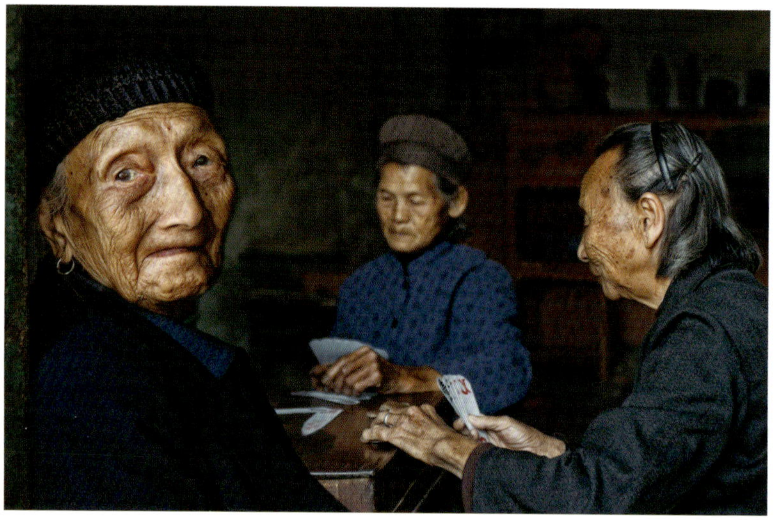

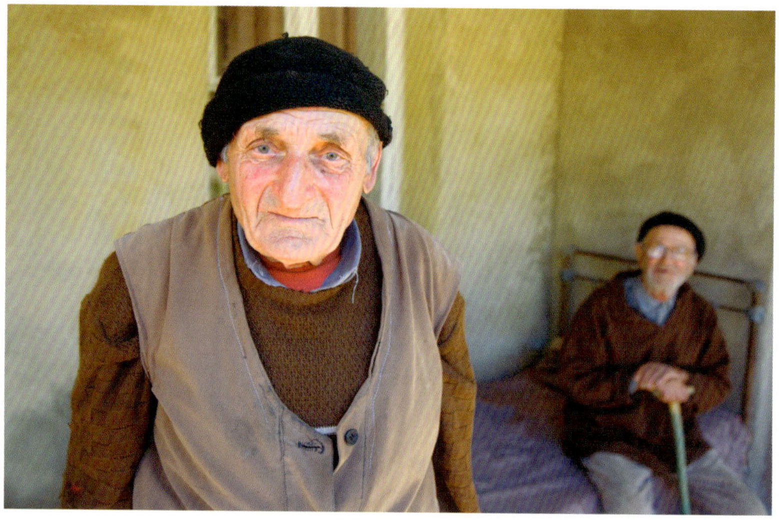

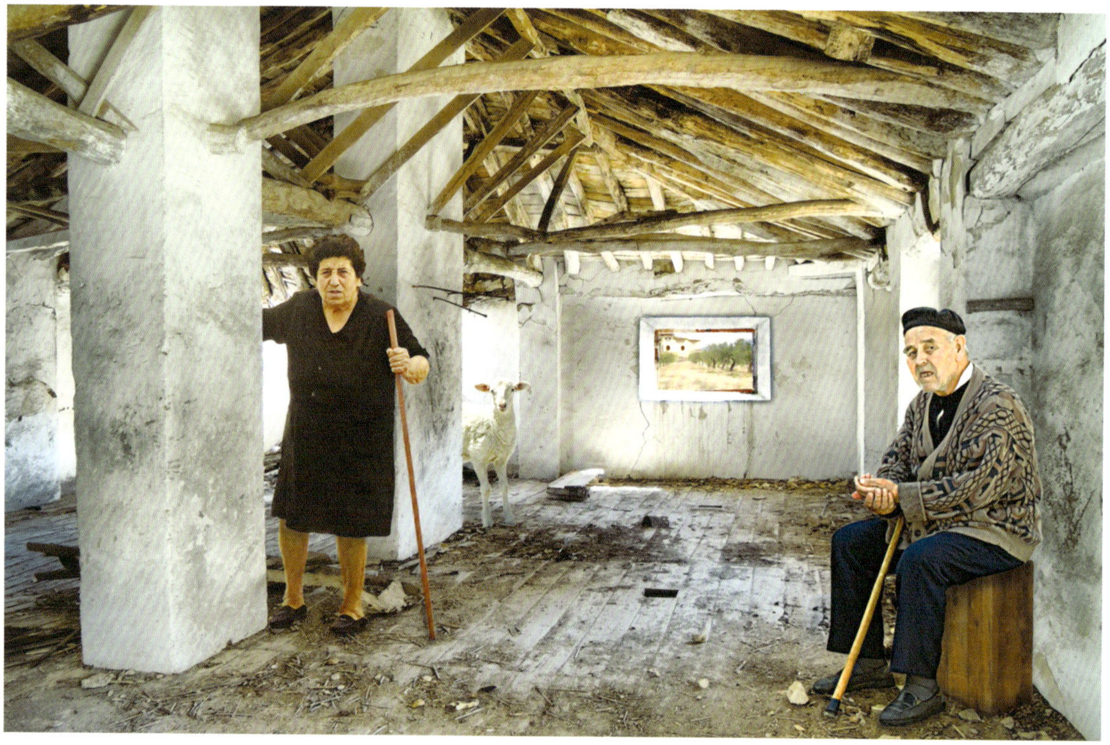

MIKE SHARPLES ARPS UK
ALAN BROWN LRPS UK

DAVID WHEELER FRPS UK

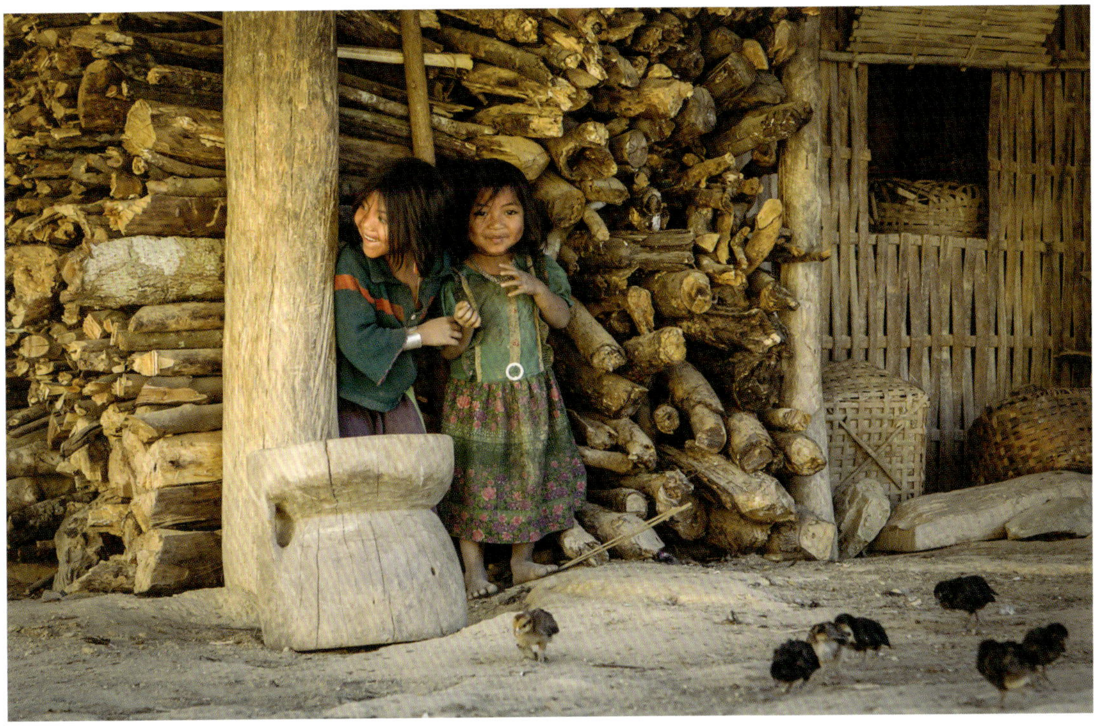

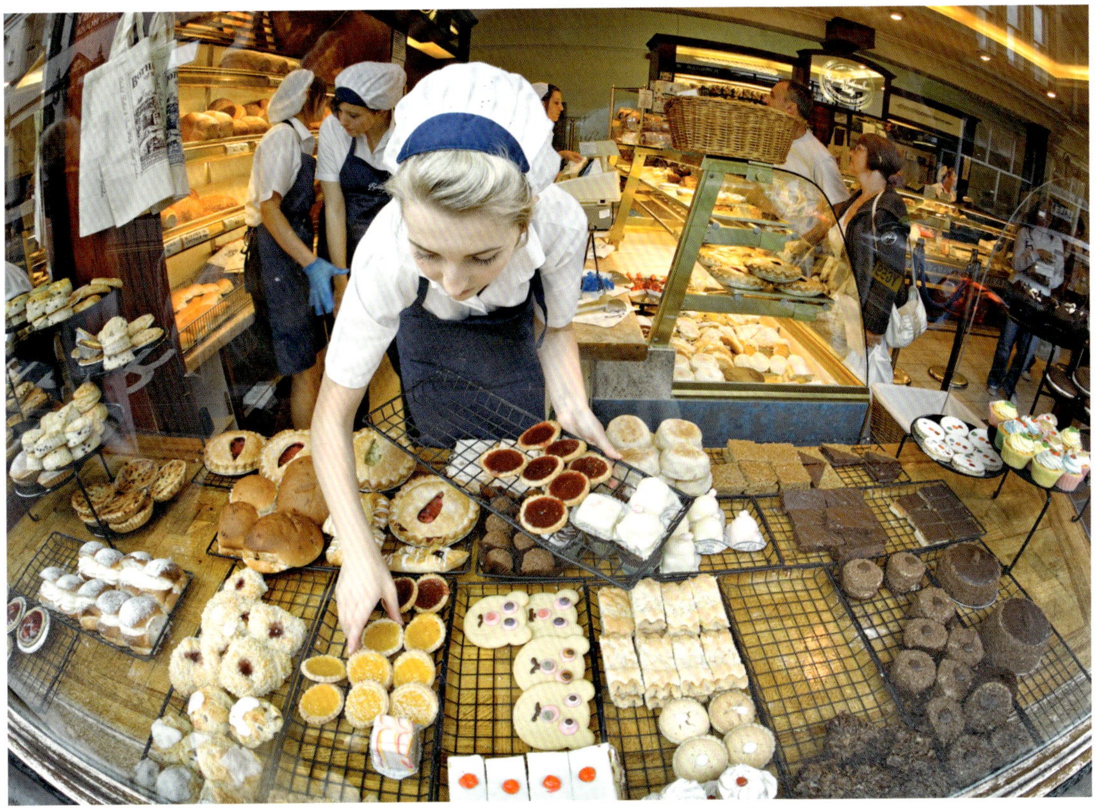

JAMES FROST FRPS UK

IAN WILSON ARPS UK

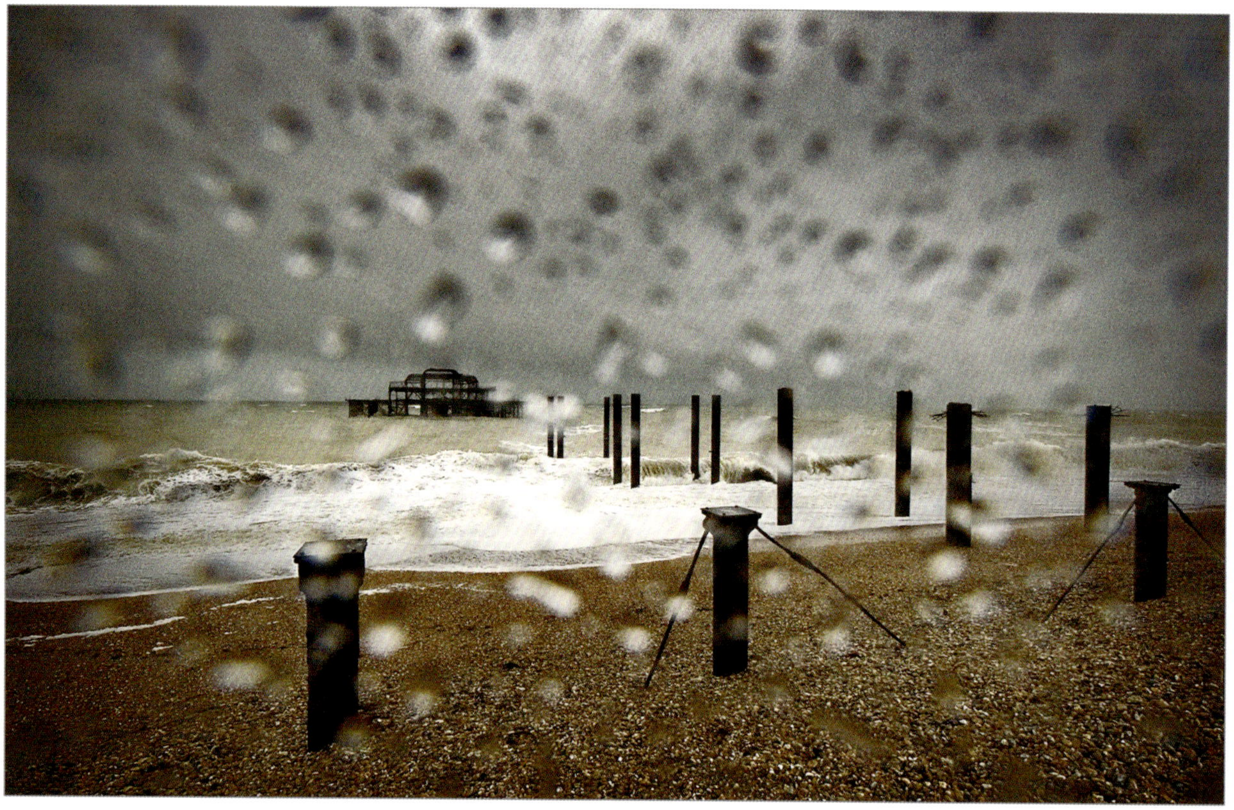

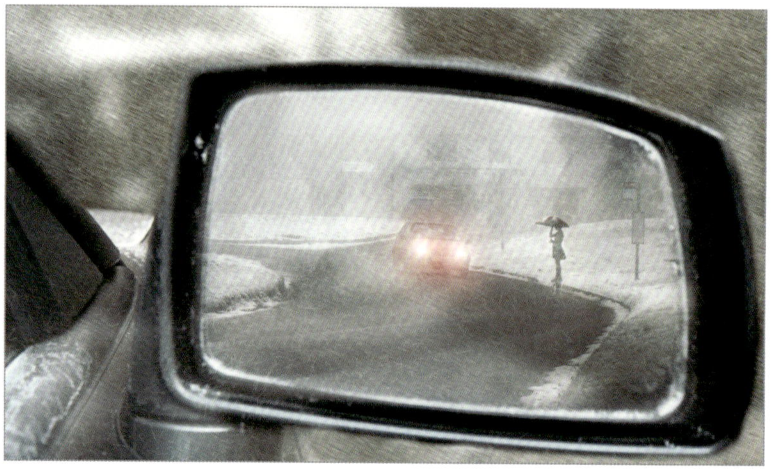

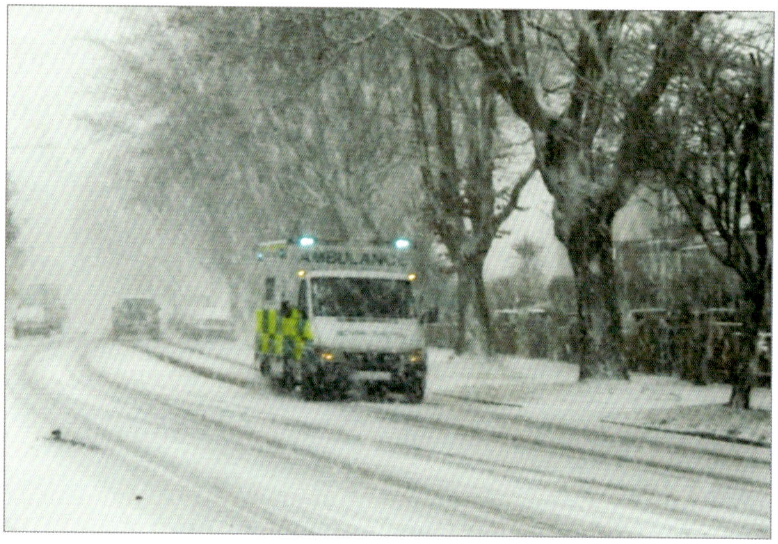

GRAHAM PORTLOCK ARPS UK

VALENTINA KULASINA ARPS UK

TOM DAVIE ARPS UK

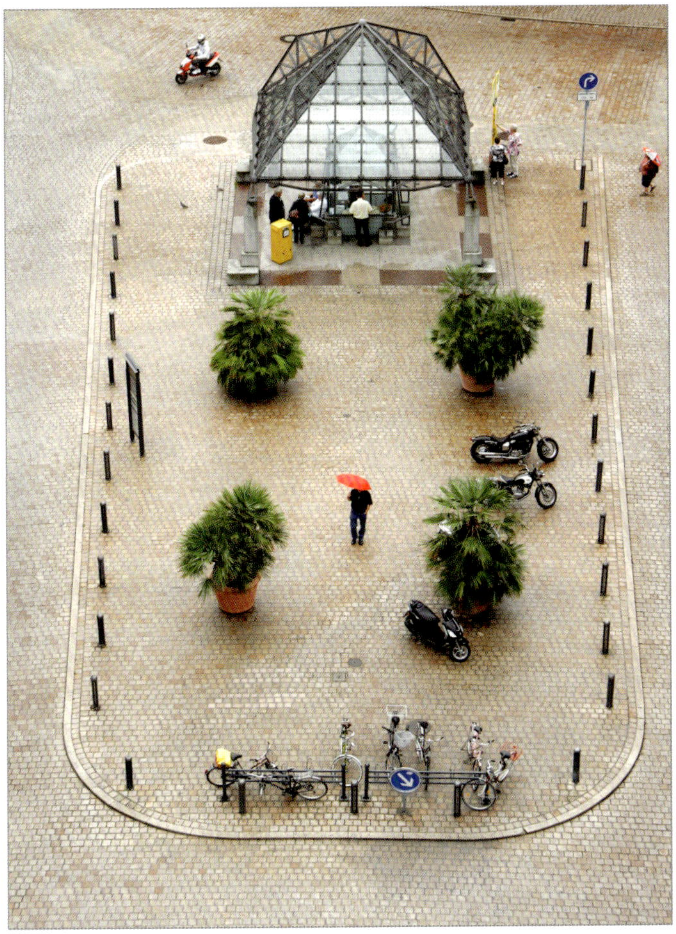

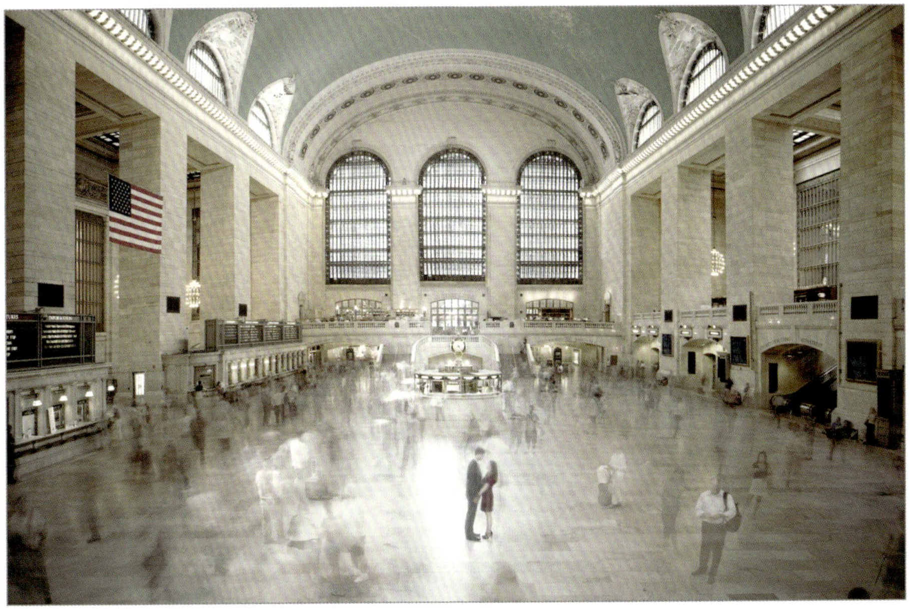

ANTHONY OLIVER LRPS UK

TIM HARRIS ARPS UK

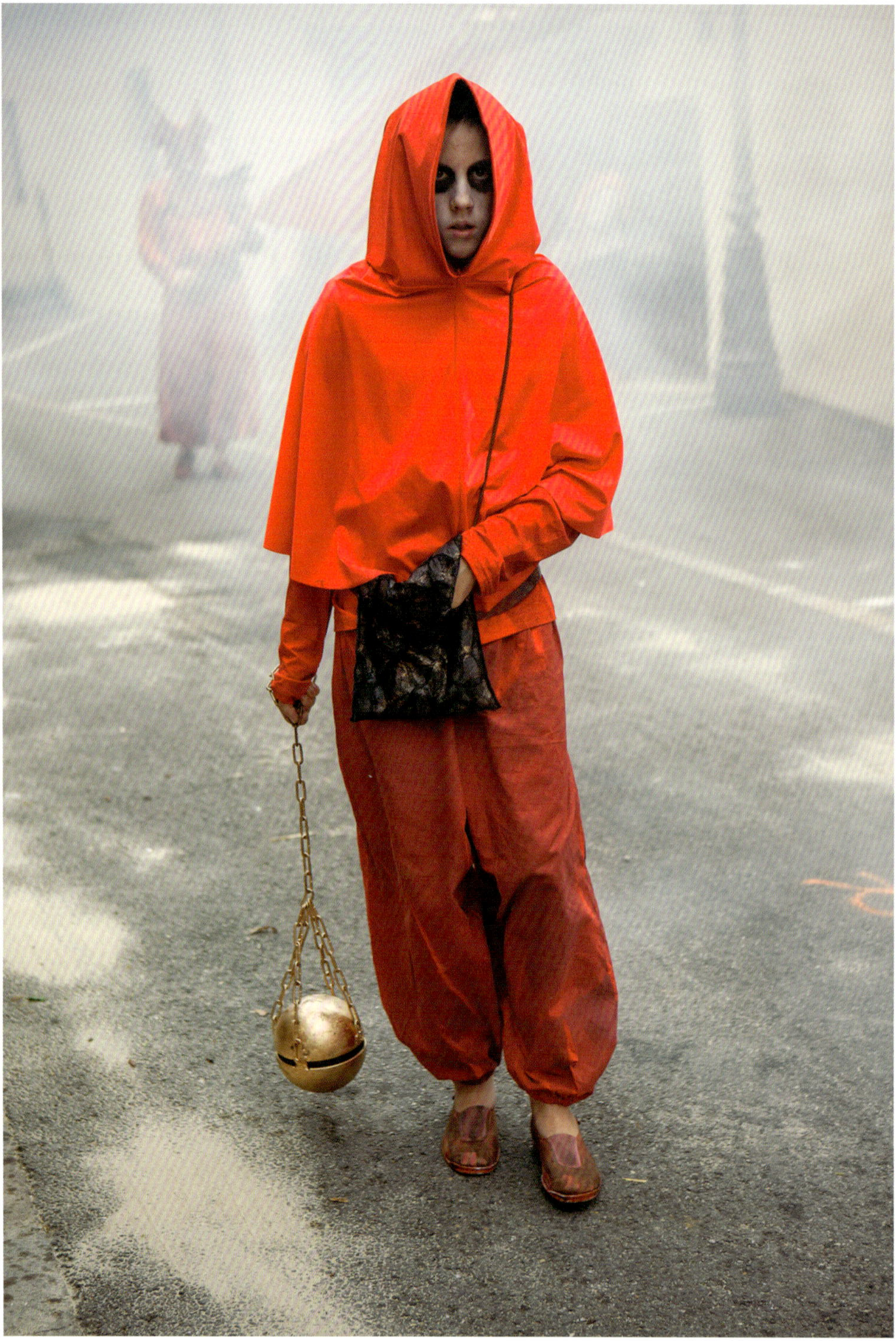

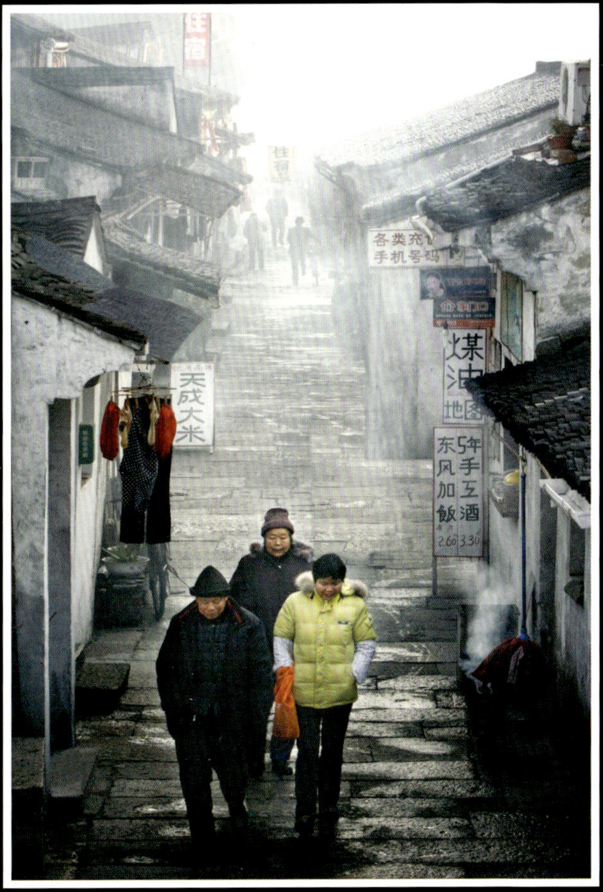

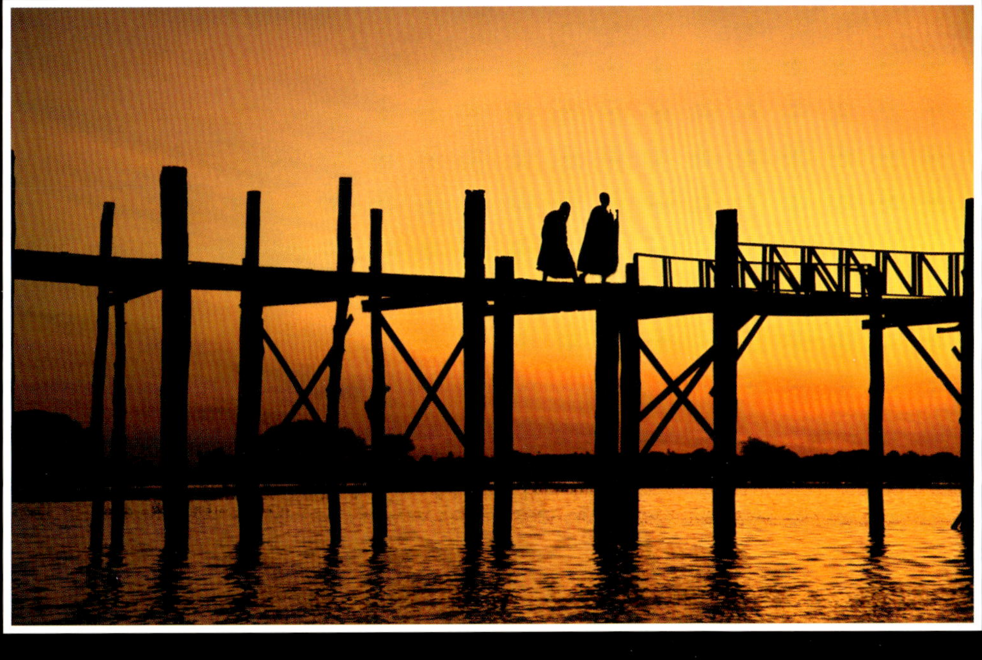

SHIU GUN WONG Hon.FRPS HONG KONG

KASUMI DOBASHI JAPAN

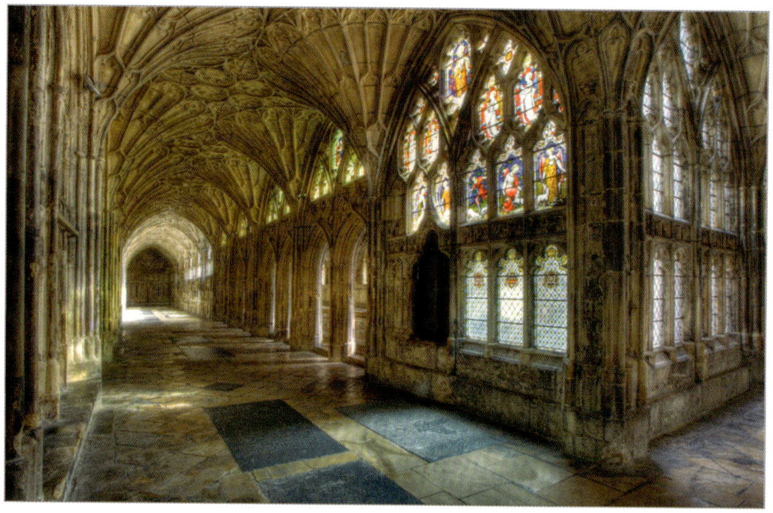

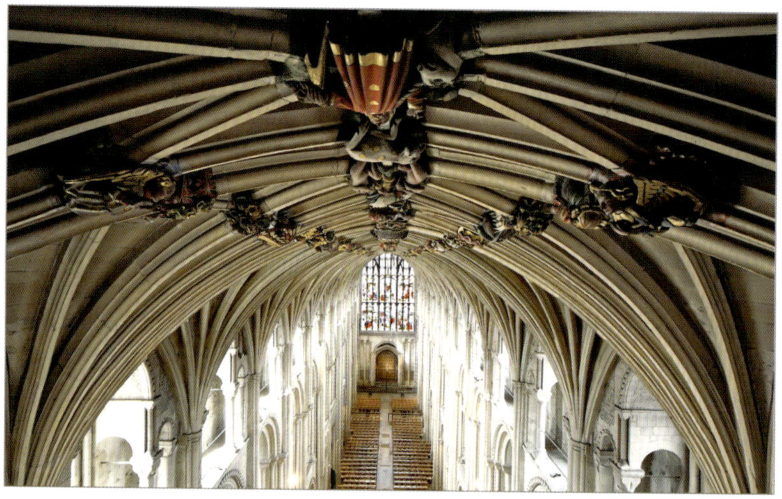

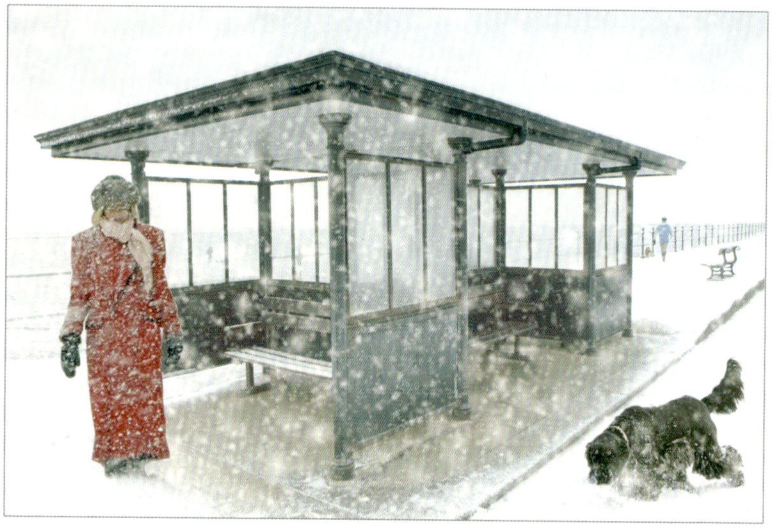

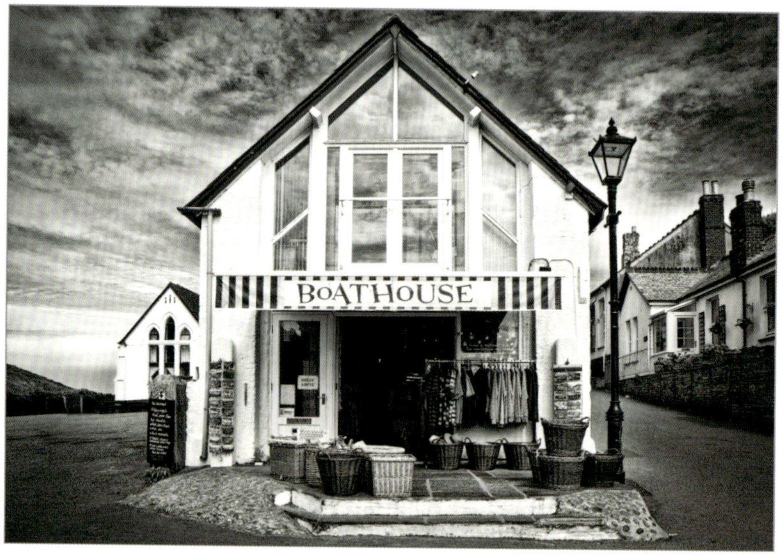

IAN O'NEILL LRPS UK
ANN MILES FRPS UK

PAUL HURST ARPS UK
SIMON HASTINGS ARPS UK

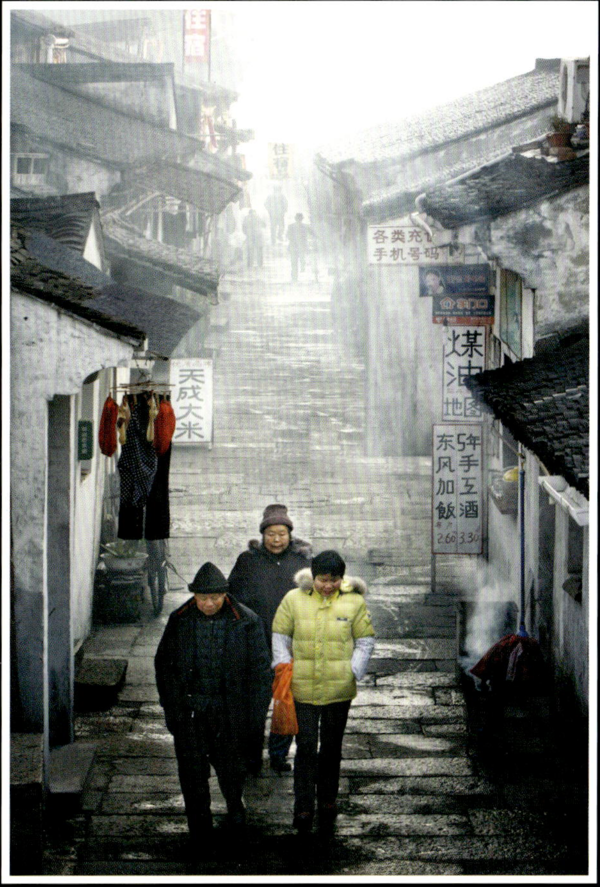

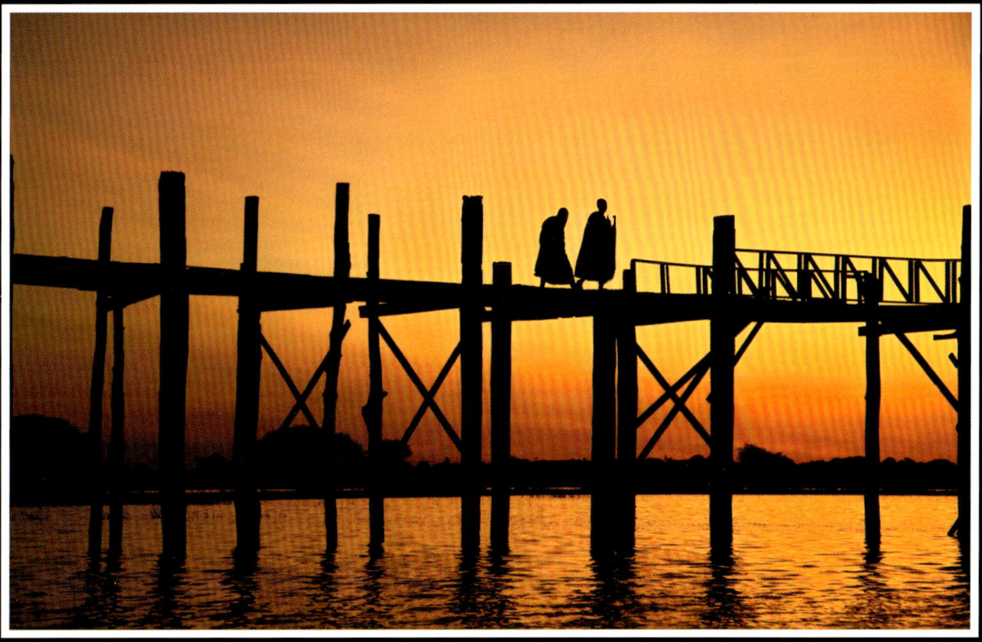

SHIU GUN WONG Hon.FRPS HONG KONG
KASUMI DOBASHI JAPAN

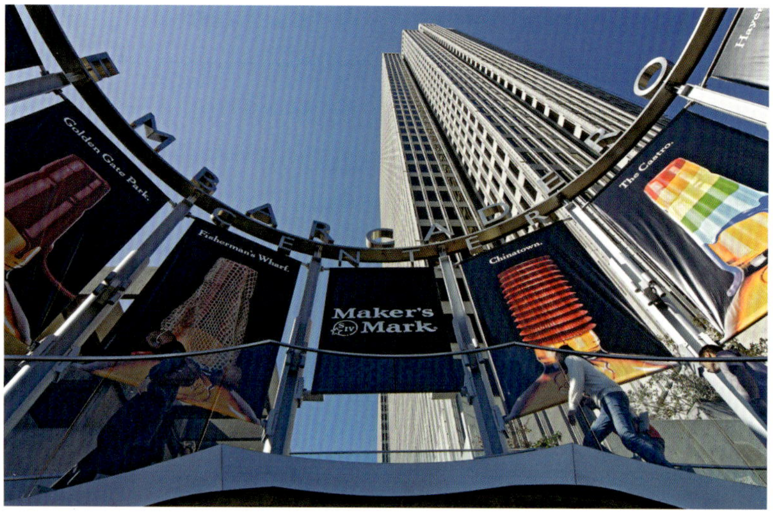

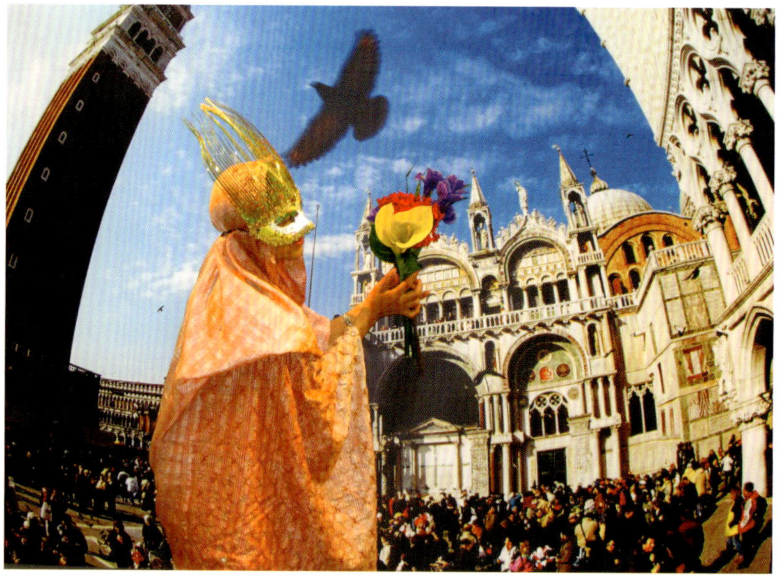

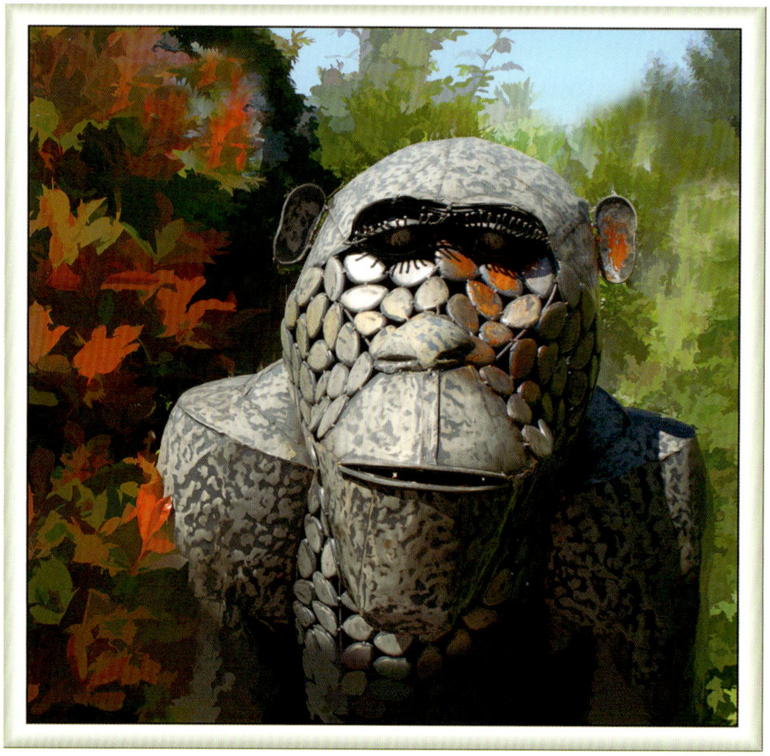

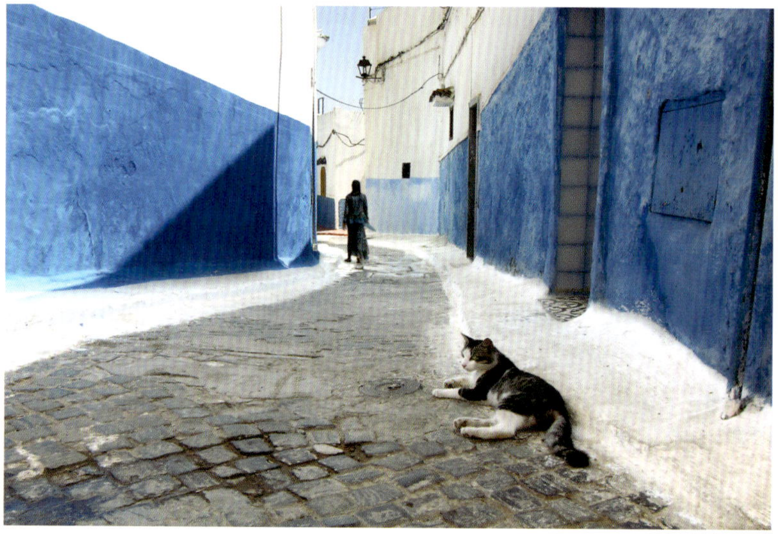

PHILIP QUARRY FRPS UK

BILL WISDEN MBE Hon.FRPS UK

MING LAI CHUNG ARPS HONG KONG

RICHARD CHERRY ARPS UK

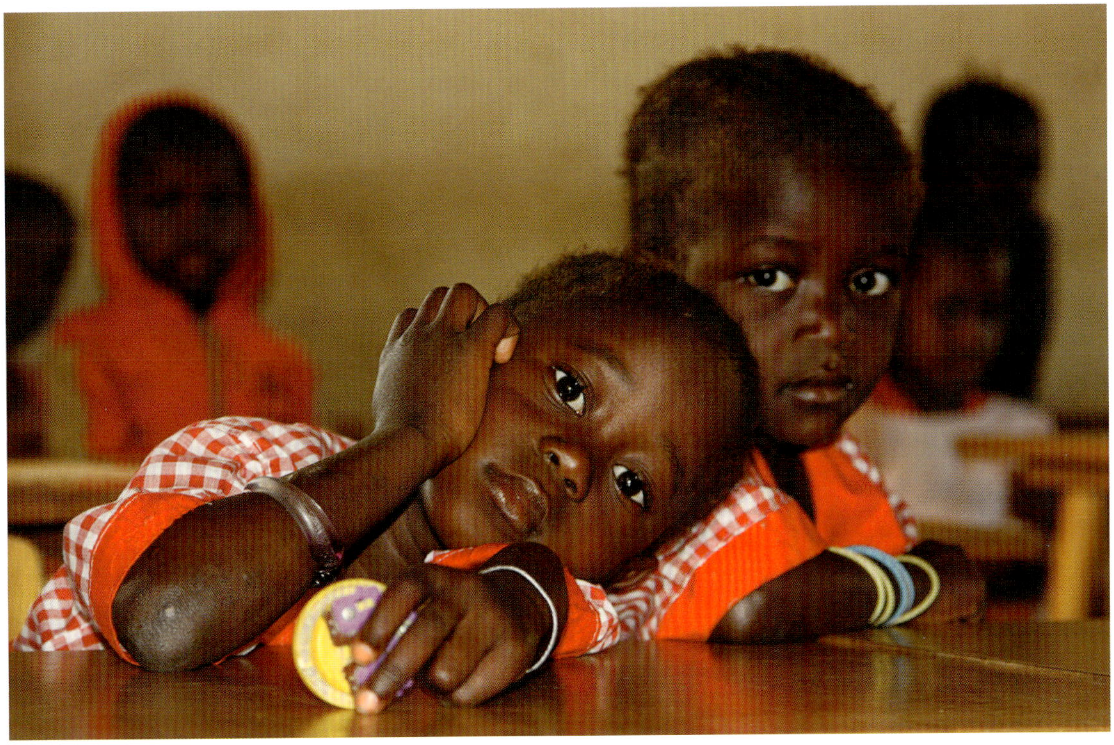

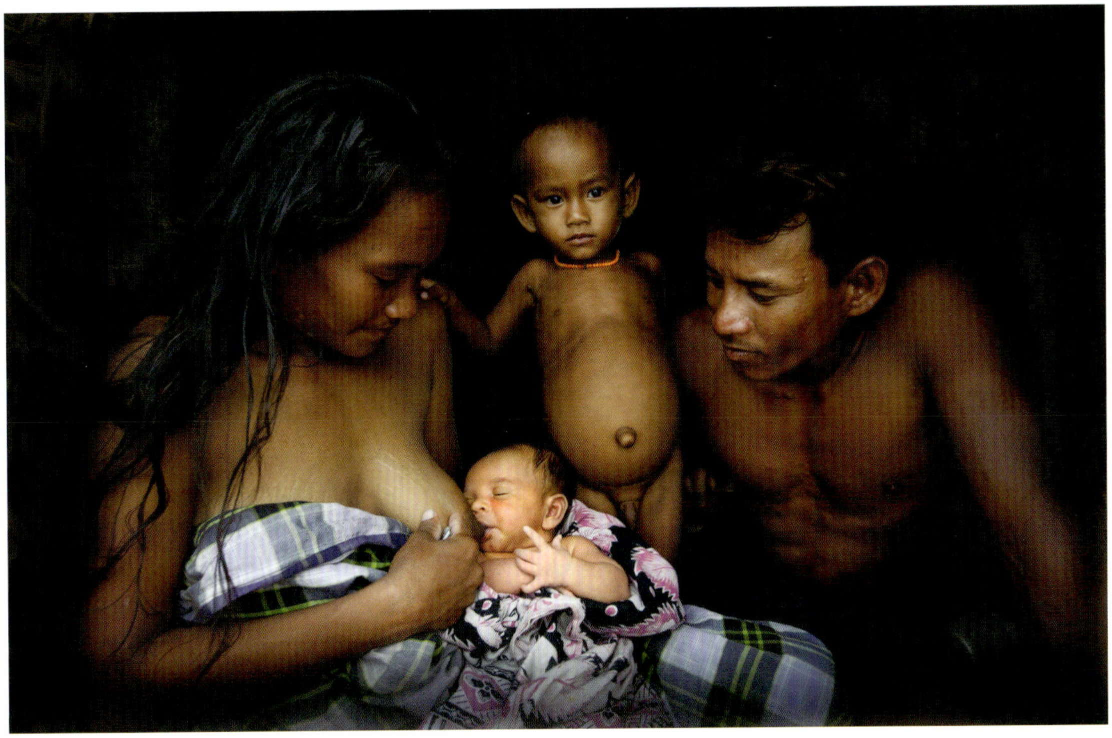

CHRIS ELLISON LRPS UK

Y.K. YEO FRPS SINGAPORE

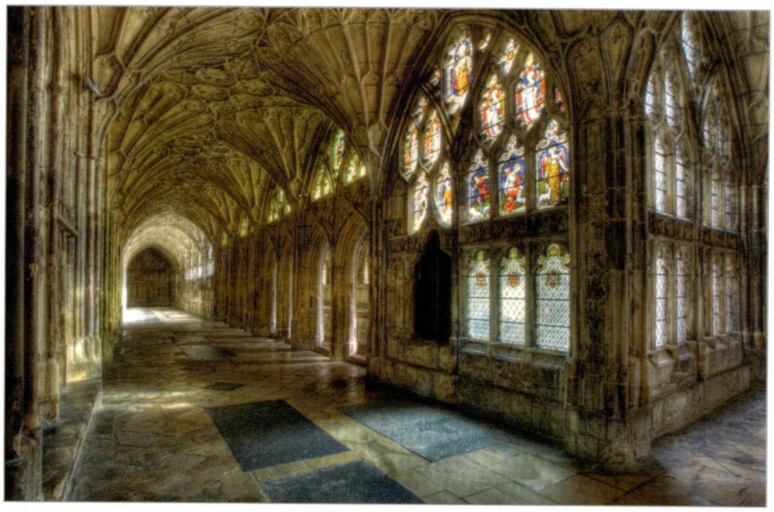

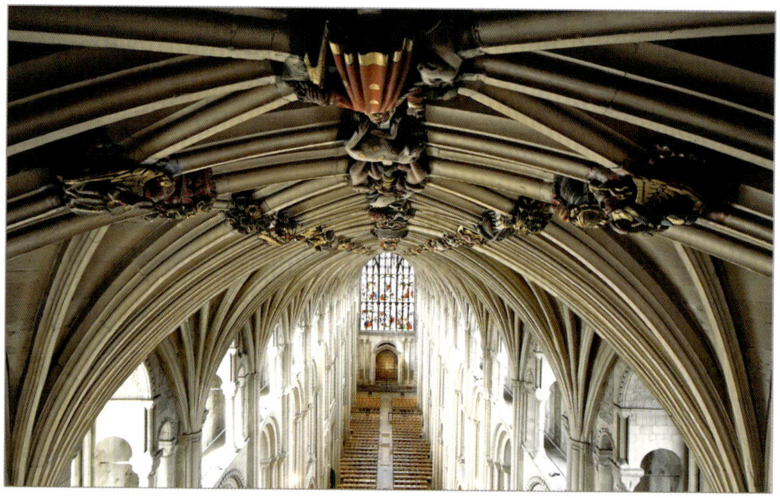

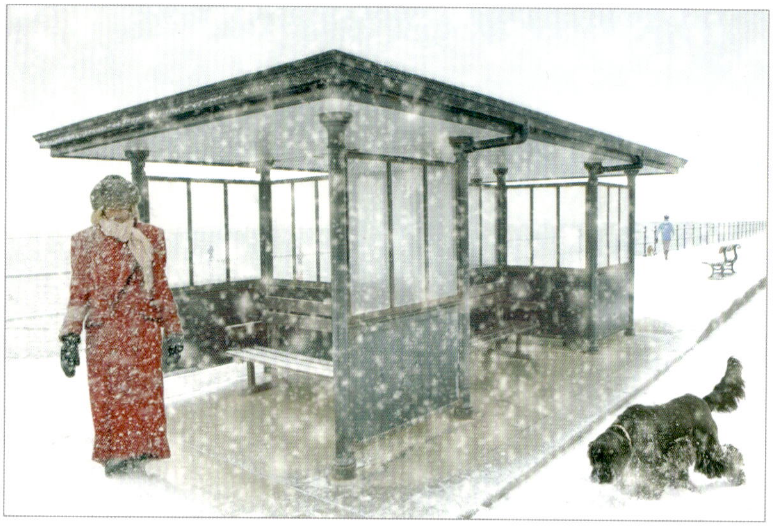

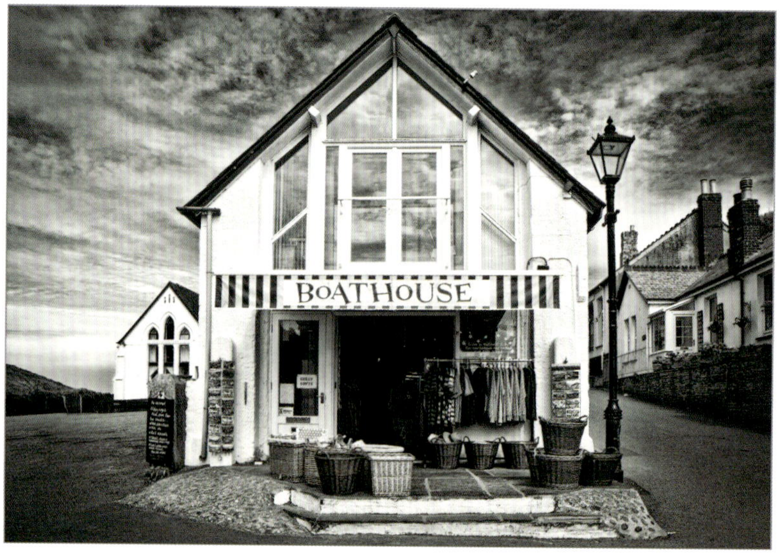

IAN O'NEILL LRPS UK
ANN MILES FRPS UK

PAUL HURST ARPS UK
SIMON HASTINGS ARPS UK

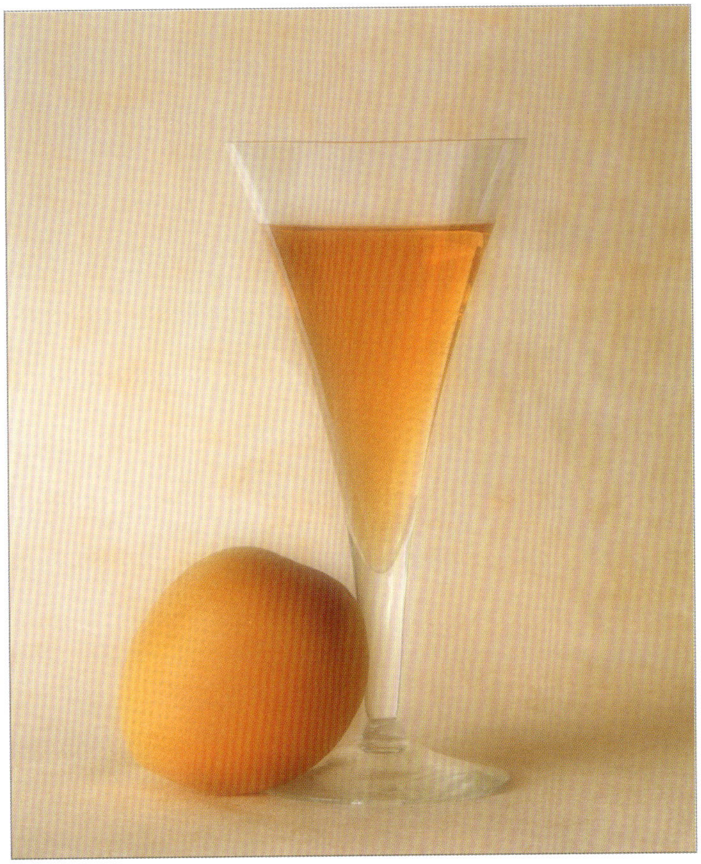

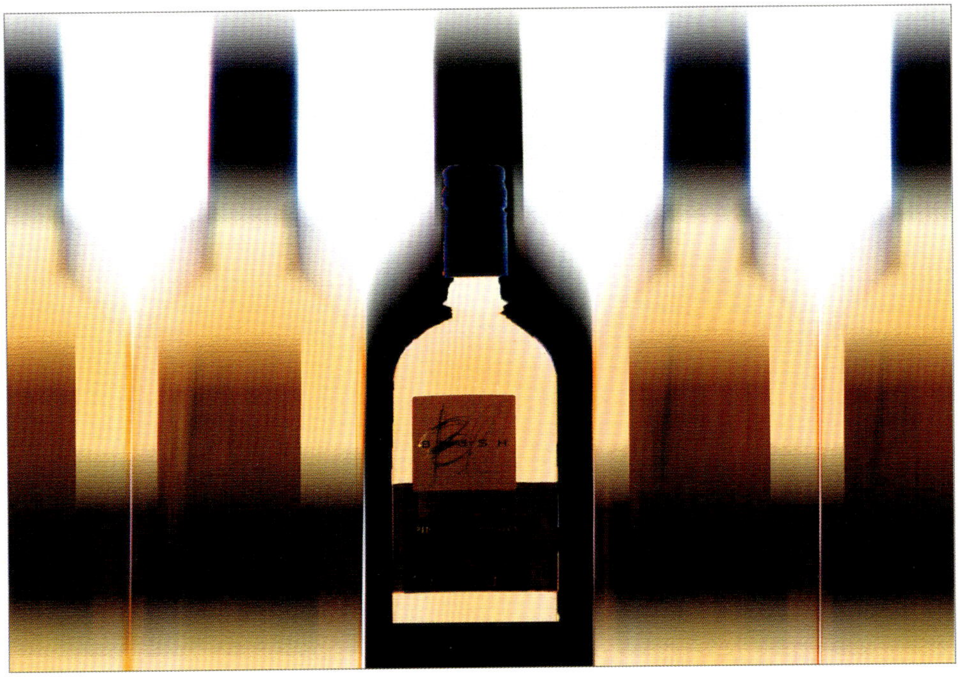

JOHN HORNE ARPS UK
ROBERT BRACHER ARPS UK

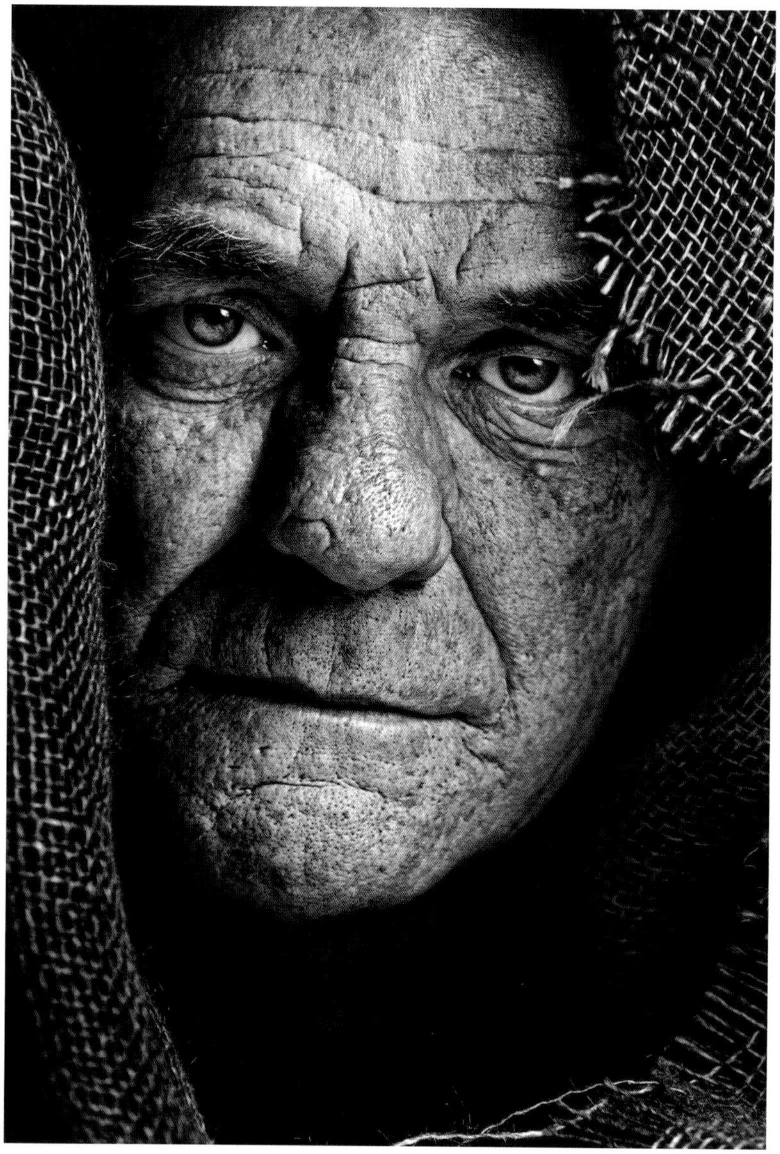

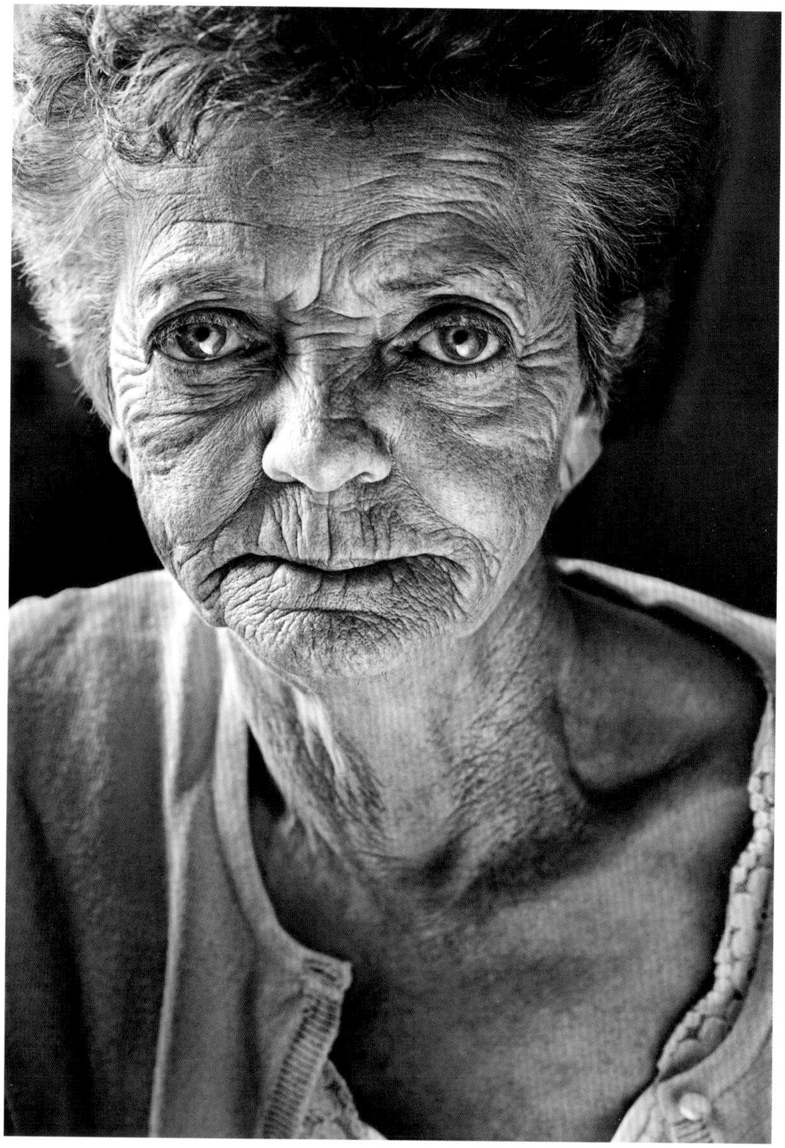

BARRY LAU ARPS UK

BARRY LAU ARPS UK

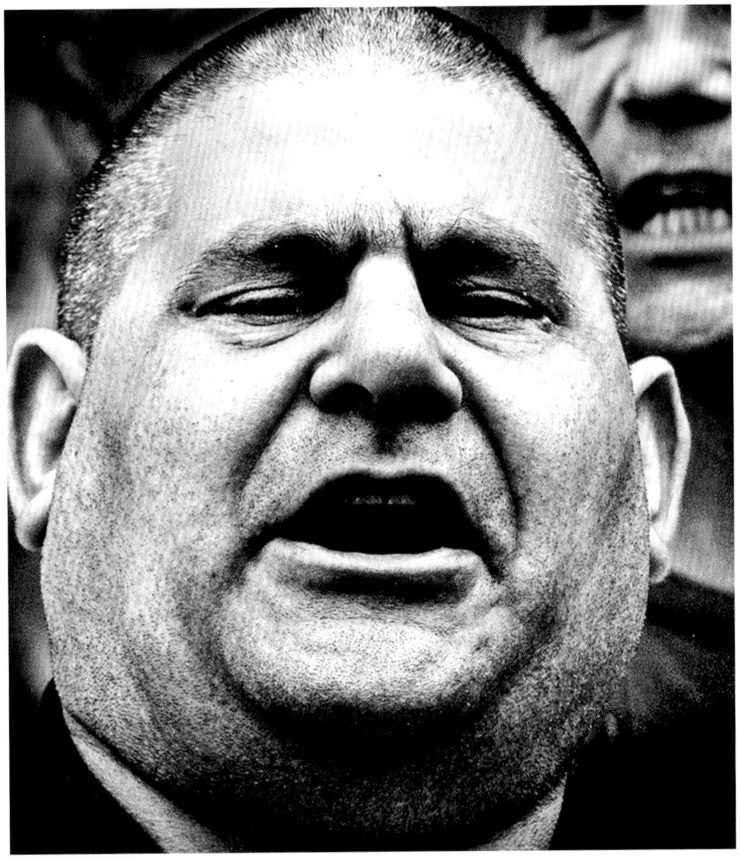

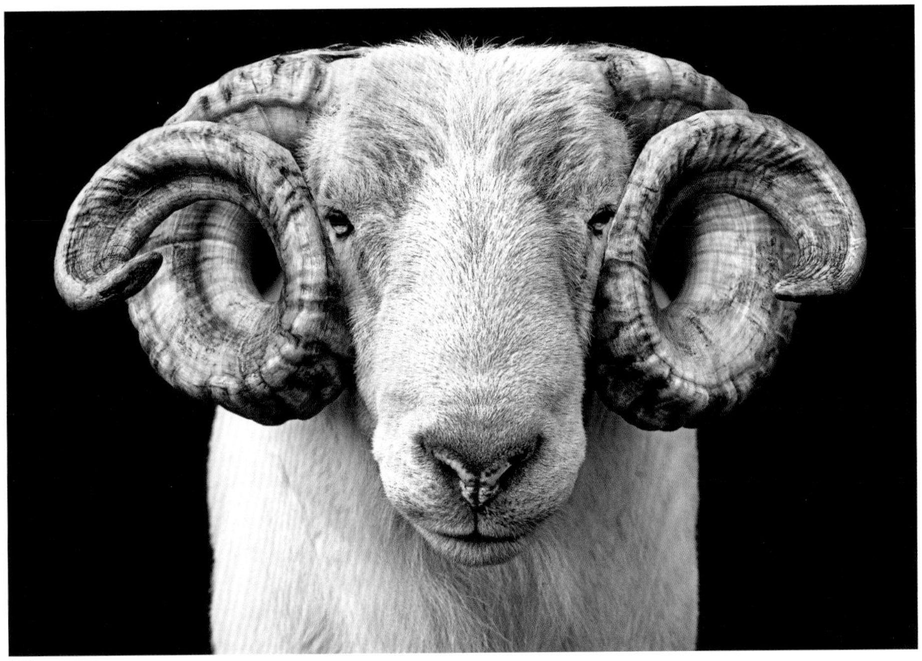

ALAN ABERCROMBIE FRPS UK
MARTIN McCORMACK LRPS UK

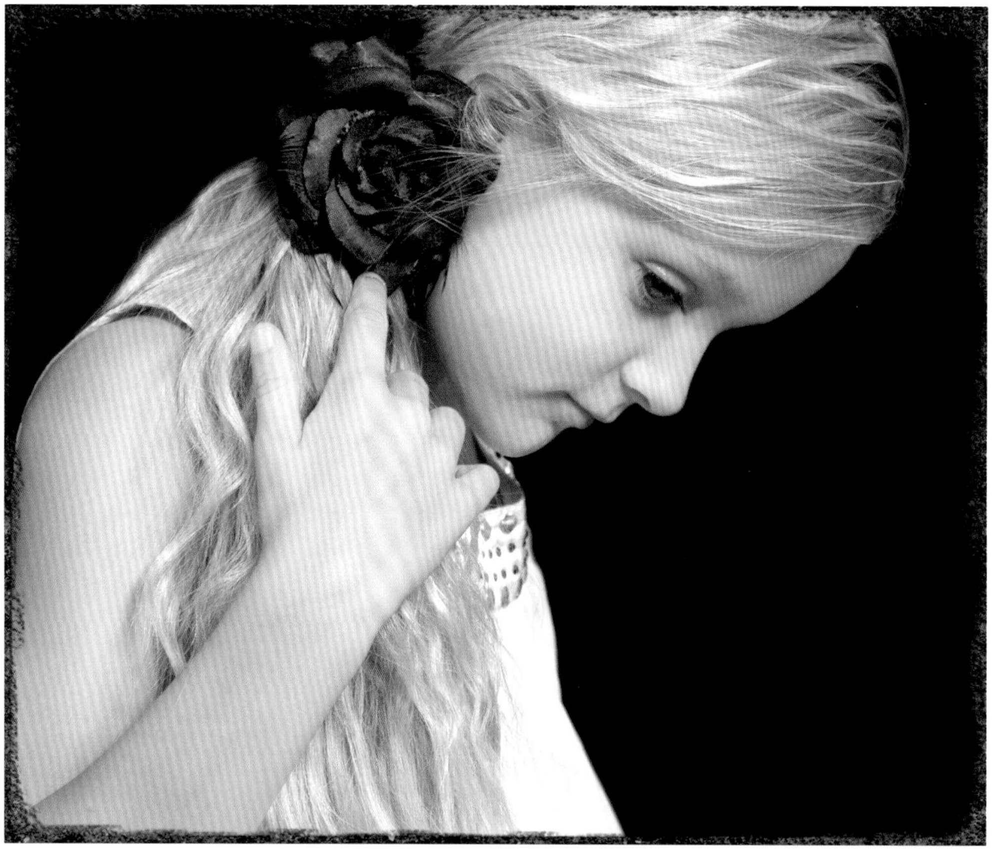

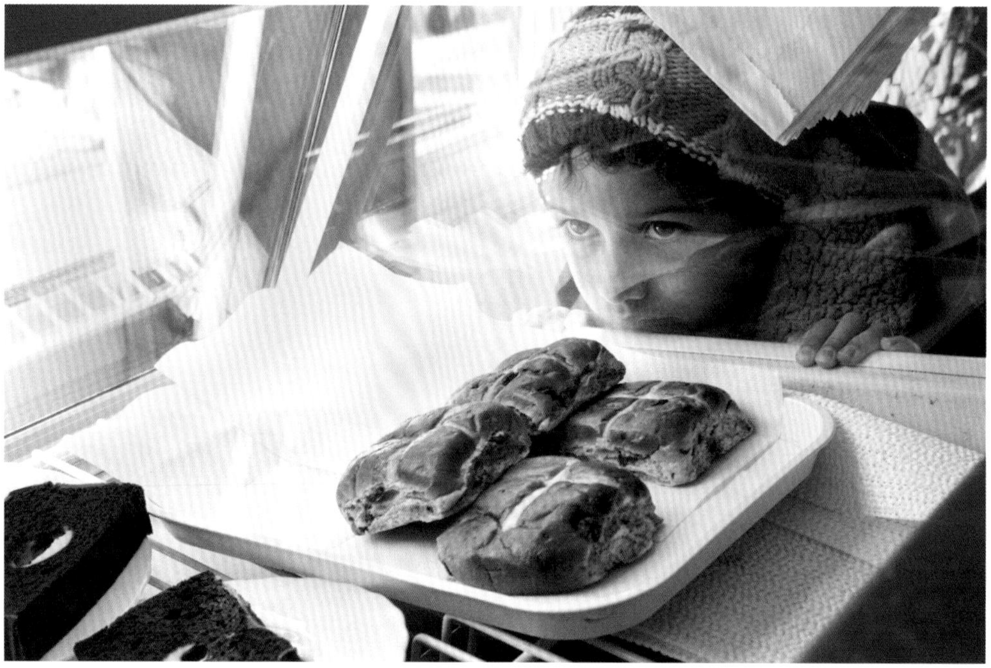

JULIA CLEAVER ARPS UK
MONICA WELLER FRPS UK

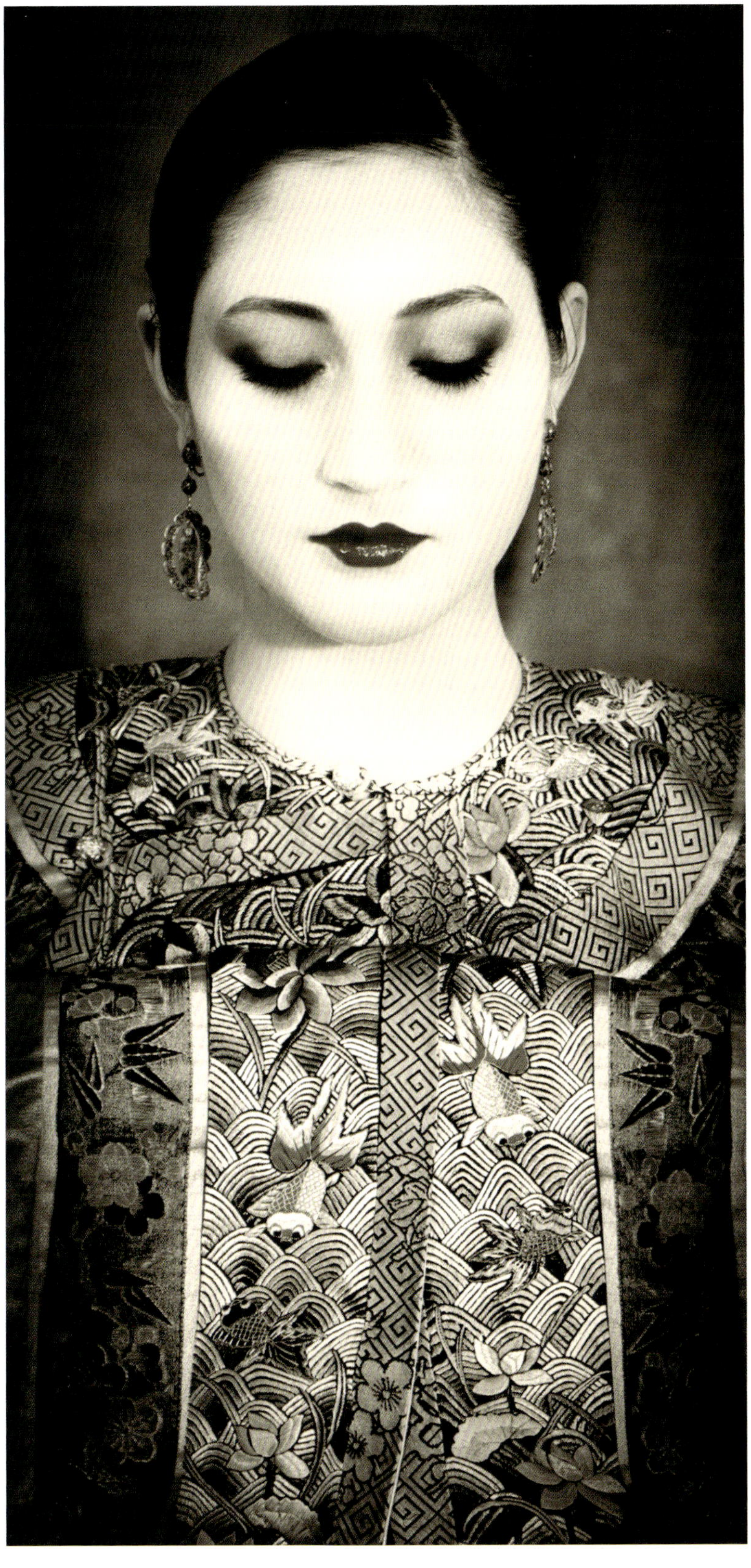

LISA POWERS LRPS NEW ZEALAND

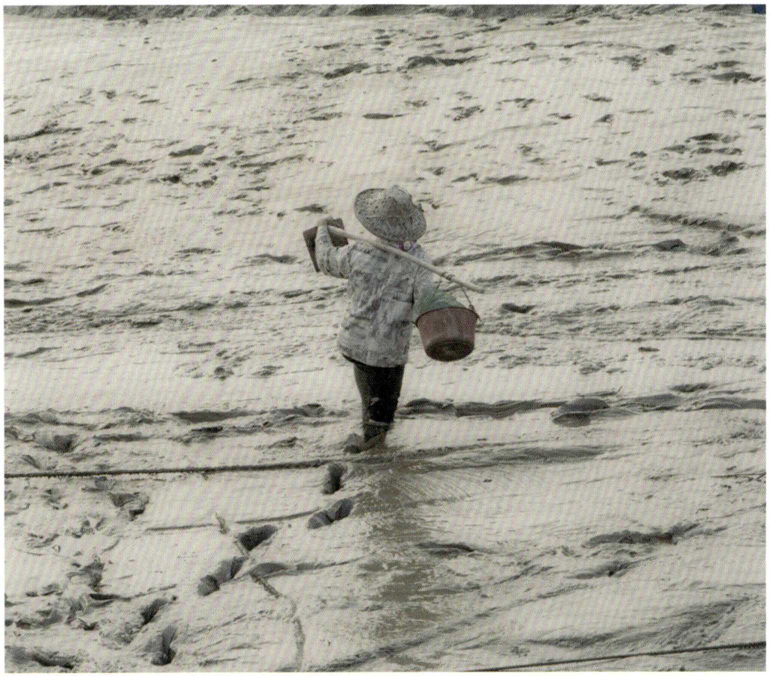

MICHAEL PRITCHARD FRPS UK

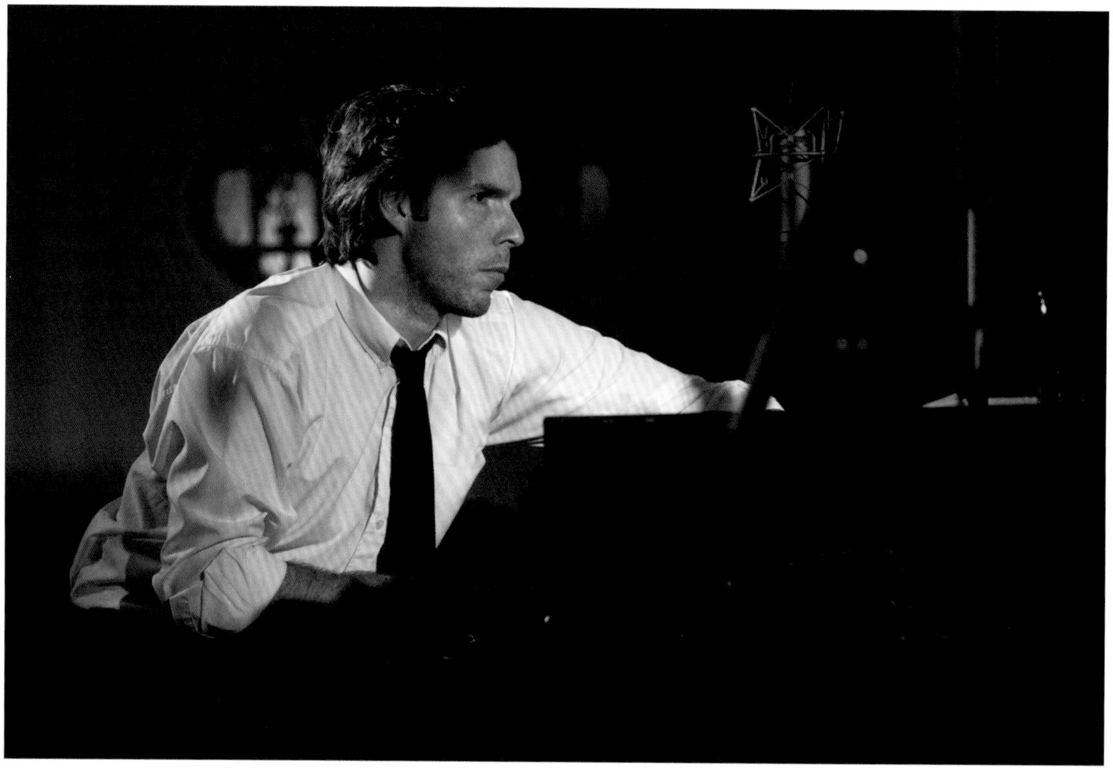

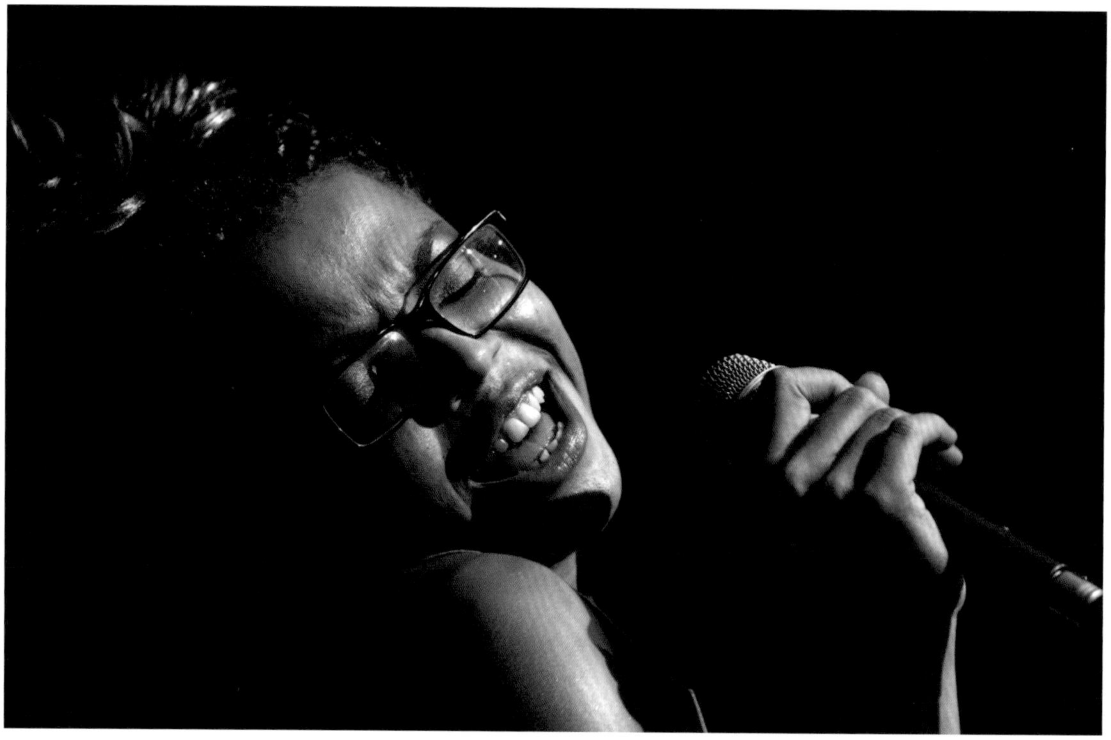

PAUL BENTLEY FRPS UK
PAUL BENTLEY FRPS UK

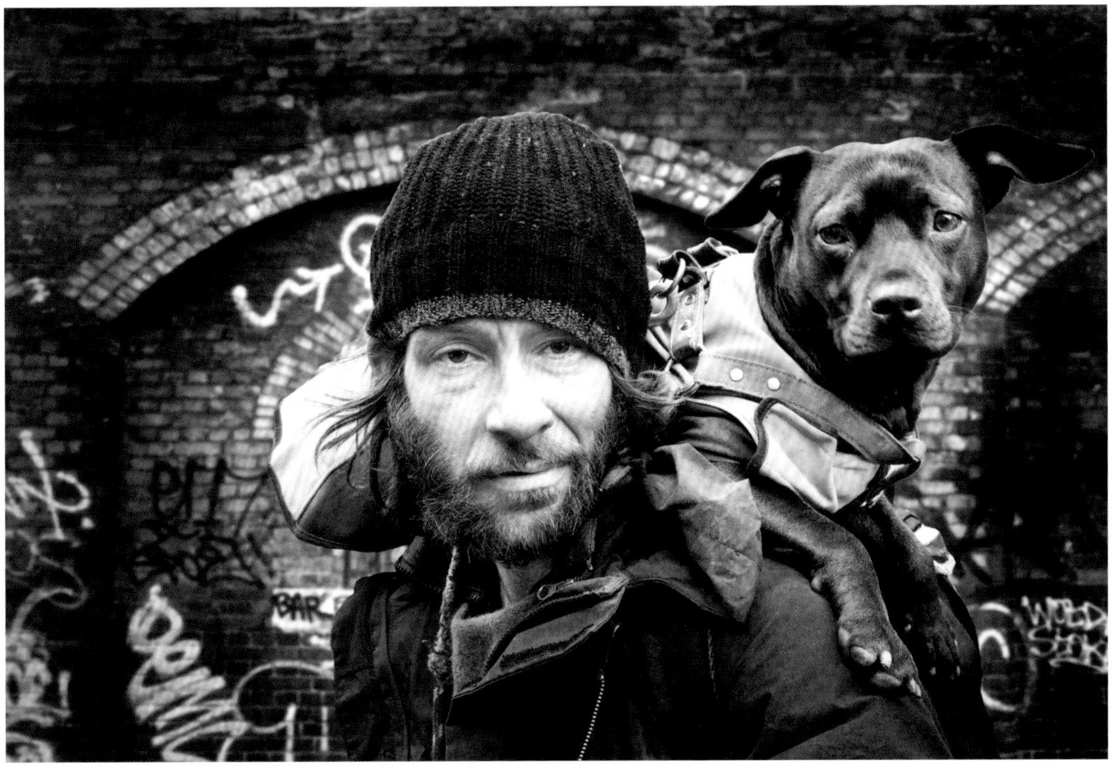

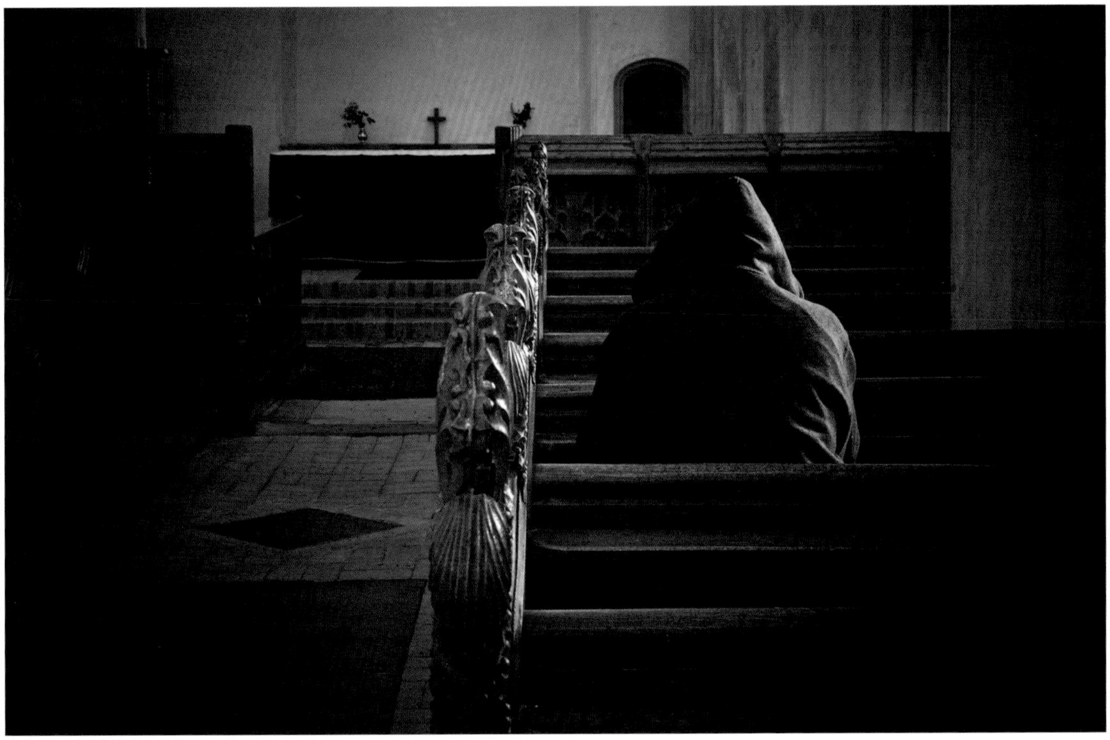

LINDA WEVILL FRPS UK

JAMES LAWS LRPS UK

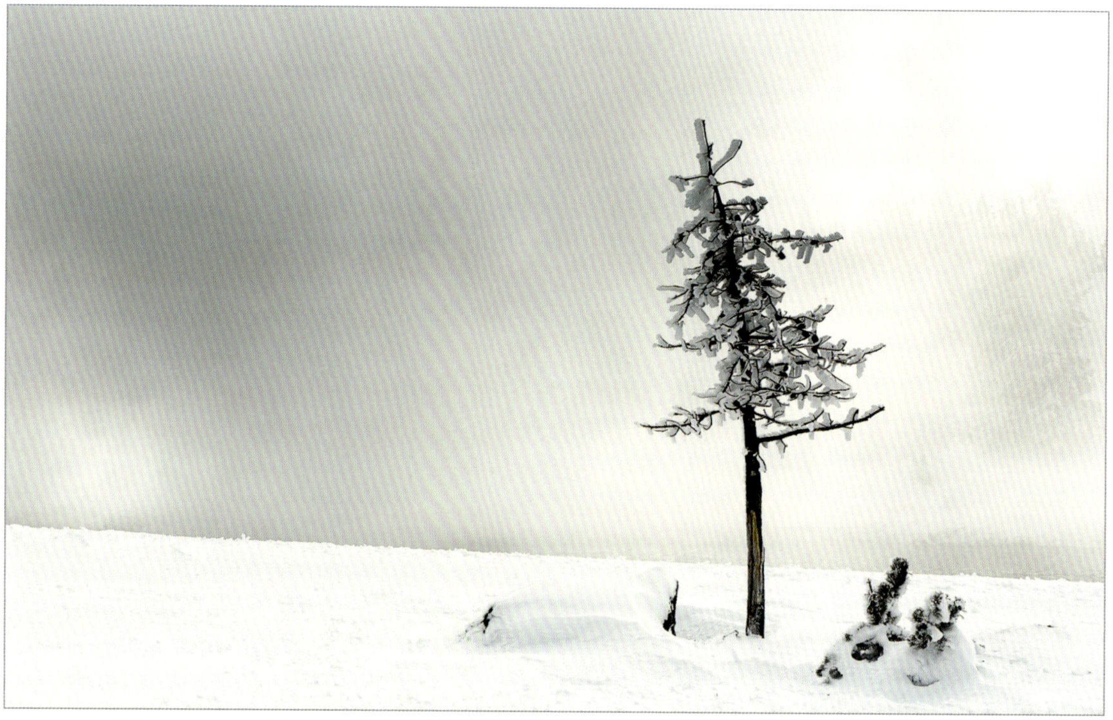

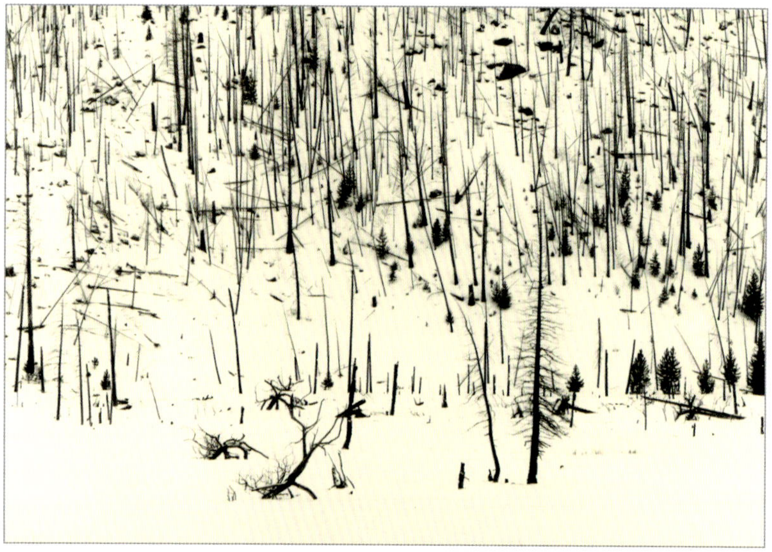

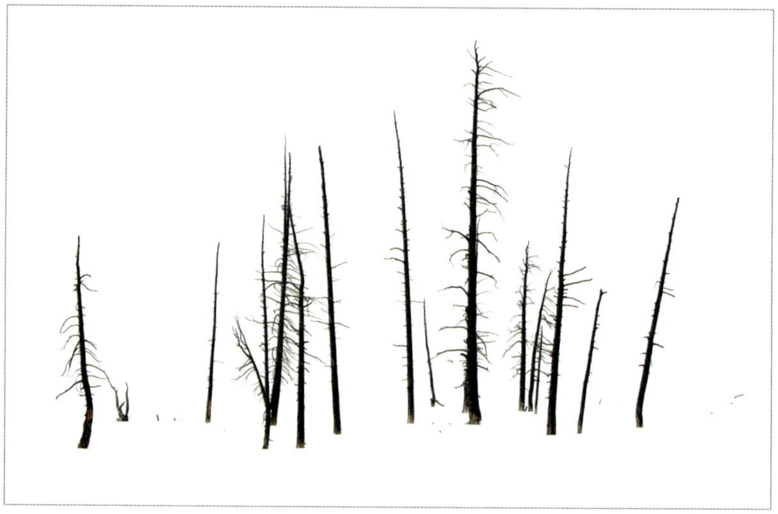

PETER PATERSON FRPS UK
TIM RUDMAN FRPS UK

PETER PATERSON FRPS UK

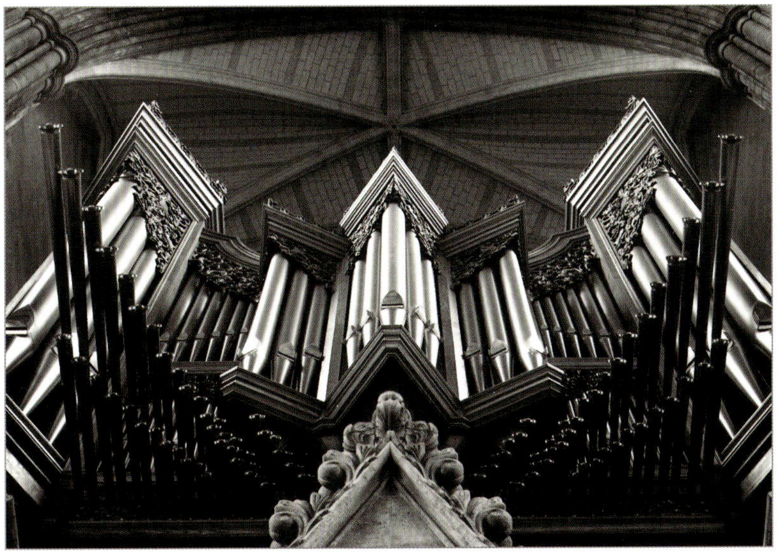

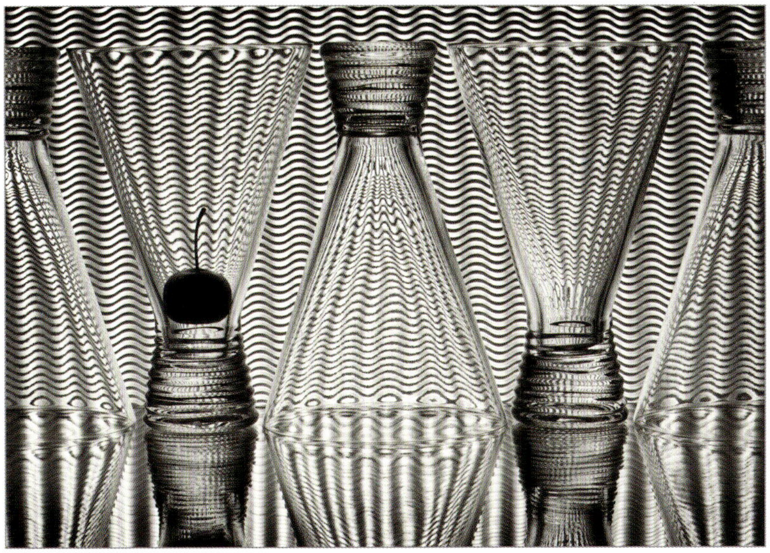

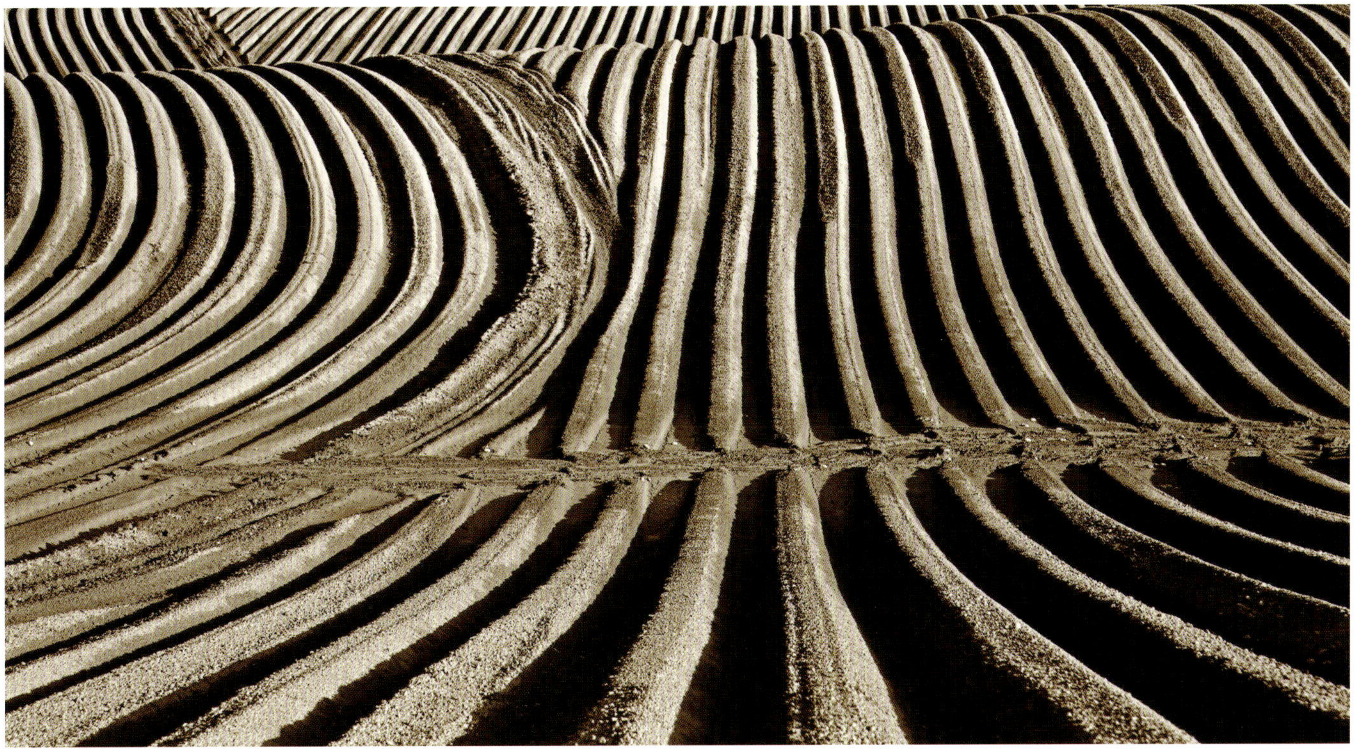

CHAS BEDFORD LRPS UK

JOHN WIDDOWS ARPS UK

ANDREW WHITE LRPS UK

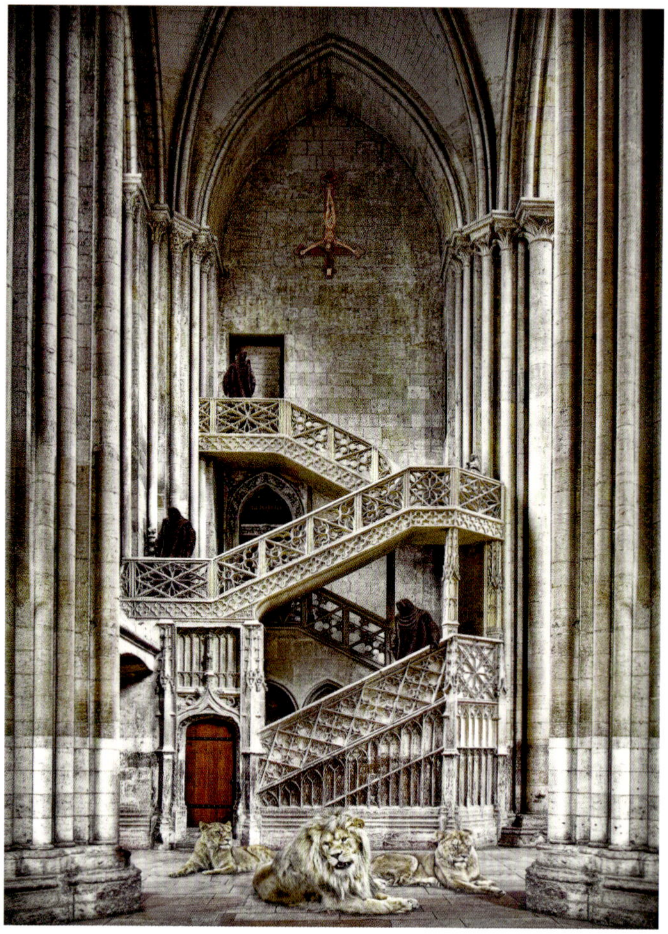

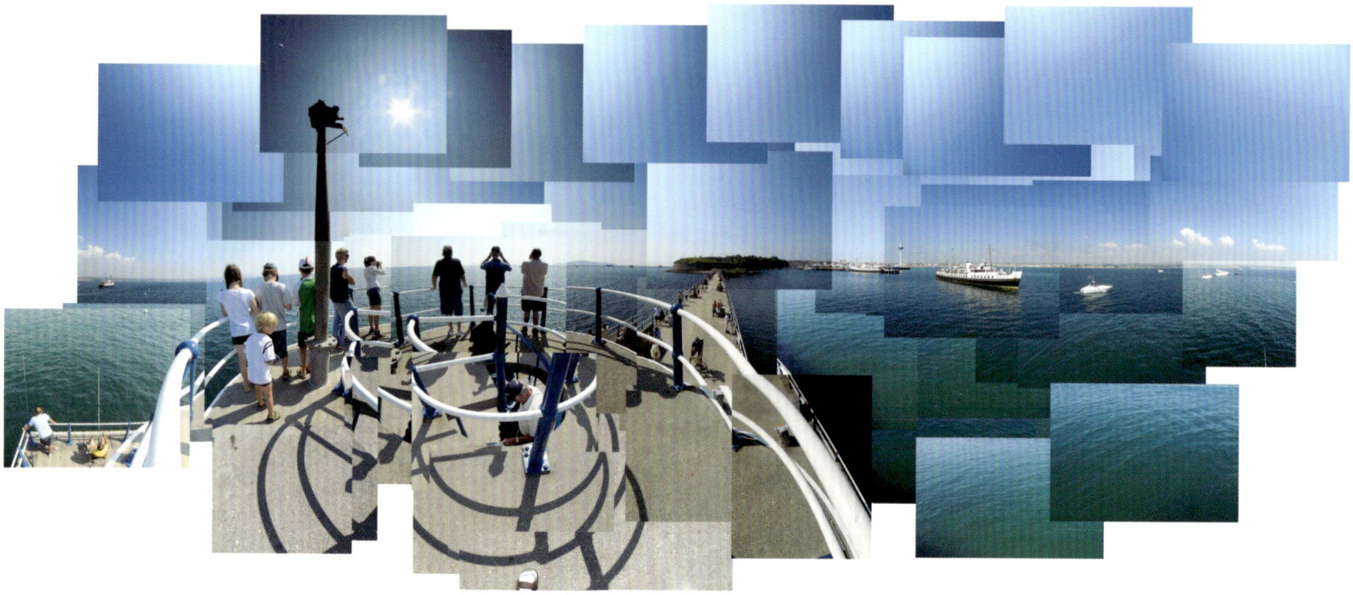

SIMON HASTINGS ARPS UK
MICHAEL HALLETT FRPS UK

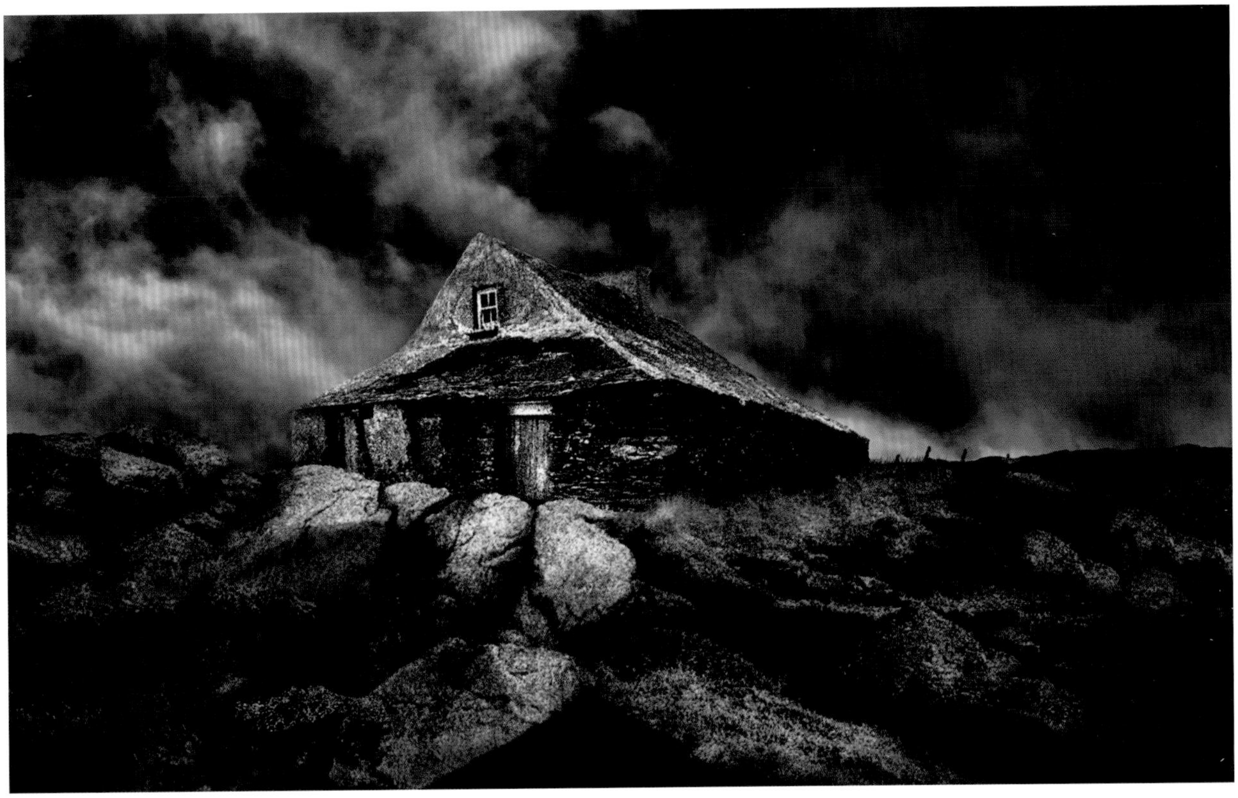

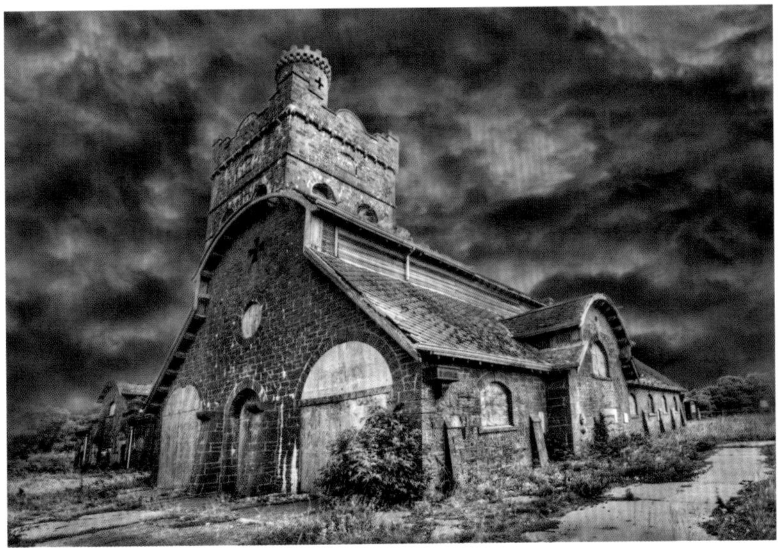

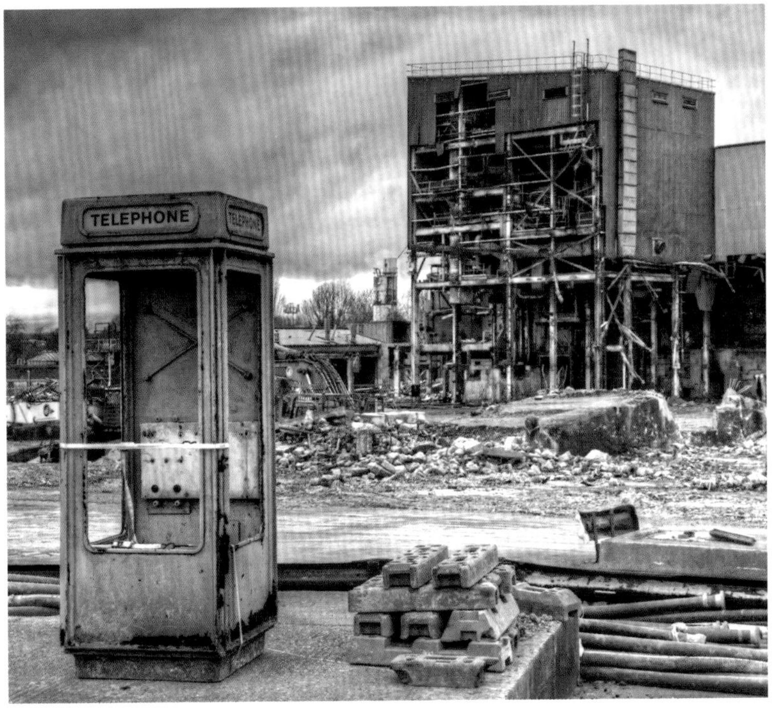

MICHAEL MAGUIRE FRPS UK

DAVID SYMONDS FRPS UK

HELEN ASHBOURNE ARPS UK

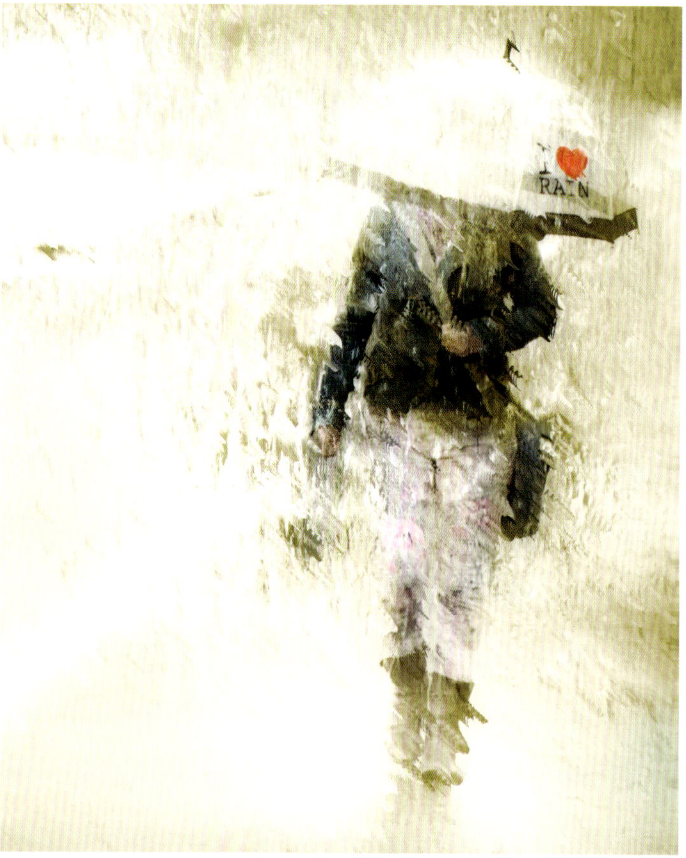

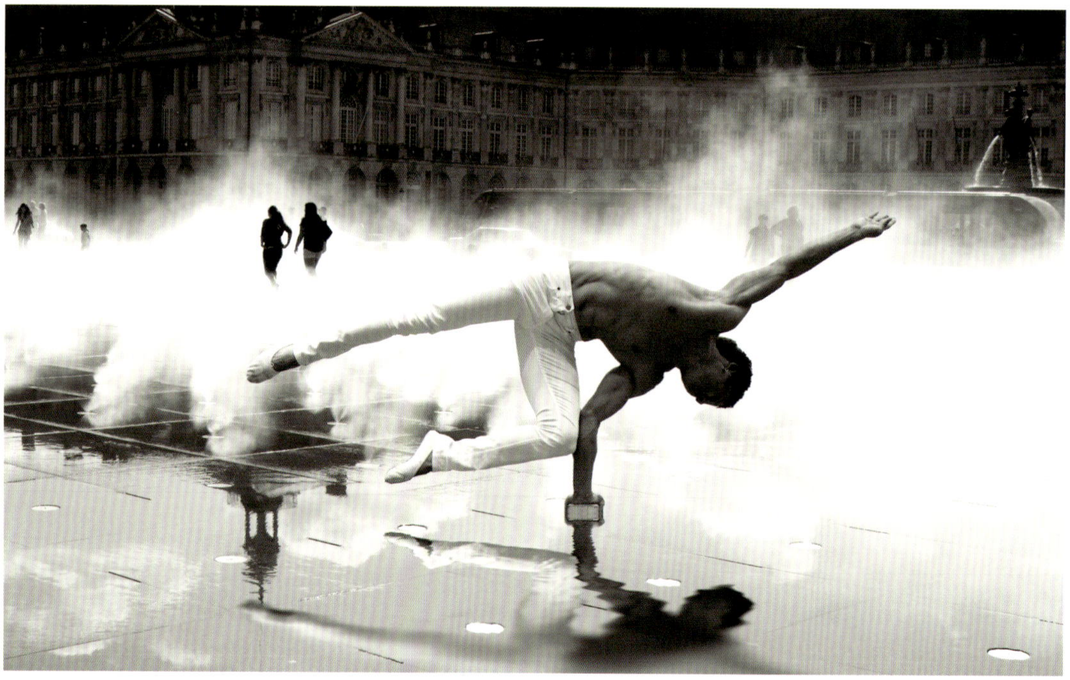

PETER STICKLER UK
BILL PRESTON ARPS UK

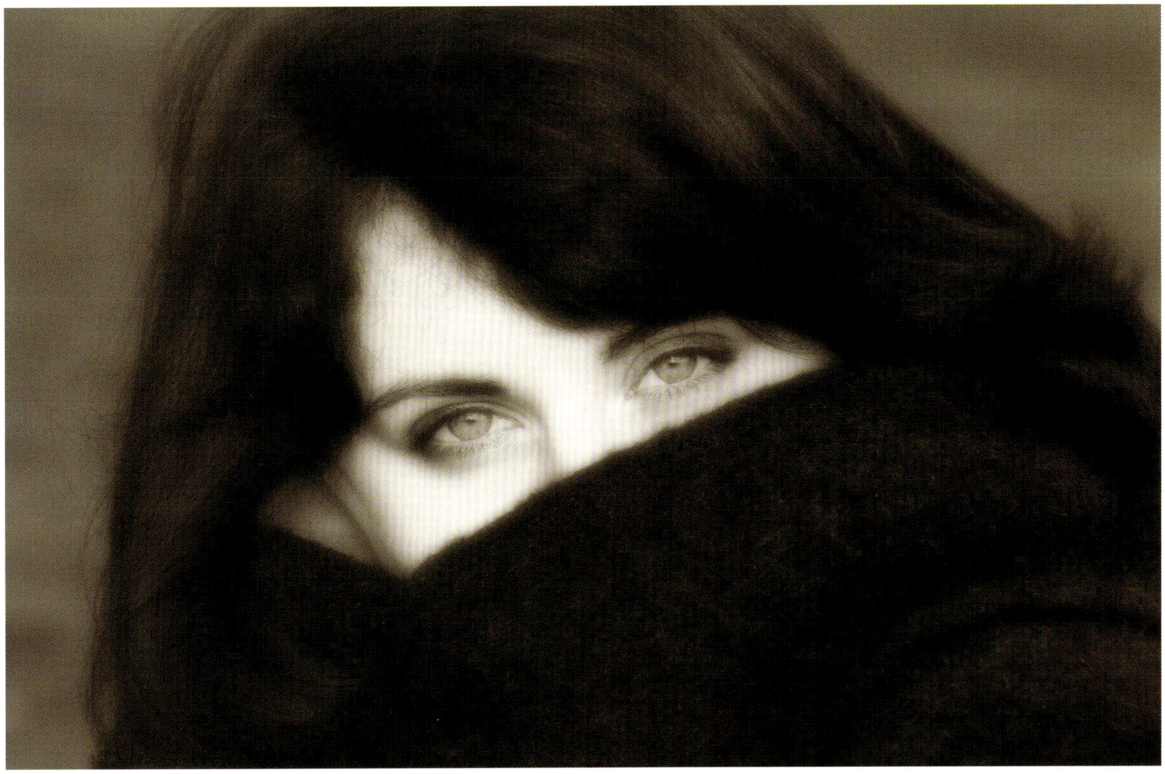

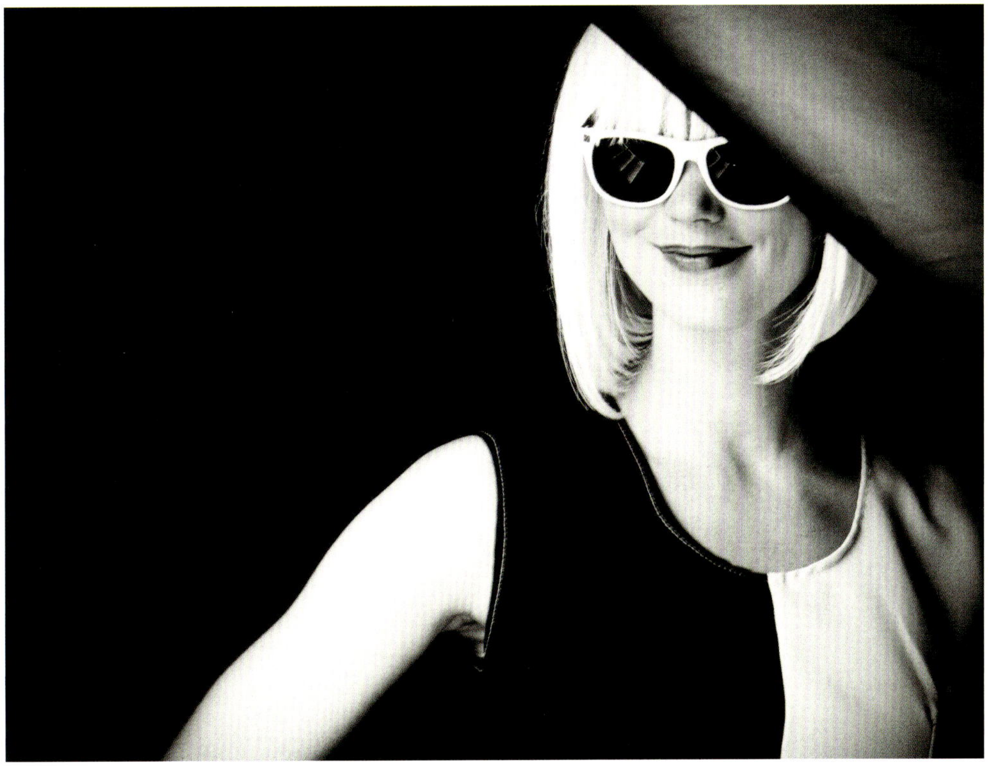

DOUGLAS VERNIMMEN LRPS UK
ROBERT BRACHER ARPS UK

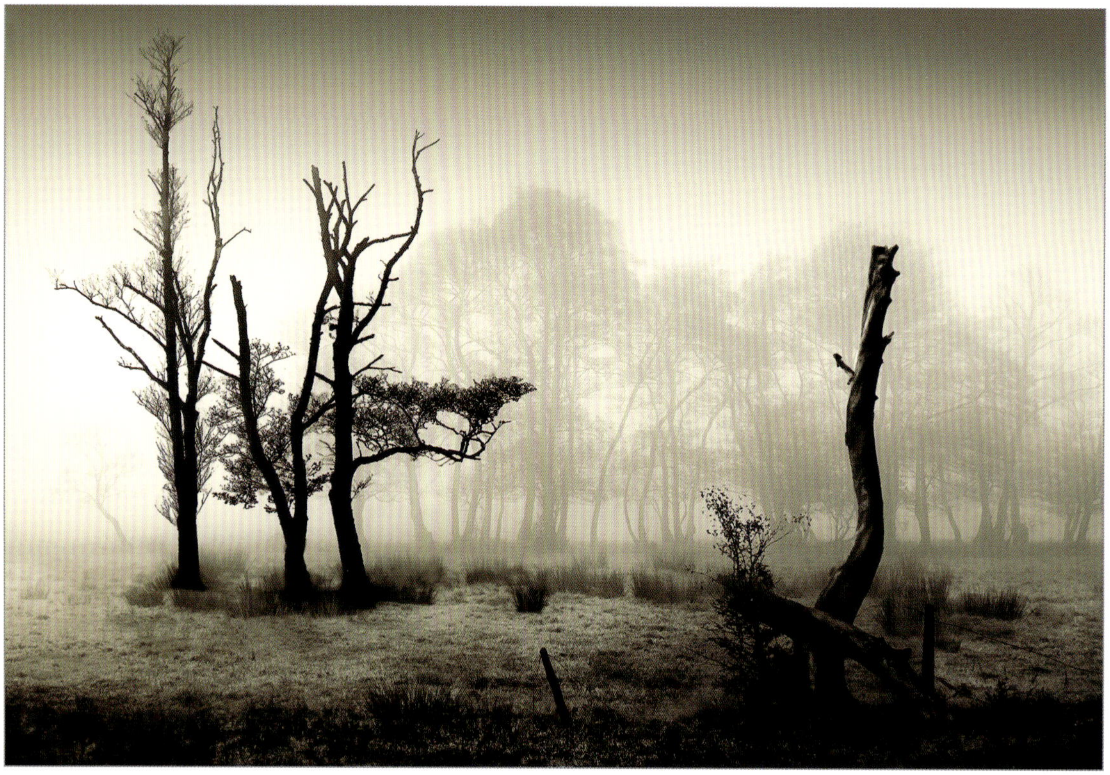

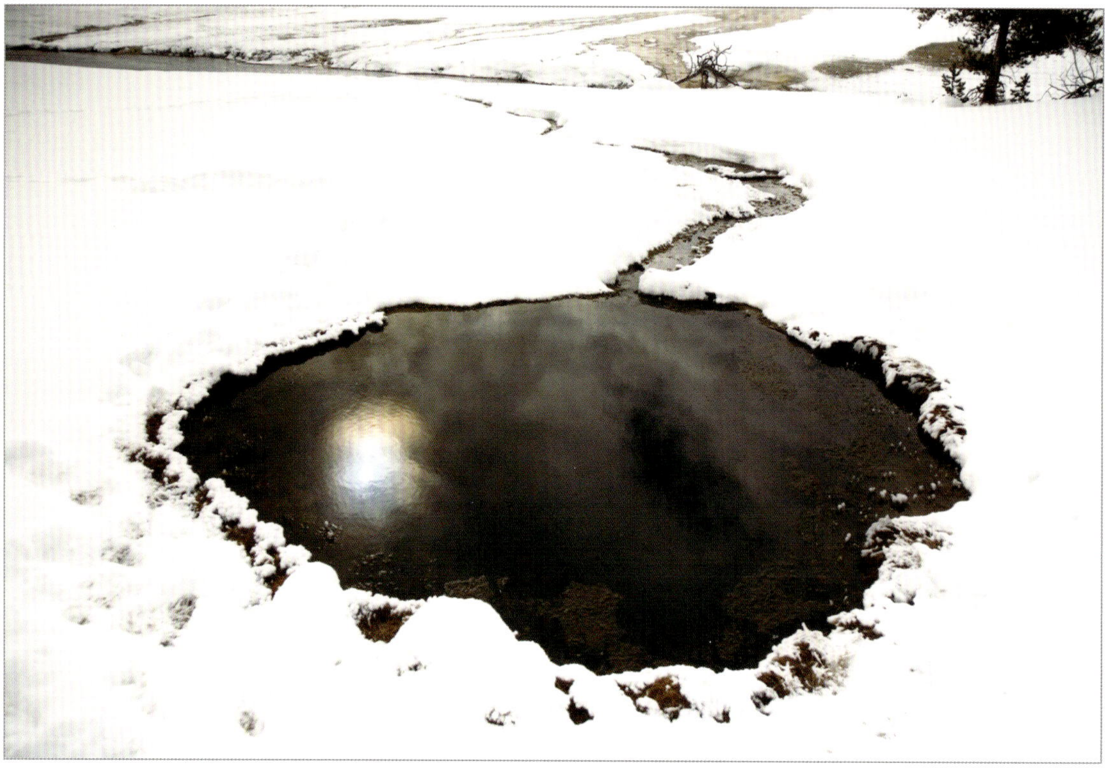

BARRY SENIOR Hon.FRPS UK
LEON KREEL ARPS UK

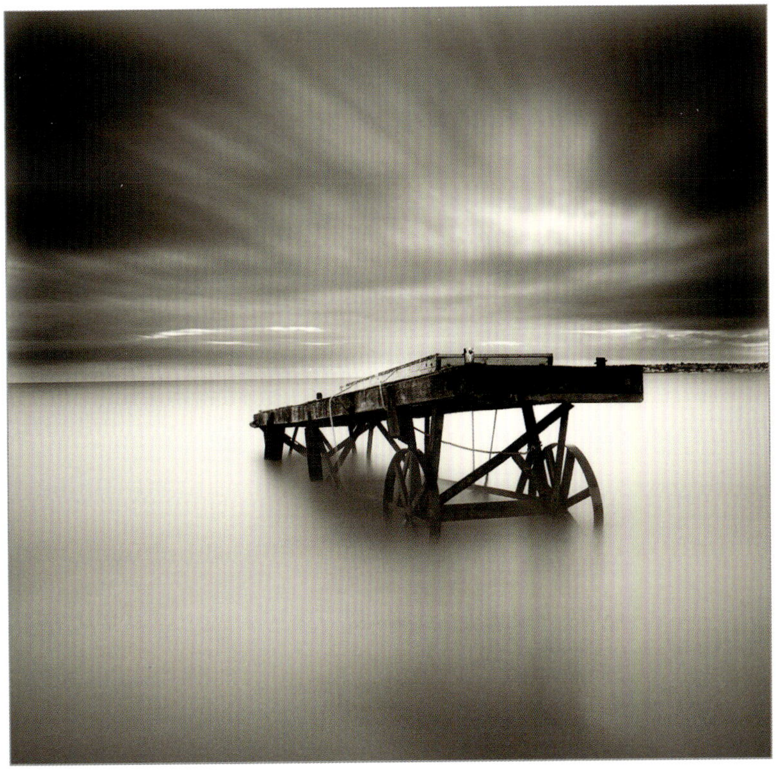

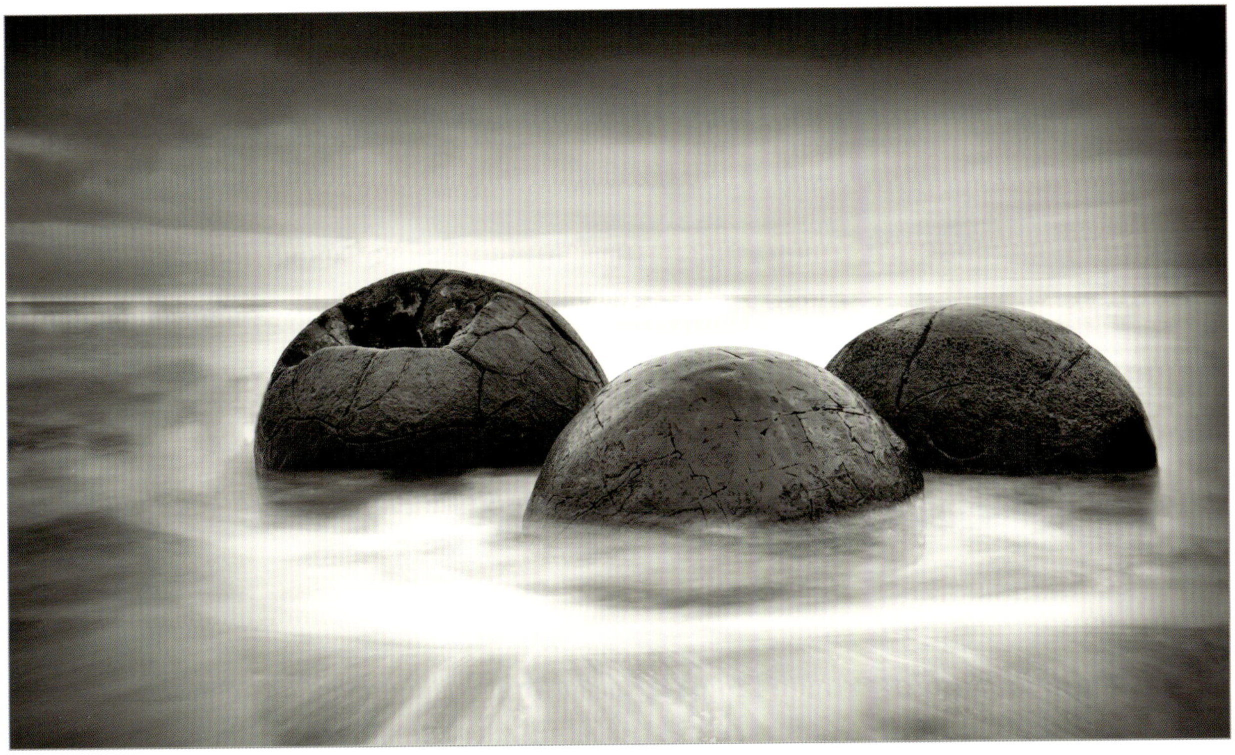

SUSAN BROWN FRPS UK
TIM HARRIS ARPS UK

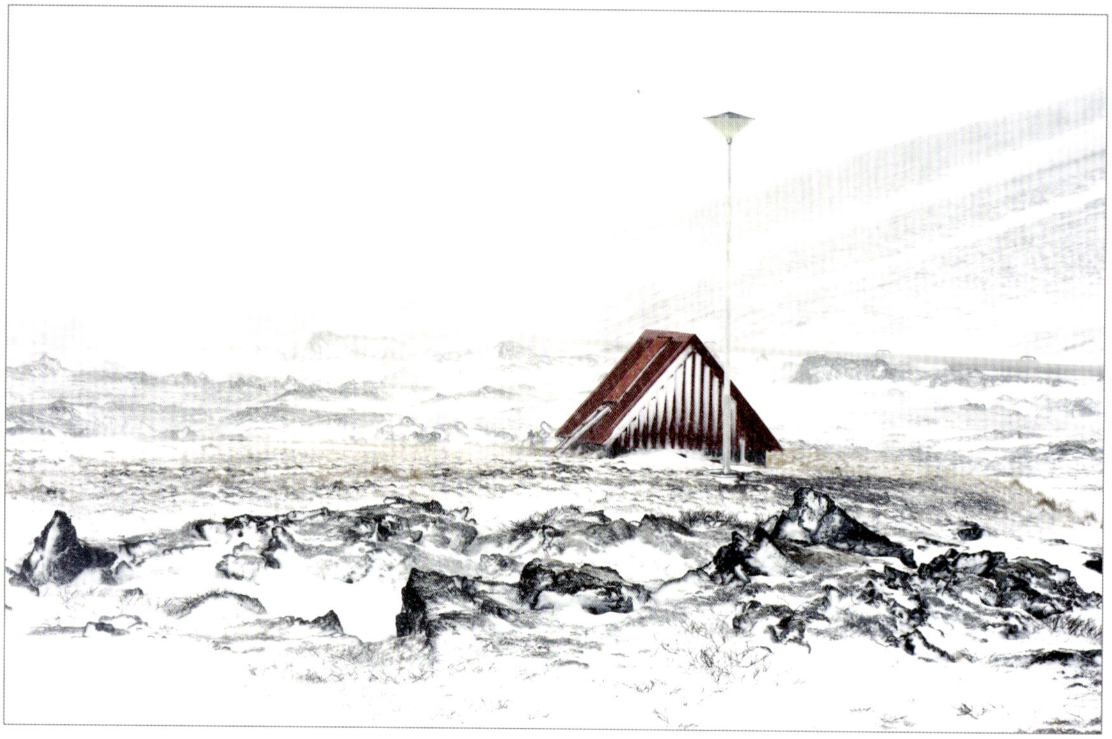

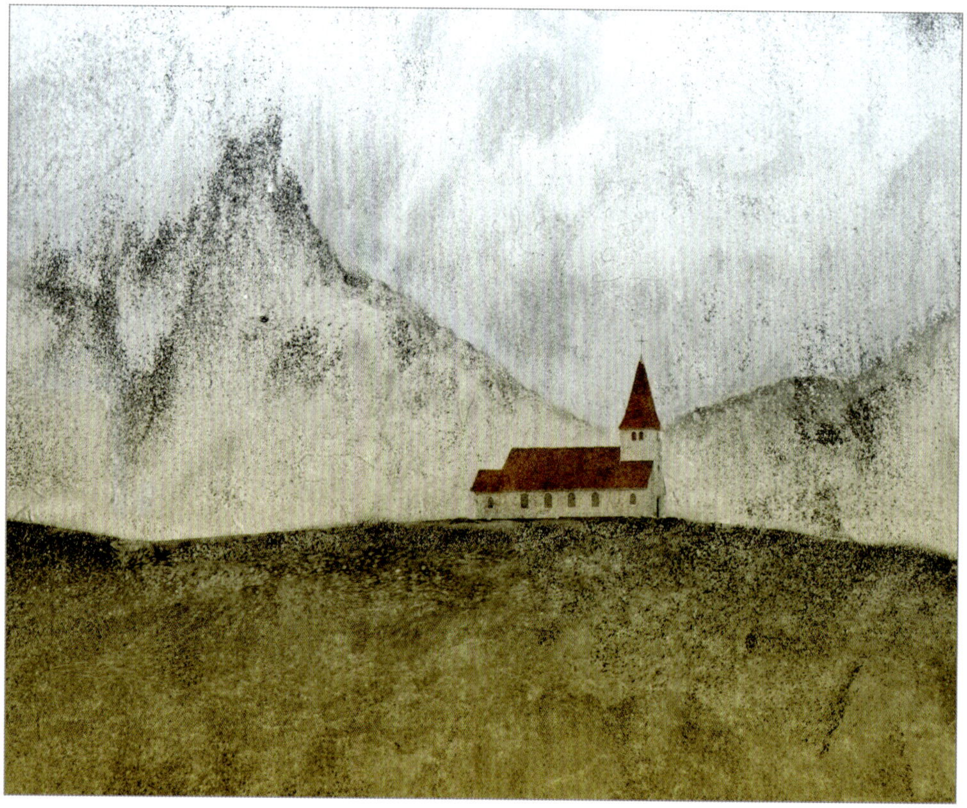

NIGEL PLANT ARPS UK

ANN MILES FRPS UK

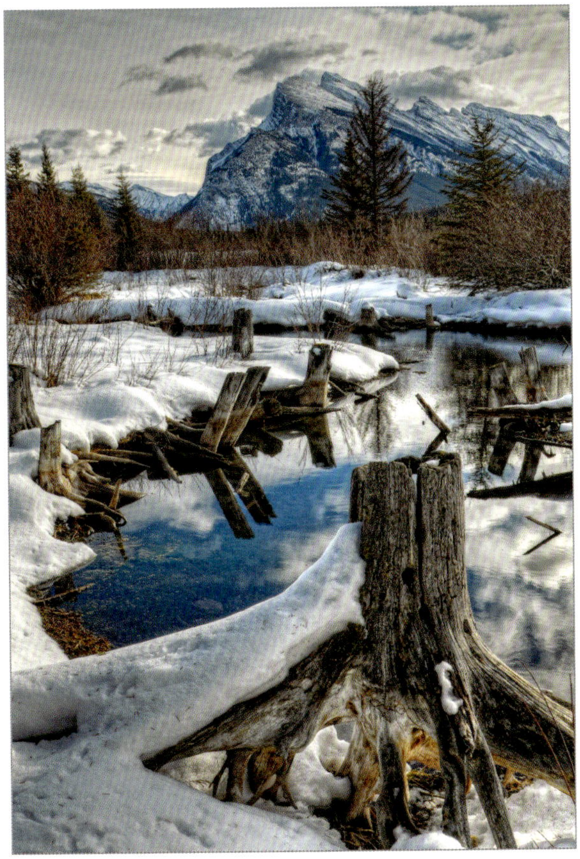

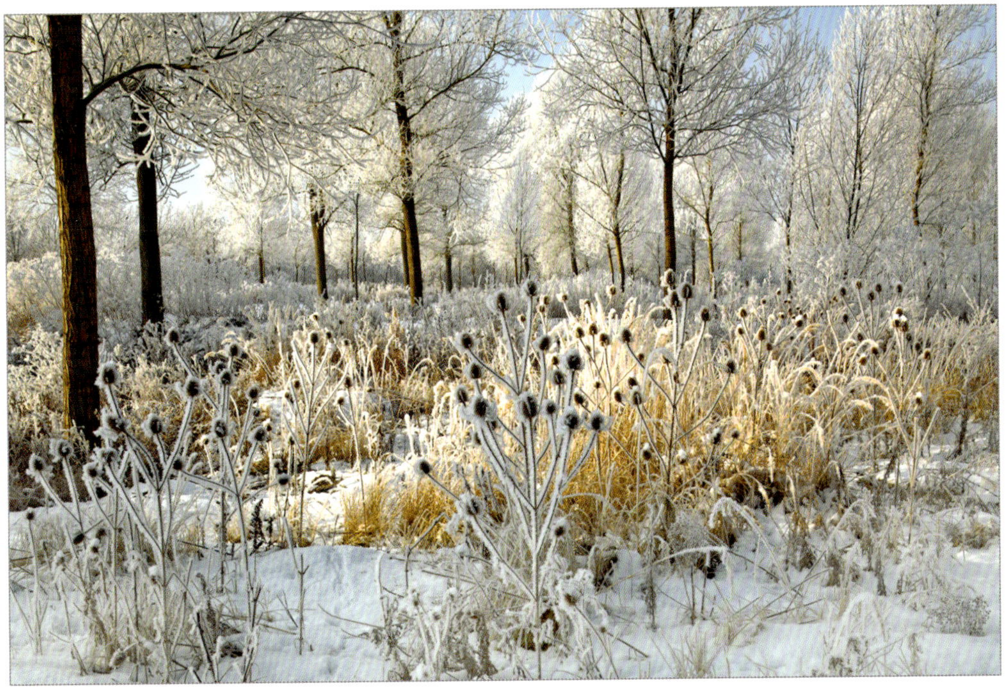

MARGARET WHITTAKER LRPS UK

ANDREW SMITH ARPS UK

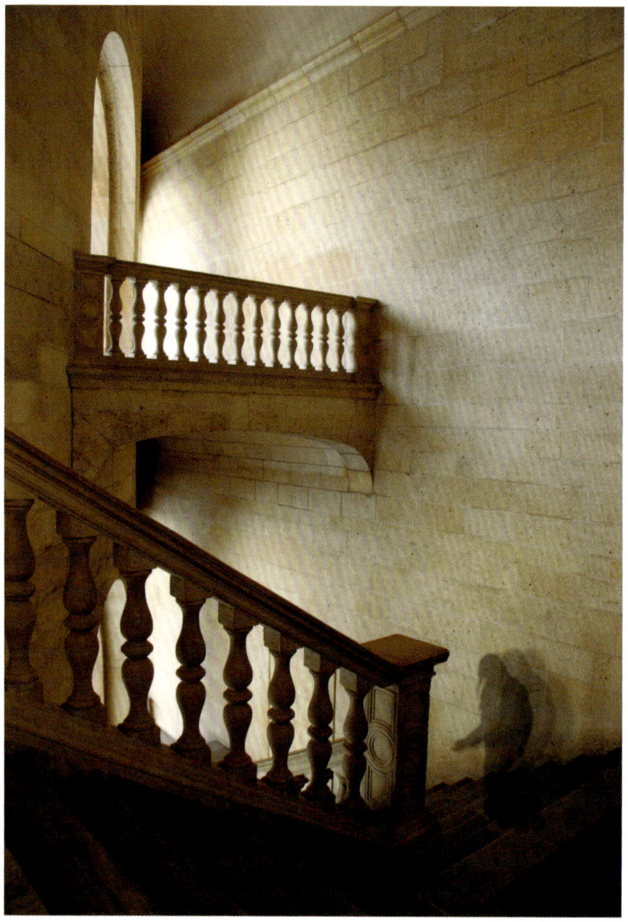

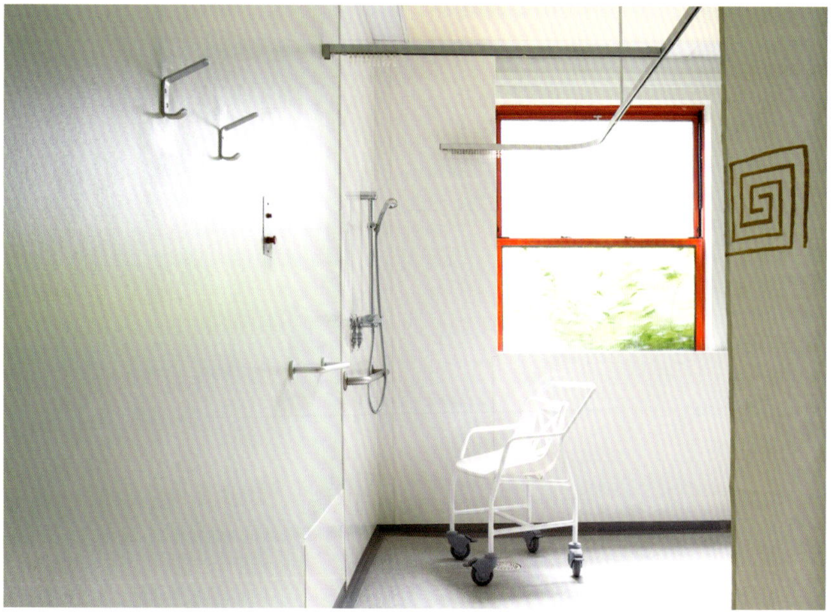

BILL PRESTON ARPS UK
ANNE CASSIDY FRPS UK

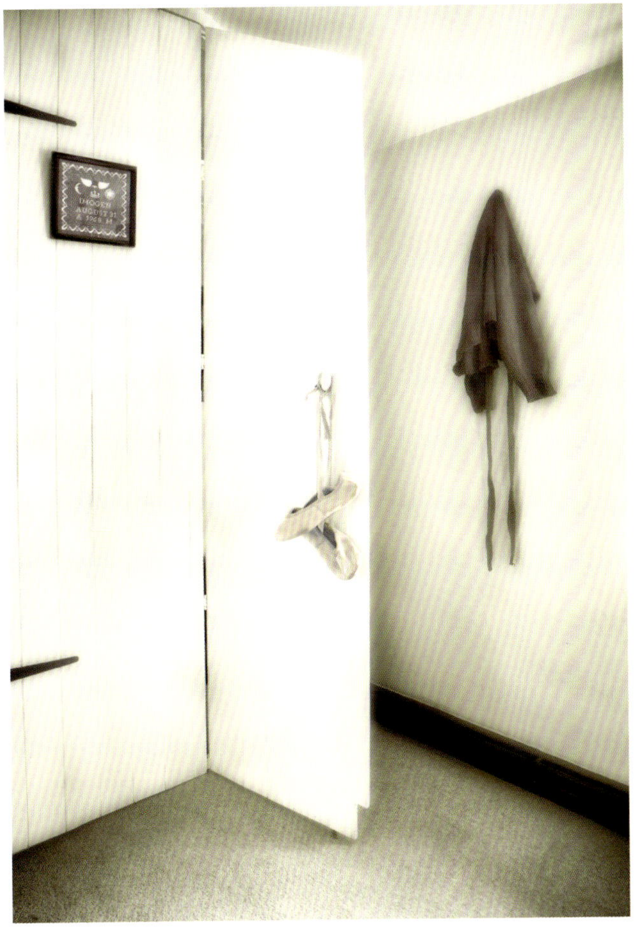

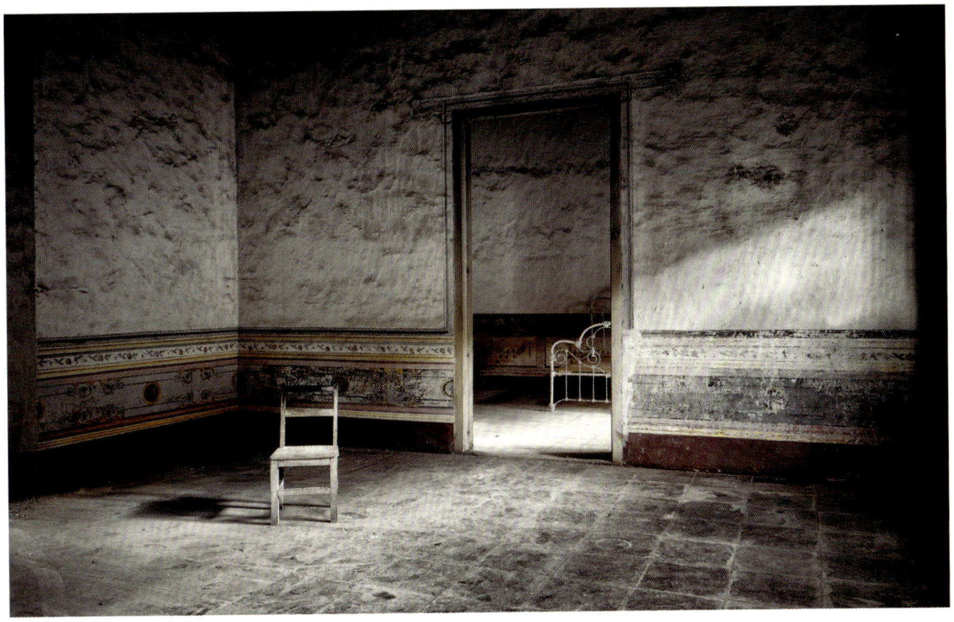

ALISON CAWLEY ARPS UK

RICHARD TICKNER ARPS UK

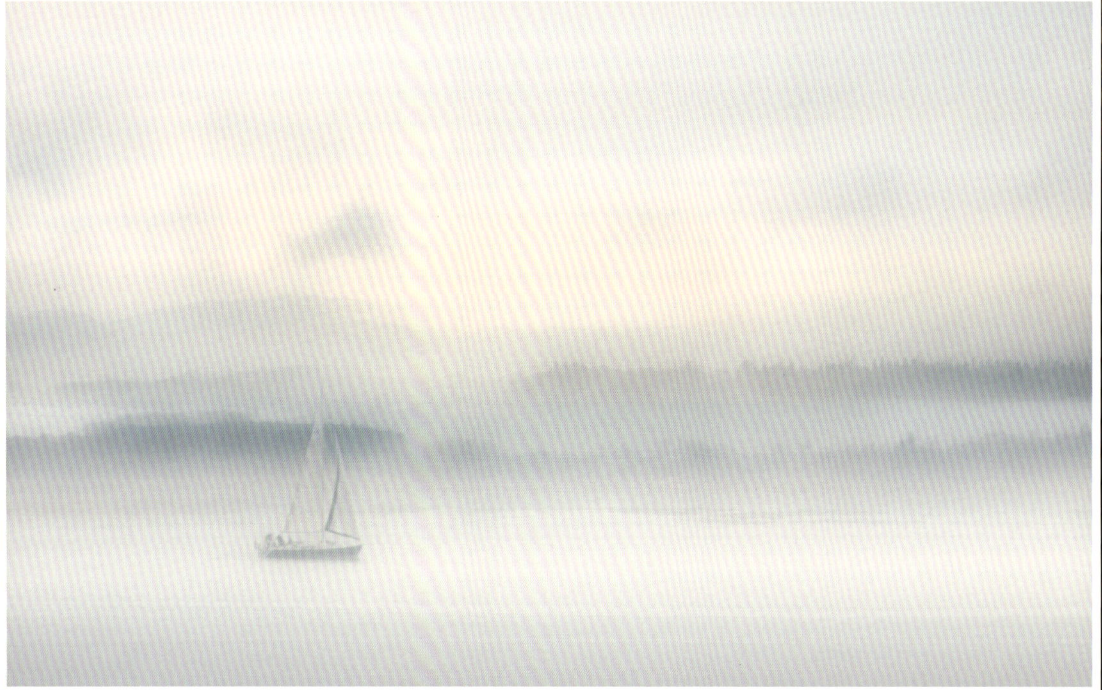

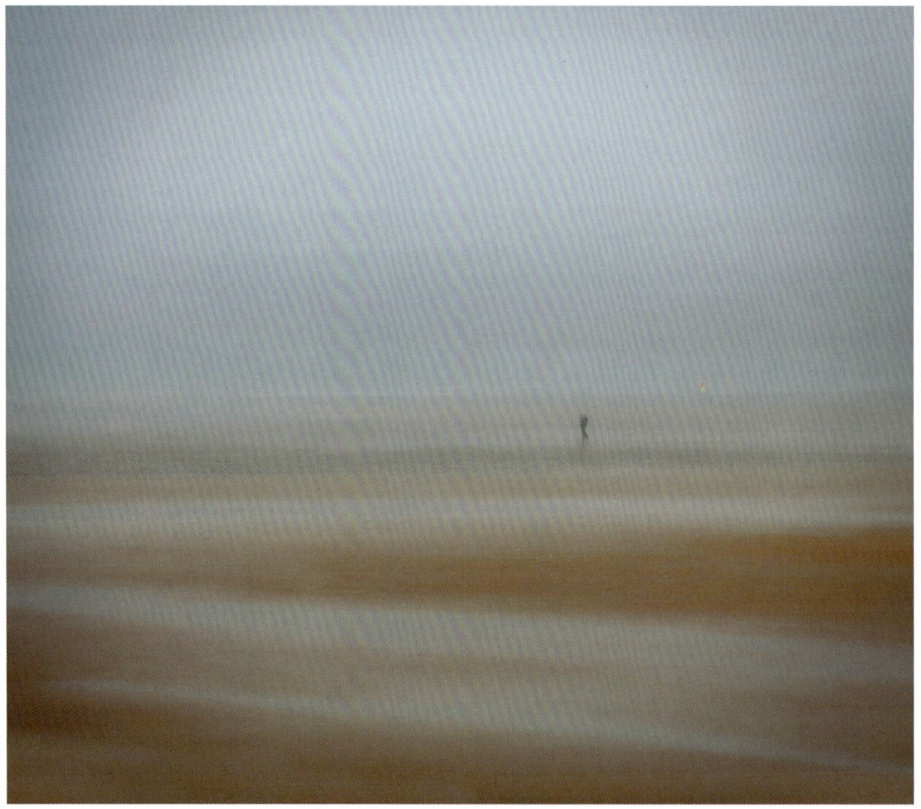

STAN FARROW FRPS UK
GINA SOCRATES ARPS CHANNEL ISLANDS

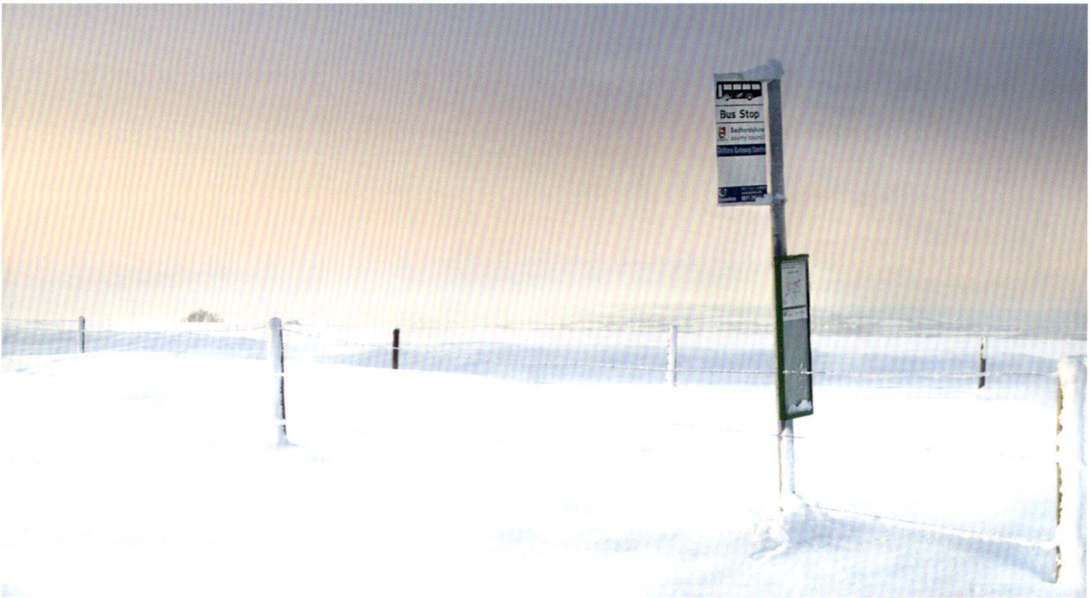
Bus Stop

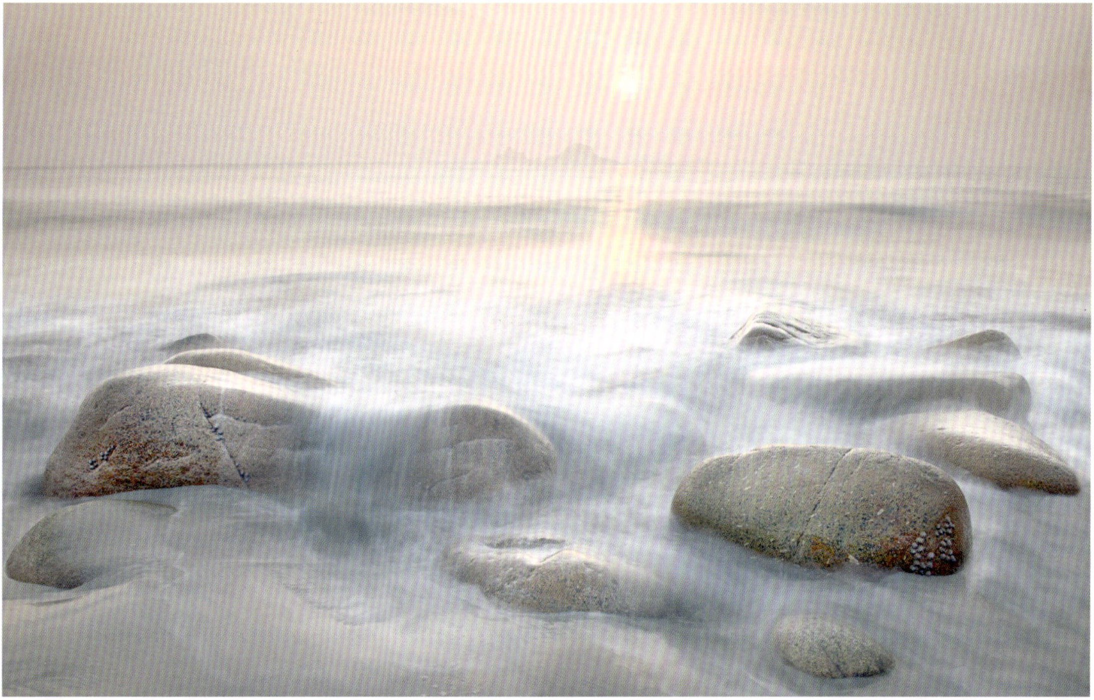

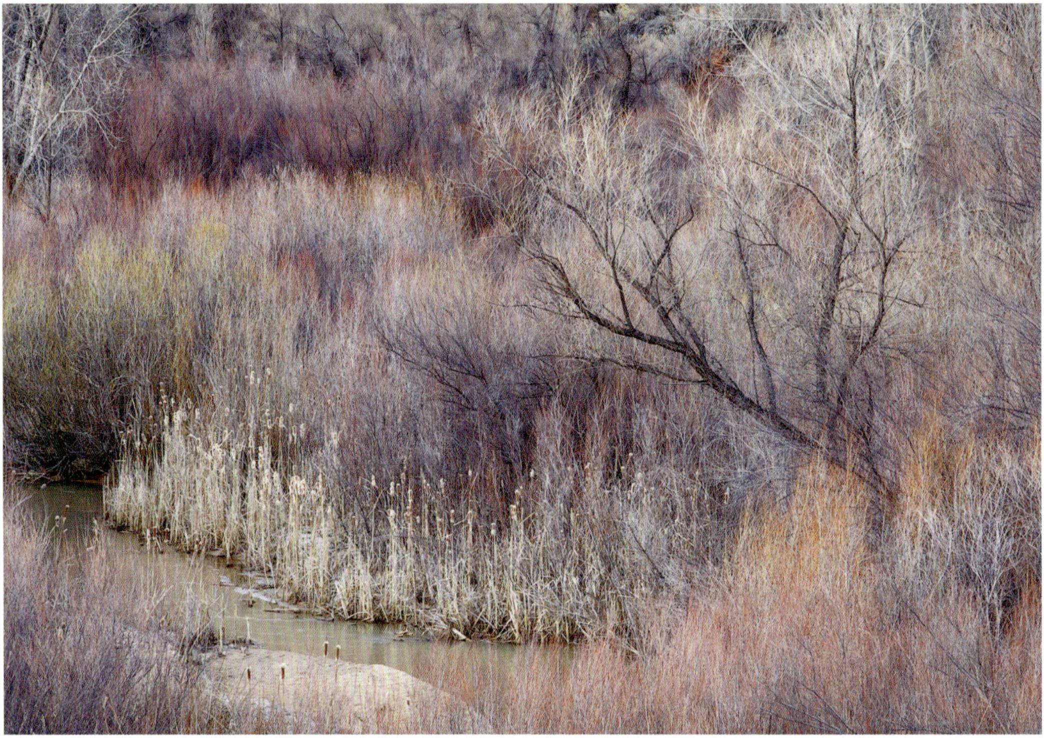

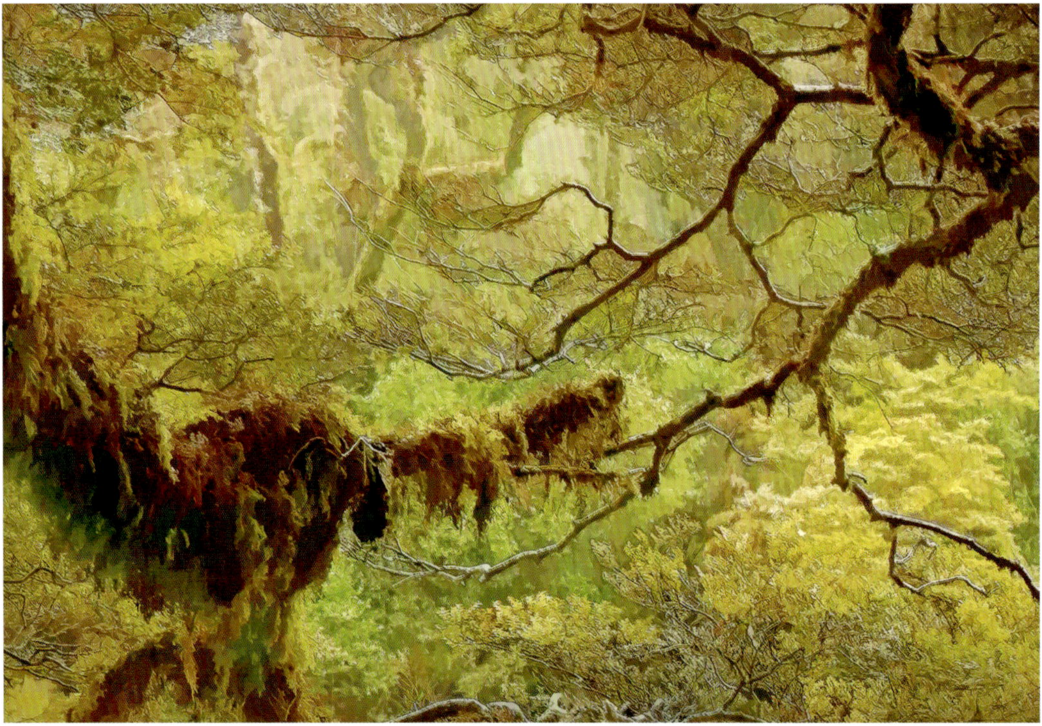

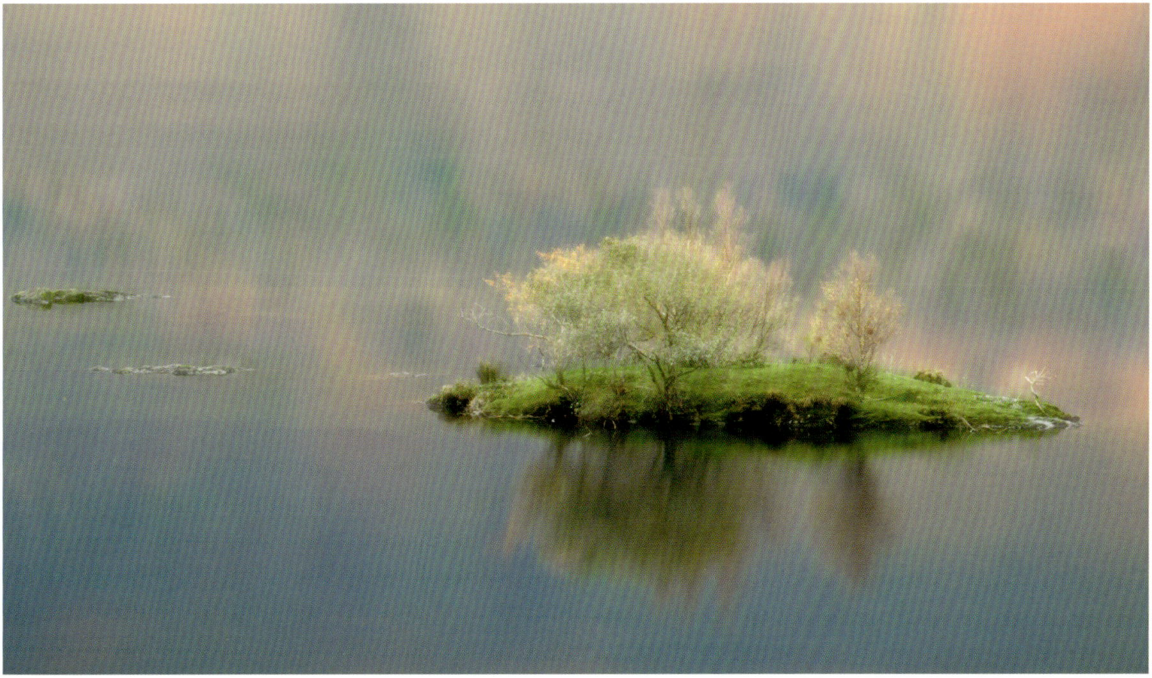

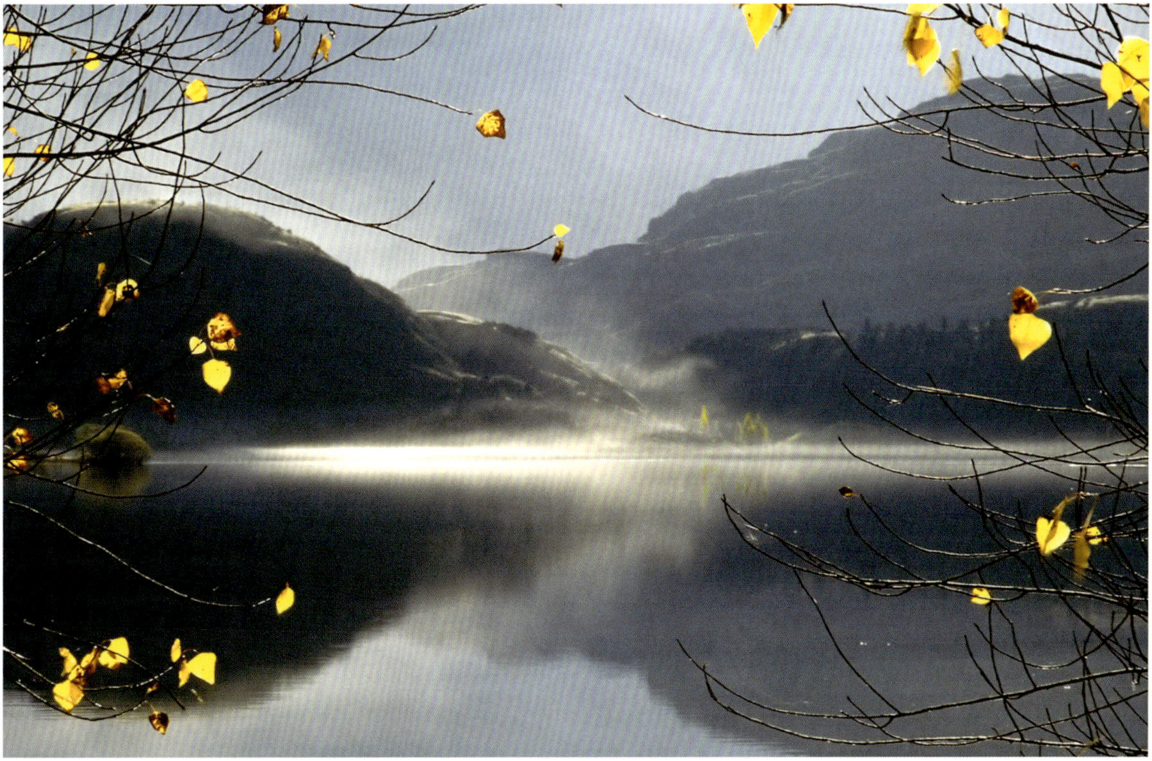

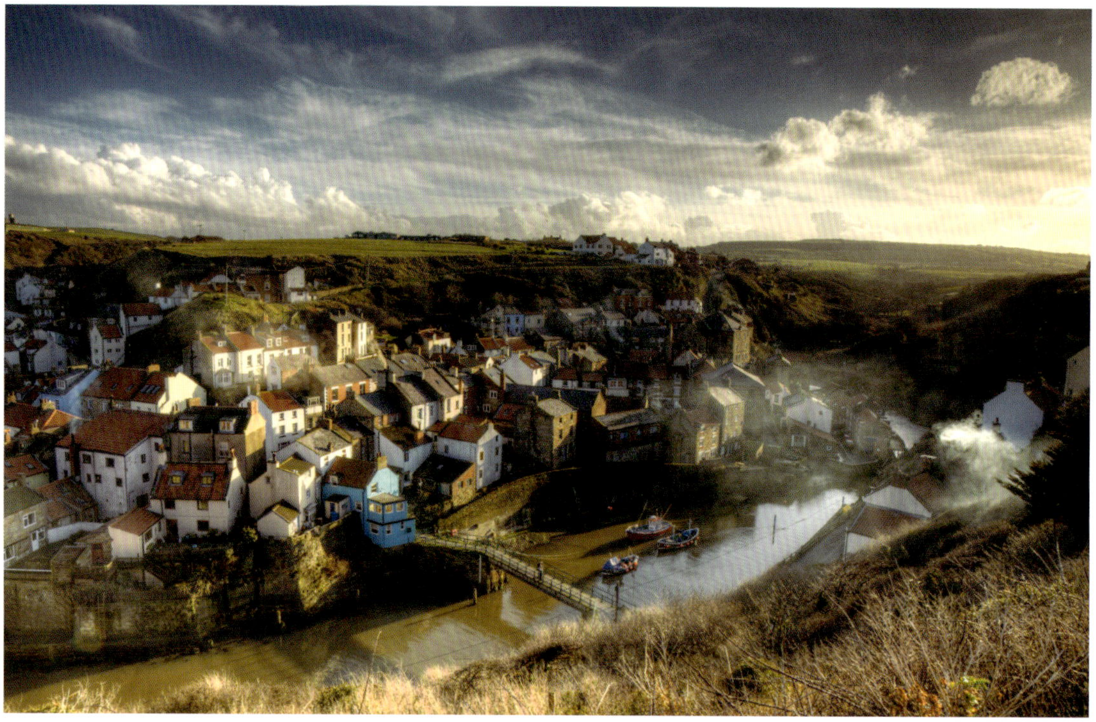

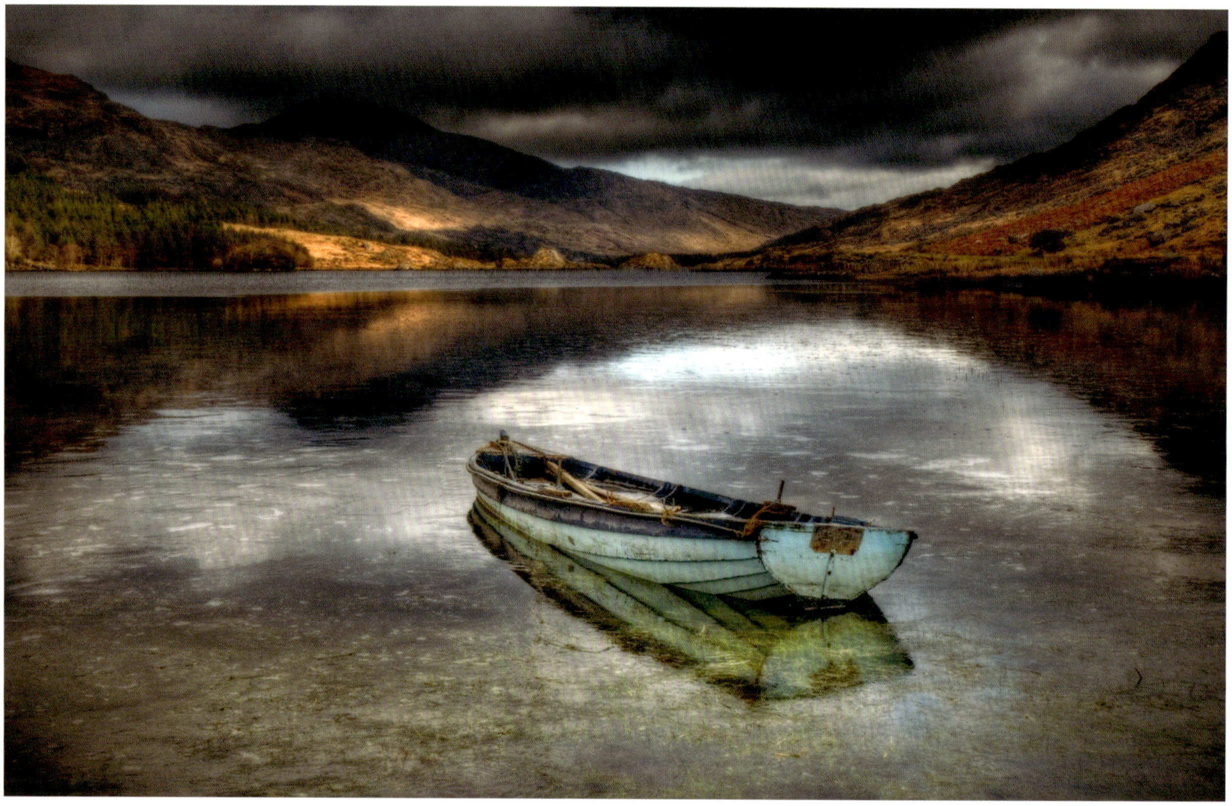

PHIL PORTUS LRPS UK
LEO PALMER FRPS UK

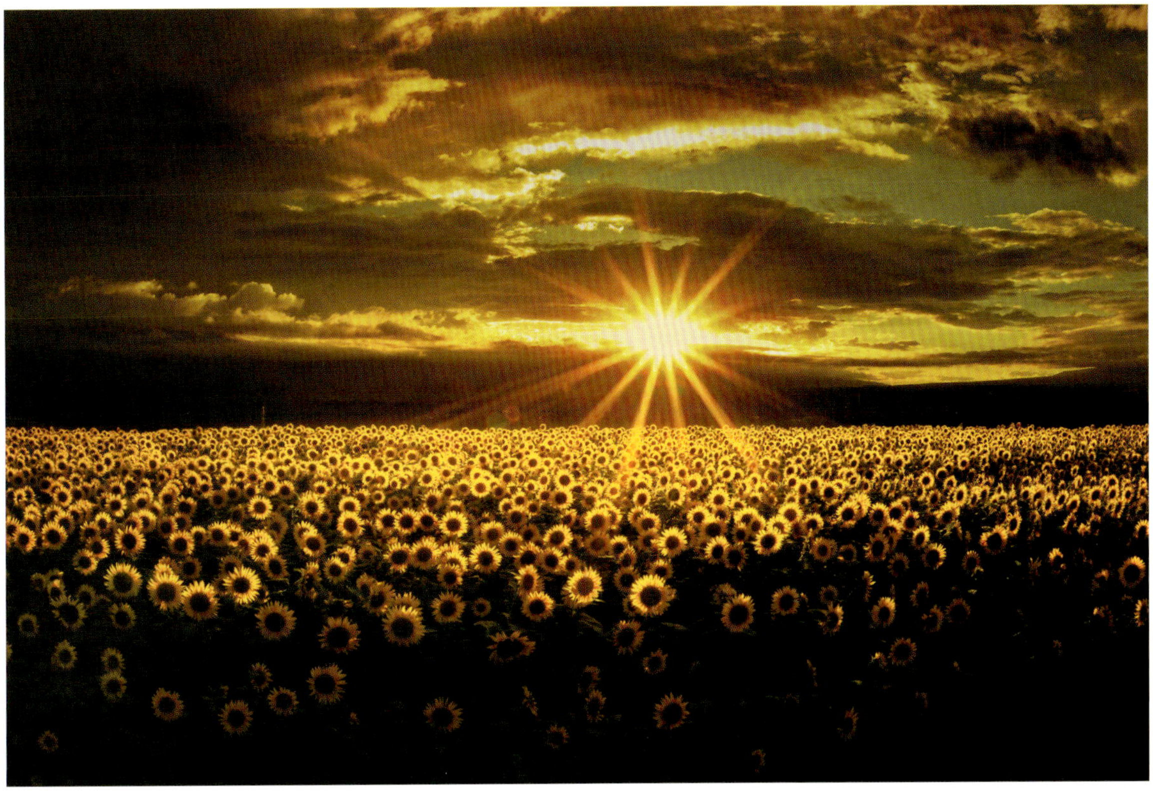

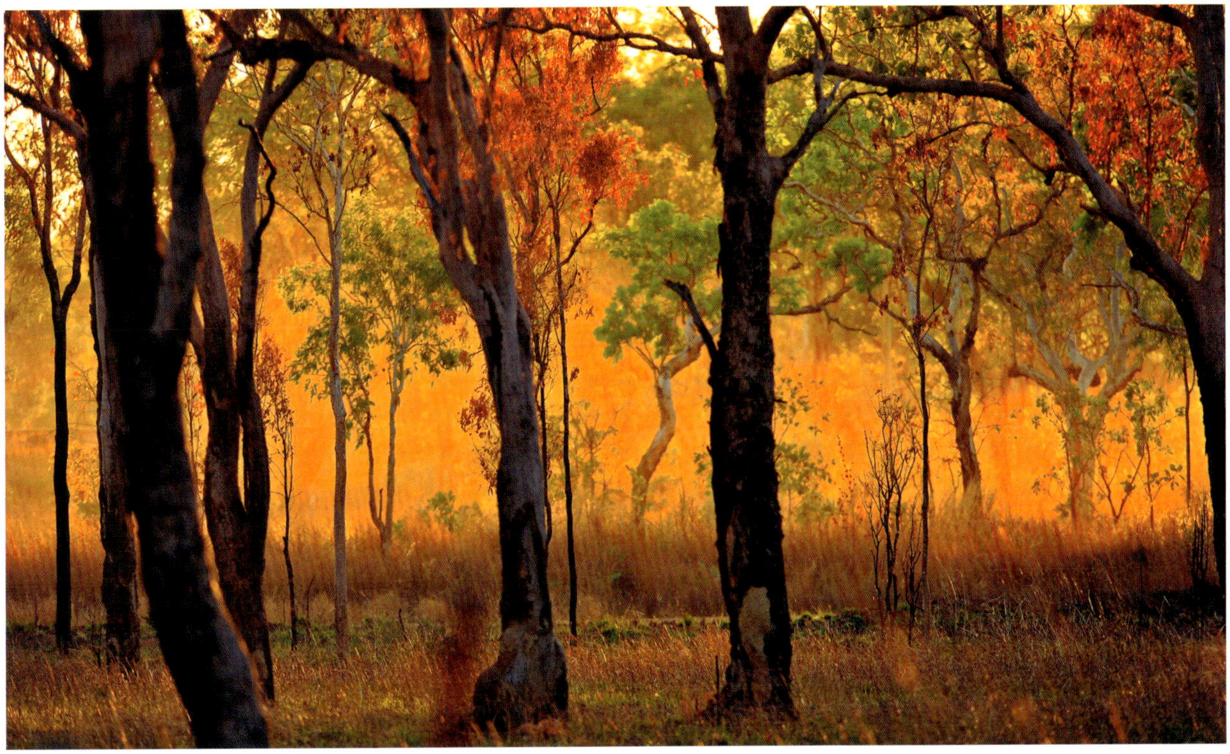

MORI SEIKO JAPAN

DAVID BIRD LRPS UK

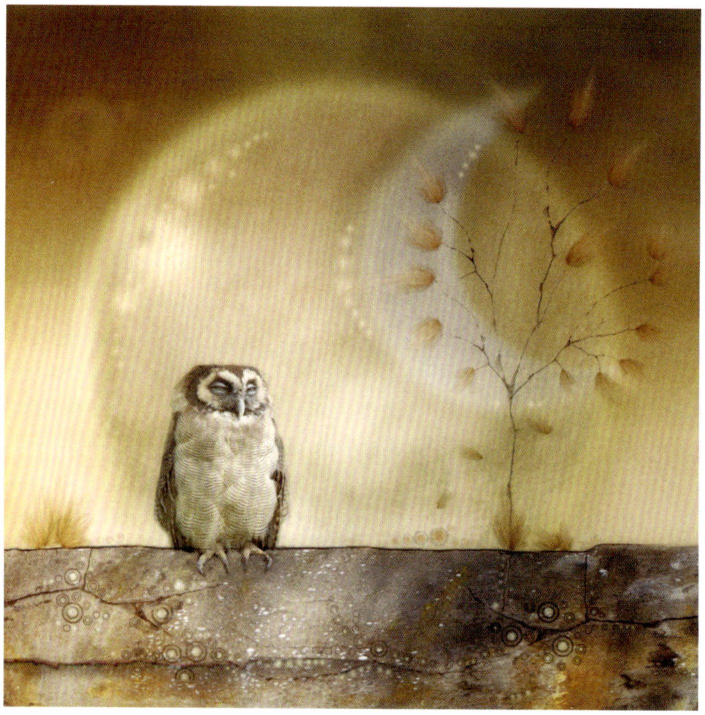

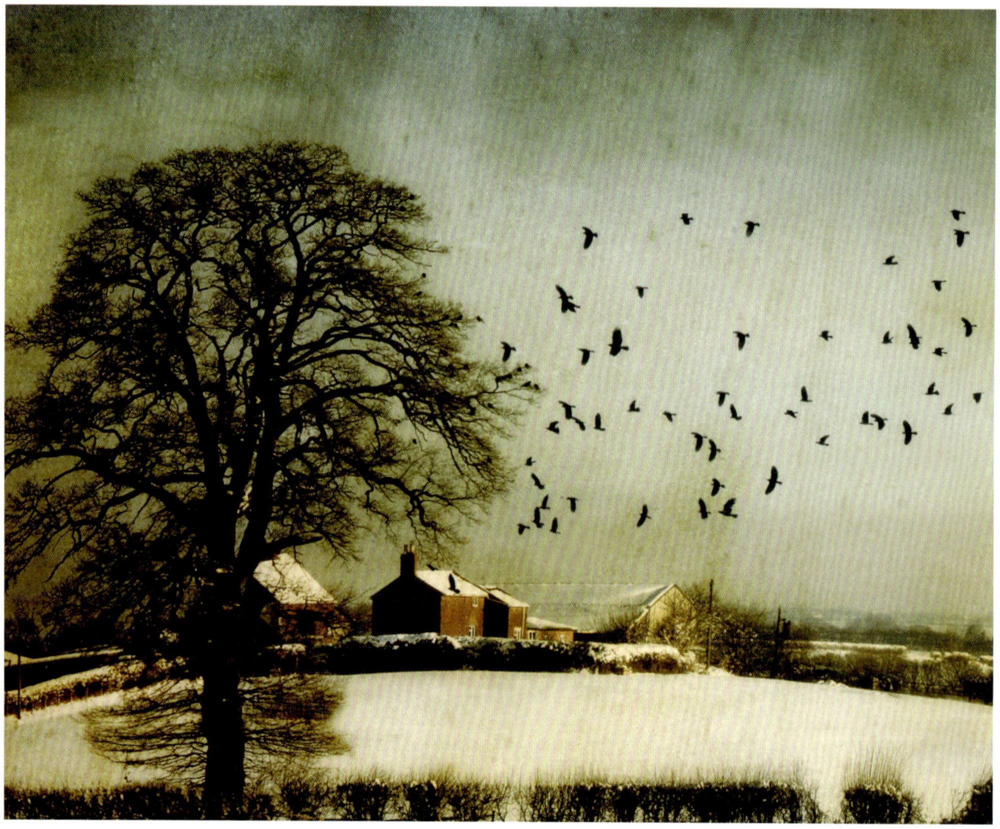

VALENTINA KULAGINA ARPS UK

DIANNE OWEN FRPS UK

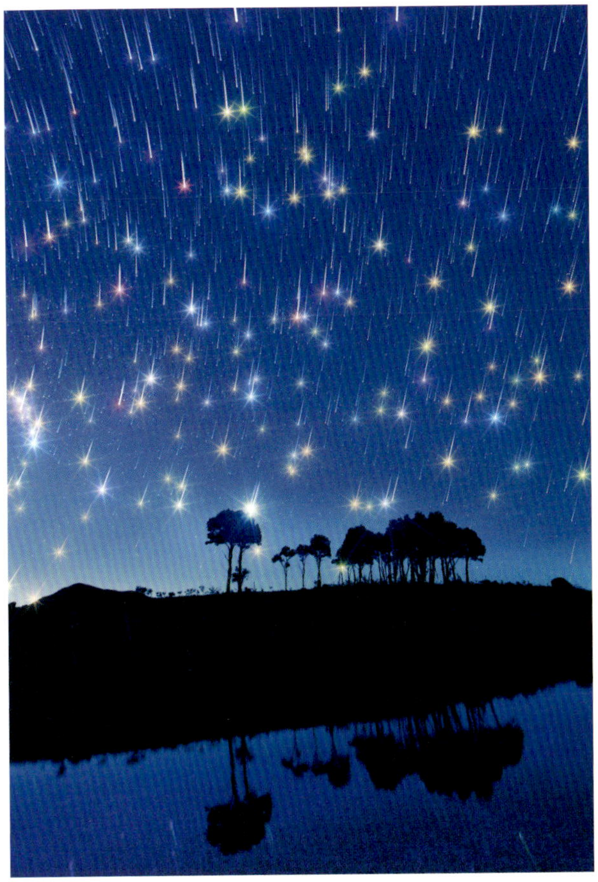

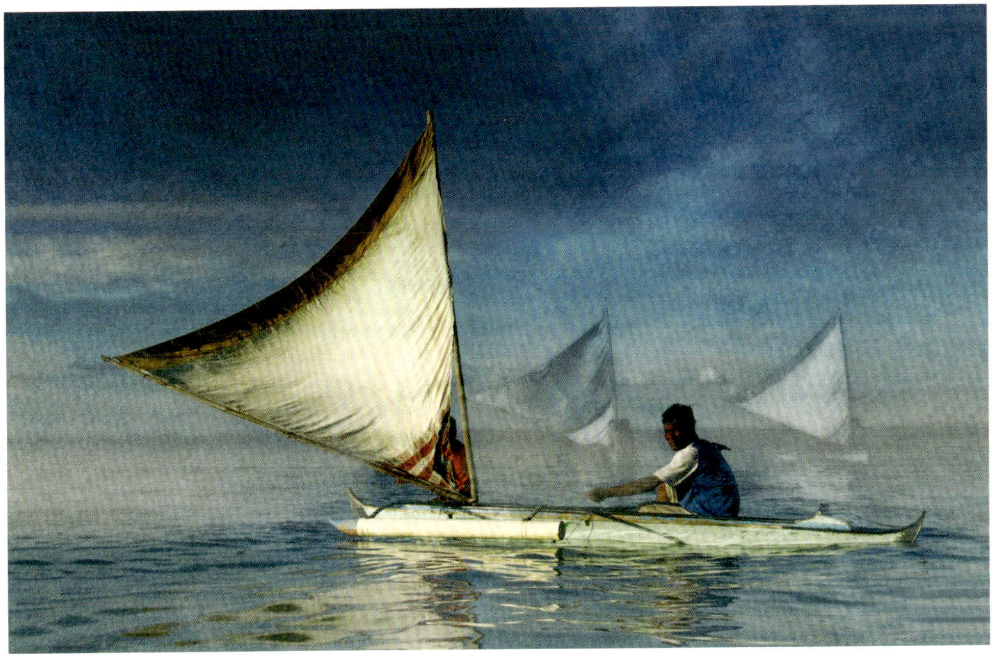

MEI TAI LO ARPS HONG KONG

Y.K. YEO FRPS SINGAPORE

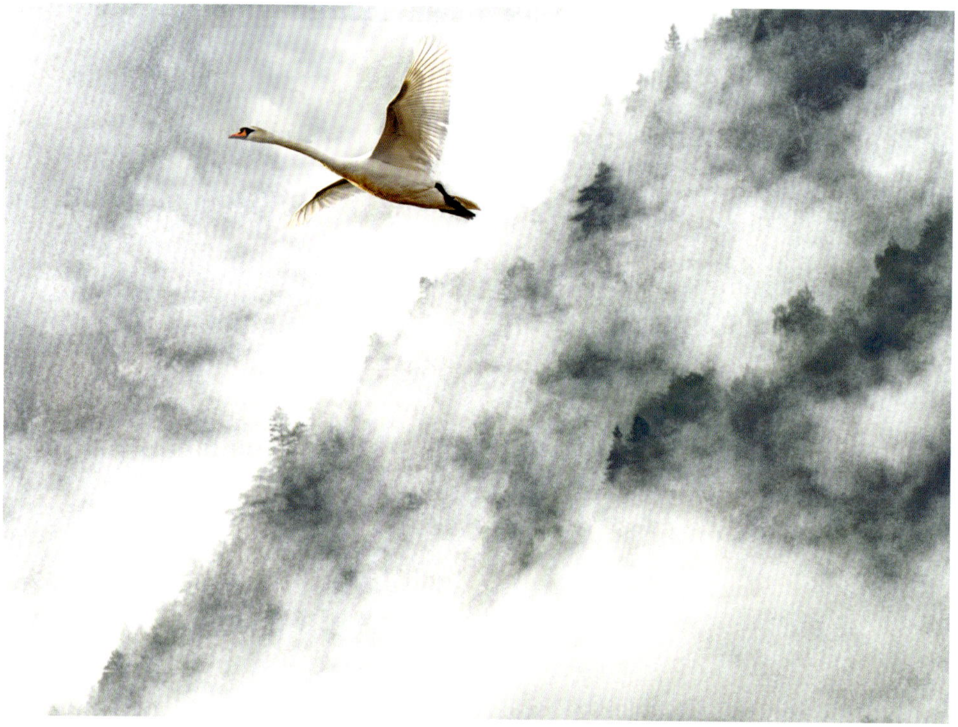

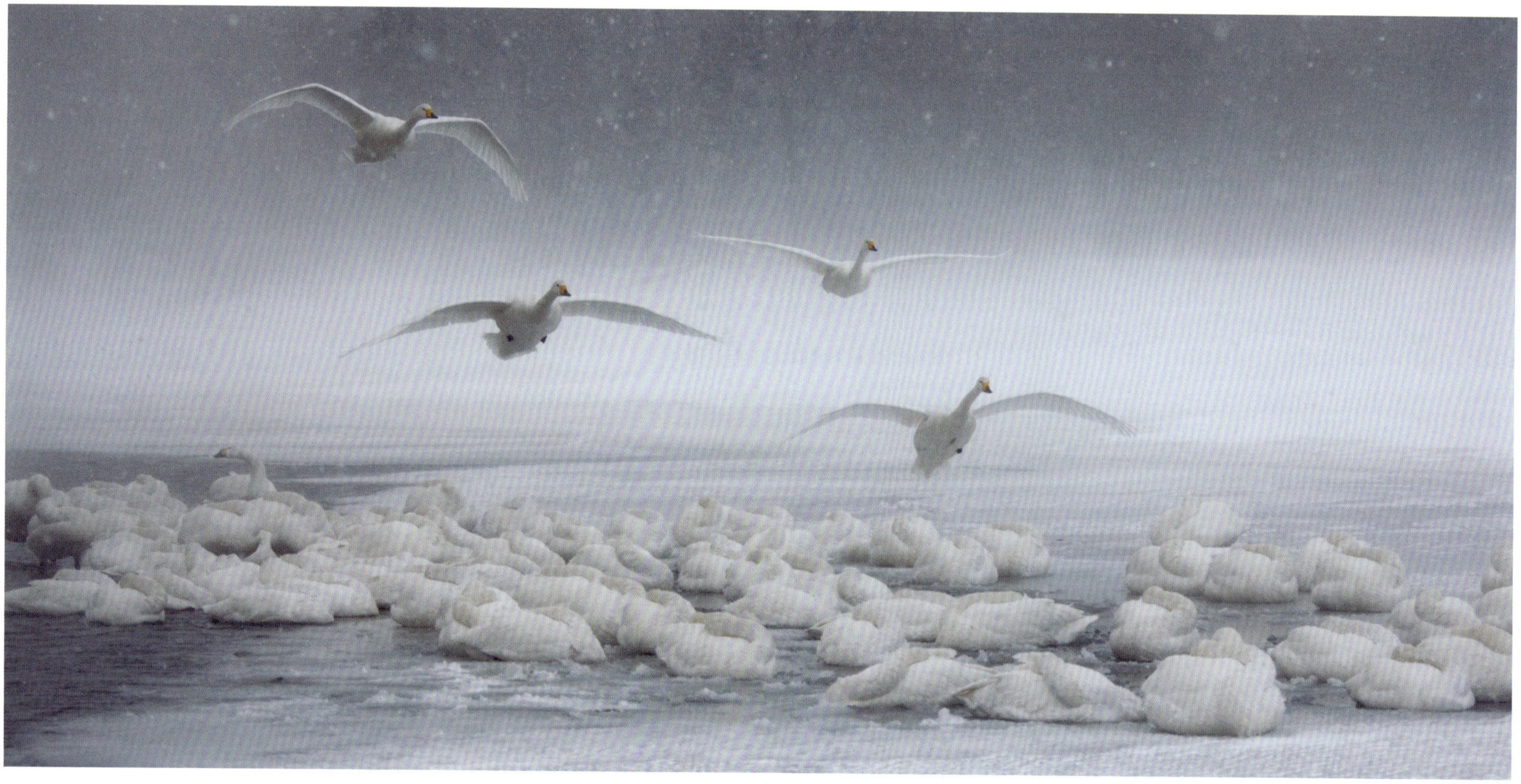

MIKE COWDREY ARPS UK
PATRICIA KEARTON LRPS UK

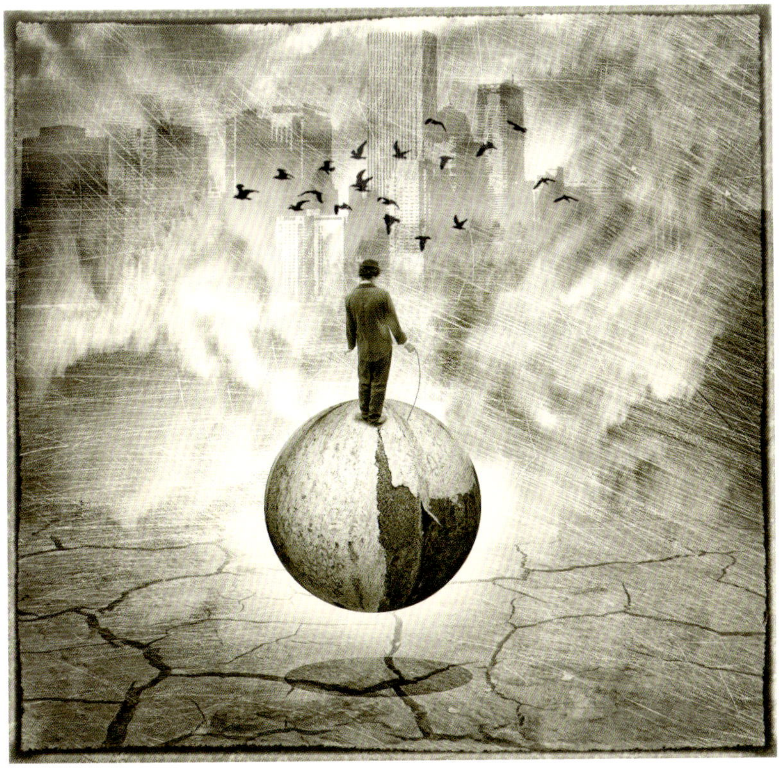

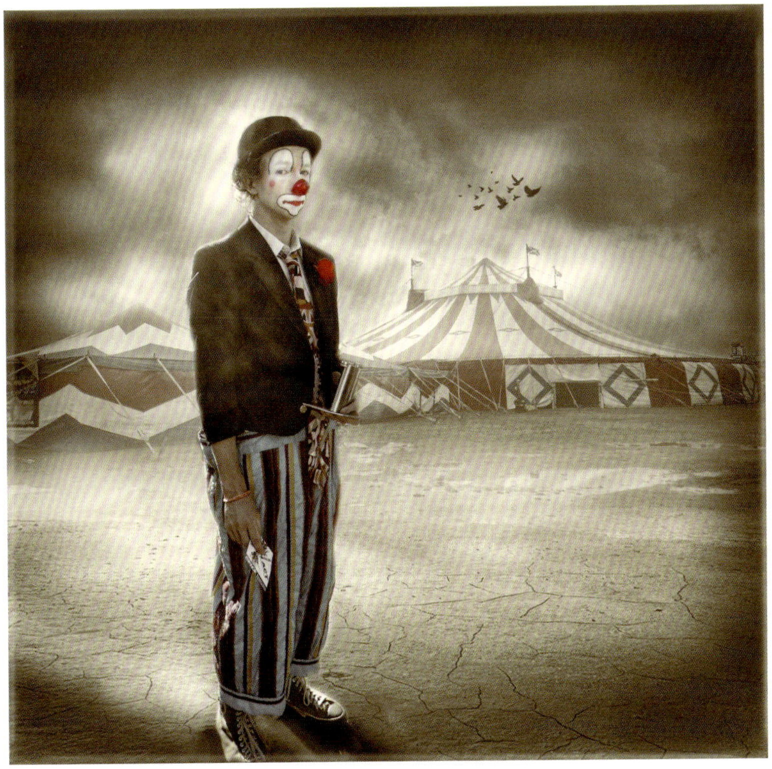

RIKKI O'NEILL FRPS UK

RIKKI O'NEILL FRPS UK

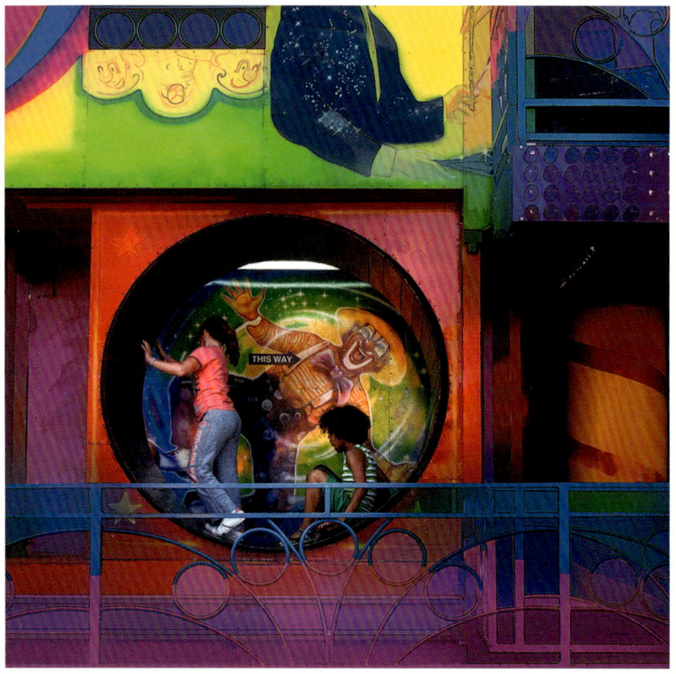
THIS WAY

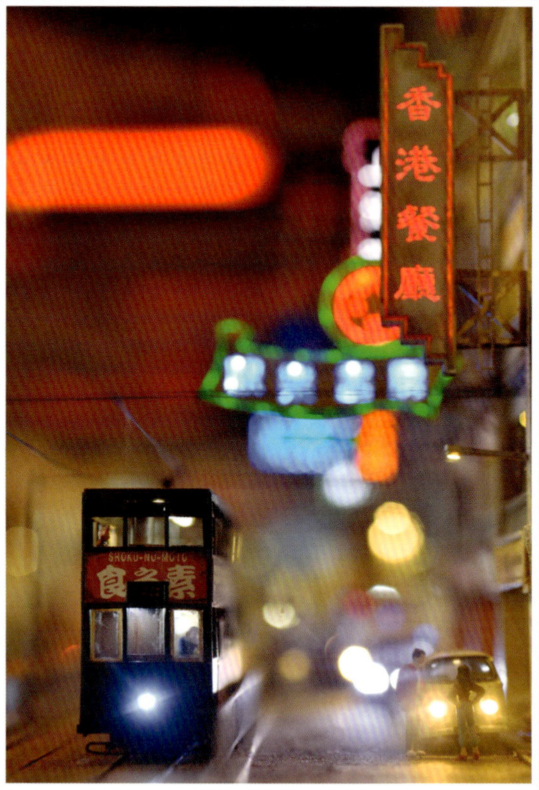
香港餐廳
SHOKU-NO-MOTO
食之素

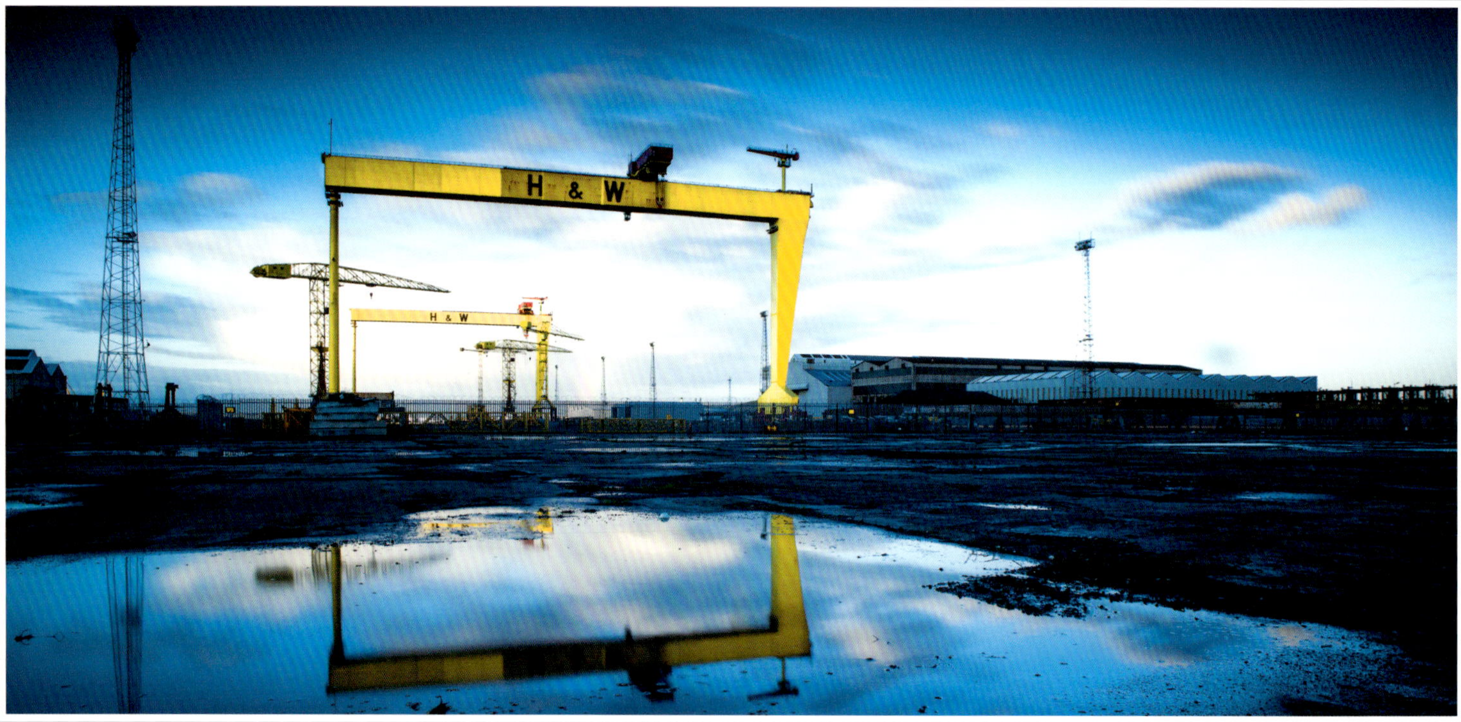
H & W
H & W

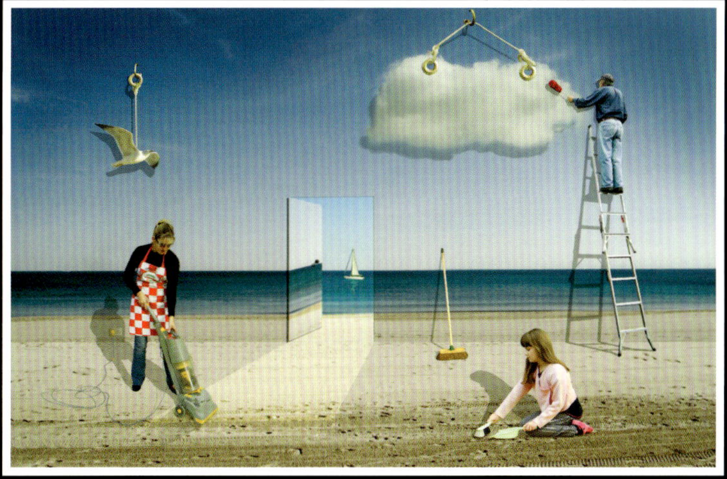

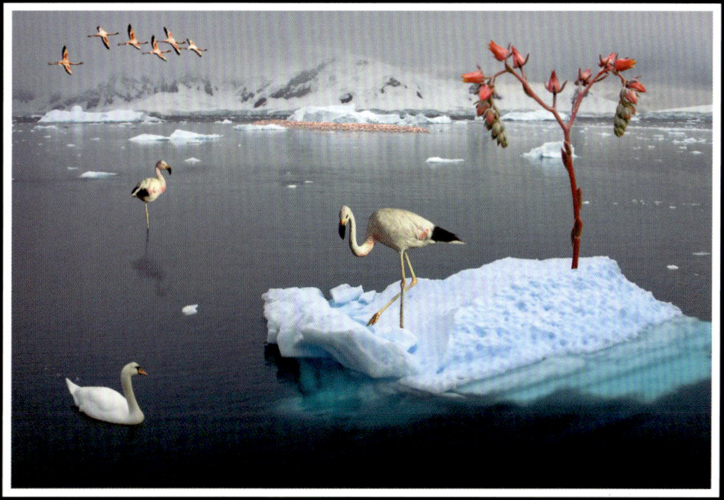

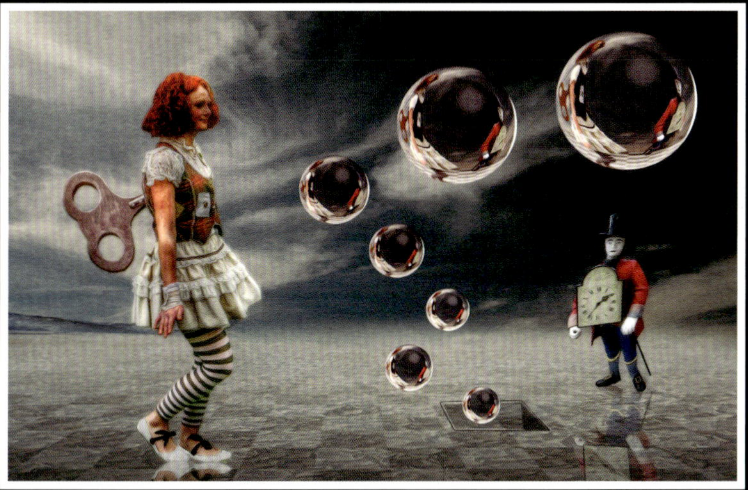

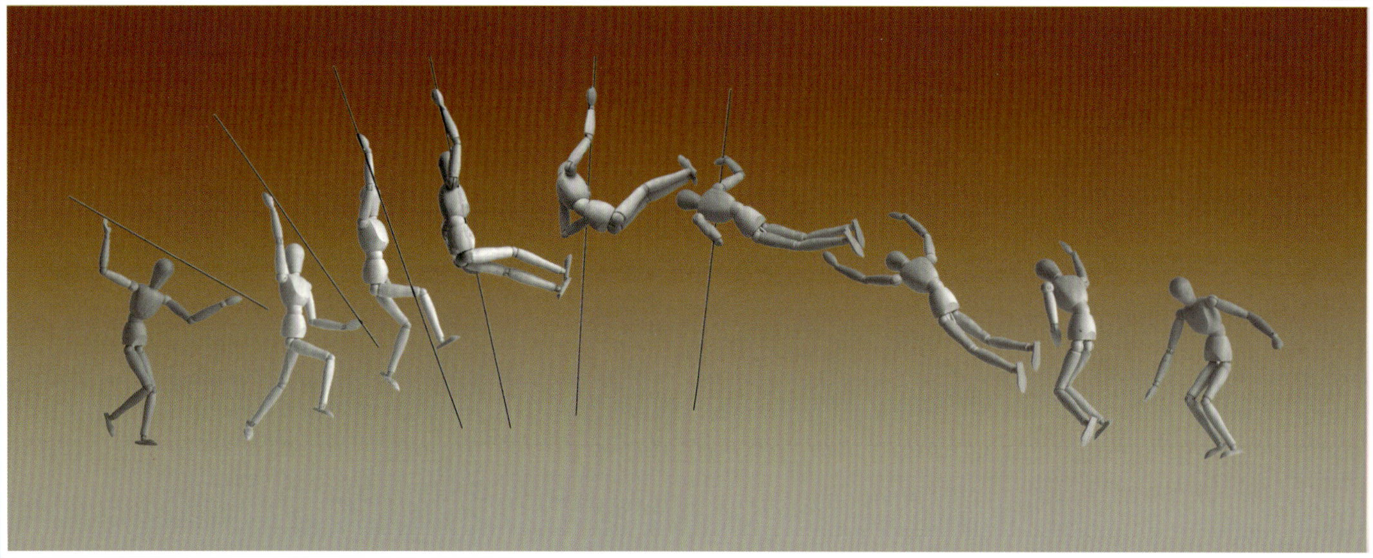

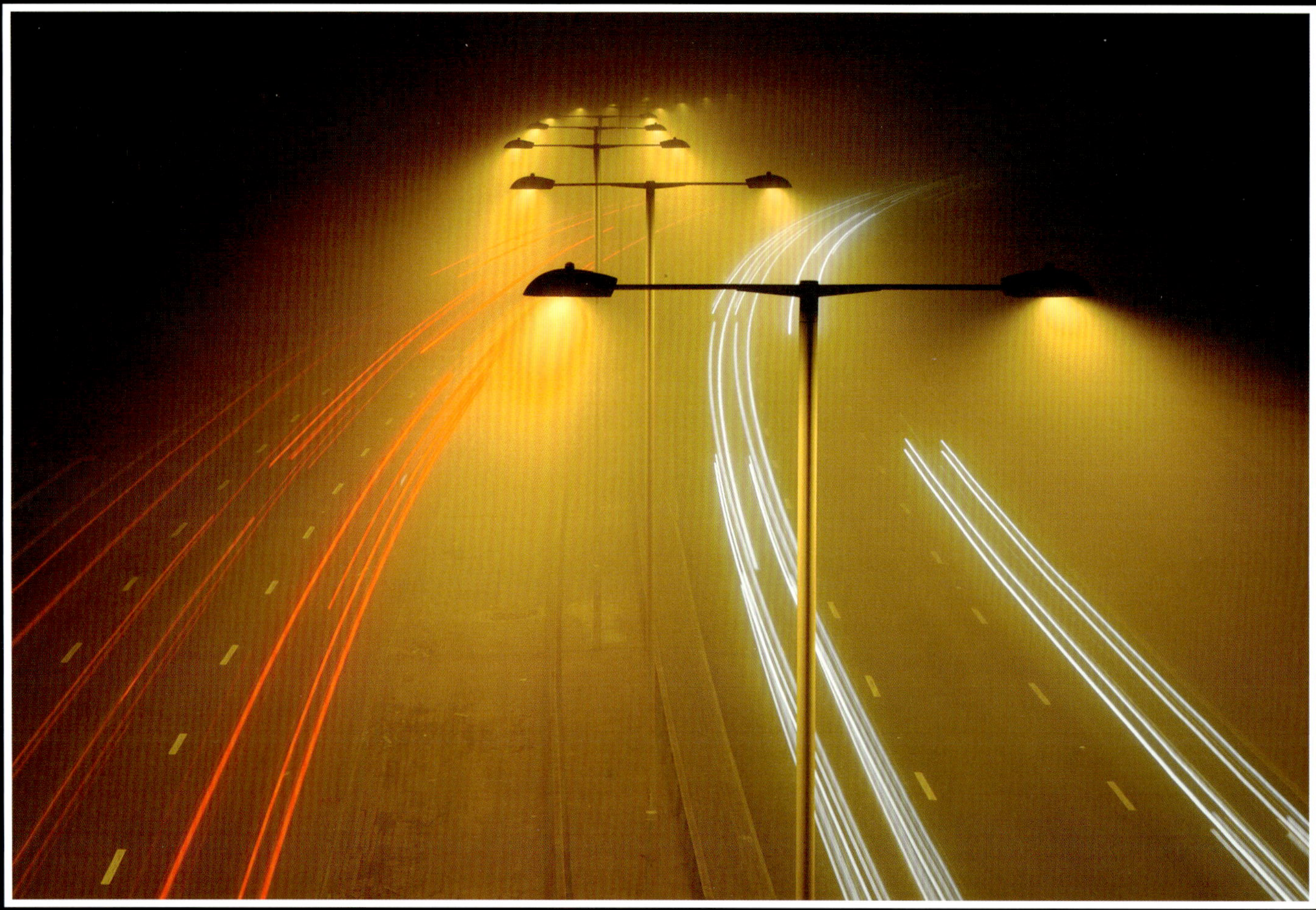

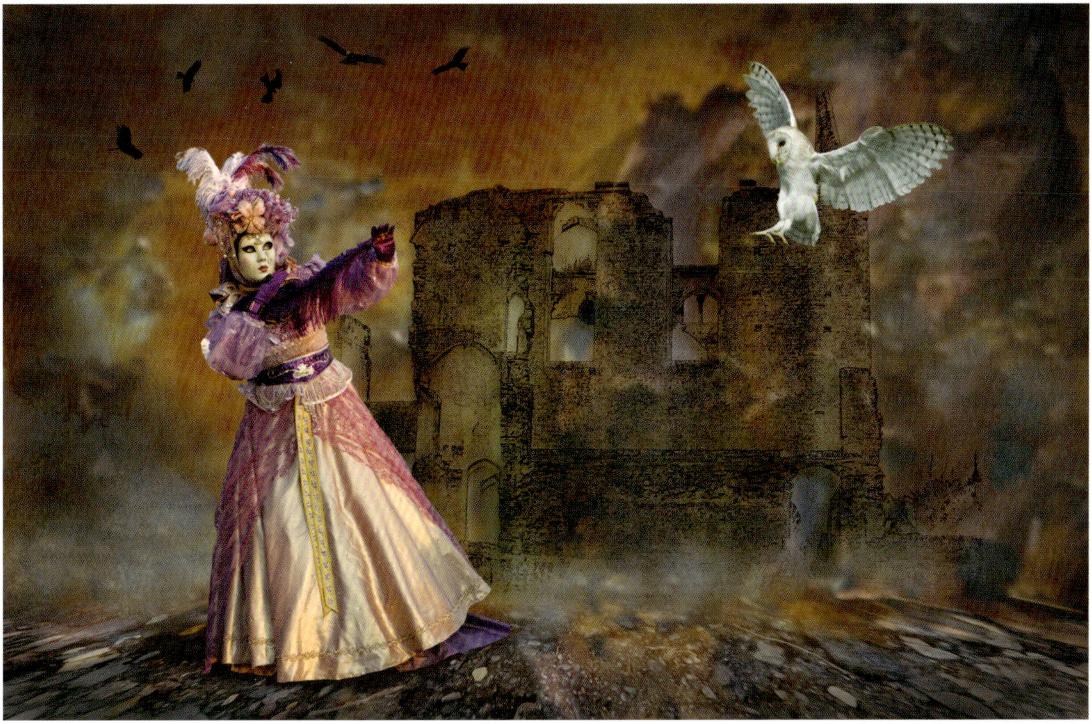

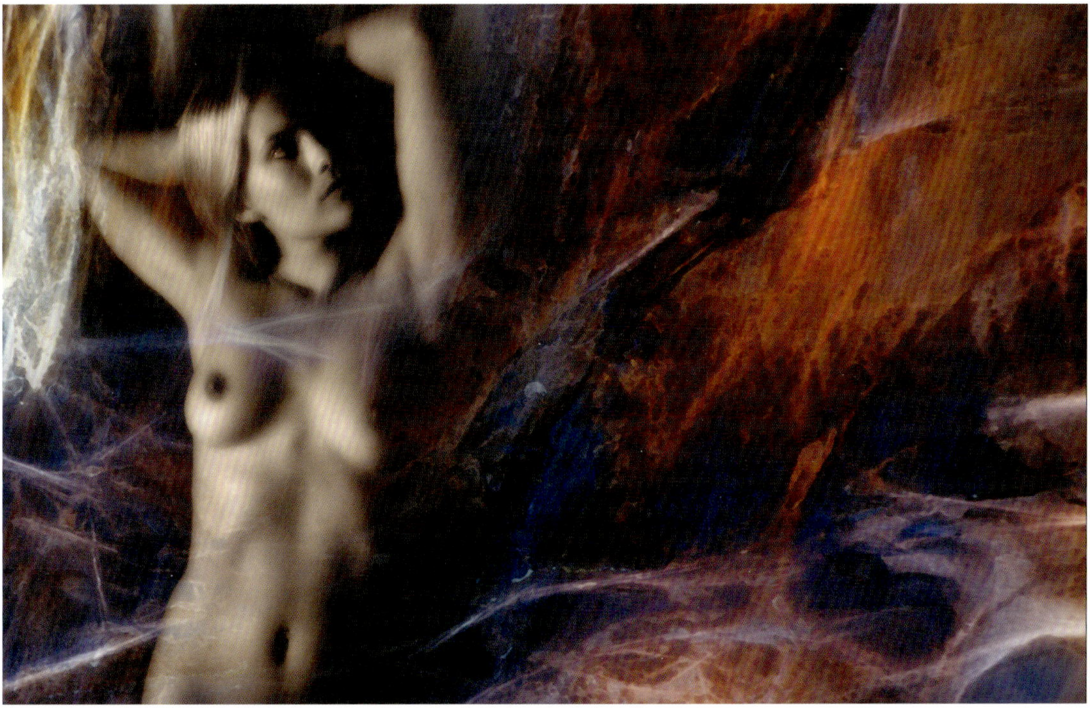

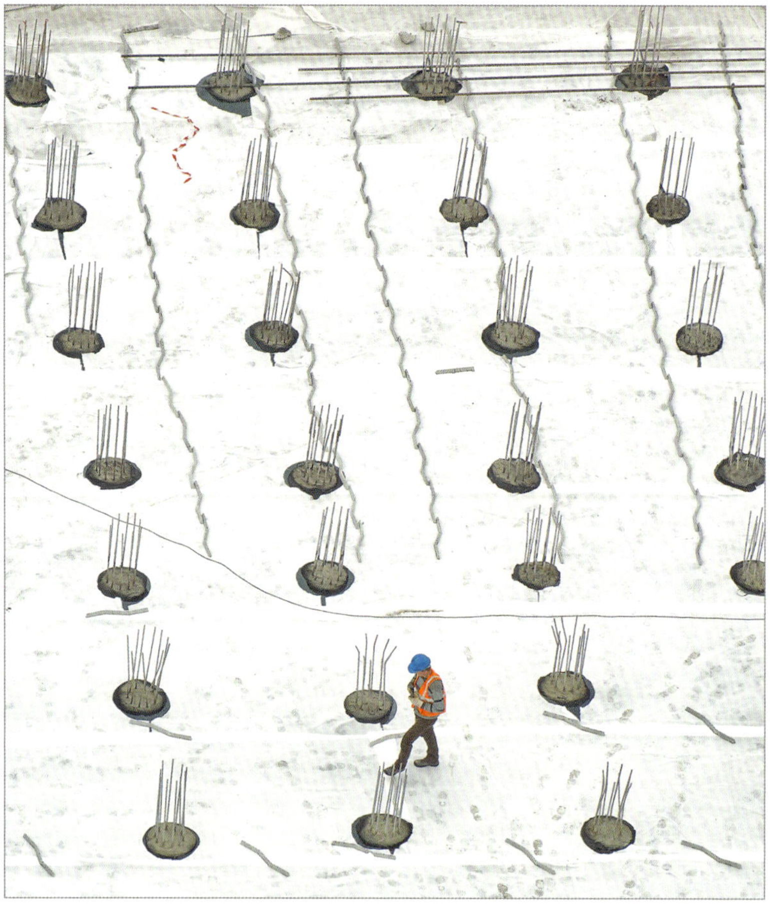

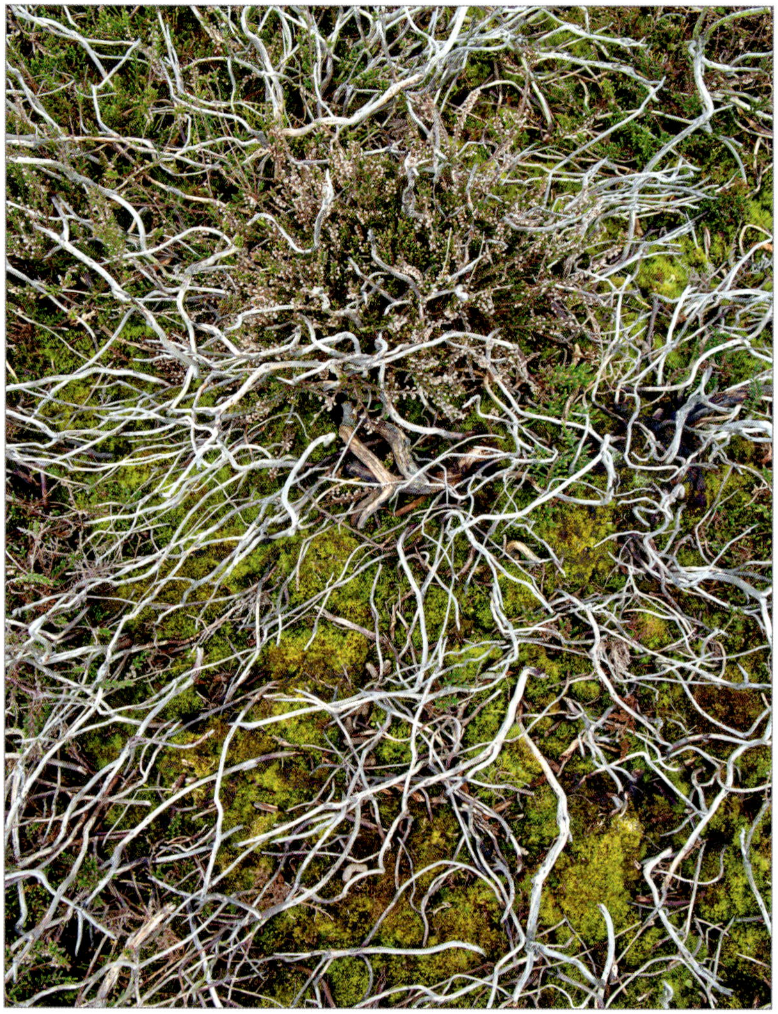

COLIN DOUGLAS ARPS UK

ANDREW SMITH ARPS UK

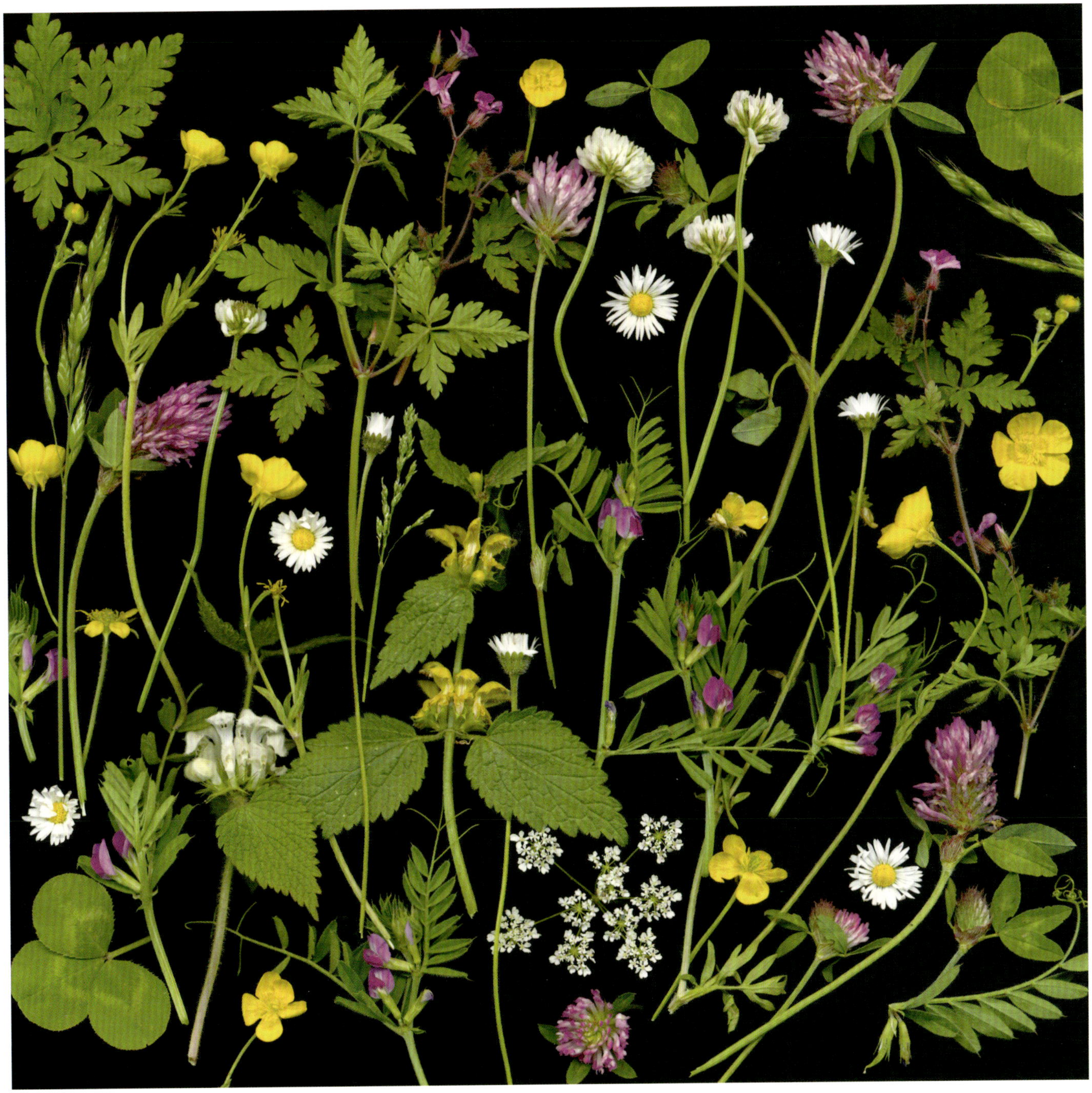

CAROLINE HYMAN FRPS UK

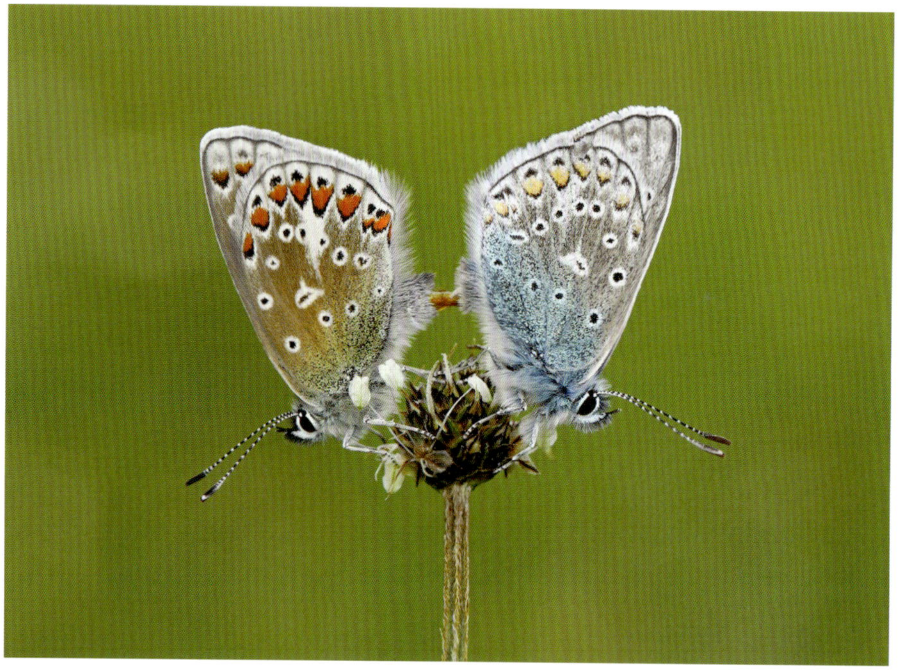

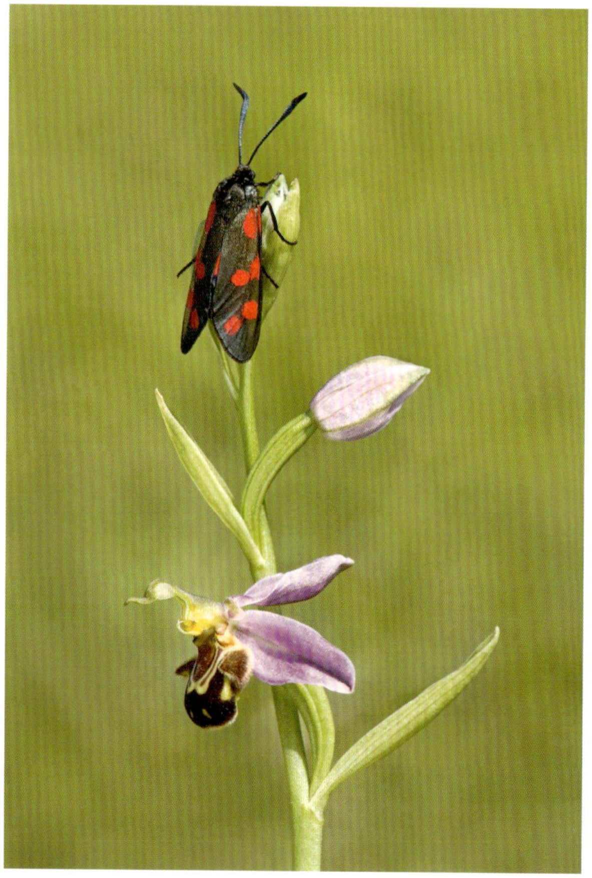

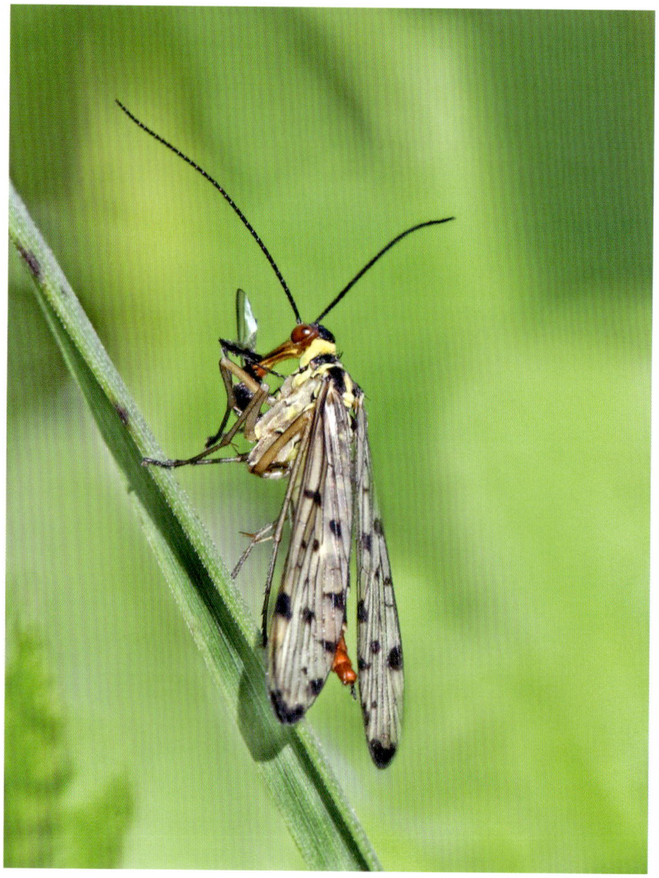

JILL PAKENHAM FRPS UK
MARK MONCKTON ARPS UK

KAREN BERRY FRPS UK

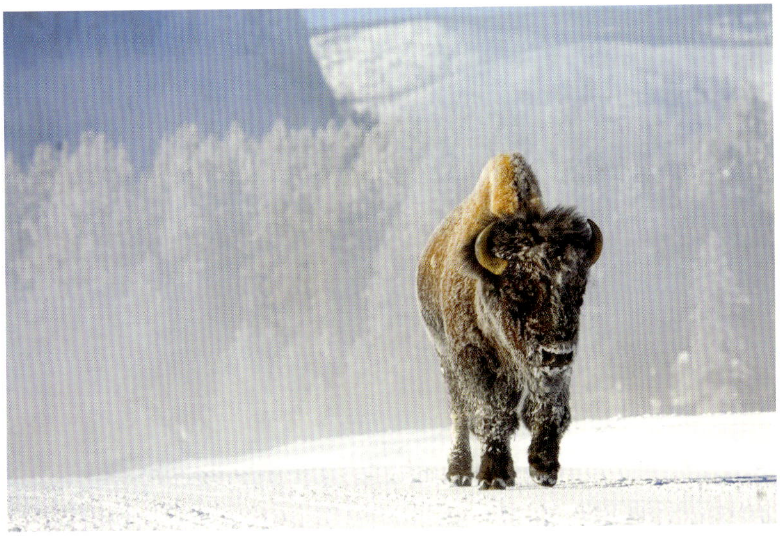

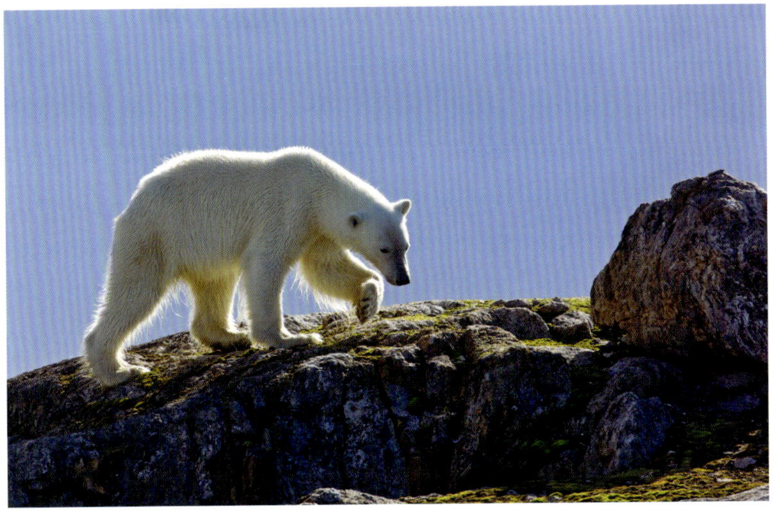

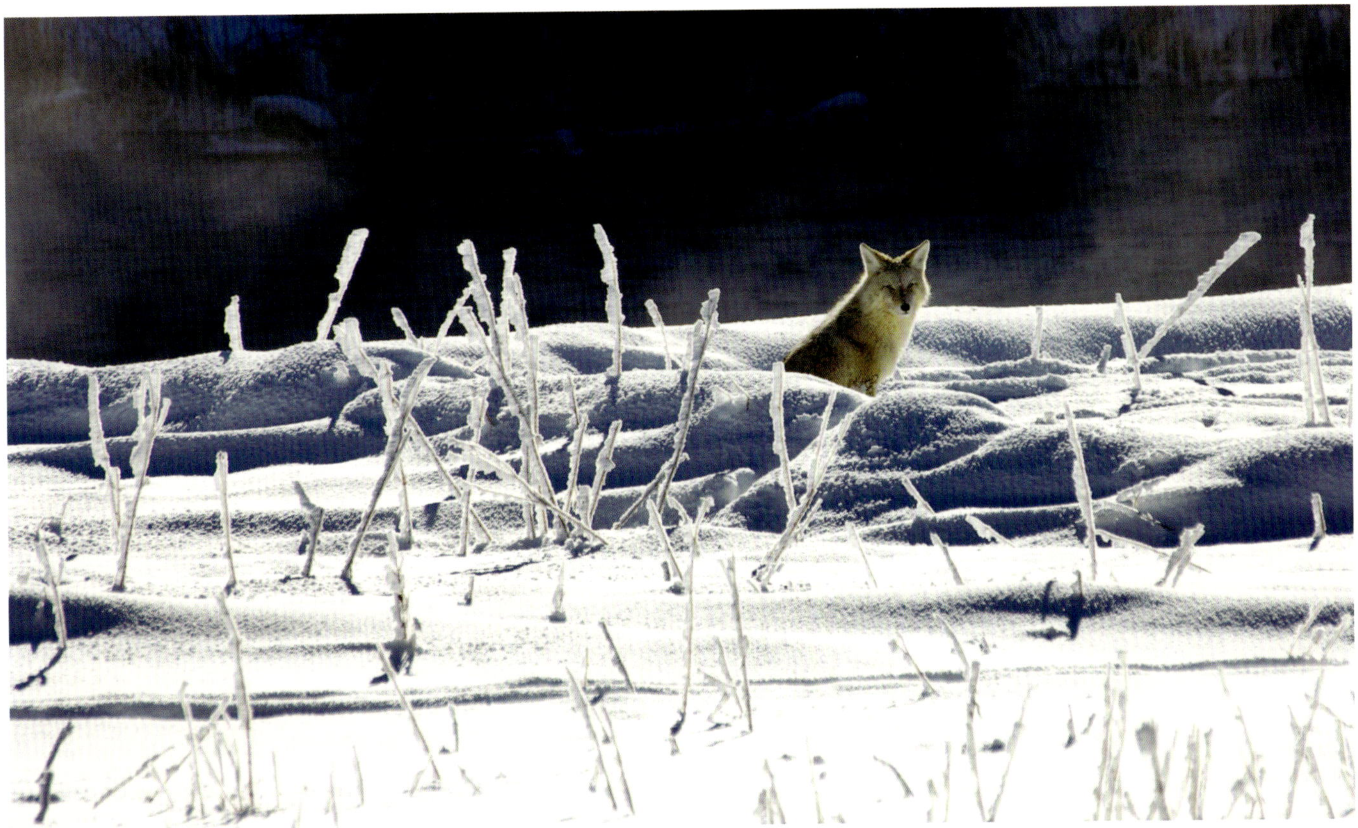

LEON KREEL ARPS UK

DICKIE DUCKETT FRPS UK

JOHN LEWIS LRPS UK

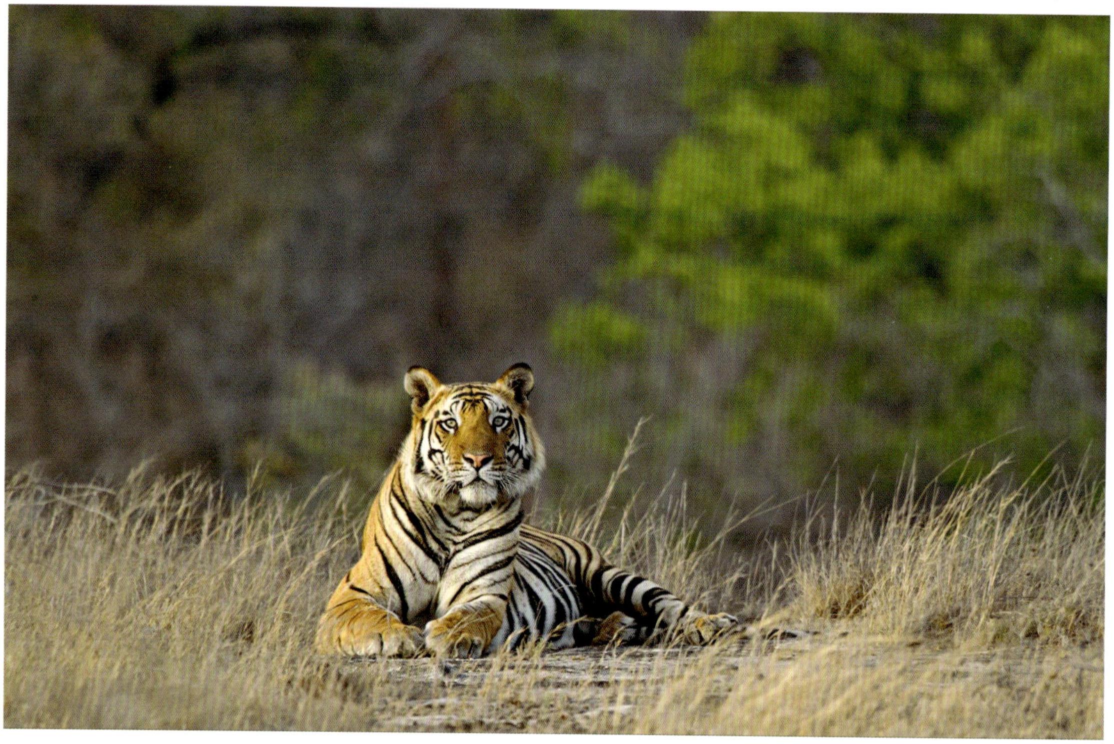

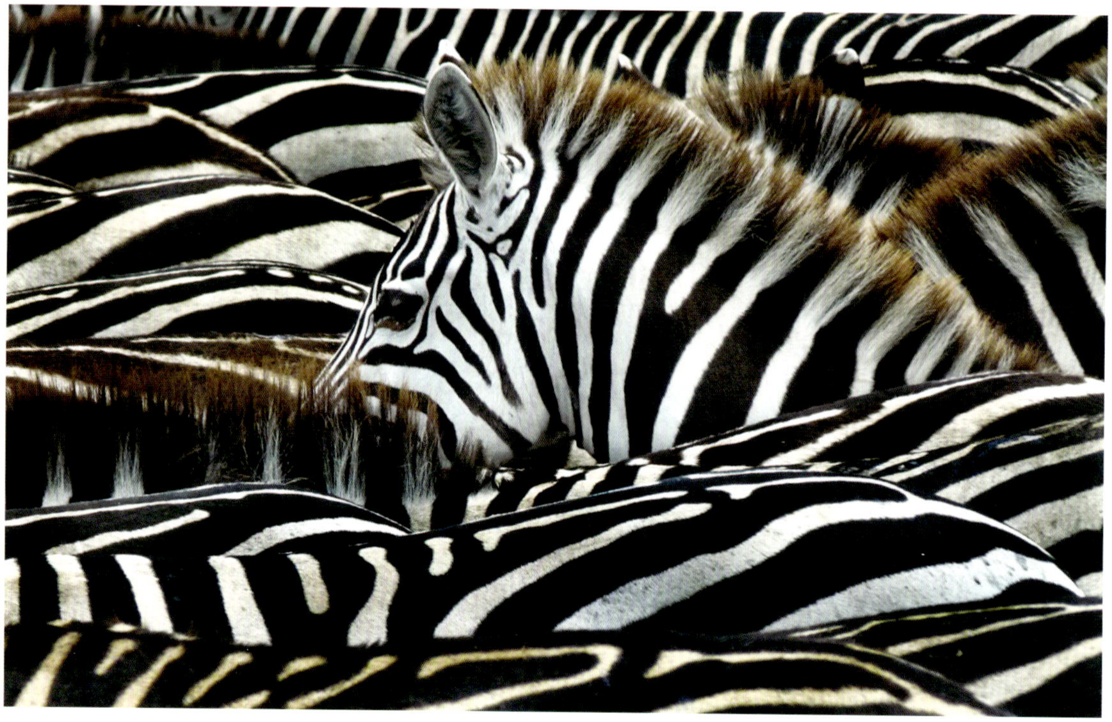

MARTIN CHAPMAN UK

ROGER HOYLE ASIS FRPS UK

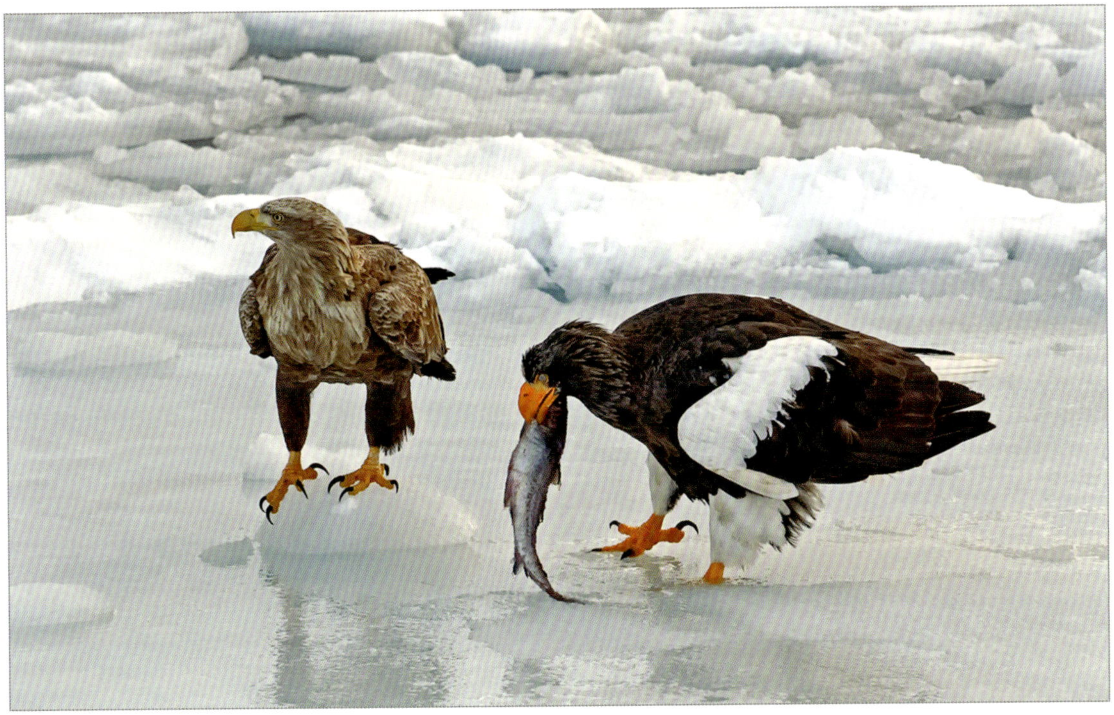

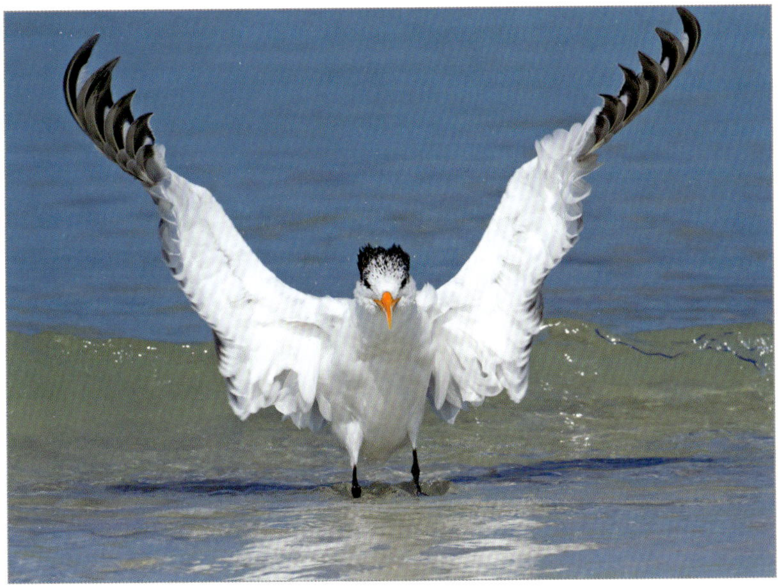

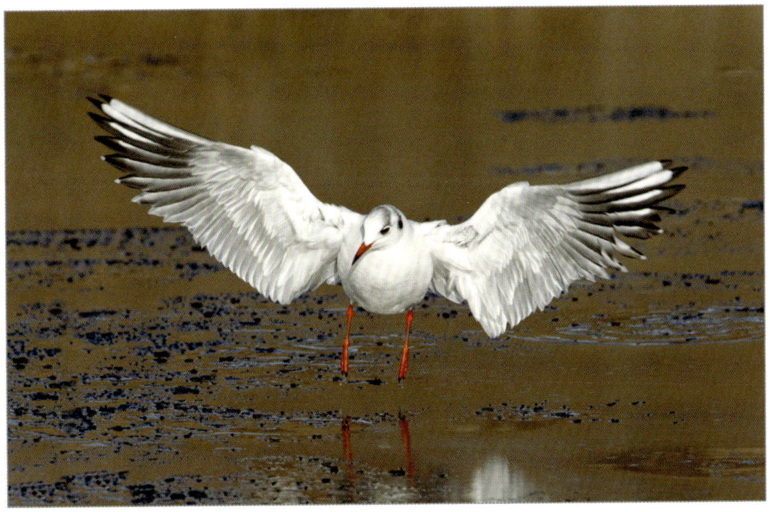

KEVIN ELSBY FRPS UK

JOHN CHAMBERLIN FRPS UK

DAVID OSBORN FRPS UK

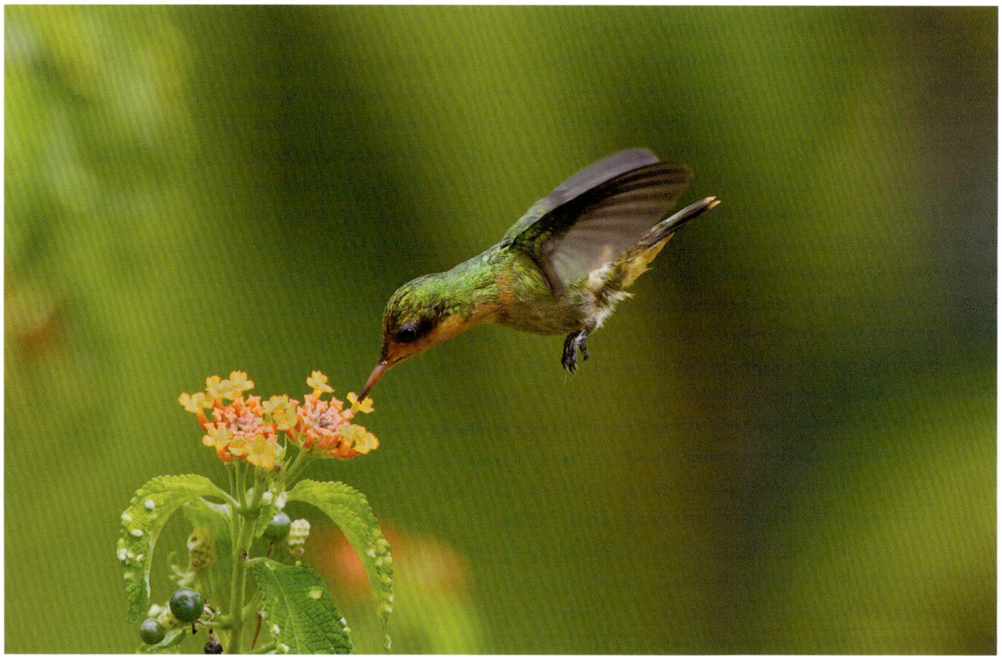

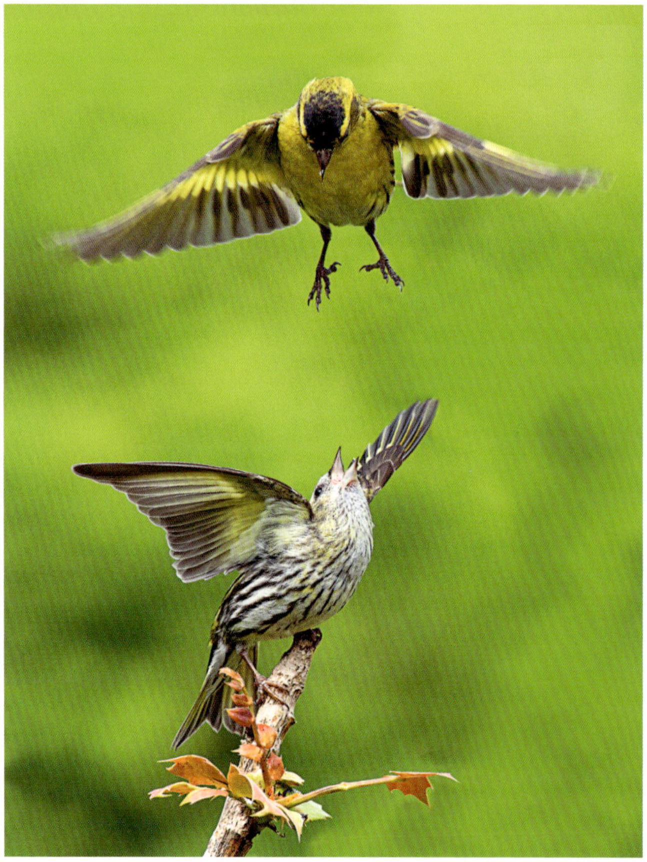

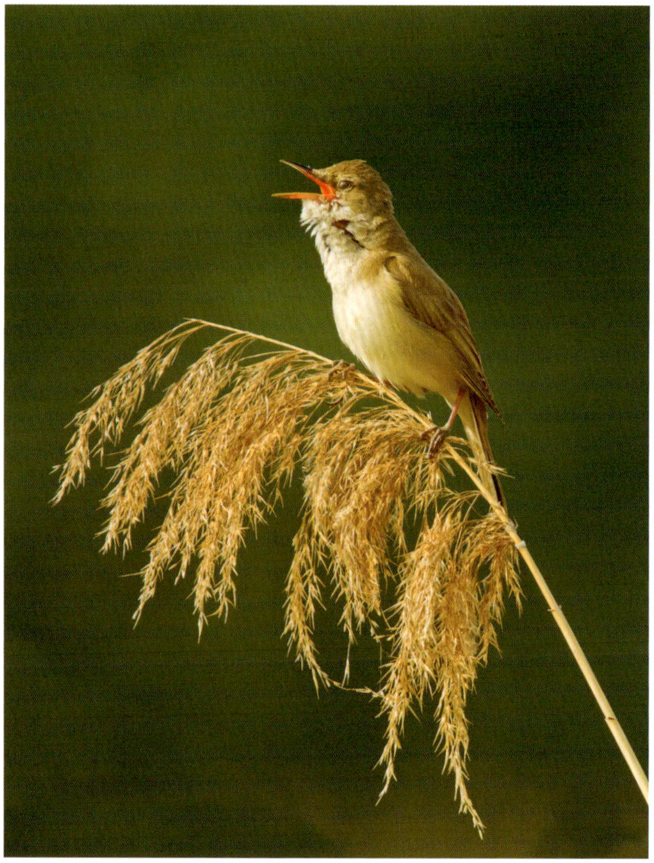

RAY COOPER ARPS UK

ANDREW CHU ARPS UK

GRAHAM HILTON LRPS UK

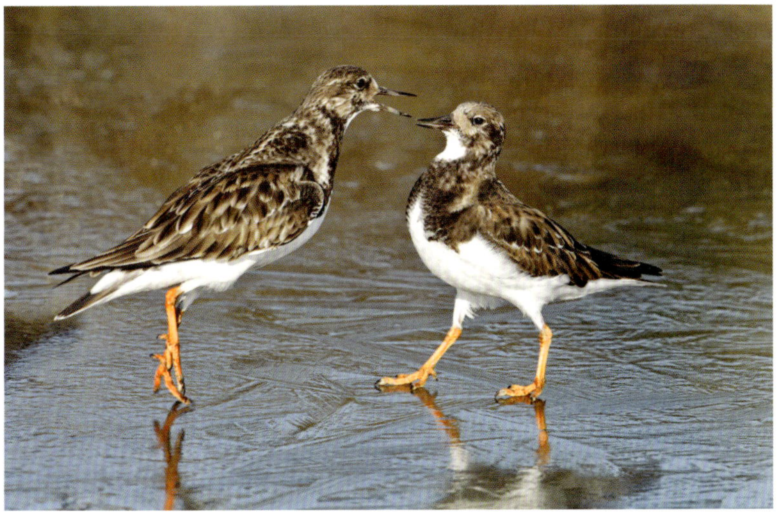

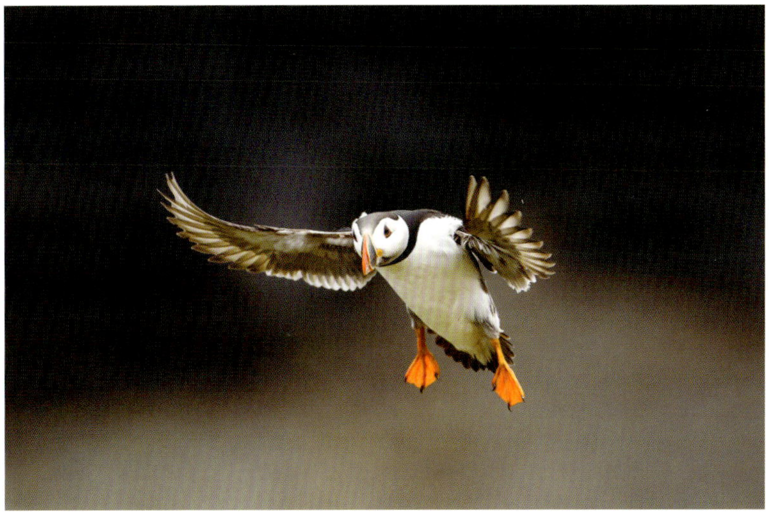

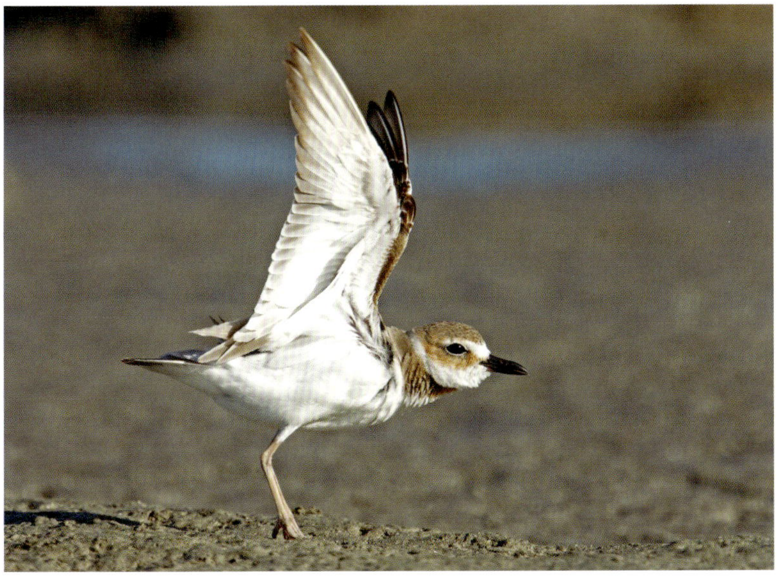

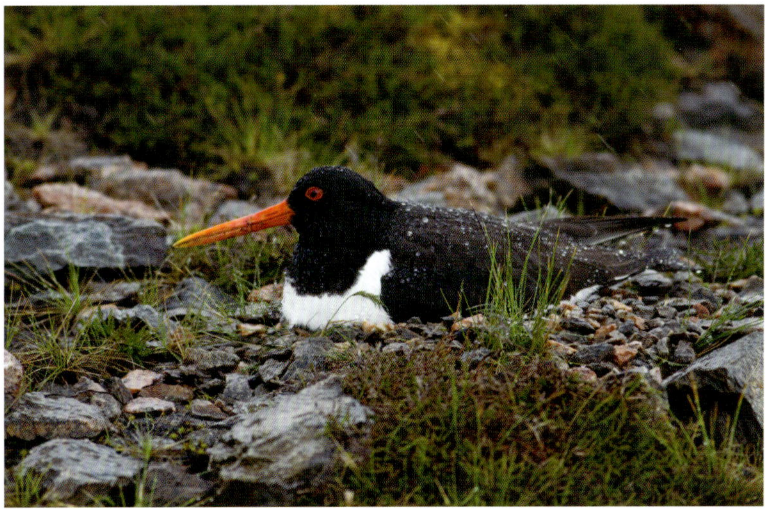

DAVID OSBORN FRPS UK
MARY CANTRILLE FRPS UK

THOMAS HANAHOE FRPS UK
JANE GREATOREX ARPS UK

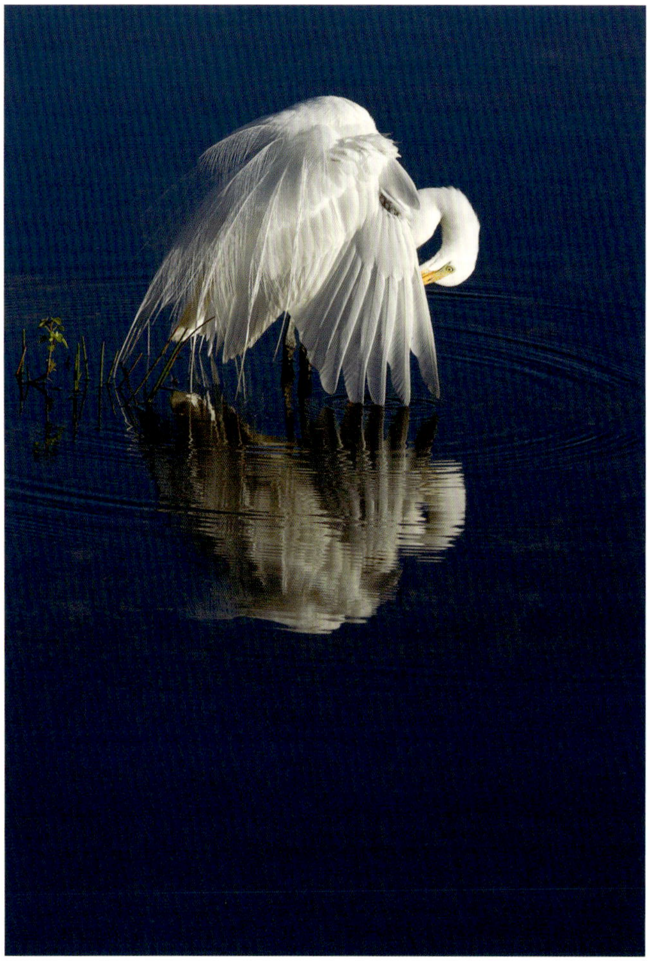

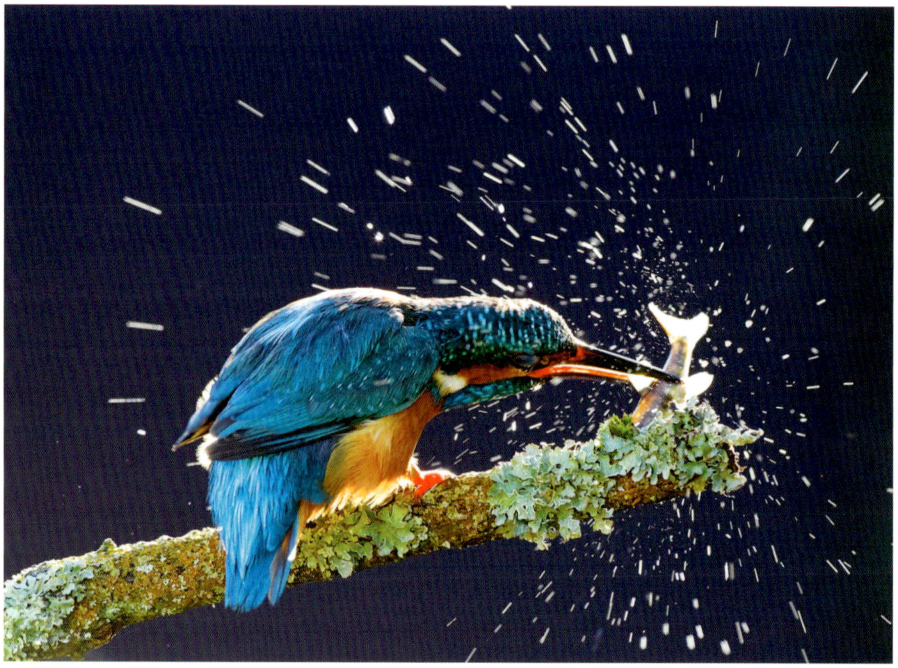

ROSEMARY WILMAN Hon.FRPS UK

KEVIN ELSBY FRPS UK

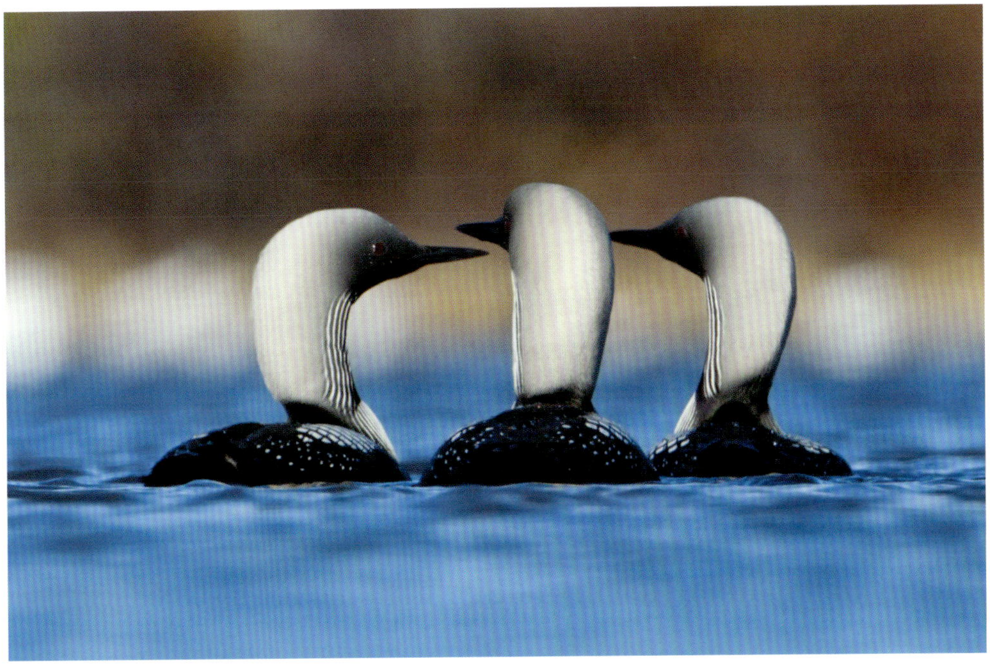

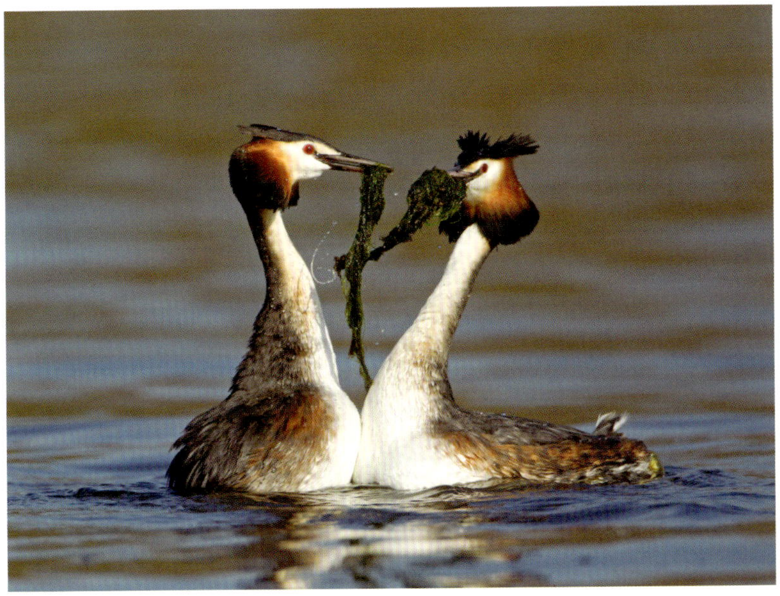

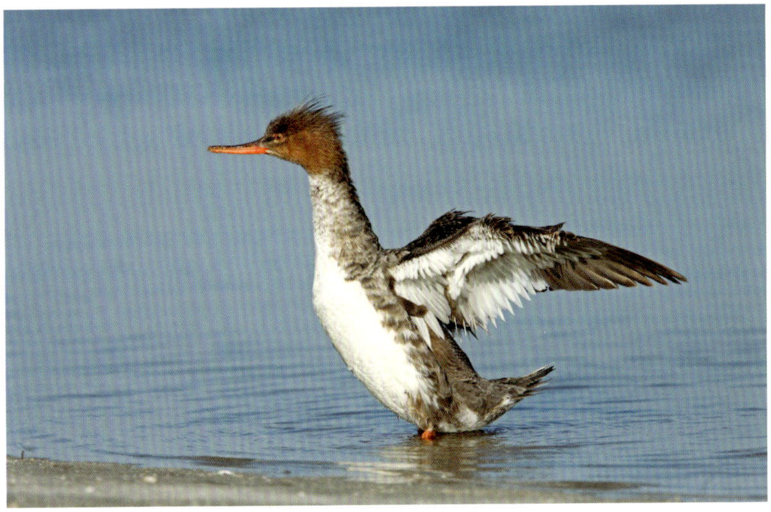

DICKIE DUCKETT FRPS UK

KWAN CHOO ARPS CANADA

MARY CANTRILLE FRPS UK

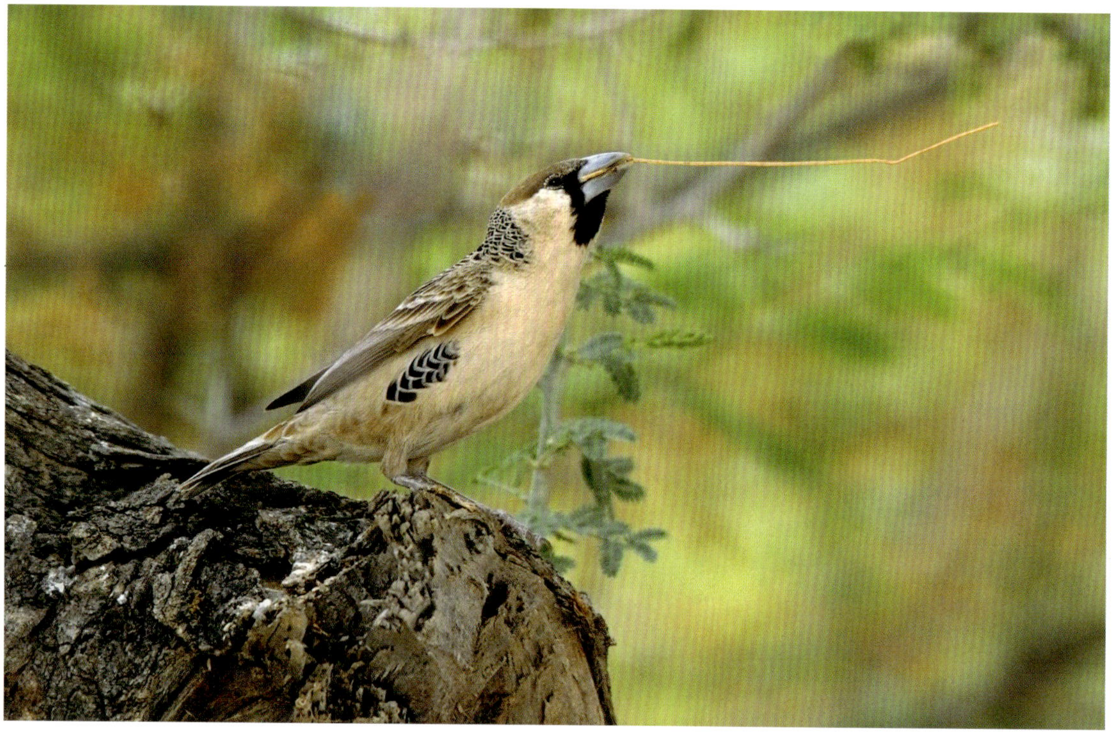

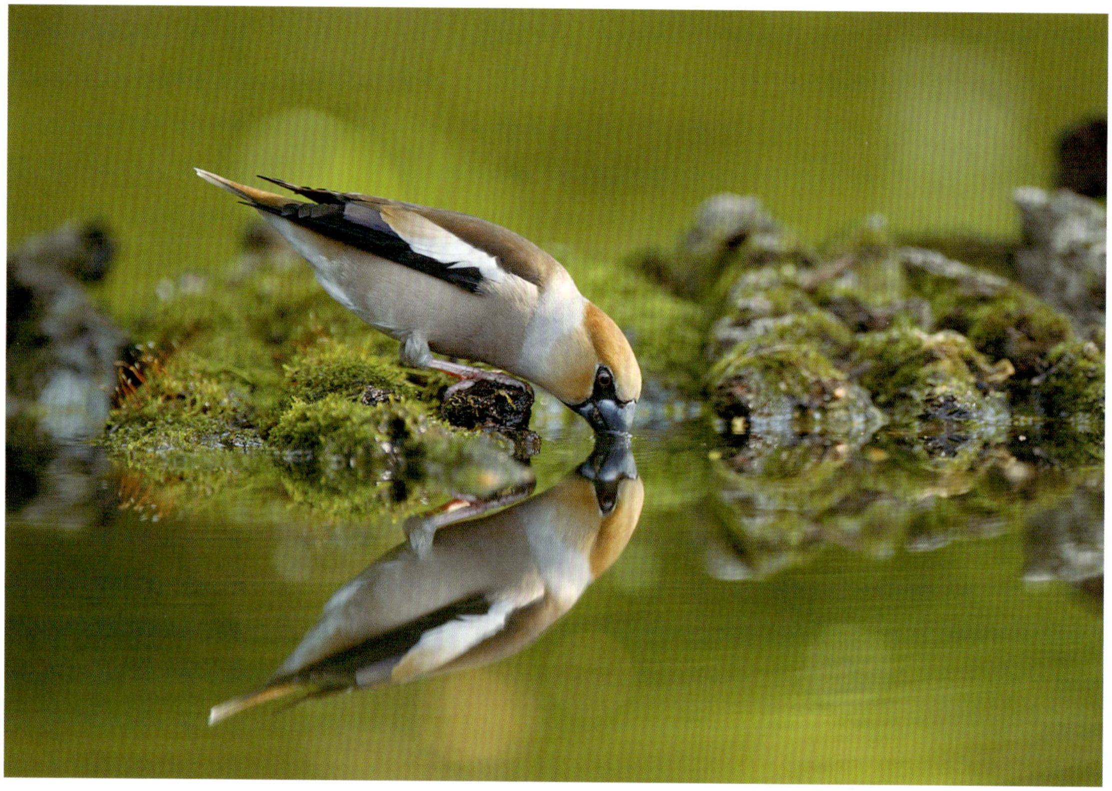

CHRISTOPHER COATES ARPS UK
MICK DURHAM ARPS UK

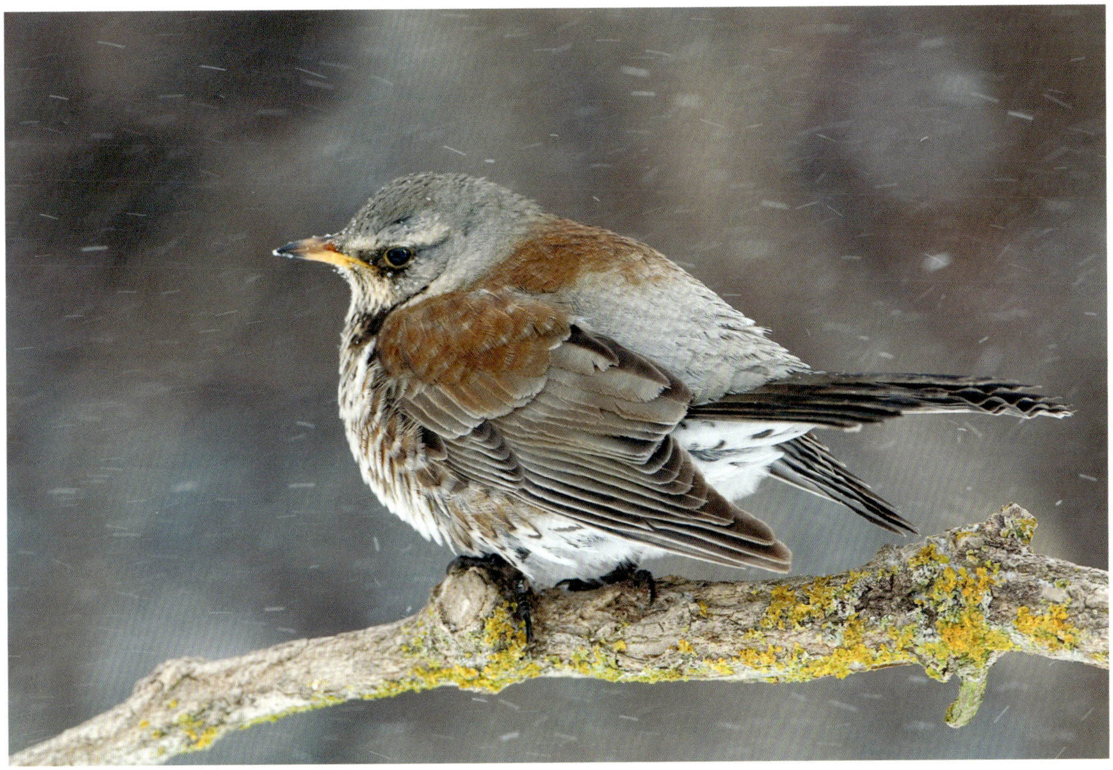

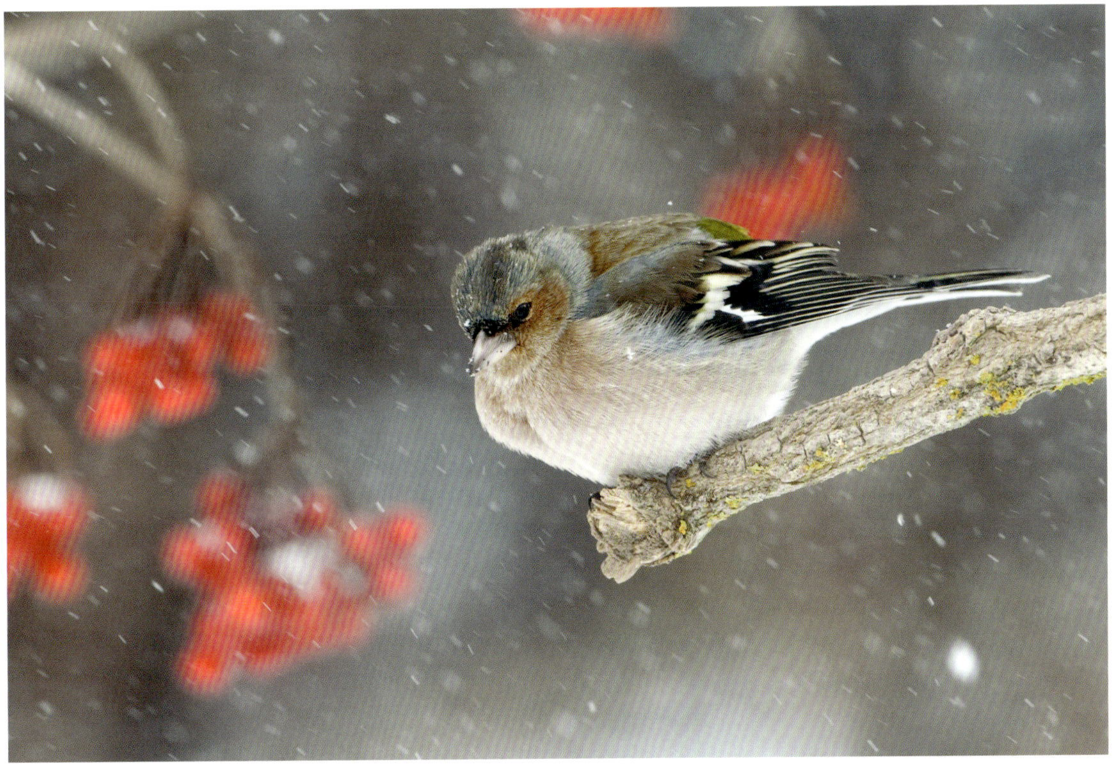

DAVID ROBINSON ARPS UK
DAVID ROBINSON ARPS UK

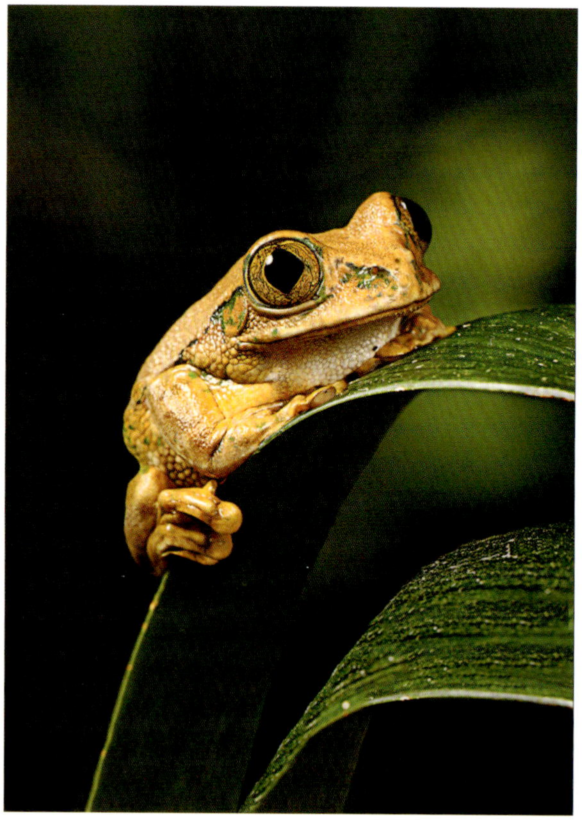

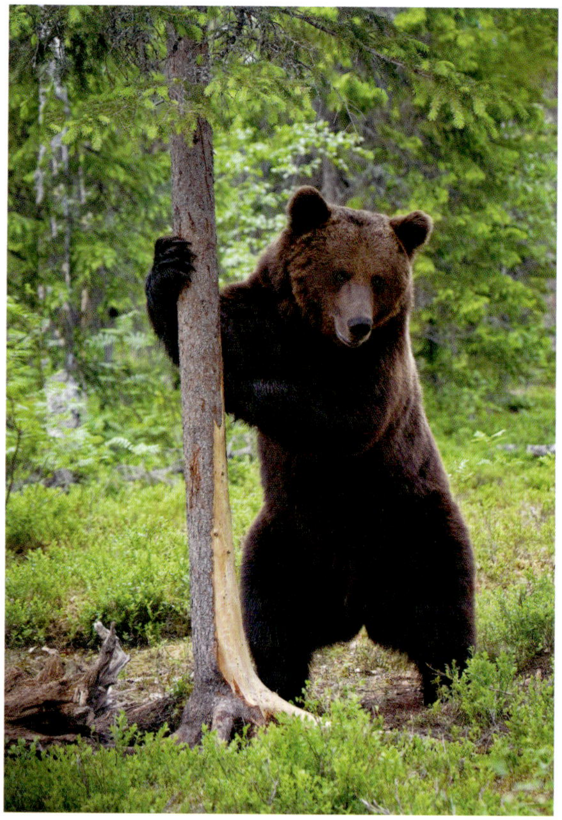

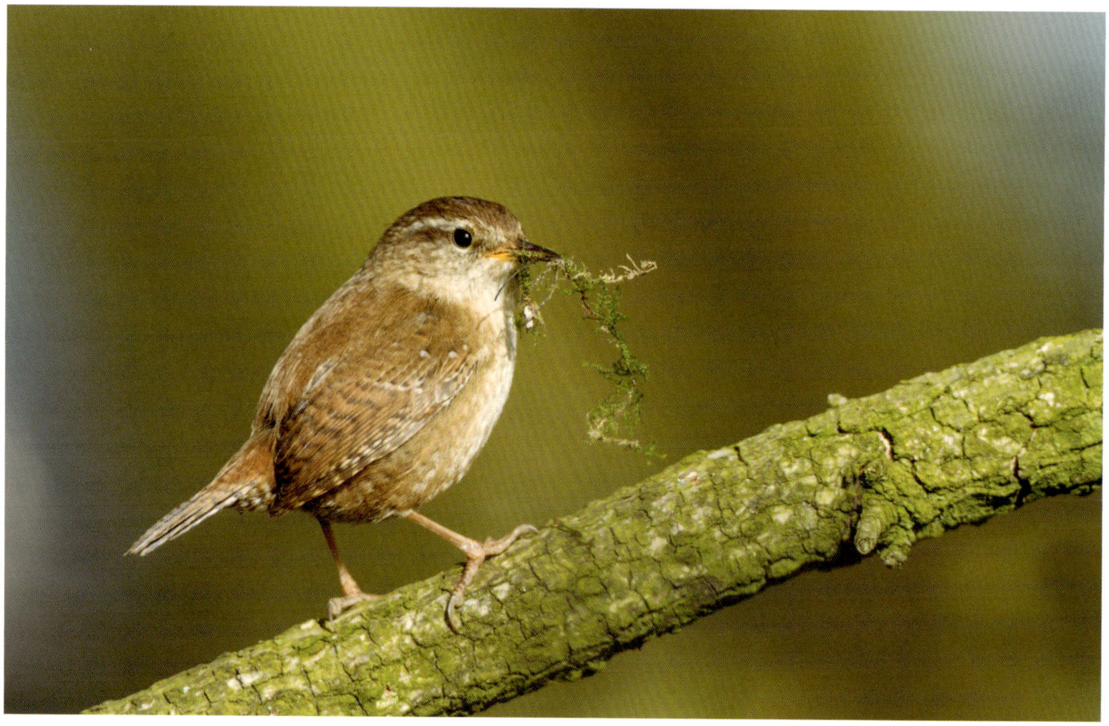

FIONA SENIOR FRPS UK

JONATHAN ASHTON ARPS UK

HELEN ASHBOURNE ARPS UK

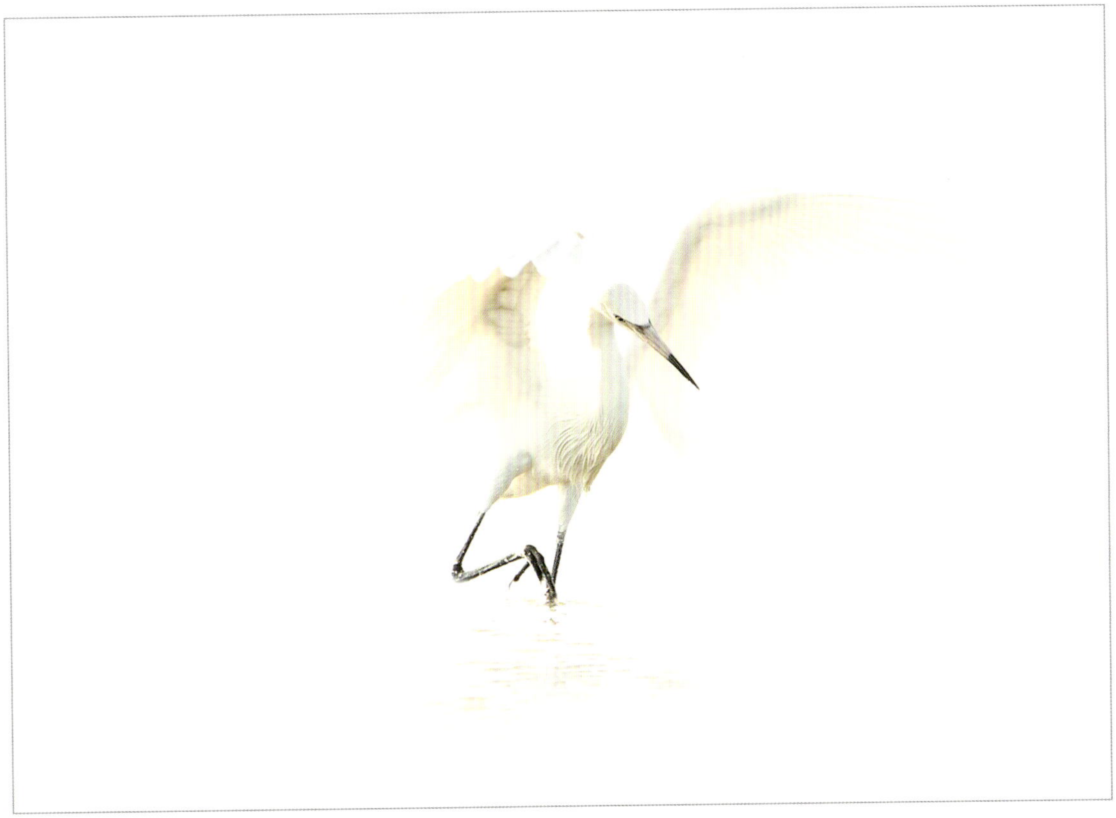

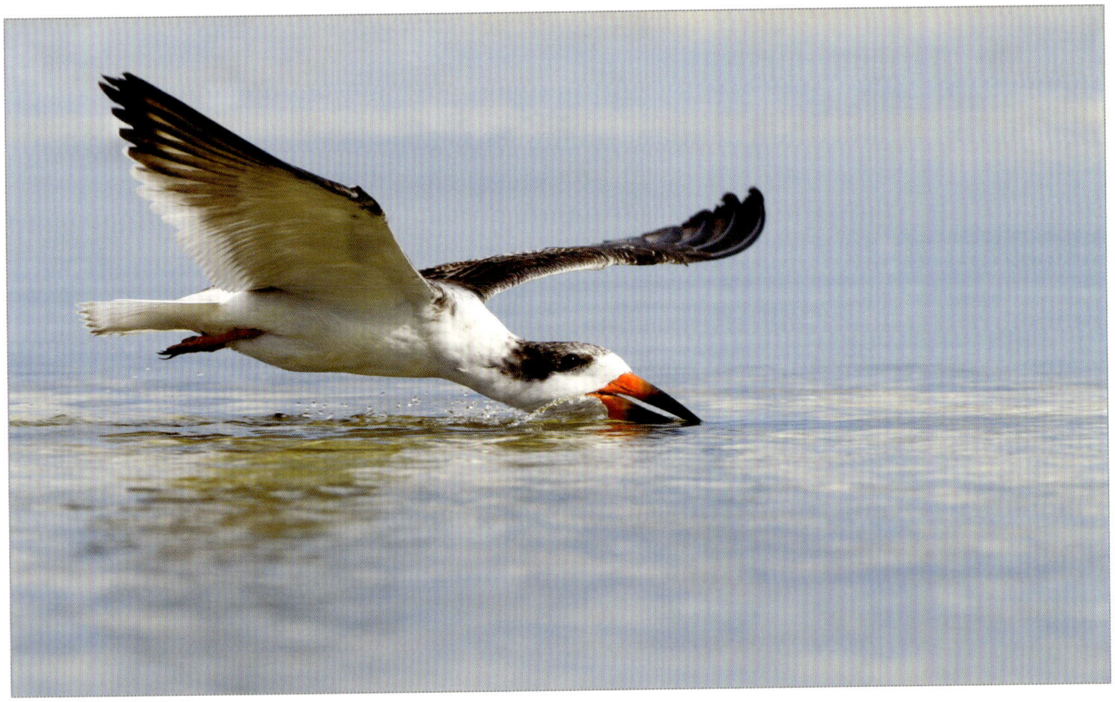

MALCOLM KINGSWELL ARPS UK

NICKI GWYNN-JONES FRPS UK

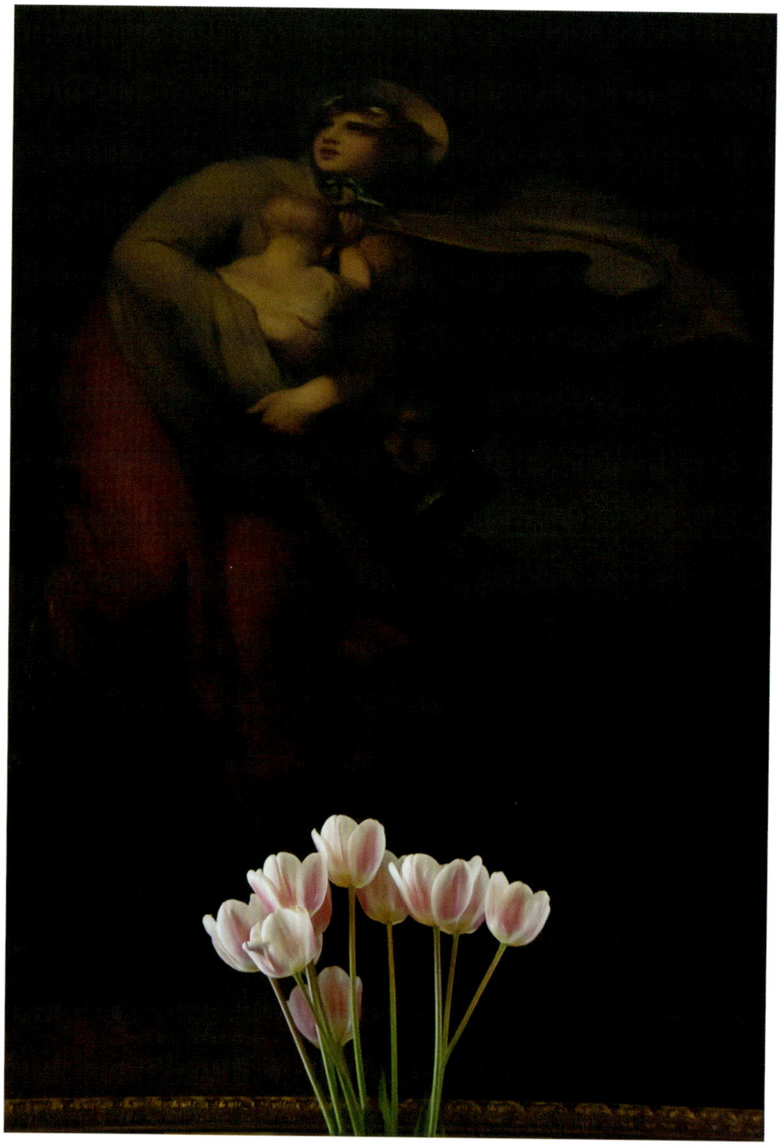

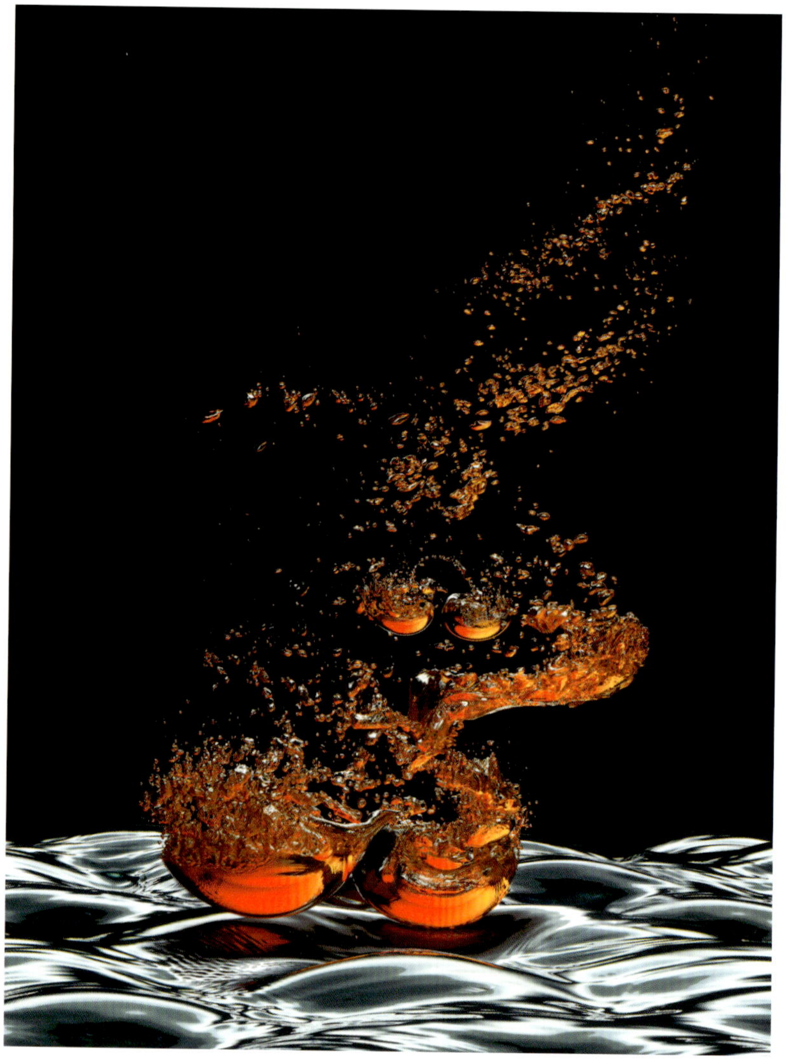

RAY SPENCE FRPS UK

RAY MASSEY FRPS UK

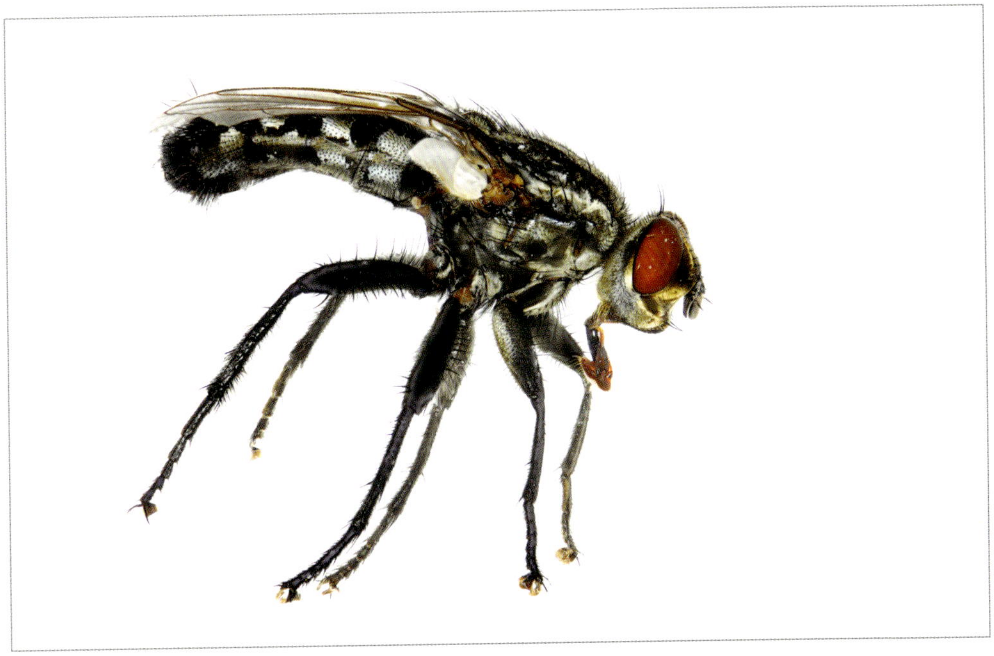

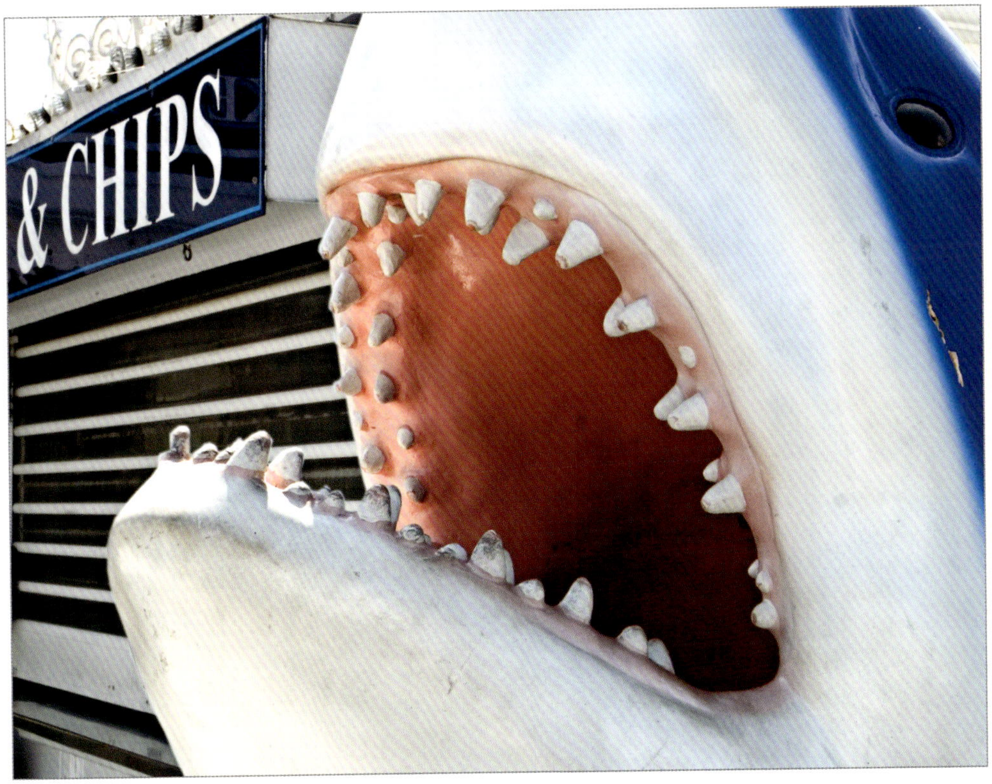

BARRY HOLMES FRPS UK

RICHARD WALTON FRPS UK

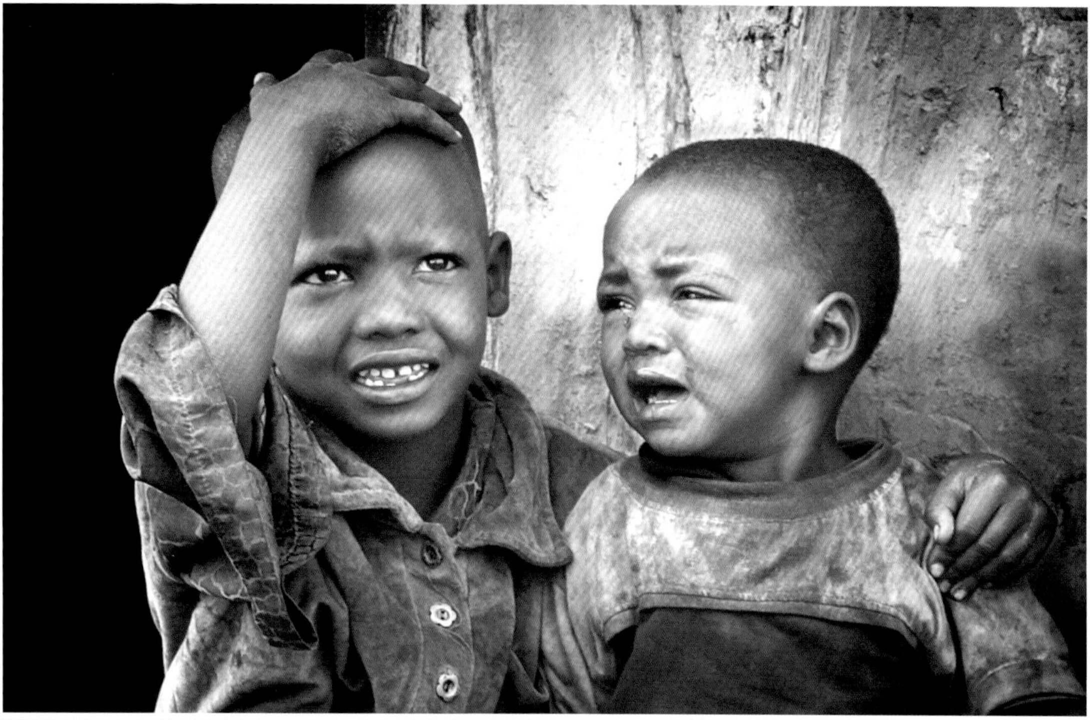

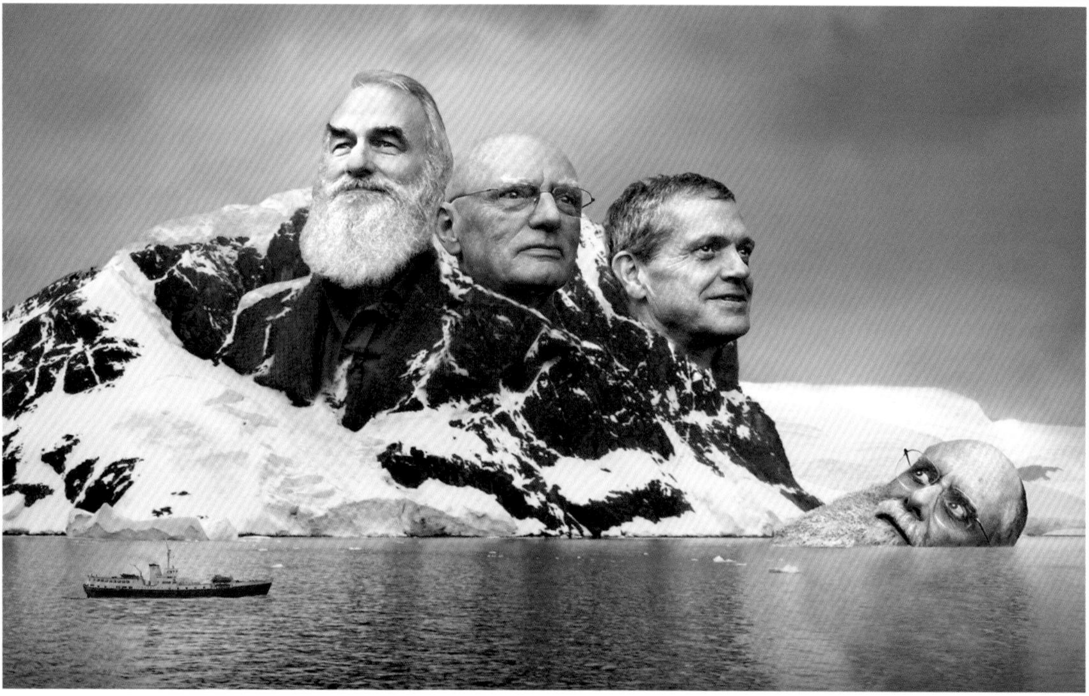

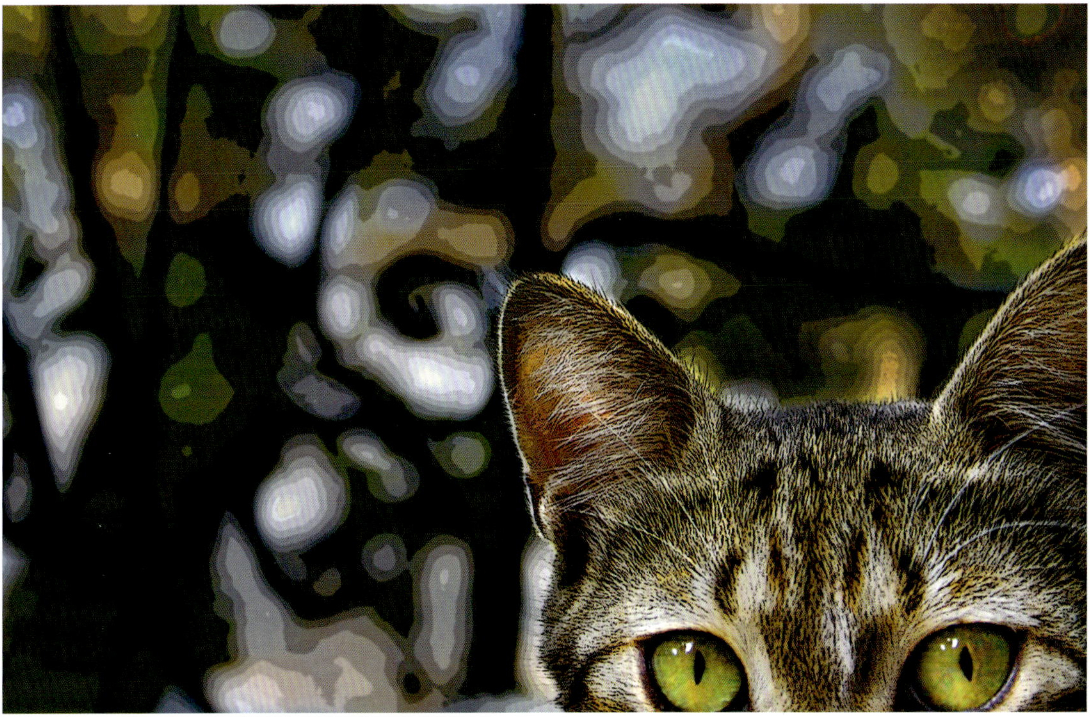

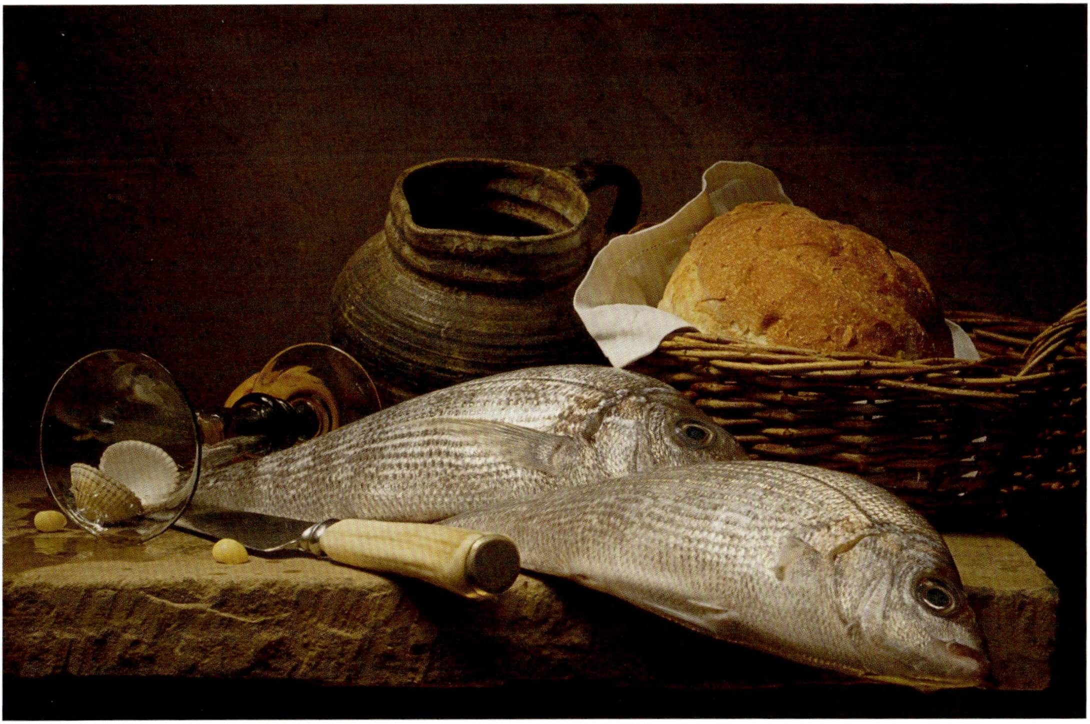

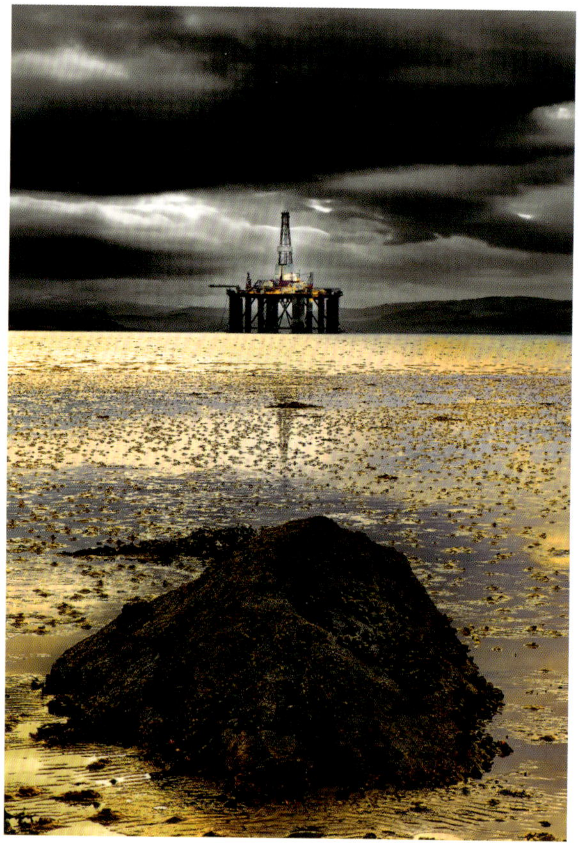

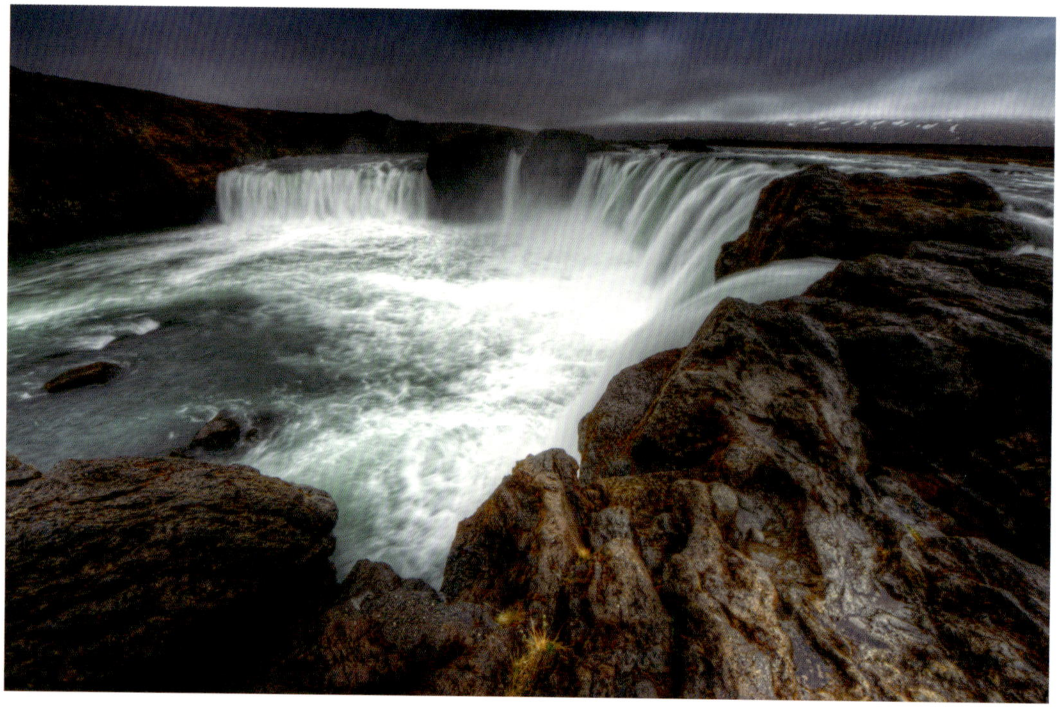

RICHARD TICKNER ARPS UK
NIGEL PLANT ARPS UK

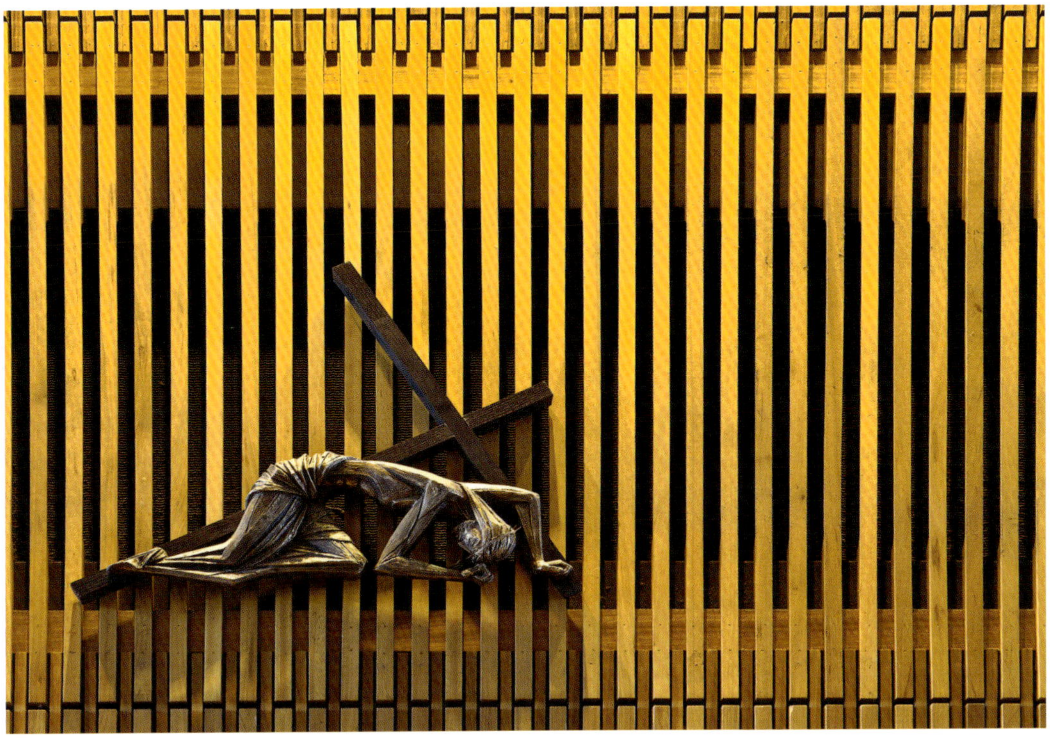

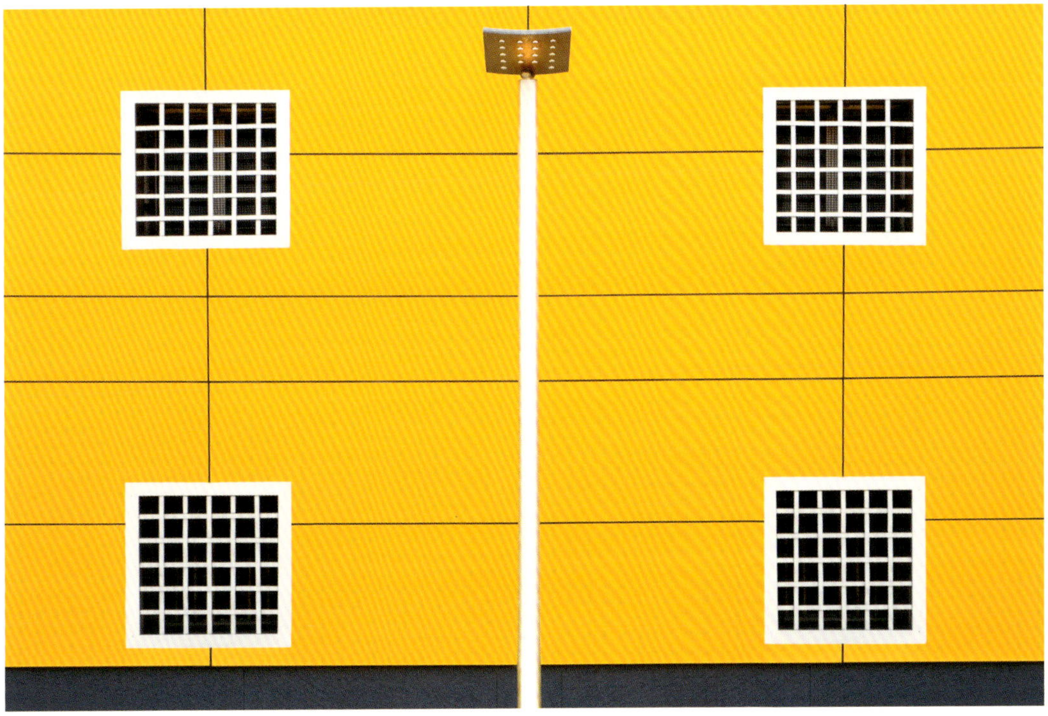

PHILIP QUARRY FRPS UK
LINDA WRIDE ARPS UK

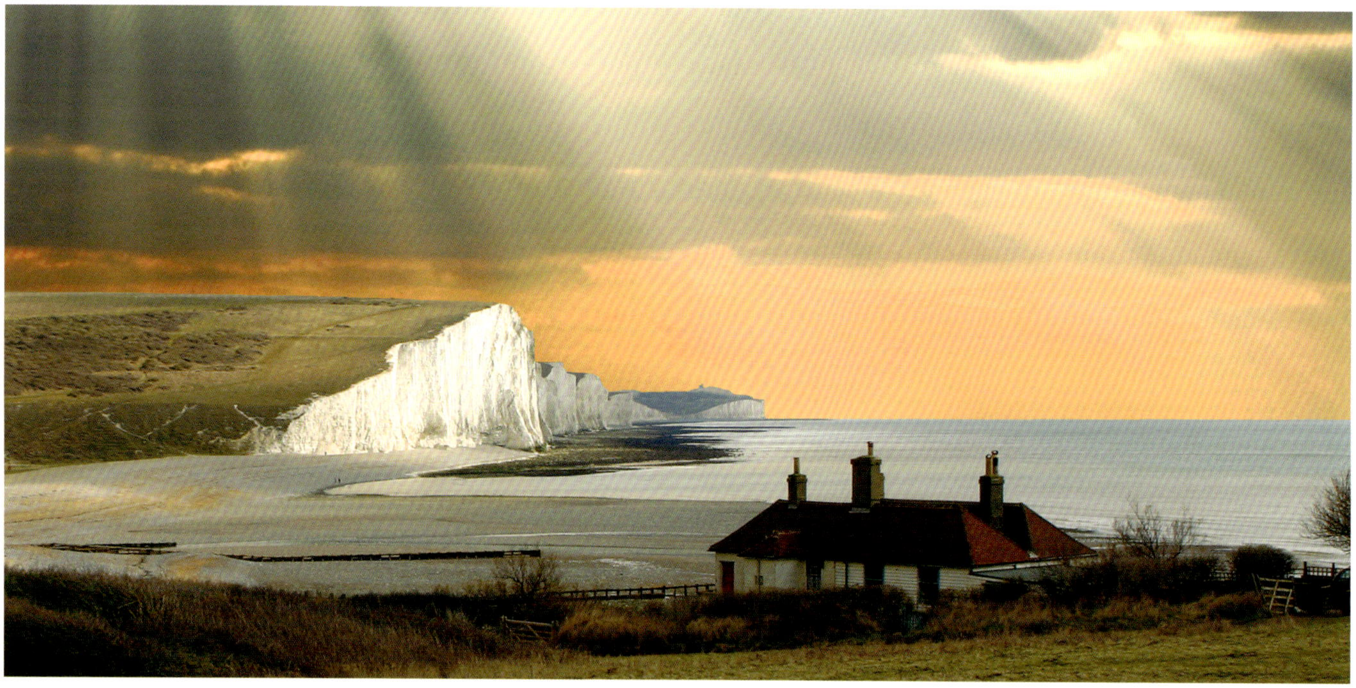

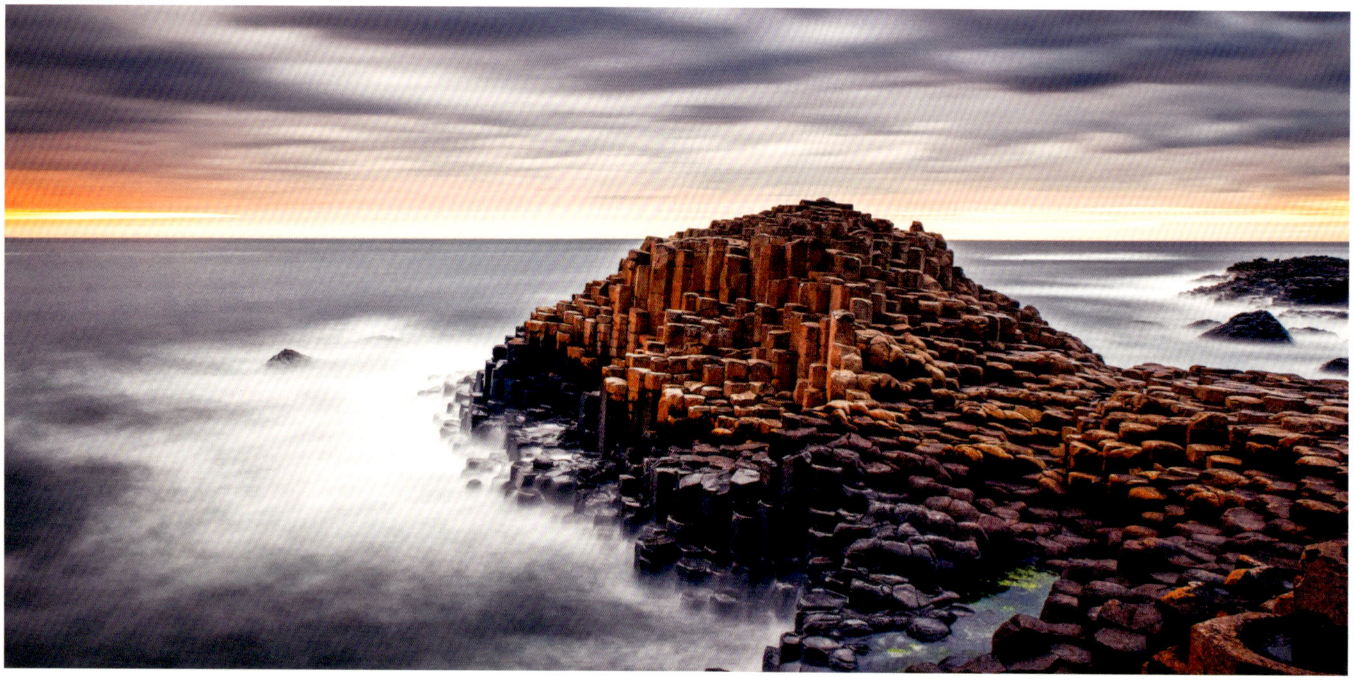

CHRISTOPHER COATES ARPS UK
JOHN MISKELLY ARPS UK

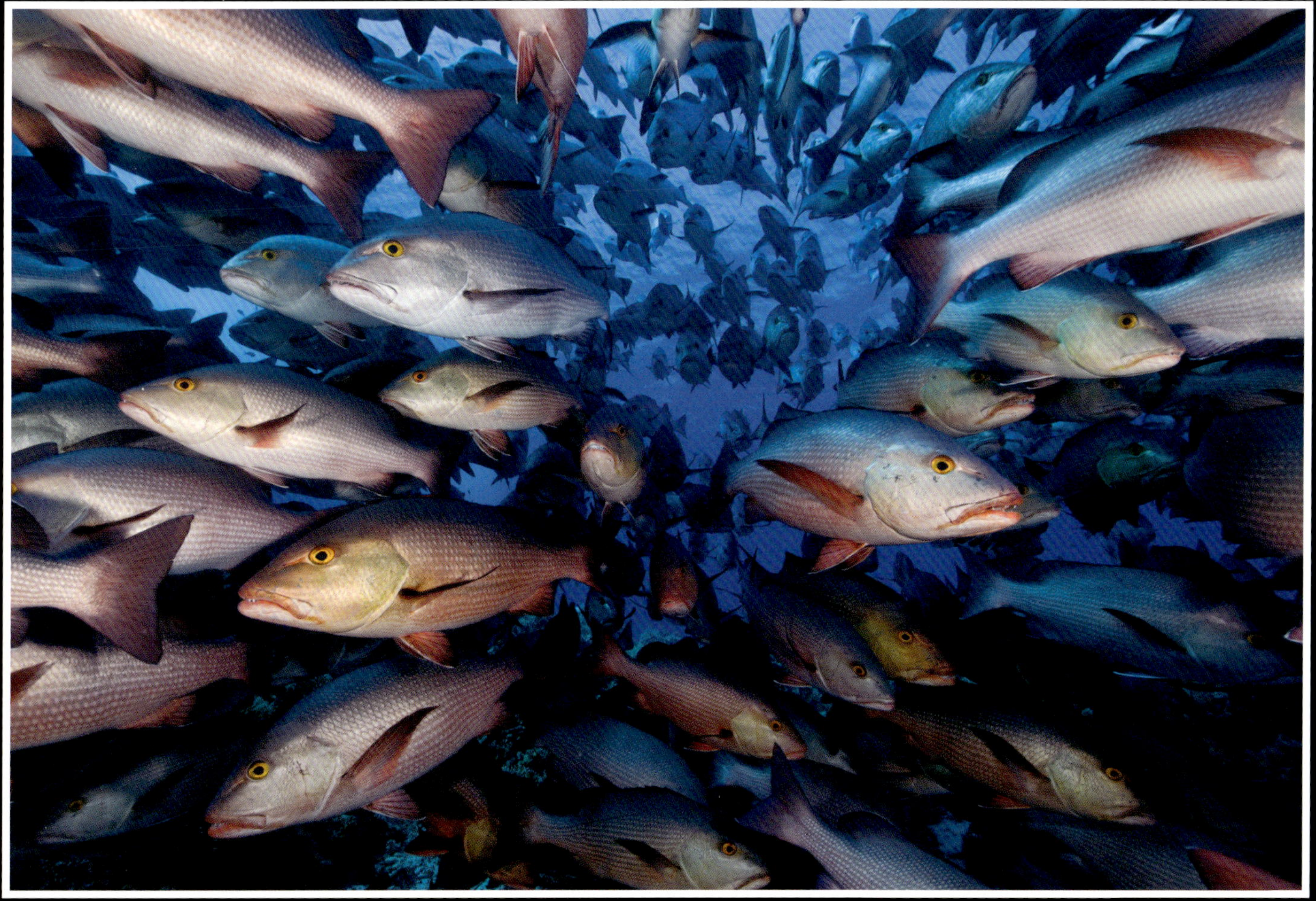

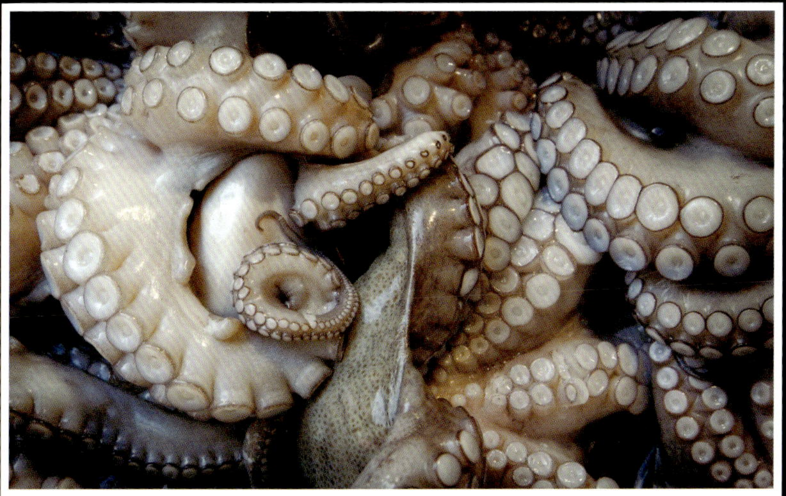

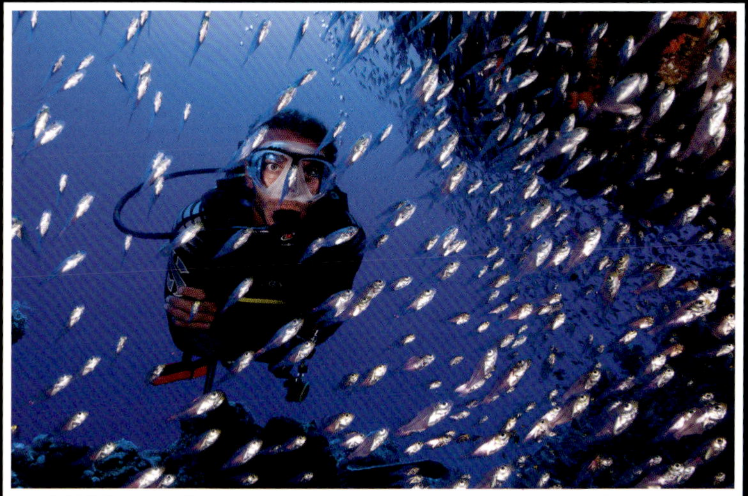

MEMBERS' GALLERY INDEX